E-Strategies for Resource Management Systems:
Planning and Implementation

Eshaa Alkhalifa
Royal University for Women, Bahrain

BUSINESS SCIENCE Reference

BUSINESS SCIENCE REFERENCE
Hershey · New York

Director of Editorial Content: Kristin Klinger
Director of Book Publications: Julia Mosemann
Acquisitions Editor: Lindsay Johnston
Development Editor: Dave DeRicco
Publishing Assistant: Casey Conapitski
Typesetter: Keith Glazewski
Production Editor: Jamie Snavely
Cover Design: Lisa Tosheff
Printed at: Lightning Source

Published in the United States of America by
Business Science Reference (an imprint of IGI Global)
701 E. Chocolate Avenue
Hershey PA 17033
Tel: 717-533-8845
Fax: 717-533-8661
E-mail: cust@igi-global.com
Web site: http://www.igi-global.com

Library of Congress Cataloging-in-Publication Data

E-strategies for resource management systems : planning and implementation / Eshaa Alkhalifa, editor.
p. cm.
Includes bibliographical references and index.
Summary: "This book offers insight into current research practices and trends in Information Resource Management strategies that are implemented electronically"--Provided by publisher. ISBN 978-1-61692-016-6 (hardcover) -- ISBN 978-1-61692-017-3 (ebook) 1. Business--Data processing. 2. Information resources management. 3. Strategic planning. I. Alkhalifa, Eshaa M., 1966- II. Title.
HF5548.2.E766 2010
658.4'038011--dc22

2010000977

British Cataloguing in Publication Data
A Cataloguing in Publication record for this book is available from the British Library.

Table of Contents

Foreword xvii

Preface xix

Section 1
Modeling Business Processes

Chapter 1
Making the Business Process Execution Language (BPEL) Flexible 1
Daniela Wolff, University of Applied Sciences Northwestern Switzerland, Switzerland
Nishant Singh, Indian Institute of Technology, India

Chapter 2
A Framework for the Use of Business Activity Monitoring in Process Improvement 21
Owen Molloy, National University of Ireland, Ireland
Claire Sheridan, Accenture Information Management Services, UK

Chapter 3
The Socio-Technical Balanced Scorecard for Assessing a Public University 47
Ramanjit Singh, University of Manchester, UK
Trevor Wood-Harper, University of Manchester, UK

Chapter 4
Planning Cooperation in Inter-Organizational Systems 61
María Laura Ponisio, University of Twente, The Netherlands
Pascal van Eck, University of Twente, The Netherlands
Lourens Riemens, Dutch Tax and Customs Administration, The Netherlands

Section 2
Standards and QOS

Chapter 5
Guidelines for Managing B2B Standards Implementation ... 86
Eva Söderström, University of Skövde, Sweden

Chapter 6
Ontology-Based Registries: An E-Business Transactions' Registry ... 106
Aikaterini Maria Sourouni, National Technical University of Athens, Greece
Spiros Mouzakitis, National Technical University of Athens, Greece
George Kourlimpinis, National Technical University of Athens, Greece
Dimitris Askounis, National Technical University of Athens, Greece
John Psarras, National Technical University of Athens, Greece

Section 3
Access Mediums to Online Services

Chapter 7
Strategic Framework for Developing a Process Model for Maximising the Potential of Radio Frequency Identification (RFID) Technology Integration in Hospitals ... 118
Chandana Unnithan, Deakin University, Australia
Bardo Fraunholz, Deakin University, Australia

Chapter 8
Sources of Legitimacy for the M-Government Initiatives in Turkey: Human vs. Technical Resource Management Concerns ... 137
N. Meltem Cakici, Gediz University, Turkey
Ronan de Kervenoael, Sabanci University & Aston University, Turkey

Chapter 9
Client Server System for E-Services Access in Business Environment ... 158
Eugen Pop, SC IPA SA, Romania

Chapter 10
Personalized Web Service Provisioning to Mobile Users USING Policy-Based Profile and QoS Management ... 172
Elarbi Badidi, United Arab Emirates University, UAE
Larbi Esmahi, Athabasca University, Canada

Section 4
Collaborative Systems

Chapter 11
Wiki-Dic 2.0: An E-Voting Approach to Exploit User-Generated Content 185
Theodorou L. Tryfon, University of Macedonia, Greece
Violettas E. George, University of Macedonia, Greece
Georgiadis K. Christos, University of Macedonia, Greece

Chapter 12
Supporting Electronic Collaboration in Conceptual Modeling 199
Peter Rittgen, University of Borås, Sweden & Vlerick Leuven Gent Management School, Belgium

Chapter 13
Collaborative Geospatial Web Services for Multi-Dimension: Remote Sensing Data....................... 212
Chunyang Hu, Beihang University, China
Yongwang Zhao, Beihang University, China
Dianfu Ma, Beihang University, China

Section 5
Information Storage

Chapter 14
Query Performance Optimization in XML Data Warehouses 232
Hadj Mahboubi, Université de Lyon, France
Jérôme Darmont, Université de Lyon, France

Section 6
Risks and Security

Chapter 15
Towards an Elastic Risk Management Methodology by Using Business to Software Unified Process (BSUP)... 254
Pooya Khosraviyan Dehkordi, Islamic Azad University, Iran
Farshad Kiyoumarsi, Islamic Azad University, Iran

Chapter 16
Knowledge for Managing Information Systems Security: Review and Future Research Directions.. 266
Ken H. Guo, McMaster University, Canada

Section 7
Project Supervision and Issues

Chapter 17
COTS Software Procurement Methodology 288
Seema Ahmed Al-Mahmood, Ahlia University, Kingdom of Bahrain
Mansoor Al-A'ali, Ahlia University, Kingdom of Bahrain

Chapter 18
Making Decisions in IS/IT Outsourcing: A Dynamic Perspective 306
Cheng-Chieh Huang, National Taiwan University, Taiwan (R.O.C.)
Ching-Cha Hsieh, National Taiwan University, Taiwan (R.O.C.)

Section 8
SME Research and Issues

Chapter 19
An Investigation into the Adoption and Implementation of Electronic Commerce in Saudi Arabian Small and Medium Enterprises 326
Sabah Al-Somali, Aston University, UK
Ben Clegg, Aston University, UK
Roya Gholami, Aston University, UK

Chapter 20
ICT Adoption in SMEs in an Arab GCC Country: Oman 351
Rafi Ashrafi, Sutan Qaboos University, Oman
Muhammed Murtaza, Industrial Management Technology & Contracting LLC, Oman

Chapter 21
Supporting Companies Management and Improving their Productivity through Mining Customers Transactions 376
Asem Omari, Jarash Private University, Jordan

Compilation of References 391

About the Contributors 428

Index 437

Detailed Table of Contents

Foreword ....??

Preface ....??

Section 1
Modeling Business Processes

Chapter 1
Making the Business Process Execution Language (BPEL) Flexible 1
Daniela Wolff, University of Applied Sciences Northwestern Switzerland, Switzerland
Nishant Singh, Indian Institute of Technology, India

Modeling business process is frequently the distinction that exists between businesses that end up being successful and businesses that fail. This chapter present an approach to increasing the flexibility of the Business Process Execution Language to increase its effectiveness in modeling process workflow that lead to the success of businesses.

Chapter 2
A Framework for the Use of Business Activity Monitoring in Process Improvement 21
Owen Molloy, National University of Ireland, Ireland
Claire Sheridan, Accenture Information Management Services, UK

At times of economic hardship, it is essential for businesses to keep a close eye on business activities and outcomes in real-time. This would enable businesses to be alerted immediately if any event requires urgent attention. This chapter, presents a framework that shows how Business Activity Monitoring can be used to improve existing business processes. This is an event driven model, so various thresholds are placed such that alerts are generated when key performance pass them. The framework uses an integrated rules engine taking advantage of semantic technology and relating it to the business processes.

Chapter 3
The Socio-Technical Balanced Scorecard for Assessing a Public University 47
Ramanjit Singh, University of Manchester, UK
Trevor Wood-Harper, University of Manchester, UK

This chapter displays how the balanced scorecard can be implemented for the benefit of nonprofit organizations. The original design of the balanced scorecard is based upon the for-profit organization so the main objective of implementing it is to maximize profit. Non-profit organizations, however, aim to optimize the level of the service, and to optimize the socio-technical principles through job enrichment using flexible work methods and empowerment strategies.

Chapter 4
Planning Cooperation in Inter-Organizational Systems.. 61
María Laura Ponisio, University of Twente, The Netherlands
Pascal van Eck, University of Twente, The Netherlands
Lourens Riemens, Dutch Tax and Customs Administration, The Netherlands

This chapter presents a framework called e-Planning to plan the cooperation between organizations on a network. This framework allows organizations to place an action plan for decision makers to determine who cooperation should be made with first according to set criteria, and to use critical problem solving approaches to reason about obstacles and opportunities for cooperation.

Section 2
Standards and QOS

Chapter 5
Guidelines for Managing B2B Standards Implementation.. 86
Eva Söderström, University of Skövde, Sweden

This chapter presents a model of a Business-to-Business implementation that is developed based upon a literature review and an empirical study. The model is also accompanied by a set of implementation guidelines derived from the study. These results may guide organizations that plan to standardize B2B processes. They may also help organization improve the efficiency of their performance as well as guide future researchers towards new possibilities.

Chapter 6
Ontology-Based Registries: An E-Business Transactions' Registry... 106
Aikaterini Maria Sourouni, National Technical University of Athens, Greece
Spiros Mouzakitis, National Technical University of Athens, Greece
George Kourlimpinis, National Technical University of Athens, Greece
Dimitris Askounis, National Technical University of Athens, Greece
John Psarras, National Technical University of Athens, Greece

This chapter presents an ontology-based e-Business transactions' Registry & Repository. An ontology is an explicit specification of a concept. The Registry and Repository presented describe the composition and publishing traditional, electronic or web services, along with relevant documents, rules, semantic schemas, and workflow notations. The repository can be used by e-businesses, enterprises, government institutions and intermediaries through automation which makes it an important tool in e-business management when that business wishes to liaise with organizations in other sectors or other countries.

Section 3
Access Mediums to Online Services

Chapter 7
Strategic Framework for Developing a Process Model for Maximising the Potential of Radio Frequency Identification (RFID) Technology Integration in Hospitals 118
Chandana Unnithan, Deakin University, Australia
Bardo Fraunholz, Deakin University, Australia

This chapter presents an implementation of Radio Frequency Identification in hospitals to protect high value equipment and to maximize the efficiency of processes. The tool utilized is a radical new technology, and implementations may go far beyond what is presented.

Chapter 8
Sources of Legitimacy for the M-Government Initiatives in Turkey: Human vs. Technical Resource Management Concerns.. 137
N. Meltem Cakici, Gediz University, Turkey
Ronan de Kervenoael, Sabanci University & Aston University, Turkey

Emerging markets have recently been experiencing a dramatic increased in the number of mobile phone per capita. M-government has, hence, been heralded as an opportunity to leap-frog the technology cycle and provide cheaper and more inclusive and services to all. This chapter explores, within an emerging market context, the legitimacy and resistance facing civil servants' at the engagement stage with m-government activities and the direct implication for resource management. Thirty in depth interview, in Turkey, are drawn-upon with key ICT civil servant in local organizations. The findings show that three types of resources are perceived as central namely: (i) diffusion of information management, (ii) operating system resource management and (iii) human resource management. The main evidence suggests that legitimacy for each resource management, at local level, is an ongoing struggle where all groups deploy multiples forms of resistance. Overall, greater attention in the resource management strategy for m-government application needs to be devoted to enablers such as civil servants rather than the final consumers or citizens.

Chapter 9
Client Server System for E-Services Access in Business Environment 158
Eugen Pop, SC IPA SA, Romania

E-services is a term which generally means the provisioning of services via the Internet. The prefix "e" stands for electronic. E-services access is a good opportunity for business developing and offer increased financial benefits for various economic agents. By the support of the Internet, the products or services can be efficiently offered to a large number of clients. Besides, the mobile communications networks give to the clients the advantage to access the informational services from anywhere and anytime. This will facilitate an increasing convergence of technological and financial interests of mobile operators, client server software developers, mobile terminals producers and e-content providers, along with a high level of integration of IT&C resources. This is a good basis and a challenging opportunity for value added services developing, in order to be delivered through the mobile communications networks. Client server architectures with mobile users are suitable for e-services providing, using mobile communications networks. Such a system is presented in this chapter, suitable for business environment access using mobile applications installed on Smartphones and PDAs (Personal Digital Assistants).

Chapter 10
Personalized Web Service Provisioning to Mobile Users USING Policy-Based Profile and QoS Management.. 172
Elarbi Badidi, United Arab Emirates University, UAE
Larbi Esmahi, Athabasca University, Canada

This chapter presents an implementation utilizing mobile technology. The expectation of employees now is that they can retain access to their corporate services as they move to new locations, using various kinds of handheld devices. This chapter proposes a broker-based Web services provisioning system for mobile users with quality of service (QoS) requirements. It describes a set of cooperative brokers, distributed over different sites, that work together to provide personalized services to mobile users while they move from one location to another in their corporate and partners' networks. Access to QoS-enabled Web services is obtained according to the users' home policies. Policies are a key component of the system as they are involved at different levels: authorization, QoS specification, QoS service monitoring, and service selection.

Section 4
Collaborative Systems

Chapter 11
Wiki-Dic 2.0: An E-Voting Approach to Exploit User-Generated Content 185
Theodorou L. Tryfon, University of Macedonia, Greece
Violettas E. George, University of Macedonia, Greece
Georgiadis K. Christos, University of Macedonia, Greece

We may define e-voting as the process of evaluating an article or ranking a translation of a specific scientific term in a relevant web site. This all process of participation and interaction is one of the Web 2.0 definitions, the collaborative knowledge. On-line dictionaries have to consider this factor in order to succeed. They have to be interactive and they have to attract and support the users' participation and contribution. In the proposed e-dictionary, namely "Wiki-Dic", some experts begin a dictionary, they start filling it with words and translations, and all users are allowed not only to look for the translation, but also to vote for it. The most voted translations go to the top. In addition, appropriate security countermeasures are used to deal efficiently with the "one vote per person" problem and to avoid malicious software. Furthermore, an intelligent algorithm that is giving weights to the voters is implemented. In this way, the weights are computed automatically from our application, based on quantitative and qualitative information as well.

Chapter 12
Supporting Electronic Collaboration in Conceptual Modeling 199
Peter Rittgen, University of Borås, Sweden & Vlerick Leuven Gent Management School, Belgium

This chapter studies collaborative modeling by analyzing conversations and loud thinking during modeling sessions and the resulting models themselves. It identifies the basic activities of the modeling teams on the social, pragmatic, semantic and syntactic levels and derives a schema for the pragmatic level. This main conclusion is that team-based modeling is largely a negotiation process. Drawing on these results an architecture of a system that supports the distributed development of conceptual models is presented.

Chapter 13
Collaborative Geospatial Web Services for Multi-Dimension: Remote Sensing Data....................... 212
Chunyang Hu, Beihang University, China
Yongwang Zhao, Beihang University, China
Dianfu Ma, Beihang University, China

Satellite remote sensing imagery data is an important Geospatial data which is playing an increasingly important role in many applications such as crisis management, military activities and government decision-making. However, it will continue to be a great challenge to organize and manage these multi-dimension massive remote sensing data for collaborative visualization services in Internet environment. In this chapter we proposed a global hierarchical data model of massive multi-dimension remote sensing data based on tiling and pyramid technologies for the organization and management of multi-source and multi-scale remote sensing data. We implemented a collaborative Geospatial data visualization system based on our proposed storage structure of data model using Web Services, WSRF and Web2.0 technologies. Finally, we evaluated the prototype system with real data sets, which demonstrated the high performance data visualization in our system.

Section 5
Information Storage

Chapter 14
Query Performance Optimization in XML Data Warehouses 232
Hadj Mahboubi, Université de Lyon, France
Jérôme Darmont, Université de Lyon, France

XML data warehouses form an interesting basis for decision-support applications that exploit complex data. However, native-XML database management systems (DBMSs) currently bear limited performances and it is necessary to research for ways to optimize them. In this chapter, we present two such techniques. First, we propose an XML join index that is specifically adapted to the multidimensional architecture of XML warehouses. It eliminates join operations while preserving the information contained in the original warehouse. Second, we present a strategy for selecting XML materialized views by clustering the query workload. To validate these proposals, we measure the response time of a set of decision-support XQueries over an XML data warehouse, with and without using our optimization techniques. Our experimental results demonstrate their efficiency, even when queries are complex and data are voluminous.

Section 6
Risks and Security

Chapter 15
Towards an Elastic Risk Management Methodology by Using Business to Software Unified Process (BSUP)............ 254
Pooya Khosraviyan Dehkordi, Islamic Azad University, Iran
Farshad Kiyoumarsi, Islamic Azad University, Iran

Riskit is a now a world-wide risk management methodology deployed by a number of expert software engineering communities since its first rollout. Business to Software Unified Process (BSUP) has been the proprietary Business to software modeling approach introduced for the first time in 2003. In this paper the goal is apply the capabilities inherent in BSUP to optimize Riskit process model. BSUP, UML 2.0 and Fuzzy Logic Concepts are widely used whenever the model is to be made.

Chapter 16
Knowledge for Managing Information Systems Security: Review and Future Research Directions............ 266
Ken H. Guo, McMaster University, Canada

Knowledge is one of the critical factors that organizations need to consider when managing the security of resource management systems or information systems (IS) in general. This is because knowledge is not only the object but also a tool of IS security management. On the one hand, IS security is about the security of knowledge (including data and information). On the other hand, IS security management is a knowledge-intensive activity that depends heavily on IS professionals' expertise and skills and end-users' awareness. Given the important role of knowledge, this chapter aims to review current security research by applying knowledge management concepts and frameworks as a tool and lens. Based on the systemic review, this chapter identifies gaps in the current IS security literature and provides some guidelines for security practices.

Section 7
Project Supervision and Issues

Chapter 17
COTS Software Procurement Methodology 288
Seema Ahmed Al-Mahmood, Ahlia University, Kingdom of Bahrain
Mansoor Al-A'ali, Ahlia University, Kingdom of Bahrain

Two of the most important COTS software acquisition processes are the COTS software solution evaluation and selection process and the COTS software solution contract management process. This chapter presents a new methodology to deal with these two phases in detail. The evaluation and selection part consists of 12 steps divided over four phases. The contract management part consists of nine steps divided over four phases. We explain each of the two parts of the methodology by describing each of the 21 steps. This research presents a solution to the difficult problems facing the vendors, users, and experts involved in COTS software evaluation, selection, and acquisition and guides them systematically to make the best educated decision. To our knowledge, this work presents the first integrated solution to the software evaluation, selection, and acquisition processes of COTS software. The research is based on real experience obtained from the analysis of three case studies of major COTS software acquisition projects in Bahrain. This chapter is a step forward in the continuous research of COTS software acquisition and procurement processes.

Chapter 18
Making Decisions in IS/IT Outsourcing: A Dynamic Perspective 306
Cheng-Chieh Huang, National Taiwan University, Taiwan (R.O.C.)
Ching-Cha Hsieh, National Taiwan University, Taiwan (R.O.C.)

Making decisions in an IS/IT outsourcing project is complex and the outcome is unpredictable. Prior research on IS/IT outsourcing decisions simply assumed the decision-making process is rational, comprehensive and independent that is not descriptively accurate, and thus, cannot be prescriptively useful in such a complex environment. In order to gain a deeper understanding of decision-making in IS/IT outsourcing processes, this chapter creates an outsourcing decision framework, derived from a dynamic perspective, to illustrate the decision-making process and how the decisions impact outsourcing results. An in-depth case study methodology is used to interpret an e-strategy transformation outsourced project. The analysis indicates interwoven decisions, knowledge as power, decision-makers' cognition, and ideologies should be the focus of future studies on IS/IT outsourcing.

Section 8
SME Research and Issues

Chapter 19
An Investigation into the Adoption and Implementation of Electronic Commerce in Saudi Arabian Small and Medium Enterprises 326

Sabah Al-Somali, Aston University, UK
Ben Clegg, Aston University, UK
Roya Gholami, Aston University, UK

Saudi Arabian Small and Medium Enterprises (SMEs) will face fierce competition from new entrants to local markets as a result of their accession to the Word Trade Organization (WTO), and electronic commerce (e-commerce) technologies can reinforce SME's competitive edge. This study investigates the state of e-commerce adoption and analyses the factors that determine the extent to which SMEs in Saudi Arabia are inclined towards deploying e-commerce technologies. This could assist future firms in designing effective implementation projects. Seven SMEs' e-commerce adoption levels are studied as a case. The Technology-Organization-Environment (TOE) framework was used as the major source of inspiration in our analysis of e-commerce adoption amongst Saudi SMEs. In addition to advancing research on e-commerce in Saudi Arabia, this chapter also highlights several directions for future inquiry and implications for managers and policymakers.

Chapter 20
ICT Adoption in SMEs in an Arab GCC Country: Oman 351
Rafi Ashrafi, Sutan Qaboos University, Oman
Muhammed Murtaza, Industrial Management Technology & Contracting LLC, Oman

This chapter reviews UN and World Economic Forum ICT indicators for assessing the adoption of Information and Communication Technologies (ICT) in Gulf Cooperation Countries (GCC). Also, it presents the results of an exploratory study carried out to learn about the adoption of ICT in SMEs in Oman. The study investigates infrastructure, software used, driver for ICT investment, perceptions about business benefits of ICT and outsourcing trends of SMEs. The study provides an insight on the barriers for the adoption of ICT. Data on these aspects of ICT was collected from 51 SMEs through a survey questionnaire. The results of the study show that only a small number of SMEs in Oman are aware of the benefits of ICT adoption. The main driving forces for ICT investment are to provide better and faster customer service and to stay ahead of the competition. A majority of surveyed SMEs have reported a positive performance and other benefits by utilizing ICT in their businesses. A number of SMEs outsource most of their ICT activities. Lack of internal capabilities, high cost of ICT and lack of information about suitable ICT solutions and implementation were some of the major barriers in adopting ICT. These findings are consistent with other studies. There is a need for more focus and concerted efforts on increasing awareness among SMEs on the benefits of ICT adoption. The results of the study recognize the need for more training facilities in ICT for SMEs, measures to provide ICT products and services at an affordable cost, availability of free professional advice and consulting services at reasonable cost to SMEs. Our findings therefore have important implication for policy aimed at ICT adoption and use by SMEs. The findings of this research will provide a foundation for future research and will help policy makers in understanding the current state of affairs of the usage and impact of ICT on SMEs in Oman and other GCC countries

Chapter 21
Supporting Companies Management and Improving their Productivity through Mining Customers Transactions 376
Asem Omari, Jarash Private University, Jordan

Selling products or services online plays an important role in the success of businesses that have a physical presence, like a retail business. For many businesses, a retail website is an effective line of communication between the businesses and their customers. Even if the business does not present all of its products and services in the website, the website may be just what the customer needs to see to choose it over a competitor. Therefore, it is important to have a successful website to serve as a sales and marketing tool to participate in meeting the core requirements of the business. Clustering and classification are two important data mining techniques that are widely used to assign customers to different categories. Those categories are used to analyze customer behavior and interestingness. In this chapter, we use clustering and classification to support web designers to have better designed retail websites. This is done during the design phase by improving the structure of the website depending on the extracted patterns in a way that makes it easy for the website's navigator to find his target products in an efficient time, give him the opportunity to have a look at some products that may be of interest for him, and encourage him to buy more from the available products which will consequently increase the business's overall profit. This approach will open the eyes of business leaders to adapt new efficient technological tool that when invested in their organizations will improve the strategic goals and meet their basic requirements to be successful, productive, and competitive. The experimental work shows very promising results that can positively change the traditional techniques of the process of designing retail websites.

Compilation of References 391

About the Contributors 428

Index 437

Foreword

Historically, managers in any organization have always used information to perform their tasks and duties as decision makers. The art of management is seen as making the best decision possible, given the incomplete nature of the underlying information. Recently, in the information industry, attention has shifted from administration, to helping executive, managers and professional to achieve the objectives of their organization.

Information Systems is the backbone and lifeblood of the organization. Today, most decision makers understand that Information Systems are crucial and have learned that it is practically impossible to manage their organizations without some knowledge of Information Systems. The state of Information Systems has improved significantly. It is well recognized both in practice and in literature that the capabilities of Information Systems presently offer management more choices in terms of alternatives than those previously available to organizations, and as a consequence, offer new options to the managers. However, the design, implementation and operation of Information Systems is a complex task, which required careful planning, commitment and involvement by appropriate managers and users.

This book explores a lot of fresh ground. It features an expansive, up-to-date survey of Information Systems and analytical approaches, plus collections of reading in profit and nonprofit organizations in developing and developed countries. The topics primarily add in-depth treatment to important areas in the field of Information Systems and also emphasize applications and illustrations of how particular organizations have used Information Systems concepts and tools to their advantage.

The book adds new materials on the latest development in Information Systems, in particular Modeling Processes, Standards and Quality of Services (QoS), Access Mediums to online Services, Collaborative Systems, Information Storage, Risk and Security, Project Supervision and Issues, and Small and Medium Enterprises Research (SME) and Issues. This book gives a "flavor" of the prosperity of the Information Systems world.

The book is intended for two audiences: first, academics, senior-level and MBA students taking a course in Information Systems and, second, practitioners in staying abreast of the fast-moving practices of Information Systems. It can also be used in conjunction with one of several Information Systems casebooks.

We have learned much from the experience of the business organizations over the recent past. Yet, in our content, especially in many exhibits, we still seek a balance of theory and practice, as well as between research findings and models.

The book you are holding is a valuable tool. The author approaches a far-reaching, complicated collection of Information Systems subjects in a truly inspiring way. It is filled with a map for the road ahead.

Adel Ismail Al-Alawi
Vice President of ISACA, Bahrain Chapter
Royal University for Women, Kingdom of Bahrain

Adel Ismail Al-Alawi *(BSc in Business Adminstration, Husson University, Maine, USA, MBA, Thomas College, Maine, USA, PhD, University of Leeds, UK) is an Associate Professor and holds a PhD from University of Leeds, UK. Previously he was Dean of School of Business and Advisor to the President for Academic Affairs at the University College of Bahrain and the Chairman of Management Information System (MIS) department at the University of Bahrain (UoB). He served UoB for more than 20 years. Dr Al-Alawi founded MIS Department in the University of Bahrain. He is also one of the founders and Board members for Bahrain Information Technology Society (BITS); Bahrain Academic Society and a Vice President of Information Systems Audit & Control Society. Dr Al-Alawi intensively participated in the Board formed by a decree from HH the Prime Minster for the development of Bahrain Internet Exchange (BIX) and substantially contributed in the Committee founded by HH the Prime Minster for the Preparation of the Government Program for Parliament. Dr. Al-Alawi's research has been published in several international journals. His main interest of research is in management in general and is more specifically in MIS.*

Preface

The main goal of the book is to offer insight onto current research practices and trends in Information Resource Management strategies that can implemented electronically. The Internet has revolutionized business practices because it is also used within organizations to allow the exchange of electronic documents and to allow processes to flow electronically rather than with old fashioned paper. Eventually, almost all, if not all information that flows or is exchanged within an organization is turning into electronic based information. That has occurred so fast that many organizations still find difficulty in shifting all processes from a paper world to an electronic paperless world.

Organizations, e-businesses, e-governments, e-learning institutions, inter-organization cooperation, inter-sector collaboration, and even international business deals take place on a daily basis through electronic means. It is not necessary for every single organization to follow the same learning curve and fall into the same pits and troughs to arrive at a successful solution that would facilitate reaching their goals.

If that is not a sufficient reason, one may add a few comments on the tough economic times everyone is going through, which spells out a clear statement. Maximum efficiency of resources is of utmost importance to maximize possible profit. The existing business environment is not a tolerant one for mistakes, so a source of information can at least present various thought and ideas that may be considered both by researchers and theorists as well as by implementers in the real world of business.

This book reveals through several different sections and topics, the state of the art theories and practice assessments in the world with respect to real issues that arise when implementing a paperless office. In other words, this book wants to fill the head of its reader with ideas that are practical, and can be implemented. It will then be the responsibility of the decision maker to make the right choices for the suitable business application.

Yet, the book does not attempt to solve all business problems on the earth, nor does it leave the choice solely to the reader without attempting to classify the presented ideas into a format that would facilitate finding relevant work. Consequently, the book is organized into several sections.

Business modeling for example includes analyzing how to implement various strategies including the Balanced Scorecard to nonprofit domains, as well as includes how to study an electronic business modeling language and make it more flexible. This, shows that the book attempts to satisfy a diverse set of needs that includes implementation of a theory described in the book, as well as includes how to adjust tools that are already available in the market to optimize modeling outcomes. The medium of modeling is therefore also placed under scrutiny and not only the messages that modeling medium delivers.

One of the modern trends is the drive towards standards because a business that wishes to exist on the Internet wishes to interact with other businesses that also exist on the Internet. If the two businesses do not speak the same language, or if this preface is write this preface in Arabic, then the author of this preface will lose the ability to communicate with readers. Standards, therefore, present themselves as the common language of communication between different systems, or electronic representations of the organizations.

Phones are resources that have grown exponentially and eventually became windows to the Internet resources. There were several different implementations that allowed phones to access web pages; of which some are more successful than others. The book presents ideas, and implementations of new technologies including phones and RFIDs to optimize resource management.

Communities were formed on the Internet, and that in turn implies that a benefit can be obtained from collaborative cooperation that was not possible without the Internet. Social media sites grew exponentially yet not enough benefit has been gained from the business world by this global presence on the Internet.

As information grows with the growth of the Internet, data stores turned into data warehouses, and that in turn implies that rules of organizing these warehouses are necessary. A warehouse crash of data, is much more alarming from a personal computer crash while searching for information in a data warehouse is much more complicated than searching on a Personal Computer folder.

When is a process at risk, and how can security of that electronic information be undermined? Every resource is worth something to the organization that owns it, so what if the resource is information that available on the Internet. Security issues are of importance to an organization which owns that information.

Information Technology Projects are by far, the most complicated types of projects to implement because once the word integration comes up, fear of failure start to creep in. Programs have grown from a few hundred lines of code, to thousands and perhaps millions making it extremely difficult to foresee the issues that may arise. The process itself may be automated.

One of the main worries that exist in the global marketplace is the Internet threat that may exist for small to medium enterprises. To form an international marketplace implies an international level competition, so businesses can no longer grow under the security and boundaries of their own countries, until they reach a size that allows them to venture to the international arena. Instead, they are at competition from the beginning, so they are encourage to also seek online presence but is this the best way to go?

People who are interested in remaining up to date with current ideas on optimizing e-business solutions as well as those in the field of implementation should find this book interesting. New ideas, and new implementations of old ideas are both included in this publication. People who are interested in learning how their organization can be better aligned to its goals, will also be interested in the modeling section of the this publication. New technological implementations and ideas are included to allow that organization that wishes to remain one step ahead of the competition to do so. Researchers will also find regional information and comparisons, as well as know what others are working on, and the hurdles that exist in this field.

The first chapter is written as a result of collaboration between a researcher from Switzerland and another from India. It presents an approach to making the business modeling language more flexible. Frequently, modeling business processes is the distinction that exists between businesses that end up being successful and businesses that fail. This chapter presents an approach to increasing the flexibility of the Business Process Execution Language to increase its effectiveness in modeling process workflow that lead to the success of businesses.

The second chapter is a result of a collaboration of a researcher from Ireland with a researcher from the United Kingdom and presents an approach to monitor businesses. This approach enables businesses to be alerted immediately if any event requires urgent attention. The chapter presents a framework that shows how Business Activity Monitoring can be used to improve existing business processes by placing event threshold levels that produce alerts when attention is required.

The third chapter originates from the United Kingdom to display how the balanced scorecard can be implemented for the benefit of nonprofit organizations. The original design of the balanced scorecard is based upon the for-profit organization so the main objective of implementing it is to maximize profit. Non-profit organizations, however, aim to optimize the level of the service, and to optimize the socio-technical principles through job enrichment using flexible work methods and empowerment strategies.

The fourth chapter, from the Netherlands, presents a framework called e-Planning to plan the cooperation between organizations on a network. This framework allows organizations to place an action plan for decision makers to determine who cooperation should be made with first according to set criteria, and to use critical problem solving approaches to reason about obstacles and opportunities for cooperation.

The fifth chapter from Sweden, presents a model of a Business-to-Business implementation that is developed based upon a literature review and an empirical study. The model is also accompanied by a set of implementation guidelines derived from the study. These results may guide organizations that plan to standardize B2B processes. They may also help organization improve the efficiency of their performance as well as guide future researchers towards new possibilities.

The sixth chapter from Greece, and presents an ontology-based e-Business transactions' Registry & Repository. Ontology is an explicit specification of a concept. The Registry and Repository presented describe the composition and publishing traditional, electronic or web services, along with relevant documents, rules, semantic schemas, and workflow notations. The repository can be used by e-businesses, enterprises, government institutions and intermediaries through automation which makes it an important tool in e-business management when that business wishes to liaise with organizations in other sectors or other countries.

The seventh chapter from Australia, presents an implementation of Radio Frequency Identification in hospitals to protect high value equipment and to maximize the efficiency of processes. The tool utilized is a radical new technology, and implementations may go far beyond what is presented.

The eighth chapter from Turkey builds on the fact that emerging markets have experienced exponential growth in mobile phones per capita causing them to contribute to Mobile Government research to provide cheaper and more inclusive and services to all. This chapter explores, the legitimacy and resistance facing civil servants' at the engagement stage with m-government activities and the direct implication for resource management. The findings show that three types of resources are perceived as central namely: (i) diffusion of information management, (ii) operating system resource management and (iii) human resource management. The goal is to identify the hurdles that have to be crossed in order to offer this type of services.

The ninth chapter from Romania, encourages the provision of eservices. The prefix "e" stands for electronic. The goal of this chapter is to present a system that allows the use of Smartphones, and PDAs (Personal Digital Assistants) to clients through client server architecture. This would allow clients to be able to access the information provided from anywhere they happen to be at any time of day that suits them.

The tenth chapter comes as a result of collaboration between the United Arab Emirates and Canada to present an implementation utilizing mobile technology. Employees expect to retain access to corporate services as they move from one location to the next using various types of handheld devices. This chapter proposes a broker-based Web services provisioning system for mobile users with quality of service (QoS) requirements. It describes a set of cooperative brokers, distributed over different sites, that work together to provide personalized services to mobile users while they move from one location to another in their corporate and partners' networks. Access to QoS-enabled Web services is obtained according to the users' home policies. Policies are a key component of the system as they are involved at different levels: authorization, QoS specification, QoS service monitoring, and service selection.

The eleventh chapter comes from Greece to present an e-voting site that ranks articles or translations of terms utilizing Web 2.0 technology and collaborative knowledge. A proposed e-dictionary called "Wiki-Dic", a few experts fill out a dictionary with words and translations and users are later allowed to look up translations and to vote for the translations. The most voted translations go to the top. Appropriate security countermeasures are used to deal efficiently with the "one vote per person" problem and to avoid malicious software. Furthermore, an intelligent algorithm that is giving weights to the voters is implemented. In this way, the weights are computed automatically from the application, based on quantitative and qualitative information as well

The twelfth chapter comes from Sweden. The architecture of a system that supports the distributed development of conceptual models is presented. This is done based on the analysis of conversations and think aloud modeling sessions that are held. The basic activities of the modeling teams are identified based upon the social, pragmatic, semantic and syntactic level, and a schema is derived.

The thirteenth chapter comes from China to present a solution to the organization and management of remote sensing data for collaborative visualization services. Satellite remote sensing imagery data is an important Geospatial data which is playing an increasingly important role in many applications such as crisis management, military activities and government decision-making. A global hierarchical data model of massive multi-dimension remote sensing data based on tiling and pyramid technologies is proposed for the organization of this class of data. A collaborative Geospatial data visualization system is implemented based on the proposed storage structure of data model using Web Services, WSRF and Web2.0 technologies. Then prototype system is evaluated with real data sets.

The fourteenth chapter comes from France to present a data warehouse solution because native-XML database management systems (DBMSs) currently bear limited performances and it is necessary to find ways to optimize them. The chapter presents two techniques. The first is an XML join index that is specifically adapted to the multidimensional architecture of XML warehouses. The second is a strategy for selecting XML materialized views by clustering the query workload. To validate these proposals, the response time of a set of decision-support XQueries over an XML data warehouse is measured, with and without using our optimization techniques. Results demonstrate the efficiency of the proposed solutions.

The fifteenth chapter comes from Iran to manage risk using Riskit methodology. Business to Software Unified Process (BSUP) has been the proprietary Business to software modeling approach introduced for the first time in 2003. This chapter applies the capabilities inherent to BSUP to optimize Riskit process model.

The sixteenth chapter comes from Canada to review current security research by applying knowledge management concepts and frameworks as a tool and lens. Based on the systemic review, this chapter identifies gaps in the current IS security literature and provides some guidelines for security practices. Knowledge about security is a critical factor in maintain the security of knowledge.

The seventeenth chapter comes from the Kingdom of Bahrain to present a solution to the difficult problems facing the vendors, users, and experts involved in COTS software evaluation, selection, and acquisition and guides them systematically to make the best educated decision. The research is based on real experience obtained from the analysis of three case studies of major COTS software acquisition projects in Bahrain.

The eighteenth chapter comes from Taiwan to show some of the problems that may arise in outsourcing IT projects. Prior research on IS/IT outsourcing decisions simply assumed the decision-making process is rational, comprehensive and independent that is not descriptively accurate, and thus, cannot be prescriptively useful in such a complex environment. In order to gain a deeper understanding of decision-making in IS/IT outsourcing processes, this chapter creates an outsourcing decision framework, derived from a dynamic perspective, to illustrate the decision-making process and how the decisions impact outsourcing results. An in-depth case study methodology is used to interpret an e-strategy transformation outsourced project. The analysis indicates interwoven decisions, knowledge as power, decision-makers' cognition, and ideologies should be the focus of future studies on IS/IT outsourcing.

The nineteenth chapter comes from the United Kingdom about Saudi Arabia. Saudi Arabian Small and Medium Enterprises (SMEs) will face fierce competition from new entrants to local markets as a result of their accession to the World Trade Organization (WTO), and electronic commerce (e-commerce) technologies can reinforce SME's competitive edge. This study investigates the state of e-commerce adoption and analyses the factors that determine the extent to which SMEs in Saudi Arabia are inclined towards deploying e-commerce technologies. This could assist future firms in designing effective implementation projects. Seven SMEs' e-commerce adoption levels are studied as a case. The Technology-Organization-Environment (TOE) framework was used as the major source of inspiration in our analysis of e-commerce adoption amongst Saudi SMEs. In addition to advancing research on e-commerce in Saudi Arabia, this chapter also highlights several directions for future inquiry and implications for managers and policymakers.

The twentieth chapter from Oman reviews the UN and World Economic Forum ICT indicators for assessing the adoption of Information and Communication Technologies (ICT) in Gulf Cooperation Countries (GCC). It presents the results of an exploratory study carried out to learn about the adoption of ICT in SMEs in Oman. The study provides an insight on the barriers for the adoption of ICT mainly represented in that only a small number of SMEs in Oman are aware of the benefits of ICT adoption. A majority of surveyed SMEs have reported a positive performance and other benefits by utilizing ICT in their businesses. A number of SMEs outsource most of their ICT activities. Lack of internal capabilities, high cost of ICT and lack of information about suitable ICT solutions and implementation were some of the major barriers in adopting ICT. These findings are consistent with other studies. There is a need for more focus and concerted efforts on increasing awareness among SMEs on the benefits of ICT adoption. The results of the study recognize the need for more training facilities in ICT for SMEs, measures to provide ICT products and services at an affordable cost, availability of free professional advice and consulting services at reasonable cost to SMEs. These findings therefore have important implication for policy aimed at ICT adoption and use by SMEs.

The twenty-first chapter is from Jordan. It uses clustering and classification to support web designers to have better designed retail websites. This is done during the design phase by improving the structure of the website depending on the extracted patterns in a way that makes it easy for the website's navigator to find his target products in an efficient time, give him the opportunity to have a look at some products that may be of interest for him, and encourage him to buy more from the available products which will consequently increase the business's overall profit. This approach will open the eyes of business leaders to adapt new efficient technological tool that when invested in their organizations will improve the strategic goals and meet their basic requirements to be successful, productive, and competitive. The experimental work shows very promising results that can positively change the traditional techniques of the process of designing retail websites.

With respect to research, this book collects a number of experiences and ideas from different parts of the world. The combination of this work into one publication was not easy, and the main goal is to produce work that is of value to people that are not able to travel to all those countries to gather experiences and knowledge. Consequently, the variety is intended, while the similarity in the overall topics of concentration is emergent. The list of topics proposed were more than those that emerged, simply because it would allow the world to tell us, what the currents trends are. True enough, the areas of researcher interest emerged as exhibited above.

With respect to organizations and businesses, this book presents a generally non-technical source of information of possible implementations that may optimize business practices. It presents implementations for mobile phone technology, RFIDs, etc. Consequently, it presents complete descriptions of implementations or ideas of how new technology can serve business goals. The book also presents how standards could be implemented, and how organizations can interact online. Document procurement is yet another business idea that is presented in this book. Existing business, as well business ideas for new businesses may emerge as a consequence of this book.

Eshaa Alkhalifa
Royal University for Women, Bahrain

Section 1

Modeling Business Processes

Chapter 1
Making the Business Process Execution Language (BPEL) Flexible

Daniela Wolff
University of Applied Sciences Northwestern Switzerland, Switzerland

Nishant Singh
Indian Institute of Technology, India

ABSTRACT

The Business Process Execution Language (BPEL) is a process modeling language which uses standard control constructs to define a workflow. But, today's enterprises need to be agile to cope with increasing change, uncertainty and unpredictability. Therefore, automating agile business processes is still a challenge as they are normally knowledge intensive and can be planned to a limited degree. The execution order depends heavily on the case, which has to be performed. So instead of modeling all possible cases and situations which might occur in a knowledge intensive process we introduced an approach which uses semantic technologies and rules. Business rules can be utilized to allow for case-specific adaptation of process steps. A component was developed which allow during run-time rules to automatically detect the state of the case and to determine the necessary process adaptations.

INTRODUCTION

Today's enterprises need to be responsive to competitors, the market, organizational changes and changing customer requirements and need to response immediately. Agile enterprises are able to scope with increasing changes, uncertainty and unpredictability in the business environment. Although, the original concept of an agile manufacturing was popularized 1991 by the Iacocca Institute (Iacocca 1991), there is still a lack in supporting agility by information systems (Mutschler, Reichert et.al. 2006; Rymer and Moore 2006).

Several workflow management systems exists, which mostly provide process definition tools that presents the knowledge about the process using standard modeling elements like activities, roles or control flows elements (Mendling and Neumann 2005). This is suitable for production oriented processes, but it is ill-suited to deal with changes (van der Aalst and Jablonski 2000). Because, change is difficult, complex and risky according

DOI: 10.4018/978-1-61692-016-6.ch001

to unintended side effects. Every change of one part of the enterprise has an impact of another part, which leads to the choice, whether to make a change or abandon the competitive benefits of innovation because of the risk (Mitra and Gupta 2008). However, change may range from complete restructuring of the process definition to ad-hoc modification of a single process instance. Especially, knowledge-intensive tasks are performed in a fair degree of uncertainty in which they have to deal with exceptional situations, unforeseeable events and unpredictable situations. If possible at all, covering all possible situations and events, the process model would be highly complex and difficult to manage containing multiple decision points. So, knowledge-intensive processes can be planned to a limited degree (Faustmann 1998). The ability to have more freedom while performing a process instance is called flexibility (Sadiq, Sadiq, and Orlowska 2001).

Knowledge-intensive processes might be structured, but often they are semi-structured or unstructured. Possibly, only parts of a process can be classified as knowledge-intensive (Heravizadeh and Edmond 2008). So, due to performance and efficiency issues it makes sense to combine workflow management approaches with a component which executes the flexible process part.

Service-oriented Architecture (SOA) inherently enables flexibility and adaptivity through choreography of services where each service can select and invoke any other web service. Hence, combining technologies of SOA- and BPM will achieve more flexibility in orchestrating tasks.

The Business Process Execution Language for Web Services (BPEL) supports the specification for coordination and composition of web services (Alonso et.al. 2004). However, by providing predefined control constructs BPEL lacks the flexibility to deal with knowledge-intensive processes. Thus, BPEL is useful for the execution of the structured part of a business process, but it has to be adapted to fulfill the requirements of knowledge-intensive processes.

The execution of knowledge-intensive tasks depends heavily on the case, which has to be performed. For instance, running a credit check in an enterprise is often only done for new customers. Depending on their amount of order several checks might be necessary ranging from requesting only a credit institute to get information about the customer to demanding several department collection services. The condition of an object and how it has to be performed is called its state. The state of an object is given by the values of all of its properties (Mitra and Gupta 2006). To make a process more case sensitive, the case with its property has to be modeled. The state of the case is then during run time used to specify the process flow for the knowledge-intensive process part.

Business rules can be utilized to allow for context-specific adaptation of process steps. During run-time rules allow to automatically detect the state of the case and to determine the necessary process adaptations.

In this chapter, we present an approach where we use BPEL for the execution of the structured part with a component, which is able to perform the knowledge-intensive process part and can adapt the process flow depending on the case. Because the data of case can be variously interpreted by different people and applications, we use ontologies, which serve as communication medium between people and applications and between different applications ontologies are used to specify the case. The Semantic Web Rule Language (SWRL) combines OWL with RuleML, which allows the definition of terms and facts in an ontology. With the use of SWRL and OWL a case sensitive execution of a knowledge intensive task can be supported.

Hence, in the next section, Modeling Approach, we discuss the business rule paradigm and SOA paradigm (basically BPEL). Thereafter, we propose our approach describing modeling of variable processes and how to execute the process model. In the following section, Run Time Approach, we describe the business rule engine RHEA, which would present the run time execution of the approach. Thereafter, we conclude with a summary and future works.

MODELLING APPROACH

As mentioned in the introduction, we still use BPEL for the structured part. BPEL provides an XML based structure to describe processes through the combination of web services. Some key notions are as follows: (Alonso et.al. 2004)

- Process Information: *<bpel:process>* tag encloses the description of the whole process. It contains information about the process like the name of the process, process namespace etc.
- Imports: *<bpel:import>* tag has the information of the WSDL files, filenames and namespaces, which have been referred in the BPEL process.
- Partnerlinks and variables: *<bpel:partnerlink>* gives the name of the partner link and its partnerLinkType. The partnerLinkType associates the ports, which in turn associate the variables to this partnerlink. *<bpel:variable>* gives the information of the variables which include messageType which is napped to a WSDL message.
- Flow: *<bpel:flow>* tag encloses the flow of the process. It encloses information of link between activities (*<bpel:link>*), copy activities (*<bpel:copy>*), receive and reply activities(*<bpel:receive>* and *<bpel:reply>*) and finally the flow tree which consists of iterative encapsulated constructs like sequences, split etc. (e.g. *<bpel:sequence>*). To be more explicit *<bpel:flow>* tag only encloses the constructs at the highest level. All the iterative lower level constructs are enclosed within the scope of the tags of their parent constructs. The constructs which are to be run in parallel can be modeled by the split construct. All conditional branches can be modeled by IF-DO construct and all the sequential activities can be modeled by sequence construct.

However, BPEL provides only predefined control constructs which is useful for structured processes but lacks flexibility for unstructured process parts. So, a component is necessary, which can be easily integrated in a BPEL process, but is responsible for the execution of a knowledge-intensive process part. Instead of modeling all possible process parts, a rule based approach is used, which is able to determine during run time the process flow for the specific business case. In this part the case, the activities which have to be invoked depending on the case and the business rules which specify the conditions and actions have to be modeled.

Business Rules are explicit statements to govern business behavior (Ross 2003), (von Halle 2002). Several classification schemata for Business rules formalization exist, but since it is well understood and comprehensive, we follow the classification of Barbara von Halle to explain the different kinds of rules. The rule classification depicts business rules into the following main components:

- **Terms:** A term is a phrase which has a specific meaning for the business in some context.
- **Facts:** A fact is a statement expressing relationships between two or more terms.
- **Rules:** Rules are declarative statements that apply logic or computation to information values.

Barbara von Halle splits rules into five subclasses. Amongst others she defines action enabling rules as rules which trigger another rule or a process (step), if the condition holds. This action

Figure 1. Simplied order process

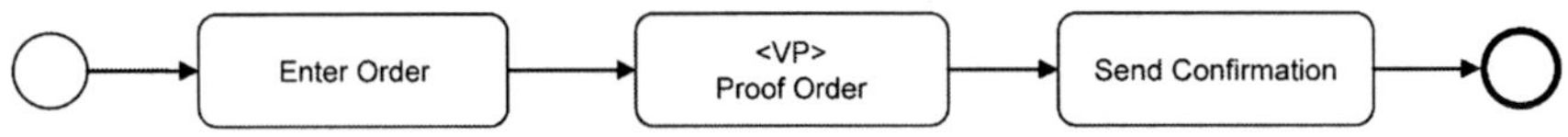

enabling rules helps to trigger the process adaptation. In the condition part of a rule the necessary property values of a case and the necessary action can be specified.

Geminiuc from Oracle proposes also a concept for combining business rules with BPEL to support decision points (Geminiuc 2006), which has the main goal to decouple the interpretation and execution of rules in application independent services. Another approach focuses on integration of BPEL with different rule-based systems, by providing a service bus (ESB) as middleware for the service-oriented architecture (Rosenberg 2005). These approaches support decision points and not to achieve flexibility in process orchestration and choreography.

Additionally, our work is related to business rule approaches. For instance, one approach using action enabling rules is represented by (Beer et.al. 2007). In their approach ECA (Event, condition, action) rules are used to provide users with tailored messages related to their current situation (context). In (Bider et.al. 2006) an approach is represented to activate knowledge using rules for planning.

To illustrate our approach we want to introduce a business process for running a credit check. The simplified process is illustrated in **Fehler! Verweisquelle konnte nicht gefunden werden.** using BPMN[1]. It contains a structured part that determines, first the order should be entered, second the order is proofed and a confirmation is lastly send to the customer. Depending on the entered data of the order, the tasks "Proof Order" can consits of several additional sub tasks have to be performed. It may range from proofing if the ordered products are in stock to checking the credit volume for a new customer. Instead of modelling every contrivable case and event, we mark this knowledge-intensive tasks by using the object type *variable process <VP>s*. This object type is related to a pool of possible sub tasks, which are related to action enabling rules. These rules determine at run time the appropriate.

For the case specific specification of the knowledge-intensive process part during run time, the actions, the case and the business rules have to be modeled. Therefore, several possible actions can be executed depending on the case, we use a task pool, which contains all sub tasks, which might be executed. To specify the condition when the actions have to be executed we use rules.

(Figure 2) shows a simplified example for such a task pool. If the customer is new he has to be added to the information system and a limit has to be set on his credit. If the order amount is lower than his limit, he will get a confirmation otherwise the order has to be rejected. This example can be modeled in the traditional way. But to make the formalization and the process execution clearer we assume that this is a variable process.

We define four activities:

- **Activity(A)CheckAndSetCreditVolume**: This activity checks and sets the high of the credit limit of the customer.
- **Activity (B) RejectOrder**: RejectOrder is invoked, if the order has to be rejected.
- **Activity (C) AddCustomerToSystem:** If a customer is not registered in the information system, he has to be added.
- **Activity (D) ApplyOrder:** ApplyOrder is executed, if the order can be applied.

Figure 2. Brief example

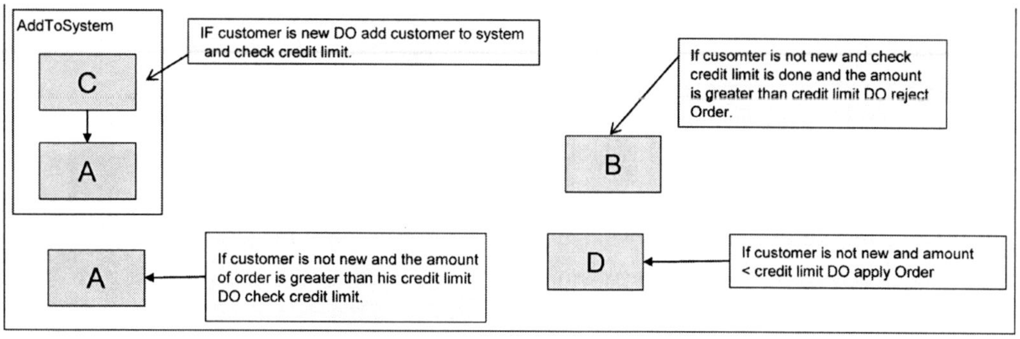

For demonstrating reasons we assume, that a new customer has submitted an order. Therefore, she is not registered in the system, she has to be added to the system and her credit limit has to be set. After invoking activity A, C needs to be executed. They can be modeled as a sequence, because this has to be done by every new customer in every case.

In order to be validated and executed, the business rules and processes have to be represented in a language with well-defined semantics. Current business rule systems only have simple formalism with weak semantics for representing facts and terms. Extending the expressiveness towards ontologies has the advantage of higher expressiveness and the chance to use inferences. As a consequence, since the procedural knowledge must be highly integrated with declarative knowledge, a rule language must be available in which all rule types can be expressed and which can be integrated with ontologies. Therefore, we use OWL and SWRL to express terms, facts and business rules, while the process models are represented in OWL-S.

Figure 3. Concepts of the case ontology

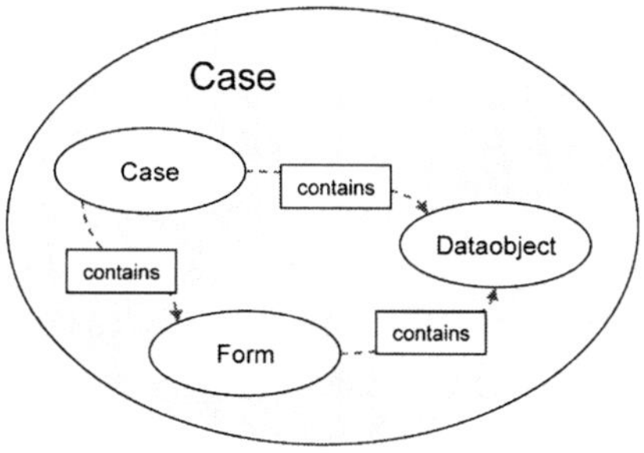

To model variable processes we use the following phases:

1. Creation of an ontology, which is used to represent the case.
2. Representation of tasks of the variable process part in OWL-S.
3. Creation of rules.

Stage 1. Creation of An Ontology To Express The Case

To be able to present the case an ontology is used. Similar to the case handling (van der Aalst and Weske 2005) we focus on the case which has to be handeld. The case contains for each knowledge-intensive process part of a process several forms which represents a view on the case. The forms contain all data objects which are necessary to perform the knowledge-intensive process part. Referring to the example, the concept form can contain as sub class the customer including the attributes name and address.

The terms represented as concepts in the case ontology and facts defined as properties are used to create the rules. These rules determine during run time depending on the state of a specific form (which is represented as an instance with its property values) the process adaptation.

Stage 2. Represent of Tasks

Now that we have defined the case, we have to model the sub tasks which might be executed depending on the state. The tasks of the knowledge-intensive process part are modeled using OWL-S. The sub tasks are represented as OWL-S atomic processes. If during build time a specific order of sub tasks can be specified, the atomic processes can be combined to a compositeProcess using control constructs like sequences or switches. Referring to our example, if a new customer should be added to the system and afterwards, her credit limit should be set is modeled as a composite process.

Regarding the four activities, the process ontology should contain four instances of the concept *atomicProcess*, *AddCustomerToSystem*, *CheckAndSetCreditLimit*, *applyOrder* and *rejectOrder*. The sequence is represented by *AddToSystemSequence*, which is an instance of a control construct Sequence.

Stage 3. Creation of Rules

After these two steps the action enabling rules can be created. On the one hand we can define the condition using the case ontology and on the other hand we can define the actions, which have to executed at a specific state. Hence, we use ontologies to express both condition and actions we use the rule language SWRL, which combines OWL and RuleML.

For the example we have created four rules. The following rule expresses if the customer is not new and the amount of the order is less than or equal to his credit limit:

```
customer(?x) and
hasOrdered(?x, ?o) and
amount(?o, ?a) and
creditLimit(?x, ?c) and
status(?x, "regular") and
swrlb:lessThanOrEqual(?a, ?cl)
   → atomicProcess(applyOrder)
```

During runtime, the state of the case is checked, and if the status of the customer is regular and the amount of the order is less than or equal to his credit limit, the atomic process (applyOrder) is invoked.

RUN TIME APPROACH

As mentioned before, we still use BPEL for the structured process part. The unstructured parts are orchestrated and invoked by an additional component which can be integrated easily into the BPEL process. So, we implement the additional component as a web service.

The component, which is able to execute the unstructured process part, was realized during the FIT-Project[2] and is called RHEA. RHEA provides the following features:

- Integration of ontological inferences with rule execution
- Invocation of rule engine for context-adaptive process execution by workflow-engine.

The structured process is executed by a BPEL engine. For testing reasons we used Active BPEL engine[3]. Everytime, a knowledge-intensive process part should be executed RHEA is integrated in the BPEL process during design time and during run time invoked. Then, RHEA controls the execution of the variable process part.

Therefore, RHEA is implemented as a web service it has to know the case, which has to be performed, the actions and the rules. So, the invocation of RHEA needs three input parameters. One input contains the rules, one the URIs of the case and process ontologies and the case relevant data must be given. These inputs are necessary knowledge to execute rules.

These inputs are transformed and used within RHEA in several steps. The first three steps transform the given data in an appropriate format, so that in step 4 the rules can be executed. Afterwards, the result is analysed and the actions given as OWL-S which have to be executed are transformed into a BPEL process. After all, the BPEL process is executed. These steps are illustrated in (Figure 4). The components are described in more detail in the next sections.

OntologyManager

The OntologyManager adds case relevant data of the current case to the domain ontology. The case relevant data is given as an array of RDF-triples.

```
//Set Order_123 as instance of
Order
data[0][0] = namespace + "Or-
der_123";
data[0][1] = rdfNamespace +
"type";
data[0][2] = namespace + "Or-
der";
//Set amount = 4.500
data[0][0] = namespace + "Or-
der_123";
data[0][1] = namespace +
"amount";
data[0][2] = namespace +
"4.500";
//Relate order to customer Paul
data[0][0] = namespace + "Paul";
data[0][1] = namespace + "hasOr-
dered";
data[0][2] = namespace + "Or-
der_123";
```

Above a triple is shown, which specifies the *Order_123* of customer *Paul*, by using RDF triples. The first part defines *Order_123* as an instance of *Order*. The second triple specifies the *amount* and the last triple relates the order to the customer *Paul*.

Figure 4. Architecture of RHEA

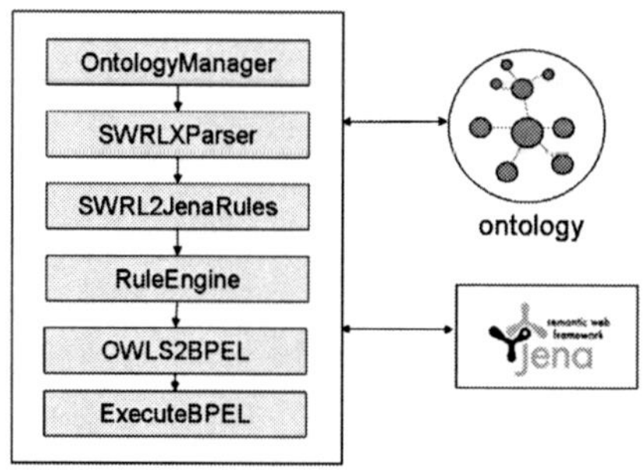

The OntologyManager adds this data as instances and property values to the case ontology by parsing the ontology and searching for the URIs. For the first triple, the manager searches for the concept with the URI <namespace> Order and adds the instance *Order_123* to this concept. After it, the *amount* is set, by adding the value at the data property of *Order_123*. After all, the *Order_123* is related to the customer *Paul*, by using the object property *hasOrdered*.

SWRLXParser and SWRL2JenaRules

Both parsers, SWRLXParser and SWRL2JenaRules, are used to parse the rule sets and to add these rules to the knowledge base of the rule engine. We have adapted the rule engine provided by the JENA2[4]-Framework. The reasoner supports rule based inference over RDF graphs and provides forward, backward chaining and a hybrid execution model (Reynolds 2007). Hence, JENA2 uses another format for expressing rules we transform SWRL to the format used by JENA2.

The header and the body of a rule are separated in JENA2 using the symbol ->. So, first all body-atoms are transferred, the narrow is added and after all, the header is created.

Figure 5. Stages of OWL-S to BPEL

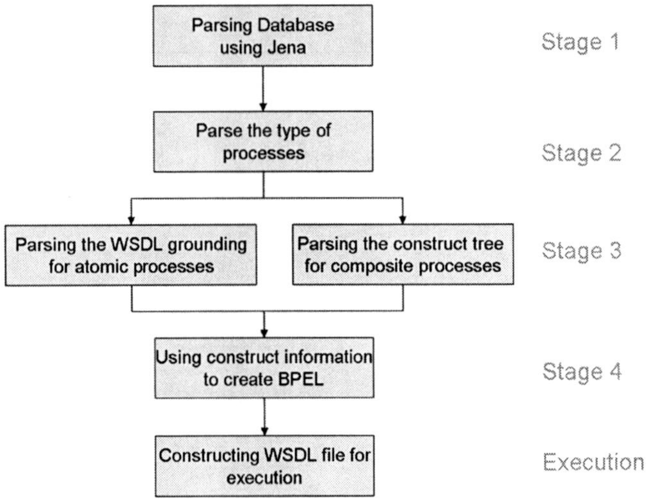

RuleEngine

After setting the knowledge, the rule engine can now be invoked. For RHEA we use forward chaining RETE engine provided by JENA2. We have extended the class RETEEngine by a functionality which stores the fired consequences for an execution in a list. If a condition holds, an instance of an atomic or composite process is fired and added to the list. According to the example shown in last sections, if the Order of Paul is less than or equal to his credit limit, the atomic process applyOrder is fired.

OWLS2BPEL

BPEL and OWL-S have a very similar process structure, and the similarity lying in the constrbucts which lay the framework for designing a process. There is a formulation of conversion from BPEL to OWL-S (Aslam et. al. 2006). Here, in lines to the goals of RHEA we propose a formulation of conversion of OWL-S processes to BPEL processes.

A complete conversion of OWL-S to BPEL requires parsing the OWL-S grounding class and creating the WSDL to be referred by the BPEL process for execution. This is explained in the next section. Assuming the WSDL has been created, here we explain the export of OWL-S process information to BPEL. (Figure 5) shows the approach which stages are described in more detail.

Stage 1. Parsing the Owl-S Ontology Using Jena2 and Storing It as RDF Triplets In A Database.

In this stage using the *DBConnection* object type we obtain a connection and then pass this connection as a parameter to the ModelMaker object type which invokes the *createModel* function with the OWL-S file as parameter and hence stores the ontology in the form of RDF triplets in the database. This database can be queried using SPARQL query language.

Stage 2. Parsing the Type of Processes

In this stage we use the following SPARQL queries.

First query:

```
SELECT ?t\n
    WHERE {
  ?t <&rdf;#type>
  <&owls;#AtomicProcess> }
```

Figure 6. (Stage 1.) OWLS file to JenaDB

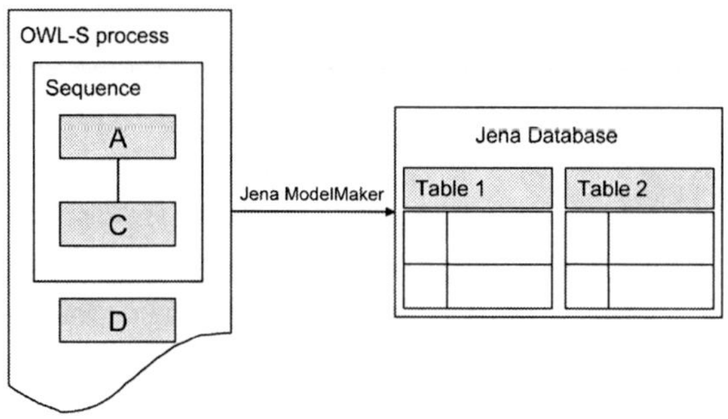

Figure 7. (Stage 2.)Table structure for each composite and atomic process

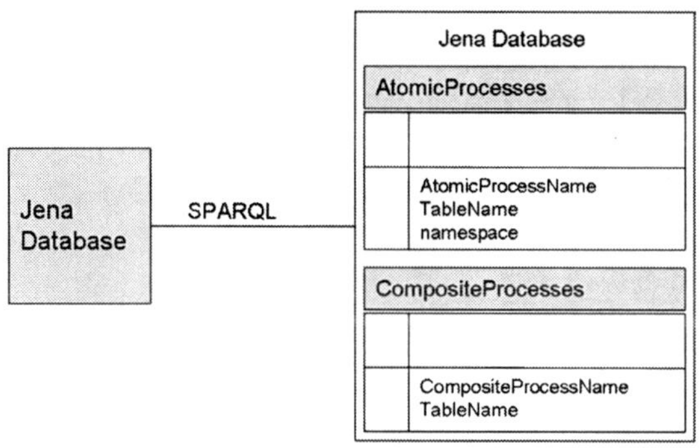

Figure 8. Querying for processes and table

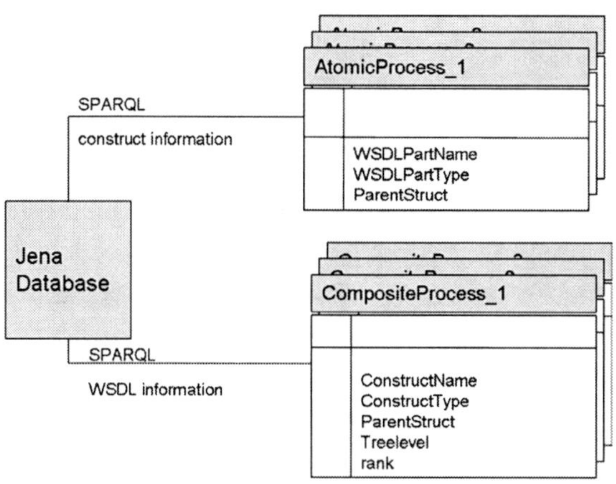

Second query:

```
SELECT ?t\n
      WHERE {
?t <&rdf;#type>
<&owls;#CompositeProcess> }
```

From the first query we get the atomic processes and store it in a table named *atomicprocesses*. For example, there would be three entries namely A, C and D. We also store the name of the table and namespace entries for the processes. Similarly, for the Composite processes we make a table named *CompositeProcesses* with entries for each composite process and their respective *TableName*. Here we will have a single entry named *CompositeProcess_1*. This structure is depicted in *QueryingForProcessesAndTable*.

For each composite process we create a table, which stores the information of the construct tree.

Stage 3. (PART 1) Parsing the WSDL Grounding for Each Atomic Processes

Each process table for the atomic processes namely *AtomicProcess i* (for ith atomic process) consists of fields namely *WSDLPartName*, *WSDLPartType* and *ParentStruct*. For instance, we assume, we have a RDF triple after parsing the WSDL Grounding through Jena2 as follows:

```
<grounding:wsdlgrounding A>
<grounding.owl#wsdlDocument> <C>
```

When we query for a document for the above grounding namely *A*, we get *C*. Now, we store the information in the respective table with *A* as the *ParentStruct*, *grounding:wsdlDocument* as the *WSDLPartType* and *C* as the *WSDLPartName*. Similarly with appropriate SPARQL queries we extract information and store it in a MySQL database.

Later on this information is used through SQL queries to generate appropriate tags and partner links which has been later explained in the document. The queries used extract the WSDL information by first identifying the *atomicProcessGrounding* for the given *AtomicProcess*. This is done by querying by keeping the predicate as *owlsProcess*. The *ParentStruct* for this information is kept as the *ProcessName*.

We also query with *hasInput* and *hasOutput* as the predicate to extract information of *Inputs* and *Outputs*. These are also stored with the *ParentStruct* as the *ProcessName*. Thereafter, the \textit{wsdlDocument}, \textit{wsdlInputMessage} and \textit{wsdlOutputMessage} are identified by keeping appropriate predicates. They have *wsdlGrounding* as the *ParentStruct*. *wsdlGrounding* also acts as the *ParentStruct* for objects queried with predicates of *wsdlOperation*. Thereafter, this object serves as the *ParentStruct* for *wsdlPartTypes wsdl:operation* and *wsdl:portType*, which symbolize the *porttype* and *operation* information.

Similarly proceeding *Input* and *Output Message maps* are also extracted. Additionally, Binding information is extracted. Once all this information is made available in the tables they are later queried through SQL to construct copy tags, partnerlinks and other relevant tags.

Stage 3. (PART 2) Parsing the Construct Tree For Each Composite Process

Each process table consists of fields namely *ConstructName*, *ConstructType*, *ParentName*, *treelevel* and *rank*. *ConstructName* depicts the name of the construct, *ConstructType* represents the type of the construct i.e. sequence, split, until or others. *ParentName* represents the name of the parent construct. *treelevel* represents the depth of this construct in the tree and *rank* represents the rank of this child among the children of the parent construct.

Hence the parsing of the tree is done through a recursive procedure, where each recursion terminates at a construct with construct type as *Perform*. *Perform* is the construct type which implies that the node is an atomic process or a composite process and not a construct and hence there is no sub tree to be traversed.

At first the *composedOf* property is checked, which gives the construct with treelevel 0.

The entry of this construct has the parentName as the processName. Thereafter the ProcessTree function is called for this construct. It checks the components property for constructs other than *ControlConstructBag*, *ControlConstructList*, *If-Then-Else*, *Until and While*. For ControlConstructList and Bag, the first and rest properties are checked and the recursion is called for both the constructs returned, with the treelevel unchanged.

The *first* has a rank entry preceding the rank entry for *rest*. For Until and While the until-process and while-process properties are checked, respectively and the recursion is called with treelevel incremented and rank as 0. For If-Then-Else, Then and Else properties are checked and next recursion invoked with incremented treelevel and each having the rank as 1. Thus the recursive traversal takes place and terminates at a leaf which implies a Perform construct type. An example run is depicted in (Figure 9).

Stage 4. Using All the Parsed Data And Putting In The Bpel Framework

First, we construct the process tag. For this each atomic process has to be associated with a namespace. This information is stored in the table atomicprocesses. At the time of exporting this data is used to construct the process tag.

Thereafter, we construct the partnerlink and variable tags. For this, we need to parse the WSDL grounding information for each atomic process beforehand. Hence, we create a table respective to each atomicprocess and store all the WSDL information like InputMessageMap, OutputMessageMap, operation, porttype and others.

Figure 9. Parsing the construct tree

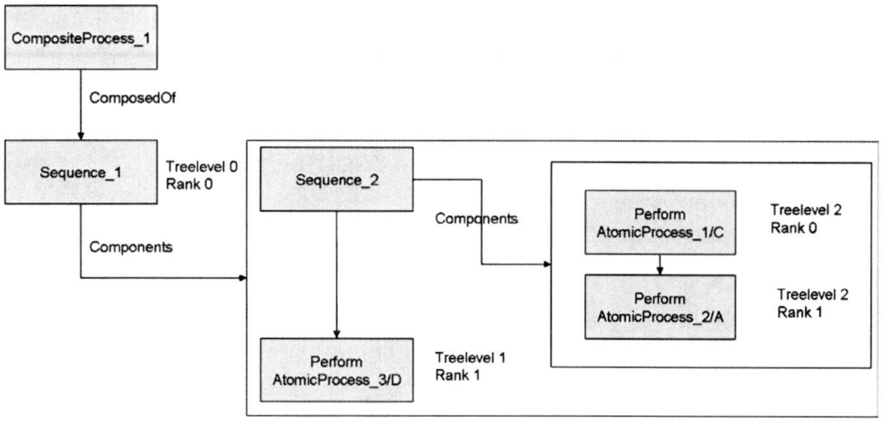

This information is stored in the table for each atomic process in the fields WSDLPartName, WSDLPartType and ParentStruct. These are the object, predicate and subject respectively in the RDF triple, for a grounding class property to the related atomic process. This is extracted for tag construction. Each atomic process in a given composite process is a partner process and each is assigned a partnerLink and PartnerLinkType which have a common basename e.g. PartnerLink_1 and PartnerLinkType_1. For getting the variable names for each partnerProcess we use grounding:wsdlInputMessage and grounding:wsdlOutputMessage. All of this information is made available in each atomic process table and is retrieved using SQL queries.

Thereafter, we generate the flow tags, which comprise of link tags, copy tags, receive and reply tags and construct tags. The Receive and Reply tags require processname, as we generate one partner link (named on the process) and use standard names for portTypes and operation, so that it can be added later in the WSDL.

As for the link tags, there are always four link tags generated with the source-target pair as ProcessName-CopyF, CopyF-MainConstruct, MainConstruct-CopyL and CopyL-ProcessName, where MainConstruct is the subject of composedOf property and CopyL and CopyF are the first and last copy tags generated. MainConstruct symbolizes the construct which envelops the whole process model. So all the inputs required by the processmodel are made available to the MainConstruct by CopyF copy tag, which copies all the inputs from the Receive process.

Similarly, all the outputs are made available to the Reply tag through the CopyL copy tag which copies the outputs form the MainConstruct to the variables of the Reply process. Thus the links are between the Receive and CopyF, CopyF and MainConstruct, MainConstruct and CopyL, CopyL and Reply and they are appropriately named as above.

The copy tags are of two types. The ones from TheParentPerform to the atomic processes and the others from the process to process. Hence checking the values of the fromProcess property for *TheParentPerform* we can generate the copy tags of the first kind. And for the other copy tags we need to query for fromProcess as the Atomic Process being considered and then check the TheVar and toParam properties to get the copy tags.

This information is already available in the respective atomic process tables, as it was parsed while extracting the wsdl information. To be explicit we extracted the binding information at that stage. Now to extract the binding information we query the table for each atomicProcess with the WSDLPartType as fromProcess and wsdl-

PartName as the name of the perform construct which executes the atomic process in question. Now as the result set we get all the processes which are providing inputs to that specific atomic process. Now, with each of these process names we query with them as the ParentStruct. We choose wsdl:TheVar and wsdl:ToParam as our predicates.

Result of these queries is the pair of variables to be used in the copy tag. Similarly, we get all the input copy tags for each process. The copy tags for the outputs are generated by taking care of as each output has to be bound to an input for a process. So, when all the processes input copy tags are generated the output tags get generated simultaneously. Now, the tags which are left are the end tags, the CopyL and CopyF tags. CopyL tags are generated in the same way. Only the destination of these copy tags is mentioned as TheEnd. As for the CopyF tags, these are generated by keeping the fromProcess object as the ParentPerform.

The construct tags are generated by using the information in the table of the composite process and the following mapping between the OWL-S constructs and BPEL constructs:

- OWL-S sequence to BPEL sequence
- OWL-S split to BPEL split etc.

Now, once we have the tags generated we order them under the flow tag. First,come the link and receive and reply tags. Thereafter, the copy tags from TheParentPerform and the tags to TheEnd. These two copy tags are though generated under the scope of a <bpel:assign> tag.

These tags are easily generated by putting the copy tag and the respective link tags under the scope of each assign tag. Thereafter, we generate the construct tags top to bottom by using the information stored earlier. At each perform we generate the invoke tag and the corresponding copy tags to that process. This way we fulfill the flow structure.

Once all the stages have been performed the BPEL file is created. But, this is still unexecutable without the WSDL file needed for reference. This is discussed in the following section.

ExecuteBPEL

For the BPEL generated to be executed we need to create the WSDL file, which comprises of all the information we have added like partnerLinks and partnerLinkType. This is the only information we have added as all the other information is already grounded in the already existing files for each atomic process.

Thus, as these are the values we have generated, we have the liberty of naming them. Hence, we have used a common base name for each partnerLinkType we have added. For instance, we have atomic processes named *A*, *C* and *D*. We have stored each one's WSDL information in a table named AtomicProcess_1, AtomicProcess_2 and AtomicProcess_3.

We have associated with them namespaces ns1, ns2 and ns3 and if two of them have same namespaces, we have given them the same namespaces and recorded the data in the atomicproceses table. Thus, now each of the above process is a partnerProcess and hence requires a partnerLink. Therefor, they are assigned the link-type pair as, PartnerLink_1-PartnerLinkType_1 and so on. These partnerlinks are also stored in the parent table which has all the data which might be retrieved later. These include namespaces and partner links and partner link types. These partner link types are stored alongside the tablename and the atomicprocessname. Hence, we know the corresponding data for each atomic process.

At the time of WSDL construction we add these partnerLinkType tags with these standardized names. The attributes of portType and operation come form the atomic process grounding information grounding:portType and grounding:operation respectively, which has already been parsed into the table for the concerned atomic process.

Hence, with this information added we have WSDL grounding for all the BPEL process information.

Thus, with the WSDL and BPEL files in place we are ready to execute the generated BPEL process.

Considering the example specified in (Figure 2), if we assume Paul is a new customer and the credit is greater than the set limit, then RHEA provides us with the OWL-S process as depicted in (Figure 10).

Hence, given the OWL-S process we parse it using the Jena2 API (Stage 1). This is depicted in (Figure 7).

Thereafter, we proceed to Stage 2, which is parsing the type of processes and creating appropriate tables. Here we have three atomic processes namely A, C and D and one composite process say CompositeProcess_1. Thus, the tables and the entries are as shown in (Table 1) and (Table 2).

Later in this stage we also create separate tables for each atomic and CompositeProcess which are filled later in stage (3) and (4).

Moving on with stage (3), in this stage we parse the construct tree for the composite process. The recursive algorithm mentioned above yields the field values for table CompositeProcess_1 as depicted in (Figure 10). To get an idea some of these values are depicted in (Table 3).

Moving on to stage (4), in this stage we fill the tables of each atomic process with the grounding information and later generate tags using the construct tree and grounding information. Here in (Figure 11) we depict the data used for generating respective BPEL tags and the operations

Figure 10. The OWL-S process

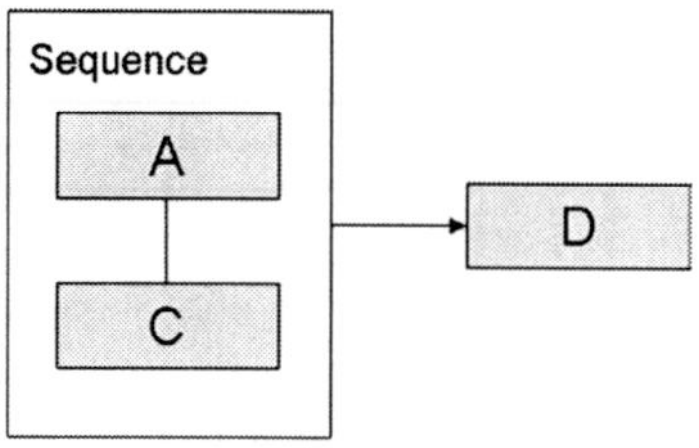

Table 1.

AtomicProcesses		
AtomicProcess-Name	**TableName**	**Namespace**
A	**AtomicProcess_1**	**ns1**
C	AtomicProcess_2	ns2
D	AtomicProcess_3	ns3

Table 2.

CompositeProcesses	
CompositeProcessName	**TableName**
CompositeProcess_1	CompositeProcess_1

Table 3.

Construct Name	Construct Type	Parentstruct	Treelevel	Rank
Sequence_2	Sequence	Sequence_1	1	0
Perform_D	Perform	Sequence_1	1	1
Perform_A	Perform	Sequence_2	2	0
Perform_C	Perform	Sequence_2	2	1

Figure 11. The BPEL tag generation, operations used and WSDL generated (it is a depiction)

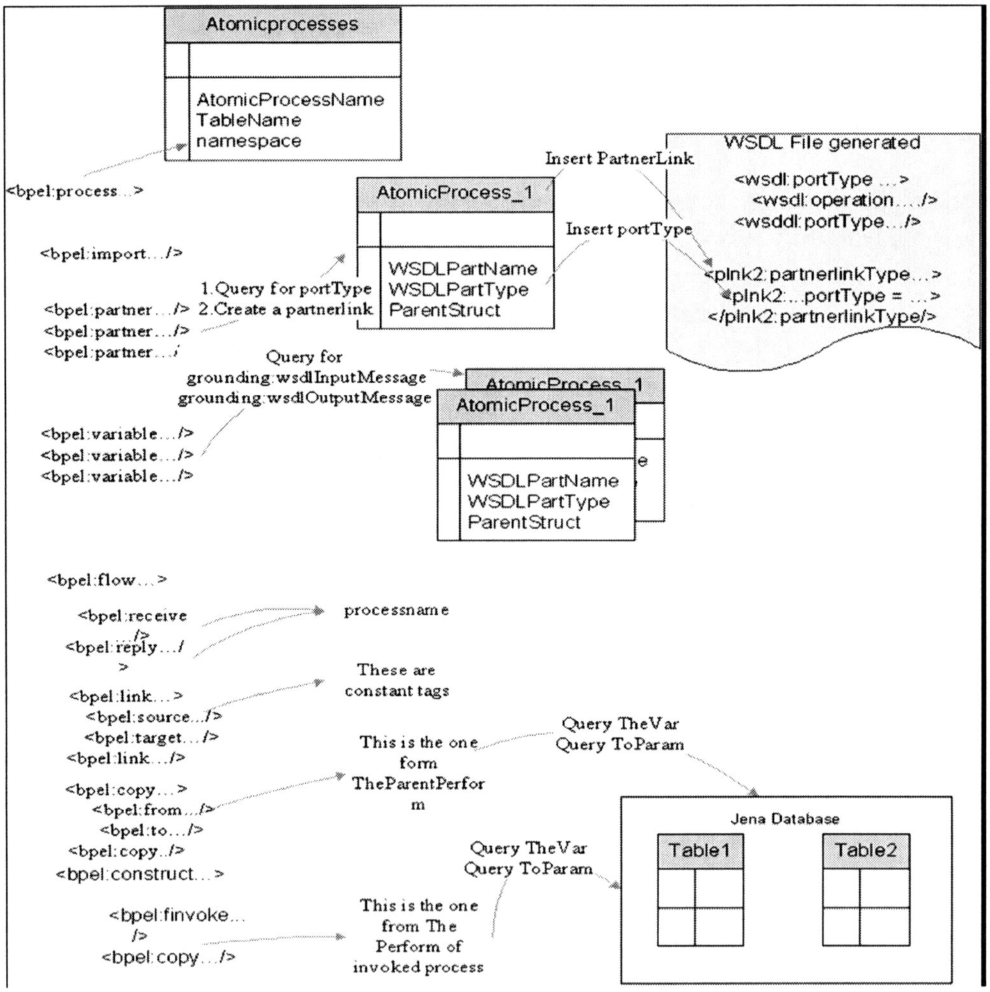

done to get the data required for constructing each tag. Please note that the <bpel:construct> used in the figure is not a real tag and is a generic notation for construct tags like <bpel:sequence>, <bpel:split> etc.

Finally, for execution we generate the appropriate WSDL file as depicted in Figure 11. It requires for us to query the portType and add it to the generated partnerLinkType tag. We also need to add new portTypes and operation for the partnerLinkType generated for Receive and Reply processes.

EVALUATION

One of the main components to make BPEL more flexible is the addition of RHEA, which supports retrieving the appropriate sub activities using rules during run time. So, RHEA has some important criteria which need to be fulfilled: the performance should be adequate, the consistency should be kept and RHEA should provide correct results.

Correctness

To evaluate the correctness of RHEA the open source JUnit[5] testing Framework was used. JUnit was originally written by Erich Gamma and Kent Beck and has been designed to write and run tests in the Java programming language.

The provided assertion methods can be used to test the correctness of RHEA, by specifying the expected results and comparing it with the actual values. If the actual value is unequal to the expected the test fails.

During the FIT project several rule sets have been created with the help of the end user. These rule sets are used to test RHEA. The workflow relevant data is specified and added to the knowledge base of RHEA. By specifying the workflow relevant data, it can be expected which conditions must be hold and therefore, which rule must be fired. The consequences of these rules are taken as expected results. After specifying all expected results all tests were executed and the results analyzed. The evaluation shows that all tests were successful and RHEA fires the rules and the results as expected.

Consistency Checking (Input and Dependency)

Another issue is to check the consistency. Rules consistency checking is similar to a source code compiler. Inconsistent rules can create errant behavior. Without a tool to check for these inconsistencies, locating the problem can be difficult in a large system.

The rule set should be provided in an xml-document according to the xml schema for SWRL provided by the W3C. If the document is not well-formed RHEA cannot execute the rules. Therefore, RHEA parses the document and errors occur an exception is thrown to the workflow engine. This is also tested using the in previous section mentioned JUnit testing framework. Instead of specifying the expected results expected exceptions can be defined. The tests shows, that an SWRLXParseException is thrown.

Also, the workflow relevant data need to be in a correct format. If the given workflow relevant data is incorrect, RHEA throws an "OntologyManagerException". This is also tested using JUnit.

If both data is given in the correct format, the data itself can be inconsistent when values should overwrite existing values. For example, if the workflow relevant data contains two times the birthday of a person. RHEA parses the workflow relevant data in the given order. So, the second data will overwrite the value of the first data. It would be better, if RHEA recognizes the action of overwriting and returns an exception.

Additionally, the consistency of rule sets must be checked e.g. if a rule set contains rules, which overwrites the results of each other. RHEA uses the first-in first-out strategy\cite{JBoss}; depth based strategy dictated by the order of activation. New activations are placed on the top of the agenda. Other strategies can easily be implemented, for example, complexity. This strategy takes into account the complexity of the conflicting rules. The more complex the rule, i.e. the more conditions it has, the more specific it is.

Performance: A Comparison with Other Semantic Rule Engines

JENA2 includes a general rule-based reasoner which is used to implement the RDFS and OWL reasoners, but is also available for general use. RHEA extends the JENA2 rule-based reasoner to support adaptive internet-based workflow engines.

In order to show the performance of the extended rule engine RHEA is tested against other semantic rule engines. Pellet and KOAN2 support also a subset of SWRL called DL-Safe-Rules.

Pellet[6] is an open source in Java OWL-DL reasoner and commercially supported by Clark and Parsia LLC[7]. Pellet is based on the tableaux algorithms for expressive Description Logics (DL) and supports the full expressivity of OWL-DL. Additionally, Pellet supports the subset of SWRL, called DL-Safe Rules. But, Pellet does not feature class atoms with anonymous classes and what is more important for the FIT-project data valued

Figure 12. Evaluation with parsing the ontology

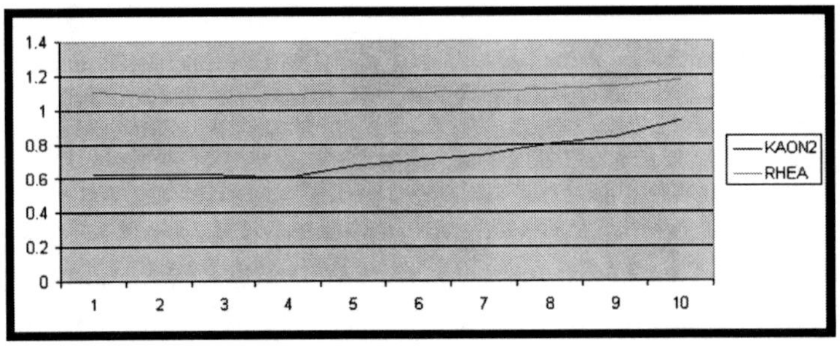

property atoms and built-in functions. SWRL files can be loaded into Pellet and rules will be parsed and processed. Rules support is enabled by default, but the rules that use one of the mentioned unsupported features will be ignored (or an exception will be thrown)[8]. However, for FIT these build-ins are very important, because comparisons have to be made. So, an adequate result cannot be reached by comparing RHEA with Pellet.

KAON2[9] is a reasoning framework, which supports OWL-DL, DL-safe SWRL rules and F-logic. It is available as a precompiled binary distribution and is free of charge for universities for noncommercial academic usage.

The test data is chosen from the end partner. For test reasons a small ontology is chosen, because the parsing of the ontology is not part of this test. The test rule sets contain first just one rule with one axiom and is enlarged to 128 rules.

For the first test, both frameworks have to parse the ontology and need to add instances and property values in their knowledge base. After it, the rules are parsed and executed.

The diagram (Figure 12) shows the comparison containing all phases. The x-axis shows the number of the rule set (rule set 1 contains only 1 rule, whereas number 10 contains 128 rules). The y-axis shows the seconds which are necessary for the execution of the rules.

It can be easily seen, that the performance of KAON2 is at the beginning much better than RHEA. But, the graphic also shows that the expanding pitch of RHEA arises not so much than KAON2.

(Figure 13) illustrates the results of the two phases, containing only the parsing and execution of the rules. The ontology is already loaded and the test data is already added. The diagram presents that RHEA performs better than KAON2.

The worse performance during the first test is due to the fact, that JENA2 is used to parse the ontology and JENA2 needs more time to parse and load the ontology than KAON. Therefore, RHEA

Figure 13. Evaluation without parsing the ontology

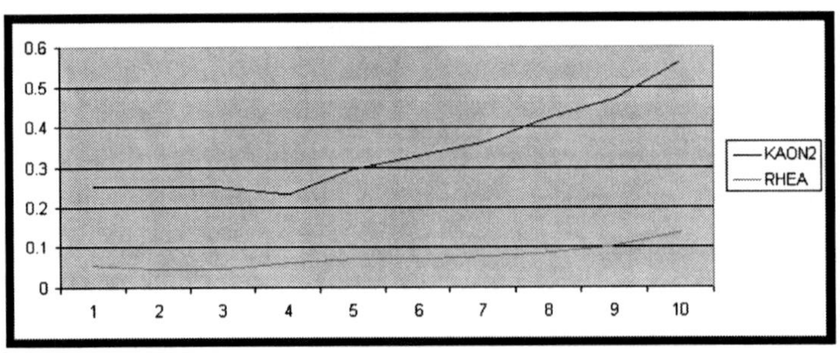

is useful for rule sets with a high number of rules and it is helpful to load the ontology only one time, which is applicable for the most processes, because a process contains more than one activity which is related to more than one rule sets.

Additionally, KAON2 does provide the DL-safe subset of SWRL, it does not support existential variables in the consequent of rules which we need in order to introduce new individuals.

To improve the performance of RHEA it is useful to combine the reasoner of Pellet with JENA2. The Pellet reasoner as the starting point is feeded with the initial ontology, where as RHEA can be used, to execute the rules. This option can be implemented in the further versions of RHEA.

To sum up, the correctness tests show that RHEA returns for the given test data the correct data. The consistency-checks are made, by throwing exceptions or using the first-in first-out strategies. The performance-test shows that RHEA is faster than KAON2, if the ontology is already loaded.

OWL-S to BPEL Optimizations

Starting with OWL-S to BPEL conversion we can observe that it is a multiple parsing algorithm. Also the construction of BPEL is serialized after the parsing. Hence here we would want to speculatively propose an algorithm which might improve the performance of the algorithm. Here we would theoretically derive the performance increase for the same.

We will break the evaluation in possible optimizations which are as follows:

1. Parallelization of atomic process identification and parsing the wsdl grounding information: Currently we have two stages in the algorithm which serialize the identification of atomic processes and the parsing of the associated grounding information for each atomic process. Currently theoretically the order of this step is as follows.

Lets say atomic process query takes 'm' time and wsdl grounding query for each atomic process takes 'n' time. Now the current algorithm time complexity for this step is O(m+K*n) where K is the no of results of the first query (i.e. the number of atomic processes in that particular tree)

Now lets say we parallelize this step. Lets say at each result of the query we parallely spawn a query for the grounding information. Hence the order complexity would look something like:

As SQL query would go serially through the database, we can assume that the time for one result would be 'm/K'. Now at (m/K) + (n) the first atomic process will finish. At 2m/K + n the second atomic process will finish. So on at m + n all results will finish. Hence this optimization will give us O(m+n) complexity. Hence if m+n is constant (as in SQL it will be) the optimization is as follows:

```
O(K) → O(1)
```

2. Top-Bottom recursive identification of nodes in stage 3 compared to bottom to top identification of nodes: Currently as explained in section 4 we use a top to bottom recursive approach of parsing the tree. Hence lets consider the given example used in section 4. In that particular example we have 5 nodes:

```
(Composite process_1)
(Sequence_1) (atomic process_d)
(atomic process_a) (atomic
process_c)
```

Another optimization could be parallelizing the tree search with the previous stage. As and when we discover the atomic processes(the end nodes) we start spawning parallel threads for discovering path to the zero node (node at tree level 0). Hence in the given example where we currently take O(4k) (where k is constant time taken to identify one edge) we would take O(2k) (as 2 is the maximum depth). Also combined with the previous optimization we move from:

```
O(K + |V| + E) -> O(1 + h)
Where H is the height of the
tree
V is the vertex set and E is the
edge set of the tree
```

Though in the current approach this is not possible as we detect nodes top to bottom. Hence we need to change the detection form bottom to top

3. Updation optimization with breadth-first search: So now this is a recursive approach which is a depth wise tree search instead of a breadth wise tree search. The first suggestion is to convert this to a breadth wise tree search. The basis of this suggestion is in the node ordering breadth wise search outputs. Currently there is an overhead of O(k) (where k is a constant) with each update of node information, in calculating the tree level information. With breadth wise search every recursion no is the tree level information. Also the node ordering is breadth based (basically all nodes on the same level are output sequentially), which is what we need as this is the order in which we update the information.

4. Parallelizing the BPEL formation with tree search: Currently once we parse the whole tree structure we do a second parse of the stored tree level information and parent-> child edges to generate tag/indent information (for xml formation). Now here we do a depth first traversal again to generate tags. This is best suited for tag generation as we go from zero to the end node to generate recursive tags. Though the optimization steps in to avoid this second traversal as in huge graphs this might be costly. Again as and when we detect atomic processes end nodes we generate atomic process tags. Thereafter we search for the parent and generate the parent tag until we reach the zero node. Doing this for each end node will cause redundant tag generation as there might be two xml tags for the same node which is incorrect. Hence to accommodate this rule we can maintain information of the opening tag created. And at the end of the formation all opening tags created should be enclosed with an ending tag. This improves the current tag generation throughput too.

Please note that this is a theoretical study of the implemented algorithm and implementation details will be disclosed as and when its implemented. Though the optimizations are very theoretical and implementable. Hence the double parse serialized algorithm can be a bottleneck when it comes to performace of RHEA. These optimizations will help us reduce the order complexity to O(|V| + E) whereas currently we can see its exponential/multiplicative in certain steps.

CONCLUSION AND FUTURE WORK

In this paper we have shown how unstructured process parts within the predefined control constructs of BPEL can be modelled, by replacing the unstructured parts using a new modelling object type.

During runtime, we have represented an approach of combining the static and dynamic parts by using BPEL, semantic technologies and business rules.

We have first explained how we can model these dynamic parts using semantic web technologies. After it we have shown, how this approach can be executed.

This approach leads to more flexible and adaptable processes, because the final process flow is determined during runtime and existing BPEL process flows can be easily adapted by calling the web service RHEA.

Further work must be done because of the return values of the executed sub tasks. If the relevant data changes because of the execution of a sub task, RHEA must be invoked again, because regarding to the changed values, other tasks can be invoked. In the approach we presented in this paper, we only invoke RHEA once.

Another problem can be recognizing by using OWL-S for our approach. We only use the two concepts AtomicProcess and CompositeProcess, so we do not use the whole standard of OWL-S.

REFERENCES

Alonso, G., Casati, F., Kuno, H., & Machiraju, V. (2004). *Web Services, Concepts, Architectures and Applications*. Berlin: Springer-Verlag.

Aslam, M., Auer, S., Shen, J., & Herrmann, M. (2006). Expressing business process model as owl-s ontologies. In *2nd International Workshop on Grid and Peer-to-Peer based Workflows (GPWW 2006)* (pp. 400 - 415).

Beer, T., Rasinger, J., Höpken, W., Fuchs, M., & Werthner, H. (2007). Exploiting E-C-A Rules for Defining and Processing Context-Aware Push Messages. In *RuleML* (pp. 199-206).

Bider, I., Johansson, L., Perjons, E., & Striy, A. (2006). *Activation of Knowledge in an Integrated Business Process Support/Knowledge Management System* (pp. 13–24). PAKM.

Faustmann, G. (1998). Enforcement vs. Freedom of Action, An Integrated Approach to Flexible Workflow Enactment. *SIGGROUP Bull*, *20*(3), 5–6.

Hammer, M., & Champy, J. (1996). *Business Reengineering, Die Radikalkur für das Unternehmen* (7th ed.). Frankfurt am Main, Germany: Campus Fachbuch.

Hao, W., Gao, T., Yen, I.-L., Chen, Y., & Paul, R. (2006). An Infrastructure for Web Services Migration for Real-Time Applications. In *Service-Oriented System Engineering (SOSE '06), Second IEEE International Workshop* (pp. 41-48).

Henbury, C. (2007). *Two definitions of agility*. Retrieved August 31, 2009, from http://www.cheshirehenbury.com/agility/twodefinitions.html

Heravizadeh, M., & Edmond, D. (2008), Making Workflows Context-Aware: A way to support knowledge-intensive tasks. In A. Hinze & M. Kirchberg (Ed.), *APCCM '08: Proceedings of the fifth on Asia-Pacific conference on conceptual modeling* (pp. 79–88).

Hinkelmann, K., Probst, F., & Thönssen, B. (2006). Agile process management framework and methodolgy . In Abecker, A., Seth, A., Mentzas, G., & Stojanovic, L. (Eds.), *Semantic Web Meets e-Government*. Menlo Park, CA: AAAI Press.

Iacocca Institute. (1991). *21st Century Manufacturing Enterprise Strategy, An Industry-Led View of Agile Manufacturing*. Bethlehem, PA: Leigh University.

JBoss. (2006). *JBOSS rules, conflict resolution*. Retrieved August 30, 2009, from http://legacy.drools.codehaus.org/Conflict+Resolution

Mitra, A., & Gupta, A. (2006). *Creating Agile Business Systems with Reusable Knowledge*. Cambridge, UK: Cambridge University Press. doi:10.1017/CBO9780511543432

Mitra, A., & Gupta, A. (2008). *Knowledge Reuse and Agile Processes: Catalysts for Innovation*. Hershey, PA: IGI Global.

Mutschler, B., & Reichert, M. (2006). Unleashing the effectiveness of process-oriented information systems: Problem analysis, critical, success factors, implications. *IEEE Transactions on Systems, Man, and Cybernetics*, *38*(3), 280–291.

OASIS. (2007). *Web Services Business Process Execution Language (WS-BPEL) Version 2.0*. Retrieved August 31, 2009, from http://docs.oasis-open.org/wsbpel/2.0/OS/wsbpel-v2.0-OS.html

Reynolds, D. (2007). *Jena2 inference support*. Retrieved August 31, 2009, from http://jena.sourceforge.net/inference/

Rosenberg, F., & Dustdar, S. (2005). Business rules integration in BPEL, a service-oriented approach. In *Proceedings of the 7th International IEEE Conference on E-Commerce Technology (CEC 2005).*

Ross, R. G. (2003). *Principles of the business rules approach.* Boston: Addison-Wesley Professional.

Rymer, J. R., & Moore, C. (2006). *The dynamic business applications imperative.* Retrieved August 31, 2009, from http://www.microsoft.com/presspassitanalyst/docs/09242007forresterdynamicbusiness.pdf

Smith, H., & Fingar, P. (2003). *BPM's third wave, based on extracts from business process management: The third wave.* Retrieved October 19, 2009, from http://www.fairdene.com/processes/BPTrendsMay2003BPM3SmithFingar.pdf

Van der Aalst, W. M. P., & Jablonski, S. (2000). Dealing with workflow change: identification of issues and solutions. *Computer Systems Science and Engineering, 15*(5), 267–276.

Van der Aalst, W. M. P., & Weske, M. (2005). Case Handling: A New Paradigm for Business Process Support. *Data & Knowledge Engineering, 53*, 192–162.

von Halle, B. (2002). *Business Rules Applied, Building Better Systems Using the Business Rules Approach.* New York: Wiley and Sons.

ENDNOTES

1 BPMN, Business process modelling notation, http://www.bpmn.org/.

2 FIT, Fostering self-adaptive e-government service improvement using semantic technologies, http://www.fit-project.org/

3 Active BPEL engine, http://www.activevos.com/community-open-source.php

4 Jena2 is a Java Framework for building Semantic Web applications. The Web Site of JENA2 is available at: http://jena.sourceforge.net/

5 Website of JUnit http://www.junit.org/

6 http://pellet.owldl.com/

7 http://clarkparsia.com/

8 http://pellet.owldl.com/faq/rules

9 http://kaon2.semanticweb.org/

Chapter 2
A Framework for the Use of Business Activity Monitoring in Process Improvement

Owen Molloy
National University of Ireland, Ireland

Claire Sheridan
Accenture Information Management Services, UK

ABSTRACT

Process performance improvement initiatives can be significantly enhanced in terms of performance measurement and diagnosis by real-time performance, quality and traceability information. Currently available Business Intelligence (BI) and Business Process Management (BPM) systems struggle to provide sufficiently lightweight or flexible solutions for the needs of process improvement projects. In addition, current process modelling languages such as XPDL and BPEL provide little or no support for the inclusion of detailed process performance metrics. This paper describes a generic framework using event-based process modelling to support the definition and inclusion of performance metrics and targets within process models, and the calculation of process performance metrics at user-defined intervals. The iWise implementation of this framework is an XML and Web services-based infrastructure that uses this event-based model for enhancing process visibility using real-time process metrics. Users can adjust alert thresholds on key process metrics in real-time. iWise also evaluates events for outlier or out-of-bounds events as they are processed. It uses an integrated rules engine, leveraging semantic technologies to write rules which are tested as process-related events occur in real-time.

INTRODUCTION

Process Improvement has been around as long as there have been processes. Since mankind has first repeated an action in order to reproduce a certain result you could argue that we have been engaged in processes. Naturally the complexity of these processes will vary – for example there is quite a difference in complexity between boiling an egg and delivering a 5-course banquet to a packed dining hall with military precision. On the other hand there is clearly a process which can be followed in both cases, with the aim of producing a result of predictable high quality, at

DOI: 10.4018/978-1-61692-016-6.ch002

Figure 1. Transformation Model of a Process

the time required, and with minimum use or waste of resources. What is also clear is that if you can't deliver to customers' expectations, they won't be coming back to you with repeat orders.

The current economic climate also highlights any internal inefficiency that a company may be carrying. With competition willing to cut costs to win orders it is vital that we are able to deliver as efficiently as possible if we are to retain a profit margin. For many companies their actual survival may depend on finding and eliminating inefficiencies in their operations. This overall goal of delivering better, faster and cheaper goods and services, that the customer actually wants, is what we are striving for when we undertake Process Improvement. The difficulty with current Business Intelligence (BI) and Business Performance Management (BPM) systems in a Process Improvement context is that they are complex, expensive and require considerable resources and time to implement. This is counter to the need in process improvement for an agile way to model, measure and analyse processes as per the requirements of individual improvement projects. While there is currently a great deal of interest in BPEL, it is normally used to automate processes within a single company or division. If we wish to monitor and measure a typical supply chain process we come up against the problems of heterogeneous systems and standards for process execution, for example across HR, CRM, ERP, Finance. Business Intelligence (BI) systems are available to pull information from such disparate systems into a coherent view of business performance, but a significant cost in terms of time and resources. In addition, BI systems are not typically *process-aware*, *lightweight* and *agile* enough to be useful in most process improvement projects. In this paper we set out the context for process improvement initiatives, before presenting a solution to the problems just outlined.

BUSINESS PROCESSES

Before looking in depth at the methods and tools of process improvement it is important to establish a clear understanding of what business processes are about. At the highest level of abstraction we can consider a process as a collection of related tasks which are initiated in response to a particular event, which achieves a specific result for the customer of that process, to paraphrase the definition of Sharpe & McDermott (2001).

Possibly the simplest model of a process is shown in Figure 1. In this transformational model of a process we see that our process must deal with certain inputs (e.g. raw material, information) and produce outputs such as goods or services. The actual transformation itself could be a *physical* transformation in that the output is created from the combination of the input; it could be a *transactional* transformation such as the generation of airline tickets or the processing of an insurance claim; it could be *locational*, such as the transportation of goods from one location to another. Other examples include *informational*, involving the generation of useful information (such as a weather forecast) from raw data (such as meteorological data). In all businesses people are now beginning to think of what they do as processes. We will see later that this process thinking is vital to beginning on the path to process improvement. What is fundamental to our understanding of a process we wish to improve is that we can clearly identify the boundaries (start, end events) and scope of that process.

As we can see from Figure 2, processes will typically cross functional boundaries within and between organizations. This simple fact often proves the most revealing when working with com-

Figure 2. Cross-Functional Nature of Processes

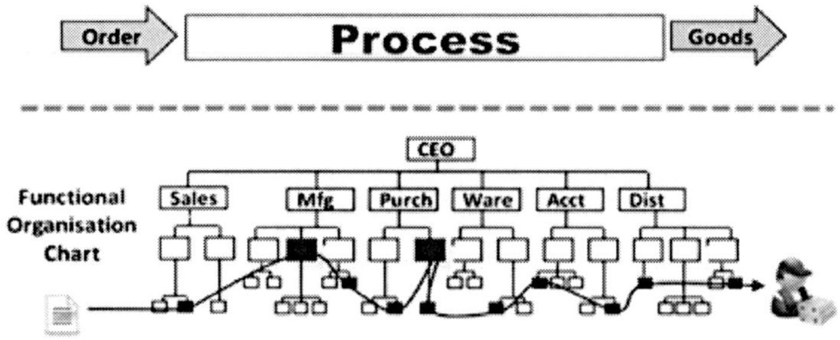

panies on process improvement initiatives. Too often, activities are optimized within functional boundaries. For example, individual departments will strive to optimize their own activities without sufficient regard to the impact on the overall process. In many instances reward mechanisms within a company are actually designed to foster such behaviour. Another result of this type of functional focus is that waste and inefficiency are more difficult to detect. In fact, lack of clarity of ownership of interfaces between departments and organizations, and poorly defined and managed service level agreements between them can contribute significantly to defects, delays and waste.

When we think of a simple example of a business process, such as ordering book through a bookshop, it is fundamentally important to remember that, while internally the process flows through multiple departments (such as Sales, Purchasing, Distribution, Accounting), from the Customers perspective it is a single process. Therefore to optimize the process requires us to optimize the end-to-end process, moving from a functional "silo" mode of thinking to a "process-oriented" approach. The difference in approaches is summarized in (Figure 3).

PROCESS TERMINOLOGY

It is useful at this point to discuss the common terminology to be used in describing process performance. As we see in (Figure 3), when we discuss processes we must remember that a process may itself be composed of a number of different sub-processes or activities which in turn may be decomposed into a set of smaller related tasks. There is no globally accepted standard terminology and it is common for some people to describe a process as an activity and vice versa. When modelling a process, the number of levels in the hierarchy must be decided on a case by case basis

Figure 3. Process vs. Functional Approach

Process Approach	*Functional (Traditional) Approach*
Emphasis on improving "how work is done"	*Emphasis on "who does what"*
Cross-functional coordination, teamwork stressed	*Frequent "hand-offs" among functions which remain largely uncoordinated*
"Systems" view – i.e., entire process is managed	*Management by function*

Figure 4. Process Hierarchy

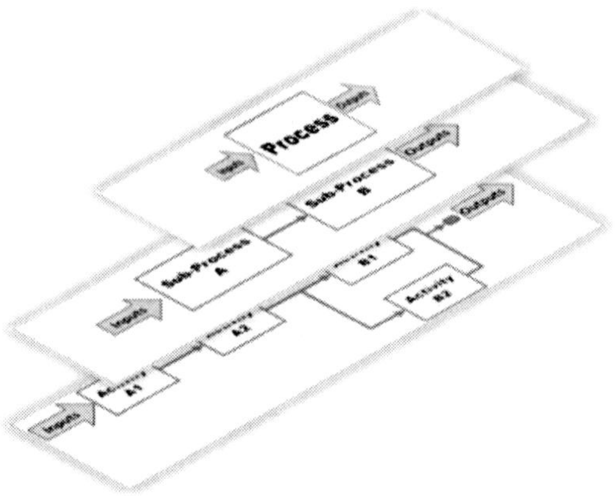

as needed. An interesting aspect of this, which is relevant from a management perspective, is that we should be able to monitor and manage performance at all levels in the hierarchy. Therefore, the concepts of yield, error rate, throughput etc. can be validly applied at all levels.

Some of the more common process measures which are of interest during the analysis of a business process are presented in (Figure 4). In a well balanced and resourced process, we would expect the process to be capable of working at the rate at which inputs (e.g. .orders) arrive. This requires each step in the process to be capable of working to this arrival "drumbeat". If not, we will have build-up of backlog of orders between process stages. Processes or activities whose capacity constrains our ability to work to this arrival rate are bottlenecks which constrain the entire process, and must be quickly identified and eliminated. Bottlenecks often have the effect of starving the following activities of sufficient work. This results in valuable resources such as people or machines being idle and underutilized. The strategies for elimination of bottlenecks will depend on our scope of action: it may be possible to add extra processing resources, or duplicate processes, or even to modify the arrival rate through negotiation with the customer.

As we will see, our focus in this work is not to dictate the improvement strategies, but to allow identification of the process performance issues. Another important measure is the delay time between activities. Time spent waiting adds to the overall throughput time (and hence customer delivery time) without necessarily adding any value. These are just few of the important ways of measuring process performance. Business Activity Monitoring (BAM) is the widely accepted term used to describe the monitoring of business activities (ideally in real time). BAM solutions normally incorporate the ability to identify process exceptions (where behaviour is outside defined limits), and to alter relevant personnel. BAM systems may be standalone or incorporate with Business Process Management (BPM) systems. BPM solutions typically include process and deployment capability as well as BAM. Van der Aalst et al. (2003) define BPM as "supporting business processes using methods, techniques, and software to design, enact, control, and analyze operational processes involving humans, organizations, applications, documents and other sources of information". A full study of BPM systems is outside the scope of this paper.

BUSINESS PROCESS IMPROVEMENT

The decision to undertake a process improvement project may be driven by a desire to improve customer satisfaction by delivering faster, cheaper products. It may be driven by the need to cut costs and drive out inefficiency, to compete or even survive. Regardless of whether an organization is purely commercial or non-profit, satisfaction of its customers' needs is fundamental to its survival and growth. Whatever the reason, organizations that decide to embark on a process improvement project will normally follow a well-defined meth-

Figure 5. Sample Process Measures

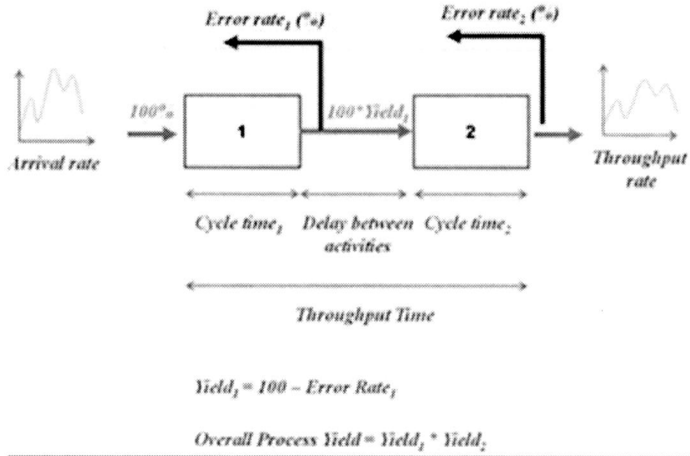

odology, such as Lean Six Sigma. Central to the notion of improvement is the need to measure. As the famous quote attributed to the physicist Lord Kelvin goes "If you can not measure it, you can not improve it".

A well-defined measurement system will provide direct and meaningful feedback for all involved with a process. With such feedback, it is possible to implement the changes necessary to further refine and improve the process. Some of the positive impacts of a measurement system listed by Harrington (1991) include:

- It focuses attention on achieving the organisation's mission.
- It shows how effectively resources are used.
- It assists in setting goals and monitoring trends.
- It provides the input for analyzing root causes and sources of errors.
- It identifies opportunities for ongoing improvement.
- It gives employees a sense of accomplishment.
- It provides a means of knowing whether you are winning or losing.
- It helps monitor progress.

Harrington identifies key characteristics of a business process that can help to identify areas where improvements can be made. Once areas are identified, specific measurement points of a process can be identified, modelled as a performance measure and measured. The key characteristics identified by him are:

- ***Flow*:** The methods for transforming input into output whilst respecting the process capacity and current supply and demand for the output.
- ***Effectiveness*:** How well customer expectations are met.
- ***Efficiency*:** How well resources are used to produce an output.
- ***Cycle time*:** The time taken for the transformation from input to output.
- ***Cost*:** The expense of the entire process.

Process Effectiveness is a measure of the quality of a process. Outcomes of an ineffective process might be unacceptable end-user products, customer complaints, re-work, backlogs, and/or late or incomplete outputs. Measurements of ***Process Efficiency*** would include *processing time*, *resources used* per unit of output, percentage of *value-added time*, percentage of *rework*,

Figure 6. Multi-dimensional categories of measurement (after Neely, 2005)

Quality	Time	Flexibility	Cost
Performance	Lead Time	Product Mix	Production Cost
Functionality	Process Time Cycle	Demand Variablity	Overheads
Reliability	On Time Delivery	Resource	Maintenance Costs
Maintainability	Demand Rate	Variability	
Value			

and *wait time* per unit. ***Cycle Time*** is an important measurement of a process. From the customers perspective it is a key measurement. It is seen as the time taken from the start of a process to completion of the process and includes all tasks involved which process, move, and store materials and information, as well as inspection and rework tasks. ***Costs*** mean normally the cost per unit of output. The actual means of assigning costs to production of goods or services will vary hugely from one organization to another, and is often difficult to compute. For example, many companies will not have sufficiently sophisticated cost models to be able to assign per unit costs by process or activity. Costs will include used of resources such as personnel and tools, other variable costs such as materials or telecommunications, and normally an allocation of fixed costs such as rent. It is important to note, however, that in the absence of a unit cost model by activity, it is difficult to accurately calculate the impact of improvements at activity level.

In performance measures, an organization must ask some important questions (Eccles, 1991): "Given our strategy, what are the most important measures of performance?", "How do these measures relate to each other?", and "What measures truly predict long-term financial success in our businesses?". Time, cost, quality and flexibility are the basic categories for assessing all business activities. Neely (2005) uses these categories to arrange individual performance measures for manufacturing processes and Forster (2006) analyzes these to propose patterns for business process improvement. It is accepted that the generic terms quality, time, cost and flexibility embody various dimensions, examples of which are listed in (Figure 6).

To illustrate the varying nature of performance measures and even the names given to annotate them, examples of metrics for measuring manu-

Figure 7. Sample performances measures in manufacturing (after Nudurupati & Bititci, 2005)

Cost	Quality	Flexibility	Delivery Reliability	Speed
Productivity	Customer Satisfaction	Response to Demand and Resource Variability	Reliability vs. Competition	Lead Time
Direct Costs	No. of Complaints		% on Time Deliveries	Cycle Time
Cost of Quality	Mean Time Between Failures		% Correct Orders	Order Processing Time
	Up-Time Percentage		Average Delay	Value Added as % of Cycle Lead Time
	Defects per Million Field			

Figure 8. KPI's Hierarchy (after Melchert, 2004)

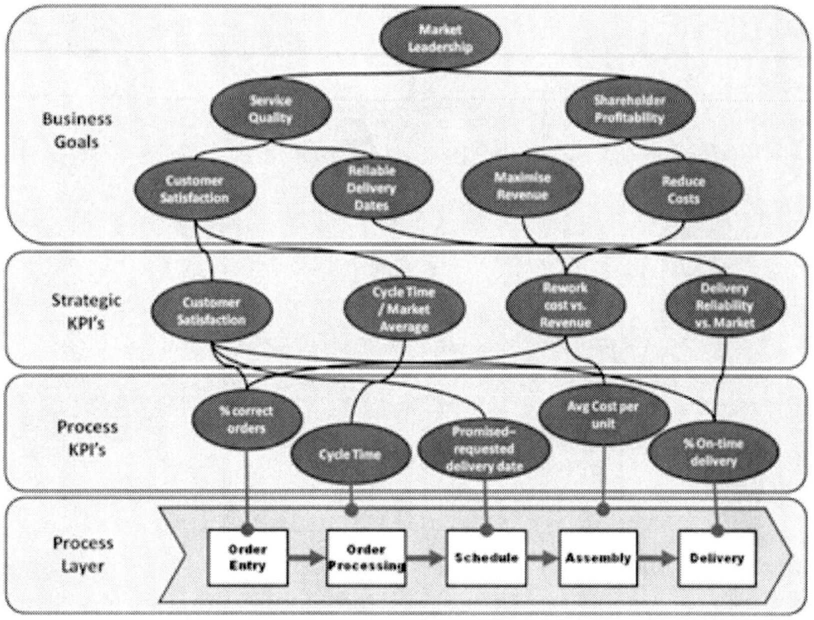

facturing performance are given in (Figure 7). These measures were collated from the research of Nudurupati & Bititci (2005) who identified 125 measures relevant to their taxonomy described above. In particular, cycle time metrics can be measured using objective data.

The question remains: what should I measure? The terms 'metric' and 'key performance indicator' (KPI) are important when discussing process performance. We understand a metric to be some measurement of a process or activity that is used to assess process performance, such as cycle time or yield. Metrics are defined in context of business objectives and they enable analysts determine if business objectives are achieved. A metric may be a simple number or form part of a more complex metric which are almost always referred to as KPIs. Devising metrics requires an intimate knowledge of relevant processes. It seems there is no universally accepted set of measures that can be directly applied to all processes. For a particular process, there can be aggregate metrics and per instance metrics. An aggregate metric is a summary view of a set of data (e.g. average throughput time). Per-instance metrics refer to a particular execution of a process (e.g. actual throughput time for a specific order).

Another important distinction is between operation and strategic metrics. There is another term tactical metrics, which is widely used without clear definition – in fact one of the most widely cited authors in this area, Melchert (2004) just uses the terms operational and strategic metrics. Juninger et al (2004) use the term Tactical Level KPI's to refer to aggregate operational level KPI's. It is more common, however, for people to understand aggregate operational level KPI's as Operational Level KPI's. The distinction between strategic and operational KPI's is an important one however. One of the key first lessons which we impart during Lean Six Sigma training to industry is to ensure that process improvement initiatives are undertaken within a strategic context. This strategic level direction and information is normally provided by senior team members and project sponsors. It is vital that we do not waste time and money optimizing a process which will be obsolete in six months, or in trying to improve

Figure 9. Lean Six Sigma (after Skalle et al, 2009)

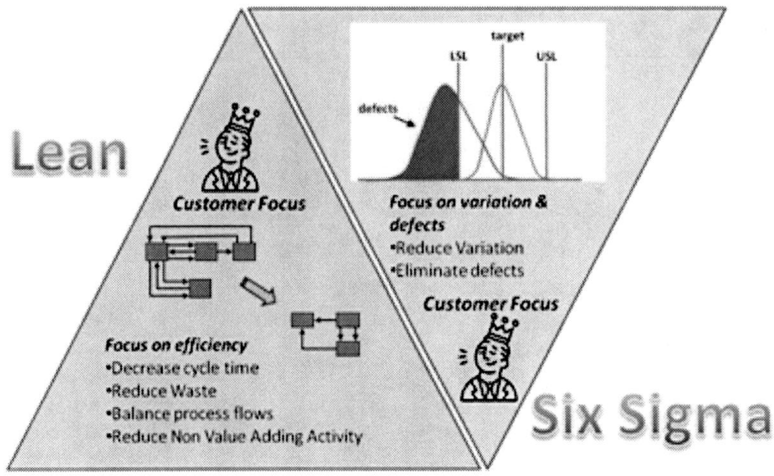

performance on a customer-focused KPI if that customer group represents a rapidly decreasing market segment!

Lean Six Sigma Process Improvement Framework

Although Lean and Six Sigma started out at different times in different situations, and were at one time considered by some as rival methodologies, more often than not they are considered as part of a joint strategy nowadays. Lean originated in the motor manufacturing industry, and is a business transformation methodology which evolved from the Toyota Production System (see Womack et al., 2007). In Lean there is strong emphasis on reduction of cycle time through elimination of waste, as well as balancing process flows. Six Sigma was developed in the 1980's in Motorola by Bill Smith (see Smith, 1993), as a quality initiative to eliminate defects by reducing variation in the semiconductor industry. However many of the concepts and tools normally used in Lean and Six Sigma have been around since the 1950's at least. These tools were developed over a number of years by the pioneers of quality such as Deming, Juran, Shewart, Taguchi, Ishikawa, Feigenbaum and Crosby. Many of their tools and techniques were originally developed and applied in Japanese industry before migrating to the US via the electronics and automotive industries. Walter Shewart for example recognized the role of variation in quality control, and he invented control charts while working for Bell Labs in the 1920's in order to differentiate between random and assignable sources of variation in manufacturing processes. He in turn inspired Deming, who pioneered Shewart's work in Japanese industry in the 1950's and 1960's.

Both Lean and Six Sigma focus on the process perspective, and strive to increase customer satisfaction while improving quality. Lean takes a holistic view, using process mapping, and workflow balancing to streamline processes, increase efficiency and reduce overall delivery times. Six Sigma takes a more analytical approach, using statistical methods to reduce variation and defects, while always keeping the customers "voice" and requirements in view.

The methodology life cycle used to implement Lean Six Sigma (LSS) is known by the acronym of the different project phases: *Define*, *Measure*, *Analyze*, *Improve* and *Control* – DMAIC. These phases of a process improvement project are normally repeated in a cyclical manner to deliver continuous improvement.

The DMAIC approach can be summarized (very briefly) as follows:

- ***Define:*** Capture the process requirements in a definable and manageable format. Include in this definition key measurements required for analyzing process execution times or other related performance information.
- ***Measure:*** Continuously calculate key process metrics as processes are executing using the model defined in the previous step. Metrics definitions may be based on cycle times and Six Sigma calculations.
- ***Analyse:*** Analyse enterprise processes for critical changes based on acceptable limits for key parameters, for example, cycle time measurements exceeding a given target. Provide analysis using applicable tools or techniques such as correlation graphs, pareto charts and cause-and-effect (fishbone or Ishikawa) diagrams. Today, more and more, Web-based dashboard portal technologies are used as a central point for process monitoring and visualization.
- ***Improve:*** Use dashboards to identify bottlenecks and inefficiencies in the process and propose improvements. Simulate suggested process improvements to evaluate effect on process design and implement as approved.
- ***Control:*** Use control charts and other techniques to verify predictable process states. If necessary, implement chosen course of action to modify process to improve performance.

In the situation where a process is implemented within a single ERP or workflow system, the generation of the data needed to analyse process performance is made easier by having only a single schema to contend with. However, even in these situations, it is often extremely difficult to extract the process-related performance data from the non-process-oriented database. This has been made simpler with the advent of BPEL-based process execution engines, wherein the process definition and process instance data are effectively co-located. Again however, in the majority of processes, and in distributed supply chains in particular, the process is distributed across multiple companies and systems. It is difficult to monitor process performance while contending with business process fragmentation and a variety of underlying systems and standards. The existence of various trading partners, standards, interfaces and infrastructure has also resulted in a fragmented information chain. Effectively marrying the myriad of systems and processes to glean the most important information will aid process performance monitoring techniques. Bolting on to in-situ applications and pulling enterprise data into a structured repository for centralised control and ownership can deliver value and benefits to an organization.

In the following section we outline the requirements for such an agile BAM solution, and look at some of the current technological challenges. In the remainder of this paper we present our solution to this problem.

BAM TECHNOLOGY

It is accepted that BI approaches provide an historical perspective on what has happened and do not provide insight into what is happening in an organization at any given moment (Nesamoney, 2004) and (Golfarelli, Rizzi, & Cella, 2004). BAM seeks to minimize decision latency by reducing the time between a business event occurring and a user making a decision about that event (Hackathorn, 2002). BAM technology is an extension of application integration and messaging technologies that taps into transactions of IT systems (Knifsend & Debb, 2005). To do so,

BAM technology relies on a robust definition of both processes and events to deliver punctual information to its end users. A BAM system must be able to (Nesamoney, 2004):

- detect events occurring in enterprise systems relevant to the activity being monitored
- calculate information for temporal processing
- integrate event and contextual business information on the fly delivering quality data
- execute business rules to set thresholds according to key performance indicators and other business-specific triggers
- provide intuitive interfaces for presenting rules and metrics

DeFee (2005) describes four important modules required for a serious BAM solution: an *event processing* module, a *process definition* module, a *monitoring* module, and a *visualization* module. To this should of course be added the ability to execute *business rules* on KPI's and their threshold levels. We will now explore in more detail this core set of BAM modules and some of the related research.

EVENT PROCESSING MODULE

Event processing refers to the extraction and collection of business data as events are detected in the source systems. The relevant event and business data, once extracted, may be loaded and transformed by the processing software or it may be manipulated by the extraction software before being loaded into a central staging area for processing. Vasilecas & Bugaite (2006) outlines the definition of events into three categories: a business event, an Information Systems event, and a software event. However, real-time event stream processing is not reserved entirely for business usage. Critical care research activity uses event processing technologies combined with SOA-based solutions to deliver critical patient data to clinicians in real-time (McGregor & Eklund, 2008), (Stacey & McGregor, 2007). Event processing modules may include Complex Event Processing (CEP) capabilities, as described by Luckham (2002). Fu et al (2005) describe an intelligent event adaptation mechanism for detecting and transforming IT-level events into a standard event format called the Common Base Event (CBE) and propagating these events to a Common Event Infrastructure (CEI) where a Business Performance Management system can process these events to generate KPIs. As it will be seen, the contribution described in this paper differs from Fu et al. in that an event payload will be defined that contains business data relevant in the context of the event. Collating events and business data means that data is held centrally for faster access.

As a new technology, EDA and CEP are lacking a formal definition process. In contrast, process modelling specifications have developed rapidly in recent years leading to overlapping efforts and the rise of de-facto standards as a result of backing from consortiums of large corporations. The OMG issued an RFI focusing on the standardization of Event definition and the relationship between EDA, CEP, BPM and SOA. Questions proposed include, amongst others:

- What is an event?
- What are the key/mandatory elements that describe an event?
- What are the major categories of events?
- Is there a standard Event ontology available/published?
- What enhancements could be made to existing modelling standards (e.g. UML) to support modelling Event Driven Architectures?

There does not seem be have been much movement on this RFI since its publication in 2006, which may be due to its highly generic nature. On the other hand, research into event ontologies for specific domains, including BAM, continues, as reported in the section on Related Work.

PROCESS AND METRIC DEFINITION MODULE

Data collected is meaningless on its own; a BAM system must provide some context for this data. Since the data is created or manipulated as part of an activity in a process, the BAM system will depend on an explicit process model to which the data can be linked. Data-warehousing technologies lack this view on business data. It is difficult to satisfy all business users with canned, pre-defined queries and reports. Business users require tools to allow them to easily define and deploy business-level metrics from process execution data. Sayal et al. (2002) developed a process monitoring tool that uses taxonomies as a means of reporting qualitative measures for its business users. A behaviour template defines generic process behaviour and this is used to allocate a process instance to a particular category in the taxonomy once completed. Using a case study approach, Telleria et al. (2002) describes the use of active monitoring techniques to improve the performance of business processes in different environments. The research study used the Integrated Performance Measurement System (IPMS) Reference Model as the basis for identifying key business processes, key performance indicators, and active monitoring systems. For each of the three case studies, the strategic focus was defined along with the key business processes supporting that strategy. Each of these was monitored from a frequency of occurrence perspective and displayed using histograms. However, the research does not document whether the initial data sets were gathered using manual or automated techniques. Zeng et al. (2005) describe a model-driven approach to business performance management. There are many business entities that need to be monitored in any company. Each entity has a set of associated metrics, each with its own expression logic. Developing a model-driven approach for performance management needs a runtime engine capable of calculating metrics in a timely fashion using enterprise events and databases. In addition, such an approach also requires an efficient method of storing and retrieving a large volume of data for metric calculation

With the exception of XPDL, business modelling and execution languages lack the semantic expressiveness required to describe a business process from a performance perspective (Thomas et al., 2005), (Mendling & Neumann, 2005). Mendling & Nuttgens (2006) note that the existence of many standards makes the "*seamless integration of the business process management life cycle a difficult task*". A common model is necessary to support and link the various stages of a process life cycle, namely, process modelling, deployment, execution and monitoring.

MONITORING MODULE

Once the data is collected and massaged, the BAM system will apply proprietary business logic to analyse the data. Jeng et al. (2004) describe a rule-based framework for active monitoring and control of business activities. Rules-based Business Activity Management (RuleBAM) uses business rules generated from high-level business policies in order to test conditions and determine appropriate actions. RuleBAM is composed of several tools and technologies for "real-time monitoring, exception handling and repair, alert and report infrastructure, process event infrastructure, monitor and configure agent deployment, [and] solution management decision support" (Jeng et al., 2004).

VISUALIZATION

Presenting the analyzed data and generating alerts for business users can be done using "dashboard" technology as named after the typical cockpit-style dashboards with dials and gauges used to present information about the immediate environment and its functions. A particular favourite with users of such technologies are the red, amber and green traffic light style of status reporting. Novel visualization techniques are also being applied to events as demonstrated by the work carried out by Suntinger et al. (2008), where visualization is based on the metaphor of considering the event stream as a cylindrical tunnel, which is presented to the user from multiple perspectives. This appears to be incorporated into the Senactive business process event analysis products.

BUSINESS RULES

At a basic level, business rules are useful for specifying process exceptions. Process monitoring software can use the rules to test current conditions and generate alerts for appropriate business users. Expert systems and business rules have been around for some time now, and it is not intended to give a full treatment of the subject here. However standards have not been widely adopted for the definition and execution of business rules across industry. While standards such as EDI, and later XML-based standards such as ebXML for business artefacts and events, were widely adopted, there are currently no widely accepted standards for business rules implementation. Much work is being carried out by the semantic research community in order to create rule languages for interoperability. Examples include RuleML and SWRL. It is important to consider the value of semantic approaches to rule modelling and the advantages that may be gained from leveraging such approaches. In particular, the ability to formally model sets of business concepts and define business rules that are a direct representation of concrete business terms will bring the business and IT communities closer in a common understanding of what really is required.

The Rule Markup Language (RuleML, 2000) initiative is the successor to BRML (which was developed in connection with IBM's Business Rules for e-Commerce project) and began in 2000 with the aim of providing a standardized format for interchanging rules anywhere on a network. Since its inception, RuleML has evolved as a rule language for the Semantic Web. The RuleML rationale and language structure are detailed by Boley et al. (2001) and Costello (2003). SWRL (Horrocks et al., 2004) is a Semantic Web Rule Language combining OWL and RuleML. SWRL facilitates rule authoring using ontology concepts as part of rule predicates. Ontologies written using OWL DL or OWL Lite are supported by the SWRL specification. Since SWRL is based on the RuleML, it inherits the RuleML rule structure.

There is value to be gained by extricating rules from the business IT infrastructure and managing these in line with business policies. Approaches for modelling and defining business rules have followed a similar path to that of process modelling and definition with formal rule syntaxes and structures developed by various research groups and governing bodies. Semantic business rule definition has advanced with the development of RuleML and SWRL. The features of these languages and the rule engines available to support these can be used to monitor business activities, and in the following section we will see how the iWise framework leverages semantic and rules technologies using SWRL.

THE IWISE FRAMEWORK

The iWise system is the result of research and development work carried out by the authors into the development of a lightweight, process-aware BAM solution which can be easily deployed in

DMAIC projects to rapidly deliver process performance information. In addition it provides some of the functionality aspired to by mainstream BPM systems in that it uses semantic technologies to allow the creation and triggering of rules defined on process performance measures. The iWise system differs from conventional Business Intelligence (BI) applications, in that it is fully process-oriented. Rather than use Extract, Transform, Load (ETL) type technology to populate complex data cubes, a system of process probes (or listeners) is deployed to deliver process event information to a central operational data store for analysis.

(Figure 11) shows the overall iWise framework approach. The modules, which will be described in the following sections, are:

- Process Capture Tool (PCT)
- Model / Event /Metric Managers
- Rules Editor and Rule Engine
- Process Dashboard

Underpinning all of the functional modules is the Process Model. It is this model which contains the process, event and metric definitions which captured in the Process Capture Tool, and used to drive all of the other functions. We will describe this model first before continuing with the description of the actual functional modules listed above.

PROCESS MODEL

In their most basic form, process modelling and execution languages describe activities and control flow of business processes. However, such languages lack the "semantic expressiveness needed to describe these activities and their performance criterion in a normative manner to support inferencing on the performance of individual activities and the overall business process", (Thomas et al., 2005), (Sivashanmugam et al., 2005). In order to address this need, an event-based process modelling approach is used. With the exception of EPCs and to some extent BPMN, process modelling does not incorporate semantics for modelling business events or even the links between processes, business events and business data. BPDM is an interchange language that caters for the concept of a start, end and exceptional events, but does not define the mechanism for handling business data as part of these events. The linking of these constructs is the contribution of this research activity as it is necessary to connect these three concepts together to reveal a more accurate picture of business operations in real-time.

Figure 10. DMAIC cycle for process performance improvement

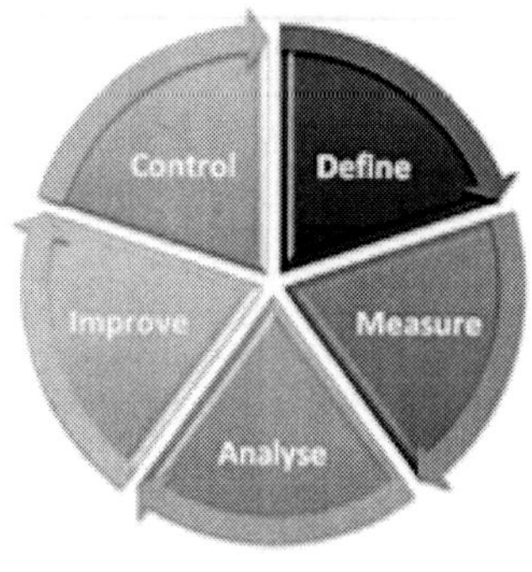

As shown in (Figure 12), a process may be modelled using a combination of event information (e.g. time of process start), hierarchy (sub-process) models, and payload data (e.g. order information). By correlating the events associated with a particular set of process instances (e.g. using Oder ID to correlated activities performed in processing a particular order), we can calculate performance metrics for that process instance. Aggregate (e.g. average) metrics can also be calculated over defined quantities of instance data to show aggregate process performance.

The fundamental unit in our process model is the "process", which is used to mean a process or activity at any level in the process model hierarchy. By correlating start and end events between parent and child processes, the same events can be used

Figure 11. The iWise Framework

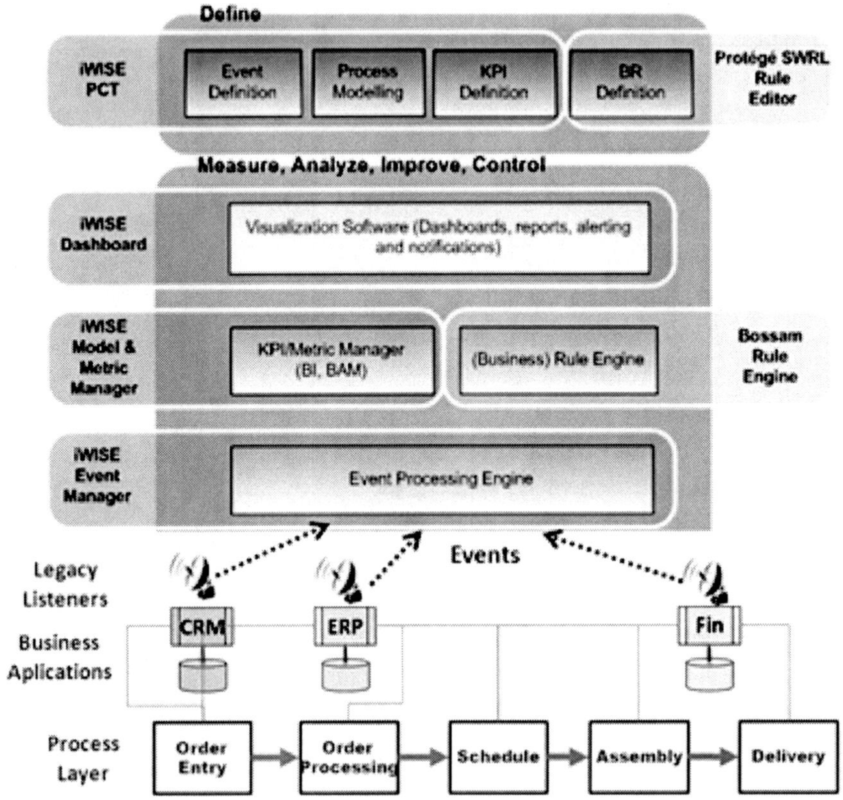

Figure 12. Process modelling concept for BAM

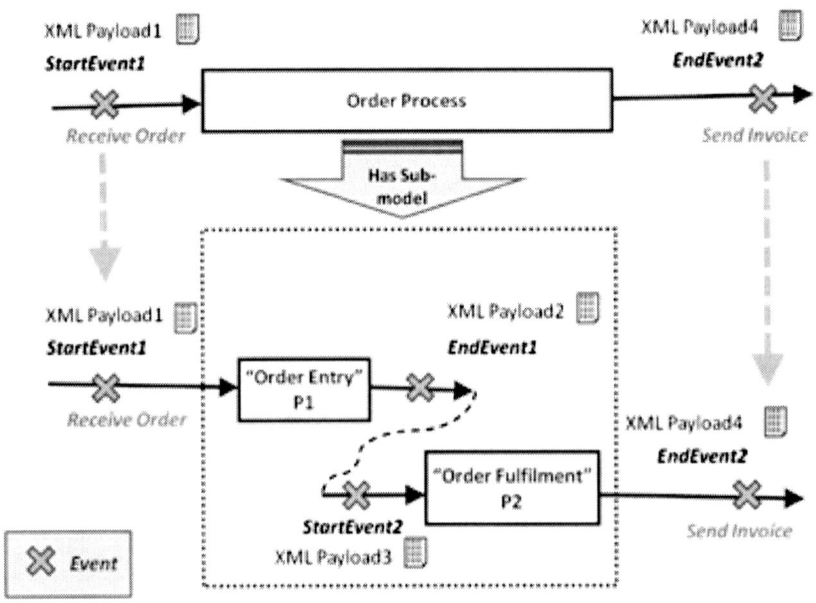

Figure 13. Event Schemas

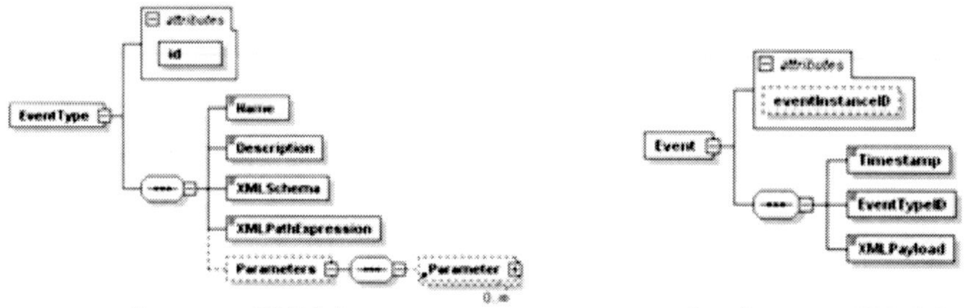

Event type XML Schema ***Runtime event XML Schema***

in the calculation of parent and child performance metrics. The set of event classifications used are:

- Queue event (assume process not yet started, but pending or queued);
- Start event (assume process has started and is executing);
- Interrupt event (assume process is in an `interrupted' state and can be resumed);
- Resume event (assume process continues executing);
- Cancel event (assume process can go from started state to cancelled, and therefore ended, state)
- End event (assume process completes successfully since it was not cancelled).

For this work, the start and end events are mandatory event types that should accompany a process definition. The remaining events are optional. In (Figure 10) we show the two types of event schemas defined. The event type is the blueprint for an event, providing meta-data about that event type. Every event type has a *Name*, *Description*, and unique *id*. The *XML Schema* describes the structure of the business data that should be packaged with any event to be consumed by an event processing engine. It is the responsibility of the Listener software detecting the events to perform the transformation necessary to produce XML that conforms to this XML Schema definition. As long as the data can be defined, captured and transformed from the source system, this approach provides a very flexible way of defining events and business data.

XMLPathExpression refers to an element or attribute from the XML document that is used to uniquely identify an event instance for a particular process instance during execution. This is known as instance correlation and is specified in order to correctly correlate start and end event instance data (or any other instance data) for particular instances of a process. For example, for an order process, the order number can be used to match start and end events, or the process *instance ID* (if transmitted in the event) may also be used. Since this information is included as part of the actual event payload, then it must be selected at design time in order to correctly correlate the event instance data at runtime. *EventTypeID* is an important element as it specifies the event type which is the blueprint for this particular event. This information is configured on the listening software when the event is defined initially. The business data is inserted into an *XMLPayload* element which conforms to the XML Schema as specified in the *XMLSchema* element in event type definition.

An event type definition may contain zero or more Parameter elements. This element is used to define business parameters not related to cycle time or utilization to allow calculation of Six Sigma type metrics on a constant basis. In its simplest terms, a parameter is a piece of business

Figure 14. Process and Model Schemas

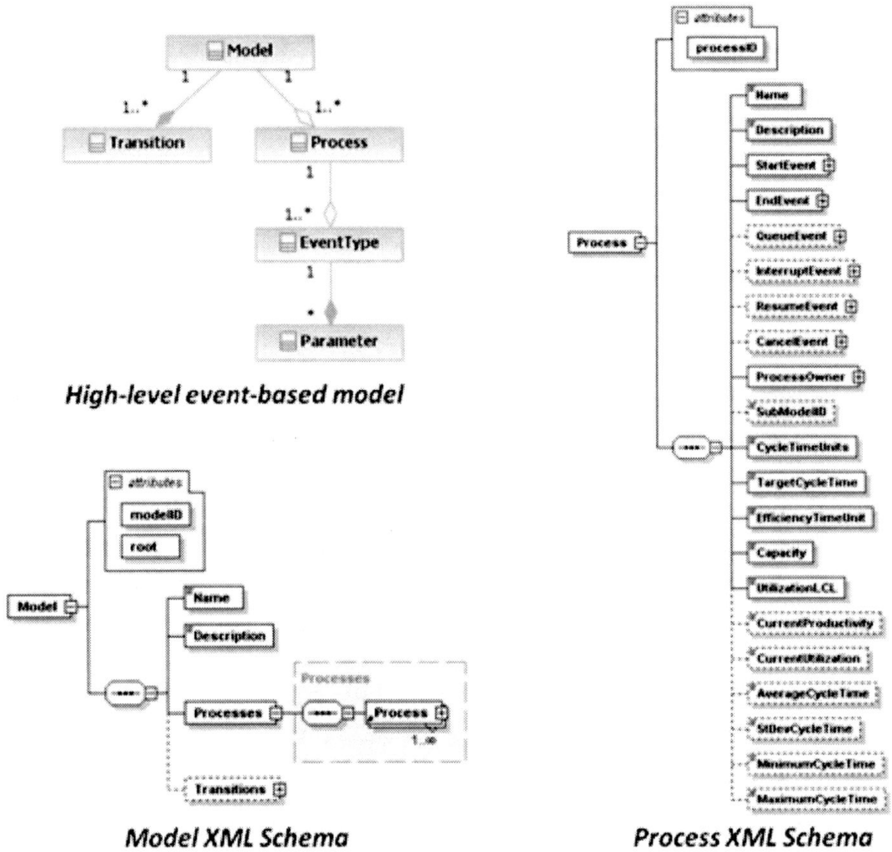

information selected for further analysis from the business content packaged as part of an event at runtime. The business data is defined by the XMLSchema element and is contained within the XMLPayload element. A user must define the business parameter during the define phase. In addition, a user must also specify an upper specification limit, USL, and a lower specification limit, LSL. These pieces of data, defined as part of the event-based process model, are used to drive the BAM solution.

Each parameter definition has its own unique *parameterID* attribute. The *Name* element contains the name of the business parameter. The following are mandatory elements of the *Parameter* element which must be captured at the define phase to fully describe a business parameter:

- *XMLPath* Contains an XPath expression indicating an element from the business data packaged as part of the event data. This must be a numeric value in order to cater for Six Sigma type calculations.
- *TargetMean* Specifies the mean target value for the XPath element chosen by the business.
- *USL* The Upper Specification Limit of the business parameter.
- *LSL* The Lower Specification Limit of the business parameter.
- *SampleSize* Configuration information to indicate the sample size for aggregate calculations for a business parameter.

Figure 15. Process Capture Tool GUI

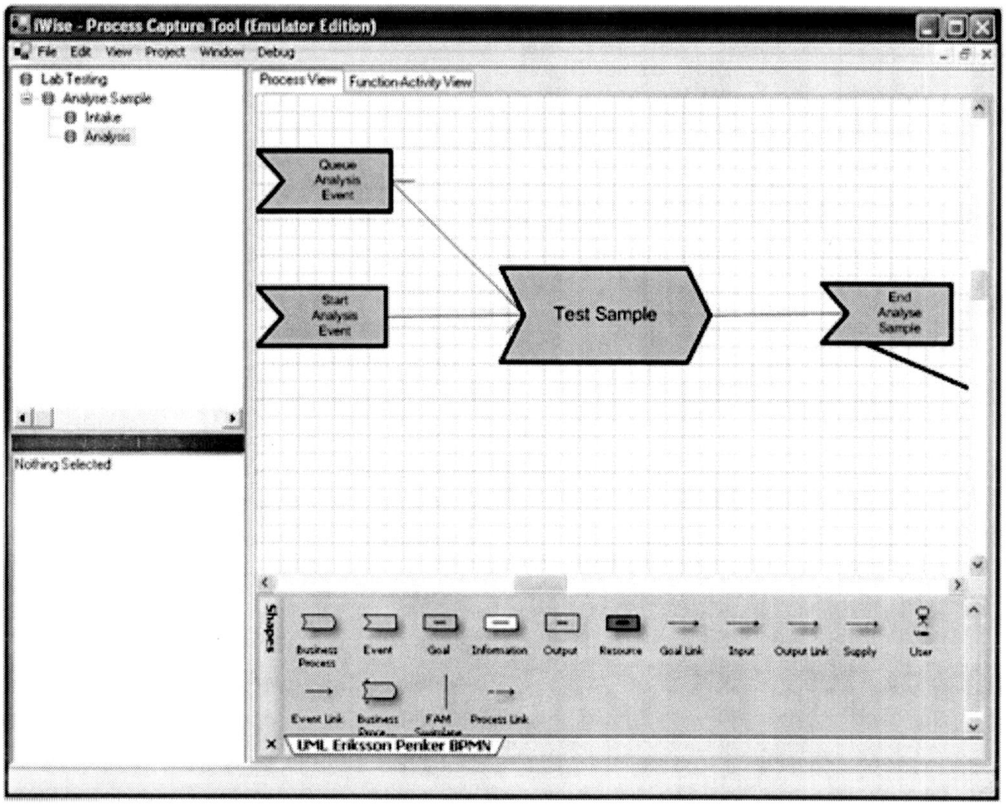

- *MeasurementUnit* The unit of measurement to be attributed to this business parameter.

The remaining elements of the *Parameter* element are aggregate level attributes describing the business parameter for a given sample size. These elements are placeholders for values calculated on the fly and represent the analysis of a business parameter over a period of time. This set of elements is based on the Six Sigma approach to process improvement. These elements include *mean*, *standard deviation*, *yield*, *capability* and others.

The schemas supporting multi-level modelling are illustrated in (Figure 14). The hierarchy of models is connected through the definition of sub-models for a particular process. Models contain processes where a Process represents a business activity or step. The level of granularity is not an issue; a process could represent a collection of other processes or anatomic task. Processes are connected via Transition elements.

The *Process* element is also described in (Figure 15). A *start event* and *end event* are mandatory for each process, as they are necessary for calculation of processing time. If a process has sub-processes they are contained within the *SubModel*. A certain number of attributes are set at design time, and used at run-time in the calculation of metrics and the evaluation of alert rules. These include the *target cycle time*, *capacity* and the *lower control limit for utilization*. A number of other attributes are calculated at run-time, using the pre-defined attributes, such as *average cycle time*.

Figure 16. Event Server Functionality

Function	Description	Collaborators
Manage Process Models	Parses and stores XML process models to underlying database. Processes requests for model information on behalf of requesting party.	Process Capture Tool
Receive Enterprise Events	Processes stream of events sent to Event Server from legacy adapter components	Legacy Adapter Components
Calculate Process Cycle Time	On receipt of events, the Event Server will calculate cycle time if the event is an end event for a process	
Calculate Process Metrics	For a process description, use all instances of process to calculate metrics such as average cycle time and number of cases above/below average.	
Update Key Parameter Metrics	For a nominated XML payload key business parameter, continuously update aggregated metrics such as average value (if numeric) and other Six Sigma metrics	
Serve Cycle Time Statistics	When requested, calculates and packages cycle time data for a process over a specified time period for presenting to the user. The iWISE Dashboard Portal requests and renders this data	Dashboard Portal
Monitor Metrics and Generate Alerts	Continuously test KPIs against threshold values defined during the process capture stage. Generate alerts to interested subscribers	Ms Notification Services

PROCESS CAPTURE TOOL

As-is business process models are captured using the iWISE Process Capture Tool (PCT) which is a standalone software application developed using Microsoft Visio libraries. The PCT allows users to construct a process map and define all important enterprise events linked to a process. The overall process flow definition is persisted using the event and metric model described in the previous section.

MODEL EVENT METRIC MANAGERS

The iWISE Event Server manages models, event streams and metric calculations using the three software packages: the Model Manager, Event Manager and Metric Manager. The Model Manager receives process models from the iWISE PCT and compiles them for further processing. The Event Manager component receives enterprise events defined in the format as specified during process capture. When raw events arrive, they are parsed and associated with the correct process. In parallel with event processing, the Metric Manager component generates metrics on-the-fly to provide both an up-to-date process view for the iWISE Process Dashboard and to generate alerts for subscribers. A listing of the most important functionality provided by the Event Server / Model Manager is shown in Table 4. The Event Server is deployed within J2EE compliant JBoss Application Server (JBoss 4.x AS).1 A combination of Enterprise Java Beans (EJBs) 2.1 and Container Managed Persistence (CMP) 2.0 is used to store information. The EJB structure comprises entity, session and message-driven beans for client software interactions. The Process Capture Tool and Non-JMS Clients interact with the Event Server using EJB Web service endpoints. All data is persisted to an underlying Microsoft SQL Server 2005 database.

The Java Message Service (JMS) is used to queue messages received from legacy listener software for further processing. The legacy listener software configures event streams which forwards enterprise events to the Event Server as they occur.

Figure 17. High-level OWL classes for a process metric ontology

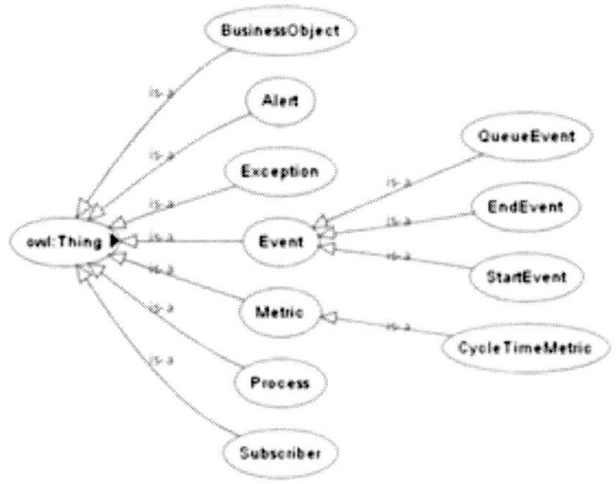

Java-based clients can place events directly on the iWISE Event Queue. Non-Java based clients use Web services to invoke a service to save the event to the data store. Regardless of the public interface access method, the Event Server places all events on a JMS queue. Each event is taken from this queue and processed individually before being stored. Process cycle time metrics are calculated by the Event Server as events arrive.

RULES EDITOR AND RULE ENGINE

Using the event-based process model described in the previous section, ontology was developed which serves as the foundation for specifying SWRL rules. The ontology was created using the Protégé ontology editor. Illustrated in (Figure 17), the ontology is a high-level abstraction of the process and metric concepts as understood by the business community. A Process represents a business process (activity, step, task etc). It can be an aggregate or atomic process. In the context of the event-based model described previously, this refers to the XMLSchema element and XML-Payload element in the Process Model. A Metric represents a process performance metric for a given business process. Events are also captured in this ontology as a step towards building event ontology. In the context of BAM and CEP, this is an aspect which may be developed further in future research.

Prior to defining alerts for business parameters, the Protégé SWRL Rule Editor provides an environment to create SWRL rules based on metric thresholds. At runtime, a monitoring com-

Figure 18. SWRL Rule Management

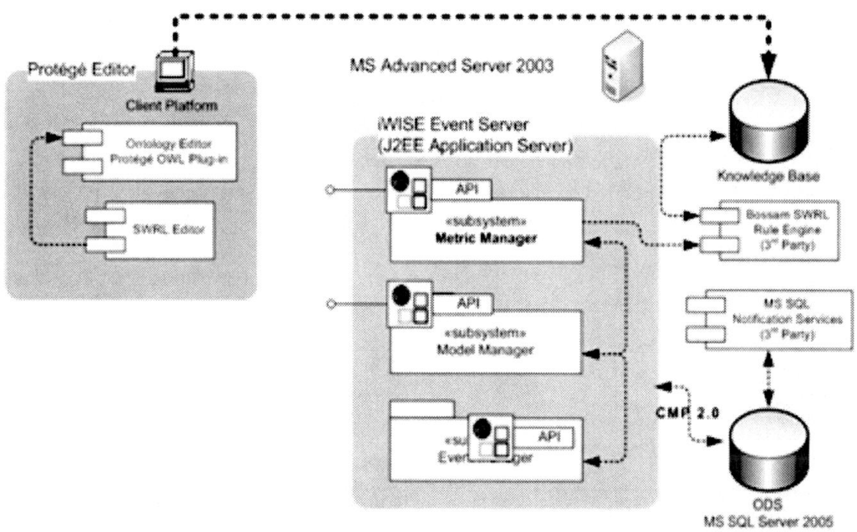

ponent calculates parameter metrics at specified intervals (configurable using application settings) and invokes the Bossam SWRL Rule Engine to test if the process parameter is beyond its limits. If certain thresholds are not adhered to, the monitoring component will create the requisite records to be picked up by MS SQL Notification Services which generates alerts to pre-configured subscribers. Bossam (Jang & Sohn, 2004) is a RETE-based, forward chaining rule engine that supports inferencing over OWL ontologies, SWRL ontologies and RuleML rules.

A sample SWRL rule for expressing when an exception has occurred with a given process is illustrated in (Figure 19). This rule enables the rule engine to test the actual utilization levels of a process against its lowest acceptable value which is defined during process capture. If the actual utilization level of a process is less than the lower limit, then the process is in an exception state. This rule has been defined based on the ontology driven by the model definition. In this way, a user can define rules based on an event-based process model for the BAM software.

PORTAL DASHBOARD

The iWISE Process Dashboard is a Microsoft (ASP .Net) portal application that provides a timely snapshot of process performance. This component converses with the iWISE Event Server to generate interactive process maps with drill-down capabilities. The portal user interface for a process model depicts each process as it is defined by the PCT. The layout of the original process diagram is preserved and rendered within the portal. This is accomplished using SVG to render the process model exactly as defined in the PCT, and it also allows us to make the process model interactive, through the addition of menus to allow drill down within the model, and direct access to process analytics for the process in the dashboard.

Figure 19. Rule Example in Protégé SWRL Rule Editor

The subscriptions page of the portal is where users of the dashboard can subscribe to Notification Services. The notification service is called "IWiseProcessAlerts". It is a windows service that the subscriptions web page hooks into. The page contains a tree view of all the models and processes in the IWise system. It allows the user to select any of these processes, select a subscription type to create a subscription and receive notifications about the subscription.

RELATED WORK

It is important to distinguish between the goals of process automation, and process analysis. At the process definition or modelling level, process modelling languages using a specific notation include the Unified Modelling Language (UML), Business Process Modelling Notation (BPMN) and Business Process Definition Metamodel (BPDM). An enormous amount of research and

Figure 20. Dashboard Process View

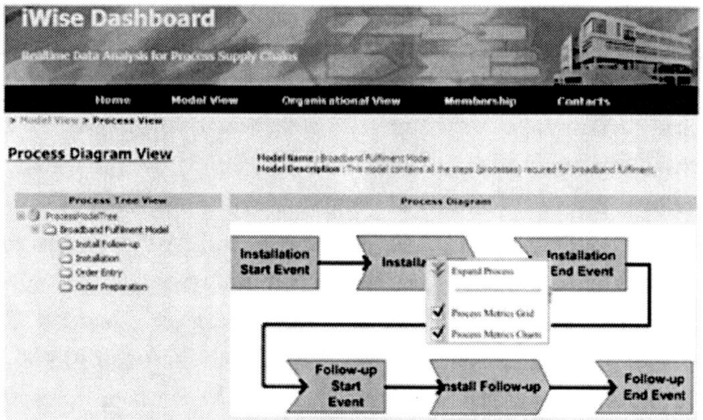

Figure 21. Dashboard SPC Analysis of Sampled Data

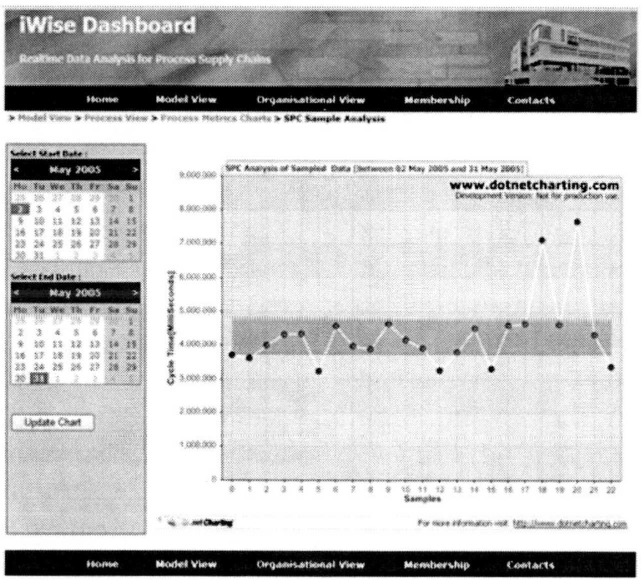

Figure 22. Dashboard SPC Analysis of Sampled Data

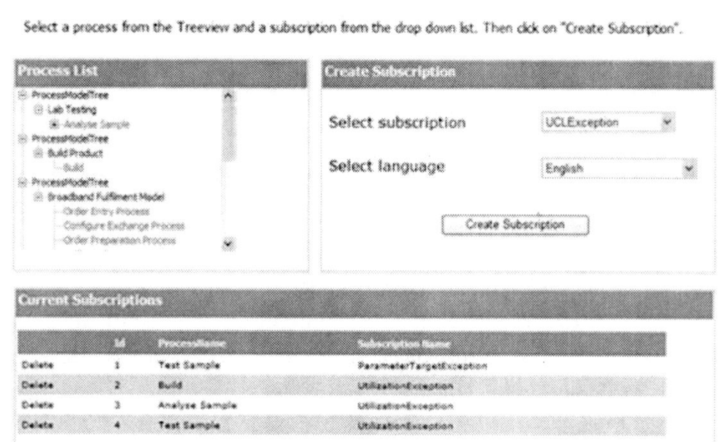

development has taken place in recent years to develop process automation standards and software, with BPEL being the notable forerunner. XPDL is also popular as both execution language and process definition exchange language between design tools. BPEL has been widely adopted and implementations are available in both standalone mode and as components of ERP and BPM systems from major vendors. Unfortunately, as an execution-oriented language, it is not suitable for use by business analysts or general business users. The actual translation between BPMN and BPEL is difficult as they are semantically and structurally incompatible. BPMN is designed for communication purposes, whereas BPEL imposes far more syntactic restrictions to ensure correctness of execution (see Ouyang et al (2006) and Recker & Mendling (2006)). Translators are available (which make certain compromises and assumptions). As yet no globally accepted standard translation exists, although XPDL may yet emerge as the serialisation format of choice for BPMN, and hence for interoperability with BPEL. To date there are over 50 major BPM and application vendors that support the XPDL standard these include IBM, Oracle, BEA, Fujitsu, Tibco and Global 360 (Pyke, 2009).

In terms of Process Analysis, which is the focus of this paper, a number of other research efforts are also ongoing in the application of semantic web technology to Business Process Analysis (for an overview see Medeiros et al, 2007). At the European level, the recently concluded SUPER project (funded by the European Commission) is to bridge the gap between the business and the technical implementation of BPM using Semantic Web Services technologies (Pedrinaci, Domingue & Brelage, 2008). On of the key outputs from this project was an ontology for Business Process Analysis (Pedrinaci, Domingue and Medeiros, 2008). Subsequent work involved the development of a metrics computation engine based on this ontology (Pedrinaci & Domingue, 2009) (Pedrinaci et al, 2008). Further work is envisaged in the support of users in defining queries.

Other work using semantics, but introducing a multi-agent approach to monitor and manage distributed processes is described by Thomas et al (2005). At the BPEL engine level there are numerous approaches published to querying and monitoring of business processes. These range from interception of SOAP messages (Moser, Rosenberg & Dustdar, 2008), to query-based systems, where the queries run as BPEL processes in parallel with the monitored process (Beeri et al, 2007). Such approaches obviously suffer the limitations of being restricted to BEPL, but can be used to generate events for consumption by other (BPA) systems.

CONCLUSION AND FUTURE WORK

The research work detailed in this paper has focused on process performance modelling for (near) real-time measurement and monitoring. Analysis of the current knowledge base with respect to process definition standards has shown that there is currently little or no standard support for process metric definition to enable process measurement and monitoring during process execution.

The first contribution of this research is a process modelling approach incorporating generic constructs for enterprise events and business parameters to support any taxonomy of events or class of business parameters. For the purpose of this research activity, Six Sigma was chosen as a significantly complex process measurement technique for understanding the requirements for the definition of the business parameter constructs.

The successful implementation and evaluation of iWISE proved that it is possible to both formally model and automate the process of data collection for monitoring a process with respect to utilization, cycle time and non-conforming process characteristics. The benefits of using a common model for both the process modelling and monitoring phases are as follows:

- Regardless of the number of underlying systems or disparate data sources required to execute the process, the common model is captured and monitored, thereby providing a single view of the process.
- The data store collects events and business data relating to processes and maintains a process-oriented, temporal data repository. The association between transactional events, business data and processes is managed through the design of the software components.
- The monitoring component uses a combination of a freely available rules engine to evaluate rules expressed in SWRL to produce convenient, timely alerts. The use of a semantic rules language to express rules is novel in this respect. This approach coupled with process constructs which are developed with an XML representation, provides a flexible approach for defining and monitoring process activities.
- The process constructs and system are flexible, providing a reusable solution independent of the industry or process type.

The following recommendations for future work relate to this research activity:

- The iWISE system has been implemented using one deployment of the Event Server. Scalability of the solution would be greatly increased through investigation of a distributed solution. Such an approach would need to consider the impact, if any, on the deployment of process models to the Event Server and potential need to propagate events to other Event Server instances. This recursive deployment scenario could also improve the message processing capabilities through aggregation of events before propagating them to other Event Server instances.
- The iWISE Event Manager module does not perform complex event processing such as pattern definition and recognition.
- The current performance ontology developed in OWL could be extended further to contain more classes and properties for Six Sigma. It could also be incorporated into other work in the area of ontologies for BPM.

REFERENCES

Beeri, C., Eyal, A., Milo, T., & Pilberg, A. (2007) Query-based monitoring of BPEL business processes. In *Proceedings of the 2007 ACM SIGMOD international conference on Management of data,* Beijing (pp. 1122 – 1124). New York: ACM.

Boley, H., Tabet, S., & Wagner, G. (2001). Design Rationale of RuleML: A Markup Language for Semantic Web Rules. In *Proceedings of the Semantic Web Working Symposium*, Stanford, 2001.

Costello, C. (2003). *Integrating Intelligence into the Business Process Management Framework.* Thesis: M.Sc. Applied Computing and Information Technology, National University of Ireland, Galway, 2003.

DeFee, J., & Harmon, P. (2005). Business Activity Monitoring and Simulation. In *Workflow Handbook 2005* (pp. 53–74). Lighthouse Point, FL: Future Strategies.

Eccles, R. (1991 January). The Performance Management Manifesto. *Harvard Business Review.*

Fillies, C., & Weichhardt, F. (n.d.). *On Ontology-based Event-driven Process Chains.* Retrieved from http://www.semtalk.com/pub/semtalkepk.pdf

Forster, F. (2006). The Idea Behind Business Process Improvment. *BP Trends*. Retrieved from http://www.bptrends.com/publicationfiles/04-06-ART-PatternFramework-Forster.pdf

Fu, S., Chieu, T., Yih, J.-S., & Kumaran, S. (2005). An Intelligent Event Adaptation Mechanism for Business Performance Monitoring. In *IEEE International Conference on e-Business Engineering (ICEBE'05)*, Beijing, China, October 18-20.

Golfarelli, M., Rizzi, S., & Cella, I. (2004). Beyond Data Warehousing: What's Next in Business Intelligence. In *Proceedings of 7th ACM International Workshop on Data Warehousing and OLAP* (pp. 1-6).

Hackathorn, R. (2002). *Current Practices in Active DataWarehousing*. Retrieved from http://www.bolder.com/pubs/NCR200211-ADW.pdf

Harrington, H. J. (1991). *Business Process Improvement: The Breakthrough Strategy for Total Quality, Productivity and Competitiveness*. New York: McGraw-Hill.

Horrocks, I., Patel-Schneider, P., Boley, H., Tabet, S., Grosof, B., & Dean, M. (2004). *SWRL: A Semantic Web Rule Language Combining OWL and RuleML*. Retrieved from http://www.w3.org/Submission/SWRL/

Jang, M., & Sohn, J.-C. (2004). Bossam: An Extended Rule Engine for OWL Inferencing. In *Rules and Rule Markup Languages for the Semantic Web. Third International Workshop (RuleML 2004)*, Hiroshima, Japan (LNCS 3324, pp. 128-138). Berlin: Springer.

Jeng, J., Flaxer, D., & Kapoor, S. (2004). RuleBAM: A Rule-Based Framework for Business Activity Management. In *SCC '04: Proceedings of the 2004 IEEE International Conference on Services Computing*, Washington, DC (pp. 262-270).

Junginger, S., Kuhn, H., & Bayer, F. (2004). Workflow-based Business Monitoring . In *WfMC Workflow Handbook*. Lighthouse Point, FL: Future Strategies.

Knifsend, F., & Debb, J. (2005). Using BAM to Empower the Organization: Unifying Events and Processes. *Business Integration Journal*. Retrieved from http://www.alignjournal.com/index.cfm?section=article&aid=54

Luckham, D. (2002). *The Power of Events*. Reading, MA: Pearson Education Inc.

McGregor, C., & Eklund, J. (2008). Real-Time Service-Oriented Architectures to Support Remote Critical Care: Trends and Challenges. In *Proceedings of 2008 Annual IEEE International Computer Software and Applications Conference (COMPSAC)* (pp. 1199-1204).

Melchert, F., Winter, R., & Klesse, M. (2004). Aligning Process Automation and Business Intelligence to Support Corporate Performance Management. In *Proceedings of the 10th Americas Conference on Information Systems*, New York, August 5-8 2004. Retrieved from http://aisel.aisnet.org/amcis2004/507

Mendling, J., & Neumann, G. (2005). A Comparison of XML Interchange Formats for Business Process Modelling . In *WfMC Workflow Handbook 2005* (pp. 185–198). Lighthouse Point, FL: Future Strategies Inc.

Mendling, J., & Nuttgens, M. (2006). XML interchange formats for Business Process Management. *International Journal of Information Systems and E-Business Management*, *4*(3), 217–220. doi:10.1007/s10257-006-0032-y

Moser, O., Resenberg, F., & Dustdar, S. (2008). Non-intrusive monitoring and service adaptation for WS-BPEL. In *Proceedings of the 17th international conference on World Wide Web, Beijing, 2008* (pp. 815-824). New York: ACM.

Neely, A. (2005). Performance measurement system design: A literature review and research agenda. *International Journal of Operations & Production Management*, *25*(12), 1228–1263. doi:10.1108/01443570510633639

Nesamoney, D. (2004). BAM: Event-driven Business Intelligence for the Real-Time Enterprise. *DM Review*, *14*(3), 38–40.

Nudurupati, S., & Bititci, U. (2005). Implementation and impact of IT-supported performance measurement systems. *Production Planning and Control*, *16*(2), 152–162. doi:10.1080/09537280512331333057

Ouyang, C., Dumas, M., Van der Aalst, W., & Ter Hofstede, A. (2006). From Business Process Models to Process-oriented Software Systems: The BPMN to BPEL Way. *BPMCentre.org*. Retrieved from http://is.tm.tue.nl/staff/wvdaalst/BPMcenter/reports.htm

Pedrinaci, C., & Domingue, J. (2007) Towards an Ontology for Process Monitoring and Mining. In M. Hepp, K. Hinkelmann, D. Karagiannis, R. Klein & N. Stojanovic (Eds.), *Semantic Business Process and Product Lifecycle Management. Proceedings of the Workshop SBPM 2007*, Innsbruck, April 7, 2007. Retrieved from http://CEUR-WS.org/Vol-251/

Pedrinaci, C., & Domingue, J. (2009). Ontology-based Metrics Computation for Business Process Analysis. *Workshop: 4th International Workshop on Semantic Business Process Management (SBPM2009) at The 6th European Semantic Web Conference (ESWC2009),* Heraklion, Greece. Retrieved from http://people.kmi.open.ac.uk/carlos/publications/ontology-based-metrics-SBPM09.pdf

Pedrinaci, C., Domingue, J., & Brelage, C. (2008). Semantic Business Process Management: Scaling up the Management of Business Processes. In *2nd IEEE International Conference on Semantic Computing (ICSC)*.

Pedrinaci, C., Domingue, J., & Medeiros, A. (2008). A Core Ontology for Business Process Analysis. In *The Semantic Web: Research and Applications*. Berlin: Springer. doi:10.1007/978-3-540-68234-9_7

Pedrinaci, C., Lambert, D., Wetzstein, B., van Lessen, T., Cekov, L., & Dimitrov, M. (2008). SENTINEL: A Semantic Business Process Monitoring Tool. In *Workshop: Ontology-supported Business Intelligence (OBI2008) at 7th International Semantic Web Conference (ISWC2008),* Karlsruhe, Germany. Retrieved from http://people.kmi.open.ac.uk/carlos/publications/obi2008.pdf

Pyke, J. (2009) XPDL - The Silent Workhorse of BPM. *BPM.com*. Retrieved from http://www.bpm.com/xpdl-the-silent-workhorse-of-bpm.html

Recker, J., & Mendling, J. (2006) On the Translation between BPMN and BPEL: Conceptual Mismatch between Process Modeling Languages. In T. Latour & M. Petit (Eds.), *Proceedings 18th International Conference on Advanced Information Systems Engineering* (pp. 521-532).

Rule, M. L. (2000). *The Rule Markup Initiative (RuleML)*. Retrieved from http://www.ruleml.org/

Sayal, M., Casati, F., Dayal, U., & Shan, M.-C. (2002). Business process cockpit. In *Proceedings of the 28th Very Large DataBase (VLBD) Conference*, Hong Kong, China, 2002.

Sharpe, A., & McDermott, P. (2001). *Workflow Modelling: Tools for Process Improvement and Application Development*. Norwood, MA: Artech House.

Sivashanmugam, K., Miller, J., Sheth, A., & Verma, K. (2005). Framework for Semantic Web Process Composition. *International Journal of Electronic Commerce*, *9*(2), 71–106.

Skalle, H., Ramachandran, S., Schuster, M., Szaloky, V., & Antoun, S. (2009). Aligning Business Process Management, Service-Oriented Architecture, and Lean Six Sigma for Real Business Benefits. *IBM Redbooks*. Retrieved from http://www.redbooks.ibm.com/abstracts/redp4447.html

Smith, B. (1993, September). Making war on defects: Six-sigma design. *IEEE Spectrum*, 43–47. doi:10.1109/6.275174

Stacey, M., & McGregor, C. (2007). Temporal abstraction in intelligent clinical data analysis: A survey. *Artificial Intelligence in Medicine*, *39*(1), 1–24. doi:10.1016/j.artmed.2006.08.002

Suntinger, M., Obweger, H., Schiefer, J., & Gröller, M. (2008). The Event Tunnel: Interactive Visualization of Complex Event Streams for Business Process Pattern Analysis. In *IEEE VGTC Pacific Visualization Symposium 2008 (PacificVis),* Kyoto, Japan, March 5-7 2008 (pp. 111-118).

Telleria, K., Turner, T., & Bititci, U. (2002). Measuring and Improving Business Process Reliability. *International Journal of Business Performance Management*, *4*(1), 76–94. doi:10.1504/IJBPM.2002.000109

Thomas, M., Redmond, R., Yoon, V., & Singh, R. (2005). A semantic approach to monitor business process. *Communications of the ACM*, *48*(12), 55–59. doi:10.1145/1101779.1101809

Van der Aalst, W., ter Hofstede, A., & Weske, M. (2003). Business Process Management: A Survey. In *Proceedings of the 1st International Conference on Business Process Management*. Berlin: Springer.

Vasilecas, O., & Bugaite, D. (2006) Business Rules Elicitation in the Process of Enterprise Information System Development. In *Eight International Conference on Enterprise Information Systems*, Paphos, Cyprus, May 2006.

Womack, J., Jones, D., & Roos, D. (2007). *The Machine That Changed the World: The Story of Lean Production-- Toyota's Secret Weapon in the Global Car Wars That Is Now Revolutionizing World Industry*. New York: Free Press.

Zeng, L., Lei, H., Dikun, M., Chang, H., Bhaskaran, K., & Frank, J. (2005) Model-driven Business Performance Management. In *IEEE International Conference on e-Business Engineering,* 18-21 October (pp. 295-304). Washington, DC: IEEE Computer Society.

Chapter 3
The Socio-Technical Balanced Scorecard for Assessing a Public University

Ramanjit Singh
University of Manchester, UK

Trevor Wood-Harper
University of Manchester, UK

ABSTRACT

The socio-technical theory is concerned with humanistic welfare paradigm. The socio-technical principles aim to improve redundant jobs and thereby benefit human work lives. Hence, jobs are enriched using flexible work methods, empowerment strategies and new technologies. Balanced scorecard is a framework that measures whether the firm is meeting its objectives in terms of vision and strategy. It assesses four perspectives: financial, customer, internal business processes and innovation & learning. Even though the balanced scorecard has proven to be beneficial in the for-profit organizations of the past, most non-profit organizations were unable to utilize the balanced scorecard. The original configuration of balanced scorecard placed financial goals on the top of the hierarchy and since maximizing shareholder wealth is not the main objective for most non-profit organizations, it was not widely applied by these organizations. Since non-profit organizations usually operate to maximize the well-being of the society, socio-technical work design principles may receive a greater acceptance in these organizations than in for-profit organizations. Thus, a socio-technical balanced scorecard for the non-profit organizations will be formulated with an emphasis on employee perspective and a public university wide assessment will be proposed.

INTRODUCTION

Socio-technical theory is half a century old. It was found by group of researchers, therapists, and consultants at the London Tavistock Clinic to assist soldiers for regaining their mental stability and health after the war. The group at Tavistock Clinic believed that treatment ideas used for healings the soldiers could be applied for enriching jobs. In line with this thinking, the Tavistock institute was developed by this group in 1946. The Tavistock institute wanted to merge disciplines such as psy-

DOI: 10.4018/978-1-61692-016-6.ch003

chology and social science in a way that enabled the organization to design jobs that lead to higher job satisfaction. Since the group originated from a therapeutic background, members were interested in "results" and also "theories". This thinking guided them to an approach that was based on action research, which resulted in the remedial changes based upon analysis and theory. The members of the Tavistock institute believed that no theory could be established without practice and no practice could thrive without theoretical influence. Upon the initial success in Britain, the socio-technical drive was internationalized in 1972, with creation of Council for the Quality of Working life. This group compromised of academics from the University of Oslo, University of Pennsylvania, York University, Centre for Continuing Education in Canberra, and the University of Michigan. Together, this group had significant influence on the development of the socio-technical theory (Checkland & Holwell, 2004; Mumford, 2003, 2006).

In the 1970s, socio-technical theory was widely applied for designing jobs. However, many firms came under pressure during the 1980s to cut costs and during these circumstances socio-technical ideas were seen as expensive and risky to implement. During 1990s socio-technical design principles continued to struggle, as there was little room for investment in the human capital. The focus was mainly on lean production methods and business process reengineering flourished. A widely accepted methodology which gained corporate awareness during the 1990s is the balanced scorecard (Robert S. Kaplan & Norton, 1992). The balanced scorecard provides an assessment on the firm's financial position, customer satisfaction, internal processes, and research & development. In other words, the balanced scorecard provides the manager with information about problems areas and invokes change to correct inconsistencies in the organization. Although the balanced scorecard has been fruitful for the for-profit organizations, its use in the non-profit sector has been rare. The original configuration of balanced scorecard placed the financial goals on the top of the hierarchy but as the non-profit organizations generally function for the well-being of the society and maximizing shareholder wealth is not the main objective, it was not widely applied by these organizations. Hence, a socio-technical balanced scorecard with an emphasis on employee perspective will be developed and proposed for assessing a public university.

HISTORICAL OVERVIEW OF THE SOCIO-TECHNICAL THEORY

The socio-technical theory was first applied in organizations in the 1970s. It was believed that socio-technical ideas could facilitate the design of jobs in a way that improve human work lives. So, jobs were enriched using flexible work methods, empowerment strategies and new technologies. Even though many organizations applied the socio-technical theory in the past, people still have jobs that are routine, closely monitored and provide little room for personal development (Checkland & Holwell, 2004; Checkland & Scholes, 1990). Perhaps, we need to ask us two but important questions. First, why did socio-technical interest decrease in the 1980s and 1990s? Second, can the socio-technical theory provide guidance for meeting challenges of the 21st century? Today, a complex economic environment surrounds the organizations and it has a significant impact on its performance and the way it functions in the society. In order to realize production efficiency, clear specification to goals need to be followed and control structures need to be in place. Even though the visionary group at Tavistock institute believed in participative goal setting, many organizations pay no attention to employee participation when designing jobs. Hence, when jobs are designed, social risks and consequences of work are often overlooked by the management (Mumford, 2003, 2006).

Figure 1. The Interacting Variable Classes within a Work System (Bostrom & Heinen, p. 25)

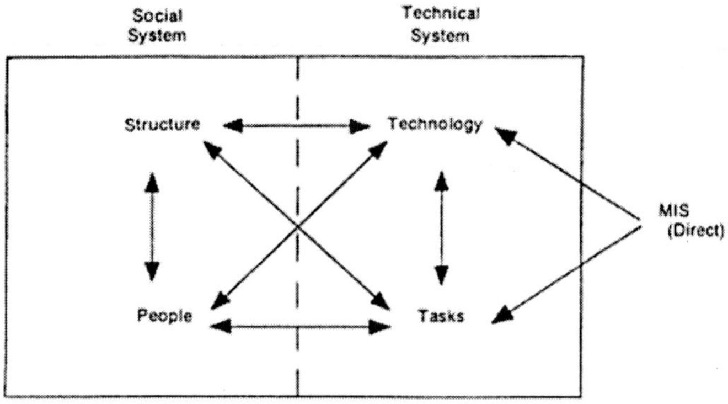

The socio-technical school of thought wanted to change this perception regarding jobs. According to the socio-technical theory, jobs should be designed in a way that fosters creativity, flexibility, and intellectual growth. In the past, practitioners at Tavistock institute have strived to reach two objectives: humanization of work and creation of democratic work policies. Similarly, the goal of socio-technical theory is the joint optimization of the social and technical elements of the organization (Mumford, 2003, 2006). Social elements of the organization are composed of work-related aspects such as task variety, task identity, and autonomy that provide job satisfaction and motivation to the organizational employees (Mumford, 2006). In addition to the work-related aspects, structural elements such as adequate workload, co-worker support, management support, career advancement opportunities and realistic performance measures and reward structures may also increase the overall job satisfaction (Seo, Ko, & Price, 2004). Technical elements, on the other hand, are concerned with the work processes, tasks, and technology needed to transform inputs into desired outputs. Also, technical elements focus on the identification of possible deviations in the transformation process and aim to control them (Wood-Harper, Fok, & Kumar, 1987). Although the two elements described above differ considerably, their interplay and harmony is essential for the organization's success in the business (Kling, 1999; Kling & Iacono, 2001).

Perhaps the most fundamental innovation in the socio-technical thinking occurred in 1976 by Albert Cherns with the development of socio-technical work design principles. As seen in (Mumford, 2003), the socio-technical design principles can be described as follows.

- Compatibility: Objectives must be compatible with the process of design. This implies that, if the goal is to establish democratic work arrangements (DWAs) then democratic processes must be used to form these DWAs.
- Minimal Critical Specification: Employees should be given clear work specifications but leaving them to determine how to attain these work objectives.
- The Socio-technical Criterion: Deviations from standards should be monitored closely in case where they cannot be eliminated. Inconsistencies of this kind must be resolved by the team that is being affected and not by the supervisors.
- The Multifunctionality Principle: Group require redundancy of functions in order to be responsive and adaptable to the changes in the environment.
- Boundary Location: Boundaries should be defined to assist the knowledge and ex-

perience sharing within the organization. Boundaries differentiate work activities of a group to another and all group members need to have multiple skill-set and be able to perform one another's work tasks.
- Information: In most organizations, information about operations is usually accessible by the upper management. However, it should rather first go to the work group whose productivity is being monitored.
- Support Congruence: Social support systems must be designed to facilitate social behaviour. If workers are to work together, management must also show supportive behaviour.
- Design and Human Values: Quality of working requires following elements:
    - Demanding job
    - Where learning occurs
    - Involves decision-making
    - Embedded with social support mechanism
    - Possibility of relating work to social life
    - Opportunity to advance and excel in the job
- Incompletion: Emergent and continual design process, leading to an iterative process of changes in environment, demanding new work structures and objectives.

Furthermore, (Pasmore, 1985) put forward a positive evaluation of socio-technical theory over the last three decades. In this study, he recommends that work systems need to be viewed as a group of activities facilitating the whole and not as a group of self-containing jobs. In addition, power sharing is important for increasing efficiency and democracy at workplace. Team members need multiple skill-set and they should be able to carry out one another's work. Lastly, jobs should be designed in a way, which facilitate variety, learning, and knowledge sharing on the job. As seen in (Mumford, 2006) Emery simplified these socio-technical principles and it was suggested that job variety, higher learning prospects, scope for decision-making, training, good supervision, recognition, and bright career prospects are important for enriching jobs. Job satisfaction may be one of the important factors of the socio-technical theory. Job satisfaction can be defined as match between the job expectations workers bring to the work and the requirements of the work as defined by the organizations. According to Mumford's framework, this can be measured under five work dimensions (Mumford & Weir, 1979).

- The Knowledge Fit: The extent to which the employee's job permits the development of skills and knowledge.
- The Psychological Fit: The extent to which the employee's job permits discretion in achieving personal goals for achievement, appreciation, development, position in the society, etc.
- The Task-Structure Fit: The extent to which the employee's job matches employee's need for task variety, task identity, and autonomy, recognition and performance assessments.
- The Efficiency Fit: The extent to which the job provides an opportunity of financial rewards and a realistic and considerate appraisal programme.
- The Ethical Fit: The extent to which the vision and mission of employer is compatible with those of the employee.

The socio-technical theory has been widely used in the organizations during the 1970s. The following discussion describes the experiences of the participating countries in more detail (Mumford, 2003).

- Norway: The Norwegian Industrial Democracy Programme was based on socio-technical design principles. It was adopted by most of the industrial firms in the country during 1970s.

- Sweden: By 1973, 500 to 1000 work improvement projects were based on the socio-technical design principles.
- Denmark: In 1970, an agreement between the Danish Employers Confederation and the Danish Federation of Trade Unions was reached. This agreement was based on principles of socio-technical theory.
- France: In 1970s, France also adopted the socio-technical design principles and subsequently became interested in "humanization of work".
- Italy: Trade union agreements between Fiat and Olivetti workers were reached on the basis of socio-technical principles.
- Germany: Humanization of work (based on socio-technical principles) initiative was introduced by the Federal Ministries of Labour and of Science and Technology in May 1974.
- Netherlands: Philips (electronics firm) was the leading socio-technical design firm in the country in the 1960s and 1970s.
- UK: Two action research projects at Tavistock Institute tested and developed the socio-technical design principles in 1949. In 1965, large scale socio-technical project was initiated at Shell UK. Upon the successful completion of this project, Shell plants in Austria, Holland, and Canada also adopted the socio-technical design principles.
- USA: During the 1960s and 1970s, the United Automobile Workers Union negotiated contracts with General Motors, Ford and Chrysler. This was performed on the basis of socio-technical theory.
- India: Prof. Nitish De, an academic in India, deployed socio-technical design principles at various Indian firms during 1960s.

It is believed that socio-technical ideas were important for two reasons during the1960s and 1970s. First, manufacturing industry was growing and firms were forced to introduce better working conditions in order to retain workers that they had. Second, increase in the number of service firms in the industry contributed to the change in work methods as workers required job variety in production process (Mumford, 2006). Approaches that work well at one time may not be so flourishing at another since both business culture and business climate can change. This change was apparent during the 1980s where many firms came under pressure to cut costs and save on the labour expenditures. Machines moved into offices to facilitate routine work processes and lean production methods became the norm in the industry (Moldaschl & Weber, 1998). During 1990s socio-technical design principles continued to struggle as there was little room for investment in human capital. The focus was mainly on lean production methods and business process reengineering flourished. To conclude this discussion, it can be implied that downsizing of the organizations in the 1980s and 1990s had a negative impact on the socio-technical movement. Nevertheless, there were a small number of firms in the United Kingdom, USA, Europe, and Australia that recognized the importance of participative decision-making, multi-skilled workforce and self-regulating autonomous work groups (Mumford, 2006).

USE OF SOCIO-TECHNICAL THEORY IN THE 21ST CENTURY

The socio-technical theory is democratic, humane, and provides autonomy and knowledge to employees at all levels. Unique to many, the ideas of socio-technical principles are not new. First, Etzioni defined a method called voluntary simplicity. This approach describes a set of ideas which limit expenditure on consumer goods while promoting quality of life, self expression and involvement in society (Elgin, 1981). Another method which is consistent with the humanistic school is associative democracy, which aims to create a participative welfare society which is cohesive and supportive in nature (Pestoff, 1999). Profit sharing and shared ownership are two approaches based on the principles of socio-technical theory. Perhaps the best example of an organization that shares profit and ownership with its employees is the Mondragon Corporation. The firm employs 20,000 workers; in addition to their basic pay, every employee gets a share from the annual profits. Another goal of Mondragon is to have employees gain ownership in the firm. Hence, the organization saves a small proportion of yearly profits for building reserve funds for its employees. Together, these financial policies help to motivate employees to attain financial goals, and also non-financial goals such as career development and long-term stable employment (Malone, 2004).

More recently, socio-technical theory has been applied in organizations to understand the social requirements of work. One such socio-technical intervention took place in 1994 in an Australian industrial site, (Garrety & Badham, 2000) involving the development of a system called AMS, designed to control a continuous manufacturing process in a plant. During the late 1990s, the AMS project group came under pressure to increase the efficiency of the AMS system, and Richard Badham and his academic panel were appointed to assist the AMS project team in reforming the system. Two major workshops were held, each attended by socio-technical specialists, technology developers, workers and management officials from the plant. Upon analyzing the findings, it was found that socio-technical principles made the AMS system more humane and responsive to changing conditions in the environment. The socio-technical approach to system development enabled identification of the role of workers in the production process, increasing job satisfaction as the workers could utilize the AMS system more effectively in their everyday work.

Another application of socio-technical theory can be found in a manufacturing organization in the UK. The first stage required the formulation of scenarios which simulate different work configurations and the second stage entailed the development of decision criteria. 12 employees participated in the scenarios and their performance was assessed by the decision criteria. It was found that intervention increased the involvement of workers in job design and was useful in creating favourable work tasks (Nadin, Waterson, & Parker, 2001). Socio-technical design principles has been used in the North Sea to make a system called Integrated eOperations fully functional and failsafe. The aim was to provide an understanding of emerging concerns that increasing complexities in the exploration of oil and gas can lead to serious vulnerabilities and long-term commercial consequences for North Sea industrial firms. The results of this intervention were the identification of appropriate technology needed to measure the risk of production errors and to manage equipment remotely (Liyanage & Bjerkebaek, 2006). Furthermore, (Jeppesen, Barfod, & Leleur, 2007) conducted a case study with a multi-national IT firm in Denmark. The main objective of this firm was to relocate its operations to the Oresund Region in Scandinavia. The principles of socio-technical design were applied to evaluate location alternatives given the strategic preferences of the firm and social needs of the workers. Although quantitative feasibility studies were an important part of case analysis, socio-technical theory proved to be equally important in conceptualizing the complex environment facing the IT firm. Although the intervention increased the participation of workers in the decision-making process, no definite decision regarding the relocation has been identified. However, authors strongly believe that the socio-technical theory can aid in reaching a solution which would benefit both the company and its workers.

USE OF ALTERNATIVE MOMC THEORIES IN ORGANIZATIONS

Even though socio-technical principles enrich jobs which benefit the overall profitability of a firm, researchers in the past have failed to find any positive correlation between socio-technical work design and a firm's profitability (Lucas Henry, 1999; Strassmann, 1990). More recently, researchers have found evidence to support the claim that socio-technical work design does increase productivity (Azoff, Jones, Rodger, & Butler, 2004; Boresson C., 2005; Butler, 2004). These findings, however, were not without controversy. Neither accounting nor economics acknowledges the fact that social elements of a firm have a positive effect on financial performance. Although accounting has recognized elements such as cost, revenue and other complex measures such as goodwill, the incorporation of intellectual assets and their worth has been poor. Traditional economics accounted for corporate social responsibility, but modern managerial economics show little concern toward the wellbeing of employees. Even the most widely cited book, *The Foundations of Corporate Success*, does not pay much regard to socio-technical job design (Land, 2000). Moreover, (Porter, 1985)'s five-force analysis does not assess employee behaviour and attitude in the firm and how it impacts the firm's performance.

Business process re-engineering (BPR), consisting of traditional and well accepted ideas of accounting and evaluation, does not recognize the need for policies and reward systems that increase job satisfaction. The furthest most authors go is to indicate the resistance of employees to accepting organizational change. Little research or discussion is taking place on why there is resistance. Business schools commonly introduce the topic of how to satisfy employees through various gain sharing and profit sharing programmes, but little attention is given to social factors that contribute to job satisfaction (Land, 2000; Mumford, 2006). To obtain wider recognition, the socio-technical approach has to show its worth and importance, in terms that are relevant to the managerial paradigm. Socio-technical evaluation may consist of two stages: first, the assesor needs to show that the socio-technical approach is likely to increase shareholder wealth and that it possesses less risk and more certainty than other approaches; second, the assesor needs to provide evidence that socio-technical iniatiatives lead to financial gains for the organization.

Technical evaluation has been widely accepted in most organizations. It is commonly performed using a set of rules that make it possible to measure performance on a single scale, the financial. The socio-technical method takes into account multiple criteria to measure the firm's performance. Hence, an assessment of the second-order impact of social changes may be required. For example, if changes introduced by socio-technical design increase job satisfaction, the likely secondary impacts might be reduced absenteeism, healthy workforce, and hopefully increased productivity. A few assessment methods are based on the multi-objective, multi-criteria (MOMC) principle. Information economics (Parker & Benson, 1988) and the balanced score card (Robert S. Kaplan & Norton, 1992) are two deviations of the MOMC concept. Information economics realizes that gains from technology-based change include factors which traditional cost/benefit calculations cannot handle, because there is a range of intangible benefits such as improved response time for handling customer complaints or ubiqutous information retrieval for on-site decision-making. According to information economics, gains are split into two categories, the technical and the social, which are assessed independently. However, no explicit guidelines are provided for assessing gains, risks and costs relating to the social aspects of work. Information economics may well be modified to incorporate a thorough evaluation based on the social aspects of work. Even though information economics has proved useful in assessing the value of information systems, it is not widely used in organizations. Perhaps its emphasis on IS assessment rather than as an organization-wide tool for assessing work design may have suppressed its acceptance (Land, 2000).

A widely accepted methodology which has gained corporate attention is the balanced scorecard (Nair, 2004). Since the balanced scorecard is concerned with the financial well-being of the firm, it may be an appropriate method for assessing the socio-technical worth of IS in the organizations. Although (Martinsons, Davison, & Tse, 1999) tailored the balanced scorecard for evaluating the worth of decision support systems, the originators never include the "social" in the scorecard. The balanced scorecard was mainly developed to measure organization's customer satisfaction, financial standing, internal business processes, and ambition to learn and grow. (Land, 2000) described balanced scorecard as: dials and indicators in an cockpit of an aeroplane. In order to navigate the aeroplane, pilot need information on aspects such as fuel, altitude, air speed, bearing, and final destination. Likewise, the complexity of running an organization requires performance information from several areas concurrently. The balanced scorecard enables the manager to answer four important questions (Robert S. Kaplan & Norton, 1992).

- How do customers view us? (Customer perspective)
- How do the shareholders perceive us? (Financial perspective)
- What must we improve and excel at? (Internal perspective)
- Can we keep on improving and creating value? (Innovation and learning perspective)
- A detailed account of the balanced scorecard is provided in the next section.

THE BALANCED SCORECARD

In order to analyze the customer perspective, the balanced scorecard requires the manager to split the mission statement into exact measures that really matter to the customer. Customer concerns commonly fall into four categories; they are quality, response time, customer service, and cost. Hence, to put the balanced scorecard at work, the manager need to define goals for quality, response time, customer service, and cost and then transform these goals into precise measurable objectives. Customer-related measurement criteria are important, but they must be transformed into specific measures of what the firm must do internally to satisfy its customers. Hence, the manager needs to identify critical success factors and improve on the operations that really matters to the customer. Factors that have the best impact on customer satisfaction include response time on customer query, product/service quality, worker skills, and productivity. To attain these goals on customer satisfaction, the manager must identify improvement areas that are influenced by workers' actions (Robert S. Kaplan & Norton, 1992).

Financial performance factors specify whether firm's strategy, performance, and implementation are improving firms bottom-line. Case flow statements, income statement, increase in assets and decrease in liabilities, and growth in share price commonly measure financial perspective. The financial objectives can be seen as guidance for the objectives and measures in the other perspectives. The primary goal for a company is to provide returns on the capital invested, to create value to its investors, hence to be profitable. The balanced scorecard aids in making the financial objectives of a company more clear and comprehensive by targeting them to specific needs of each business unit in the organization (Robert S. Kaplan & Norton, 1992).

Internal business process measures factors that a firm considers essential for its competitive success. Defining objectives and measure for the internal business process perspective is generally done after the formulation of financial and customer perspective. This is done in-order to emphasize that the metrics developed in the internal business process perspective support the objectives established for customers and shareholders. Kaplan and Norton argue that even though companies have moved beyond just relying on traditional financial measures to supplement them with measures such as quality, yield, throughput, and cycle time, they still focus on improving performance of individual departments rather than integrated business processes. In order to encourage collaboration among the different departments in a company and better monitor the cross-functional performance, it is essential to assess various business operations such as order fulfillment, procurement, and production planning and control. Cost, quality, throughput and time measures can be defined and assessed for theses operations (Robert S. Kaplan & Norton, 1992; R. S. Kaplan & Norton, 1996).

Competition in the market requires the firm to introduce new products/services and continue to improve its offering to stay competitive in the industry. A firm' measurement factor to learn, improve, and innovate is directly tied to the firm's ability to introduce new products and services, add more value for the customer, and improve internal operations, target new markets, develop foreign operations and in so doing increase shareholder wealth. The innovation process consists of two stages. In the first stage, the company has to identify the market, by discovering emerging and latent needs of existing and new customers. In the second stage, the company has to produce product/service offering (Robert S. Kaplan & Norton, 1992).

THE SOCIO-TECHNICAL BALANCED SCORECARD

The four perspectives of the balanced scorecard are inter-linked since satisfied customers and production efficiencies leads to financial well-being of the organization. In order to develop a balanced scorecard, the assessor needs to sketch a table with a list of goals and their respective measures. Thus, under customer perspective a goal might be to "reduce service time for repairs". The appropriate measure might be average time to make a repair. Based on the measurement data, the evaluator can perform standard deviation analysis to identify delays in service and which factors might have contributed to the delay. The selection of goals is an important process and stakeholder input is essential in identifying high priority goals and ranking them according to their inherent risk and organizational mission and strategy.

The critics of balanced scorecard indicate lack of many other important perspectives. For instance, one could incorporate stakeholder perspective to identify how firm is perceived by its suppliers, investors, and society at large. Nevertheless, it may be subtle to measure goals that firm cannot fully control, reducing the original significance and viability of the balanced scorecard (Martinsons et al., 1999). It is believed that the balanced scorecard can be extended to include employee (socio-technical) perspective. With the incorporation of employee perspective, the organization could identify how the employees may perceive it. Since today's employee require autonomy, freedom, safe working conditions, it is essential that appropriate measures are defined to assess employee satisfaction. Highly motivated and satisfied workforce is often linked with excellent customer service, in that, if enthusiastic staff approaches the customers, it is likely that they will return or do business again with the firm. Also, it is believed that motivated workforce is more likely to learn and improve internal operations and make the organization more competitive in the industry. Hence, employee perspective is linked with firm's major functions and it is important that the organization focus on improving its employees' work environment (Horton, Davenport, & Wood-Harper, 2005; Land, 2000). Moreover, the socio-technical balanced scorecard can be used to define goals that are important from both managerial as well as the employees social welfare.

Three areas are particularly important to include in this perspective. First, "employee competencies and skills"; do employees have the right mix of skills to complete their work tasks? Second, "the flow of information"; do employees have the tools and information they need to make timely decisions? Lastly, "the organizational climate"; do employees have incentives and rewards upon the successful completion of a task. With the incorporation of employee perspective, it is believed that goals such as higher job satisfaction, stress reduction; increase in participative decision-making may materialize. Assessment measures could include first order measures such as changes in work-satisfaction and secondary measures such as decline in absenteeism and improvement in behaviour and physical health may also be fruitful. The process of defining goals and measures in the employee perspective can be regarded as a socio-technical one. The principles of socio-technical theory may be valuable in this process. That is, they can help define goals that intend to improve employee job satisfaction (Robert S. Kaplan & Norton, 2001).

Although the balanced scorecard has been fruitful in non-profit organizations, most non-profit organizations had difficulty applying the balanced scorecard. One success example can be found at the Mecklenburg County in the USA, the balanced scorecard has transformed the company from where accountability was unclear to a few balanced scorecard experts, to a system of widespread accountability and transparency based on data -driven decision-making processes. Another was found at Northwest Fire District, Pima County in the USA. The district problem was to develop a system that would enable them to see how the organization was performing. A group of 40 employees representing all levels of the organization was formed to guide the enhanced strategic planning process for the next five years. In addition, given the communication challenges between fire services labour/management process, the balanced scorecard guided the communication process that bring along key players in the organization toward the enhanced strategic planning process. More recently, the application of the balanced scorecard can be found in US government. In nominating Jeffrey Zients to be Chief Performance Officer, US president Obama emphasize that federal government would continue to develop upon performance focus, re-invent processes, cut costs, and discover best practices in the entire government.

Not all non-profit organizations have been successful in applying the balanced scorecard. The problems facing non-profit organization using balanced scorecard originate generally from the increased complexity of stakeholder requirements and the potential variability of these demands over time. Not limited to the failures at NGOs, translating the balanced scorecard to the complex world of academia is a challenge. Since the 1990s accountability has become a challenging issue in the higher education sector. Universities are required to provide performance indicators (i.e. evidence of their value in the society) to government, alumni, prospective students and external stakeholders. Numerous state and board agencies have developed "report cards" that grade universities according to the performance on various categories. Surveys in the main stream press and Web rank universities based upon their graduation rates, resources, reputation, publications, and more. However, these performance indicators make little or no reference to the goals of the universities and literally no reference is given to the teaching methods and programme quality with respect to the specified results of teaching and research.

The original configuration of balanced scorecard placed financial goals on the top of the hierarchy but since maximizing shareholder wealth is not the main objective, it was not widely applied by these organizations. The socio-technical balanced scorecard may be useful in assessing for-profit organization's mission and vision strategy, but its application in a non-profit organization can be even greater. As non-profit organizations commonly operate on humanistic welfare paradigm and well-being of the society, the ideas of socio-technical job design may receive greater acceptance in these organizations. Universities can be defined as private or public institutions. Private universities are generally for-profit and public universities are of non-profit nature (Wikipedia, 2007). The University of Manchester is a non-profit institution and it is mainly funded by the council grants (government), academic fees (students), research grants (donors), and other operating income (accommodation) (The University of Manchester, 2004). Moreover, in a for-profit university, students pay entirely for the education that they receive. But in a public university, government and donors predominantly provide financial resources for supplementing students' tuition fees. Here one could ask, who the customer is-the student or government or donor agencies. Rather making a choice, public universities may consider government, donor agencies and students as a customer when applying the socio-technical balanced scorecard. An extensive framework for accessing a public university is developed next for a complete illustration of the socio-technical balance scorecard.

CONCLUSION

Socio-technical theory has been used in the organizations to design jobs that provide work satisfaction and motivation to the organizational employees. Although socio-technical theory has been fruitful in many organizations, it has not been applied widely due to the need for cost savings in the past. The balanced scorecard is a methodology that has been used extensively in the organizations. The balanced scorecard enables the organization to assess its strategy and whether it's meeting its financial goals. The balanced scorecard has been beneficial in the for-profit organizations; its use in the non-profit organizations has been poor. The original configuration of balanced scorecard placed financial goals on the top of the hierarchy and since maximizing shareholder wealth is not a main objective for most non-profit organizations, it was not widely applied by these organizations. Thus, the socio-technical balanced scorecard was developed to include the employee perspective.

With the incorporation of employee perspective, work-related factors that have a negative impact on the employees work performance may be identified and enable the organization to design jobs that promote employee task variety, discretion, participation in the decision-making process, training, realistic performance measures, and rewarding pay structures. Next, a framework for accessing a public university was proposed for an illustration of the socio-technical balance scorecard. The employee perspective was included to assess the academics/staff's productivity, absenteeism, and job satisfaction whereas customer perspective takes into consideration multiple measures that include student/government/donor viewpoints and goals. The internal business perspective relates to the goals that measure a university's academic as well as administrative processes including IT infrastructure. The innovation and learning perspective, on the contrary, is concerned with financial support for the students and the number of new courses developed including e-learning courses per year. Lastly, the financial perspective relates to the increase in university graduates and funding obtained from the government and donor bodies each year.

Figure 2. The Socio-technical Balanced Scorecard for a Public University Wide Assessment (The University of Manchester, 2004)

Employee Perspective

Goals	Measures
Increase in Academics' Productivity	- Number of course given per year. - Number of MSc/PhD students supervised per year. - Response time to a work-related email - Number of journal and conference papers published per year.
Reduction in Staff Absenteeism	- Number of sick days per year
Increase in Academics/Staff's Work Satisfaction	- Number of new skills acquired per year. - Amount of freedom in conducting work. - Amount of participation in decision-making. - Amount of balance between work and social life. - Number of reward/ promotions received per year.

Customer Perspective

Goals	Measures
World Class University-Student Perspective	- Number of faculties in the university. - Number of applications per year. - Number of national and foreign students enrolled per year. - Amount ICT support for the students.
World Class University-Government/Donor Perspective	- Number of degree certificates awarded per year. - Number of research awards per year. - Amount of technology support for the faculty and staff.

Internal Business Perspective

Goals	Measures
Highly Knowledgeable Academics	- Number of academics with a PhD degree
Online Course Administration	- Number of online support tools available for course management (WebCT/First Class).
Broad Selection of Literature	- Number of libraries available at the university.
Secure Internet/Intranet Access	- Number of intrusions per year.
Efficient ICT Infrastructure and Support	- Number of Computer Clusters in the University. - Number of wireless hot spots in the campus. - Number of helpdesk support staff available.

Innovation and Learning Perspective

Goals	Measures
Increase in Financial Support.	- Number of students receiving scholarships.
Industry Relevance	- Number of new courses developed per year.
Increase in e-learning initiatives.	- Number of online courses introduced per year.

Financial Perspective

Goals	Measures
Increase in University Graduates	- Number of university degrees provided per year
Increase in Donor Funds	- Amount of funding obtained from outside bodies per year

REFERENCES

Azoff, M., Jones, T., Rodger, A., & Butler, G. (2004). *IT Performance Optimisation: Realising Best Value from IT Investments*. Hull, UK: Butler Direct.

Boresson C., J. (2005). *Good Enough! IT Investment and Business Process Performance in Higher Education*. Educause Center For Applied Research.

Bostrom, R. P., & Heinen, S. (1977). MIS problems and failures: a socio-technical perspective, part 1: the causes. *Management Information Systems Quarterly*, *1*(3), 17–32. doi:10.2307/248710

Butler, G. (2004). *Managing Costs in IT: Achieving Best Value from IT Investments*. Hull, UK: Butler Group.

Checkland, P., & Holwell, S. (2004). *Information Systems and Information Systems-Making Sense of the Field*. Chichester, UK: John Wiley & Sons.

Checkland, P., & Scholes, J. (1990). *Soft System Methodology in Action*. Chichester, UK: Wiley.

Elgin, D. (1981). *Voluntary Simplicity: Toward a way of life that is Outwardly Simple, Inwardly Rich*. New York: Morrow.

Garrety, K., & Badham, R. (2000). The politics of socio-technical intervention: an interactionist view. *Technology Analysis and Strategic Management*, *12*(1), 103–118. doi:10.1080/095373200107265

Horton, K., Davenport, E., & Wood-Harper, A. T. (2005). Exploring sociotechnical interaction with Rob Kling: five big ideas. *Information Technology & People*, *18*(1), 50–67. doi:10.1108/09593840510584621

Jeppesen, S. L., Barfod, M. B., & Leleur, S. (2007, April 11). *Comparing a soft and hard multi-methodology approach: location of an IT company in the Oresund region*. Paper presented at the ISOneWorld 07, Las Vegas, USA.

Kaplan, R. S., & Norton, D. P. (1992). The balanced scorecard: measures that drive performance. *Harvard Business Review*, *70*, 70–79.

Kaplan, R. S., & Norton, D. P. (1996). *Translating strategy into action: the balanced scorecard*. Boston: Harvard Business School Press.

Kaplan, R. S., & Norton, D. P. (2001). *The strategy-focused organization: how balanced scorecard companies thrive in the new business environment*. Boston, MA: Harvard Business School Press.

Kling, R. (1999, January). What is Social Informatics and Why Does it Matter? *D-Lib Magazine*, 5.

Kling, R., & Iacono, S. (2001). *Information technology and organizational transformation: history, rhetoric, and practice*. Thousand Oaks, CA: Sage Publications.

Land, F. F. (2000). *Evaluation in a socio-technical context*. Paper presented at the Organizational and Social Perspectives on IT 2000, Aalborg, Denmark.

Liyanage, J. P., & Bjerkebaek, E. (2006). Use of advanced technologies and information solutions for North Sea offshore assets: ambitious changes and socio-technical dimensions. *International Journal of International Technology and Information Management*, *15*(4), 1–10.

Lucas Henry, C. (1999). *Information Technology and the Productivity Paradox: Assessing the Value of the Investment in IT*. Oxford, UK: Oxford University Press.

Malone, T. W. (2004). *The Future of Work: How the New Order of Business Will Shape Your Organization, Your Management Style, and Your Life*. Boston: Harvard Business School Publishing.

Martinsons, M., Davison, R., & Tse, D. (1999). The Balanced Scorecard: A Foundation for the Strategic Management of Information Systems. *Decision Support Systems*, *25*, 71–88. doi:10.1016/S0167-9236(98)00086-4

Moldaschl, M., & Weber, W. G. (1998). The three waves of industrial groups: historical reflections on current research on group work. *Human Relations*, *51*, 347–388. doi:10.1177/001872679805100307

Mumford, E. (2003). *Redesigning Human Systems*. London: IRM Press.

Mumford, E. (2006). The story of socio-technical design: reflections on its successes, failures and potential. *Information Systems Journal*, *16*, 317–342. doi:10.1111/j.1365-2575.2006.00221.x

Mumford, E., & Weir, M. (1979). *Computer Systems in Work Design-The ETHICS Method: Effective Technical and Human Implementation of Computer Systems: A Work Design Exercise Book for Individuals and Groups*. London: Associated Business Press.

Nadin, S. J., Waterson, P. E., & Parker, S. K. (2001). Participation in job redesign: an evaluation of the use of a sociotechnical tool and its impact. *Human Factors and Ergonomics in Manufacturing*, *11*(1), 53–69. doi:10.1002/1520-6564(200124)11:1<53::AID-HFM4>3.0.CO;2-F

Nair, M. (2004). *Essentials of balanced scorecard*. New York: Wiley.

Parker, M. M., & Benson, R. J. (1988). *Information Economics: Linking Business Performance to Information Technology*. Englewood Cliffs, NJ: Prentice-Hall International.

Pasmore, W. A. (1985). Social science transformer: the socio-technical perspective. *Human Relations*, *48*, 1–22. doi:10.1177/001872679504800101

Pestoff, V. A. (1999). Social empire and civil democracy in Sweden: developing a participatory welfare society in the twenty-first century. In W. E. Halal & K. B. Taylor (Eds.), *21st Century Economics*. London: Macmillan.

Porter, M. E. (1985). *Competitive Advantage: Creating and Sustaining Superior Performance*. London: Collier Macmillan Publishers.

Seo, Y., Ko, J., & Price, J. L. (2004). The determinants of job satisfaction among hospital a model estimation in Korea. *International Journal of Nursing Studies*, *41*, 437–446. doi:10.1016/j.ijnurstu.2003.11.003

Strassmann, P. A. (1990). *The Business Value of Computers: An Executive's Guide*. New Canaan, CT: Information Economics Press.

The University of Manchester. (2004). *Introducing The University of Manchester*. Manchester, UK: University of Manchester.

Wikipedia. (2007). *Public University*. Retrieved March 19, 2007, from http://en.wikipedia.org/wiki/Public_university

Wood-Harper, A. T., Fok, L. M., & Kumar, K. (1987, December). *Methodologies for socio-technical systems (STS) development: a comparative review.* Paper presented at the 8th International Conference of Information Systems, Pittsburgh, USA.

Chapter 4
Planning Cooperation in Inter-Organizational Systems

María Laura Ponisio
University of Twente, The Netherlands

Pascal van Eck
University of Twente, The Netherlands

Lourens Riemens
Dutch Tax and Customs Administration, The Netherlands

ABSTRACT

The purpose of this chapter is to present a systematic reasoning framework (called e-Planning) to plan cooperation between organizations in a network. Thorough assessment of opportunities for and obstacles to cooperation is of paramount importance, as setting up electronic networks usually requires considerable up-front investments in information technology (IT) specific for this cooperation. E-Planning offers an action plan for decision makers to determine with whom to establish cooperation first, and on which topic to cooperate more closely. Following a method for critical problem solving, e-Planning provides guidance to analyze different potential partners and to reason about obstacles to and opportunities for cooperation. To illustrate and validate the framework, it is applied in the area of cooperation between customs organizations of member states of the European Union. Applying the reasoning framework in practice revealed several potential benefits, such as fast and successful assessment of cooperation needs that result in increased re-use of knowledge and software applications. In particular, this way of reasoning may prove to help decision makers cut down unnecessary expenses by, for instance, avoiding duplicated projects.

INTRODUCTION

More and more organizations cooperate in networks to perform increasingly complex tasks. Rather than managing their resources in isolation, organizations construct inter-organizational networks in which flows of information support joint value-creating processes. Organizations participating in such networks need to understand how closer cooperation with selected members of that network can be fostered. Decision makers such as business analysts and IT architects use

DOI: 10.4018/978-1-61692-016-6.ch004

this understanding to decide which investments to make, e.g., developing or acquiring inter-organizational systems.

Consider a (potentially large) network of organizations. The members of this network know each other and are probably already cooperating in some way, or have recently done so. However, the current way of cooperation is no longer sustainable, for example due to new laws or increased transaction volumes. Consequently, one member organization in this network is interested in intensifying cooperation with one or more other members of the network (potential partners). This organization starts a process in which it tries to identify opportunities for closer cooperation, as well as potential problems in such cooperation. In other words, it tries to identify those other member organizations with which closer cooperation is feasible, together with cooperation topics for which closer cooperation is mutually beneficial. Finding these candidates for closer cooperation within the (existing) network is a large part of the problem of planning an inter-organizational network. We name this the partner selection problem. In this chapter, we present a reasoning framework that helps decision makers to solve this problem from an IT resource management perspective.

The partner selection problem comprises the first step in developing and implementing closer cooperation with selected members of a network. In this endeavor, several challenges have to be taken into account (Ponisio et al., 2008a): issues related to distribution of power and opportunistic behavior (Williamson, 1993) have to be considered, IT development processes for the inter-organizational systems needed for cooperation have to be planned, and sustainable gains have to be measured. Moreover, a network may have very ambitious joint aims, but there is no way it can accomplish all those aims at once for all members. Thus, the issue is to identify the first steps towards these aims that have a reasonable chance of being successfully implemented. Decision makers are, therefore, in need of an approach that helps them to plan closer cooperation with selected partners in a systematic and integrated way. Unfortunately, current systems development and IT project management methods do not provide such an approach. Focusing solely on one challenge at a time, they fall short in integrating the challenges mentioned above in one comprehensive and systematic assessment method.

The objective of this chapter is to present a reasoning framework (called e-Planning) that enables an organization to plan selection of partners for closer cooperation. Decision makers can use it as a systematic technique to assess opportunities for closer cooperation with candidate organizations. Furthermore, e-Planning helps decision makers to identify the most suitable topic for cooperation.

The reasoning framework leads us through the steps needed to solve the partner selection problem (i.e., problem investigation, solution design, validation, implementation and implementation evaluation) in a systematic way. The reasoning framework is based on a critical problem solving method that was chosen for a number of reasons. First, it makes the problem solving task less daunting, by splitting a large problem into smaller ones that are easier to deal with. Second, it helps decision makers to focus their attention on the most relevant issues. Third, it adds a degree of flexibility, promoting asking questions pertinent to the specific characteristics of the network. Finally, it disentangles nested problems in a logical way.

To illustrate and evaluate our reasoning framework, we use e-Customs, a case study about customs in the European Union. This example is particularly interesting because it is not a commercial business network but a *governmental* network, demanding a more complex analysis of similarities and matches between organizations to identify obstacles to and possibilities for closer cooperation. Compared to commercial business, in government organizations goals are more fluid, political benefits are intangible, and the dynamics of inter-organizational cooperation are harder to capture. The e-Customs case study precisely addresses a partner selection problem because the network consists of all member states of the EU, and, as we explain later in the chapter, implementers have considerable freedom to select partners for closer cooperation within this network.

In our case study, we applied our reasoning framework to create a plan for assessing opportunities for and obstacles to closer cooperation between customs organizations. The fifth section of this chapter, called "E-Planning illustrated: the e-Customs case study", presents a blueprint of this plan. We learned that applying our framework resulted in several benefits. According to experts from the customs domain, the reasoning framework facilitates traceability by linking IT solutions to cooperation goals. This, in turn, may prevent costly mistakes, for instance by avoiding duplicated projects. Moreover, because applying the framework creates insight in which knowledge and experience is available at which member organizations of the network, decision makers may work more efficiently than before by re-using this knowledge and experience.

This chapter extends work reported earlier (Ponisio et al., 2008a,b) with a more elaborate problem investigation and a description of the mechanisms behind the benefits of applying our framework as found in practice.

The chapter is structured as follows. In the next section, we provide the necessary background by discussing related work and relevant problems of cooperation in inter-organizational networks. After that, we present the research method applied to develop our reasoning framework. The framework itself is then presented in its own section. We then illustrate the reasoning framework by applying it to e-Customs. We wrap up by reflecting on the results of the case study and by providing directions for future research.

BACKGROUND

In this section, we discuss existing research and approaches to the partner selection problem. We start with elaborating the concept of inter-organizational systems. Then we discuss the problem of partner selection and its importance to network resource management. After that, we present the challenges of resource management in inter-organizational networks that have been identified in the literature.

Inter-Organizational Systems and Alliance Formation

Current organizations operate in networks, using services of suppliers and providing services to customers. It is not uncommon for one organization to maintain relations with hundreds if not thousands of other organizations. Such networks of relations have been studied from several perspectives. Eisenhardt and Schoonhoven (1996) and Das and Teng (2000) explain organizational network formation from the perspective of resource dependence: organizations participate in networks as a means to acquire resources that they need, but cannot acquire in another way. Networks have also been regarded as business partnerships (Rosenkopf et al., 2001; Hagedoorn, 2002; Belderbos et al., 2004). Here, networks are viewed as a way to "[obtain] access to and control of technical and strategic knowledge as well as opportunities to increase visibility as legitimate actors and potential partners in the technological community." (Rosenkopf et al., 2001, p. 750).

Not all of these relations among organizations are equally strong. Within a network, an organization selects some organizations with which it cooperates much more closely than with other organizations in the network: transaction volumes (the number of instances of cooperation) are higher, more information is exchanged, and partners adapt some of their information systems to meet requirements specific for this cooperation. We view the development of such closer cooperation relationships as alliance formation. Gulati (1998) discusses alliance formation from many perspectives and identifies a number of issues that organizations have to address, such as whether to start forming an alliance, which partners to choose, how to govern the alliance, and how to deal with its evolution. In this chapter, we focus exclusively on one of these issues: how to select other organizations that are already member of a network to develop closer cooperation relationships?

Nowadays, close cooperation between organizations requires that these organizations connect the operational systems that support this cooperation. This leads to the development of inter-organizational systems, which we define as collections of connected operational systems of more than one organization that jointly support value-creating processes in the cooperation (adapted from Ponisio et al., 2008a). Inter-organizational systems ensure that all information that is needed for close cooperation actually flows between the participating organizations. To that regard, each participating organization commits a number of its IT resources when it joins an inter-organizational system. In particular, it commits a set of information systems that includes application software, databases, computer hardware and diverse (possibly manual) procedures.

The Partner Selection Problem

We define the partner selection problem as the task of finding opportunities for cooperation and potential problems in cooperation among organizations that are member of an inter-organizational network. In other words, the problem consists of, given a particular, concrete network of organizations, identifying a priori those member organizations that have the most potential for successful closer cooperation, and identifying the most suitable topic for cooperation. Potential for successful cooperation, in turn, is defined as the extent to which development of the required inter-organizational system can be expected to be feasible. According to our observations of inter-organizational networks, this problem is an important part of the problem of planning cooperation in inter-organizational systems.

Efficient management of an organization's resources demands that organizations cooperate closely. Close cooperation, in turn, demands that participating organizations invest in the development of supporting systems, which we have called inter-organizational systems in the previous subsection. These investments are usually specific for the cooperation relation for which they are made, and they carry considerable risk. Therefore, most organizations cannot afford to enter into very many close cooperation relations with very many partners at the same time. Thus, partners for closer cooperation need to be selected carefully.

This, however, is not easy, as is perhaps best illustrated by the well-documented case of the failure of Covisint. Covisint was a very prominent online auction set up by the Big Three USA car manufacturers. Recent research (Gerst and Bunduchi, 2005) has shown that in this particular network (of car manufacturers and their suppliers), the introduction of this particular form of cooperation generated a shift in power that was too much for the network to accept. Overlooking one aspect of cooperation (in this case: power distribution) resulted in a loss that may be as high as 250 million US dollars and committed IT development resources for several years without reaching the desired outcome (Supply Chain Digest, 2009).

IT decision makers currently address the partner selection problem relying solely on the experience of stakeholders, and using ad-hoc methods and tools available to the stakeholders such as text documents, tables and graphs. Thus, the quality of partner selection depends solely on the discipline and creativity of the stakeholders involved, not on the use of a systematic reasoning framework. In addition to this, current results in the academic study of alliance formation generally take the form of correlations of quantities aggregated for a particular industry or market-segment. For example, Eisenhardt and Schoonhoven (1996) found that the rate of alliance formation increases with the number of competitors in a market. Aggregated correlations help to understand how the phenomenon of alliance formation is related to other phenomena, such as competition. However, for managerial decision making, this is not enough: a manager needs to decide precisely which members of the network are suitable partners for closer cooperation. In spite of the existence of a large body of research on inter-organizational networks, there is (to the best of our knowledge) no solution to the partner selection problem that covers all the challenges and all the perspectives involved.

What we learn from this is that in order to understand how closer cooperation can be fostered, we have to find a way to systematically reason about the characteristics of network members and the opportunities and difficulties they may create for closer cooperation. A systematic action plan would help organizations to create understanding of which issues are more important and should be considered first. Better understanding of characteristics of potential partners, their similarities and differences helps stakeholders to improve detecting potential problems and opportunities for cooperation and thus make better partner selection decisions. For instance, if we could prioritize concrete issues that affect the cooperation process (such as misaligned IT capabilities, or misaligned goals and needs), we could rule out potential partners for which cooperation is not likely to succeed due to differences in power and opposite interests.

Challenges of Planning Cooperation in Inter-Organizational Networks

Managing resources of current inter-organizational networks involves addressing the challenges of planning inter-organizational networks. Solving the partner selection problem requires understanding these challenges. This is a complex task because these challenges are rooted in different dimensions. In other words, careful assessment demands decision makers to take into account different challenges of planning inter-organizational networks and these challenges have been identified and described in different research areas.

In the previous subsections, we have called for an integrated approach to facilitate understanding of partner selection in inter-organizational networks, i.e., an approach that takes all relevant dimensions into account. In this section, we review some challenges that have been reported in the literature: alignment in inter-organizational networks, evaluation of IT development processes, distribution of power, and possibilities for opportunistic behavior. They are all challenges of our problem, however observed from different research fields.

Alignment in Inter-Organizational Networks

In recent work, Derzsi and Gordijn (2006) argue that inter-organizational cooperation needs the alignment of multiple perspectives. In their paper, they identify four levels that need to be aligned: the information systems of the organizations, the processes supported by them, the value proposition of each organization, and the strategic goals of each organization. Each organization in the network uses a set of information systems (i.e., computer hardware, application software, databases and possibly manual procedures), called the IT portfolio of the organization, to process the information flows mentioned. This portfolio includes both organization-specific information systems as well as general IT infrastructure components (e.g., email servers); this IT portfolio comprises what Derzsi and Gordijn call the information systems layer of the organization.

The alignment that Derzsi and Gordijn (2006) call for refers to the need to assess how much each partner has to change to meet the needs of the network. Consider the IT portfolios of two organizations. We do not assume that potential partners need to have identical portfolios, and thus there is no need to determine how much each partner must change to reach a situation where IT portfolios are identical. However, for close cooperation, parts of the portfolio may need to change, and this has to be determined. For instance, if A and B are organizations planning to cooperate more closely, then systems of A and B must match before cooperation can take place. In other words, to cooperate more closely, information systems of A and B must have already reached a certain maturity level and A and B must be willing to invest in their systems. For example, if A is mature enough to manage electronic transactions, but B cannot, the process of A transacting with B will not run as smoothly as if B were able to process electronic transactions.

In practice, we observe that much of the discussion is indeed about the information systems level and the levels above it such as strategic goals. However, the model of Derzsi and Gordijn lacks a concrete description of specific properties of attributes to study when planning closer cooperation. In particular, it lacks descriptors to characterize participants in the network, which is needed to compare participants. Comparing participants is a way to spot differences between them, as participants may run their organizations in different manners. Differences between participants indicate spots of possible problems even before closer cooperation starts.

Evaluation of IT Development Processes

IT development processes in inter-organizational networks are complex and risky, and, in general, lack the means to measure sustainable gain. In some cases they have a political benefit as driver of the evaluation. Political benefits are intangible and not measurable in monetary units. Therefore, evaluating processes in inter-organizational networks becomes a key skill with yet unclear descriptive concepts.

Maturity models can be used to evaluate and improve processes. In the area of collaborative work, examples of maturity models are the interoperability maturity model of Clark and Jones (1999), the supply chain management maturity model of Lockamy III and McCormack (2004), and the maturity framework for managing distributed development of Ramasubbu et al. (2005). However, existing maturity models do not sufficiently address inter-governmental networks and practice shows that descriptive concepts that are more expressive for inter-governmental networks are still missing. We need to extend existing models with concepts specific for inter-governmental networks.

Distribution of Power

Previous work derived a theory of power relations that explains power balancing operations (Emerson, 1962) and recognized the importance of addressing power relationships to coordinate inter-organizational networks (Evermann, 2006). If power relations are unbalanced in a network of power-dependency relations, there are mechanisms to restore the balance. For instance, the weaker actor may withdraw his interest in the relationship, or two weak actors may form an alliance against a stronger actor. Balancing alterations change the power relationship, tending to reduce the power advantage (Emerson, 1962).

Understanding the distribution of power is not straightforward. Working out efficient plans for cooperation includes determining which aspects are to count. If power is concentrated in some actors, which perspective will be used to detect them? Which operational definitions will connect generalizing concepts from theory with concrete features of a specific system?

Our problem and the perspective of analysis chosen in this chapter suggest to seek better understanding of opportunities and challenges of cooperation rather than to focus on determining who are the most powerful players per se and the impacts of power-dependence in corporate or conventional network (as, e.g., by Cook, 1977). We add distributing of power as a challenge of planning cooperation because understanding the distribution of power might highlight dimensions to take into account when selecting partners to cooperate with, improving thus our understanding at the time to make a decision.

Opportunistic Behavior

Coase (1937) and Williamson (1975, 1981) have developed a micro-economic theory rooted in a view of the world in which economic actors have bounded rationality and are not inherently 'good'. Bounded rationality means that an economic actor has only limited knowledge and reasoning power at its disposal when assessing a situation and choosing what to do to reach its goals. Therefore, its behavior is suboptimal from the perspective of full information and unlimited reasoning/computational power (Simon, 1985). In addition to their bounded rationality, economic actors are willing to bend the rules, breach contract, cheat, or engage in any other activity that advances them toward their goal, even if this harms other economic actors. Williamson (1993) calls this 'opportunism'.

Williamson (1975) identified opportunism as a critical transactional factor steering activities between business or governmental organizations. In partner selection, it is therefore important to understand whether a potential partner can exploit certain advantages for its benefit and in detriment of other participants in a collaboration (Williamson, 1975).

Lessons Learnt

In this section, we have seen that planning closer cooperation in a network is all about understanding. Participating organizations need to carefully assess the partners they may cooperate more closely with. In particular, they need to know needs and goals of the potential partners. Moreover, organizations need this information early in the process of forming closer cooperation relations, before significant investments have been made or legal obligations have been created. Finally, we have seen that understanding network partners involves a number of dimensions and decision makers experience little support from existing frameworks and methods in reasoning about opportunities and potential problems in a systematic way.

The current situation calls for an integrated approach to facilitate reasoning about challenges that involve multiple dimensions. What is needed is a framework that helps decision makers to reason about the problem in terms of all the dimensions discussed above in coherence, not in isolation. This can be very complex, and that is why the framework should also facilitate breaking down the complex problem into a number of steps that are easier to manage. Providing a reasoning tool to gather the necessary understanding in a logical and systematic way forms the basis of our approach.

RESEARCH METHOD

To develop our reasoning framework, we followed a design research (Hevner et al., 2004) method for software and information engineers (Wieringa, 2007) called the engineering cycle. In this section, we first present the necessary background and motivate our choice for this method. After that, we discuss how we applied this method to design and validate our reasoning framework. The reasoning framework itself is presented in the next section.

Figure 1. The engineering cycle (adapted from Wieringa, 2007)

It is then illustrated and validated by applying it in a case study in the section after that.

Solving Design Problems: The Engineering Cycle

The goal of this chapter is to provide IT decision makers with a systematic technique to assess opportunities for closer cooperation with other organizations in a network. We view this as a design problem: an artifact (our reasoning framework) that currently does not exist has to be designed.

We follow a standard design research method called the engineering cycle (Wieringa, 2007). We have chosen to follow this method for a number of reasons. First, applying a systematic technique such as the engineering cycle makes a design problem less daunting, by splitting it in smaller problems that are easier to solve. Each step in the engineering cycle may lead to new problems, which can themselves be solved using the engineering cycle. Discovering these nested problems helps us to organize our reasoning because it facilitates disentangling hidden questions. Second, the engineering cycle helps us to focus on the most relevant (nested) problems. Third, the engineering cycle is flexible, as it is easy to adapt the design process to the situation at hand. Fourth, the engineering cycle is sound, as it disentangles nested problems in a logical way.

As depicted in Figure 1, the first step to solve a design problem is problem investigation, in which characteristics of the problem are investigated: who are the stakeholders, what are their desired characteristics (requirements) of the solution, and which solutions already exist? The next step is solution design, in which one or more solutions are identified, elaborated, and/or possibly realized (e.g., created by engineers, acquired from a supplier). After that, solutions created in the previous step are validated: it is established to which extent the solutions comply with the requirements of the stakeholders. One or more of the solutions are then implemented. By implementation, we mean that the solution is placed in its usage environment, and that end-users start using it. If the solution was not already built or acquired in the solution design step, then building it, or acquiring it from a vendor, is also part of this step. Evaluating the implementation then closes the engineering cycle. This amounts to establishing whether the solution, as implemented, actually solves the original problem. Implementation evaluation may lead to new insights in the problem and new, or refined, requirements, thus starting a new iteration of the cycle.

Problem Investigation

We have performed a review of existing literature on inter-organizational networks. We focused on areas such as alliance formation, micro-economics, and inter-organizational systems development. We did not limit ourselves to recent work. Rather, we valued work on inter-organizational networks a couple of decades old. Even though today's inter-organizational networks are shaped by advances in technology, they also share characteristics and problems with networks that predate modern information technology.

Existing theoretical frameworks, methods and techniques address aspects of the partner selection problem in isolation, but do not provide a systematic, integrated technique. While there is a clear need for such a technique, the partial solutions that we found (and that are described in the Background section) provide valuable

Figure 2. Putting together quantifiable descriptors to characterize participants of inter-organizational networks

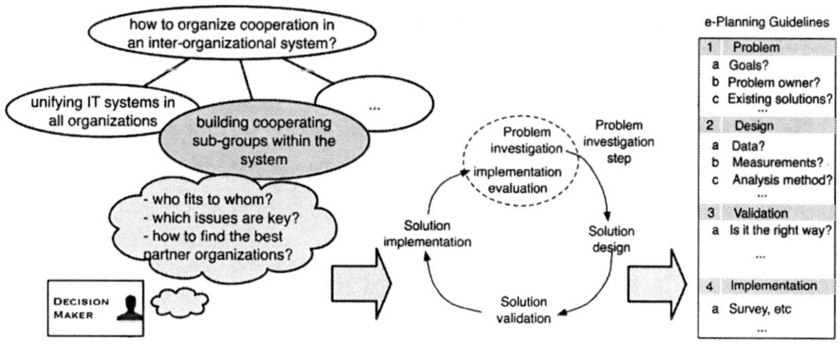

lessons learnt and form the basis of the problem investigation of our research.

In line with results of existing research, our problem investigation suggests that what is needed is a reasoning framework that facilitates reasoning about the partner selection problem in terms of all relevant dimensions in coherence. As this can be very complex, the reasoning framework should facilitate splitting the partner selection problem into a number of (presumably easier to solve) subproblems.

Solution Design

As stated in the previous subsection, our problem investigation suggested that our reasoning framework should enable organizations to split the partner selection problem into a number of subproblems. This way, our reasoning framework helps organizations to identify the steps to take to address partner selection. We realized that, therefore, our reasoning framework could itself be structured according to the engineering cycle, as it is itself a tool to solve a design problem (Hevner et al., 2004). The problem being finding those steps to take to address partner selection in a particular context.

Put in other words, in this chapter, we use the engineering cycle in two different ways. In the current section, we describe how we use the engineering cycle as a research method to address the partner selection problem (first way). The outcome of this is a reasoning framework (called e-Planning), which we present in the next section and illustrate and evaluate in the one after that. Second, this reasoning framework is a framework for the design of action plans to address partner selection in a specific context and is itself structured according to the engineering cycle (second way). Figure 2 illustrates the relation between the problem addressed in this chapter, the engineering cycle, and e-Planning. Figure 3 shows how the engineering is used in two ways in this chapter.

Solution Validation

After presenting the e-Planning reasoning framework in the next section, we present an illustration in the domain of cooperation between customs organizations of the European Union. This illustration serves two purposes. First, it is an example of how the e-Planning reasoning framework can be applied in a specific domain. Second, it serves as a validation of the framework. To validate our solution, we applied our framework to data provided by "Benchmarking Customs IT Architecture" (Netherlands Tax and Customs Administration, 2005) and i) we reasoned about potential cooperations (together with the opportunities and challenges they present) and ii) we looked for mechanisms behind cooperation in inter-organizational networks. We then derived our

Figure 3. The engineering cycle, its steps and their mapping to our approach

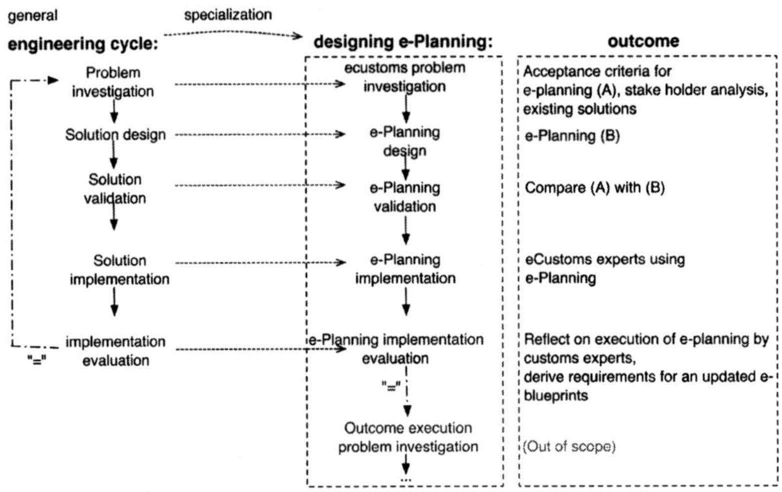

conclusions independently from the conclusions obtained by customs experts. At a later step, we compared our conclusions regarding opportunities for cooperation with those of customs experts (the benchmarking report provided a source of valuable guidelines against which to compare the results that we obtained with our approach). The conclusions derived from using our approach matched the conclusions of the customs experts who performed the benchmarking, which validated our solution.

We obtained the list of properties (the validation criteria of the action plan resulting from our application of the e-Planning reasoning framework) that would be desired in the solution directly from architects interested in the problem. According to what we learnt from customs architects, they need a framework to assess the possibilities of cooperation among customs. Customs architects perceive the need to have only one framework, rather than a clashing set of cooperation-analysis plans. The framework should help them to reason about where to start observing, how to do this in practice and about the impact of leaving areas out of the analyses. It must facilitate creating solutions. It must guide the experts towards identifying important spots for further analyses, but not constrain their freedom (it must be flexible). It should be able to help architects to detect the status of IT systems and best practices used, and it should serve as a conceptual framework that also architects from foreign countries can use.

Solution Implementation and Evaluation

The application of e-Planning in the customs domain has been developed by the authors of this chapter (one of whom is a customs architect). Implementation of the solution is outside the scope of this chapter. To implement the solution (the final step in the engineering cycle), the solution would have to be placed in its usage environment and other customs decision makers (not only the authors) would have to adopt the reasoning framework.

THE E-PLANNING REASONING FRAMEWORK

The e-Planning reasoning framework is a systematic approach to design an action plan for solving partner selection problems in a particular context.

As the framework is thus essentially a tool to solve a design problem, it follows the structure of the engineering cycle discussed in the previous section. The engineering cycle helps us to determine which are the relevant questions to ask, and we present these questions in the list below. These questions follow directly from the documentation of the engineering cycle as proposed by Wieringa (2007). Our contribution is that we apply the engineering cycle in a new problem domain. The engineering cycle as described by Wieringa (2007) is usually applied to design technical artifacts such as software systems. In our research, however, we use the engineering cycle as a guiding principle in the design of an action plan for decision makers. The questions that applying the engineering cycle proposes are as follows (the questions in italics were taken from the documentation of the method):

1. **Problem investigation**. In this step we investigate what the problem is. We address the following questions. *Who are the stakeholders?* Which factors are relevant to plan electronic customs cooperation? What are the desired characteristics (requirements) of the solution, and which solutions already exist?
2. **Solution design**, or plan for solving our problem. In this step we analyze the issue of how we can design a solution. First we ask: *which solution alternatives are available?* We can use an existing solution when it is satisfactory, adapt it if needed, invent a new solution or assemble a new solution from existing elements (this last option is what we do in this chapter).
3. **Solution validation**. *Which alternative best solves the problem?* In this step we are interested in the properties that our solution has in the environment where it is deployed. This is a different kind of problem because we have to gather knowledge rather than producing a design and it can be decomposed in several subproblems, such as property prediction, prediction validation, property evaluation (i.e., do the predicted properties of our solution agree with the goals of our stakeholders? Does our solution satisfy the goals of our stakeholders? To which degree?), etc.
4. **Solution implementation**. *Which significant milestones can be defined? Which strategy do we apply, big bang or iterative? How do we migrate procedures to the new situation? What are the risks we have to manage?* This step and the following one are outside of the scope of this chapter. We plan to address these issues in future work.
5. **Implementation evaluation**. *How well does our solution solve the problem?* This is in itself another problem investigation that is nested within our problem of finding a systematic technique to assess electronic cooperation between customs.

We have now all the elements of our reasoning framework. Table 1 presents the step-by-step structure of the reasoning framework.

E-PLANNING ILLUSTRATED: THE E-CUSTOMS CASE STUDY

In this section, we illustrate and validate e-Planning by applying it to the domain of electronic cooperation of customs organizations in the European Union (EU). The objective of illustrating e-Planning is twofold. The first objective is to help the reader make action plans for partner selection by exposing details of the situation in electronic customs cooperation in the EU. Readers can, thus, compare their situation with the one presented here and learn how the steps presented in Table 1 can be applied in a concrete case. The second objective is to contribute to the validation of e-Planning: we show how applying e-Planning in a concrete domain gives domain experts new insights in mechanisms that play a role in partner

Table 1.The e-Planning reasoning framework

1. e-Planning problem investigation phase guidelines In this phase, decision makers identify the specific cooperation situation that they have to analyze.	
(a) Identify goal	What is the exact goal of the action plan, why is the action plan needed in the first place?
(b) Identify stakeholders	Who is influenced in any way by carrying out the action plan to analyze cooperation?
(c) Identify problem owner	Whom of the stakeholders is responsible for carrying out the action plan?
(d) Identify unit of study	*What do we want to know something about?* What are the 'things' analyzed by carrying out the action plan? E.g., does the action plan cover all business processes, or only some of them?
(e) Identify questions	*What do we want to know about the unit of study?* Which questions should be answered by carrying out the action plan?
(f) Build conceptual framework	Determine key concepts that may indicate obstacles to cooperation. The criterion to use to decide whether a concept should be included in the framework is that the concept should be observable as a property of the inter-organizational systems needed for closer cooperation.
(g) Identify relevant knowledge	Identify which relevant tools, techniques, and knowledge (also in people's minds) are already available for reuse.
(h) Determine solution acceptance criteria	What properties must the action plan have to be considered useful?
(i) Analyze validation of results	How are the decision makers going to validate the results obtained by carrying out the plan? Decision makers have to double-check that the observations they make correspond with properties of the real world. In this step, they think about how they will do that.
2. e-Planning design phase guidelines So far, decision makers have analyzed the problem. In this phase, decision makers choose the techniques that comprise the action plan, based on knowledge about the specific cooperation situation obtained in the previous phase.	
(a) Choose units of data collection	What is the sample of organizations that has to be studied? Is data about these organizations available?
(b) Choose environment of data collection	Is data collected from the field, or from an artificial environment?
(c) Choose measurement instruments	Data about a unit of study can be obtained by reading documentation, interviewing experts, inserting probes in the steps of the process, or by any appropriate measurement instrument.
(d) Identify possible interactions of the person(s) executing the action plan with data collection	Experience and biases of experts may influence the results derived from data collection.
(e) Choose data analysis and visualization methods	How are decision makers going to analyze the data gathered from other organizations in the network analyzed?
3. e-Planning validation phase guidelines In this phase, decision makers reason about how they can show that the action plan designed in the previous phase can be expected to meet the acceptance criteria identified in the first phase.	
4. e-Planning implementation phase guidelines In this phase, decision makers carry out the action plan designed in the design phase. This may include solving a new set of design problems such as designing a questionnaire and getting access to (usually confidential) data.	
5. e-Planning implementation evaluation phase guidelines In this phase, the results obtained by carrying out the action plan are evaluated. What are the answers we obtained? How can we use them? What are the explanations for these answers? Are there other explanations? Do they solve the problem, or did the plan deviate from it? Are there areas that should be investigated in detail?	

selection. The fact that new insights were obtained illustrates that e-Planning is valid in the sense that it helps to find opportunities for and obstacles to closer cooperation.

In this section, we first present some background on the case study. After that, we illustrate the application in the form of an elaborated, domain-specific version of Table 1. We also discuss in detail the problem investigation step, and report on the feedback we obtained from domain experts.

The E-Customs Case Study: Background and Motivation

The European Commission aims to improve ensuring safety of the external borders of the European Union, and to facilitate trade. Therefore, it has established a network of customs organizations of all its member states. As a result, customs organizations of the 27 member countries of the European Union have to act as if they form one virtual customs organization. The network has been in place for many years, but new demands make it necessary to cooperate closer in order to fulfill these demands.

The E-CUSTOMS case study is a useful case study because it involves partner selection for closer cooperation with the ultimate aim of developing inter-organizational systems, which is exactly the focus of this chapter. For instance, a new goal of the European Union was to provide to companies a single point of contact (a 'single counter' in the form of a web portal or connection point for Electronic Data Interchange). With a 'single counter', exporting or importing companies only need to deal with one customs organization (the virtual customs organization of the EU), no matter which countries the goods travel to, from or through. The Dutch Tax and Customs Administration was interested in identifying other customs organizations in the EU to jointly develop the inter-organizational systems needed to create this virtual customs organization. Other potential topics for cooperation included: (i) sharing software applications; (ii) joint outsourcing of application support to a single vendor; (iii) taking over a solution already built by another customs organization, and (iv) selling a solution to another country.

The reader may think that the e-Customs case study is not a valid case study because each customs organization of the EU has an obligation to cooperate with precisely all other customs organizations of the EU, and consequently, there is no partner selection problem. This is true at what we may call the policy or legal level. However, this is not true at the implementation level. The virtual customs organization that all member states together have to join is not created solely top-down, by a central EU agency. Many topics for cooperation are not determined top-down. Instead, the existing customs organizations of the member states can choose these topics themselves, in a bottom-up fashion. This gives each customs organization the freedom to form small groups of member states (for example, consisting of 3-5 member states) to jointly work on a particular topic within the overall task of creating the virtual customs organization. The choice for a bottom-up implementation process to be performed by all member states is what creates partner selection problems for each member state. The alternative, to create the entire, 27 member state virtual customs organization centrally and at once, is considered far too risky if not completely infeasible by the customs organizations. For these reasons, applying our reasoning frameworks in the e-Customs domain is valid.

As a starting point, the Dutch Tax and Customs Administration conducted between January 2005 and October 2005 a study that compared the current organizational context, business processes, systems and future ambitions of ten member states (Netherlands Tax and Customs Administration, 2005). This study – called "Benchmarking Customs IT Architecture" – showed the customs networking profiles of each country, providing high-quality data suited to analyze opportunities for cooperation. In fact, this study solved the problem of lack of information required to find opportunities for cooperation.

To be useful, the e-Customs case study needs to provide good data. We found that the benchmarking study provided the data needed to analyze opportunities for cooperation. Customs organizations revealed their profiles by answering questions about their organization, transactions, technology, and processes and systems. In particular, each of these profiles contained information on organizational context, including staff size, transaction volumes, number of inspections, IT architecture (in the form of landscape maps, which we discuss below), ambitions, and best practices.

The customs experts who used the benchmarking report analyzed the data of the report solely using their experience. It was intuitive for the experts and very structured, but it did not follow a defined method. For example, the experts considered the landscape maps visualization technique (explained below) suitable to compare foreign customs organizations because they had used landscape maps successfully in their own organization. Moreover, the factors or variables enquired upon during the benchmarking (such as processes in place, transaction volumes and IT architecture) were chosen intuitively before knowing if they would be relevant variables to select partners. Applying e-Planning to e-Customs therefore 'makes sense': it is potentially useful not only to illustrate the research reported in this chapter, but also for the customs experts themselves. Moreover, the e-Customs case study can serve as a validation: if applying e-Planning leads to avoiding misunderstanding and problems, then we may conclude that e-Planning indeed improves current practice.

Problem Investigation in E-Customs

In the e-Customs partner selection problem we need to identify which elements are relevant to plan the assessment of possibilities for and obstacles to customs cooperation. This is the problem investigation phase of the case study. The problem investigation section of the critical thinking research approach (Wieringa, 2007) we are following guides us by proposing which questions to ask. In E-CUSTOMS, the fundamental questions that needs to be answered in this step are related to the main goal behind the cooperation, the real stakeholders involved, and the relevant knowledge about the problem (such as existing partial solutions and crucial properties of customs organizations.)

We follow the substeps indicated for the first step in e-Planning as presented in Table 1. First, we ask what the *goal* to achieve in closer cooperation is. Why exactly is closer cooperation required? Which need is supposed to be fulfilled? Part of the problematic phenomena are the inter-organizational elements such as the need to understand foreign customs architectures and aspirations across distance and cultural differences. Getting access to information and communication about, and understanding of, e.g., foreign legacy applications and processes is not straightforward. Moreover, a foreign customs organization may have different unexpected aspirations: there are historical, political and geographical reasons for customs to be different (Ponisio et al., 2008a). All this generates the need to look for potential common goals. When we start analyzing (and decomposing) goals, we may find that each goal uncovers a complex matter itself.

Second, we ask who the *stakeholders* are. In the case of e-Customs, the stakeholders are customs IT decision makers, e.g., managerial levels of customs organizations of different countries, people implementing the operational level in each customs, architects of e-Customs, groups of countries (such as the European Union), and the European Union itself.

We also determine the goals of each stakeholder individually. For instance, the goal of the European Union for e-Customs is to obtain unified electronic customs throughout the EU. Specifically, the goal is to "make custom clearance more efficient, reduce administrative burdens, combat fraud, organized crime and terrorism, serve fiscal interests, protect intellectual property and cultural heritage, increase the safety of goods and the security of international trade, enhance health and environmental protection and allow for a seamless flow of data between export and import countries", as stated in the strategic plan of the European Commission. However, the goal of a custom organization of a member state may be different. A customs organization that is experiencing capacity problems can, for instance, be more focused on closer cooperation with other customs to increase efficiency of inspections, reducing redundant control. Customs organizations from smaller countries may, for instance, focus on decreasing maintenance cost of software applications.

Third, we determine who the *problem owner* is. In the case of e-Customs, the problem owner is the customs architect.

Fourth, we determine the *unit of study*, which is a crucial element to understand a problem. In e-Customs, the unit of study is a customs organization. In particular, we are interested in the organization's interaction with other customs organizations (the peers in the inter-organizational network) and in the organization's interaction with organizations that do not participate in the network. In e-Customs, these are organizations that support and work together with customs within the country such as the agriculture ministry and the police.

Fifth, we *identify questions* that nail down precisely what we want to know about the unit of study. In other words, once we carry out our assessment plan, along which lines are the answers we should get?

Sixth, with the questions above we are gathering insight about the problem. It is now the turn to start *building a conceptual framework* to categorize our knowledge about the problem. We identify the main concepts that we use to reason about obstacles for closer cooperation.

Seventh, we *identify relevant knowledge* in terms of tools, techniques and knowledge that are already available for reuse. In the case of e-Customs, we found that customs experts already use metrics, visualizations, and so-called landscape maps. We discuss these after completing this list in the section 'Existing solutions to plan e-Customs'.

Eight, we determine the *solution acceptance criteria*: the properties that a good solution for the E-CUSTOMS problem should have. We identify the following criteria: (i) the resulting action plan should facilitate understanding opportunities for and potential problems in cooperation; (ii) the resulting action plan should be logical: it must be characterized by clear, sound thinking so that decision makers can explain to higher management the rationale behind the choices they made (why they have to support this investment); (iii) The plan must be fast to implement, portable (being easy to adapt to different groups of customs organizations), and scalable (to allow customs architects to compare groups of customs of different sizes), and (iv) it must facilitate communication (e.g., visualizing the current architectural process, data and application mappings), without involving complex notations that experts of foreign customs might have trouble learning or find ambiguous.

Ninth, we have to analyze *validation of results* by determining a sound plan to check validity of the results of applying e-Planning. As implementation of the action plan is outside the scope of this chapter, we skip this step.

Existing Solutions to Plan E-Customs

Metrics

Metrics have proved to be helpful to plan inter-organizational cooperation in the context of e-Customs. An example are the number of electronic import declaration forms received in one year by a country as a percentage of the total number of forms for all countries in the sample, and likewise for import inspections and staff size; the ratio of inspections over declarations, and the number of declarations per 1000 inhabitants. As we showed in earlier work (Ponisio et al., 2008a), this metric is very helpful to divide customs organizations into groups where members of a group are alike and, therefore, potential candidates for closer cooperation.

Visualization

One aspect of metrics is visualization of the numerical data obtained (Tufte, 1997, 1990; Ware, 2000) to gain understanding of complex systems.

In earlier work (Ponisio et al., 2008a), we show that a solution that has proven to be helpful is to aggregate metrics into simple shapes to visualize the system. Visualization (derived from metrics) together with non-quantifiable information has proven to be a valuable aid to understand partner selection for closer cooperation in a network of electronic customs (Netherlands Tax and Customs Administration, 2005).

Landscape maps

Landscape maps (Van der Torre et al., 2006; Van der Sanden and Sturm, 2000) are tabular representations that can be used to visualize the IT portfolio of an organization. A landscape map clusters the information systems that comprise an organization's IT portfolio according to two dimensions, which can be chosen arbitrarily. They are used to visualize the allocation of business functions to software applications per case: which applications support which systems for which cases. Customs experts (architects) use landscape maps as an effective way to communicate. This technique has the advantage that experts from other customs organizations do not need to be familiar with notations such as the Unified Modeling Language.

All in all, the outcome of the problem investigation step is deep knowledge about the problem. In e-Customs we have clarified goals, we know who the actual stakeholders are and we know which methods, tools and techniques are available for re-use. Moreover, we have acceptance criteria for a potentially usable solution. We use this knowledge to answer the questions and perform the rest of the activities indicated in e-Planning.

E-Planning Illustrated: Answering The Questions for E-Customs

The discussion of the problem investigation step in the previous section shows how in applying e-Planning to e-Customs we go systematically through the list of issues to consider (the questions in the e-Planning table). This adds a priority order over the task to be done. Moreover, we decompose the problem in smaller problems, which are easier to solve. Using expert interviews and e-Customs documents, we also elaborated the other four steps of e-Planning. Table 2 presents the answers obtained.

The objective of explaining e-Planning by showing Table 2 is to help the reader make such plans by exposing details of the situation in e-Customs. Readers can, thus, get an idea of the kind of answers to look for in the answers presented here.

What Does E-Planning Show Us?

As stated before, one of the aims of applying the e-Planning reasoning framework in a case study is to validate the reasoning framework by assessing its usefulness. To this end, in the current subsection we report experiences of customs experts with the outcome of our e-Planning application (as presented in Table 2). We group these experiences in three categories, which we call 'oversight through traceability', 'oversight through problem decomposition', and 'network use'. For each of these categories, we first present the benefits that customs experts reported, and after that explain these benefits in terms of the mechanism that we see behind it. Finally, we validate the outcome of applying e-Planning to the acceptance criteria identified earlier.

Oversight Through Traceability

In this chapter, we view closer cooperation as a process that starts with partner selection and eventually leads to one or more projects to develop the organizational systems needed to support closer cooperation (see section 'background'). When successful, these projects in turn result in implemented inter-organizational systems, which we refer to as 'solutions'. According to e-Customs experts, e-Planning facilitates traceability from goals to these solutions and from solutions to the initial goals. In an arena where decisions are made but their rationale soon forgotten, the ability to explain why a decision was made earlier prevents unnecessary and costly backtracking.

The kind of traceability offered by e-Planning facilitates smarter resource management because it links (connects) solutions with goals. Solutions tell *how* to achieve a goal, while goals explain the rationale behind a solution (*why* it is needed). When the time comes to question whether to continue a project, we can explain why we do things and why we do not have to do other things. Thus, we can avoid costly mistakes. A case in point is that e-Customs experts reported that the traceability provided by e-Planning might help in preventing duplicated projects (i.e., building a new system that is not needed because the functionality desired from it has already been implemented). Duplication not only unnecessarily commits resources; it also generates consistency problems and makes maintenance very difficult.

The mechanism behind these benefits is that following the e-Planning steps forces an organization to document the questions and answers to each of the steps. The traceability provided by e-Planning is based on the oversight created by the documentation stream resulting from e-Planning. The discipline enforced by e-Planning to work systematically and to document each step contributes to increased maturity of the organization, which in turn leads to the benefits presented in this section.

Oversight through Problem Decomposition

E-Planning offers a sound way to decompose partner selection problems in smaller problems. This is crucial because, as discussed in the background section, partner selection problems tend to be very complex (one e-Customs expert stated that "one could write a book about each point involved in the problem"). When customs experts follow e-Planning they go systematically through a list of prioritized questions and fill the empty slots with answers, which helps them not to loose track. Taking the lead in making decisions about systems that impact inter-organizational cooperation involves a high responsibility, as systems of partners are affected by these decisions. Under these circumstances, the ability not to loose oversight in finding an acceptable solution is essential.

The mechanism that creates this oversight is the same one as the mechanism that creates traceability benefits: e-Planning forces decision makers to clearly document the goals, the questions and the answers that led to a certain solution. It helps experts to reason through the layers of why and how, giving oversight of projects in which closer cooperation is developed (i.e., what has already been implemented, what needs to be done?).

Network Use

The third category of benefits that e-Customs experts reported is related to knowledge transfer in the network as a side effect of applying e-Planning. Customs experts reported that using the action plan created by e-Planning, they should be able to work more efficiently: e-Planning offers a way to identify partners with similar interests or useful knowledge and experience and to find the stakeholders involved in a particular issue. In short, "you know whom to ask". They knew which other customs organizations have which valuable knowledge and experience. The ability to find the right experts in an inter-organizational network helps decision makers to make better use of that network.

For instance, when the Dutch Tax and Customs Administration was planning to acquire a particular new system for managing declarations, customs experts were able to identify another EU member state that was already using that particular system. This led to considerable efficiencies as the Dutch Tax and Customs Administration applied the knowledge acquired by this other member state when buying and deploying the system.

Table 2. e-Planning illustrated

1. e-Planning problem investigation phase	
(a) Identify goal	The goal is to understand potential electronic cooperation with customs organizations. The results of the analysis will be used for diagnosis and prediction of possibilities for and obstacles to cooperation.
(b) Identify stakeholders	Stakeholders identified are customs officers, customs section managers, and customs architects. We also determine the goals of each stakeholder.
(c) Identify problem owner	The problem owner is the customs architect.
(d) Identify unit of study	The unit of study is the customs organization.
(e) Identify questions	Customs architects need to plan electronic cooperation between customs organizations. The following questions need to be addressed: What are similarities and differences of the customs organizations studied? Which opportunities and obstacles can be identified? With whom are we going to cooperate? Which are the ambitions of the customs organization?
(f) Build conceptual framework	A large set of concepts to compare and contrast customs organizations can be identified. The unit of study suggests the following concepts, which are well suited for analysis using landscape maps: customs processes and process categories, IT functions, data availability, and IT applications.
(g) Identify relevant knowledge	Customs experts already use metrics, visualizations, and so-called landscape maps. Moreover, questionnaires from a previous analysis are available.
(h) Determine solution acceptance criteria	The solution acceptance criteria are: (i) the resulting action plan should facilitate understanding opportunities for and potential problems in cooperation, (ii) it should be logical, (iii) it must be fast to implement, portable and scalable, and (iv) it should facilitate communication.
(i) Analyze validation of results	Implementation of the action plan is outside the scope of this chapter; therefore, we skip this step.
2. e-Planning design phase In our case study, the main elements of the action plan are the factors to analyze and the tools to use for the analysis.	
(a) Choose units of data collection	The units of data collection are a sample of countries (selected via a convenience sampling). A good sample is one that includes customs with different properties, but that belongs to the same geographical group and can provide 'standard' qualitative and quantitative data, as customs architects have to be able to compare them to analyze possibilities for cooperation.
(b) Choose environment of data collection	Data collection will be performed by Dutch customs in the field, i.e., in the natural environment of customs rather than in an artificial/simulated environment.
(c) Choose measurement instruments	Data will be collected via interviews with customs experts of the countries studied.
(d) Identify possible interactions of the person(s) executing the action plan with data collection	To avoid invalid analysis results, teams of architects from every customs in the sample will conduct the interviews. Moreover, architects not only interview other architects, but also section managers and customs officers. The function of the person interviewed will be recorded in order to include this information in the final analyses.
(e) Choose data analysis and visualization methods	Quantifiable data will be analyzed using visualization techniques (Ponisio et al., 2008a; Netherlands Tax and Customs Administration, 2005). Information about IT portfolios will be analyzed using landscape maps as presented in this chapter. Landscape maps, after years of use, are the basic units of understanding and communication for customs architects, and therefore they are an important element. We count on the experience of architects with years of expertise in customs to interpret these visualizations from the perspective of understanding inter-organizational networks, such as spotting possibilities for opportunistic behavior.
3. e-Planning validation phase The issue here is to check whether the action plan is likely to meet the acceptance criteria identified in item 1(h) above. Although not conclusive, what we have learnt (see below) from applying e-Planning gives enough confidence that our action plan meets the acceptance criteria.	
4. e-Planning implementation phase The action plan will be carried out by a team of customs experts over several weeks time. To acquire data as described in the design phase, they will have to develop a questionnaire, decide which visualization technique to use, get access to data, perform interviews, etc. These are design problems on their own.	
5. e-Planning implementation evaluation phase The main question to answer in this phase is whether sufficient information has been acquired about the customs organizations involved to plan closer cooperation. If the information acquired leads to concrete examples of opportunities for cooperation, and if it helped architects to detect concrete potential obstacles, then the information acquired was sufficient.	

The mechanism that creates this side effect is that e-Planning requires an organization to record and maintain data about peers in the network. In particular, the questions to identify stakeholders, problem owners and the unit of study help to create an overview of interests, knowledge and experience of various members of the network.

Validating the Outcome of Applying E-Planning Against The Original Acceptance Criteria

We check whether the result of applying our reasoning framework meets the acceptance criteria identified in step 1h in the problem investigation phase. According to this, applying e-Planning should produce a plan that is logical, fast to implement, portable, scalable, and that facilitates communication.

The support for traceability that experts witnessed indicates that the plan resulting from applying our framework is indeed logical. Table 2 shows that it is fast to implement, as most of the time is invested in gathering data. The resulting plan seems to be portable, as it does not contain any steps that are specific for a particular group of customs organization and therefore, there should be no problems in applying the resulting plan to other groups of customs organizations. It also seems to be sufficiently scalable, as there are no steps that become intractable when applying the resulting plan to large groups of customs organizations. Finally, the plan seems to facilitate communication: experts report that they re-use knowledge and experience from the network, which requires that there is communication.

Summary

In summary, e-Planning is useful for decision makers in the domain of electronic customs cooperation, as it may help them to identify opportunities for and potential problems in closer cooperation. They are able to do so because, for a number of reasons, e-Planning provides them with oversight of the problem at hand. First, e-Planning provides traceability, which helps to prevent costly misunderstandings such as duplicated projects. Second, decision makers can explain the rationale behind a project (or behind cancellation of a project), which contributes to the maturity of the organization. Third, applying e-Planning facilitates knowledge transfer: for instance, e-Planning may lead to increased knowledge reuse because decision makers are aware of similar interests and relevant knowledge and experience in the network.

RESULTS

In a previous section, we illustrated our reasoning framework by applying it to the domain of cooperation of customs organizations. This illustration also served as a validation by showing that the action plan thus obtained turned out to be potentially useful for decision makers in this domain. In the current section, we reflect on our case study by discussing internal and external validity of our research.

Internal Validity

Internal validity is the extent to which, in the domain of our application in the case study, our proposed solution (the e-Planning reasoning framework) meets the acceptance criteria. In the Research Method section, we listed a number of acceptance criteria for e-Planning that we obtained from IT decision makers in e-Customs. According to them, the reasoning framework should help them to reason about where to start observing, how to do this in practice and about the impact of leaving areas out of the analyses. It must facilitate creating solutions. It must guide the experts towards identifying important spots for further analyses, but not constrain their freedom (it must be flexible). It should be able to help decision makers to detect the status of IT systems and best practices used and it should serve as a conceptual framework that also decision makers from foreign countries can use.

Our e-Planning reasoning framework meets most of these criteria and therefore, we consider the case study internally valid. Our reasoning framework facilitates creating action plans that can help decision makers to detect potential problems in and opportunities for closer cooperation. These action plans guide decision makers in ordering the observations to make in the network and thus to determine where to start. However, it does not inform automatically about the impact of not analyzing specific areas such as communication skills.

The reasoning framework facilitates creating solutions by supporting traceability as explained in the previous section. The approach has room for flexibility by incorporating existing successful partial solutions. It also allows decision makers flexibility by letting them adapt the plan to the specific situation at hand. The framework calls for gathering data about many aspects of the organizations in the network. This way, knowledge about the status of the IT systems and best practices used is obtained. As explained in the previous section, in the case studied this in itself may lead to re-use of knowledge and experience already available in the network. Whether decision makers from foreign countries can use e-Planning as a conceptual framework has not been tested.

External Validity

External validity is the extent to which the results obtained by applying our reasoning framework in the customs domain can be generalized to other domains. According to e-Customs experts, the application of our reasoning framework to the case study forms a "kind of reverse engineering" process that is useful to detect opportunities for cooperation with potential partners. On the one hand, such reverse engineering must be possible in domains other than cooperation between customs organizations. In fact, the notion of reverse engineering is well-known in other domains. Hence the case study gives circumstantial evidence that this planning technique can be used to detect potential partners for cooperation in other domains.

On the other hand, in previous work (Ponisio et al., 2008a), we did find a peculiarity of the customs domain that may be specific for networks of customs organizations: the role of the European Union. In the customs domain, the European Union acts as a body that defines legislation and implementation provisions that are mandatory for all participants. Not all networks have that type of actor involved.

FUTURE RESEARCH DIRECTIONS

We identify four directions for future research: alignment of cooperation in a network with cooperation outside that network, cooperation with organizations that are not IT-driven, cooperation mechanisms, and generalizability. Alignment of cooperation in a network with cooperation outside that network refers to an aspect of inter-organizational cooperation that we have left out of the current e-Planning framework. In this chapter, we only consider cooperation with partners in one specific network. However, organizations usually cooperate in more than one network simultaneously. For instance, in the domain of customs organizations, a customs organization of one country not only cooperates with those of other countries, but also with other government agencies in its own country (e.g., the bureau of statistics, the agriculture ministry). How to extend e-Planning such that this is taken into account is one direction for future research.

Cooperation with organizations that are not IT-driven refers to the fact that organizations not only cooperate in IT-driven processes, but also in other processes. The reasoning framework presented in this chapter focuses on elements supporting inter-organizational cooperation such as IT architecture, software applications, data and processes, which are all relevant for IT-driven cooperation. However, the work that an organization performs together with other agencies that are not IT driven (e.g., co-ordination of inspections) needs to be addressed because it can impact the relationship between the organization and the network.

Cooperation mechanisms are another direction for future research. Currently, success of applying our reasoning framework depends heavily on knowledge of the expert that is planning closer cooperation. For instance, there might be valid reasons for choosing not to include certain aspects that only experts can identify. Therefore, future work would be to identify mechanisms that decision makers can use as guidance in applying e-Planning. In recent work (Ponisio et al., 2009), we have presented one such mechanism. This mechanism describes why it is important to join new groups of cooperating organizations as early as possible. Future research should be directed at uncovering more mechanisms like this.

Finally, future work should as well follow the line of analyzing more case studies in depth to further investigate generalizability (external validity) of our reasoning framework.

CONCLUSION

In this chapter, we present an approach to systematically investigate opportunities for and problems in cooperation in inter-organizational networks. Our approach, called e-Planning, helps decision makers to plan selection of partner organizations with which to establish closer cooperation such as connecting operational information systems. When decision makers need efficient and careful assessment of opportunities for cooperation, e-Planning supplies an action plan to determine which key factors need to be analyzed first. Identifying these key factors helps decision makers to make correct investment decisions for new IT systems that support closer cooperation.

The reasoning framework has been illustrated and evaluated using a case study called e-Customs, a network of customs organizations of member states of the European Union. Our evaluation suggests that e-Planning provides the focus and guidance needed to create a systematic and sound action plan. In particular, this way of reasoning brings several benefits such as increased re-use of knowledge and prevention of duplicated development projects. The mechanisms we identified that explain these benefits are support for traceability and problem decomposition provided by the reasoning framework.

ACKNOWLEDGMENT

We gratefully acknowledge the financial support of the Dutch Jacquard program (Netherlands Organization for Scientific Research) for the project nr 638.004.609 (QuadRead).

REFERENCES

Belderbos, R., Carree, M., Diederen, B., Lokshin, B., & Veugelers, R. (2004). Heterogeneity in R&D cooperation strategies. *International Journal of Industrial Organization*, *22*, 1237–1263. doi:10.1016/j.ijindorg.2004.08.001

Clark, T., & Jones, R. (1999). Organizational interoperability maturity model. In *Proceedings of the 1999 Command and Control Research and Technology Symposium*. Newport, RI: United States Naval War College.

Coase, R. H. (1937). The nature of the firm. *Economica*, *4*(16), 386–405. doi:10.1111/j.1468-0335.1937.tb00002.x

Cook, K. S. (1977). Exchange and power in networks of interorganizational relations. *The Sociological Quarterly*, *18*(1), 62–82. doi:10.1111/j.1533-8525.1977.tb02162.x

Das, T. K., & Teng, B.-S. (2000). A resource-based theory of strategic alliances. *Journal of Management, 26*(1), 31–61. doi:10.1016/S0149-2063(99)00037-9

Derzsi, Z., & Gordijn, J. (2006). A framework for business/IT alignment in networked value constellations. In T. Latour & M. Petit (Eds.) *Proceedings of the workshops of the 18th International Conference on Advanced Information Systems Engineering* (CAiSE 2006) (pp. 219–226). Namur, Belgium: Namur University Press.

Eisenhardt, K. M., & Schoonhoven, C. B. (1996). Resource-based view of strategic alliance formation: Strategic and social effects in entrepreneurial firms. *Organization Science, 7*(2), 136–150. doi:10.1287/orsc.7.2.136

Emerson, R. M. (1962). Power-dependence relations. *American Sociological Review, 27*, 31–41. doi:10.2307/2089716

Evermann, J. (2006). Organizational paradigms and organizational modelling. In T. Latour & M. Petit (Eds.) *Proceedings of the workshops of the 18th International Conference on Advanced Information Systems Engineering* (CAiSE 2006) (pp. 230–239). Namur, Belgium: Namur University Press.

Gerst, M., & Bunduchi, R. (2005). Shaping IT standardization in the automotive industry – the role of power in driving portal standardization. *Electronic Markets, 15*(4), 335–343. doi:10.1080/10196780500302872

Gulati, R. (1998). Alliances and networks. *Strategic Management Journal, 19*(4), 293–317. doi:10.1002/(SICI)1097-0266(199804)19:4<293::AID-SMJ982>3.0.CO;2-M

Hagedoorn, J. (2002). Inter-firm R&D partnerships: an overview of major trends and patterns since 1960. *Research Policy, 31*, 477–492. doi:10.1016/S0048-7333(01)00120-2

Hevner, A., March, S., Park, J., & Ram, S. (2004). Design science in information systems research. *Management Information Systems Quarterly, 28*(1).

Lockamy III, A., & McCormack, K. (2004). The development of a supply chain management process maturity model using the concepts of business process orientation. *Supply Chain Management Journal, 9*(4).

Netherlands Tax and Customs Administration. (2005). *Benchmarking customs IT architecture. exploit commonality, manage variability.*

Ponisio, M. L., Sikkel, K., Riemens, L., & van Eck, P. (2008a). Combining visualisation techniques to understand cooperation in inter-organisational systems. *Journal of Systems and Information Technology, 10*(2), 159–179. doi:10.1108/13287260810897774

Ponisio, M. L., van Eck, P., & Riemens, L. (2008b). Using critical problem solving to plan inter-organisational cooperation in e-customs. In *Proceedings of the International Association for Development of the Information Society (IADIS) International Conference e-Commerce 2008* (pp. 28–39). Amsterdam: IADIS Press.

Ponisio, M. L., van Eck, P., & Riemens, L. (2009). Ecustoms case study: mechanisms behind cooperation planning. In *Proceedings of the International Association for Development of the Information Society (IADIS) International Conference e-Commerce 2009*. Algarve, Portugal: IADIS Press.

Ramasubbu, N., Krishnan, M., & Kompalli, P. (2005). A process maturity framework for managing distributed development. *IEEE Software, 22*(3), 80–86. doi:10.1109/MS.2005.69

Rosenkopf, L., Metiu, A., & George, V. P. (2001). From the bottom up? Technical committee activity and alliance formation. *Administrative Science Quarterly, 46*(4), 748–772. doi:10.2307/3094830

Simon, H. (1985). Human nature in politics: the dialogue of psychology with political science. *The American Political Science Review*, *79*, 293–304. doi:10.2307/1956650

Supply Chain Digest (2009 May). The Greatest Supply Chain Disasters of All Time 2009. *Supply Chain Digest.*

Tufte, E. R. (1990). *Envisioning Information.* Cheshire, CT: Graphics Press.

Tufte, E. R. (1997). *Visual Explanations.* Cheshire, CT: Graphics Press.

van der Sanden, W., & Sturm, B. (2000). *Informatie-architectuur: de infrastructurele benadering* (2nd ed.). Rosmalen, The Netherlands: Panfox/Ordina.

van der Torre, L., Lankhorst, M. M., ter Doest, H., Campschroer, J. T. P., & Arbab, F. (2006). Landscape maps for enterprise architectures. In E. Dubois & K. Pohl (Eds.), *Advanced Information Systems Engineering. 18th International Conference, CAiSE 2006* (LNCS 4001, pp. 351–366). Berlin: Springer-Verlag.

Ware, C. (2000). *Information Visualization.* San Francisco: Morgan Kaufmann.

Wieringa, R. (2007). *Research and design methodology for software and information engineers.* Internal report. Retrieved from http://www.cs.utwente.nl/~roelw

Williamson, O. E. (1975). *Markets and hierarchies, analysis and antitrust implications: a study in the economics of internal organization* (1st ed.). New York: The Free Press.

Williamson, O. E. (1981). The economics of organization: The transaction cost approach. *American Journal of Sociology*, *87*(3), 548–577. doi:10.1086/227496

Williamson, O. E. (1993). *Opportunism and Its Critics* (*Vol. 14*). New York: Emerald Group Publishing Limited.

ADDITIONAL READING

Boonstra, A., & Devries, J. (2008). Managing stakeholders around inter-organizational systems: A diagnostic approach. *The Journal of Strategic Information Systems*, *17*(3), 190–201. doi:10.1016/j.jsis.2008.04.001

Granovetter, M. (1985). Economic action and social structure: The problem of embeddedness. *American Journal of Sociology*, *91*(3), 481–510. doi:10.1086/228311

Granovetter, M. S. (1973). The strength of weak ties. *American Journal of Sociology*, *78*(6), 1360–1380. doi:10.1086/225469

Kraut, R. E., & Streeter, L. A. (1995). Coordination in software development. *Communications of the ACM*, *38*(3), 69–81. doi:10.1145/203330.203345

Kumar, K., & van Dissel, H. G. (1996). Sustainable collaboration: Managing conflict and cooperation in interorganizational systems. *Management Information Systems Quarterly*, *20*(3), 279–300. doi:10.2307/249657

Sabherwal, R. (2003). The evolution of coordination in outsourced software development projects: a comparison of client and vendor perspectives. *Information and Organization*, *13*(3), 153–202. doi:10.1016/S1471-7727(02)00026-X

Star, S. L., & Griesemer, J. R. (1989). Institutional ecology, 'translations' and boundary objects: Amateurs and professionals in Berkeley's museum of vertebrate zoology, 1907-39. *Social Studies of Science*, *19*(3), 387–420. doi:10.1177/030631289019003001

KEY TERMS AND DEFINITIONS

Decision Maker: Business analysts, IT architects, domain experts and other stakeholders who are responsible for selecting organizations for closer cooperation.

Engineering Cycle: A systematic technique to solve design problems proposed by Wieringa (2007). The engineering cycle comprises five steps: problem investigation, solution design, solution validation, solution implementation, and implementation evaluation.

External Validity: Given a problem and a solution for that problem, the extent to which the results obtained by applying the solution to a particular problem instance can be generalized to other instances.

Inter-Organizational System: Collections of connected operational systems of more than one organization that jointly support value-creating processes in the cooperation (adapted from Ponisio et al. (2008a)).

Internal Validity: Given a problem and a specific application domain, the extent to which a proposed solution for that problem meets solution acceptance criteria in that domain.

Partner Selection: The task of finding opportunities for cooperation and potential problems in cooperation among organizations that are member of an inter-organizational network.

Section 2
Standards and QOS

Chapter 5
Guidelines for Managing B2B Standards Implementation

Eva Söderström
University of Skövde, Sweden

ABSTRACT

This chapter presents a model of a Business-to-Business implementation that is developed based upon a literature review and an empirical study. The model is also accompanied by a set of implementation guidelines derived from the study. These results may guide organizations that plan to standardize B2B processes. They may also help organization improve the efficiency of their performance as well as guide future researchers towards new possibilities.

INTRODUCTION

Predictions are often made stating that Business-to-Business (B2B) endeavours will grow in numbers extremely fast, but little is known about real-world standards usage and implementations (Chan and Swatman, 2002; Edifecs, 2000). B2B refers to "*...the use of the Internet and Web-technologies for conducting inter-organizational business transactions.*" (Teo and Ranganathan, 2004). It is focused on streamlining transactions both internally within an organisation, and externally with others (Ersala et al, 2002). Coordination across systems in an organisation is even part of how enterprise systems can be defined, as an integrated planning and resource management system that coordinates information across all enterprise functions (Bendoly et al, 2009). B2B implementation is a complex issue, and much of it is still unknown (Teo and Ranganathan, 2004; Jap and Mohr, 2002; Baghdadi, 2004). This is shown by organisations still having problems in implementation, in spite of the advantages brought about by standards (Premkumar et al, 1994). Hence, simply investing in B2B technology does not automatically lead to improved performance. Previous studies have shown that each IT implementation includes additional concepts (or assets) that impact IT, and finally also the organisation (Kohli and Devaraj, 2004; Lee and Lim, 2003). According to Swann

DOI: 10.4018/978-1-61692-016-6.ch005

Figure 1. A simple overview of B2B exchanges

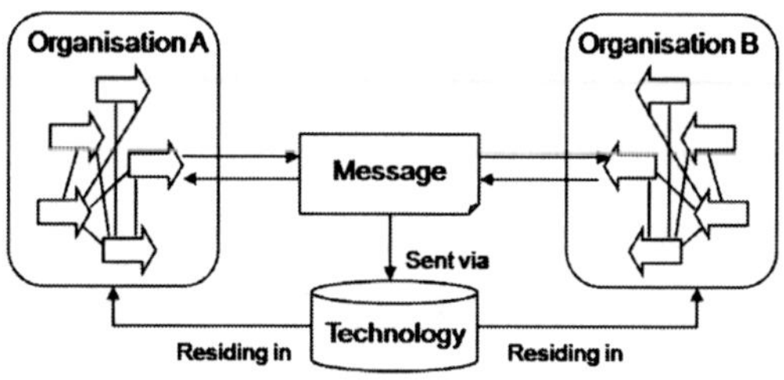

(2000), the value to business and the economy at large comes not from standards publication, but from standards usage. A model of the implementation process could spur improved planning of B2B standards implementation projects. Potential implementation problems and the kinds of available support need to be described as well. Many standards are complex and difficult to interpret. Implementation knowledge may mean that problems can be reduced and catered for already in the planning process.

Since implementation is complex, research is needed into e.g. how organisations are affected by standards, how the implementation process is structured, and what factors affect it. In this chapter, we present a model of B2B implementation developed from a combination of a literature review and an empirical study. A model alone will not do the trick, since there still would be issues in how organizations can apply the model and what issues to consider when doing so. Therefore, the model is accompanied by a set of guidelines also derived from the study. These results may help organisations about to enter into standardisation to think ahead and to avoid making mistakes. It may also help already experienced organisations to improve their implementation performance, as well as give researchers additional insight by developing novel results. The research thus has a potentially broad application, since results would be of interest to different kinds of standards stakeholders, such as users, developers, researchers, and software providers. The results could help bring research and practice together, as well as help standards stand a greater chance of actually being used. Before travelling further upon the path of B2B implementation, let us first unravel some background information on B2B and standards.

BUSINESS-TO-BUSINESS (B2B)

There are different levels in which companies can engage in B2B. Egan et al (2003) divide endeavours into primitive or advanced B2B. The primitive level includes for example internal integration of operational databases, and customer transactions over the Internet. The advanced level, or full electronic commerce, refers to integrated fulfilment cycle of ordering, shipping, billing, etc. Many organisations strive for the advanced level, but most are still on their way there (Egan et al, 2003). A similar division of B2B is made by Lee et al (2003), who claim that B2B can be either basic or collaborative. Basic refers to automation of simple exchanges; while collaborative include entire networks of organisations and channel partners. In any case, B2B is focused on streamlining transactions both internally within an organisation, and externally with others (Ersala et al, 2002). Therefore, B2B exchanges are at the heart of high technology markets (Zolkiewski and Littler, 2004). We illustrate a typical B2B scenario in figure 1. This figure will be explained in more detail when introducing standards.

B2B is anticipated to greatly exceed the future of B2C as a means to increase sales and reduce operational costs (Kaefer and Bendoly, 2004). Kaefer and Bendoly's reasons are two-fold: Large volumes of sales typically take place between business partners rather than between an organisation and individual consumers; and there is an opportunity to gain in efficiency in inter-organisational communication by exploiting emerging IS technologies. This would mean that many organisations feel pressured into B2B. Pressured or not, organisations involved in B2B must form relationships with one another, whether actors are individuals, companies, agencies or other entities (Kotok, 2002). These relationships include communication and transactions between the business partners. Relationships can be classified in short-term or long-term relationships. Short-term refers to single trading occurrences, or transactional exchanges (Jap and Mohr, 2002), where the customer and supplier both want to maximise their own profits. Long-term, or relational exchanges, refer to long-lasting business relationships, and where competition is replaced by co-operation in order to increase mutual benefits (Jap and Mohr, 2002). B2B adoption is a strategic decision as well as a technology decision, which means relationships must be carefully managed (Teo and Ranganathan, 2004). B2B can thus be considered an important enabler for competitiveness (Lee et al, 2003), where competition is based on the use of resources that are unique, rare, valuable, and not easily imitable or substitutable (Tarafdar and Gordon, 2007). Resources are part of an organisation's flexibility along with coordination (Lengnick-Hall et al, 2009). The reason is that B2B can facilitate relationships and transactions between partners and hence enable them to faster respond to market needs. However, managerial time is a finite resource (Bendoly et al, 2009), and is crucial in all organisations. Furthermore, B2B relationships improve efficiency and competitiveness by linking business processes from several partners. The systematic consideration of relationships can thus create larger payoffs (Jap and Mohr, 2002).

STANDARDS

In a competitive business environment, organisations must be able to connect, collaborate and communicate with both partners and customers. Standards are enablers of communication and network set-up. Organisations conduct B2B using standards (Ersala et al, 2002). In fact, the most important factors in achieving integration between organisations are standardisation and digitalisation (Shin and Leem, 2002). The authors motivate this based on all the various hardware, software, documents and trading customs that exist in B2B trading. Inter-organisational systems help improve links between partners, and standards are a natural form of such systems (Soliman and Janz, 2004). In this paper, a B2B standard is defined as guidelines for how communication and information sent between companies should be structured and managed.

Figure 2. Business process standard in a relatively simple context

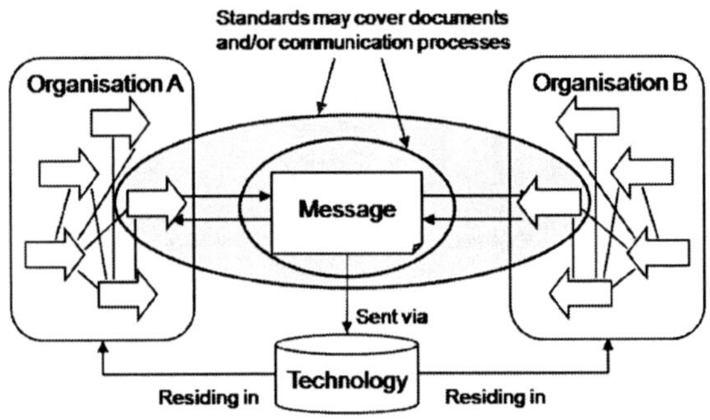

Illustrative Example

We have two organisations, *A* and *B*. Organisation *A* is a manufacturer of product *X*. *X* is used as a part of product *Y*, which is manufactured by organisation *B*. Whenever product *X* is evolved and improved, organisation *B* wants information about the changes made. *A* and *B* decide to invest in B2B in order to automate the information exchange between them (Figure 2). As a result of *B*'s interest in product *X*, the first process[1] to automate was product information update exchange[2] using a standards-based approach to speak a common language. The standard guides the organisation in how to structure both the messages to be exchanged, and the communication processes performing the transaction. In our example, the selected standard makes it possible for the organisations to include automatic recognition of and response to e.g. an incoming order. This means that whenever *B* places an order, *A*'s information systems recognise that the incoming message is an order, and automatically sends a confirmation message back that the order has been received. Standards thereby create a more fair way of accessing and managing resources, since all incoming and outgoing messages are treated and structured in the same way. However, reaching the goal of fairness is still something of a dream, and many resource management techniques fall short in ensuring fairness in this way (Han and Youn, 2009).

The Role of Standards

Standards are not the same as the technology used. Instead, messages created based on the standards are sent using the technology. The standard is the "glue" enabling alignment and co-ordination of the communication. Two differently organised processes with different input and output can communicate regardless of their respective environments. The scope of standards may vary depending on the type of information to be exchanged. Some focus only on the structure and content of messages and/or documents to be sent, while others focus on entire processes for this communication. The common language usually consists of either Electronic Data Interchange (EDI) or the eXtensible Mark-up Language (XML). As Figure 2 shows, some standards are *document-centric*, which means that they focus on describing guidelines for how the messages to be sent should be structured and what they should contain. One example is cXML, which aims to be an open language for transaction requirements (of B2B e-commerce documents). Others are *process-centric*, which means they focus on sequences of transactions, i.e. on organizing not only the documents but also the order in which to

Figure 3. Moving to electronic- and standards-based communication

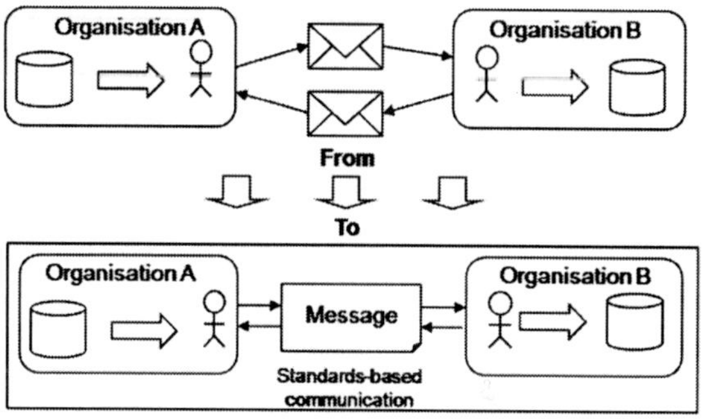

send them and how to organise the work around them. One example is RosettaNet, which aims to establish common standard processes for the electronic sharing of business information.

Standards are implemented to facilitate inter-organisational communication and co-operation. Making the communication electronic-based is an important factor, as is enabling automation (Graham et al, 2003). In this sense, standards make it possible to remove much of the manual, paper-based communication, and replace it with electronic and partly automated communication (see Figure 3). Thick arrows within the organisation depict business processes, while "cans" depict systems. As described, standards guide organisations in message and/or business processes structuring, using the organisations' ICT.

The example illustrates a simple case. In more complicated ones, parallel processes with multiple communication points may exist, and more than two organisations may be involved in the communication. In summary, standards provide the glue through which communication and information flow is enabled regardless of used platforms. Organisations may use standards for communication between internal systems as well as with partners.

Standards Affect Organizational Resources

Standards can, if implemented consciously and correctly, affect the availability and use of organizational resources. For example, they can reduce lead, set-up, preparation and processing time (Ollner, 1988; Premkumar et al, 1994), such as speeding up the time required to connect with other organisations. Furthermore, Lee (1996) claims that standards usage improves product compatibility, hence making new investments and products more cost-effective. In this way, standards also bring a more efficient use of IT in companies (Burrows, 1999; Seminiero, 2000), for example by removing the need to translate between document formats. Standards may also simplify the method of working. One argument is that they can help remove or lower barriers to trade (Ghiladi, 2003; Mörschel, 2003). This has clear connections to increased product range and price competition, since the lowered cost of entry due to competition makes it simpler for small companies and third world countries to enter B2B. There is also simplicity on another level, in that neutral data standards enable preservation of internal systems (Ishikawa, 2003).

Organisations can be more efficient when standards are used. One motivation is that they enable connection and automation (Ousterhout, 2000; Burrows, 1999; Folmer et al, 2003), thus removing unnecessary manual work. This can also be a way to increase productivity (Mähönen, 2000). Finally, standards make it easier for organisations to get access to existing knowledge and they will not have to start from the beginning when e.g. implementing a standard. Through automation, much unnecessary manual work can be avoided. This means that repetition and unsatisfying work can be reduced (Gelete et al, 2003; Capers et al, 2001). This is regarded as positive by many employees, since they can spend more time focusing on core competencies.

RESEARCH APPROACH

The B2B Standards Implementation Model

The research was designed using a combination of literature review of relevant sources, and empirical data collection. Literature sources were primarily scientific, complemented by descriptions in industry white papers, where specific focus was placed on descriptions of various implementation activities.

Empirical data was gathered in interviews with three stakeholder perspectives: Standards Development Organizations (SDO, 6 respondents), Standards User Organizations (SUO, 4 respondents) and Standards Software Organizations (SSO, 3 respondents). The SDOs were both industry consortia and formal standards bodies. The SUOs are those who implement and use B2B standards in real life. Finally, SSOs create standards-based software for B2B. In the latter case, the respondents were responsible for the standards product management in their companies. Each respondent was assigned an identification number (SUO1, SSO2, etc) to allow for some level of identification in quotes.

The material was compiled and merged into one document. First, the text was analyzed searching for descriptions of an implementation approach or steps taken during implementation. Identified activities were noted in a special document, for further text-based analysis as a second step. Results were merged into a general implementation model. A first step towards validation was conducted by discussing the model with two companies, in order to investigate the appropriateness of the steps.

Since these companies only are starting their B2B ventures, the discussion did not concern a specific case that can be presented.

The Guidelines

As mentioned, each implementation phase is accompanied by a set of guidelines. A "guideline" describes aspects of B2B standards implementation that should be taken into consideration by those organisations who perform implementation of said standards. For example, the guidelines may serve as input into standards implementation planning and preparation.

The guidelines were formulated following a review of the results from the B2B standards implementation mode. In deducting potential guidelines, the phases and steps were reviewed and analysed. The data collection was combined with a data analysis and two interviews with companies for validation purposes. Even if result triangulation would have been preferred, this was not possible due to respect for the respondents' time available for participation. The interviews gave a first insight into the applicability of the guidelines, but additional validation is adviced as future research.

THE B2B STANDARDS IMPLEMENTATION PROCESS

Explicit models provide organizations with a path forward when doing development work. Today, however, few standards are asssociated with an explicitly formulated implementation process: "*Well, that's a good question. That's a very good question. And unfortunately, I'm not sure I can give you the response it deserves, because [standard X] is so new that we're not really...we haven't got a well worn path in that area yet.*" (SDO5). Even so, most respondents were able to say something about included phases and steps. As in literature, results show that implementation

Figure 4. The implementation process model

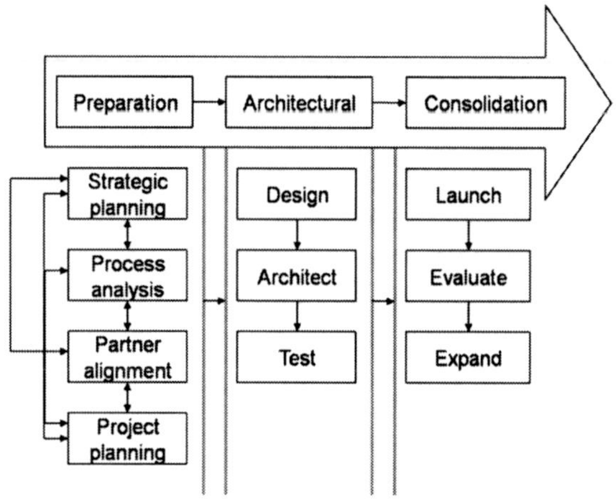

of Internet business systems is complex (Lee et al, 2004). Without enablement[3], organizations may not be able to realize the potential of e-business (Edifecs, 2000). This may prove disastrous, since organizations more and more rely more on collaboration with partners to enhance their position in the business world (Lu et al, 2006).

The B2B standards implementation process (Figure 4) consists of three phases (Söderström, 2008): *Preparation* concerns activities for the planning of projects and architectural work, negotiation with partners, etc. *Architectural* work concerns making changes to processes and technology to incorporate the standard into the existing infrastructure. Finally, *consolidation* concerns launching the standards and putting it into work, as well as evaluating and maintaining the system and expanding its use in the organization. In some respect, the implementation model represents an ideal case. However, since the experiences from practice are included, we argue that the included phases and steps are realistic, and that organizations will benefit from being prepared for them. Some of the steps may be undertaken in parallel. Implementation with individual partners requires a significant amount of time. Thus it is essential all the details of the co-operation are completed before actual implementation begins.

Each phase in Figure 3 will be elaborated on in separate chapter sections. In some respect, the implementation model represents an ideal case. However, since the experiences from practice are included, we argue that the included phases and steps are realistic, and that organizations will benefit from being prepared for them. The principles for implementation are furthermore more or less the same for all standards.

The Preparation Phase

As mentioned, the preparation phase of standards implementation contains all kinds of activities for planning everything from the strategic level, partner alignment, and a detailed project schedule. The preparation phase can be further divided into four steps: strategic planning, process analysis, partner alignment, and project planning. The order of these steps is not necessarily the same in all e-business projects, and there is no pre-defined order to follow. Thus, the model is descriptive rather than prescriptive.

Strategic Planning

A key starting point in any e-business venture is for organizations to make some strategic decisions. Several respondents emphasized this as a crucial first step, to make standards part of the B2B strategy. The same is emphasized in literature (see e.g. Dubelaar et al, 2005). Thus, standards have become a strategic tool for delivering innovation, reducing costs, improving the quality of goods and services, and for opening new business opportunities (Kotok, 2002). Organizations need to clearly identify how technology (and standards) can assist them in achieving their business plan, create new markets, redefine old ones, and enable interoperability (Ramsey, 1998; Bolin, 2004). In fact, the lack of a strategic vision is a major barrier to justifying IT investments (Love and Irani, 2004). Top management support is necessary, but clear ownership is also required from the user departments (Teo and Ranganathan, 2004). Users should hence be involved early. The necessity of management support has also been highlighted in other studies, e.g. Attaran (2004), where Business Process Re-engineering (BPR) efforts were unnecessary due to the failure of connecting them to company goals. One motivation for strategic planning, highlighted throughout our study, was to facilitate the understanding of business needs: "*[SUOs] need to look at, you know, also at their interaction with their customers and their business partners and decide whether [standard X] offer them an ability [...] that they need.* " (SDO5). Organizations must have a clear objective for considering standards. Olson and Williams (2001) describe how planning for strategic changes was conducted firstly by developing an integrated strategy which contained a business strategy, a process approach and technology planning; and secondly the engagement of business and technology groups by involving process owners, technology experts and a cross-functional team leadership. Organizations must set the internal expectations to move to standards (RosettaNet, 2003).

Process Analysis

An analysis of the business processes aims to identify, prioritize and orchestrate which processes to include in B2B collaborations (RosettaNet, 2003; Nucleus, 2002; respondents). These analyses enable a deeper understanding of what really happens in business activities (Kosanke and Nell, 1999). It also helps to identify business transaction requirements and determine if a chosen standard covers these requirements (Rukanova et al, 2003) Business processes also help define the scope of projects, and to identify which processes need support (Ersala et al, 2002). Once the processes are identified and established, one respondent recommended performing a gap analysis to determine how the processes are designed today, and what may need to be changed. Standards must be selected before processes can be changed for the changes to have effect. This is often the case when organizations make internal changes before integrating with each other. During this process, it is essential for the business partners to communicate about internal changes: "*We expect our business partner to openly communicate any internal preparation or implementation efforts, which could impact the overall success of the project.*"(SUO2). Lastly, by defining which processes to standardize, organizations obtain an overview of what parts of them will be affected by the change, e.g. in terms of ways of working. If employee participation is allowed in relating process change to their work, reluctance to change may decrease.

Partner Alignment

By definition, there are at least two organizations involved in a B2B standards implementation. Participating organizations may have different levels of maturity, which in this case means varying experience in doing business using standards. It is essential for a company to identify with whom to trade (Olson and Williams, 2001; RosettaNet, 2003; Intel, 2003; RosettaNet, 2002; respondents). There is much on which to agree, e.g. what, where, how, and which scope to have (webMethods, 2003). Common goals must be set, responsibilities, time span and resources established, and a commitment given by each partner. Trading Partner Agreements (TPA) can be used, in which all of these issues are negotiated and agreed upon. Again, management support is essential: "*Both sides need to ensure that the necessary management support for this project is given and that all participants bring up the commitment for a collaborative and professional execution of the project.*" (SUO2). Trust is important, and mutual agreements are needed. Commitment with signed documents enhances the chance that all partners adhere to their promises. It provides concrete evidence should problems arise. The formation of cross-functional implementation teams with employees from all trading partners may enhance project success. Alignment and implementation speed varies depending on partner readiness (eMarketer, 2002).

Project Planning

Detailed project planning must be completed before the technical architecture work can be initiated. If not done before, standards must be selected here. Details about required technology and infrastructure are also determined (RosettaNet, 2002; RosettaNet, 2001; respondents). Based on the process analysis and technological requirements, the remainder of the implementation process can be carefully planned. Planning is in fact the key to implementing IT (Ramsey, 1998). Agreements between project participants are important: "*It is rather difficult to give out a detailed project schedule without reflecting the specific needs of the implementation. Thus, we recommend that both trading partners work out and agree on a joint project plan with a detailed timeline and clear responsibilities.*" (SUO2). A project plan includes established goals, milestones, and the necessary material and human resources aligned to the time-plan. Open issues must be resolved, and execution options prepared to avoid failure. In fact, one important criteria for implementation success is people with adequate resources and authority to implement the plan (Joseph et al, 2008).

The Architectural Phase

When all necessary preparations and negotiations are complete, the architectural implementation work is initiated. The included steps are: design, architect, and test. Some may argue that design and architect mean the same thing. We separate the two and assign the meaning of organization-internal changes to the design step while integration issues between organizations are assigned to the architect step.

Design

Internal design refers to the establishment of the technological infrastructure or framework inside each organization. Any internal changes to and alignments of e.g. back-end systems should be communicated to the partners. The key to effective standards use is to integrate standards-based information with internal applications to improve the effectiveness and efficiency of the organization's ways of working (Lee et al, 2005). This should be done based on the project plan and scope agreements. Both SUOs and SSOs mention that few user organizations bother with technical details, and that they therefore often outsource the entire architecture phase to the SSOs.

Architect

Once internal changes have been made, the focus turns to external links to partners. Back-end systems are aligned to match standards specifications. Pilot projects are common here. These include a few organizations only, mostly two or three, doing a test implementation for parts of their co-operative venture before attempting larger scale advancement. Many components requiring mutual interoperability are quite immature, which may cause problems (Teo and Ranganathan, 2004). Attention must hence be paid to details, especially if the desire is to create IS resources. Such resources can be created when processes and structures are applied in non-transparent ways to combinations of information systems resources (Tarafdar and Gordon, 2007). The final implementation of business rules into the system is made, including system level rules for databases. Systems are connected and also executed for the purpose of ensuring they work as intended. This touches upon the final step, which is testing.

Test

Standards are only meaningful if implemented in a consistent way (Skall and Rosenthal, 2000; Dssouli et al, 1999). Testing is therefore important, since standards in themselves are not enough to ensure inter-operability. Standards ambiguity is actually one contributing factor. Determining whether or not a product faithfully implements a standard is essential in creating robust, inter-operable solutions (NIST, 2001). If companies do not undertake proper testing, it may cause people to misunderstand the complexity of integration work (Meehan, 2002). Tests are needed both against the standard and against other implementations. Assessment against the standard refers to ensuring the implementation follows the standard's specifications properly, while assessment against other implementation is for connectivity, that the systems can exchange information. Testing can be conducted by different organizations (ISO, 2003): First-party assessment by the supplier itself; Second-party assessment by a customer; and Third-party assessment by a party independent of both customers and suppliers. Assessment is then made against the requirements of the standard. Regardless of which party performs the tests, conformance assessment increases the probability of software products conforming to a specification to be implemented correctly (NIST, 2001).

The Consolidation Phase

Consolidation is the final implementation phase, and refers to all kinds of activities occurring after the technical architectural work has been completed. There are three identified steps: launch, evaluate, and expand. There are considerable variations in what this phase contains according to the interview as well as the literature. The description is a merger of all sources, and will therefore most likely differ depending on the project at hand.

Launch

The first step is to put the newly created standards-based system into the organization, and to initiate it into the daily work. Launch may begin with a plan for how the launch itself is to take place and how to monitor the system's initial performance (webMethods, 2003). Some describe launch using the term "go live" instead. In either case, the step includes submission of actual messages and/or the exchange of actual production data.

Evaluate

After the implementation has been launched and the initial operation has been monitored, the results must be evaluated. Such evaluations include a validation of bandwidth sufficiency, an investigation that sent messages and/or documents have been successfully received, and that the possible automatic responses have been sent and received. Log files will also be scrutinized to ensure the successful exchange of messages.

Expand

If the evaluation period yields a successful result, the pilot organizations may decide to expand the standards-usage to other partners as well. This means the existence of the expand step depends on the intentions to use standards with other organizations. One factor that may influence the expansion decision is if previous experience with standards exists or not. Chau and Hui (2001) identified prior experience as a significant determinant for EDI adoption, for example. If there is a positive decision to expand, new pilot projects start, initiating a new implementation process.

GUIDELINES FOR B2B STANDARDS IMPLEMENTATION

The B2B standards implementation model need, for usability purposes, to be accompanied by a set of guidelines (summarized in table 1).

Organisations get help in issues related to implementation. They can thereby enter into standardisation more easily, think ahead and to avoid making mistakes.

The Preparation Phase

The guidelines for the preparation phase will be presented according to the four steps contained in the phase.

Strategic Planning

As mentioned, incorporating standards plans into the business strategy is a necessary condition for implementing standards. Management should therefore review the existing strategy, and ensure relevant changes are made. Assigning appropriate strategy levels and resources contributes to improving management commitment. In fact, resources should be considered in both strategy formulation and in implementation (Lengnick-Hall et al, 2009). In deciding if standards make sense, management may use the lists of potentials and problems derived in this thesis in order to weigh arguments for and against standards use. Additional aspects from other sources may also be included. Many existing project planning tools relate to strategic planning as well, including functions for estimating personnel resources and assignments. Many organisations already utilise such planning tools today, in which case they can also be used for standards implementation. Detailed plans for staff assignments should be made at a project planning level, while management must review the skills needed to facilitate educational requirements. Finally, managers must prepare for employee involvement, in order to facilitate adop-

Table 1. Guidelines for B2B standards implementation

Phase	Step	Guidelines
Preparation	Strategic planning	Updated business strategy
		Resource allocation discussions
		Multifaceted view of standards consequences
		Resource planning across borders
		Competence identification
		Employee participation plans
	Process analysis	Process models (AS-IS, TO-BE)
		Process priorities
		Different skills in process analysis
		Financial implications
	Partner alignment	Partner readiness descriptions
		Contract/trading partner agreements
		Cross-functional implementation teams
	Project planning	Detailed project plans
Architectural	Design	Standards documents for internal changes
		Communicating internal changes
	Architect	Security requirements update
		Usability aspects in interface design
		Updated maintenance plans
	Test	Selection of test cases, methods and actors
		Test results
Consolidation	Launch	Logs and monitor reports of transactions
		Comparison between tests and reality
	Evaluate	Launch documentation input
		Lessons learned for organisational learning
	Expand	Evaluation report input
		Comparison between strategy and evaluation

tion of the standard. One method may comprise a system of incentives which promote employee involvement in the project. Another involves one or several kick-off meetings which celebrate the new method of working. Different kinds of checklists can aid organisations by ensuring proper attention to the right aspects. Such checklists should at least consider the following: what standards are, why they should be used in the organisation, which standard to use, how standards may affect existing systems and methods of work, and how employees at different organisational levels can be included and motivated.

The guidelines for strategic planning thus are:

- An updated business strategy that takes B2B standards into consideration helps organisations ensure successful standards implementation
- Resource allocation discussions that include the co-operative setting of B2B standards implementations improve the

chances of estimations being relevant and accurate
- Insight into the possible potentials of, and problems with, standards, and documentation of their relevance assist organisations in obtaining a multifaceted view of any possible consequences standards may have
- Explicit documentation and task assignment for the employees involved in the implementation work facilitates the resource planning of a project that spans multiple organisations
- Establishing the competence required to conduct the new method of working facilitates the identification of educational needs
- Explicit plans which engage and motivate the participation of an organisation's employees in the implementation project increase their acceptance of and faith in the forthcoming standards-based system

Process Analysis

The number of approaches to concepts modelling is vast, and the same holds for process modelling. Many organisations, particularly large ones, have an adopted tool for this purpose, which can be used to model both current business processes (AS-IS), and how they should be structured (TO-BE) once the standard has been implemented. Existing process models are usable, provided they are up-to-date. The gap between the two models should be reviewed to identify actions required in order to properly align processes. Furthermore, the organisations' economists can provide appropriate instruments that facilitate estimations of the financial implications such as Return-On-Investment (ROI) calculations. Finally, the creation of checklists which should at least consider the following: which business processes to include, how to rank the processes in order of importance, their current status, what their future status should be, what the gap between the current and future status is and the actions needed to bridge the gap, the competences required for the new method of working, and how the changes best can be communicated to employees. Competencies are considered to develop when resources are combined to create specific organisational abilities (Tarafdar and Gordon, 2007). Careful consideration to personnel resources is therefore needed and appropriate competencies should be combined in team efforts.

The guidelines for process analysis thus are:

- Process models of both the current and the future situation enable organisations to identify the changes required in the current situation in order to facilitate the new method of working. This can be achieved via a gap analysis in which both the current and future status of business processes should be reviewed
- Process priorities assist organisations in limiting an implementation project's focus by identifying processes of the highest priority, and reasons for their inclusion
- The co-operation of personnel with different skills ensures process analysis will result in a multi-faceted view of the situation
- The calculations of experienced professionals on the financial implications of standards implementation provide organisations with more informed arguments for the importance of the standard within and between organisations

Partner Alignment

Organisations about to engage in B2B standards implementation have different levels of knowledge and preparedness. In order to facilitate implementation project planning and to establish, for example, the level of education required for all the partners, explicit descriptions of the readiness of each partner are essential. Some standards include checklists for this purpose, but other methods of documentation may also be used. Such checklists should at least include: the selection of partners with which to conduct B2B, the scope of an implementation project, the readiness status of the partners, the project goals, the assignment of the project leader from which partner, time allocations of the project, the legal aspects of the business relationships, and the resources each partner can contribute with. Trading partner contracts which explicitly govern the business co-operation venture must be formed jointly. These contracts should be drawn up with legal expertise. Cross-functional teams can be created by forming groups of staff members from each trading partner. The personnel should have a diversity of skills as well as different department or organisational level origins.

The guidelines for partner alignment thus are:

- Descriptions of partner readiness enable organisations to more accurately calculate time allocation for standards implementation. These descriptions should e.g. indicate the inclusion of standards in the business strategies, resource allocation preparedness, and checklists of important activities
- Contracts or trading partner agreements are explicit statements on the commitment and conditions for the joint project. The contracts should at least include responsibility agreements, resource allocations, and legal implications
- Cross-functional implementation teams enable the co-operating partners to quickly solve business and technical problems, and to orchestrate implementation activities

Project Planning

Existing project planning methods should be used when applicable. It is important to consider the overall co-ordination requirements for resources, staff and skills when more than one organisation is involved. Checklists can be created, that at least consider the following: commonly agreed upon time boundaries, resources, staff allocation and responsibilities, milestones, the structure of follow-ups, and how project progress will be reported. This facilitates standards implementation projects by providing a frame of reference.

The guideline for project planning thus is:

- Detailed project plans developed jointly by the co-operating partners assist in the consideration of the entire B2B standards implementation project, as well as each partner's business situations

The Architectural Phase

Similar to the preparation phase, the guidelines for the architectural phase are presented for each step in the phase.

Design

Internal systems and business processes are the starting points for the technical work. Input should be gathered from the steps in the preparation phase in terms of the documents and results presented. These provide instructions regarding necessary changes in the processes and systems architecture, and with which processes to start. The cross-organisational team, provided one has been created, can meet at inter-operability events. Such events provide the venue for resolving any technical issues with standards, and are common for both the architectural work and for testing. Prototype environments are used as test beds for this purpose, and models are designed to illustrate the new common approach. Several standards development organisations also provide such events, but primarily for standards compliance activities. Internal changes can be communicated via the cross-organisational implementation group and/or the project manager. This is important for synchronised and professional project management. Checklists can be created that should at least include: how internal process and system changes should be documented and tested, and which changes to communicate to partners.

The guidelines for the design step thus are:

- Documents concerning the selected standard, process gap analysis results, and partner agreements assist organisations in conducting internal changes to documents and/or processes and/or systems to establish them into the new method of working
- Communicating internal changes to partners improves the organisations' synchronisation of the joint implementation project

Architect

Security issues are one of the main problems for B2B and other inter-organisational solutions. Standards for security are currently evolving, and new versions and developments occur frequently. Information about updates is often obtained from the organisations that develop them, or from security and B2B related journals and magazines. End-user inclusion during systems and interface design has also been emphasised in our study and in the literature. One approach is to include end-users in the cross-organisational implementation team, and to perform usability tests on the alternative interfaces and designs. This is also important when dealing with systems that link externally. Checklists can be created, that should at least include: which security mechanisms to incorporate, how usability features can be incorporated in the architecture, how to involve users in the work, and which business rules to consider.

The guidelines for the architect step thus are:

- Attention to updated security requirements and to research progress in relevant areas enable organisations to design their architectures for the purpose of ensuring secure transactions
- Attention to usability aspects in interface design enables organisations to create systems that are easier to learn, use and adopt, and hence shorten the implementation process
- Documents concerned with future process structures and internal technical infrastructure updates facilitate successful external links

Test

A completed architecture must be tested. An organisation should develop test cases that simulate actual transactions or business situations. Testing can be conducted internally or by using a third party. The latter is gaining preference, as test results are considered more reliable, and test methods more up-to-date if the testing is conducted by a specialist third party. However, if the necessary knowledge and skills reside within an organisation, testing can very well be conducted internally. In either case, tests must be conducted against both the standard and partner implementations. The motivation is that standards can be interpreted differently, and therefore implementations that conform to standard are not necessarily interoperable. Checklists should be created that at least include: by whom the tests should be conducted, test methods to use, the relevant test cases, and how to document and report the test results.

The guidelines for the test step thus are:

- Careful attention to the selection of test cases, the test methods and the type of testing organisation help focus on aspects that may affect the credibility and relevance of the test results
- Tests performed with regard to an implementation's conformance to the standard, and of implementations' mutual compatibility with each other improve chances of the resulting connected infrastructure to work

The Consolidation Phase

The guidelines for the consolidation phase and its included steps will be presented in this section, similarly to the previous phases.

Launch

Once a standards-based architecture has been launched and used in live business relationships, logging and monitoring must be conducted. Existing methods for this purpose may be used here, but cross-organisation co-ordination is needed in order to check for success in all the partners. All employees may not be possible to include, however, since that is a very resource-consuming task (Finnegan and Currie, 2009). A possible cross-organisational implementation team can be assigned the responsibility for this task. Both our study and the literature emphasise that a cross-organisational team should remain operational for logging, monitoring, evaluation (see the next list of guidelines) and regular maintenance. Checklists should be created that include at least: where, when and how the launch should take place, how it will be advertised both internally and externally, how to monitor operations, and how to document launch results.

The guidelines for the launch step thus are:

- The logging and monitoring of live business transactions by using the standard facilitate the control of correct operations and provide a better basis for the evaluation of the success of the implementation
- The comparison of results from real-life use with those from tests enable organisations to track potential problems and obstacles

Evaluate

The evaluation can be conducted at seminars where representatives from all the partners review various documents and discuss the level of contentment. Internal as well as external evaluation should involve the cross-organisational teams, management for all partners, and end-users in order to provide a multifaceted view of the results. All the lessons learned should be documented in some form of knowledge base, which could be utilised for future projects and educational needs. The bank can be either electronic or paper-based. Checklists should be created that include at least: how the evaluation should proceed, how it should be documented, if the results correspond to the expectations and the business strategy, how maintenance should be conducted, and if the benefits justify cost.

The guidelines for the evaluate step thus are:

- Launch reports, project plans, test reports, updated business strategies, financial calculations, updated infrastructures, and the results of the implementation provide input in the evaluation of the conducted implementation
- Documentation of lessons learned provide an improved basis for organisational learning, to be used in future standards implementation projects

Expand

The final step of the implementation process involves management deciding whether or not to proceed with standards usage with new business processes and/or with new partners. The report generated from the evaluation step is input. The list of ranked business processes indicate with which processes to proceed, if processes remain that were eliminated from the scope of the first project. Furthermore, input can be gathered from new partners, providing such exist who are willing to engage in standards-based B2B with the organisation in question. Finally, the business strategy needs to be reviewed to ensure implementation results correspond with it. Checklists should be created that at least take into account:

if all necessary evaluation documents have been reviewed, if additional partners exist that wish to conduct B2B, and if a decision has been reached.

The guidelines for the expand step thus are:

- The evaluation report provides an organisation's management with a tool for deciding whether or not to expand the standards usage to further parts of the organisation's B2B relationships
- A comparison of the business strategy with the evaluation report enables organisations to ensure that business operations and standards use correspond with their overall goals

CONCLUSION

The B2B standards implementation model was developed using a blend of theoretical and empirical material. It has not been empirically implemented as of yet, but was validated internally as well as using external theoretical validity, and a primary step towards external empirical validity. *Internal validity* is shown by the results being non-contradictory to each other and to previous research. *External theoretical validity* concerns the extent to which the research material is compliant with existing relevant theories. In the paper, related work has been discussed in order to position the research, and validating its similarities and differences from that of others. *External empirical validity* refers to the results being reviewed externally by two independent organisations about the potential usefulness and quality of the guidelines. In future work, the model will be used for implementation in an ongoing B2B project. Also, it will be explicitly related to other existing software lifecycle models in order to provide a more complete process roadmap. Careful planning of implementation is essential, since the success of the implementation provides the foundation for the success of the entire B2B standards effort. This has been verified by both literature and the respondents. Guidelines may therefore make planning more realistic and focused. Our guidelines can be used to elaborate, compare, and analyse different aspects of standards, as well as implementation. In addition, effective implementation of plans is one of the primary challenges in for example resource and environmental planning (Joseph et al, 2008). Guidelines thus provide a simple way of achieving an overview of relevant aspects to consider. They facilitate for organisations to raise their level of knowledge about standards and their planning for standards implementation projects. So far, only little strategic guidance has been developed for B2B standardisation, and our guidelines can be considered a contribution in this respect. Not the least since the implementation process itself is largely unknown with only few guidelines and tools.

REFERENCES

Attaran, M. (2004). Exploring the relationship between information technology and business process reengineering . *Information & Management*, *41*, 585–596. doi:10.1016/S0378-7206(03)00098-3

Baghdadi, Y. (2004). ABBA: an architecture for deploying business-to-business electronic commerce applications. *Electronic Commerce Research and Applications*, *3*, 190–212. doi:10.1016/j.elerap.2003.09.006

Bendoly, E., Rosenzweig, E., & Stratman, J. (2009). The efficient use of enterprise information for strategic advantage: A data envelopment analysis. *Journal of Operations Management*, *27*, 310–323. doi:10.1016/j.jom.2008.11.001

Bolin, S. (2004). *The Nature and Future of ICT Standardization*. Retrieved June 21, 2004, from http://www.sun.com/software/standards/natureandfuture_ICT.pdf

Burrows, J. (1999). Information Technology standards in a changing world: the role of the users . In *Computer Standards & Interfaces* (pp. 323–331). Amsterdam: Elsevier Science B.V.

Capers, C., Bartels, A., Wilson, R., & Rugullies, E. (2001 November), *B2B Exchanges: Future Hopes, Current Doubts*. Booz Allen Hamilton and Giga Information Group.

Chan, C., & Swatman, P. (2002), Management and business issues for B2B eCommerce implementation. In *Proceedings of the 35th Hawaii International Conference on System Sciences*.

Chau, P., & Hui, K. (2001). Determinants of Small Business EDI Adoption: An Empirical Investigation. *Journal of Organizational Computing and Electronic Commerce*, *11*(4), 229–252. doi:10.1207/S15327744JOCE1104_02

Dssouli, R., Saleh, K., Aboulhamid, E., En-Nouaary, A., & Bourhfir, C. (1999). Test development for communication protocols: towards automation. *Computer Networks*, *31*, 1835–1872. doi:10.1016/S1389-1286(99)00063-8

Dubelaar, C. (2005). Benefits, impediments and critical success factors in B2C e-business adoption. *Technovation*, *25*, 1251–1262. doi:10.1016/j.technovation.2004.08.004

Edifecs. (2000). *Solving the B2B Ramp-up Challenge: Key to Realizing Widespread e-Commerce Adoption*. Research Report, Edifecs Inc.

Egan, T., Clancy, S., & O'Toole, T. (2003). The Integration of E-Commerce Tools into the Business Processes of SMEs. *Irish Journal of Management* (pp. 139-152).

eMarketer. (2002). *Europe eCommerce: B2B & B2C*. Executive summary, eMarketer Inc.

Ersala, N., Yen, D., & Rajkumar, T. (2002). Enterprise Application Integration in the electronic commerce world . *Computer Standards & Interfaces*, *2189*, 1–14.

Finnegan, D., & Currie, W. (2009). *A multilayered approach to CRM implementation: An integration perspective*. European Management Journal.

Folmer, E., Hinderer, H., & Otto, B. (2003). The openXchange framework for ebXML-based business process integration . In Jardim-Gonçalves, R. (Eds.), *Concurrent Engineering: Enhanced Interoperable Systems* (pp. 447–453). Amsterdam: A. A. Balkema Publishers.

Gelete, S., Coscuellala, C., & Garcia, J. (2003). Agent assisted concurrent process engineering system for design support . In Jardim-Gonçalves, R. (Eds.), *Concurrent Engineering: Enhanced Interoperable Systems* (pp. 463–467). Amsterdam: A. A. Balkema Publishers.

Ghiladi, V. (2003). The Importance of International Standards for Globally Operating Businesses. *International Journal of IT Standards and Standardization Research*, *1*(1), 54–56.

Graham, I., Pollock, N., Smart, A., & Williams, R. (2003). Institutionalisation of E-Business Standards. In J. L. King & K. Lyytinen (Eds.), *Standard Making: A Critical Research Frontier for Information Systems, Pre-conference workshop for International Conference on Information Systems (ICIS 2003)*, December 12-14, 2003, Seattle, USA (pp. 1-9).

Han, Y., & Youn, C.-H. (2009). A new grid resource management mechanism with resource-aware policy administrator for SLA-constrained applications. *Future Generation Computer Systems*, *25*, 768–778. doi:10.1016/j.future.2008.11.005

Intel. (2003 October). *Collaborative RosettaNet Implementation: Intel and Fujitsu streamline e-Business automation across the supply chain*. Intel Information Technology White Paper.

Ishikawa, Y. (2003). Concurrent Engineering: Part 1: Business requirements, life cycle activity, key agenda for success and challenge with ISO standards . In Cha, A. (Eds.), *Concurrent Engineering: The Vision for the Future Generation in Research and Applications* (pp. 523–532). Lisse, Portugal: Balkema Publishers.

ISO. (2003). *How conformity assessment works*. Retrieved June 2, 2003, from http://www.iso.org/iso/en/comms-markets/conformity/iso+conformity-02.html

Jap, S., & Mohr, J. (2002). *Leveraging Internet Technologies in B2B Relationships*. California Management Review.

Joseph, C., Gunton, T., & Day, J. (2008). Implementation of resource management plans: Identifying keys to success. *Journal of Environmental Management*, *88*, 594–606. doi:10.1016/j.jenvman.2007.03.028

Kacfcr, F., & Bcndoly, E. (2004). Mcasuring the impact of organizational constraints on the success of business-to-business e-commerce efforts: a transactional focus. *Information & Management*, *41*, 529–541. doi:10.1016/S0378-7206(03)00088-0

Kohli, R., & Devaraj, S. (2004, March). Realizing the Business Value of Information Technology Investments: An Organizational Process. *Management Information Systems Quarterly*, *3*(1), 55–69.

Kosanke, K., & Nell, J. (1999). Standardisation in ISO for enterprise engineering and integration. *Computers in Industry*, *40*, 311–319. doi:10.1016/S0166-3615(99)00034-2

Kotok, A. (2002). *Standards-Based Methodology for U.S. E-Government Initiatives. Data Interchange Standards Association*. DISA.

Lee, K. (1996, June). Cooperative Standard-Setting: The Road to Compatibility or Deadlock? The NAFTA's Transformation of the Telecommunications Industry. *Federal Communications Law Journal*, *48*(3).

Lee, S. (2005). Efficiency analysis of controls in EDI applications. *Information & Management*, *42*(3), 425–439. doi:10.1016/j.im.2001.09.001

Lee, S., & Lim, G. (2003). The impact of partnership attributes on EDI implementation success. *Information & Management*, *41*, 135–148. doi:10.1016/S0378-7206(03)00043-0

Lee, S. C., Pak, B. Y., & Lee, H. G. (2003). Business value of B2B electronic commerce: the critical role of inter-firm collaboration. *Electronic Commerce Research and Applications*, *2*, 350–361. doi:10.1016/S1567-4223(03)00003-6

Lengnick-Hall, M., Lengnick-Hall, C., Andrade, L., & Drake, B. (2009). Strategic human resource management: The evolution of the field. *Human Resource Management View*, *19*, 64–85. doi:10.1016/j.hrmr.2009.01.002

Love, P., & Irani, Z. (2004, December). An exploratory study of information technology evaluation and benefits management practices of SMEs in the construction industry. *Information & Management*, *42*(1), 227–242.

Lu, X.-H. (2006). Critical success factors of inter-organizational information systems – A case study of Cisco and Xiao Tong in China. *Information & Management*, *43*, 395–408. doi:10.1016/j.im.2005.06.007

Mähönen, P. (2000). The standardization process in IT – Too slow or too fast? In Jakobs, K. (Ed.), *Information Technology Standards and Standardization: A Global Perspective* (pp. 35–47). Hershey, PA: IDEA Group Publishing.

Meehan, M. (2002, January 1). Users Say Lack of IT Integration Hurts B2B. *ComputerWorld.* Retrieved from http://www.computerworld.com

Mörschel, I. (2003). Standardization of and for services: opportunities, risks, best practice. In K. Jakobs (Ed.), *Proceedings of the 8th Euras Workshop on Standardization,* Aachen, July 11-12, 2003 (pp. 59-60).

NIST. (2001 January). What is this thing called Conformance? *NIST.* Retrieved March 10, 2004, from http://www.itl.nist.gov/

Nucleus. (2002). *Microsoft BizTalk Server: A Nucleus Research Report.* Research report C30, Nucleus Research Inc. Retrieved from http://www.NucleusResearch.com

Ollner, J. (1988). *The Company and Standardization* (3rd ed.). Stockholm, Sweden: Swedish Standards Institution.

Olson, E., & Williams, P. (2001). E-Commerce with Web-Based Standards: A Case Study in Implementing RosettaNet Process Standards at Avnet, Inc. *PriceWaterhouseCoopers.* Retrieved April 2001, from http://www.rosettanet.org/RosettaNet/Doc/0/BMHE9II7VRKK916EJ4DPI6I635/avnetwhitepaper.pdf

Ousterhout, J. (2000 October). Managing Trading Partners. *EAI Journal*, 89-92.

Premkumar, G., Ramamurthy, K., & Nilakanta, S. (1994). Implementation of Electronic Data Interchange: An Innovation Diffusion Perspective. *Journal of Management Information Systems, 11*(2), 157–186.

Ramsey, J. (1998 August). Developing an IT Strategy. *Computer Bits, 8*(8). Retrieved from http://www.computerbits.com

RosettaNet. (2001). *Case Study: Arrow and UTEC replace EDI-based purchase order process with RosettaNet standards.* Retrieved February 20, 2004, from http://www.rosettanet.org/RosettaNet/Doc/0/D074294MUC4KJD8GF7HQL8RE67/Arrow_case_study.pdf

RosettaNet. (2002). *Achieving Streamlined Operations Through Collaborative Forecasting and Inventory Management: STMicroelectronics E-Chain Optimization (eChO) Project.* Retrieved February 10, 2004, from http://www.rosettanet.org/RosettaNet/Doc/0/63NGGI61LP84P753UQ28VBMLA3/STMicroelectronics+White+Paper.pdf

RosettaNet. (2003). *Intel and Shinko to use RosettaNet standards to build forecase-to-cash procurement process.* Case study report. Retrieved from http://www.rosettanet.org/RosettaNet/Doc/0/FSG4VFMC6RA4B47H0FJB0NNPED/IntelShinkoROICaseStudy.pdf

Rukanova, B., van Slooten, K., & Stegwee, R. (2003). Beyond the Standard Development and the Standard Adoption. In K. Jakobs (Ed.), *Proceedings of the 8th Euras Workshop on Standardization,* Aachen, July 11-12 (pp. 133-143).

Seminerio, M. (2000). B2B 2 The World. *eWeek, 17*(35), 51-55.

Shin, K., & Leem, C. S. (2002). A reference system for internet based inter-enterprise electronic commerce. *Journal of Systems and Software, 60*, 195–209. doi:10.1016/S0164-1212(01)00092-9

Skall, M., & Rosenthal, L. (2000). *Conformance.* Presentation from the ebXML Tokyo Meeting in November, 2000.

Söderström, E. (2008). Towards a general model of the B2B standards implementation process. In *Proceedings of the IADIS E-Commerce conference 2008*, Amsterdam, 22-24 July, 2008 (pp. 151-158).

Soliman, K., & Janz, B. (2004). An exploratory study to identify the critical factors affecting the decision to establish Internet-based inter-organisational information systems. *Information & Management*, *41*, 697–706. doi:10.1016/j.im.2003.06.001

Swann, P. (2000, December 11). *The economics of standardization*. Final report for Standards and Technical Regulations Directorate, Department of Trade and Industry, Manchester Business School.

Tarafdar, M., & Gordon, S. (2007). Understanding the influences of information systems competencies on process innovation: A resource-based view. *The Journal of Strategic Information Systems*, *16*, 353–392. doi:10.1016/j.jsis.2007.09.001

Teo, T., & Ranganathan, C. (2004, December). Adopters and non-adopters of business-to-business electronic commerce in Singapore. *Information & Management*, *42*(1), 89–102.

webMethods. (2003 February). *GEAR 6 RosettaNet Implementation Guide: Project Planning Guide* [Whitepaper].

Zolkiewski, J., & Littler, D. (2004). Future business relationships – traditional, electronic, virtual or hybrid? *Telematics and Informatics*, *21*, 183–196. doi:10.1016/S0736-5853(03)00056-X

KEY TERMS AND DEFINITIONS

B2B Business-to-Business: the use of the Internet and Web-technologies for conducting inter-organizational business transactions

Standards: Guidelines for how communication and information sent between companies should be structured and managed

Implementation: All activities and actions taken in an organisation to operate the standard in the inter-organisational communication

Guideline Aspects of B2B: standards implementation that should be taken into consideration

SDO: Standards development organization, responsible for identifying, formulating and issuing standards

SSO: Standards software organizations, takes standard specifications to construct an organization's software

SUO: Standards user organization, implement and use the standards to collaborate and conduct business activities

ENDNOTES

1. Processes are depicted by thick arrows in (Figure 2). Relationships between internal processes are depicted by straight lines.
2. Inter-organisational exchange is depicted by the thin arrows in (Figure 2).
3. Enablement is defined as the process of preparing a company and its customers and suppliers to transact business electronically.

Chapter 6
Ontology-Based Registries: An E-Business Transactions' Registry

Aikaterini Maria Sourouni
National Technical University of Athens, Greece

Spiros Mouzakitis
National Technical University of Athens, Greece

George Kourlimpini
National Technical University of Athens, Greece

Dimitris Askounis
National Technical University of Athens, Greece

John Psarras
National Technical University of Athens, Greece

INTRODUCTION

In the dawn of 21st century, there has been substantial technological progress in the area of e-Business. However, despite the fact of e-Business evolution, the adoption of new internet-based technologies in the business environment is still limited, especially in the sector of small and medium (SMEs) or very small enterprises (VSEs), (Androutselis, 2005). In parallel, the to-date efforts for developing and adopting e-Business solutions has been targeted more towards the Business-to-Consumer (B2C) and the Business-to-Business (B2B) of same interests –same business sector– area and not so vitally towards the area, which this chapter addresses to. This area comprises the Business to Business (B2B), Business to Government (B2G) and Business to Intermediaries (B2I) –such as Banks and Public Insurance Institutions– transactions between Entrepreneurial, Governmental and Banking Organizations of different countries (cross-border) or of different interests/operation domains (cross-sector).

DOI: 10.4018/978-1-61692-016-6.ch006

Background to Ontologies

The term of Ontology derives from Philosophy's domain, meaning a systematic assessment of existence. A short interpretation of the term "Ontology", that T.R. Gruber has provided and R. Studer improved is the following (Gruber, 1995): "An explicit and methodological specification of a conceptualization". With the term of conceptualization T.R. Gruber (1995) defines an abstract aspect of the real world that needs to be modelled and represented.

Last decades ontologies have entered the area of the Computer Science and nowadays comprise a manifold and effective approach for electronic information. The major sectors for potential commercial applications of ontologies are (TOVE Project):

- Information and Knowledge Management, such as World Wide Web, knowledge sharing etc.
- E-business, such as in the Supply Chain Management field.

The object-oriented software systems are usually based on an ontology. So, in the case of software tools and applications, Ontologies can be used at different levels (Gruninger, 1995), such as:

- During the design and development of application systems, contributing particularly to the specification, reliability and reusability of the systems.
- At the communication level providing easy data exchange.
- At the Interoperability level, facilitating Data, Function and Process Interoperability.

Related Efforts and Scope

As many renowned scientists and academics state, in modern economy the key question for an enterprise is not whether to deploy electronic transaction solutions and internet technologies – since this may already be considered a necessity – but how to deploy it in order to realize the biggest possible benefits (Porter, 2001).

Towards realizing this goal a number of research initiatives are already undergoing within the scope of the sixth and seventh framework programme (FP6, FP7) aiming at providing solutions in key areas, such as enterprise modelling, ontologies, enterprise applications, interoperability and information and communication technology (ICT) standards, that may enable electronic transactions. Such initiatives constitute the (INTEROP), (ATHENA) and (GENESIS) projects. Nevertheless, when it comes to developing such systems – both at research and industrial level – the focus remains concentrated in providing technological solutions that will cater for features such as the interconnection of heterogeneous IT infrastructures, the ability to execute static and dynamic workflows, the exchange of standardized or generic business documents and the incorporation of high security standards to the implemented systems, putting aside important semantics and key factors that influence and shape the functional operation of the enterprise.

Process modelling is a traditional topic in Information Systems research, thus the various possible motivations for modelling a process, the various sources of models, and the resulting variety of requirements on the formalisms used for representing processes are often not considered. This contributes to the dominance of a simplified, workflow-centric view on business processes, i.e. business processes are reduced to the sequencing of activities. Evidence of this workflow-minded notion of processes is that languages and tools for modelling business processes and also used for e-business transactions modelling focus on control flow patterns. (Hepp, 2007). Additionally, semantics and business knowledge cannot be clearly represented and managed.

For this reason, this chapter presents an ontology-based e-Business transactions' Registry & Repository, devoted to the formal description, composition and publishing of traditional, electronic, or web services, together with the relevant documents, rules, resources and the process descriptions in an integrated schema of semantics and workflow notation. Through this repository, the discovery of e-business transactions by users –enterprises, government, intermediaries- or systems can be automated, resulting in an important tool for managing e-Business transformation towards achieving cross-sector and cross-border interoperability.

DEFINING THE E-BUSINESS TRANSACTIONS ONTOLOGY

Motivation

The representation means of the proposed system have to capture the core elements of the domain, together with their main relationships. Although ontologies for the e-Business domain exist, most approaches cover abstract or sub-domains (Osterwalder, 2002). The work presented to this chapter has been oriented towards a generic e-Business ontological approach incorporating predefined core e-business concepts and terms.

In order to identify these concepts, a survey for the e-business transactions conducted by European SMEs, has been carried out. This survey has intended to identify the most common and important transactions conducted within the European Union and then to recognize the core concepts and elements necessary for these transactions' modelling and definition. This survey has been based on the (UBL standards 2.0), (eEurope2005), (IDABC initiatives) and (IFX), standards which are briefly presented below:

- UBL 2.0: A Standard for Government e-Procurement. The OASIS Universal Business Language (UBL) is intended to help solve these problems by defining a generic XML interchange format for business documents that can be extended to meet the requirements of particular industries. UBL is designed to provide a universally understood and recognized commercial syntax for legally binding business documents and to operate within a standard business framework such as ISO 15000 (ebXML) to provide a complete, standards-based infrastructure that can extend the benefits of existing EDI systems to businesses of all sizes. UBL is freely available to everyone without legal encumbrance or licensing fees.
- eEurope 2005 Action Plan was launched at the Seville European Council in June 2002 and endorsed by the Council of Ministers in the eEurope Resolution of January 2003. It aimed to develop modern public services and a dynamic environment for e-business through widespread availability of broadband access at competitive prices and a secure information infrastructure.
- IDABC Initiatives in the context of Interoperability:
- European Interoperability Framework (EIF) v2.0: the new set of interoperability guidelines for European Member States.
- SEMIC.eu: The European Semantic Interoperability Centre, an infrastructure for reusing semantic components.
- NIFO, A National Interoperability Frameworks Observatory, currently under development by Gartner, for IDABC.
- Interactive Financial eXchange (IFX) specification is a mature, well-designed XML-based, financial messaging protocol, built by financial industry and technology leaders incorporating decades of combined experience and best of breed design principles.

Design

After studying the above standards and approaches, the proposed e-Business Interoperability-oriented Ontology has concluded to comprise nine top-level entities in order to integrate the multifaceted concepts of e-business transactions.

1. Sector, referring to the environment – domain in which a "Party" operates, such as Entrepreneurial, Governmental, Banking sector.

Figure 1. The Upper E-business Transactions Ontology

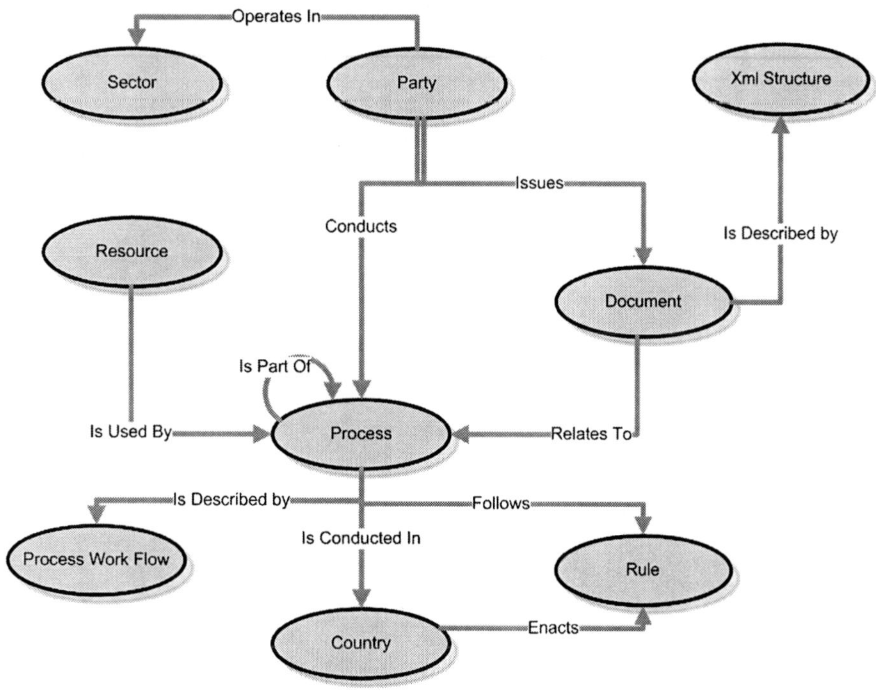

2. Party, nested at infinite levels, being an enterprise, public organization, bank or one of its divisions and departments.
3. Document, representing electronic or paper form – application involved in processes as input or output of them.
4. Xml Representation, being an XML or XSD file with the typical, standard structure of a Document.
5. Process, being an e-business transaction or a sub-transaction conducted between Parties, utilizing Resources, involving Documents and following the defined legislation.
6. Process Work Flow, being a BPMN (Business Process Modelling Notation) model with aim to link a Process with its work-flow illustration.
7. Resource, referring to medium used in order to facilitate a Process execution, such as an information system, a web-portal.
8. Rule, representing important factors and parameters which influence and assign an e-business transaction – Process, such as legal rules or best practices.
9. Country, representing a Country where specific rules are enacted and Processes are conducted following them.

The unified picture of the proposed e-Business Ontology is presented in Figure 1, enhancing the nine main entities with the relationships defined among them. Therefore, the proposed e-Business Ontology is a process-centric modelling approach based on relational and semantic conceptualization, beyond the step-by-step flow details.

The identified metadata definitions cover all the important facets for classifying and querying the elements of the ontology, so as to provide answers to important questions around the status of electronic conduction of transactions, existence and structure of documents, relation of transactions

Table 1. Process Metadata

Field	Description, Type
Code	The Process Code, Unique, String
Title	The Process Title, Unique, String
Engaged Parties	Organisations (Enterprises, Public Administrators, Banks etc.), taking part in the process flow, Multi-Element
Type	The Process Type, List
Category	Process Category, according to the theme, Element
Starting Event	The associated Starting Event, Element
Authentication Type	Type of Authentication, the engaged parties need when the process is conducted (e.g. username/password, token, digital signature),, List
Frequency	Frequency the process is conducted, by means of High-Medium-Low, List
Information Source	The source(s) of information for the process conduction, String
Date of last Update	The date of last information sampling, Date

Table 2. Rule Metadata

Field	Description, Type
Code	The Rule Code, String
Title	The Rule Title, Unique, String
Type	The type of the Rule (law, directive, best practice etc), List
Legal Framework	The superseding legal framework if exists, Element
Date of last Update	The date of last sampling, Date

with organisations, characteristics of the various information systems and so on. Table 1 shows an initial sample used as the metadata definitions for the Process element, indicating which of them are represented as strings, numbers, list of values or structured elements themselves.

Relevant, extensive metadata description fields exist for Documents and Parties, providing an indication of the descriptive power of the Ontology. In lower level of description, elements e.g. Rule have simpler metadata descriptions, as shown in Table 2.

THE ONTOLOGY-BASED E-BUSINESS TRANSACTIONS REGISTRY

Overview

The Ontology-based e-Business Transactions Registry is a web platform devoted to the formal description, composition and publishing of entities of the defined e-Business Ontology, such as B2B,B2G and BNK transactions and services, together with the relevant documents, rules and the process descriptions in an integrated schema. By using the Registry, enterprises, organizations and Communities establish ontologies, or shared conceptual models, to provide a framework for sharing a precise meaning of symbols exchanged during traditional, electronic and automated transactions. The Registry is responsible for storing and managing entities which contain descriptions of services. It allows for typical database operations, such as adding new data, updating existing documents and searching for services that meet specific requirements, as well as more composite operations such as process workflow management, ontology visualization and XML composition.

Design and Architecture

The e-Business Transactions Registry comprises of four layers:

- The Web Interface: The Web Interface layer consists of all the necessary elements that enable the user to interact with the Registry. More specifically, this layer includes typical Web forms with both basic and extended graphical user interface (GUI) controls for managing the entities of the e-Business Transactions Registry. The main goal of the Web Interface is to hide the complexity from the users by providing them ease to use yet flexible user interface controls and utilities that deal with common difficulties met in ontology management applications and repositories, such as structural complexity and anomalies, disambiguation of terms and incomplete coverage of ontology entities. The custom-developed OntoGrid control, for instance, provides a ubiquitous control panel for managing (insert, update, save, delete) instances of the Ontology Entities that appear in the data grid as well as an integrated navigational module that facilitates querying and traversing ontology information. Moreover, the Views module of the OntoGrid control allows the representation of the listed entities into a variety of forms and formats such as OWL diagrams and XML. Furthermore, the Registry's Search control allows users to easily find and explore entities based on keywords that are related to their properties. The Registry search control ensures that users only ever create "meaningful" queries (queries that could possibly return at least one result) and can avoid the need for users to know the underlying identifiers assigned to the types in the ontology. The Web Interface has been developed with ASP.NET 2 web application framework running in integrated mode on Internet Information System 7.0.
- The Registry Core Engine: The core engine of the Registry is the layer where the application logic lies. The engine of the registry includes the Entity Library provider, the Business logic of the web interface, and the Rule Validation module. The Entity Library is responsible for managing the classes representing the entities of the e-Business Ontology. The library includes the entities' definition in terms of properties, constraints and class axioms, and the related data providers for communicating with the database component. The Entity library is used in the business logic of the Registry platform which interconnects the Web Interface with the database system. The rule validation module manages the integrity and consistency of the e-Business Ontology's entities. It provides the framework for managing entity business rules and custom error information that the web interface can bind to. Controls such as the OntoGrid automatically detect this interface and provide error icons along with descriptions about the error
- Supporting Tools API and Engine: The supporting tools layer includes complete third-party utilities and tools that are seamlessly integrated to the e-Business Ontology Registry .More specifically, for defining and maintaining process workflow entities, the Registry platform takes advantage of BOC ADONIS process modelling application. Additionally, XML properties or elements, such as the XML representation of business documents that are exchanged in an e-business transaction are managed through Altova's XML suite capabilities. Lastly, additional third-party tools are used for data visualization and reporting. The registry core engine retrieves events from the web interface and communicates with

the corresponding tool, providing an end-to-end user-experience.

- Database: The database layer provides all the necessary components and modules for communicating with the database management system of the e-Business ontology Registry. The database engine that has been used is Microsoft SQL Server.

Platform's Functionality

The e-Business Transactions Ontology Registry is a portal for managing elements of the e-Business transactions ontology. The registry's functionality can be categorized as follows:

- e-Business Transaction Entities Management

The platform provides standard management functionality (create, edit, delete) for all the entities of the e-Business Transaction Ontology, each of which corresponds to menu item. Thus, the items of the entities management menu are Sector, Party, Document, Process, Resource, Rule and Country. Users can list all the available entities, view the details of any entity (properties, versioning, constraints, related legal directives and laws, etc), search for a defined entity and of course create, update and delete an instance. In order to find an entity the user is asked to provide search words describing the entity s/he wants to search for. The search request goes through the matching modules. The search query is matched with the appropriate context semantics specified in the e-Business Transaction Ontology. Typical operations involve "New" and "Edit" buttons, where as more complex operations involve entity inheritance, entity creation based on a stored template and class axioms realization.

- e-Business Process Workflow Management

In order to efficiently describe business process workflows a formal representation is achieved

Figure 2. e-Business Transactions Registry – Process Edit Form

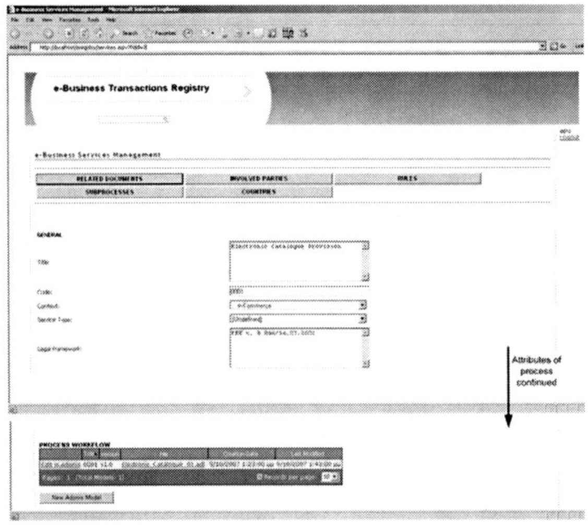

through the ADONIS business Process Management Application (ADONIS BOC), seamlessly integrated within the Registry platform. By activating the process workflow item in the Registry, the ADONIS modelling environment shows up in order to create or update a process workflow according to the BPMN Methodology. When the modelling process is over, changes are saved in the Registry database and the user can return back to the platform's web interface. A key thing to note is that all the necessary elements involved in the workflow diagram (Documents, Resources, Process properties) are directly referenced to the entities created by the Registry's web interface. For example, the available "Documents" in the Adonis environment are only the documents created through the Registry's "Documents" Management.

At this point, it should be cleared that the Registry does not intend to replace or compete business process modelling languages, standards or other work-flow representation tools. However, through the utility of e-Business Process Workflow Management, this approach adopts the BPMN methodology as an established standard and it uses it through a widely-recognised BPM tool

Figure 3. e-Business Transactions Registry Work flow Model

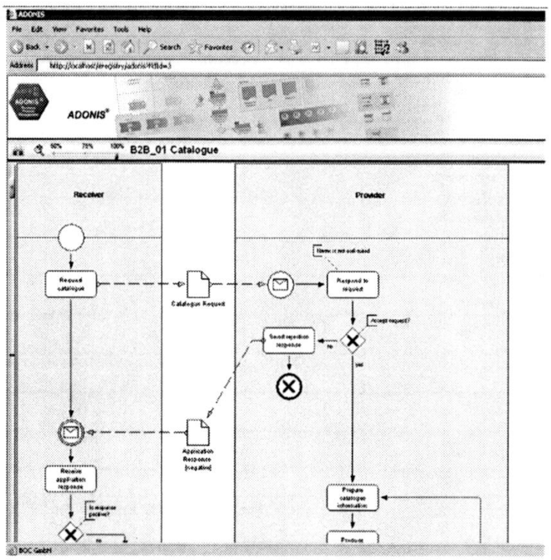

(ADONIS) and combine this way the workflow representation with the semantics and business knowledge of the transactions into an integrated schema.

- XML Management

Similar to the workflow modelling functionality, by activating an entity that involves XML representation (typical the XSD or XML of a business document), Altova's XMLspy shows up in order to proficiently edit the XML files. The created XML files are thereafter been referenced with the corresponding business documents of the ontology.

- Process Change Management

The proposed approach does not include a fully-automated change management process. However, the architecture and the methodological approach of the proposed repository provide some features that enable a kind of automated or semi-automated change management activities. The reporting mechanism facilitates consistency check notifications. The affected processes by modified legal issues (for example) are in this way located in order to undergo maintenance activities. Additionally, few automated cascading effects are invoked.

Pilot Testing

A list of selected common B2B, B2G and B2I transactions used by enterprises of different sectors and countries in EU are presented in Table 3. Each one of these transactions has been modelled into the Registry as a pilot testing of its potential and usability.

Transactions of the above list (Table 3) have been modeled up to a generic process view, by taking into consideration the different processes from the different counties. More specific, as far as it regards the B2B transactions, 6 countries were selected for generating the generic interoperable transaction models (Greece, Turkey, Romania, Bulgaria, Lithuania and Czech Republic), whereas B2G and Banking generic models were based on the process models of 4 countries (Greece, Cyprus, Italy and Turkey). For each sector, a mix of EU member states, newly added members and candidate members was selected. (Sourouni, 2007)

During modelling many issues had arisen, which mainly involved the legal rules and the data entities that accompany each transaction in each country. Moreover, the way each transaction is carried out differs from country to country as the business logic is not the same. Those issues are by defacto not taken into consideration when trying to design interoperable systems for conducting transaction in country specific domains, as all enterprises operating in the same country follow the same legal rules and have the same data requirements.

However, when trying to extend the environment of e-business by comprising cross-border and cross-sector transactions, all the above issues come up to the surface. Therefore, we have created

Table 3. List of Modelled Transactions

Category	Business Process / Transaction
B2B	Catalogue Provision (Request, Issue/Get, Handle)
	Quotation (Request, Issue/Get, Handle)
	Order (Request, Issue/Get, Handle)
	Packing Slip (Issue/Get, Handle)
	Invoice (Issue/Get, Handle)
	Billing (Credit/debit, Reconcile, Handle)
	Fulfillment Collaboration (Despatch/Receive through 3rd Party)
B2G	VAT Statement (periodic)
	VAT Statement (annual or cumulative)
	Enterprise Income TAX Statement (annual)
	INTRASTAT Statement (annual)
	Social Security Statement – Contribution (periodic)
	Transactions Reporting (intra-EU/national, periodic)
	Various VAT sub-statements and reports
	Declaration of hiring new employee
B2I (Banking)	Account Status
	List of Account Transactions
	Fund Transfer (intra-bank, inter-bank)
	Specific Payment (VAT, tax, other)
	Payment Check (Credit Note) Issuing
	Payment Check (Credit Note) Status
	Loan Status Inquiry

a consolidated generic process model, which has to respect all the underlying exceptions and has to aggregate all the underlying business logic, legal rules and data requirements into a unique model so as to satisfy all the needs which spring out of the public processes.

In order to meet these demands and to finally reach the ultimate goal which is no other than proposing an approach for cross-border and cross-sector interoperability, those generic process models have to be designed at the highest abstraction level that could be reached. This way, the generic models represent the service orchestration which has to be established between the different parties in order to carry out their transactions successfully. The abstraction level chosen defines the obligatory business document exchange which must take place but at the same time does not interfere with the different internal processes of each party. However, several rules regarding the legal issues or the data entities have to be applied, which may or may not affect the internal of the parties' processes, depending of the architecture that will be selected upon the system implementation process.

As far as the execution way or the process flow of a transaction itself are concerned, based on the examined countries there seem to be only small differences in the business logic of the transactions. Therefore the generic models could easily fit to all the examined countries, as the chosen abstraction level is able to cover the core process flow of the examined transactions.

CONCLUSION

This chapter presented the definition, the design and the development of an ontology-based e-Business Transactions registry for the description, composition and publishing of transactional business services, together with the relevant documents, rules and the process descriptions. The Registry can be further utilized for e-Business transactions execution standardization, administrated by the authorized organization of the EC, or a specific country.

However, e-business systems are subject to a continual change. Better change management is nowadays more important due to the evolution of Europe towards a multicultural, more open and international society. With respect to the presented approach, an inference engine is under study and design. Such an engine has to be built in order to use rules and implement reasoning capabilities of the underlying approach. Subsequently, there are plans for implementing extra modules, especially focused on content population of the ontology.

Future steps of this work include further research based on the findings and results of the Registry's pilot application in Greece, in cooperation with the General Secretariat of Research and Technology of Greek Ministry of Development. This future research should certainly deal with process change management and inference mechanisms, which could extremely advance our approach's features.

ACKNOWLEDGMENT

The work described in this chapter was carried out as part of GIC project (FP7), "Greek Interoperability Center".

REFERENCES

ADONIS. (n.d.). Retrieved from http://www.boc-group.com/documents/ products/bptrens_boc_adonis_ reportshort_eng.pdf

Androutsellis-Theotokis, S., Karakoidas, V., Gousios, G., Spinellis, D., & Charalambidis, Y. (2005 October). *Building an e-Business Platform: An Experience Report.* Paper presented at the eChallenges 2005 Conference, Amsterdam, Netherlands.

ATHENA Project. (n.d.). Retrieved from http://www.athena-ip.org

eEurope. (2005). Retrieved from http://europa.eu/information_society/eeurope/

GENESIS Project. (n.d.). Retrieved from http://www.genesis-ist.eu

Gruber, T. R. (1995). Toward principles for design ontologies used for knowledge sharing. *International Journal of Human-Computer Studies*, *43*(5/6), 907–928. doi:10.1006/ijhc.1995.1081

Gruninger, M., & Fox, M. S. (1995 August). *Methodology for the Design and Evaluation of Ontologies.* Presented at the Workshop on Basic Ontological Issues in Knowledge Sharing, IJ-CAI-95, Montreal Quebec Canada

Hepp, M., & Roman, D. (2007 February). *An Ontology Framework for Semantic Business Process Management.* Presented at the 8th international conference Wirtschaftsinformatik 2007, Karlsruhe, Germany.

IDABC European eGovernment Services. (n.d.). Retrieved from http://ec.europa.eu/idabc

IFX (Interactive Financial Exchange) Forum. (n.d.). Retrieved from http://www.ifxforum.org/home

INTEROP Network of Excellence. (n.d.). Retrieved from http://www.interopnoe.org

Osterwalder, A., & Pigneur, Y. (2002 June). *An e-Business Model Ontology for Modelling e-Business.* Presented at the Bled Electronic Commerce Conference, Bled, Slovenia.

Porter, M. (2001, March). Strategy and the Internet. *Harvard Business Review*, 63–78.

Sourouni, A. M., Koussouris, S., Charalabidis, Y., Askounis, D., & Kalaboukas, K. (2007 December). *A generic process modelling approach for interoperable e-business transactions.* Paper presented at IADIS International Conference e-Commerce 2007, Algarve, Portugal.

TOVE Ontology Project. (n.d.). Retrieved from http://www.eil.utoronto.ca/enterprise-modelling/tove/

UBL (Universal Business Language). (n.d.). Retrieved from http://www.oasis-open.org/committees/ubl/

Section 3

Access Mediums to Online Services

Chapter 7
Strategic Framework for Developing a Process Model for Maximising the Potential of Radio Frequency Identification (RFID) Technology Integration in Hospitals

Chandana Unnithan
Deakin University, Australia

Bardo Fraunholz
Deakin University, Australia

ABSTRACT

Radio Frequency Identification is a radical technology that is being experimented in hospitals commonly for tracking high value equipment, in order to maximize the efficiency of processes. RFID deployment and integration is mostly vendor and business driven, and hence its potential is not maximized. In this chapter, we propose a strategic framework to develop a process model, that will assist in maximizing the potential of RFID in hospitals.

INTRODUCTION

Radio Frequency Identification or RFID is a broad term that is used for classifying technologies that use radio waves to automatically recognize objects and people (Greene, 2005). This radical concept came into existence in 1940s (Landt, 2001), when it was first used in World War II by British aircrafts to identify friendly airplanes returning from their missions. RFD has the ability to track signals and store data, which helped its commercialisation through RFID tags -- small silicon microchips, which may be as small as a half a millimetre square, attached to antennae and can be placed anywhere (Taghaboni-Dutta, Velthouse, 2006). RFID tags are able to store unique serial numbers and other

DOI: 10.4018/978-1-61692-016-6.ch007

information, which can be read by readers a few or hundreds of meters away.

For the manufacturing industry, RFID was an evolution from bar coding technologies. While bar coding required line of sight, requiring a scanner to see the code - so as to read it, RFID systems did not require the line of sight (Greene, 2005). RFID improved the efficiency of the supply chain management simply by its ability to track goods from the factory to retail stores. Fisher and Monahan (2008) contend that RFID systems draw upon their successful utilisation in manufacturing and retail environments – for more efficient management of resources in organisations; and they drew upon their military applications to offer potential for heightened identification functions.

Hospitals globally began to realise the benefits of adopting RFID into their operations, to enhance efficiency and provide better services, in the last decade (Cavoukian, 2008; Cangialosi, Monaly, Yang, 2007). RFID systems has been trialled to track medical equipment and supplies more efficiently, enabling the authenticity and administration of drugs, and improving patient safety via the use of RFID bracelets. Hospitals are interested particularly in tracking high value equipment, and frequently used equipment, to optimise their utilisation in emergency settings such as surgeries (Nagy et al., 2006).

The rationale for RFID adoption was quite simple. In the dynamic world today, hospitals are finding it increasingly complex to provide care to an adequate standard, due to resource constraints (Hoskins, 2006). Surgical procedures are delayed due to missing high end critical equipment or regularly used assets, as well as clinician time spent on tracking them. In an emergency, it is not uncommon to find doctors and nurses hunting for an IV stand or defibrillator, although the hospital may have numerous supplies. Large hospitals spend significantly on stocking equipment that is used frequently. Yet, medical staff spend hours searching for patient care assets, including medical devices (such as infusion pumps, portable x-ray machines and patient monitoring devices), as well as other mobile assets such as wheelchairs, laptops, stretchers and gurneys.

Poor utilisation and slow device cycle times cause many high-value assets to go underutilised while these hospitals continue to overspend on new and rental assets (Hoskins, 2006). Meanwhile, nurses sacrifice time with patients (especially in surgeries) to seek equipment they need and maintenance staff lose productive hours searching for specific items that need maintenance. As a result, the efficiency of processes in the hospitals reduce, costs and complexities continue to rise (Hoskins, 2006, Nagy et al., 2006). Managing the processes efficiently, enhancing quality of care and controlling costs are seen as the rationale for adopting RFID systems.

Relatively inexpensive RFID technology is perceived to optimise utilisation and support appropriate allocation of scarce material resources. Current seminal research into drivers for RFID in hospitals (Nagy et al. 2006; Chen, et al., 2008) indicated that the use of RFID tags may lead to reduction in clinical errors, reduced costs and increased efficiencies. Many hospitals have initiated the use of RFID tags on wristbands (or bracelets) which store data and can be scanned with a reader to identify a patient, and what surgical procedure is required (Hancox, 2006; Cangialosi et al., 2007). For example, RFID tags embedded in patient bracelets can help medical staff identify patients before surgery and before administering medications or blood transfusions – reducing possible clinical errors. RFID systems have been implemented such that patient movements can be traced through hospital services. Medical staff is often given RFID tags on their badges in order to collect data on workflow to find inefficiencies in current operations of the hospital. These systems are particularly useful in emergency settings where there is high patient volume, and heightened risk of medical error. Conversely, tracking equipment takes less time, leaving practitioners to spend more time with the patients (McCarthy, 2004). Hospitals can lower expenses on rental equipment and over supply inventories, with the implementation of RFID systems often known as *indoor positioning systems* (Fisher, 2006).

Current research (Fisher and Monahan, 2008) concur that due to its many dimensional uses, RFID is rapidly becoming the standard for hospitals to track inventory, identify patients, and manage personnel. The potential of RFID has been explored for asset tracking and process enhancements in hospitals, worldwide. The technology has now been accepted in such environments, as it is relatively inexpensive and, in principle, uncomplicated to integrate with other clinical support systems. It is perceived to offer many benefits to currently resource critical/strained hospitals. However, the research also indicate that RFID systems do not easily adapt to hospital settings because of the infrastructure in terms of space, equipment, personnel and patients, making it much more complicated than a factory or warehouse setting. The authors' opinion that privacy concern of patients/staff and the possible work intensification for nursing and other hospital staff, as a result of efficiencies experienced by this technology, should be taken into account from the onset, particularly during design and implementation stages.

Fisher and Monahan (2008) are of the opinion that healthcare can be improved through better implementation of RFID although it is important to know what effects the technological system have upon organisational roles and relations; and the surveillance potential of the system – as the evolving nature of the technology may alter the conditions within hospitals, as different groups adapt to and define their roles in relation to the innovation. There is a possibility that the outcome of RFID implementation may become more invasive and less efficient than intended. For example, RFID systems may have a valence toward surveillance, such that nurses may feel overtly scrutinised by the tracking technologies.

According to Scott Wallace, President and CEO of Chicago based National Alliance for Health Information Technology, process improvements and cost savings are motivations for investment in RFID. However, the challenge is how quickly workflow processes can be transformed (H&HN, 2004). The Spyglass Consulting Group (eWeek, 2005) argues that uncoordinated efforts between hospitals, vendors, shippers and suppliers are restricting RFID adoption in hospitals. In many hospitals, the implementation of RFID is vendor driven and implemented, often not in consultation with all the staff concerned. For example, RFID implementation is always done with a pilot project. An RFID pilot may begin with a vendor providing the equipment, handling installation and testing, which may be quite sudden and not known to all the people concerned. In a resource constrained hospital, it is also more difficult to inform everyone, as many staff work part time. Effectively, this lack of coordination or minimal coordination, results in underutilisation of the system as such. Specifically, if every employee who works part time is not aware of RFID tracking being available, they may not be using it during their shift hours. Conversely, when a pilot implementation begins, all the equipment to be tagged may not be available at one time to be tagged. And all tags may not have arrived at one time in stock, to enable the tagging from the vendor. This results in less accuracy of tracking, poor adaptation of the systems and also encourages a certain level of resistance from the users.

Two major themes emerge from current research on RFID implementation in hospitals: (1) RFID design and implementation should be a coordinated and consultative effort, driven by users; and (2) since the technology is constantly evolving, a process model that considers all aspects of integration of RFID systems into current processes and workflows, within a hospital, is required to maximise the potential of this technology. While undertaking research into the maximisation of RFID technology potential in hospitals, the researchers were motivated to build a process model that maximised the potential of

RFID integration in hospitals. In this chapter, we offer a strategic research framework used in the making of this process model.

CONTEXTUAL TAXONOMY

As Radio Frequency Identification emerges as a useful technology for hospitals, it also keeps evolving. For clear understanding of this technology, as it is applied to the context, in this section we provide some basic technologies that comprise of the broad term, RFID.

"*RFID is a generic term of technologies that use radio waves to automatically identify people or objects. The most common method is to store a serial number on a microchip attached to an antenna*"(Greene, 2005:30).

RFID is commonly known as an evolution from Bar Coding Technologies in the manufacturing and retail sector. However, these are different technologies. The bar code technology requires line of sight i.e. require a scanner to "see' the code to read it, which is not required by an RFID reader (Greene, 2005). In the USA, Food and Drug Administration Agency had ordered that most prescription drugs and blood products meant for transfusion carry bar codes for some time and it is pushing for RFID, for safety reasons (H&HN, 2004). According to the agency, converting all US hospitals to bar codes could cost $2 billion or more by 2014. Nevertheless, according to Accenture, if there is an existing bar coding project, the financial justifications for RFID is already met and bar coding technology was serving as a platform to move to RFID (H&HN, 2004).

The RFID technology consists of two components: a tag that acts as a data transponder; and an RFID reader. While the number of tags can range a few thousands in small RFID systems, the number of readers can increase in large scale systems, to create a more accurate three dimensional positioning system for the tags. In healthcare, the RFID tags take many forms including badges, pendants, labels, cards and even implants (Wicks, Visich & Li, 2006).

There are 4 types of RFID tags available; passive, active semi passive and semi active (Mehrjerdi, 2008). Passive tags react when the signal is received they are powered by an electronic reader and store small amount of data. They receive energy from a remote RFID reader. They have a 3 feet range of 3 feet approximately (Roark and Miguel, 2006). Semi passive tags are similar to passive tags except they have an internal power source that increases the storage capacity and the range. They use a small onboard battery to power the chip and are priced at about USD6 to USD50 depending on the capabilities. The read range for a passive tag depends on various factors such as the power of the reader, interference from metal objects or other RF devices.

In general, low-frequency tags are read from a foot or less, while high frequency tags are read from about three feet and Ultra High Frequency (UHF) tags are read from 10 to 20 feet. Where longer ranges are needed, active tags are used to boost read ranges to 300 feet or more. Active tags have an internal lithium battery power source that continuously receives and transmits signals on various different frequencies. It uses a battery for both the chip and the transmission of data on the antenna. It has an internal data storage capability (Roark DC & Miguel, 2006). Active tags have a limited life, are heavier and more expensive when compared to passive tags. Semi-active tags use the battery for powering the antenna but the chip relies on the RF energy from the reader (Mehrjerdi, 2008).

The RFID system is based on miniaturized transponders and readers for connection to information systems (Mehrjerdi, 2008). Each RFID tag has a unique identification number stored in it, which identifies the object to which the tag is attached. The communication between the tag and reader begins when the tag enter the electromagnetic field of the reader. The reader interrogates the tag using a modulated carrier and the tags reply by modulated backscattering. The reader that acts as a transceiver can read and write information on the tag. Greene (2005: 30) summarises as follows:

"Active tags have a transmitter and their own power source (typically a battery). The power source is used to run the microchip's circuitry and to broadcast a signal to a reader (the way a cell phone transmits to a base station). Passive tags have no batteries, instead they draw power from the reader, which sends out electromagnetic waves that induce a current in the tag's antenna".

One of the issues pointed out in seminal research (Nagy et al., 2006) is the lack of common global standard for RFID. There are existing and proposed RFID standards that deal with the way tags and readers communicate, the way data is organised or formatted, ways to test that product meets the standard and how standards are used on applications (such as labels, for example). The International Standards Organisation has created different standards that apply to each of these. The situation became complex because the Auto-ID Centre at MIT Labs, in USA, which developed the Electronic Product Code (EPC) technologies, chose to also create its own air interface protocols for tracking good through the international supply chain (RFID Journal, 2005:1).

Specifically, the Auto-ID Center was set up in 1999 at MIT, in USA, to develop the Electronic Product Code (EPC) and related technologies that could be used to identify products and track them through the global supply chain. Its aim was to develop a low-cost RFID system, based on global and open standards. It developed its own protocol and licensed it to EPCglobal. A set of classes of tags, with different memory and capabilities were proposed and eventually, two were retained: a Class 0 tag, which was a read only tag that was programmed at the time the microchip was made and Class 1 tag, which used a different protocol and was also a simple, passive only, backscatter tag, with one time field programmable, non volatile memory. Since the Class 0 tag used a different protocol from the Class 1 tag, end users had to buy multiprotocol readers to read both. The reason to retain these non-interoperable tags was because of the prohibition of one type of tags in Europe as compared to North America. For example, Class 0 sent out a signal at one frequency, and received a signal back at different frequency within the UHF band; which was prohibited in Europe (RFID Journal, 2005:2).

In 2003, the Auto-ID Center transitioned into two separate organizations. While Auto-ID Labs and other universities continued primary research on EPC technologies, the technology itself was licensed to the Uniform Code Council, which set up EPCglobal as a joint venture with EAN International, to commercialise EPC technology. Finally, in September 2003, the Auto-ID Center handed off the Class 0 and Class 1 protocols to EPCglobal. Subsequently, the board of EPCglobal approved Class 0 and Class 1 as EPC standards. However, the issue remained that it is still not a global standard and therefore, could not be submitted to ISO. Subsequently, in 2004, EPCglobal began developing the second-generation protocol (Gen-2), in an effort to create a single, global standard that aligns with ISO standards and it was approved in December, the same year (RFID Journal, 2005:3).

In the process of this transition up until the year 2005, many organisations had already adapted the previous standards. The new generation RFID tags were not backward compatible and therefore, those organisations had to either mover forward and upgrade their RFID systems, replace them or continue with the existing standards issues. To a large extent, this had restricted RFID adoption in various sectors, particularly in healthcare and hospitals.

Conversely, RFID implementation worldwide seem to be driven by vendors. A survey based report from Frost and Sullivan, in 2005 (O'Conner, 2005), revealed that the vast majority of RFID education – for users – are vendor driven and lacking in technological detail. The same report also suggested that it is process efficiencies that is driving the mandate for RFID. According to the report, the views of vendors and systems integrators on the need for end-user training were divergent. Most vendors felt that informing the users was a key component for success, while some integrators felt that end-users could be trained throughout the implementation. However, even the vendors did not find it necessary to involve the end-users in the whole implementation process.

The first author of this chapter explored an RFID integration pilot implementation in Australia, which revealed that the technology being vendor driven was not accepted completely by end users. When the pilot was implemented, there was no user involvement with the implementation team – which was mainly consisting of vendor related teams. The implementation was mostly product/technology driven. Therefore, the processes which were affected, after RFID implementation, were based on conceptual knowledge of the vendor – rather than informed by active participation by end users from the hospital. In hospitals, where processes are time critical, and if these were to be made more efficient, by RFID integration, the end user involvement is imperative from the onset.

RFID IN HOSPITALS

RFID applications in hospitals in developed nations demonstrate the value of the technology. Tracking is an activity in hospitals that is pivotal to its operations. There are varied items that would need to be tracked including people: doctors, nurses, patients, visitors etc; equipment that needs to be prevented from being stolen; medicines that need to be administered in time, in the correct proportions, from the correct packages and so forth (Pappu et al., 2004). According to H&HN (2006:28), hospital staff has always reported trouble in tracking down ventilators, intravenous pumps and similar medical devices. With the increased reliance on shared handheld devices and laptop computers – the scenario is further complex. Therefore, a growing number of hospitals are beginning to combine their existing wireless communication networks, with RFID, to create real-time location systems.

In hospitals, RFID tags can be attached to equipments and people, such as newborns whose security can be better ensured with an RFID wristband. Clinicians in a hospital also can be traced and reached quickly in an emergency, while emergency departments can use RFID tags to follow patient charts and improve efficiencies. According to the managing Director of a large health care practice in California, hospitals should adopt RFID in such manner that the technology is compatible in different parts of the hospital (Greene, 2005). For example:

"*RFID tags could be used by materials management to track portableX-ray machines and also by the pharmacy to track a unit dose of an expensive drug*" (Greene, 2005: 32).

A survey in 2005 (Baker, 2005) revealed that 10 percent of health care organisations in the USA use RFID tags to track expensive equipment and 45 percent are expected to have systems in place. As reported in H&HN (2005:23), in 1993, St Elizabeth Medical Centre in Edgewood, Ky, deployed an early form of RFID to prevent baby thefts in the maternity ward. Since then, it upgraded the technology and extended its use to some patients – mainly those with psychological or substance abuse problems- who are likely to hurt themselves or someone else if they are left untreated. The same report also pointed out the early use of patient tracking in Boston based Beth Israel Deaconess Medical Centre which outfitted its 48,000 square foot emergency department with RFID tags to track clinicians, patients and equipment (H&HN, 2005:24).

RFID has a major advantage that might justify any additional cost - it is automatic and so does not require manual intervention to work, which removes the potential for human error. In a frenzied operating room environment, inventory control cannot get in the way of taking care of the patient

(Nagy et al., 2006). A Frost and Sullivan report (Simpson, 2007) indicated that RFID tracking can save hospitals time and money which could be expended in tracking lost equipment. Page (2007) reported that pilot testing of RFID tracking had already given way to implementation, with hospitals moving ahead with dependable uses of RFID such as asset tracking. For example, O'Connor (2006) reported on the results of an RFID pilot implementation of RFID in a Toronto area hospital, Hamilton Health Sciences Acute Care Center, Canada. The pilot implementation tagged 200 pumps, as well as diagnostic equipment and other high value mobile assets in the nursing ward. Although the upfront costs were substantial, the full implementation is expected to bring high ROI, as it extends to infant tracking, adult patients or geriatric patient monitoring. The pilot was successful in identifying the shortfalls and leading to broader implementation.

The Shelby County Regional Medical Center in Memphis, implemented RFID patient tracking systems to reduce overcrowding in the emergency department (HFM, 2005). Until that time, the centre could only account for 25 percent of the typical patient stay in the trauma unit. After implementation of RFID, it now accounts for 80 percent of the patient time. The Heart Hospital Baylor Pano, Texas, has implemented an RFID network, which automates tracking and cataloguing of the hospital's high end equipment (Godinez, 2007). Staff in the hospital had embraced this technology well and very satisfied with its performance. Subsequently, the President of the Dallas Fort Worth Hospital Council declared that all hospitals in the region plan to deploy RFID systems. Baldwin and Larkin (2008) find that asset tracking systems can help hospitals keep tabs on their mobile inventories. They comment that RFID monitoring can fit into a hospital's strategic priority. However, which tracking solution and infrastructure is needed can vary widely depending on the context. They comment that one RFID solution do not fit all hospitals, nor countries.

Bacheldor (2006) reports that Rockhampton Base Hospital In Queensland, Australia, is using RFID to improve safety of nurses, during a renovation that has left holes in mental health ward building. Specifically, nurses in the hospital's mental-health ward are using Alarm Cards, which combines a long-range wireless duress transmitter, a photo ID and proximity access control in one device, which is credit-card-sized.. The duress transmitter features a battery-powered RFID tag, operating at 433 MHz. Any nurses in danger or in need of assistance can push a button built into the back of the card, causing the transmitter to send a signal to an RFID reader to alert coworkers. To make the process convenient, nurses receive the cards when they sign in at the beginning of their shifts, and the tags' unique ID numbers are correlated in a database with the nurses' names and photos.

RFID may have much more potential in developing nations where healthcare systems even in advanced hospitals are strained by inefficient utilisation and the shortage of expensive equipment. The need is therefore higher in finding solutions that enable optimum utilisation of assets, resources and increasing the quality of care. For example, in India, where there are a multitude of small, medium and large hospitals that are struggling to assimilate and use expensive, higher technology equipment that is increasingly being demanded by both physicians and their patients. This creates significant shortages in hospitals, leading potentially to denial of the highest standard of care, even when, in theory, the device or equipment in question is part of the hospital inventory.

Since 2006, the Bhagwan Mahaveer Jain (BMJ) Heart Center – a cardiac hospital in Southern India, is using passive UHF RFID tags to assist with maintaining patient records, monitoring patient flows and tracking assets throughout the outpatient department (Bacheldor, 2007). An average of 100 patients is tracked in a day, which includes returning patients as they check into the outpatient department. Patients checking into the outpatient

Figure 1. RFID based Patient Management Systems (Adapted from Chowdhury and Khosla, 2007)

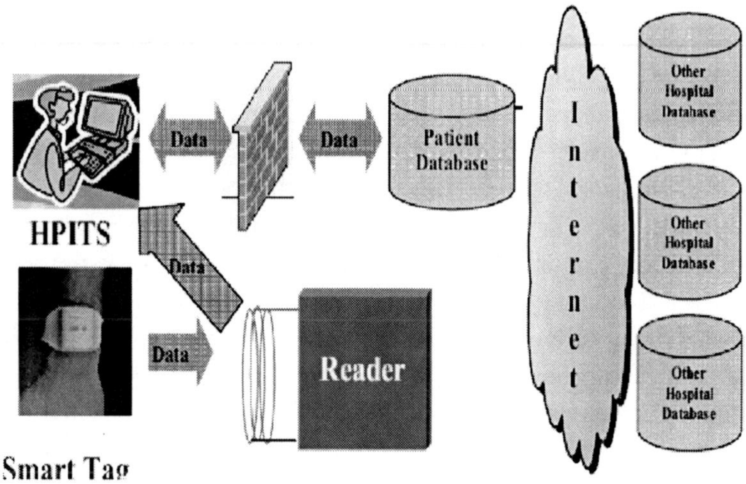

department receive RFID tagged cards. The unique ID number on each tag is associated with that of the patient electronic records in the Clinical Information Processing Platform (CLIP) – a system that includes software and RFID interrogators and tags. The RFID interrogators or readers are positioned in the waiting room, consultation rooms and labs and they document whenever a patient enters, leave and how long they stay in the area. The CLIP system is also integrated with hospital billing system, enabling the staff to use patient care and workflow information for accurate billing. The manual effort of paper registration and use of paper forms has been eliminated.

With respect to asset tracking using RFID, the hospital is attaching EPC Gen 2 RFID tags to stents, pacemakers, wheelchairs, gurney and other high value items, as well as certain mobile devices used in diagnostic labs. The CLIP AssetLIVE application, which uses a mapping technology, is used to track the location of these assets. The system, instead of tracking tagged objects in real time, documents their location by analysing RFID data reads and render their last known position in a graphic (Bacheldor, 2007). The hospital has benefitted from the technology in that it has increased patient throughput, reduced paper work and added visibility to supplies. However, the hospital is still in the process of finding if RFID is providing cost savings and improving workflow processes in the hospital, especially in the asset tracking area.

Chowdhury and Khosla (2007) provided an overview of the main components of an RFID based patient management system, as illustrated in the Figure 1, based on a model built for hospitals in Australian context. According to them, hospitals can track patients accurately and efficiently, improve the safety of clients by capturing basic data such as drug allergies, prevent and reduce medical errors as well as build a more collaborative environment with varied departments such as wards, medication and payments.

Early applications of RFID such as infant tracking is now giving away to staff tracking, combined with time and motion studies to optimise workflows in areas such as radiology and surgeries (Cox, 2008). The author reported few instances where RFID has been beneficial with reshaping processes within hospitals, resulting in reduced errors, cost savings and better patient care. Harrisburg Hospital in Pennsylvania deployed a range of RFID applications from a patient tracking system for surgical patients to a 433MHx wireless infrastructure able to track wheelchairs and a range of portable medical gear. In Christiana Hospital, Newark, Delaware, the emergency department has 76 treatment rooms that handle 100,000 patients annually. Nurses were losing track where patients were in the treatment process, as they were moved among diagnostics and treatment facilities. This resulted in patient stay spiking above normal levels and resulted in 4-5% leaving without treatment. The hospital combined a tracking system with infrared sensor network for locating hardware assets. A web based application showed tagged patients, staff and medical assets and created a visual workflow for patient progress. The data is filtered through various subset views so departments can expect and manage the number of patients and streamline their progress. According to the report, the length of patient stay has been reduced (Cox, 2008).

Chen et al., (2008:286) imply that while an increased number of vendors, hospital administrators and caregivers are advocating the relative advantages of RFID, the adoption seems to have slowed, which can be attributed to technology resistance, expensive system costs and disparate standards. Their research, which addressed RFID adoption in hospitals from the expectation-confirmation perspective, revealed that Healthcare providers who have a high perception of the usefulness in front-end interoperability and of performance expectancy affirm a positive confirmation experience with the use of RFID technology. However, for its continues use and progress,

...hospital administrators and equipment vendors need to address those factors that have been revealed as significant such as increasing the perceived frontend interoperability by using experienced consultants and integrators to implement systems that are proven to be interoperable at the front-end. They may also intervene via training and education to increase caregivers' performance expectancy of RFID (Chen et al., 2008:286).

An investigation was conducted post the pilot implementation of an RFID based real time location system integration, at St Vincent's Private Hospital in Sydney, Australia (Unnithan, Smith, Fraunholz, 2009), supported by Intel, to track movable equipment such as wheel chairs, infusion pumps, and oxygen regulators. On the basis of the success of the pilot, the hospital now plans to implement RFID in the emergency department of St Vincent Public Hospital, in Australia. The investigation revealed that this intended project requires much user involvement, coordinated process redesign, hospital readiness and project management. We also find that this may be the case for many other hospitals which are in a similar situation of RFID integration into their existing processes.

Therefore, we proposed to build a process model where deployment and integration of RFID can be done in a manner such that its potential is maximized. Such a process model will be dynamic to evolve with the technology and adapt to the context, and continue to build on learning based on implementations/integration. The rest of this chapter would illustrate the strategic framework, used in the development of this process model, adapting the action framework and justifying that the case study can inform Phase 1 of the cycles i.e. Discovery and Modelling, as illustrated in the next section.

THE STRATEGIC FRAMEWORK

As revealed in the literature as well as ongoing research investigation by first author in the Australian context, RFID implementation in hospitals seem to be an arbitrary process, often untimed, based on particular needs of a department/section, and often driven by vendors who would like to push the technology. We also find that many RFID implementations in hospitals require specific process changes within the departments, which are unique to them. Therefore, what is applicable in an emergency department, may not be the same in an out-patient facility. A one size fits all integration approach cannot be envisaged, if the ultimate benefits have to outweigh costs of implementation. Therefore, we find the action research framework is useful for the iterative learning and informing another implementation.

ACTION RESEARCH

Action research is an iterative process, with researchers and practitioners acting together, diagnosing problems, actively intervening to achieve enhancement and reflective learning (Susman, 1983). Fraunholz (2001) who contextualized action research to trade sector concurs that it draws from the synergy created by the co-operation of researchers and practitioners in particular settings. Some early citations (Avison et al., 1999) recommend action research as a means of making academic research relevant, in order to explore theories and assumptions with practitioners in real situations and real organisations. During the last few years, the method has been applied in health care settings, which often deploy innovative technologies. It has endorsed as a suitable method in health settings, as reported in academic journals (Hampshire 2000, Dick, 2006).

The role of action research was demonstrated by the PRIDE project which developed, deployed and redesigned a technological innovation for use in primary health care setting of UK (Waterman et al., 2007). From their experiences, they uphold that:

action research can be employed successfully to diffuse innovations that need a high level of adaptation in each new setting or where there is high complexity and mismatch between groups of people in an organisation, providing there is an established need for researching the said innovation further (Waterman et al., 2007:380).

The participatory approach helped the researchers understanding the cultural context in which the innovation had to be developed, thus effectively helping them develop, test, redesign, and deploy the innovation.

Hospital environments are chaotic, with time being the most crucial asset. Consultation and involvement with staff was found to be an essential ingredient in developing this research framework. Even for a pilot implementation, using a vendor solution, sufficient involvement, training and adaptation may be required by the users. Therefore, we found the action research framework is one of the methods by which the researchers can develop a process model.

Action research is a continuous cyclical approach (Susman, 1983) which involves the cycles of *situation diagnosis-action planning-action taking-evaluating-specifying learning*. The cycle continues until the researcher and practitioners are satisfied of the outcome of the project. Fraunholz (2001) built a preliminary framework based on this cyclical approach, for the virtual management of projects in the German trade sector, re-labelling them as *awareness raising-action planning-action taking-evaluating-specifying learning*.

From these fundamental research frameworks, we adapted the cycles of Action Research, relabeling them as illustrated in (Figure 2) and explained as follows.

In the process of learning via action research, Fraunholz (2001) cautions that the researchers need to ensure that learning occurs such that it will enhance the proposed models and facilitates theory generation, without being accused of influencing the context via consulting. However, the cyclical process of action research that facilitates meticulous documentation could facilitate the process. With this view, we propose the following.

Phase 1: This phase was the starting point known as "*Situation Diagnosis*" (Susman, 1983). Fraunholz (2001) had renamed this phase as "*Awareness Raising*", as the domain of trade sector required that a certain level of awareness had to be

Figure 2. The Iterative Process of Action Research (Adapted from Susman (1983) & Fraunholz (2001))

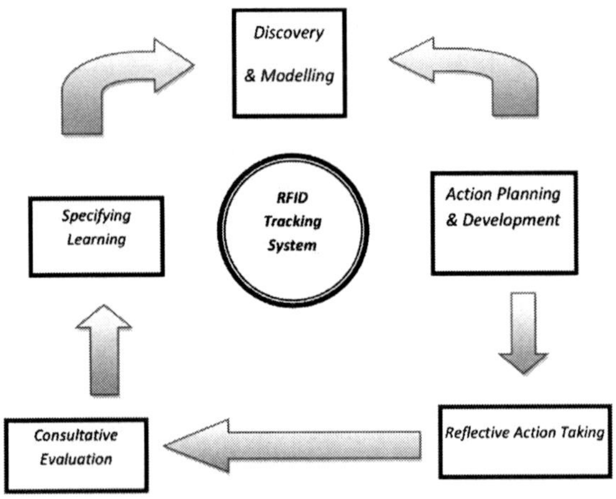

created among them, that they are performing sub optimally and that improvements are necessary. In hospital contexts, the key stakeholders and medical practitioners are aware that certain processes, such as asset tracking, can be enhanced using RFID tracking systems. Nevertheless, the researchers feel that the level of awareness also need to be raised among the staff of the hospital, who are directly involved in the day-to-day processes of the hospital. By developing a process model in consultation with the key staff involved or rather end users, will enable the researchers to identify and map the processes, evaluate how they will change post the RFID implementation and then based on this, build a process model for implementation. Specifically, during this phase, researchers, practitioners, hospital staff and other stakeholders will be involved in a discovery process which will effectively result in a model – that can be enhance with RFID implementation. Therefore, the researchers propose to re-label this phase as a ***Discovery and Modelling***.

This phase will include extended literature reviews in the health care domain, with a particular focus on hospitals and their utilization of RFID, as it is being implemented worldwide. Extant best practices of RFID deployment and existing gaps can be identified through this process. Subsequently, the researchers will focus on the context, or the current processes in the hospital that relate to the specific departments and assets concerned in order to model the processes. This modelling process will be iterative, in consultation with the key people/end users who are involved in the processes. As part of this phase, the researchers propose a requirements engineering exercise using cross functional teams within the departments involved. It is envisaged that the issues identified by the participants may fill the research gaps identified, such as inconsistencies or lack of knowledge of processes involved by all people negating the process enhancements envisaged. This requirements engineering exercise will also be part of the *discovery* process, which will lend itself to *modelling* the processes efficiently as well as contribute to identifying a suitable RFID implementation design. At the end of the phase, the researchers expect to have modelled the existing situation, gathered requirements for improving the situation and prepare the new process model i.e. specifically, how the processes will be post RFID implementation.

Phase 2: Susman (1983) called this cycle "*Planning*" and Fraunholz (2001) labelled the phase as "*Action Planning*". In this phase, the researchers propose to draw from phase 1 and building on the learning, prepare a requirements gathered document (with specifications discovered by the staff) and propose an RFID implementation design, which can be communicated via a strategic plan document. The researchers will also identify metrics of performance and prepare for appropriate data collection processes that will contribute towards development of a theoretical model that will inform academic research. During this phase, the researchers will also identify a suitable RFID vendor, in consultation with the organisational stakeholders involved and obtain a solution which can be mapped against the requirements document, and the existing process model, to introduce any changes to the proposed design. A final specifications document that will guide the prototypical implementation, periodic evaluation of results and also communicated in the strategic plan of the hospital will be developed. The researchers propose to label this phase as "***Action Planning and Development***" phase, maintaining that action is not only planned, but also developed through relevant documentation.

Phase 3: This phase is better known as "*Action*" by Susman (1983) and "Action Taking" by Fraunholz (2001) who suggested that this is the phase when the first change is introduced into an organisation, with the intention of enhancing the current processes. In this context, there are 2 stages of action that have been identified. In Stage 1, the RFID prototype based on the design (phase 2) will be rolled out, guided by the final specification document. Before any process change is implemented, the researchers will baseline the current asset tracking performance using RFID tags, based on the metrics of performance and associated analysis developed in phase 2. From the time of the roll out, it is expected that this activity will take a month of data collection. After the baseline, all relevant staff members will be trained by the vendor, as advised by the researchers. Changes may be suggested and introduced by the researchers, who will continue to make observations, which will thereafter contribute to the final theoretical model development.

In Stage 2, based on best practice and the existing process model of the organisation, the researchers will analyse processes to continuously refine/optimise them to derive maximum benefit from RFID technology. This includes *ex ante process* such as allocation and planning of asset use as well as *ex post analysis* such as financial controlling to reflect if assets are used cost efficiently and usage cost is allocated/budgeted correctly. The metrics of asset tracking performance employed to baseline performance prior to deployment of modified RFID tracking processes will again be collected, following full process deployment and enhancement, over an extended period of time (estimated to be three months). The data so collected will be compared with that collected pre-implementation and analysed. In parallel with the above analysis, affective measures of performance (i.e. measures based upon stakeholders' perceptions of ease of use and the extent to which they believe RFID asset tracking has affected clinical workflow) will be assessed using focus group techniques, during stage 2. Given the iterative nature of this cycle, where the researchers have to take action, after reflecting on the change introduced, we re-label the stage as "***Reflective Action Taking***". We concur with Fraunholz (2001) that the aim of this phase is to ensure that the tracking system is optimised for use on a day-to-day basis.

Phase 4: Regarded as "evaluating" phase (Susman, 1983: Fraunholz, 2001) -- this phase involves the researchers and all others involved undertaking an evaluation, to determine if the result has been achieved and the introduced change was successful (Fraunholz, 2001). It involves extraction of all findings and documentation. Observations extracted from Phase 4 will be reviewed to extract key findings relevant to the process framework. The final framework will be revised and built iteratively, drawing from key learning, inputs and analysis. Focus groups to validate the framework are envisaged at this stage. During this time, the researchers will communicate clearly to all key stakeholders and staff of the hospital that the researchers are trying to get objective feedback to validate the framework. As Fraunholz (2001) cautions, it is possible that the people involved are hesitant to be critical due to fear or may want to avoid another change altogether. In many occasions, any change introduced would be viewed as a tedious task, especially in a hospital environment, where time is of critical value. However, the researchers have to ensure that the framework of implementation, from phase 1, will involve all the staff involved in the process, are taken into consultation, so that they are not only aware of the implications, but can also make positive contributions to the change. Rather than a directed change, a participatory change is proposed in this context. We re-label this phase as "***Consultative Evaluation***" to reflect that all people concerned are involved in this cycle.

Phase 5: This is regarded as the final phase of the action research (Susman, 1983) and labelled as "Specifying Learning". Fraunholz (2001) considers that this is an ongoing process which will occur during all the phases. However, the researcher had formally placed it at the final stage, as it is regarded as the most important phase, which will determine whether the research was successful. If the research was unsuccessful, it is recommended that the knowledge gained then feeds into the next iterative cycle for future research. Conversely, if the outcome is success, the next action would then be for the organisation to adapt the knowledge gained by the research.

In this context, if the outcome was unsuccessful, it would then feed into the next cycle for future research into RFID. If it is successful, the whole hospitals and all departments could then adapt RFID using the framework developed. Furthermore, the generic process model could then be used to implement RFID in other hospitals as well. This phase establishes a future strategy, no matter what the outcome was. While the researchers are essentially the key people in specifying the learning, the people involved may offer independent points of view, which can then be considered by the researchers for enriching the learning.

According to Fraunholz (2001) the iterative process of data gathering and theory building will repeat, until it is proven that a clear hypothesis cannot be drawn, or there is a clearly defined hypothesis (or framework in this context). The researcher also confirms that there has to be documentation for each phase and each cycle, which will consist of participants, documents, models, aims, possible issues and key learning. Building on these recommendations, we propose that the phase continues to be labeled as "***Specifying Learning***" phase for this framework.

Furthermore, Fraunholz (2001) contextualized the Susman (1983) action research framework and provided a thematic diagram for the virtual management of projects in trade. We built on this schema, contextualizing it to the context of RFID deployment in hospitals, and provide the adapted framework in (Figure 3). The framework indicates the aims of each phase, people involved and documentation proposed. Each phase will also have issues that will be identified and key learning, which will be documented at the end and drawn upon for specifying learning in the final iteration of the project and for the development of the process model.

CASE STUDY AS A LINEAR CONDUIT TO INFORM (PHASE 1)

In the process of building the model, using this framework, the researchers find that the case study method can be useful to inform Phase 1, Discovery and Modelling. To illustrate this, a case study investigation was conducted in St Vincent's Private Hospital in Sydney, where a vendor and technology driven implementation of RFID was already piloted. In this instance, the learning from the pilot implementation was to form a linear conduit for informing Phase 1 of the framework, for implementing the second project. Effectively, the key learning post implementation was to be taken into account, while planning for the next implementation, planned for St Vincent Public Hospital, emergency department.

The St Vincent Private Hospital had a web based clinical information system. One of the key modules of this system is the clinical support resource management system that books, tracks and manages patient orderlies to efficiently move patients and equipment between wards, operating theatres and clinic appointments. This module was to be integrated with a real time location system or RTLS (using RFID technology), to enable a more efficient real time view of hospital resources. The

Figure 3. A Framework for RFID Facilitated Processes in Hospitals(Adapted from Fraunholz (2001))

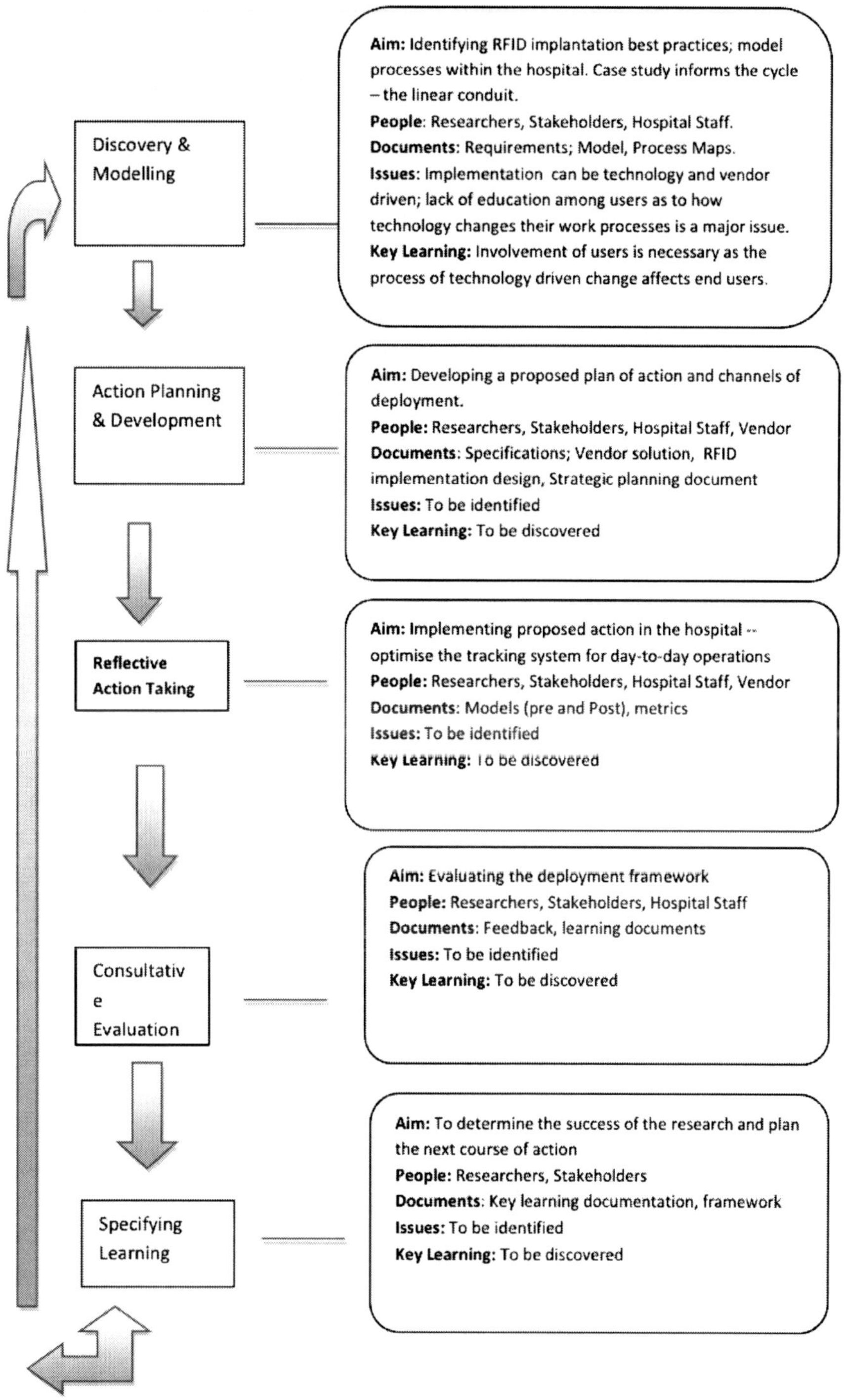

Table 1. Internal User/Manager/Technology Integrator Views on RFID implementation: A Post Implementation Review(Adapted from Unnithan, Smith, Fraunholz, 2009)

St Vincent's and Mater Health, Sydney, Australia	*Intel Australia Pty Ltd, Sydney, Australia*
Mr David Roffe (Chief Information Officer) Ms. Beryce Walsh (Customer Relations Manager) Mr Glenn Eliott (Integration Manager) Mr P Leel (Systems Analyst – Implementation Projects) Mr Vincent Cox (Nursing Unit Manager) Mr.Jeremy Gowing (Manager, CSU) Mr Mathew Dwyer (Patient Care Orderly) Mr Daniel Hermann (Patient Care Orderly)	Mr Leopoldo Irribarren Senior Solutions Architect Worldwide Data Centre Solutions Enterprise Solution Sales
The Alfred (Hospital), Melbourne, Australia	
Ms. Cathie Steele General Manager Centre for Health Innovation	

project had the objective of evaluating RFID integration so that the key learning and issues can be considered for deploying a similar system, within the emergency department of St Vincent Public hospital (Unnithan, Smith, Fraunholz, 2009). Since the pilot was vendor and technology driven, the end user were not really involved in the setting up of the system, but was rather informed/educated by the integrator – from outside of the hospital.

Since the project was a pilot, the hospital felt that the tracking system should not be immediately integrated with the existing Hospital Information System. The rationale was that a separate pilot would cause minimal disruption and existing processes can continue, while the system can be tested for effectiveness. Therefore, the Real Time Location System (RTLS), with its own web interface was piloted to be used by Patient Care Orderlies and Sterilizing Services Unit members to locate resources within the hospital. The pilot was acclaimed as successful by the hospital and also reflected in the post implementation report of the technology integrator.

After this report, an investigation was conducted as a post implementation review with the project team and end users (hospital staff) involved, with a view to: understand the process integration of RFID in the clinical context and the achievements of the technology in this context as well as validating the review that was conducted immediately post deployment of the pilot (Unnithan et al., 2009). The interviews focused on the processes that were targeted for enhancement, the actual changes to processes observed; and the extent to which the technology has aided in reshaping the clinical processes and enhancing process efficiencies. Specifically, users/user managers, project/strategic managers and technology implementers were interviewed on the effectiveness of the RFID tracking system – on its perceived and experienced benefits in regard to cost and time savings, better efficiencies and process enhancements for better quality of patient care. The focus of the research investigation was to find the extent of process integration achieved and if the potential of this technology has been achieved.

In the process of the interviews, some significant facts emerged. First, the end users were not involved in the conceptualization of this RFID implementation, and their view, which was critical for the successful integration therefore, was not considered. It was evident that if the pilot were to become the norm (RFID integration with Hospital Information System) to become successful, user involvement is crucial as illustrated in (Table 1), for better process integration.

As can be seen from these summarised views, the users feel that they were not involved in conceptualisation, while the internal technology integrators felt that the potential of RFID could be much more, and accuracy could be better handled, if user involvement was more than of the external vendor. The senior managers of the units also felt that more could be achieved if the technology and needs of the hospital were better aligned, through user involvement. Therefore, we find that the case study formed an informative tool to inform the Phase 1 of our research framework, which would then lead into the new implementation. Thus the case study informs Phase 1, and the follow on effects the whole framework and helps build the final model.

SUMMARY OUTLOOK AND CONTRIBUTIONS

This chapter is dedicated to presenting a strategic framework used for developing a generic process model for deploying and integrating RFID technology, in hospitals, which can be adapted to the context, in a manner that the potential of the technology is maximized and dynamic sufficiently to evolve, with the technology.

In reviewing current literature it was revealed that for RFID integration to be successful and ongoing in hospitals, the implementation need to be more user driven. Processes within a hospital are more complex, and any technology induced change, such as RFID is bound to change the existing processes – perhaps for the better, but with certain disruptions on its day-to-day operations. The researchers also conducted a post implementation review of a successful RFID integration at a hospital, and found that the user involvement is the key to success.

Subsequently, we proposed the strategic framework, adapted through the Action Research Lens, in order to build a generic process model, for best implementation of RFID in the future so that it's potential is maximised in the context. In addition, the authors propose that the case study method can be a very useful tool, in informing the phase 1 – Discovery& Modelling, of the action research cycles – as it can form a linear conduit for the next implementation.

This chapter offers the following contributions to academia: (1) The strategic framework will be used to build the process model, for achieving best RFID integration into hospital processes, which may be validated by other researchers in hospitals (2) the literature review of current issues and gaps may be followed up by other researchers (3) other strategic frameworks may be similarly developed using the model. The framework suggested in this chapter has been tested and found applicable. Hence there is significant contribution of academic work, that is applicable to the practical context i.e. RFID integration in hospitals for maximum efficiency.

For the industry or practice i.e. vendors and external technology providers of RFID and integrators, it offers significant learning. For example, health/hospitals are more complex and there needs to be adaptation of the technology to fit the context. This can only be achieved by user involvement from hospitals. This key finding from ongoing research has been valuable for the major technology providers involved in this research, as they had piloted RFID as a vendor driven exercise with minimal result. The development of a process model has therefore found to be significant in the hospitals and technology provider context, to enable them work together for a win-win result.

The research also offers significant learning and possibilities to be explored by hospitals, providing new horizons for experimentation to effectively improve their quality of care. Specifically, it is notable that improving workflow efficiencies is possible through RFID, but the framework for deployment and integration had to involve users significantly. If the users rejected this radical technology, as it is perceived to be hampering day-to-day work, no doubt, the potential of this technology is not optimal. If the users are willing to experiment and integrate the technology, offering suggestions for improved usage, the potential can be maximised. This strategic process framework offered a conduit for effectively achieving the same. Hence, the chapter has contributed significantly to informing academia and practice with enriched theoretical and applied knowledge.

ACKNOWLEDGMENT

The authors would like to thank the following people and their respective institutions for their support.

REFERENCES

Avison, D., Lau, F., Myers, M., & Nielsen, P. A. (1999). Action Research. *Communications of the ACM*, *42*(1), 94–97. doi:10.1145/291469.291479

Bacheldor, B. (2006, October 24). RFID Fills Security Gap at Psychiatric Ward. *RFID Journal*. Retrieved from http://www.rfidjournal.com/article/articleview/2750/1/1/

Bacheldor, B. (2007, August 21). RFID documents surgery at Huntsville hospital. *RFID Journal*. Retrieved from http://www.rfidjournal.com/article/articleprint/3572/-1/1/

Baldwin, G., & Larkin, M. (2008 January). Where did we put that wheelchair? *HealthLeaders*, 33-34.

Cavoukian, A. (2008). *RFID and Privacy - Guidance for Health Care Providers* [Report]. Toronto, Canada: Information Privacy Commissioner of Ontario and Hewlett Packard Company.

Chen, C. C., Wu, J., Su, Y. S., & Yang, S. C. (2008). Key drivers for the continued use of RFID technology in the emergency room. *Management Research News*, *31*(4), 273–288. doi:10.1108/01409170810851348

Chowdhury, B., & Khosla, R. (2007 July). RFID based Real Time Patient Management System. *Computer and Information Science*, 363-368.

Collins, J. (2005, July 5). India adopts 865-867 MHz for RFID. *RFID Journal*. Retrieved from http://www.rfidjournal.com/article/view/1703/1/1

Cox, J. (2008, August 25). RFID proving to be Rx for hospitals. *New World (New Orleans, La.)*, *25*(33), 24.

Fisher, J. A., & Monahan, T. (2008). Tracking the social dimensions of RFID systems in hospitals. *International Journal of Medical Informatics*, *77*(3), 176–183. doi:10.1016/j.ijmedinf.2007.04.010

Fraunholz, B. (2001) Project Management in the German Trade Sector – A (preliminary) framework for computer assisted management of Projects in Small and Medium Sized Enterprises. In *Proceedings of Australasian Conference on Information Systems,* Coffs Harbour, NSW, Australia.

Godinez, V. (2007, April 29). RFID tracks hospitals devices: System improves heart facility's care. *Dallas Morning News*.

GOI. (2002). National Health Policy. *Government of India*. Retrieved from http://mohfw.nic.in/np2002.htm

Greene, J. (2005 September). Is your Hospital Ready for Radio Frequency Identification? Above Board Technology. *Trustee*, 30-32. H&HN. (2004 May). Beyond Bar Codes. *Hospitals and Health Networks Magazine*, 26. H&HN. (2005 June). Behind the Hype. *Hospitals and Health Networks Magazine*, 22-24.

Harrop, P. (2006). Rapid Adoption of RFID in Healthcare. In *RFID in Healthcare 2006-2016,* [White Paper]. Retrieved September 24, 2008, from http://www.idtechex.com

HFM. (2006, August). RFID tracks ED overcrowding. *Health Facilities Management*, 8.

Hoskins, R. (2006). *InfoLogix Announces Health-Trax RFID Asset Tracking Software for Hospital Mobile Assets Management*. Retrieved from http://www.bbwexchange.com/pubs/2006/02/11/page1395-98309.asp

Journal, R. F. I. D. (2005). A summary of RFID standards. *RFID Journal*. Retrieved from http://www.rfidjournal.com/article/view/1335/1/129

Kahn, M. (2008, June 25). RFID in hospitals could pose risks. *PC Magazine Online*.

Landt, J. (2001 October). Shrouds of Time: The history of RFID. *Association for Automatic Identification and Mobility*.

Lee, C. P., & Shim, J. P. (2007). An exploratory study of radio frequency identification (RFID) adoption in the healthcare industry. *European Journal of Information Systems*, *16*, 712–772. doi:10.1057/palgrave.ejis.3000716

Mehrjerdi, Y. Z. (2008). RFID enabled systems: a brief review. *Assembly Automation*, *28*(3), 235–245. doi:10.1108/01445150810889493

Nagy, P., George, I., Bernstein, W., Caban, J., Klein, R., Mezrich, R., & Park, A. (2006). Radio Frequency Identification Systems Technology in the Surgical Setting. *Surgical Innovation*, *13*(1), 61–67. Retrieved from http://sri.sagepub.com/cgi/content/abstract/13/1/61. doi:10.1177/1553350606013001 10

Nahas, H. A., & Deogun, J. S. (2007). Radio Frequency Identification Applications in Smart Hospitals. In *Proceedings of the Twentieth IEEE International Symposium on Computer-Based Medical Systems (CBMS'07)*.

O'Connor, M. C. (2005, August 25). Efficiencies Drive RFID adoption. *RFID Journal*. Retrieved from http://www.rfidjournal.com/article/articleview/1833/1/1/

O'Connor, M. C. (2006, November 26). Toronto area hospital kicks off asset tracking pilot. *RFID Journal*. Retrieved from http://www.rfidjournal.com/article/articleview/2848/1/1/

Page, L. (2007, August). Hospitals tap into RFID to track patients and equipment. *Health Facilities Management*, 5–6.

Page, L. (2007 May). Hospitals tune into RFID – Testing gives way to implementation. *Material Management in Health Care*, 18-20.

Pappu, M., Singhal, R., & Zoghi, B. (2004 September). *RFID in hospitals: Issues and Solutions*. A report from the Consortium for the Accelerated Deployment of RFID in Distribution.

Roark, D. C., & Miguel, K. (2006). Bar coding's replacement? *Nursing Management*, *37*(2), 29–31. doi:10.1097/00006247-200602000-00009

Simpson, G. (2007, August 27). Hospitals need RFID injection. *ZDNet Asia*. Retrieved from http://www.zdnetasia.com/news/communications/0,39044192,62031433,00.htm

Thomas, K. (2008, May 30). Radio wrist tags that make for smoother operations, A technology for tracing consumer goods may help save lives and keep track of hospital equipment. *Financial Times (North American Edition)*, 12.

Unnithan, C., Smith, R., & Fraunholz, B. (2009). Maximising the Benefits of Radio Frequency Identification Technology (RFID) Integration in Clinical Contexts: a Linear Conduit. In *HIC'09 Conference*, August 19-21. Canberra, Australia: Health Informatics Society of Australia.

Waterman, H., Marshall, M., Noble, J., Davies, H., Wakshe, K., Sheaff, R., & Elwyn, G. (2007). The role of action research in the investigation and diffusion of innovations in health care: The Pride Project. *Qualitative Health Research*, *17*(3), 373–381. doi:10.1177/1049732306298976

Wicks, A. M., Visich, J. K., & Li, S. (2006). Radio Frequency Identification Applications in Hospital Environments. *Hospital Topics*, *84*(3), 3–8. doi:10.3200/HTPS.84.3.3-9

KEY TERMS AND DEFINITIONS

RFID: Radio Frequency Identification.
EPC: Electronic Product Code
UHF: Ultra High Frequency

Chapter 8
Sources of Legitimacy for the M-Government Initiatives in Turkey:
Human vs. Technical Resource Management Concerns

N. Meltem Cakici
Gediz University, Turkey

Ronan de Kervenoael
Sabanci University & Aston University, Turkey

ABSTRACT

Emerging markets have recently been experiencing a dramatic increased in the number of mobile phone per capita. M-government has, hence, been heralded as an opportunity to leap-frog the technology cycle and provide cheaper and more inclusive and services to all. This chapter explores, within an emerging market context, the legitimacy and resistance facing civil servants' at the engagement stage with m-government activities and the direct implication for resource management. Thirty in depth interview, in Turkey, are drawn-upon with key ICT civil servant in local organizations. The findings show that three types of resources are perceived as central namely: (i) diffusion of information management, (ii) operating system resource management and (iii) human resource management. The main evidence suggests that legitimacy for each resource management, at local level, is an ongoing struggle where all groups deploy multiples forms of resistance. Overall, greater attention in the resource management strategy for m-government application needs to be devoted to enablers such as civil servants rather than the final consumers or citizens.

INTRODUCTION

Mobile government (m-government hereafter) has been heralded as an imperative for administrative processes' modernization in emerging countries (Kushchu, 2007). Although several m-government services are already available in emerging markets, provided by both private and public organizations, little is known about the formative

DOI: 10.4018/978-1-61692-016-6.ch008

stages and the legitimacy/ resistance (positive and negative) civil servants are encountering in their everyday activities, from a resource management perspective, in order to implement m-government applications and strategies (Abanumy & Mayhew, 2005; Ghyasi & Kushchu, 2004; Sundar & Garg, 2005; Tozsa & Budai, 2005; Prins, 2001). In this chapter, m-government is defined as the development of new technologies, applications and services in order to create an "able society" (Kushchu, 2007). Digital technologies as resource management tools used in public administration have contributed to an improved understanding of many aspects of everyday practices, especially at local level, including digital strategies (Kahraman et al., 2007; Ferguson, 2001), impact of e-culture on e-governments (Hazlett & Hill, 2003), m-government policy issues (Yildiz, 2007; Lam, 2005), service architecture (Sharma & Gupta, 2004; Abramowicz et al., 2006), e-governance (Saxena, 2005; Stahl, 2005; Holliday & Kwok, 2004) and e-government models (Heeks, 2002).

In turn, legitimacy of ICT and mobility within public administrations at local level, in an emerging market context, point to multiple possible sources (m-GovLab, MGCI, www.mgovernment.org). The literature highlights two important aspects: (i) the difference between the meanings of mobility: mobility which is driven by personal motivation/resistance and by social factors; and (ii) the difference between mobile technological innovation and the legitimacy of institutional changes.

Consecutively, mobile technologies have attracted interdisciplinary interest centered around three main areas: domestication (Goggin, 2008; Weilenmann, 2001); mobile technology and user practices (Fortunati et al., 2003; Katz, 2003); and, at a societal level, adoption with engagement in wider spheres including politics and social policies (Brown et al., 2002; Rheingold, 2002). Further related aspects include status symbols (Dedeoglu, 2004; Ozcan & Kocak, 2003), MMS/SMS social and pragmatic aspects (Chapman & Schofield, 1998; Lin & Tong, 2008; Rettie, 2007; Sharma & Sturges, 2007), networked society (Ling, 2004, Goggin, 2008), mobile devices as fashion items (Katz & Sugiyama, 2006; Hulme & Peters, 2003) and m-entertainment (Ha et al., 2007; Harmer, 2003; Pagani, 2004).

The negative aspects of mobile technologies have also been studied including issues relating to health (Foster & Moulder, 2000), addiction (Bianchi & Phillips, 2005), lack of concentration while driving or multitasking (Esbjornsson et al., 2007), increased reaction time, psychological impact of mobile consumption on children and adolescents (Döring & Gundolf, 2005) and miss-appreciation of cognitive and/or physical demand while multitasking (Goodman et al., 1999; McEvoy et al., 2005).

Based on the above characteristics, three partial gaps have been identified from the literature. First, few, if any, studies have been conducted in the context of the public services and the role of m-services. Second, most studies examining digital resource management strategies have usually been conducted at macro level rather than at local level. Third, published work on digital resource management strategy has almost exclusively focused on the so-called 'first tier' countries, with concentration on the central North American and European perspectives. Examples of the 'second tier' or peripheral regions of Europe such as Turkey are limited.

This book chapter presents the findings of a total of 30 phone interviews which were conducted with the key civil servants working within local government organizations in Turkey during the introduction of the first concrete m-government strategy in 2008-2009. This key period coincides with the recent transition and creation of the central e-government platform, which was launched only few months before in December 2008, in order to centralize the digital government strategy.

While the e-government activities have yet to be fully understood and implemented by all local organizations, deeper technological transitions are already requiring further evaluation, attention and changes. In this context, this chapter draws on a number of concepts such as organizational development, innovation management, strategic management, and evolutionary theory of the firm and development studies (Marcelle, 2004).

This chapter is organized as follows: Section II provides a summary about digital and m-government resource management in general and regarding Turkey in particular. Section III presents the literature review on legitimacy and the impact of the forming stage framework in shaping legitimacy and resistance to new strategies. Methodology and findings are explained in Section IV and Section V, respectively. Finally, Section VI presents the conclusion.

M-GOVERNMENT BACKGROUND

Digital government is defined as the provision of traditional government services to citizens through electronic tools such as computers, telephone and other hand held devices. The Internet is increasingly becoming the channel for delivering government services to citizens and sharing information among various administrative layers and civil servants (Melitski et al., 2005). Digital databases have been created to support back-end operations that are able to provide instant and up-to-date services which are accessible anywhere and at anytime. Recent developments in mobile technologies, especially the introduction of internet enabled mobile phones (3G), PDAs, Wi Fi and wireless networks, are creating a sustainable alternative model for managing, updating and retrieving government information and knowledge towards creating the civil administrations and administrators of tomorrow. These developments are opening a new era in public service delivery practices which is often called as New Public Management (NPM) (McIvor et al., 2002).

M-government is further defined as a strategy and its implementation, which involve the utilization of all kinds of wireless and mobile technology, services, applications and devices for improving services to the parties involved in digital government, including citizens, businesses, NGOs and all government units. In particular, mobile government gives extra added value when compared to previous methods of public service delivery, in terms of (i) lowering costs (Holden et al., 2003), (ii) increasing the efficiency of work practices, and providing the transformation/modernization of public sector organizations (Larsen & Rainie, 2002), (iii) increasing convenience and flexibility (Klein, 1999), and (iv) increasing range and types of applications (Kushchu & Kuscu, 2003). In emerging markets, active initiatives and engagements can be found in countries such as Hungary Latvia Estonia, Bulgaria, and Croatia with local referendum, road planning debate, infrastructure building competition, procurement and public health information, public administration and job advertisements as examples (http://www.epractice.eu/en/factsheets/).

More than four billion mobile subscriptions worldwide signal a great opportunity to reach and interact with broader audiences both for final user service delivery and more importantly for day-to-day resource management within public administration. For example, in Turkey, the total number of wireless subscribers is estimated to increase from 66.4 million in 2008 to 76 million in 2013 (Research and Markets, 2009). In effect, many citizens will own more than one handset.

Concurrently, examples of governance and policy delivery related activities, through which mobile phones have been used (Briseno, 2009), include: i) SMS communication to empower people in places where censorship and violence are present; ii) social participation and advocacy purposes (the protest against former president Estrada in the Philippines, women in Kuwait advocating for the right to vote -which they ultimately won - and pro-democracy demonstrations in Ukraine and Burma are examples that have been replicated in the rest of the world); iii) voting and participatory decision making (e.g. civil society organizations have been using mobile phones for monitoring electoral processes in several countries; m-voting will soon be possible in Estonia where the Parliament approved the use of mobile technology for the 2011 elections); iv) m-government for public service delivery, which is making its case as a complementary way to reach people that remain unconnected, leads to new applications such as information consultations and requests, parking payment mechanisms and payment for local services in Malaysia and the Philippines; v) m-government is also used in data monitoring and collection in remote rural areas; vi) mobile technology has made it easier to increase civil participation and enforcement of laws; the reporting of crime in Ireland and Peru by providing real-time exchange of information between citizens and law enforcement units: In Ireland, MMS (multimedia SMS) has been used to send the photos of suspects to law enforcement agencies. In Peru, crime reporting systems have helped in the reduction of drug related crime; vii) finally, mobile technologies are also now widely used as enabling tools to save time and to be closer to citizens; benefit check, neighborhood task forces, services for the disabled and the old, as examples.

Our attention is now turned specifically to m-government in Turkey which will provide a more specific background to the analysis. The main initiatives center in the newly implemented E-government gateway (www.turkiye.gov.tr) which is a single and centrally managed website with a standard format and set of services. This platform provides detailed information about government services electronically to citizens (Table 1) and is divided into two main sections; (i) the e-government portal itself and (ii) the array of interactive e-services available.

At local level, further efforts have been made in creating and developing initiatives that provide day-to-day applications such as SMS for public announcements (e.g. regarding school activities, weather warnings, roadwork, and utilities cut) which also give information about the status of the services (Ghyasi & Kushchu, 2004). These

Table 1. E-Government gateway services in Turkey

	Service	Subjects
1	Birth	Notification of birth, registration, maternity leave
2	Education	Preschool education, primary, secondary and higher education
3	Military service	Enrollment of soldiers, military man and reserve officer operations, operations abroad
4	Job and career	Job search, employment, legal provisions, unemployment insurance
5	Social security	
6	Family	Marriage, health, register of births operations, children and young, children's rights
7	Individual and society	Women's rights, housing, traffic, civil defense activities
8	Health	Family and society health, nutrition
9	The disabled	Health, education, employment, employee benefits and services
10	Social relief and public spirit	Welfare subjects, project support programs, welfare services, the old
11	Travel and tourism	General information about Turkey, railway and highway transport
12	Environment	Forestry, nature protection and national parks, forestation, erosion check, fight against desertification
13	Culture, arts and sports	Cultural heritage, cultural activities, theaters, festivals, fairs, sports activities
14	Legal issues and rights	Legal affairs, being elector, protection of consumer rights, address registration, public notary
15	Turkish citizens abroad	e-consulate, diploma equivalence, military service, marriage
16	Foreigners	Visa and passport, travel, habitation, birth, marriage

Source: https://www.turkiye.gov.tr/portal/dt?provider=HomePageContainer&channel=icerik

interactive types of services allow citizens to directly receive information, updates and feedbacks.

At institutional level, rather than providing services directly to citizens, a series of initiatives and strategies such as infrastructure enabling tools (Ghyasi & Kushchu, 2004), Mobile Electronic System Integration, Traffic Information System, Mobile information Project (Ministry of education), G2G applications (mobile intranet for ministry personnel), and modernization of the National Judicial Network have been implemented (Court system integration) (Cilingir & Kushchu, 2004). After setting the scene in Turkey and demonstrating similar examples of services in other emerging countries, we now focus on the theoretical basis of this study which is formed by the concepts of legitimacy and front-loading.

LITERATURE REVIEW

Our work takes into account theories and models such as: (i) Rogers' (1995) adoption of innovation framework which identifies desirable factors for the success of a new product or innovation including relative advantage, compatibility, complexity, communicability observability and triability; (ii) theories such as the Theory of Reasoned Action (TRA) and the Theory of Planned Behaviour (TPB) (Ajzen, 1985, 1991; Ajzen & Fishbein, 1980) which provide a theoretical framework for understanding individuals' behavioral patterns; (iii) Studies by Davis et al. (1989) that consider users' acceptance of technology (Holak & Lehmann, 1990; Pagani, 2004; Venkatesh et al., 2003).

Following on from these theories and models, we now present the theoretical constructs of legitimacy and frontloading framework and link them to ICT resource management in public administration. We take a first step towards understanding: (i) how legitimacy is derived from m-resources; (ii) why civil servants decide to use or resist to certain m-resources?; (iii) how m-ICT is shaping the relationship between civil servants and formal government structures.

Legitimacy

Legitimacy, within the context of this chapter, is defined as "a generalized perception or assumption that the actions of an entity are desirable, proper, or appropriate within a socially constructed system of norms, values, beliefs and definitions" (Suchman, 1995, p.574). Legitimacy is a multifaceted construct; both positive and negative, short term and long term. Its meaning, opportunities and limits are located both within technological development, resource management strategy and human technology relationship (Prins, 2001). These are often depicted as contentious issues whereby a polarization occurs where winners or losers have to be defined. Technology is seen, not simply as a body of practice, but as a body of understanding. As a consequence, the nature of the evaluation (deterministic modus operandi) and selection choice become more dynamic and recurrent (multi-period) and increase in scale and scope as the initial investment grows (Ziman, 2000). Furthermore, civil servants and all other types of stakeholders in the power structure, who support the acquisition or reject certain forms of technology, ought to be explicitly perceived as part of the legitimacy rationalization. They are, in effect, legitimating the intangible investment and are the guardians of the technical knowledge and cultural learning that form the ethos of the organization (Marcelle, 2004).

Shaping new forms of governance in the mobile information age requires knowledge of dynamics of hardware (back-end) processes and structures in the public sector as well as sufficient information about the capabilities associated with information and communication technologies in order to respond to everyday needs. At this point, the degree of relative advantages, benefits and consequences of the new innovation need to be addressed. These advantages range from increase in profits to gain in social status. As an extreme position, over-adoption, which is defined as "adoption of an innovation by an individual (or organization) that experts feel he/she should reject" (Rogers, 1995, p. 215) is also found to be relevant. From a different perspective, ethical and practical obstacles, which are related pragmatically to security, fraud, liability, free access, equality and privacy, should not be underestimated (Prins, 2001, p.3).

Following Dacin et al.'s (2007) study, five dimensions of legitimacy are presented: market, relational, social, investment and alliance legitimacy. The first type of legitimacy, "market legitimacy", refers to an organization's expanding or maintaining its place in a market. When an organization enters a new market or aims to enhance its place in a new environment, strategic alliances with already successful, experienced partners approved by the local market increase the company's legitimacy in a geographical area, technology or product market. The second aspect, "relational legitimacy", is perceived as the worthiness of an organization to attract alliance partners. Once an organization is high in relational legitimacy, it is able to attract high-quality partners whose market share and experience can be shared. "Social legitimacy" as the third type leads to getting approval from others for using resources. By engaging in strategic relationships with favorable partners, one increases in social legitimacy. Social legitimacy is more important for the organizations practices of which are questioned or are undergoing radical change. These organizations contribute to further services within given communities in order to reduce opposition and boycotts. "Investment legitimacy" means that an organization is more likely to be supported by external parties by demonstrating an increased level of investment in the particular objectives sought (i.e. hardware, software and skills provision), which in turn makes the future goals more feasible to accomplish. Finally, "alliance legitimacy" is especially crucial for the markets where a history of competition and rivalry is prominent. The use of strategic alliances for increasing legitimacy in particular technologies enables organizations to reduce risk. The legitimacy interactions of an organization or an individual determine how well the resources are: (i) deployed, (ii) integrated with other activities, (iii) reducing the risk of pervasive acts, and (iv) allowing the creation of competitive advantages (Dacin et al., 2007). Legitimacy becomes central to the engagement process. Our attention now turns to the notion of front-loading.

Front-Loading

Front-loading activities are defined as being part of a strategy that seeks to improve pre-service activity performance by identifying and solving current and potential problems in the early phases of the transition process. Front loading, as a philosophy, has been applied successfully in the automotive industry and has been particularly associated with lean production methods championed by Toyota (Thomke & Fujimoto, 2000). In other areas such as team management, front-loading activities are linked to the forming stage which includes the engagement of agents or teams in specific activities (Tuckman, 1965). Other examples, where preparatory stages have been recognized as crucial, are: (i) technology acceptance, (ii) attitude towards smoking, alcohol and drugs, (iii) encouragement towards greener disposition of garbage, (iv) systematic wearing of seat belts and bicycle helmet, and (v) fishing quotas.

Front-loading strategies concentrate on 'preliminary/preparation needs' which are crucially important to legitimize engagement and logic in future cooperation and to lower potential resistance. Themes such as project scope, investment expectations, management roles, time frame, benefits, external and internal supports as examples are assessed. Reflecting this, micro-strategies are deployed to encourage civil servants' engagement in new technologies at early stages that ought to increase the likelihood of the overall outcome success (de Kervenoael et al., 2010). Significantly, individuals want to minimize unpleasant changes during the transition process towards new ICT usage and reproduce traditional processes that allow them to retain control over their everyday work routines. In turn, hierarchical setting and historical relationships between technological services and individuals have a memory effect on learning opportunities and communication style directly shaping the transition and acquisition of novel communication know-how (Gudykunst, 1993).

In most of the organizations, the conceptualization of innovation as a learning process is rather loosely applied. The precise nature of the learning that takes place, as well as how it occurs and who learns, are matters that often remain largely unexamined (Ziman, 2000, p.119). According to Holm et al. (2002), the role of ICT for the national economies is constantly increasing and careful selection of human resource management (HRM hereafter) practices has become crucial in managing the growing population of information professionals. Studies show that there have been several alternative approaches to consider depending on how the effectiveness of HRM is defined and what the expected outcomes of the best HRM bundle are.

It is further underlined that how people identify and commit to their groups and organizations should be understood from an individual point of view. Higher management strategy, on the other hand, traditionally only tackles technological transition and change issue from a deterministic functional process. A miss-match is often found between HRM strategy at individual and organizational levels shaping illegitimacy and causing resistance to engage in m-ICT before it is deployed. How individuals' future expectations are aligned with the business strategy and how they support each other are often overlooked (Holm et al., 2002).

Rousseau's (1995) model of psychological contracts provides an interesting unifying framework for simultaneous analysis of both managerial and individual views. Two fundamental terms of psychological contracts are developed namely transactional and relational. Transactional contract is based on close-ended time frame and mutual profitability. Relational contract on the contrary is based on confidence, stability and commitment. Organizational commitment is one key element which makes the difference between transactional and relational contracts. Subsequently, commitment is defined as; i) acceptance of an organization's goals and values; ii) willingness to exert considerable effort on behalf of an organization; iii) desire to maintain organizational membership (Porter et al., 1974). Furthermore, this framework contains an additional performance requirement dimension in addition to the time frame that relates to the duration of the employment relationship (Holm et al., 2002).

Front loading activities are traditionally broken up in a series of iterative steps ranging from; (i) the learning and understanding of the current standing and relationships during change; (ii) the critical evaluation and re-evaluation of current processes benchmarked against industry leaders; (iii) the design of novel structure to allow collaborative problem solving and quicker identification of emerging problems often involving feedback loops; (iv) the evaluation of expectations regarding possible outcomes; (v) the proactive recognition that individuals are fundamentally different and that more than one outcome or solution ought to be considered before finding a solution to complex dynamic issues; and (vi) setting achievable goals for the coming periods. The concept of legitimacy and front loading will now be discussed together within the specific context of m-government.

ICT Resource Management Considering Digital Government Services

As the availability and the accessibility of information improve and cost declines, many governments are considering the Internet as the efficient way to reach to a large group of citizens. Indeed recent reforms have lead to the introduction of approaches putting greater emphasis on ICT 'as a transition from passive to an active welfare state'. Significantly, despite the importance of technologies, it is estimated that governments' ICT spending for the 2000-2010 period stands at over $3 trillion but that between 60 to 85 percent of e-government projects will fail to deliver their expected outcomes (Gubbins, 2004). On the other hand, how this dynamic setting affects the way through which government services are accessed and offered remain unanswered. What cultural and organizational changes are needed in order to manage the transition are also important issues to be addressed which remain controversial especially in emerging market conditions.

Several key characteristics are shaping the debate including: (i) civil servants' control over the interface choice in their daily administrative work at local level; (ii) human machine synergies and the re-organization of activities and tasks; (iii) co-operation, negotiation and deliberations between administrative layers, arm length public private partnerships, NGOs and the business world; (iv) regulation and standards regarding information depository, storage and access; (v) rights that protect civil servants' privacy, promote ethical and transparent practices, and create a learning organization which maximizes the common use of ICT services across all government layers. Guarantee of an acceptable level of service quality, both by individual civil servants and new hardware and software providers, has become paramount. The integration of pre-ICT era information, the translation of administrative jargon and processes, and the match of jurisdictional structure with the new emerging ICT back end infrastructure, along with possibilities for tracking, correcting and upgrading services, are required to take full advantages of the new digital opportunities. m-ICT ought to allow, following the French example, the true creation of "the Administration á accés pluriel" (plural access to administrative services) with a greater "service de proximité" (local services or where citizens are "in the field").

In particular, m-government has been described as limiting: (i) demand to interpretation, (ii) hidden discretion, and (iii) political influence (Lenk, 1997). Such m-opportunities in turn allow a better decision making process which includes: (i) substantiation of facts by data, (ii) decision as a result of information processing, (iii) clear execution of strategy and corrective mechanisms. Significantly, m-government allows administrative cooperation: (i) over distances, (ii) across organization boundaries, and (iii) across hierarchical echelon. Technology should not be seen as the reason for resistance but only the tool which allows organizational changes (Gerst & Bunduchi, 2005).

From these perspectives, the idea of hegemony and control of power remain important. Technologies often bring radical change within organizations and power and politics are issues that cannot be neglected in the domain of m-services for municipalities (Emerson, 1962). The multiple types of shareholders ought to develop a strategic framework regarding m-governance. From this point of view, legitimacy can be re-defined as positive resistance. Resistance is, in this context, the sum of "those behaviors and cultural practices by subordinate groups within the context of hegemonic social formation that threaten to unravel the strategies of domination" (Haynes & Prakash, 1991, p.3). Legitimacy, as an m-governance issue, needs to be analyzed along a continuum including public administration history, culture and power (Hall, 1990, p 225). As a result, a novel definition of power is emerging that is transitory, flexible and ambivalent abolishing previous boundaries and creating new territories (Law, 1997, Sack, 1986). These schematics are also utilized in Actor Network Theory giving a greater role on non-human agency and contingency (Heeks & Stanforth, 2007). Contingency represents the language, connections, flows, speed and lines of contestations. At this point, the significance of apparently apolitical standpoints cannot be overstressed. In other words, following Canel (1992), the traditional state centered locations of politics and new emerging civil society voices should not be seen as separated.

Lastly, new technical infrastructures have to be created that often involve third parties from private sector. The services and processes which are required include: (i) payment procedures, (ii) certifying agencies, (iii) protocol and interface control systems, (iv) m-signature and (v) m-legislation regarding complaints and errors. In addition, m-applications include resource management such as voice over IP, moving images, file transfer, web browsing, collaborative working, electronic agents, job dispatch, information services and still images which are all requiring 3G or GPRS technologies. Other examples of SMS/GPRS applications are email, chat, remote monitoring, instant messaging, electronic commerce, customer service and vehicle positioning.

From this perspective, the m-platform function appears more complex than originally perceived by civil servants. Simultaneously, clearer divergences from other forms of digital government such as e-government become more prominent. Indeed, many of these requirements will only become apparent during the trial period of these applications which escalate the financial risk faced by local authorities. As stated by Phipps, (2000) p 41: "A risk is acknowledged that ICT developments may reinforce polarisation and create additional division through people and communities who are 'information rich' or 'information poor', whereby the failure to get plugged-ins leads to a downwards spiral of economic activity with associated fall outs. ICT can be seen as neutral in themselves, as an enabler. Positive and beneficial applications, enhancing democracy and accountability, are an active choice and responsibility for our society". Furthermore, increase in information intensity, access reliability, urgency of information and data interactivity need to be considered within this context.

METHODOLOGY

This research is based on a series of semi-structured interviews which were conducted in 2008-2009 as being part of a wider project. This period coincides with the initiation of the first Turkish e-Government gateway portal. Phone interviews, using the notable people methodology (Kempster, 2007), were conducted with a total of 30 ICT officers within local government organizations (municipalities) in Turkey. Each respondent was interviewed in four waves. This methodology enabled us to talk to the civil servants sufficiently despite their work load. Respondents did not receive any feedback on previous surveys' results or other respondents' comments. Each interview lasted in total between 40 and 90 minutes and was audio taped.

For each respondent, a separate within case analysis was conducted (Each author's own observation). This follows Yin's (1989) ideas of pattern matching. Second, cross case comparisons to offer consistency on the issues, themes and a holistic appreciation of the data were made (Miles & Huberman, 1994). In order to operationalize the coding based on the original broad constructs identified in the literature, the authors developed and reinterpreted their coding to reach a consensus, via a series of iterative discussions with a focus on flexibility and contextual sensitivity (Merriam, 1998).

Each wave of interviews builds on the findings of the previous interviews. Following Lee and Cadogan (2009), "analysis proceeds concurrently with data collection and theorizing, with each having an impact on the procession of the others". Moreover, this methodology is used to determine the moment of "theoretical saturation" (Strauss & Corbin, 1998) where respondents do not add any further aspects or new themes.

Themes investigated included: (i) the current usage of ICT by the municipalities and the civil servants' awareness and perception of m-services, (ii) organizational process and day to day civil practices in terms of m-ICT, (iii) mobility and ICT capability building, and (iv) m-services resource management issues in local governments (see Appendix 1 for the survey).

FINDINGS

Three broad resource management dimensions, leading to legitimacy for adopting or rejecting to the new initiatives related to m-government, emerged as the most enduring aspects; i) *Awareness and diffusion of information management,* ii) *Operating system and resource management, and* iii) *Skill, strategy and human resource management.*

Awareness and Diffusion Of Information Management

The first group of findings was related to the concepts of awareness and information diffusion among civil servants about the current and future potential of m-municipality services (investment and market legitimacy). First, interoperability was described as key to any engagement likelihood. As compatibility, the degree at which the innovation was perceived as consistent with the existing value, past experiences and needs of potential adopters remained fundamental. Fragmentation was depicted as present both from a technical perspective (e.g. back-end architecture, middleware integration and individual applications level) and from a broader cultural organizational perspective (e.g. process, practices, praxis). Indeed, technology was not viewed singular by civil servants. The adoption, resistance or legitimacy of a technological tool was an important precedent for current and future strategies. The boundaries around an initiative or an activity were often not clear cut which caused the perception of threats rather than benefits, at least in the short term.

Transferability is an important issue to be solved. Coordination among the departments within the municipality is crucial; I think, m-municipality may benefit a certain group of citizens or civil servant, but I do not know what shall be done to widen the scope of the target audience.

Second, scalability to all services in all aspects of municipality life was not perceived as straight forward. Third, a re-engineering process towards a seamless m-municipality was required. To achieve the integration and automatic workflow services, IT offices and floor level civil servants needed greater and better communication channels. For m-government, the positioning of the innovation and the strategy at national level made an implementation difficult at local level. Not all stakeholders (e.g IT, financial, Technical providers) were indeed available in the local environment. While benefits were perceived for the civil servants acting in the field, it was recognized that few civil servants were leaving their offices. Traditional process required a citizen to come physically to the local office and not vice versa.

Mobile government does not provide any advantage for municipalities compared to e-government. I still need to have the same technology, servers etc. But from a civil servant "in the field" perspective, it will provide a time saving practice.

Subsequently, it was felt by some of the respondents that indigenous local knowledge and specificity were forgotten. As described by Rogers (1995) p. 240, "An innovation often commit the empty vessels fallacy by assuming the potential adopter are blank slates who lack relevant experiences with which to associate the new idea". Furthermore, cross national services provision through better content management is yet to be achieved in Turkey in other areas (e.g. school management). It was felt that the complexity of the changes was not appropriately understood as negatively related to potential legitimacy. This element was compounded by a lack of trialability and observability. These were highlighted by a number of respondents with issues such as:

Cultural factors are important; all civil servants should adopt these mobile services, but what about local differences?; I think other civil servants know m-government services but I don't know whether they use them or not; does it fit what they need to work with?

From the present perspective, further organizational integration was emerging as an underlying requirement. In parallel, a certain categorization of civil servants regarding to whom and when m-government would have impact on seemed to become a compelling necessity. The question of m-government initiatives' including all civil servants (exhaustive method) based on innovativeness degree to which a unit/jurisdiction has been subject in the past or using other methods such as starting in one service based on urgent needs and moving organically towards all services should be addressed.

My colleagues are not knowledgeable about mobile services that much. As the IT office, we are more informed and knowledgeable now, my team (IT) knows but most of the people working in our municipality do not have detailed information about the mobile services; We are already using mobile devices and my colleagues know m-applications. I have information about the activities of other municipalities. My friends know the applications which are developed by Istanbul Metropolitan Municipality. But in general I can say that there is a trust and security concern; Most of the civil servants are not aware of these mobile services since they are very old. Those who are aware of these services don't have detailed information about the services offered to citizens.

In particular, a strategy needed to be devised regarding private sector's roles in supporting m-municipality applications, the role of interpersonal (political) network and its influence on both individuals and organizations. Defining leaders and champions (opinion leadership) seemed particularly relevant for the informal integration of m-government and its automation components of resource management. Legitimacy was found to be important in driving m-government through clear policy statements, official documentation and political discourse.

Operating System and Resource Management

The second group of findings centered on operating system and resource management within the set of local level activities (technology robustness legitimacy). First, the cost of running back-end services for mobile applications was described as unknown. This feeling was reinforced by a lack of homogenous pricing structure for similar services by the three m-providers in Turkey. Second, supporting m-services through mobile phones was described as tricky due to the great variety of devices and operating systems. This lack of interoperability became a psychological barrier as well as a technical limit for the civil servants. Third, mobile government activities' value added was still not perceived as superior than other traditional delivery methods by most of the civil servants. This resulted in confusion over priority and usage of technological tools such as mobile phones and traditional computers. These were described by our respondents with the concerns such as:

There are technical issues such as the variety of mobile phones in terms of design, operating systems, technical limits and capabilities. Therefore, it is problematic to build a common m-application base structure; I don't think there is problem in terms of government, actually government supports m-applications. But institutions differ a lot in their policy and attitudes towards resource management. Public institutions except municipalities are dependent on national government funding waves and therefore their ability to generate m-applications is so limited; "The problem here is that each mobile phone does not support m-services. There is a limitation, so it is not like a computer on internet. So, even if one person likes to use the m-service, he cannot do it because of his old generation mobile phone.

Another emerging issue was linked to the level of decentralization or centralization of m-government strategy. The experience of the e-Government gateway was a move towards a centralized application in Turkey. From this perspective, peer diffusion of innovation and experimentation couldn't be sufficient and the order of service priority didn't reflect local needs. Furthermore, user self reliance was encouraged in a decentralized process which is not the case currently. Yet, it was perceived that technical expertise or quality of m-service as a proxy could be easier to standardize at central level. Cost was also perceived as high; hence an impediment in a decentralized system.

Emerging m-service quality is good but the price level limits its usage along with security issues. Mobile signature application should also be improved; In mobility, cost of using a service is important (3G phone acquisition and daily use). Besides, I do not prefer to use my mobile phone for a service if I can have access to the same service free of charge through a municipal (work phone) provided device. I think the main problem is the cost also for us civil servants. Similar to e-government, m-government will also provide labor cost reductions. It provides a better allocation of government resources. Moreover, compared to e-government, m-government will enable us to deliver public services to everyone, even to those who cannot use computers.

While implementations at local level within day to day activities were emerging, stronger strategic perspectives were required to allow legitimacy of investment both in terms of ICT resources and service range and depth. Civil servant layers within any country should not been seen as homogenous. Civil servants at public administrations, rather than the ones at organizations, do not always work together to achieve common goals. The hierarchy of power is having a deep impact on the politics that shapes each layer. M-government is related not only to internal organizational structure, characteristics of organizations and public administrations' adoption of change but also to individuals' uniqueness. We now turn our attention to this.

Skill, Strategy and Human Resource Management

The third group of findings included concepts which were related to individuality, level of confidence with ICT and strategic tools that were used to persuade civil servants to engage in m-technologies' tools and services for their daily activities at the municipalities (social and relational legitimacy). Easy learning, convenience and accessibilities were important factors. Compared to usual computers, m-devices were described as: (i) accessed anytime and anywhere, (ii) always switched on and carried around, (iii) more precise at delivering instant up to date content to relevant individuals, and (iv) more confidential since a person does not usually share mobile phone. Implications were profound in terms of responsibility and control mechanism. The older generation perceived risk as they traditionally did not engage in technological changes and had control over the tasks.

I think Turkish civil servants will be able to adapt to any technological developments On the other hand, technology improves so fast that older colleagues do not follow. We are curious to learn about new technological tools but usually we do not have the education and technical background to learn quickly how to use these tools efficiently, immediately.

As a secondary perspective, the findings highlighted that civil servants could be convinced to invest in m-services if a series of themes were clarified at strategy level; (i) both the civil servant users and the technical service providers need to demonstrate readiness to implement m-applications; (ii) the timing or intensity of change needed to be made by consensus; (iii) the issues such as the ranking of m-services within the whole array of digital services and the people who will make the decision regarding adoption or rejection were perceived to be political rather than technical; (iv) the impact on municipalities' service delivery regarding efficiency and effectiveness remained too vague. Evaluation of the progress or the consequences of failure on the achievement of the targets were important. Typically respondents described issues related to skills and strategy making in the following ways:

If a municipality has budget to train us and qualified employees are recognized, then it is easy to build the required infrastructure for m-municipality. In addition, young personnel can learn technological tools more easily than the old can do that should accelerate the change in culture towards ICT resource management; How is all that going to be assessed? Against which criteria and by whom?; How fast will decisions be taken?

Interestingly, these issues were echoed in other countries as a source of legitimization for engaging in m-government. In Turkey, the changing working patterns of civil servants regarding more 'in the field' and 'closer to the citizens' as opposed to the traditional 'behind desk' position need progress.

CONCLUSION

One of the greatest pains to human nature is the pain of new ideas. It ... makes you think that after all, your favorite notions may be wrong, your firmest beliefs ill founded ... Naturally, therefore, common men hate a new idea, and are disposed more or less to ill treat the original man who brings it (Bagehot, 1999 as cited in Rogers, 1995, p. 335).

This chapter proposed an approach that examined civil servants as resisting gate keepers of the new promising applications of m-government. Civil servants' perspectives on the concepts surrounding legitimacy and resistance in the early stages of an m-government strategy were presented including market investment, technological robustness, social and relational legitimacy. The findings of this exploratory study indicated that the legitimacy of m-government services -in Turkey- is multi-factorial. Thus, it should be better understood that m-government resource management ought to take into account the emotional management of civil servants at local level as well as the overall organizational change brought by the concept of mobility both at national and local level. Mobility is understood more as how local governments can provide a better social infrastructure through mobile applications and services than technological tools per se. While digital government has been an important step taken by most of the governments, provision of services through mobile technologies is now inevitable and needs to be managed not only from a citizen centric perspective but also taking into account civil servants' expectations. Although previous research concentrated mainly on macro strategy level from a citizen perspective, we argue that more interest should be given on civil servants and ICT supply chain issues.

From these perspectives, it is pertinent to consider the global policy landscapes and the convergence between countries in the widening of ICT usage which makes the engagement in innovation more important for Turkey and other emerging countries. At this moment, it is obvious that mobile services are rapidly emerging as the new frontier of change in transforming government from within. As more advanced mobile devices are becoming common and faster rates of data transfer are possible, more useful and higher value-added mobile services will be expected from all levels of governments. For this reason, understanding civil servants' legitimacy and resistance to mobile technologies and applications has become more important. Furthermore, from a resource management perspective, an evolution needs to occur that takes into account both human and technical issues which are related to change in non-homogenous organizations.

In a nutshell, the objective of this chapter was to investigate the perception of the civil servants, who are working at local level, regarding the potential for m-government services. Our findings indicated that there are many issues that influence civil servants' legitimacy to engage in or resist to m-government services. Frontloading activities at local level and national level were found to be important steps towards making m-governments' resource management initiatives successful and beneficial for both the citizens and the civil servants. Legitimacy regarding the perception of m-municipality services, mobile tools and technologies, as prerequisites for further improvement and growth in information communication technologies, was emphasized. More action is needed in order to increase the awareness and knowledge of civil servants currently delivering m-municipality services. Thus, further research should look at various types of civil servants from a qualitative perspective in order to elicit detailed issues in practice which are related to the emerging mobility phenomenon.

ACKNOWLEDGMENT

We are very thankful to TUBITAK for funding part of this project (grant number 107K272).

REFERENCES

Abanumy, A., & Mayhew, P. (2005). M-government implications for e-government in developing countries: The case of Saudi Arabia. *European Mobile Government Conference*. Mobile Government Consortium International LLC

Abramowicz, W., Bassara, A., Filipowska, A., Wisniewski, M., & Zebrowski, P. (2006). Mobility implications for m-government platform design. *Cybernetics and Systems: An International Journal*, *37*(2-3), 119–135. doi:10.1080/01969720500428255

Ajzen, I. (1985). From intentions to actions: A theory of planned behavior . In Kuhl, J., & Beckman, J. (Eds.), *Action-control: From cognition to behavior* (pp. 11–39). Germany: Springer.

Ajzen, I. (1991). The theory of planned behavior. *Organizational Behavior and Human Decision Processes*, *50*, 179–211. doi:10.1016/0749-5978(91)90020-T

Ajzen, I., & Fishbein, M. (1980). *Understanding attitudes and predicting social behavior*. Englewood Cliffs, NJ: Prentice-Hall.

Bianchi, A., & Phillips, J. G. (2005). Psychological predictors of problem mobile phone use. *Cyberpsychology & Behavior*, *8*(1), 39–51. doi:10.1089/cpb.2005.8.39

Briseno, A. G. (2009). *From m-euphoria to m-governance: Thinking about the potential of mobile technology*. Retrieved from http://blogs.worldbank.org/governance/from-m-euphoria-to-m-governance-thinking-about-the-potential-of-mobile-technology

Brown, B., Green, N., & Harper, R. (2002). *Wireless world: Social, cultural and interactional issues in mobile communications and computing*. London: Springer.

Canel, E. (1992). New social movement theory and resource mobilization: the need for integration . In Carroll, W. (Ed.), *Organizing Dissent: Social Movements in Theory and Practice* (pp. 22–51). Toronto, Canada: Garamond.

Chapman, S., & Schofield, W. N. (1998). Lifesavers and Samaritans: emergency use of cellular (mobile) phones in Australia. *Accident; Analysis and Prevention*, *30*(6), 815–819. doi:10.1016/S0001-4575(98)00034-7

Cilingir, D., & Kushchu, I. (2004). E-government and m-government: Concurrent leaps by Turkey. In D. Remenyi (Ed.) *Proceedings of European Conference on E-Government (ECEG 2004),* Trinity College, Dublin, June 17-18 (pp. 813-821). Reading, UK: Academic Conferences International.

Dacin, M. T., Oliver, C., & Roy, J.-P. (2007). The legitimacy of strategic alliances: An in-stitutional perspective. *Strategic Management Journal*, *28*, 169–187. doi:10.1002/smj.577

Davis, F. D., Bagozzi, R. P., & Warshaw, P. R. (1989). User acceptance of computer technology: A comparison of two theoretical models. *Management Science*, *35*(8), 982–1003. doi:10.1287/mnsc.35.8.982

De Kervenoael, R., Palmer, M., & Cakici, N. M. (2010). Exploring civil servant resistance to m-government: A story of transition and opportunities in Turkey . In Abdel-Wahab, A. G., & El-Masry, A. A. (Eds.), *Mobile Information Communication Technologies Adoption in Developing Countries: Effects and Implications*. Hershey, PA: IGI Global.

Dedeoglu, A. O. (2004). The symbolic use of mobile telephone among Turkish consumers. *Journal of Euromarketing*, *13*(2/3), 143–163. doi:10.1300/J037v13n02_08

Döring, N., & Gundolf, A. (2005). Your Life in Snapshots. Mobile Weblogs (Moblogs) . In Glotz, P., Bertschi, S., & Locke, C. (Eds.), *Thumb Culture. The Meaning of Mobile Phones for Society* (pp. 211–224). Bielefeld, Germany: Transcript.

Emerson, R. (1962). Power-dependence relations. *American Sociological Review*, *27*, 31–41. doi:10.2307/2089716

Esbjornsson, M., Juhlin, O., & Weilenmann, A. (2007). Drivers using mobile phones in traffic: An ethnographic study of interactional adaptation. *International Journal of Human-Computer Interaction*, *22*(1-2), 37. doi:10.1207/s15327590ijhc2201-02_3

Ferguson, M. (2001). *e-Government- A strategic Framework for public services in the Information Age*. London: Society of IT Management.

Fortunati, L., Katz, J. E., & Riccini, R. (2003). *Mediating the human body: Technology, communication, and fashion*. Mahwah, NJ: Lawrence Erlbaum.

Foster, K. R., & Moulder, J. E. (2000). Are mobile phones safe? *IEEE Spectrum*, ▪▪▪, 23–28. doi:10.1109/6.861774

Gerst, M., & Bunduchi, R. (2005). Shaping IT standardisation in the automotive industry - the role of power in driving portal standardisation. *Electronic Markets*, *15*(4), 335–343. doi:10.1080/10196780500302872

Ghyasi, A. F., & Kushchu, I. (2004). m-Government: Cases of developing countries. *Mobile Government Lab* (*mGovLab*).

Goggin, G. (2008). *Mobile phone cultures*. London: Routledge.

Goodman, M. J., Tijerina, L., Bents, F. D., & Wierwille, W. W. (1999). Using cellular phones in vehicles. *Transportation Human Factors*, *1*, 3–42. doi:10.1207/sthf0101_2

Gubbins, M. (2004). *Global IT spending by sector*.

Gudykunst, W. B. (1993). Toward a Theory of Effective Interpersonal and Intergroup Communication . In Wiseman, R., & Koester, J. (Eds.), *Intercultural Communication Competence*. Newbury Park, CA: Sage.

Ha, I., Yoon, Y., & Choi, M. (2007). Determinants of adoption of mobile games under mobile broadband wireless access environment. *Information & Management*, *44*, 276–286. doi:10.1016/j.im.2007.01.001

Hall, S. (1990). Culture identity and diaspora . In Rutherford, J. (Ed.), *Identity: Community, Culture, Difference* (pp. 222–237). London: Lawrence and Wishart.

Harmer, J. A. (2003). Mobile multimedia services. *BT Technology Journal*, *21*(3), 169–180. doi:10.1023/A:1025175518841

Haynes, D., & Prakash, G. (1991). Introduction: The entanglement of power and resistance . In Haynes, D., & Prakash, G. (Eds.), *Contesting power: Resistance and everyday social relations in South Asia*.

Hazlett, S. A., & Hill, F. (2003). E-government: The realities of using IT to transform the public sector. *Managing Service Quality*, *13*(6), 445–452. doi:10.1108/09604520310506504

Heeks, R. (2002). *Failure, Success and Improvisation of Information Systems Projects in Developing Countries. Institute for Development Policy and Management (IDPM)*. University of Manchester.

Heeks, R., & Stanforth, C. (2007). Understanding e-government project trajectories from an actor-network perspective. *European Journal of Information Systems*, *16*(2), 165–177. doi:10.1057/palgrave.ejis.3000676

Holak, S. L., & Lehman, D. R. (1990). Intentions and the dimensions of innovation: An exploratory model. *Journal of Product Innovation Management*, *7*(1), 59–73. doi:10.1016/0737-6782(90)90032-A

Holden, S. H., Norris, D. F., & Fletcher, P. D. (2003). Electronic government at the local level: Progress to date and future issues. *Public Performance & Management Review*, *26*(4), 325–344. doi:10.1177/1530957603026004002

Holliday, I., & Kwok, R. C. V. (2004). Governance in the information age: Building e-government in Hong Kong. *New Media & Society*, *6*(4), 549–570. doi:10.1177/146144804044334

Holm, J., Lähteenmäki, S., Salmela, H., Suomi, R., Suominen, A., & Viljanen, M. (2002). Best practices of ICT workforce management –a comparable research initiative in Finland. *Journal of European Industrial Training*, *26*(7), 333–341. doi:10.1108/03090590210432688

Hulme, M., & Peters, S. (2003). Me, my phone and I: The role of the mobile phone. *3GSM World Congress*. Cannes, France: Teleconomy Research House.

Kahraman, C., Demirel Cetin, N., & Demirel, T. (2007). Prioritization of e-government strategies using a SWOT-AHP analysis: The case of Turkey. *European Journal of Information Systems*, *16*, 284–298. doi:10.1057/palgrave.ejis.3000679

Katz, J. E. (2003). *Machines that become us: The social context of personal communication technology*. New Brunswick, NJ: Transaction.

Katz, J. E., & Sugiyama, S. (2006). Mobile phones as fashion statements: evidence from student surveys in the US and Japan. *New Media & Society*, *8*(2), 321–337. doi:10.1177/1461444806061950

Kempster, S. J. (2007). Echoes from the past: An exploration of the impact of 'notable people' on leadership training. In *Academy of Management Annual Meeting Proceedings- Best Papers*, Philadelphia, PA.

Klein, H. (1999). Tocqueville in cyberspace: Using the internet for citizen associations. *The Information Society*, *15*(4), 213–220. doi:10.1080/019722499128376

Kushchu, I. (2007). *Mobile government: An emerging direction in e-government*. Hershey, PA: IGI Publishing.

Kushchu, I., & Kuscu, H. (2003). From e-government to m-government: Facing the inevitable. In *Proceedings of European Conference on E-Government (ECEG 2003),* Trinity College, Dublin, July 3-4 (pp. 253-260). Reading, UK: Academic Conferences International.

Lam, W. (2005). Barriers to e-government integration. *The Journal of Enterprise Information Management*, *18*(5), 511–530. doi:10.1108/17410390510623981

Larsen, E., & Rainie, L. (2002). *The rise of the e-citizen: How people use e-government agencies' web sites*. Washington, DC: Pew Internet & American Life Project.

Law, L. (1997). A matter of choice: discourses on prostitution in the Philippines . In Manderson, L., & Jolly, M. (Eds.), *Sites of Desire/Economies of Pleasure: Sexualities in Asia and the Pacific* (pp. 233–261). Chicago: University of Chicago Press.

Lee, N., & Cadogan, J. W. (2009). Sales force social exchange in problem resolution situations. *Industrial Marketing Management*, *32*(3), 355–372. doi:10.1016/j.indmarman.2008.02.002

Lenk, K. (1997). Business process re-engineering in the public sector: Opportunities and risks . In Taylor, J. A., Snellen, I., & Zuurmond, A. (Eds.), *Beyond BPR in Public Administration* (pp. 151–163). Amsterdam: IOS Press.

Lin, A., & Tong, A. (2008). Text-messaging culture of college girls in Hong Kong: SMS as resources for achieving intimacy and gift-exchange with multiple functions . In Goggin, G. (Ed.), *Mobile Phone Cultures* (pp. 158–170). London: Routledge.

Ling, R. S. (2004). *Mobile connection: The cell phone's impact on society*. San Francisco: Morgan Kaufmann.

Marcelle, G. M. (2004). *Technological learning*. Cheltenham, UK: Edward Elgar.

McEvoy, S. P., Stevenson, M. R., McCartt, A. T., Woodward, M., Haworth, C., & Palamara, P. (2005). Role of mobile phones in motor vehicle crashes resulting in hospital attendance: a case-crossover study. *British Medical Journal*. Retrieved July 12, 2005, from http://www.bmj.com/cgi/content/abstract/bmj.38537.397512.55v1

McIvor, R., McHugh, M., & Cadden, C. (2002). Internet technologies: Supporting transparency in the public sector. *International Journal of Public Sector Management*, *15*(3), 170–187. doi:10.1108/09513550210423352

Melitski, J., Holzer, M., Kim, S., Kim, C., & Rho, S. (2005). Digital government worldwide: An e-government assessment of municipal websites throughout the world. *International Journal of E-government Research*, *1*(1), 1–19.

Merriam, S. B. (1998). *Qualitative research and case studies applications in education*. San Francisco: Jossey-Bass Publications.

Miles, M. B., & Huberman, A. M. (1994). *Qualitative data analysis: An expanded sourcebook*. Newbury Park, CA: Sage Publications.

Ozcan, Y. Z., & Kocak, A. (2003). Research note: A need or a status symbol? Use of cellular telephones in Turkey. *European Journal of Communication*, *18*(2), 241–254. doi:10.1177/0267323103018002004

Pagani, M. (2004). Determinant of adoption of third generation mobile multimedia services. *Journal of Interactive Marketing*, *18*(3), 46–59. doi:10.1002/dir.20011

Phipps, I. (2000). New communications technologies: A conduit for social inclusion. *Information Communication and Society*, *3*(1), 39–68. doi:10.1080/136911800359419

Porter, L. W., Steers, R. M., Mowday, R. T., & Boultian, P. V. (1974). Organizational commitment, job satisfaction, and turnover among psychiatric technicians. *The Journal of Applied Psychology*, *59*, 603–609. doi:10.1037/h0037335

Prins, J. E. J. (2001). *Designing e-government: On the crossroads of technological innovation and institutional change*. Amsterdam: Kluwer Law International.

Research and Markets. (2009). *Turkey mobile operator forecast, 2009-2013*. Retrieved from http://www.researchandmarkets.com/reports/1087690/

Rettie, R. (2007). Mobile phones as network capital: Facilitating connections. *Mobilities*, *3*(2), 291–311. doi:10.1080/17450100802095346

Rheingold, H. (2002). *Smart mobs: The next social revolution*. New York: Perseus.

Rogers, E. (1995). *Diffusion of Innovations*. New York: Free Press.

Rousseau, D. M. (1995). *Psychological contracts in organizations-Understanding written and unwritten agreements*. London: Sage.

Sack, R. D. (1986). *Human territoriality: Its theory and history*. New York: Cambridge University Press.

Saxena, K. B. C. (2005). Towards excellence in e-governance. *International Journal of Public Sector Management*, *18*(6), 498–513. doi:10.1108/09513550510616733

Sharma, G., & Sturges, P. (2007). Using ICT to help the poor access public services: An action research programme. *Information Development*, *23*(1), 15–24. doi:10.1177/0266666907075623

Sharma, S. K., & Gupta, J. N. D. (2004). Web services architecture for m-government: Issues and challenges. *Electronic Government*, *1*(4), 462–474. doi:10.1504/EG.2004.005921

Stahl, B. C. (2005). The ethical problem of framing e-government in terms of e-commerce. *The Electronic .Journal of E-Government*, *3*(2), 77–86.

Strauss, A., & Corbin, J. (1998). *Basics of qualitative research techniques and procedures for developing grounded theory*. London: Sage.

Suchman, M. C. (1995). Managing legitimacy: Strategic and institutional approaches. *Academy of Management Review*, *20*(3), 571–610. doi:10.2307/258788

Sundar, D. K., & Garg, S. (2005). M-governance: A framework for Indian urban local bodies. *European Mobile Government Conference*. Brighton, UK: Mobile Government Consortium International LLC

Thomke, S., & Fujimoto, T. (2000). The effect of front-loading problem-solving on product development performance. *Journal of Product Innovation Management*, *17*, 128–142. doi:10.1016/S0737-6782(99)00031-4

Tozsa, I., & Budai, B. (2005). M-government in Hungary. *European Mobile Government Conference*. Brighton, UK. Mobile Government Consortium International LLC

Tuckman, B. W. (1965). Developmental sequences in small groups. *Psychological Bulletin*, *63*, 384–399. doi:10.1037/h0022100

Türksat. (2008). Retrieved from http://www.turksat.com.tr/english/v2/e-government-gateway

Venkatesh, V., Morris, M. G., Davis, G. B., & Davis, F. D. (2003). User acceptance of information technology: Toward a unified view. *Management Information Systems Quarterly*, *27*(3), 425–478.

Weilenmann, A. (2001). Negotiating use: Making sense of mobile technology. *Personal and Ubiquitous Computing*, *5*(2), 109–122. doi:10.1007/PL00000015

Yildiz, M. (2007). The state of mobile government in Turkey: Overview, policy issues, and future prospects . In Kushchu, I. (Ed.), *Mobile Government: An Emerging Direction in E-Government* (pp. 252–268). Hershey, PA: IGI Publishing.

Yin, R. (1989). *Case study research: Design and methods*. Newbury Park, CA: Sage Publishing.

Ziman, J. (2000). *Technological innovation as an evolutionary process*. Cambridge, UK: Cambridge University Press.

APPENDIX 1. SUMMARY OF THE SURVEY INSTRUMENT

Wave one investigated the ICT adoption by the municipalities and civil servants' awareness and perception of m-services?

Q0 Can you provide us general information about your municipality's characteristics regarding ICT usage?

Q1 Can you summarize your municipality's ICT activities over the last 5 years?

Q2 How do you evaluate if there is a demand for mobile services?

Q3 How do you perceive the use of mobile phones for your daily tasks?

Q4 What is the most important benefit of being mobile as a civil servant?

Q5 What may be the key problems related to using mobile phones for public administration work, and from an individual user perspective?

Wave two explored organizational processes and possible causes of resistance to ICT.

Q0 What are the effects of the following barriers on your municipality's usage of ICT?

- Errors/defects in supplied equipment hardware and software
- Lack of flexibility considering ICT suppliers
- Lack of integration between applications
- Lack of qualified staff in the municipality
- Difficulties to recruit or retain ICT qualified staff
- Reluctance among staff to use ICT
- Municipality's lack of updated ICT strategy
- Lack of commitment by management
- Cost of adoption of ICT

Wave three investigated the concept of ICT capability building relating to m-services in particular.

Q0 What types of initiatives have been undertaken to introduce m-government to civil servants in your municipality?

Q1 At an individual municipality level, how are you preparing to explain the future development of m-government services? Why? Why not?

Q2 Can you describe the current ICT capabilities from a technical perspective and from a civil servant user perspective? How is technological change rationalized?

Q3 Set of questions on ICT expertise location*

Q4 Set of questions on trust in other knowledge regarding ICT*

Q5 Set of questions on coordination of ICT knowledge*

*Q3-5 adapted from Kanawattanachai, P. (2002). Formation and development of socially-shared cognition and its impact on performance of virtual teams over time. Doctoral Thesis, Department of Information Systems. Case Western Reserve University.

Wave four concentrated on the concept of m-services' resource management issues in local governments.

Q0 In your opinion, which factors influence the management and legitimacy of m-services resources, both considering technical and human factors?

Q1 How does civil servants' perception of mobility affect the resource management process?

Q3 How do you think the political pressures are shaping m-government adoption? Why? Why not? Benefits/problems?

Q4 Do you perceive any power-control issues arising from the new possibilities and opportunities offered by m-government?

Chapter 9
Client Sever System for E-Services Access in Business Environment

Eugen Pop
SC IPA SA, Romania

ABSTRACT

E-services is a term which generally means the provisioning of services via the Internet. The prefix "e" stands for electronic. E-services access is a good opportunity for business developing and offer increased financial benefits for various economic agents. By the support of the Internet, the products or services can be efficiently offered to a large number of clients. Besides, the mobile communications networks give to the clients the advantage to access the informational services from anywhere and anytime. This will facilitate an increasing convergence of technological and financial interests of mobile operators, client server software developers, mobile terminals producers and e-content providers, along with a high level of integration of IT&C resources. This is a good basis and a challenging opportunity for value added services developing, in order to be delivered through the mobile communications networks. Client server architectures with mobile users are suitable for e-services providing, using mobile communications networks. Such a system is presented in this chapter, suitable for business environment access using mobile applications installed on Smartphones and PDAs (Personal Digital Assistants).

INTRODUCTION

Data transmission through mobile networks became very attractive for many business agents, in the purpose of promoting and offering electronic services to their clients. This chapter presents a client server architecture, which offers to the mobile users the possibility of GPRS (General Packet Radio Service), UMTS, 3G, or WLAN (Wireless Local Area Networks) access to electronic services, through mobile data terminals like Smartphones and PDAs. As a representative example for a business environment service, a stock market transactions electronic service, based on client server architecture, was developed and presented. The functionality of the system can be

DOI: 10.4018/978-1-61692-016-6.ch009

extended for a larger number of s applications: e-commerce, e-banking, e-health, e-learning, location based services, e-government, etc.

An informational service is a software application that can be accessed by the users, through the Internet or mobile communication networks, which gives to the client the mobility advantage. The 3G networks offer significant channel bandwidth for increasing data traffic. In the last years a spectacular evolution of the communication technologies took place, which offered to the mobile communications operators the possibility to implement high performance networks and services.

UMTS (Universal Mobile Telecommunication System) was established by interconecting the 2G local networks in a functional universal system, based on roaming concept. In Europe and Japan, for example, the UMTS standard will be implemented through 3G networks. This evolution to UMTS starts with the great number of GSM users in the world, then passes through GPRS (2,5G) and EDGE (2,75G). The 3G standard IMT2000 was created by the International Telecommunication Union to join all the networks in the world with the general roaming functionality. The main wide area 3G standards that acomplish this target are: W-CDMA, CDMA2000, şi TD-SCDMA.

E-business cover online transactions, but also extends to all Internet based interactions with business partners, suppliers and consumers; monitoring and exchanging information, auction surplus inventory, collaborative product design. The term e-commerce refers to online transactions, buying or selling goods and/or services over the Internet.

Potential e-business benefits include:

- improved accuracy, quality and time, required for updating and delivering information on products and/or services;
- access of customers to catalogues and prices, 24 hours x 7 days;
- improved access, speed and immediacy of customer ordering;
- enhanced market, industry or competitor intelligence, acquired through information gathering and research activities;
- new distribution channels via the electronic delivery of some products and services, for example product design collaboration, publications, software, translation services, banking, etc.
- expansion of customer base and growth in export opportunities;
- reduces routine administrative tasks, (invoices and order records), freeing staff to focus on more strategic activities.

SYSTEM ARCHITECTURE AND TECHNOLOGY

Hardware Architecture

System's hardware architecture is presented in the (Figure 1), consisting of the server and mobile clients terminals. The general block scheme of the client server system is adapted for data transmissions, using various mobile channels. The server hardware structure basically consists of an IBM PC compatible computer, Core2Quad, 2,8 GHz, Windows XP Professional operating system with an Internet/Intranet cabled IP connection. The laptop can be connected at the Internet using modems, through CSD, GPRS, 3G and CDMA channels. The connection between the laptop and modems can be made by USB, serial cable or Bluetooth channels.

The system's mobile terminals are SE P990i Smartphone, with Symbian v. 9.1 operating system [Liming, S, D.], and QTEK 2020i PDA, with Windows Mobile 2003 operating system respectively. The GSM/GPRS, 3G and WLAN – Wi-Fi channels are used for TCP/IP data transmissions. Also other types of Smartphnes, PDA's or Java enabled phones, can be used [Douglas, B].

Sony Ericsson P990i mobile terminal has two important modules:

Figure 1.

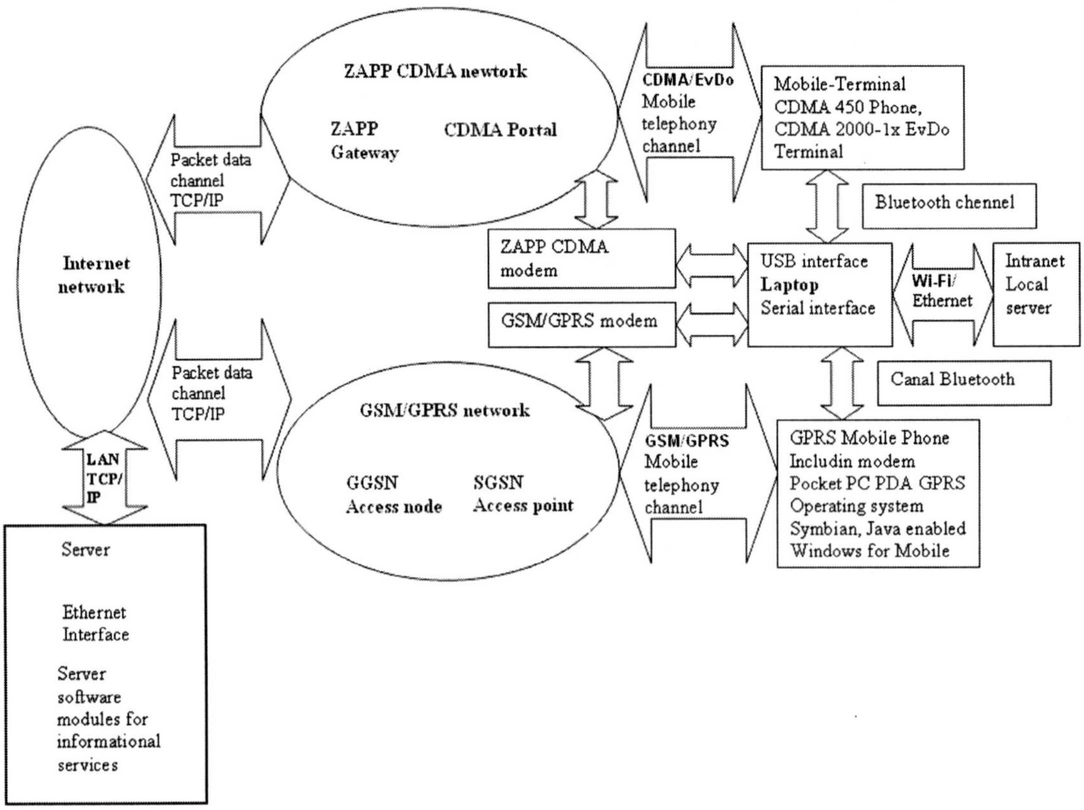

- the GSM phone with a flash memory, developed in a conventional structure;
- an "Organizer" module, where the operating system is stored and launched, having Important resources of flash and RAM memory and possibilities to transfer files to the PC.

The RAM memory is controlled by the Symbian OS, it is not involved for data or program storing but performs a Reset when the SE P990i phone is started. The available 128 flash memory is divided into two parts: 68 MB for operation and respectively 60 MB for user's data storing, for example audio files, figures, images, documents, settings. The flash memory preserves the data, even when the phone battery is empty. This is an advantage with respect of different types of PDA's, because a back-up battery for the memory isn't necessary. Sony Ericsson P990i has the following basic technical specifications:

- communication networks: Tri-band GSM, GSM 900, GSM 1800, EGSM, WCDMA, UMTS, FDD;
- operating system: Symbian OS v9.1, UIQ 3.0;
- data rate: 12 Mbps.

The basic mobile communications and data transmission parameters of a SE P990i smartphone are presented in the following table.

The Pocket PC PDA, QTEK 2020i, with the Windows Mobile 2003 OS, has the following basic technical characteristics:

Table 1. Communications and data transmission parameters for a SE P990i **Smartphone**

Parameter	GSM 900/ E-GSM 900	GSM 1800	GSM 1900	WCDMA
Frequency (MHz)	TX: 880-915 RX: 925-960	TX: 1710-1785 RX: 1805-1880	TX: 1850-1910 RX: 1930-1990	TX: 1920-1980 RX: 2110-2170
Channel spacing	200 KHz	200 KHz	200 KHz	5 MHz spaced 200 KHz
Channel number	174 purtătoare x 8 (TDMA)	374 carriers x 8 (TDMA)	299 carriers x 8 (TDMA)	277
Modulation	GMSK	GMSK	GMSK	QPSK
Phase stability	< 5° RMS	< 5° RMS	< 5° RMS	< 17,5° Magnit.
Duplex spacing	45 MHz	95 MHz	80 MHz	190 MHz
Frequency stability	+/- 0.1 ppm	+/- 0.1 ppm	+/- 0.1 ppm	+/- 0.1 ppm
Biasing	3,6 V	3,6 V	3,6 V	3,6 V
Emission power	33 dBm 2W Cl1	30 dBm 1W Cl1	30 dBm 1W Cl1	24 dBm 1W Cl3
RF impedance	50Ω	50Ω	50Ω	50Ω
Spurious emissions	<-36 dBm	<-30 dBm	<-30 dBm	<-36 dBm
RF sensibility	>-102 dBm	>-102 dBm	>-102 dBm	>-106 dBm
Reception BER	<2,4%	<2,4%	<2,4%	<0,1%

- access networks and data transmission: GSM 900/GSM 1800 / GSM 1900, class 10, WLAN 802.11b, Bluetooth:
- memory SDIO/MMC, 128 MB RAM;
- Intel processor Bulverde 520 MHz;
- data messages: SMS, MMS, e-mails, Instant messaging;
- browser WAP 2.0/xHTML, HTML (PocketIE);
- PC conectivity, using Microsoft Active Sync tool, MP3, album video, audio.

Based on these facilities, the PDA can realize point to point data transmissions and corporate telephony data connections, so is suitable for Microsoft Windows Mobile applications development.

Other Windows Mobile OS based PDA, like HPiPAQ hw6515 or HTC TyTN, can be used for e-service development. Shortly, the HPiPAQ hw 6515, has the following parameters:

- Windows Mobile 2003 Second Edition OS, for Pocket PC – Phone Edition;
- Intel processor PXA 272, 312MHz, on 32 bits, Xscale nucleus, ARM architecture, comply with the V. 5TE sytandard;
- 64MB SDRAM volatile memory and 64MB FLASH ROM memory;
- user available memory 55MB, 12MB of which unvolatile, for iPAQ File Store directory.

The system's software architecture and possibilities are adequate to perform the e-serviceaccess by socket to socket type data transmission, suitable for Smartphones and PDAs. E-serviceaccess can also be achieved using embedded Web browsers for 3G mobile terminals, Web services or database query applications [Delaney, K].

Software Architecture

Several server software modules must be developed, for e-service access using laptop, or PDA;

- the electronic service WEB site;
- the stock market exchange web service;

- server database for e-service information storing;
- server application, installed in the operating system;
- server software applications for serving mobile connections requests, and TCP/IP data transmission;
- client applications, suitable for mobile data terminals [Darie, C.];

The e-service WEB site represents the collection of related web pages, images, videos, or other digital assets, that are addressed with a common domain name or IP address in an Internet Protocol based network. The service's web site can be hosted on one web server, or can have a distributed architecture, accessible via the Internet/Intranet.

A suitable architecture for a business environment e-service is generally based on three sections, or tiers: the presentation, the commercial and the data section [Darie, C.]. This architecture is advantageous because it groups the software modules according to their logical functions and assures the scalability and configurability of the application.

The presentation section represents the fix or mobile user interface, containing software modules that reflect the client interaction with the e-service. Generally, it consists of dynamically web pages and is very important for the e-service's attractiveness.

The commercial section receives the requests from the presentation section and returns a result to it. Almost any event that takes place in this section rises up an event in the presentation section. For example, if the user is looking for a certain company stock exchange data, he will call the commercial section asking for this. Consequently, the commercial section will call the data section, in order to answer to the client's request.

The data section stores, manages and administrates the service's data and send them to the commercial section, when a request is received. The database has an adequate number of informational tables and a request from a client leads to a database query.

These sections are logically defined and separated, and there are no restrictions with respect to their physical locations. The information between these sections is sequentially transferred. This means that the presentation section never can access the data section directly, but only through the commercial one. That is why the commercial section represents the "brain" of the web site's architecture.

The architecture based on three sections is efficient for the stock exchange service web site. Sometimes, in complex projects, the commercial section can be divided into several levels and the result is "n section" architecture.

The stock market exchange WEB service is developed to offer stock exchange market information, to the client. Besides, the web service is also a public software interface, which can be accessed through the Internet, by suitable mobile client applications. The WEB service offers to the client fourteen WEB methods, which allow the mobile clients to:

- realize web transactions, following the evolution of Bucharest Stock Exchange market quoted societies;
- create, administrate of user accounts, available on the server, which permit stock-exchange market demo transactions;
- processing the orders placed by users with the maximum delay of 15 min.

The query protocols used by the web methods are: Soap 1.1, 1.2, Http Post, Get.

A standardized description of operations and web service supported data types must be published, to be accessible on the main server, in the form of a WDSL - Web Services Description Language - file. The presence of the WDSL file is not necessary for SOAP interrogation of the server, but it allows client side code generating and using, for various integrated development environments (ex. MS Visual Studio, Netbeans etc.).

Through the web service [Hirsch, F.], the platform provides to the client software developers the possibility to integrate stock exchange market information in their own applications, using standard tools, instruments and protocols. The web service can be accessed through the platform's Symbian and Windows Mobile client applications, or by third parties developed applications.

The stock market exchange data upgrade operation is done through the Stock Exchange information resources access, at the market closing moment, when the current day transaction reports are published.

The New Account Statement method of the WEB service is presented, as an example. This method allows the client to open user accounts, in order to utilize the interactive components of the web service. An e-mail address must be specified by the client. The New Account statement operation will be recorded, and will have effect in the local database. Automatically, an e-mail message will be transmitted to the client, containing the account data, User Id and Password.

The method's input variable, which must be provided by the user for invoking, reflects the personal data: name, address, country, town, zip code, telephone number, e-mail, etc.

The output variable is an Account class object, whose member variables comprise the user account data.

The stock exchange electronic service database contains several societies, currently listed at the stock exchange first category. The database can be accessed in two modes: by WEB service and through PHP scripts, containing the SQL queries. The database is continuously updated, by an adequate software module.

The client software applications can be available on the server, for downloading and installing in the adequate mobile terminals of the user: Smartphones and PDA's.

The server "listens", to the client connections requests, at the suitable logic port and allows a Request Identifier to the client request and registers it.

The server database can be created in the following steps:

- starting the IIS service in the PC's Windows XP OS;
- in PhpMyAdmin folder, the index.php file is opened in a web browser;
- logging as a "root" user, with adequate password, for security reasons, to access the application main interface;
- defining a new database using "Create New" menu;
- embedding the scripts in Php type files, so they can be accessed directly on the site, as web pages.

SOFTWARE DEVELOPMENT TOOLS

Server Applications Development Tools

The server was created using the IIS service and can be local accessed in a Web browser, through the index.php file, in the PhPMyAdmin folder. Logging is necessary as a "root" user and password, to access the PhPMyAdmin main interface. The database is created using the "Create New" menu and contains one table, with the corresponding fields. With Insert tab the information insertion is performed. The scripts are embedded in php files and represent the SQL queries, accessed directly on the site, as Web pages. The database contains several societies, currently listed at the stock market first category. The query has the following general form http://localhost/query.php?parameter=value.

Several steps must be performed in order to create an e-service site. A web site folder must be created at the beginning, and then a virtual folder, pointing out to the physical one. The realization of the web page must begin with the index.html page, located in the web site folder. Any editor, even Notepad, can be used to create the index. html page. Since thee-servicesfolder is configured as a virtual directory, the .html files can be accessed using a web browser, and entering the URL address of the web site, ex: http://localhost/website/ index.html. Visual Studio .Net is a tool that automates a lot of work, in the background, to create a web site or web application, for example a web service, by the following steps:

- create the application, or service's folder and than converts it into a virtual directory;
- automatically creates the virtual directory in the IIS;
- creates a lot of default files and code, compile and build all WEB pages;
- offer the possibility to design user controls, like text boxes, button controls, etc.

The e-service site contains static and dynamic pages. For the static web pages, the content is written in the page itself as plain html. The content remains the same in the static pages until the author of the web page updates the content. The content of a static web page remains always the same. In fact, static web pages are meant for providing information which does not change often. For example, the content can be always the same, until the provider updates the content, by uploading a new html file to the web server. HTML files are used to create static web pages.

The Dynamic WEB pages get content from database and they are created using "serverside code", when the page is loaded every time. When the URL is typed in the browser, the page is dynamically created from database, based on the id specified in the URL. The quotation information content is stored in the database, not in the file itself. When the page is accessed, the server side code will check what represents the query. php?parameter=value in the URL. Based on the Id, it will retrieve the appropriate information content from the database and dynamically create the web page. One can change the value in the query.php?parameter=value part of the URL to some very large number and try again. If the specified ID does not exist, the page will give an error because the code will fail to get the corresponding information content from the database. This entire e-service site can have several files like index.aspx, tutorial.aspx etc. Dynamic web pages are created using technologies like ASP, ASP.NET, PHP etc. All html files are static pages.

ASP.Netis a very useful and complex tool to develop WEB pages. An html file has the .htm or .html extension, meanwhile the ASP.NET page has the .aspx extension. So, the main difference between an html and an ASP.NET page consist in the file extension. By looking at the file extension, the web server understands what type of file it is, and decides how to process it. An html file and ASP.NET need to be processed differently by the server.

An index.aspx file can be accessed by opening it with a web browser, and entering the URL address of the web site, ex: http://localhost/website/index.aspx. There are also another technologies which can be used to develop dynamic web sites and pages, for example Php.

Whatever technology is used to develop the dynamic web pages, a standard browser should be able to display the page to the visitors. The only thing a browser can understand is "HTML". A browser does not know ASP.NET or PHP so, even if the web site is developed using ASP.NET, still the browser understands only HTML. Whatever technology is used to develop web pages, what is sent from server to browser is just plain HTML. Depending on various conditions, ASP. NET generates different HTML.

The service's database information can be accessed by queries. For example, entering the following URL address in the browser: http://localhost/website/query.php? parameter=value. aspx, will cause the browser to compose a request for this page and send it to the web server in Internet. The web server analyzes the request and it understands that the request is for a page called "query.php?parameter=value.aspx". So, the web server hands over the request to the ASP. NET service, running as part of the web server. If the page is .php file, then there must be a php service running on the web server.

The ASP.NET service loads the page "query. php?parameter=value.aspx". Inside this page is written the code necessary to read the query. php?parameter=value passed as a parameter (parameters are called "Query String"). The code gets the id and then retrieves the corresponding content from the database. Then the code embeds this content into the page and returns the dynamically modified page content to the e-service web server. Web server returns the dynamically generated page to the browser. It can be seen that this dynamically generated page has only HTML in it, even though this HTML came from database. When the browser receives the page, it has only HTML. The web server generates the dynamic content from database or whatever and gives only HTML page content to the browser.

The server side code realizes the server functionality and it can be developed using, for example, C# or VB.NET (or any other .NET compatible code). Server side code is used to retrieve and generate content for the dynamic pages. The code retrieves the content from database or something like that. When a dynamic page is requested, the server side code is executed on the server and a page is generated. Once the generated page comes to the browser, the connection with the server is established. The server side code is written between the special tags: <%, %> Also, the language code used to develop the server application must be specified. For example, the specification <&@Language="C#"%>, which represents the first line, on top of the index.aspx file, means that the C# compiler must be used. More than one language in page, cannot be used. For example, if a page uses C# syntax, then VB.Net syntax cannot be used for some portion of the code in the same page [10]. Any .Net programming language can be used to write server side code in ASP.Net. The following are the .Net languages provided by Microsoft: C#, VB.Net, C++, J#.

The client side code realizes basic operations in the browser when the page is displayed to the user and it cannot be used to access the server or database on the server. The WEB data traffic is very important for such applications. It is achieved through WEB requests and and responses. The client side code initiates the data requests from the server. In simple words, a web request is sent from a client to the server, asking for a specific web page. When the e-service's URL is typed in a web browser or when a hyper link is clicked in any component web page, the client side code actually makes a Request to the server, for the specific URL. It composes a request in the proper format that the server can understand and sends the request to the server using the HTTP protocol.

A request usually includes the URL which is requested and other information like:

- details about the browser that makes the request (version number, browser type etc), is the request is made by browser;
- computer information like screen resolution, IP address, etc.;
- cookies, which is information stored in the client machine by the same web site;
- user registration details from the input field, sent to the server as part of "Request".

To implement all the functionality stated before, an almost complete list of the software development tools can be the following:

- HTTP application server IIS 5.1;
- DNS installed on a server of the local network.
- Microsoft Visual Studio 2008, ASP.NET, VISUAL C#;
- .Net Framework 3.5;
- Adobe Dreamweaver CS3;

Figure 6.

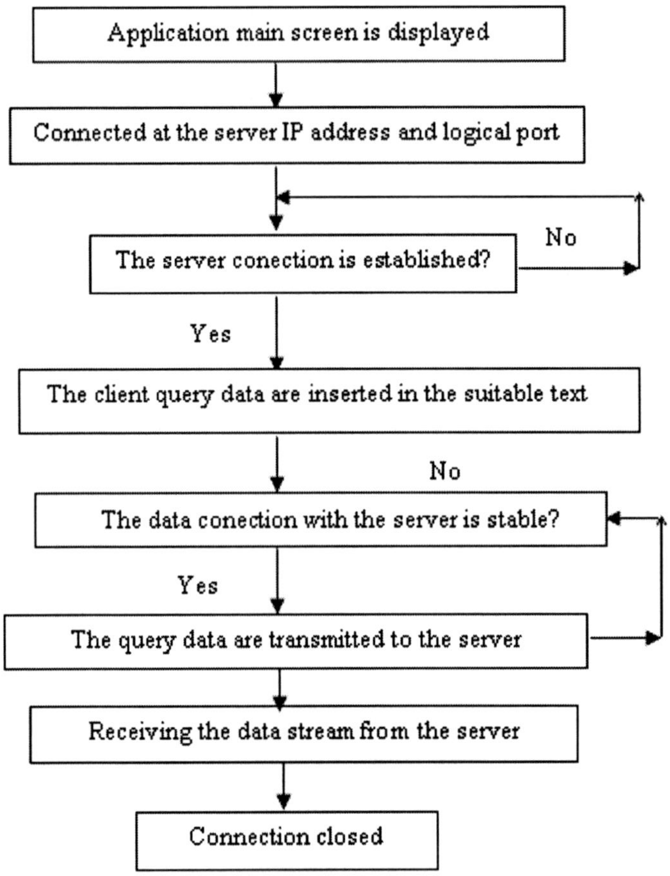

- MySQL server for storing the e-content of the service;
- PhpMyAdmin tool, for developing and administrating the database of the service;
- HTML language, using the Get, Head, Post, Push, Put functions, for data transfer;
- Php language for the project site developing.

The client software application diagram is presented in the (Figure 6). In the application main screen the user specifies the server IP address and logical port, for connection. After the connection is established, the query data is inserted in an input box, then is transmitted to the server. If the connection is stable, the data is transmitted to the server. After receiving the information stream, the client may close the connection. Dedicated client software application, for Smartphones and PDA must be developed [9]. These applications achieve direct database queries, without using a Web browser.

The Client Software Applications Development Tools for Sony Ericsson P990i

Adequate tools can be used to develop client applications, according to the SDK GUI platform and the mobile phone operating system [Harrisson, R]. In case of SE P990i Smartphone, the following tools, installed on a Windows XP OS PC were used:

- the UIQ 3.0 SDK GUI platform, for Symbian v 9.1, containing the Windows XP OS compatible phone emulator, header files and ARM processors libraries;
- the CodeWarrior Professional 3.1 IDE, based on C++ language, for object oriented programming, compatible with UIQ 3.0 SDK, containing tools for application and SIS file development and debugging;
- utility software, for file transfer from PC in the Smartphone's internal or card memory.

The Codewarrior IDE, is based on C++ programming language, for Symbian OS, Palm OS, etc. and is available in different editions: Personal, professional and OEM. It works well on the Intel Pentium and AMD K6 processors, requiring at least 128 MB RAM and 250 MB free memory space on the hard disk. Memory space must also be available for UIQ 3.0 SDK. The applications can be developed on Windows 2000, NT, and XP PC OS. The IDE complies also with the C and Java programming languages, for a large variety of mobile phones: Nokia, Sony Ericsson, Motorola, Siemens, Panasonic, etc.

The CodeWarrior IDE for Symbian OS contains suitable compilers for the phone emulator, as well as for real hardware and processors files. The WINSCW and GCC-E compilers were used for UREL devices.

The Codewarrior IDE Graphical User Interface proviodes the user efficient menus and submenus. The basic menus and interface functionality are shortly described in the following:

- the Project Manager, allows the project resources and files access and handling;
- the Editor, allows the user to create and modify the source code;
- the Search Engine, allows text frames finding and processing in source code files;
- the Source Browser, facilitates the management and visualization of the symbols and variables, declared in the software application;
- the Build System tool converts the source code into an executable file;
- the Debugger is a very useful tool that helps at software error correcting.

The Codewarrior graphic interface allows the user to open a New file, or to import a .MMP file. The program compilation is performed according to the mobile platform and the GUI SDK that is finaly aimed for instalation and launching.

The Symbian project files are called „makemake files" and have allways the .MMP extension. The Importing MMP files command converts a Symbian OS project, created with a suitable SDK, like UIQ for example, in a CodeWarrior project.

For a new Codewarrior project creation, the user has two options: the Symbian Stationary Project Wizard.

The Create from Stationary menu offers all the necessary resources to obtain an executable file, without importing any .mmp file. A Stationary Project represents a template for an efficient application developing. The suitable commands succesion, executed in the IDE GUI is the following:

- File, New, Project Tab, followed by the project type selection;
- specification of the new project name and installation location;

For link editing the CodeWarrior IDE uses source, hearder files and the available software libraries. The information regarding the mobile platforms available for compiling and building the solution is stored in the device.xml file.

The Empty Project option allows the user to create the project file that helps for source code organizing. The Symbian Stationary Wizard option selection offers to the programmer an application development template.

After the project development model selection, the user must select the target mobile platform type.

The project files will be automatically generated, the project window will be opened, containing source files templates and libraries. Importing a .MMP project file is performed by the commands: .MMP Symbian OS File > Import Project from the suitable directory. This will make the Symbian Importer dialog window to appear. The user will select the GUI SDK (UIQ, S60 or S80, etc.) and the directory location of the .MMP file. Codewarrior will create a .mcp file, representing the Symbian OS development frame, including the suitable emulators and debuggers.

In the IDE Preferences Window, the project efective resources handling options can be specified (target and global settings). These can also reffer to the project editing or debugging. The Editor window offers word processing facilities for the project's source files and assistance for the variables and commands syntax. Also browsing for specific text items, code lines, functions and files is an available facility.

The project window interface facilitates the visualization, changing, handling and controling of all the project's files. The File menu offer information about the project resources, allow new files adding, selecting the compilation location and attributes visualization.

The Codewarrior browser interface allows classes, data, variables, function creation and visualisation, including the relations among them. A contexual help sis asisteng these operations. For classes structure vizualisation the Class Hierarchy or Single class hierarchy windows can be used. The Browser Contents window can display information regarding the database stored symbols, in alphabetical order.

Codewarrior IDE programes linking and compliling

The compiler translates the source code into the object code, pointing out the syntax error. For ARM processors executable files, a suitable compiler, like GCC-E must be used, started from the Codewarrior IDE project or from the command window. The link-editor combines the sorce files, the DLL object codes and other associated files, to create the application binary file.

After compiling and editing, the package files creation is necessary, followed by instalation of the deployment files in the mobile phone, under the Symbian operating system (these files have .pkg extension). They are created using the IDE editor and then are integrated in the project. The IDE combines all the applications components and the header file, in a single .sis file, that will be transfered in the Symbian mobile phone, using a suitable tool. If the mobile phone is already connected at the PC, the IDE can realize the „upload".

The integration of the .pkg files in the application project is realized by the following comands:

- in the editing window the commands: Add FileName to Project Menu;
- selecting Project, Add Files;
- localization and selection of the .pkg files, using Select and Open submenus;
- launching Symbian SDK's Connect followed by starting of the mobile phone PC connection driver;
- the .sis file selection and „upload" in the mobile phone;
- instalation of the application on the target Symbian OS mobile phone.

The Codewarrior IDE contains compilers and „debug" utilities, both for the emulator and for the files that are developed for the OEM type hardware. In this case a Symbian OS adequate cross compiler is used.

The Symbian UIQ SDK emulator is a Windows application which emulates on the PC the mobile phone's hardware platform. The application will be developed on the PC and, finally, the file destinated to be installed on the PC is obtained. In the first development phases the emulator has time developing efficiency, becouse the IDE provides data visualization, error corection and application functioning. The emulator reduces the time necessary for application development, testing and instalation of the application on the mobile phone. The emulator processes are almost identical with those of the real phone, but differences appear due to the memory amount of the mobile device. That is why the same code cannot be executed on the emulator and on the phone and the emulator is not usefull in all of the development phases. The files that are strictly dedicated to a hard device, cannot be emulated.

One of the important differences between the mobile phone and an emulator is the information display, becouse it depends of the pixel dimensions. Sometimes, the code can be very well executed on the emulator, but the mobile phone can have dificulties in displaying the whole information. The final applications must be anyway tested directly on the mobile phone.

The emulator is started by the Run or Debug commands, from Codewarrior, or by >epoc at the Command Promt. In fact, EPC is the first name of the Symbian OS, which appears now in the executable files name, like epoc.exe, in the SDK working directory, \epoc32\release\winscw \udeb. There is also a directory where the execution generated files are stored: \epoc32\release \ winscw\urel.

The Client Software Applications Development Tools for QTEK 2020i PDA

In order to develop client applications and Web service interfaces for QTEK 2020i Phone Edition PDA, running Windows for Mobile 2003, the following tools can be used: .NET Compact Framework SDK libraries, MS Visual Studio 2005 IDE, installed on Windows XP Professional. Active Sync 4.0 for PC connection.

EXPERIMENTAL RESULTS

Stock Market Exchange Web Service Access Using Browser

It is useful to test the web service's functionality before consuming it through mobile channels. This allows us to establish that the web service works properly and the extension on wireless channels is possible. The call and response for all the WEB service's methods, using the browser, it is useful to be tested.

Stock Market Exchange Web Service Access Using Windows Mobile and Symbian Client Application

The specific software instalation kits for PDAs and Smartphones, developed for Windows Mobile and Symbian operating systems respectivelly, are stored on the server side, and are directly downloadable in the mobile terminals. To obtain them, the interested users can access the WEB server by browsing. By registration in the database, they will receive a „User name" and a password that will allow them to access the platform site private section, where the client application kits are stored. The mobile applications can be installed in the terminal and used to invoke the web service methods.

The main GUI window of the mobile SE P990i, client application, for stock exchange service access is opened by the commands: Main Menu – Tools – Mobacces, Info Companies, Figure 2 (a) and Figure 2 (b);

- in the Company field, the symbol of the company is introduced, than is clicked Done and Go;
- in the Ready window the connection status is shown: Connecting, Connected, Data re-

Figure 2. (A) and (B)

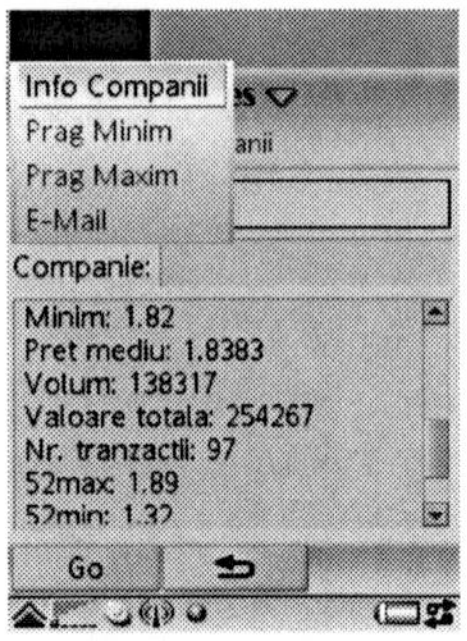

Figure 2(A)

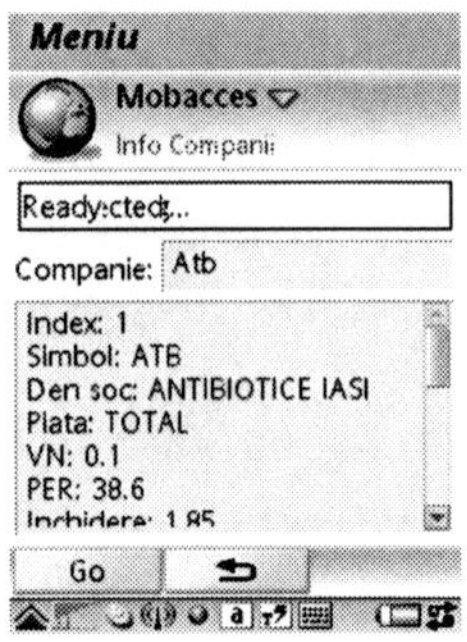

Figure 2(B)

Figure 3.

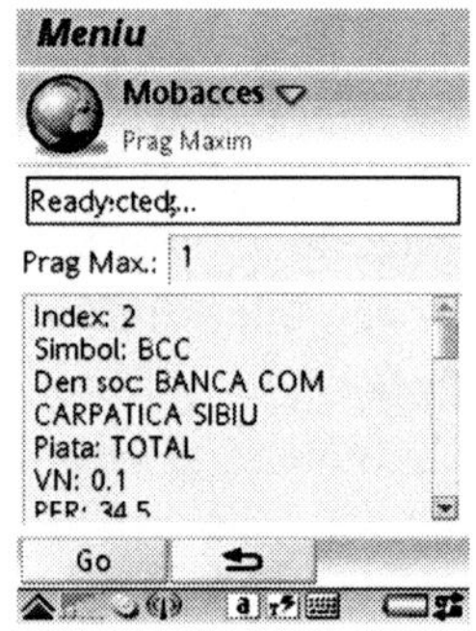

Figure 4.

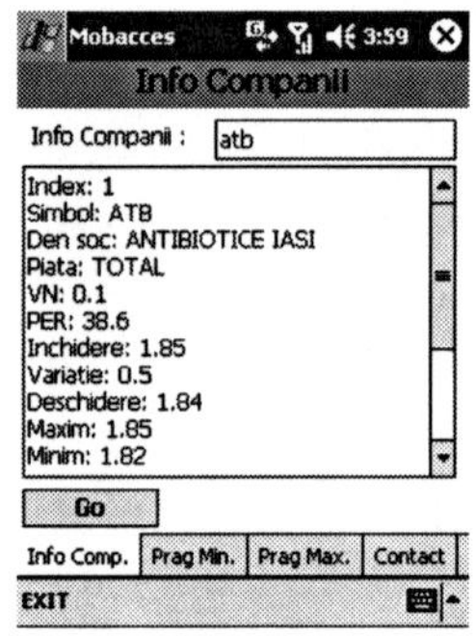

ceived, Successful transaction, then the requested company information is displayed.

The list of companies whose quotation variation is under the maxim threshold "x", or minim threshold "y" is obtained by entering the commands:

- in the main screen, select Menu – Maxim Threshold, or Minimum Threshold ;
- the cursor is placed in Threshold Maxim window, or Threshold Minim window, the virtual keyboard become active and the desired maximum value can be typed, "1" or "0" for example; than press Done, Go;
- in the informational field, the companies that had a quotation variation under, or above the introduced value, are displayed, (Figure 3).

The project database, transactions_summaries (1), stores the listed company quotations, which can be observed by browsing on a PC, at the URL http://localhost/phpmyadmin/index.php. The stock exchange information regarding the company's maxim and minim threshold is available to the **e-service**'s client by next steps:

- open the browser and enter the URL:http://localhost/query3.php?symbol= ATB;
- open the browser and enter http://localhost/ query1.php?above=x; or sub=y;
- open the browser and enter the address http://localhost/query2.php?sub=y.

The same applications should be tested on a PDA terminal [Darie, C.], QTEK 2020i (See Figure 4 and Figure 5). Based on these applications, the user can efficiently decide to sell or buy shares.

Figure 5.

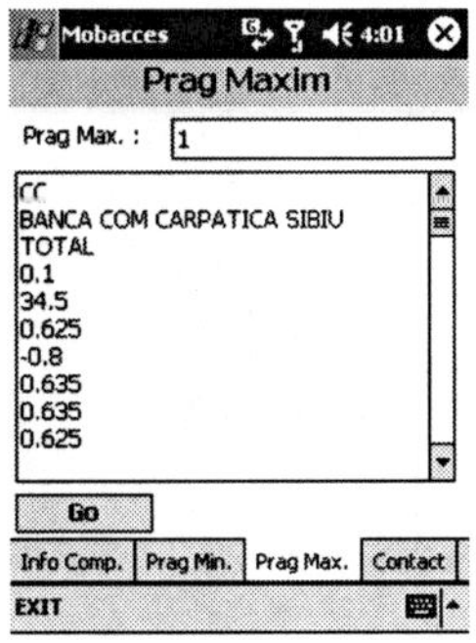

CONCLUSION

A client server system for a stock market transactions e-service was realized and presented. The e-service can be accessed using mobile data terminals like: Smartphones, PDAs, and laptop, on GSM/GPRS, CDMA or WLAN channels. A Web service is implemented, to provide the answers to the client's queries: selected companies stock transactions information, list of companies whose quotation variation is under, or sub, the maxim, or minim threshold, introduced by the user. The stock market information is available to the client by direct and dedicated applications, which is significantly reducing the access time and data traffic cost. The service's site offers to the client executable access files for SE P990i and QTEK 2020i mobile terminals. These samples, can be downloaded on a PC, and then installed on the mobile phone, using ordinary Sync tools.

REFERENCES

Darie, C., & Bucica, M. (2006). WEB services connections . In *PHP5 and MySQL for Electronic Commerce* (pp. 506–534). Bucarest, Romania: Teora.

Darie, C., & Watson, K. (2006). Credit card transactions: creating customer accounts. In *Beginning ASP.Net 2.0 E-Commerce in C#2005: From Novice to Professional* (pp. 593-624). New York: Apress.

Darie, C., & Watson, K. (2009). Creating customer accounts. In *Beginning ASP.Net E-Commerce in C# 2008: From Novice to Professional* (pp. 465-530). New York: Apress.

Delaney, K. (2008). Tracing and profiling . In *Inside Microsoft SQL Server 2005* (pp. 57–103). Redmond, WA: Microsoft Press.

Douglas, B. (2008). Device to device communications . In *Programming Windows Embedded CE 6.0* (4th ed., pp. 469–535). Redmond, WA: Microsoft Press.

Harrison, R., & Shackman, R. (2007). Communications and messaging services. In *Symbian OS C++ for Mobile Phones Vol. 3, Application Development for Symbian OS v9* (pp. 605 649). Upper Saddle River, NJ: John Willey & Sons, Ltd.

Hirsch, F., & Kemp, J. (2006). Introduction to service oriented architecture . In *Mobile WEB Services* (pp. 21–25). Upper Saddle River, NJ: John Willey & Sons, Ltd.doi:10.1002/9780470017982.ch3

Liming, S. D. (2003). Development requirements . In *Windows XP Embedded Advanced* (pp. 9–12). San Clemente, CA: RTC Books.

Sharp, J. (2008). Creating and using a WEB service. In *Visual C# 2008 Step by Step* (pp. 623-645). Redmond, WA: Microsoft Press.

Templeman, J. (2003). The.Net framework class library. In *Microsoft Visual C++.Net Step by Step, Version 2003.* Redmond, WA: Microsoft Press

Chapter 10
Personalized Web Service Provisioning to Mobile Users USING Policy-Based Profile and QoS Management

Elarbi Badidi
United Arab Emirates University, UAE

Larbi Esmahi
Athabasca University, Canada

ABSTRACT

In the last few years, a rising proportion of the workforce is becoming more and more mobile, meaning that organizations must consider this new trend in their corporate and IT strategies. The expectation of employees now is that they can retain access to their corporate services as they move to new locations, using various kinds of handheld devices. This chapter describes our proposed broker-based system for Web services provisioning to mobile users with quality of service (QoS) requirements. It describes a set of brokers collaborating to provide tailored services to mobile users while they move from one site to another in their corporate and partners' networks. Access to QoS-enabled Web services complies with the policies of the user's home site. Policies are a key component of the system as they are involved at different levels: authorization, QoS specification, QoS service monitoring, and service selection.

INTRODUCTION

With the emergence of service oriented computing and the ubiquitous deployment of enterprise applications on the Web to reach a wide base of customers, many organizations have moved their business online. Service oriented computing aims to promote business collaboration and application integration on a global scale. It is increasingly changing the way designers and architects develop software applications. Furthermore, it is changing the way these applications are delivered and used by consumers. It enables organizations to exhibit their main capabilities programmatically over the Internet and a variety of networks, e.g., cable, Universal Mobile Telecommunications System (UMTS), Digital Subscriber Lines (xDSL), Blue-

DOI: 10.4018/978-1-61692-016-6.ch010

tooth, etc., using standard languages and protocols, and implementing self-describing interfaces.

Services are computational elements that can be described, published, and discovered using standard protocols. Providers build their services in a way that is independent of consumers' context. This means that service providers and consumers are loosely coupled. Web services technology is currently the most promising paradigm relying on the concept of service oriented computing. It provides the foundation for developing and executing business processes that are distributed over the Web and accessible via standard interfaces and protocols. By using Internet-based standards, such as the Business Process Execution Language (BPEL), the Simple Object Access Protocol (SOAP), and the Web Services Description Language (WSDL), it becomes possible to orchestrate Web services into business processes.

Another development in the area of service oriented computing is the unprecedented rise in the number of mobile workers using a variety of devices including laptops and handheld devices, such as PDAs and SmartPhones, to consume online services. Modern mobile devices are often fully equipped with broad capabilities. Most of these devices support several wireless communication options including Wi-Fi, Bluetooth, General Packet Radio Service (GPRS), and Enhanced Data GSM Environment (EDGE). They also come with advanced multimedia capabilities including streaming, and the ability to play several audio and video formats. These devices present now browsing capabilities that go beyond the simple Wireless Application Protocol (WAP), to support HTML-based Web sites.

As a result of this proliferation of mobile devices, wireless enterprise applications, i.e., messaging and voice services, are increasingly built and deployed using Web services technology. Therefore, using the service oriented computing paradigm in mobile environments considerably enlarges the range of accessible business applications and enables delivering integrated services across wireless networks. The current drive towards using mobile devices is due to several factors. First, there are more wireless networks, services, and devices than ever before. Second, consumers are demanding better mobile experiences than ever before. Third, people want 'anytime, anywhere' connections more than ever before. Mobile workers are increasingly requiring services tailored to their needs as they move from one site to another in their corporate and partners' networks. They are also requiring retaining access to their corporate services as they move to new locations.

In this chapter, we describe our broker-based framework, which allows mobile users to use home services as they move to new locations in their corporate or partners' networks. These networks are divided into several domains; and each domain has a broker, which is the key component for services' selection and delivery to mobile users. Our framework takes advantage of the World Wide Web Consortium (W3C) and the Open Mobile Alliance (OMA) standards for describing device capabilities (hardware, software, and characteristics of supported networks). Such standards allow providers to tailor service provisioning to mobile devices by adapting content presentation to their capabilities.

MOTIVATION AND RELATED WORK

Our motivation in this work is the desire to support mobile users with services tailored to their needs and to their home profiles as they move from one site to another in their corporate or partners' networks. To attain this goal, three main aspects need to be considered. First, we need to identify the mobile worker's device in use at any particular time and its capabilities. Second, we need to identify the mobile user preferences and functional and non-functional service requirements, such as the minimum level of QoS he/she is willing to accept. Third, a close cooperation between home and visited locations needs to be established to negotiate and agree on issues related to the user profile.

Our framework is relying on a QoS broker at each site to negotiate the mobile user profile and the level of service to be delivered to the mobile user. Brokers have been extensively used in multimedia systems and in mobile computing systems to deal essentially with the issue of QoS management. In the Service Oriented Architecture, brokers are used to mediate between service providers, service consumers, and partners. Next section describes some research works in which brokers had been previously used, as well as the issue of consuming services on mobile devices.

Several research works have studied the issue of service delivery to mobile users. Ganna et al. (Ganna, 2003) proposed a policy-based approach for service provisioning and a mobile agent-based approach for users' management. Their architecture is based on the notion of a domain that represents an administrative authority with its own behavior, policies, and users. Policies govern the behavior of agents and decide on the actions to take when a mobile foreign user connects into the domain. QoS and security levels are negotiated when a mobile user requests a service from the domain. Harroud et al. (Harroud, 2003) described an agent-based service provisioning system for mobile users. Their system comprises a set of cooperative agents, distributed over different sites, that work together to provide personalized services to mobile users. Access to services by mobile users is governed by their home policies as well as by their current location policies. An Adaptive Service Presentation agent was used to adapt the service presentation to the capabilities of the users' mobile devices. Toivonen et al. (Toivonen, 2004; Riva, 2007) described a two-tier model for providing personalized services to mobile users. The model presupposes that the system is aware of the users' profiles and contexts as well as available services and can match them with each other. Besides, it enables sharing information about services among users to harness user-to-user communication for the purpose of service provision. Ballon et al. (Ballon, 2008) described and analyzed four potential business models for emerging mobile service platforms. A business model is a framework that describes how a company or a group of companies intend to create strategic value with a service. In the context of mobile service platforms, the following roles have been identified: 1) Profile/Identity management, 2) Service provisioning/Service brokerage, 3) Charging and billing, and 4) Service creation environment.

These works share some common goals with our proposed work. However, they were done in other contexts other done the service oriented environment, which currently represents the most-predominant environment for service delivery. Our work takes advantage of the various standards that have been developed in the last few years for both Web services and mobile computing especially the standards for describing the capabilities of mobile devices.

BACKGROUND

QoS Brokers in Multimedia Systems and Mobile Computing

QoS Brokers have been proposed in several research works in mobile computing as well as in distributed systems. Stattenberger et al. (Stattenberger, 2001) proposed a signaling protocol to allow mobile users to negotiate QoS for a flow with a bandwidth broker. This protocol may also be used to negotiate QoS for traffic aggregates between two bandwidth brokers. The mobile user may roam between several domains, each managed by a different bandwidth broker. Marques et al. (Marques, 2002) described an end-to-end QoS architecture with user mobility for telecommunication systems beyond 3rd generation. The network is divided into several domains, and each domain has a QoS broker, which is the key component for resource management and resource allocation to customers. A broker may negotiate with its peers in other domains the QoS to be provided to a user. There are several limits and constraints in the mobile environment that poses challenges for QoS support, including the effect of link quality on QoS, the effect of movement on QoS, and the limitations on Portable devices (Chalmers, 1999).

QoS Brokers in Web Services Environments

QoS brokers had also been proposed in many research works in QoS management for Web services. Yeom et al. (Yeom, 2005) designed and implemented a Web Service QoS broker system, which monitors QoS, in terms of availability, performance, and reliability, of Web services. Tao et al. (Tao, 2005) proposed a broker-based framework for the composition of QoS-aware Web services with QoS-constraints. The broker's components implement dynamic service composition, service selection and adaptation. Zuquim et al. (Zuquim, 2006) described a Web service architecture providing QoS management using QoS brokers. Interaction with the Universal Description Discovery and Integration (UDDI) is performed through the brokers, which publish QoS information obtained from providers in the UDDI and assist customers select services according to their functional and QoS requirements. In (D'Mello, 2008; Gang, 2009), a broker-based architecture had been proposed to deal with the issue of dynamic Web services selection with QoS-constraints.

Services on Mobile Devices

Several service providers currently offer services that allow information to be pushed to a mobile device, or offered via a limited Web-browser interface. With the service oriented architecture, it is becoming possible to offer services that fully use the power of the mobile device. Nevertheless, mobile services access is still suffering today from interoperability and usability problems. This is to some extent attributable to the small physical size of the screens of mobile devices. It is also due to the incompatibility of several mobile devices with not only the structure of much of the information conveyed to mobile devices, but also with computer operating systems.

The W3C Mobile Web Initiative (MWI) is a new initiative, established by the W3C, to develop best practices and technologies for creating mobile-friendly content and applications. The goal of the initiative is to enable access to the Web from mobile devices and to make it more reliable and accessible. This typically requires the adaptation of Web content based on the device capabilities. The W3C has published guidelines (Best Practices, W3C mobileOK checker service) for mobile content (W3C, 2008). The MWI Device Description Working Group is actively tackling the problem of device diversity by setting up a repository of device descriptions (W3C Mobile Web Initiative, 2005). Authors of Web content may use the repository to adapt their Web content to best suit the requesting device.

The OMA specification defines the User Agent Profile (UAProf) to describe capability and preference information of wireless mobile devices (Open Mobile Alliance, 2001). This information is to be used mainly by content providers to generate content in a suitable format for the device. It is based on the generic framework W3C CC/PP (Composite Capabilities/ Preference Profiles) (W3C, 2007). CC/PP defines a schema for the description of a device's profile, which is composed of components that describe characteristics of hardware, software, network, and so on. A CC/PP profile can be used to adapt Web contents to a specific device.

A UAProf file describes the capabilities of a mobile device, including Vendor, Model, Screen size, Multimedia Capabilities, Character Set support, and more. It consists of seven components, which are *Hardware Platform*, *Software*

Platform, *Network Characteristics*, *Browser UA*, *WAP Characteristics*, *Push Characteristics*, and *MMsCharacteristics*. A server called the Profile Repository stores user agent profiles. Frequently, mobile device manufacturers manage their profile repositories. For instance, Nokia manages its own profile repository in which it maintains user agent profiles describing the capabilities of Nokia smartphones. The x-wap profile header of requests sent from a given mobile device contains the URL that points to the user agent profile of that device. For example, the the x-wap-profile header created by a Nokia N80 cell phone has the following value:

http://nds.nokia.com/uaprof/NN80-1r100.xml

SERVICE PROVISIONING FRAMEWORK

Service Provisioning Requirements

To provide mobile workers with tailored services while they move from one location to another in their corporate networks or their partners' networks, several issues need to be addressed.

1. Authentication and authorization control to identify the user and his/her authorized services at the home site.
2. Identification of the mobile user device so that the service presentation is tailored to the capabilities of the device.
3. Exchange of the user profile between home site and visited sites to identify the user preferences, and to provide him/her with access to local services using these preferences.
4. QoS monitoring and management to provide the user with his/her required and authorized QoS.
5. Design and implementation of Web services so that that they may be consumed on mobile devices to respond to the needs of organizations.

To address these issues, our proposed framework is relying on a brokerage service, which mediates, on one hand, between the mobile user home site and the visited site, and, on the other hand, between the mobile user and a local Web service at the visited site. Normal operations of a company may be implemented as Web services so that they may be consumed by its customers using different platforms and operating systems. Brokers cooperate and communicate with each other. They also communicate with mobile users and services. A key component of the broker is the *Policy Manager*, which is responsible for maintaining authorization policies, and policies for monitoring services and their QoS. A policy-based management and control approach can contribute to addressing these issues. Indeed, it had been previously used to allocate resources, primarily network bandwidth, QoS, and security, according to defined business policies. The use of policies greatly reduces the system's complexity, while still permitting the user's activities to be efficiently controlled.

Policy-Based Management

Policy-based management had been mainly used for network management. A policy is a set of conditions imposed on a subject that permits or prohibits actions. These conditions may apply to the subject, the target, or the state of the system. A policy may be the trigger that allows actions to be performed when conditions are appropriate.

The IETF Policy Framework Working Group has developed a policy management architecture, which is considered as one of the best approaches for policy management on the Internet (IETF Network Working Group, 1999). The framework components are: *Policy Management Service*, *Dedicated Policy Repository,PDP (Policy Decision Point)*, *PEP (Policy Enforcement Point)*,

Figure 1. Framework components

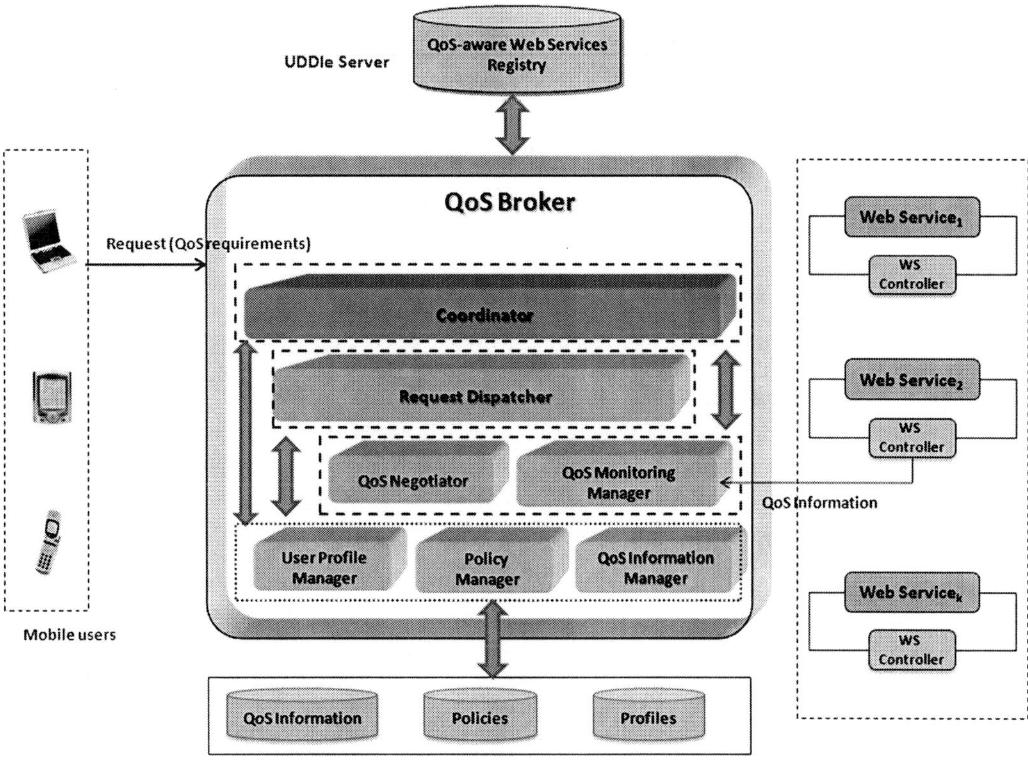

and *LPDP (Local Policy Decision Point)*. Policy-based management may play a crucial role in the management of Web services in general and management of their QoS in particular. Web services are, however, different from the network context as the intrinsic components are different from one context to the other. Management of policies typically requires a Policy Manager and a Policy Repository.

Having policies in Web services environments has been recognized since the specification of the first standards for Web services. The WS-Policy specification was proposed later by leading software companies to define the means for building policy expressions. These expressions allow describing the requirements for accessing a Web service (Vedamuthu, 2007). In this policy-based model for Web services, particular requirements or capabilities of a policy subject are declared using XML policy assertion elements. Each assertion describes an atomic aspect of service requirements (e.g. authentication scheme, authorization scheme, QoS characteristics, etc.). A policy expression can include one or more policy assertions, which are assembled in Policy alternatives using logical policy operators. This policy expression may be associated with a Web service resource, like a service or endpoint, using mechanisms defined in WS-PolicyAttachment (W3C, 2006).

Framework Components

Figure 1 depicts the main components of the framework at a given site. These components cooperate to deliver personalized services to mobile users with various devices across interacting sites. They are under the control of the *Coordinator* component and allow carrying out several management operations: Admission control, QoS negotiation, QoS-based service selection, QoS monitoring,

Figure 2. Example of a QoS policy

```
<wsp:Policy>
        xmlns:wsp= "schemas.xmlsoap.org/ws/2004/09/policy"
        xmlns:qosp-"garnize:8080/schema/qospolicy"
                <wsp:ExactlyOne>
                        <wsp:All>
                                <qosp:ResponseTime
                                        xmlns:qosp="garnize:8080/schema/qospolicy"
                                        operation="get"
                                        specification="uddi:uddi.org:qos:attribute:responsetime">45
                                </qosp:responseTime>...
                        </wsp:All>
                </wsp:ExactlyOne>
</wsp:Policy>
```

User profile management, and policies management. The back-end databases maintain information about policies, user profiles and preferences, and dynamic QoS information.

QoS Specification

Specification of QoS that providers can deliver may be performed by incorporating QoS parameters, such as response time, throughput and cost, into the WSDL service description. This is the QoS model supported by the UDDIe (Shaikh Ali, 2003). Recent works (Zuquim, 2006; Ganna, 2003) have proposed extensions to the Web services Policy Framework (WS-Policy) to represent QoS policies of Web services. WS_Policy does not describe the mechanisms by which policies are discovered or attached to a Web service. The WS_PolicyAttachment specification (W3C, 2006) describes the mechanisms for associating policy with WSDL artifacts and UDDI elements. Figure 2 depicts an example of a QoS policy defined with a policy assertion representing the response time supported by a Web service.

In our framework, the policies repository stores QoS policies together with other policies concerning authentication, authorization, user profile and preferences management, and mobile devices profile management.

Admission Control and QoS-based Service Selection

The *Request Dispatcher* is in charge of the admission control of incoming requests. It is responsible for determining whether incoming requests are allowed to use the requested services. This means that Web services access is denied to requests from users who did not negotiate the level of QoS with the selected Web services providers.

Moreover, the *Request Dispatcher* is in charge of implementing diverse policies for selecting appropriate Web services to deliver user required QoS. Various policies for service selection have been extensively described in the literature. Random and round-robin are examples of simple static selection policies. Complex selection policies, however, consider the current state of servers, such as availability and load, in their selection decision. The Request Dispatcher performs matchmaking between the required QoS and the QoS that is stored in the UDDIe and/or in the policies repository.

QoS Negotiation

The *QoS Negotiator* carries out QoS negotiation to reach a Service Level Agreement (SLA) between the selected service provider and the user. The SLA specifies the service to be provided, the guaranteed

Figure 3. Web service controller

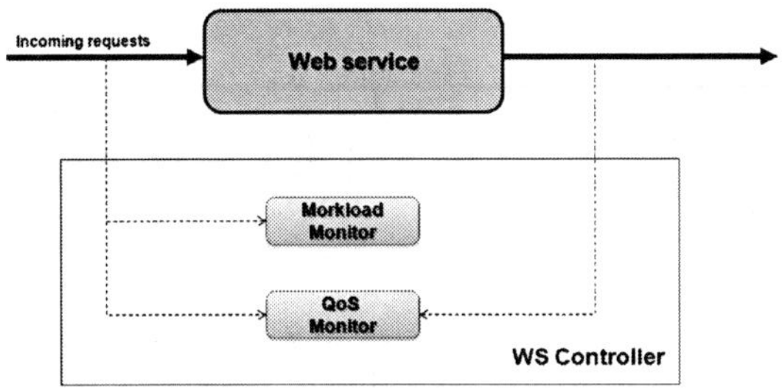

QoS, the cost of the service, and the actions to take when a violation of the agreed QoS is detected. Section 5 details the SLA negotiation protocol.

QoS Monitoring

The QoS Monitoring Manager and the Web Service Controller, as illustrated in Figure 3, are in charge of monitoring the QoS of Web services. They continually observe the level of QoS level rendered to clients. The service contract specifies the QoS parameters, such as response time and availability, which need to be observed through periodic measurements at the server side and/or at the client side. QoS violation occurs when measured values of a QoS parameter do not meet the requirements of the contracted QoS. Both the client and the provider are notified of the occurrence of any QoS violation. Moreover, details about QoS violations are stored in the broker QoS Information Base and may be used to perform eventual dynamic QoS adaptation. Violation details include information on the violation type, name of violated QoS parameters, period during which the violation occurred, and cause of the violation.

Profile Management

The *Profile Manager* at a given site is responsible for managing users' profiles at that site. A user profile mainly describes the user preferences in terms of personalized services, current location, and required QoS. When a mobile user moves to

Figure 4. Policy Manager components

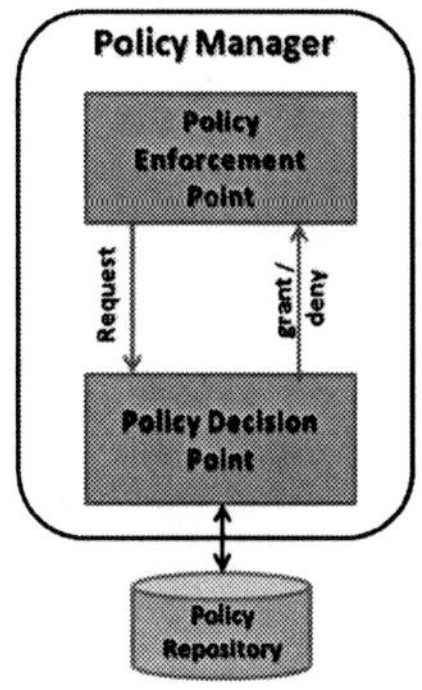

a visited site, the *Profile Managers* at home and visited sites start negotiating the user profile along with his/her authorized services at the visited site prior to service provision. Section 5 describes the profile negotiation protocol.

Policies Management

The *Policy Manager* is responsible for maintaining authorization policies, and polices for monitoring services and quality of service. It receives access control requests, processes them against a set of policies, which describe how users can use services, and returns access control responses. Figure 4 depicts the architecture of the *Policy Manager*. The *Policy Decision Point* (PDP) is the component that grants or denies access to services. It encompasses a rule engine that determines the policies to apply when a user has issued a request for service. When a user attempts to access a service, with QoS requirements, the *Policy Enforcement Point* (PEP) component sends a message to the PDP asking whether to accept or not the user request. It then replies with approval or denial of access to that service depending on the service rules and the request parameters.

The Policy Manager allocates services by taking into account the mobile user privileges, the availability of services, and any other factors that the administrator may specify when composing the policy. It controls the extent to which a user

Figure 5. Inter-site profile negotiation

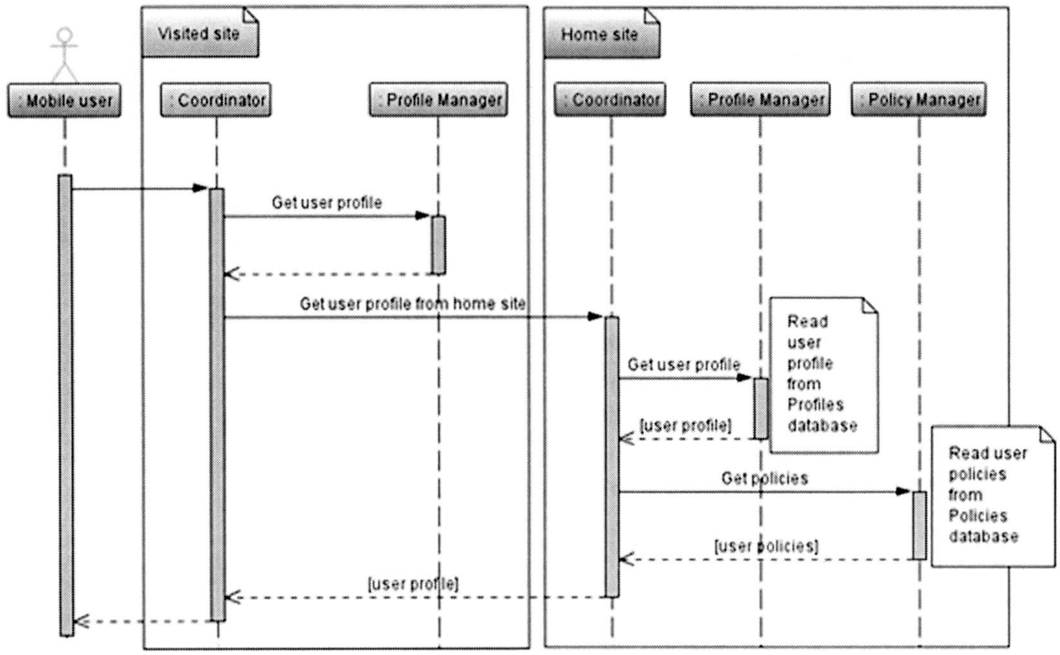

(eventually a mobile user) can use the service (e.g. access to limited functions or access to the whole functions of the service). A Policy Manager is particularly crucial for protecting the mobile user privacy.

INTER-SITE NEGOTIATION

The QoS Broker can initiate and control interactions with Web services, within its domain of control, and with service requestors by exchanging information messages using the SOAP protocol. Reliable exchange of messages may be implemented using WS-ReliableMessaging specification (OASIS, 2007).

Profile Negotiation

Figure 5 depicts the interactions between the brokers, at both the visited site and the home site of a mobile user, to create a user's profile at the visited site.

1. The mobile user submits a request, which includes the CC/PP of the mobile device in use.
2. After processing the user's authentication on an authorized device, the *Coordinator* at the visited site requests the user profile from its *User Profile Manager*. If the user profile had been previously stored in its profile repository, the *Coordinator* starts negotiating the terms of service with the mobile user as described in the next section. Otherwise, the following steps are accomplished.
3. The *Coordinator* sends a request to its peer in the *home site* of the mobile user in order to get the user profile. This is achieved through the following steps.
4. The *Coordinator* at the home site of the mobile user forwards, then, the user profile request to its *User Profile Manager*.
5. The home *User Profile Manager* reads the mobile user profile from the profiles database.

Figure 6. SLA negotiation protocol

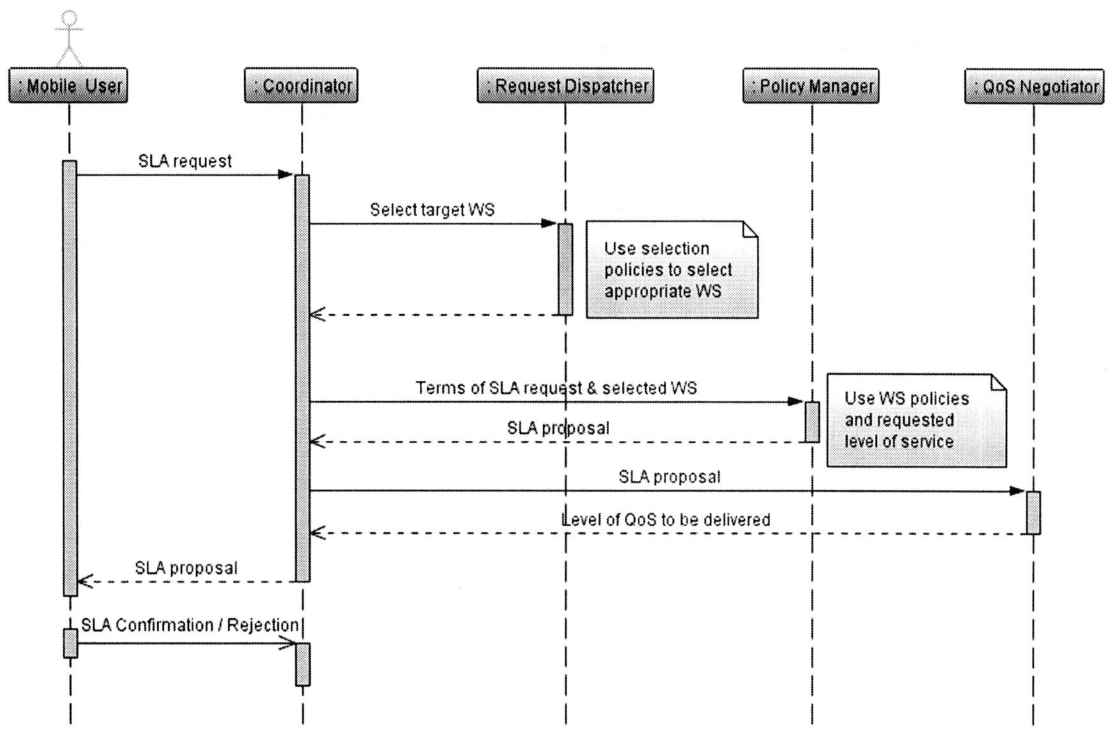

6. The home *User Profile Manager* requests from the home *Policy Manager* the policies regarding the user, such as authorization policies to services available at other sites to which the user may have access and the type of access.
7. The home *Policy Manager* reads the policies regarding the mobile user from the policies database.
8. The home *User Profile Manager* returns the requested profile of the mobile user to its *Coordinator*.
9. The home *Coordinator* returns the user profile to its peer at the visited site. After getting the final profile of the user, the *Coordinator* at the visited site starts negotiating the terms of the SLA as described in the next section.

Policy-Driven SLA Negotiation Process

Once the user profile has been determined, the mobile user and the QoS broker at the visited site start negotiating the terms of the SLA according to the following protocol, which is illustrated by Figure 6:

1. The mobile user formulates a SLA request, which details the service provisioning request, and sends it to the *Coordinator* component at the visited site.
2. The *Coordinator* may decide whether the SLA proposal can be processed or not. This decision relies on the user profile that has been obtained in the previous process. If, for instance, the requested service is not among

the services that the user can access, then the *Coordinator* rejects the user request.

3. The *Coordinator* requests, then, the selection of a target Web service from the *Request Dispatcher*.
4. Upon receiving the reference of the selected Web service, the *Coordinator* sends that reference and the SLA proposal to the *Policy Manager* to decide whether this selected Web service can handle or not the mobile user request, on the basis of the requested level of service and the Web service policies.
5. The *Coordinator* and the mobile user start negotiating the specific terms of service provisioning, relying on the policies of the selected Web service and the SLA requirements. Then, the *Coordinator* requests from the *QoS Negotiator* to determine the final profile of the user by negotiating the level of QoS to be delivered.
6. Proposals are returned to the mobile user, who can accept or reject offers – rejections typically trigger renegotiation.

CONCLUSION AND FUTURE WORK

In this chapter, we have presented a cooperative broker-based system for service provisioning to mobile users while they move from one location to another in their corporate and partners' networks. Access to QoS-enabled Web services is obtained according to the users' home policies. Policies are a key component of the system as they are used at different levels: authorization, QoS specification, QoS service monitoring, and service selection. The components of QoS brokers at the visited site and the home site are involved in determining the mobile user profile and in negotiating a final SLA. This final SLA details the terms of service at the visited site according to several policies: Web service policies, selection policies, and QoS policies.

A prototype of our proposed framework is under development. The implementation platform includes: NetBeans 6.8, the UDDIe registry with MySQL, and Apache Neethi, which provides a general framework for developers to use WS-Policy. As a future work, we intend to test the prototype using real-life services and policies, and extend our proposed architecture with security policies related to SOA using standards such as WS_Security and WS_Policy.

REFERENCES

W3C. (2006). *Web services policy attachment*. Retrieved from http://www.w3.org/Submission/WS-PolicyAttachment

W3C. (2007). *Composite Capability/Preference Profiles (CC/PP): Structure and vocabularies 2.0*. W3C Working Draft 30 April 2007. Retrieved from http://www.w3.org/TR/2007/WD-CCPP-struct-vocab2-20070430/

W3C. (2008). *W3C mobileOK Checker [Beta]*. Retrieved from http://validator.w3.org/mobile/

W3C Mobile Web Initiative. (2005). *MWI device description working group*. Retrieved from http://www.w3.org/2005/MWI/DDWG/

Ballon, P., & Walravens, N. (2008). Competing Platform Models for Mobile Service Delivery: The Importance of Gatekeeper Roles. In *Proceedings of the 7th International Conference on Mobile Business (ICMB '08)*, (pp. 102 – 111).

Chalmers, D., & Sloman, M. (1999). A survey of quality of service in mobile computing environments. *IEEE Communications Surveys & Tutorials, 2*(2).

D'Mello, D. A., Ananthanarayana, V. S., & Santhi, T. (2008). A QoS Broker Based Architecture for Dynamic Web Service Selection. In *Proceedings of the Second Asia International Conference on Modeling & Simulation (AICMS 08)*, (pp. 101 – 106).

Gang, Y., Chanle, W., Jun, Y., & Shi, C. (2009). A QoS-Aware Model for Web Services Discovery. In *Proceedings of the First International Workshop on Education Technology and Computer Science (ETCS '09)* (Vol. 3, pp. 740–744).

Ganna, M., & Horlait, E. (2003). Policy-based service provisioning and users management using mobile agents . In Horlait, E., Magedanz, T., & Glitho, R. H. (Eds.), *Lecture Notes in Computer Science* (*Vol. 2881*, pp. 53–66). Berlin: Springer.

Harroud, H., & Karmouch, A. M. (2003). A Policy-driven personalized multimedia services for mobile users. *IEEE Transactions on Mobile Computing*, *2*(1), 16–24. doi:10.1109/TMC.2003.1195148

IETF Network Working Group. (1999). *Policy framework architecture*. Retrieved September 2008, from http://tools.ietf.org/html/draft-ietf-policy-arch-00

Marques, V., et al. (2002). An architecture supporting end-to-end QoS with user mobility for systems beyond 3rd generation. In *Proceedings of IST Mobile and Wireless Telecommunications Summit 2002*.

OASIS. (2007). *Web services reliable messaging (WS-1 ReliableMessaging) Version 1.1. OASIS Standard*. Retrieved March 2009, from http://docs.oasis-open.org/ws-rx/wsrm/200702/wsrm-1.1-spec-os-01.pdf

Open Mobile Alliance. (2001). *WAG UAProf, version 20-Oct-2001*. Retrieved from http://www.openmobilealliance.org/tech/affiliates/wap/wap-248-uaprof-20011020-a.pdf

Riva, O., & Toivonen, S. (2007). The DYNAMOS approach to support context-aware service provisioning in mobile environments. *Journal of Systems and Software*, *80*(12), 1956–1972. doi:10.1016/j.jss.2007.03.009

Shaikh Ali, A., Rana, O. F., Al-Ali, R., & Walker, D. W. (2003). UDDIe: an extended Registry for Web services. In Proceedings of *The IEEE Symposium on Applications and the Internet Workshops, (SAINT 2003)*, pp. 85-89.

Stattenberger, G., & Braun, T. (2001). QoS provisioning for mobile IP users . In Afifi, H., & Zeghlache, D. (Eds.), *Applications and Services in Wireless Networks*. New York: Hermes Science Publications.

Tao, Y., & Lin, K. J. (2005). A broker-based framework for QoS-aware Web service composition. In *Proceedings of The 2005 IEEE International Conference on e-Technology, e-Commerce and e-Service (EEE'05)* (pp. 22-29).

Toivonen, S. (2004). Hybrid Service Provision Model for Mobile Users: Prospects for the DYNAMOS Project. In Hyvönen, E., Kauppinen, T., Salminen, M., Viljanen, K., and Ala-Siuru, P. (Eds.): Proceedings of the *Web Intelligence Symposium of the Finnish Artificial Intelligence Conference (STeP 2004)*, (pp. 183-192).

Vedamuthu, A. S., et al. (2007). *Web services policy 1.5 – framework*. W3C Recommendation 04 September 2007. Retrieved February 2009, from http://www.w3.org/TR/ws-policy/.

Yeom, G., & Min, D. (2005). Design and implementation of Web services QoS broker. In *Proceedings of The International Conference on Next Generation Web Services Practices (NWeSP 2005)* (pp. 454- 455).

Zuquim, D., Guimares, G., & Felgar de Toledo, M. B. (2006). A Web service architecture providing QoS management. In *Proceedings of The Fourth Latin American Web Congress (LA-WEB '06)* (pp. 189-198).

Section 4
Collaborative Systems

Chapter 11
Wiki-Dic 2.0:
An E-Voting Approach to Exploit User-Generated Content

Tryfon L. Theodorou
University of Macedonia, Greece

George E. Violettas
University of Macedonia, Greece

Christos K. Georgiadis
University of Macedonia, Greece

ABSTRACT

We may define e-voting as the process of evaluating an article or ranking a translation of a specific scientific term in a relevant web site. This all process of participation and interaction is one of the Web 2.0 definitions, the collaborative knowledge. On-line dictionaries have to consider this factor in order to succeed. They have to be interactive and they have to attract and support the users' participation and contribution. In the proposed e-dictionary, namely "Wiki-Dic", some experts begin a dictionary, they start filling it with words and translations, and all users are allowed not only to look for the translation, but also to vote for it. The most voted translations go to the top. In addition, appropriate security countermeasures are used to deal efficiently with the "one vote per person" problem and to avoid malicious software. Furthermore, an intelligent algorithm that is giving weights to the voters is implemented. In this way, the weights are computed automatically from our application, based on quantitative and qualitative information as well.

INTRODUCTION

Web 2.0 is basically the transition of a web site from an isolated information silo to interlinked platforms. According to the user, those platforms look and feel like locally available software. Moreover, in Web 2.0 people can easily generate and distribute content (Wikipedia, 2008).

Web 2.0 is already heavily using e-voting. Indeed the implementations of e-voting are many nowadays, and they can vary from simple local plebiscites (asking users to vote for expressing their opinions on certain issues, e.g. for the location of the new polluting Power Factory), to the elec-

DOI: 10.4018/978-1-61692-016-6.ch011

tion of the president of the United States. Internet voting goes beyond the classical voting models having the ability to dynamically present in real time the aggregated ranking (Tennenholtz, 2004).

We can easily extend the definition of e-voting to the participation of the users of a web site or portal, on just choosing the most preferable translation of a word, or even choosing the candidate they prefer as local representative in city council or elsewhere.

One of the major problems faced by various dictionary producers is the factor of time change. By the time a dictionary is finished it is almost outdated. New things, new definitions have arisen, plus some of the old ones do not exist (or are not accurate) any more. The dictionary has to be revised, re-print, publish the errata etc. Another issue is that such a work is subjective to the author (field of expertise, community subjective etc). All these issues require an adequate solution: the dictionary may be published on-line and the users-readers should be given the ability to place new words/translations and to vote for every translation they see. Thus, the more ballots one particular translation gets, the more rises to the scale of the available translations for this specific term-word. Users can simply use (read) the translation on the top of the list (obviously the most popular one), or they can vote for one of the less accepted ("lower") ones.

The basic idea is this: a dynamic web page is launched and the administrators provide the basic terms. As users visit the page, they add new definitions or new words for translation. Other users add a translation, or vote for an existing one. The only thing the administrators have to do is to make sure that the page runs smoothly. No irrelevant suggestions (on purpose), no sexual discrimination, use of proper language etc. As the dictionary grows, the web page attracts more users who add more definitions, and so on.

E-VOTING PERSPECTIVES

E-voting is under study of the Council of Europe (Remmert, 2004). Application types (categories), motives/advantages, and requirements may provide three major perspectives for analyzing critical e-voting issues.

E-Voting process may fall in one of the following four categories (Mitrou, Gritzalis, & Katsikas, 2002):

a. public elections and/or referenda at state and/or local level (with binding effects),
b. internal elections and similar decision procedures,
c. advisory polls for decision-making and advisory referenda, and
d. internet polls.

As declared in the 2004 Council of Europe recommendation for electronic voting, the most important motives for implementing e-voting are (CoE, 2004):

1. enabling mobility of the voters,
2. facilitating the participation in elections from abroad,
3. raising voter turnout by offering additional channels,
4. widening access for citizens with disabilities,
5. reducing cost,
6. delivering voting results reliably and more quickly.

The first four are obviously helping and serving the voters, while the last two are significantly reducing the cost and the labor needed to perform any kind of an election.

Finally, it must be noticed that the elimination of direct physical intervention entails a careful management of the implications of virtual par-

Table 1. e-Voting Requirements

S/N	Constitutional requirements	Generic (first-level) requirements list
1	General	1.1 Institutionally equivalent to traditional 1.2 Eligibility (registration and identification)
2	Free	2.1 Uncoercibility 2.2 No propaganda in the e-voting site 2.3 Non-valid voting capability
3	Equal	3.1 Equality of candidates 3.2 Equality of voters 3.3 One voter – one vote
4	Secret	4.1 Secrecy 4.2 Balance security vs. transparency
5	Direct	5.1 Not monitored ballot recording and counting
6	Democratic	6.1 Trust and transparency 6.2 Verifiability and accountability 6.3 Reliability and security 6.4 Simplicity

ticipation (Anane, Freeland, & Theodoropoulos, 2007). Depending on the importance of the specific e-vote, a number of questions and issues arise. The most important (CoE, 2004) are demonstrated in the following (Table 1).

It is widely-accepted that e-voting has spread throughout the world without sufficient attention to security, transparency, or reliability. E.g., current e-voting systems use proprietary code and vendors have often asserted the confidentiality of this code when independent reviews of certified systems are what transparency requests (Bishop & Wagner, 2007). Many efforts indeed still share the criticism by the public in regard to the lack of transparency of the application itself. Oostveen and van den Besselaar (2005) have shown that trust in the e-voting process is not dependent on the actual level of security but on the user's belief how secure the system is. This belief is largely dependent on the transparency of a system and thus the main challenge for electronic voting is actually the lack of transparency. A remarkable attempt towards a detailed catalog of checkable requirements for e-voting, and measures for evaluation against the requirements is recently released (Volkamer & McGaley, 2007).

E-POLL, USER-GENERATED CONTENT AND WIKI APPLICATIONS

E-Voting potentials do find practical implementations at Web 2.0. This brand new Web requires the participation of users and their interaction. Those capabilities are giving developers the ability to build up new applications or improve the existing ones. Following this trend, the "Wiki-Dic" application was developed, bringing all this new era, to the ordinary dictionary applications. The application may be categorized as a hybrid e-voting type: a combination of an Internet poll and of an advisory referendum for decision-making.

In fact, the application developed uses e-poll functionality to support and enhance user-generated content contributions. It is a "wiki" application, whereas the term "wiki" is recently used to define the type of Web applications and sites that allows site visitors to easily add, remove, edit and change the site's content. The most well-liked of "wiki" sites is Wikipedia, which is the most popular education-reference Web site in the UK (according to Hitwise statistics, May 2006). Collaborative content and knowledge sharing models receive increasing awareness in both the research and the business communities (Nov, 2007), although Wikis are not (yet) adequate for a professional environment, and several things have to be changed to have companies adapt the power of wiki-based knowledge sharing too (Spek, 2008).

The purpose of developing this case study was to have a better view on how to apply e-poll mechanisms to old fashioned applications, exploring the outcome. The strength of "Wiki-Dic" is that it is using e-voting functionality and as such it inherits the advantages and the disadvantages of these systems. In detail, the e-voting advantages of cost reduction, speed and reliability that were mentioned earlier, do find a perfect much to this case study. These advantages make that new application a new proposal for the dictionary applications in the future.

Moreover, "Wiki-Dic" is expected to enjoy all advantages related with contributors' motivations of collaborative, user-generated content applications. Therefore, the significant role of users-volunteers has to be underlined, who offer their talent and time for supporting collaborative knowledge sharing. According to Nov (2007), content contribution (as a volunteering activity) can be explained by the factors emphasizing volunteering behavior:

- values: opportunity to express humanitarian concerns for others
- social: chance to engage in activities viewed positively by important others
- understanding: chance to learn new things and exercise skills and abilities
- career: opportunity to achieve job-related benefits
- protective/enhancement: chance to eliminate negative ego-based factors (e.g. guilt) and to increase positive features of the self
- fun and ideology: opportunity to simply have a good time or to 'fight' for setting information free (the main motivations of open source software development).

On the other hand, developing the application several problems and requirements arisen, such as who is eligible to vote and how to identify the user. For example, the first version of "Wiki-Dic" (Theodorou, Violettas, & Georgiadis, 2008) had serious problems like "One voter one vote" and "Verifiability and Accountability" which are solved in the current version of the case study. Nevertheless, the particular e-voting type of "Wiki-Dic" application (e-poll for supporting user-generated content contributions) decreases the importance of several requirements of Table I (such as uncoercibility, no propaganda in the e-voting site, or secrecy to a certain level).

CASE STUDY: THE "WIKI-DIC" VERSION 2.0 APPLICATION

The "Wiki-Dic" dictionary is a dynamic web-based application (Figure 1). Its main functionality is to provide translations from English to Greek words and vice versa. The innovation that "Wiki-Dic" introduces is that the word translations are not introduced by professors or linguistics only. Towards the implementation of more democracy at the internet (literally stated from Descy (2006) as "…true democracy that works…") the "Wiki-Dic" users can also introduce words and word translations. What makes "Wiki-Dic" information accurate and accepted is the e-voting functionality that is integrated with the dictionary. Any user, even the anonymous one (not logged in), has the right to ballot for any of the translations. The e-voting results are visible in real time for any translation. As a result, the most accepted translations climb up to the translation list and the next user gets a clear view of the most popular translations.

Architecture and Implementation

The requirements of the application developed are basic and minimal:

- The system should be a web-based application in order to provide access to the system to everyone using an internet web browser.
- Online information using dynamic web pages based on client-server technology.
- Minimal look and buttons, so any kind of computer user (naive or expert), should be able to use the system.
- Multi-language support, (both languages English & Greek should be supported).
- Simple structure in order to be upgraded easily.

The system architecture is divided into three main modules:

1) Client Side - User Interface Module is the webpage where users interact with the application. The "Wiki-Dic" is a user-driven application where user interactions are accomplished using the mouse and the keyboard. From the design point of view, there was a great effort to keep the application interface as simple as possible and easy to use. As a result, the application uses one central Web page where users can have all the needed functionality to operate the dictionary without getting lost by moving from one page to another back and forth one page to another. Moreover, there is a great deal of defensive programming that protects and keeps the user informed about the state and the actions that one can take while using the application. Color, size and the position of the form components was taken in to account following basic user interface design rules. For example, red color warns the user about wrong

Figure 1. Application Basic structure: The database is stored on a Server (It can be different from the web server), and the users connect over the Internet or Intranet. The Administrators can connect from the Internet or the local network

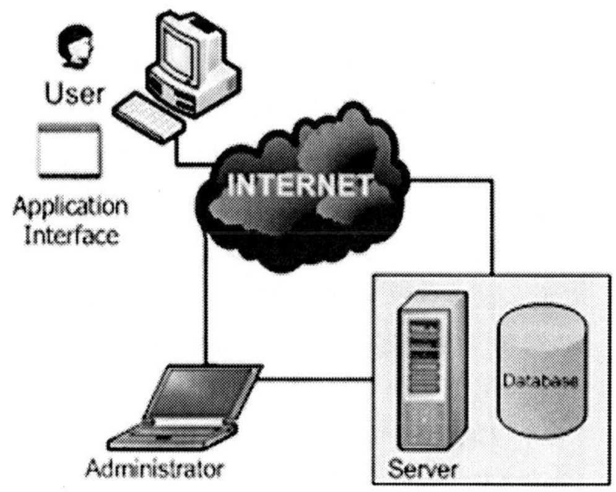

actions or deletion, while green colour awards and informs the user about successful operations.

2) Database Module is the heart of the application, since it is the main receiver of all the dictionary-sustained data. As it can be seen from the entity relationship diagram (ER) in Figure 2, the database has four main entities:

- Word categories entity is used in order to divide the set of words into main categories of interest. For example category "engineering" has words that are only used in engineering related fields. Use of word categories narrows the word search and helps the user to concentrate in a specific set of words and translations. Word categories can be introduced and altered only from the administrator users since they are crucial for the dictionary operation.
- Words entity is the centre of the system. Words are associated with the word categories, the translations and the users. The system allows a word insertion or modification only if a certain number of criteria is satisfied:

  - only authorised users can insert, update and delete words
  - users can modify only the words inserted by them
  - a word that already has at least one translation, cannot be modified (for maintenance reasons administrators are excluded)
- Translation entity contains information about the word that it refers to and the user id of the user who introduced it. Moreover, it saves information about the votes. The system accepts a new translation if a certain number of criteria is satisfied:
  - only authorised users can insert, update and delete translations
  - users can modify only the translations inserted by them
  - a translation that already has at least one vote, can be modified only by administrators for maintenance reasons
- Users entity is used to store user profile and specific information about the user actions.

Through unique key ids the relational database can associate words with translations, divide words in categories and keep track of user actions.

The system also uses log files to keep track of every change in the database using trigger technology. As a result, whenever something changes e.g. new word insertion, new translation, new vote etc., then the database system logs it automatically. Log data are used for the translation order algorithms that are described later in this chapter.

The application's structure was made in such a way that it could easily be altered for other resembling uses.

3) Server Side - Administration Module is used to help the dictionary administrators to manage, supervise and support the operation of the dictionary.

The webpage has three user access levels:

- The first access level is the "anonymous user access level". At that level anyone can access the "Wiki-Dic" application and get information about word translations. Moreover, everybody can vote for the best translation in their opinion.
- The second access level is the "user access level". That level gives the user the ability to insert new words or new translations to existing words. In order to access that level one needs a login name and a password provided by the application administrators. The user is confirmed valid by a unique e-mail address that is obligatory submitted during the registration procedure.
- The third access level is the "administrator access level". The administrators are actually the users who supervise the proper use of the dictionary application/site. Their main responsibility is to attend and protect the application. Since the "Wiki-Dic" is an application based on user collaborative knowledge, there is a great deal of work to be done, in order to protect the dictionary from mischievous users.

Ensuring One Vote per User Per Translation

Having the anonymous vote as a milestone in the system, the "one vote per person" problem had to be solved, a problem present in all the anonymous voting systems. Since the system does not keep the voter's personal information, there is a drawback that allows users to submit more than one vote for the same choice. This problem creates great bias and credibility problems for that type of systems (Lieshout, 1999), (Kramer, Gregorowicz, & Iyer, 2008).

Theoretically the best solution to that problem is to keep track of the IP address of the voter for each vote. That solution is impossible to be used today, first of all because of the limitations of the IP addresses available worldwide. Internet protocol IPv4 forces nearly every local network to use one gateway IP for more than one station. Secondly, the Internet Service Providers (ISPs) are

Figure 2. Application ER-Diagram

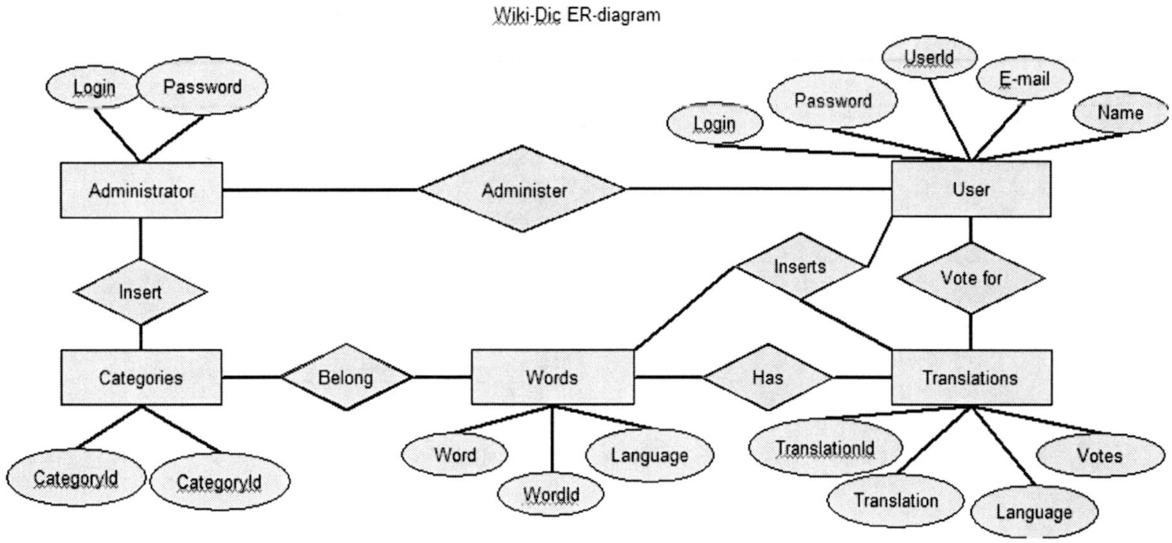

using DHCP Servers altering the IP addresses of the home users every single time they re-connect. This problem may decay when Internet IPv6 will be globally functional since it supports static IP for each station.

In "Wiki-Dic" system, in order to solve that kind of problem, a most common and popular technique in Internet programming was used: Cookies. For each anonymous user that connects to "Wiki-Dic" and votes, there is a cookie file stored into the user's computer. The cookie holds information like a unique user id and the word translation id. That information is updated for each vote each user submits. Moreover, before each vote submission, the system checks the user's cookie file for already submitted votes earlier for the current translation of the same user.

Although in practice the above approach may solve the problem in the 90% of situations, there are certain drawbacks as well. The most common is the deletion of the cookie files from the user's computer or the deactivation of the cookies technology from user's computer due to security reasons.

Furthermore, in order to avoid malicious users or malicious software, CAPTCHA question technology was added to the system. As a result, users has to answer the CAPTCHA question before the submission of their votes.

It is important to be stated here that the user is free to submit a vote to other translations of the same word since it is common for someone to change his/her mind over time.

System Development and Installation

The system was developed using the C# programming language, the Hypertext Markup Language (HTML) and ASP code. The development environment was Microsoft Visual Studio 2005. The source code compilation produces dynamic Active Server (.aspx) web pages and dynamic linked libraries which are the runtime environment of the application. Structured Query Language (SQL) was used for the communication between the database and the application web pages. The relational database management system Microsoft SQL Server 2005 was used for data storage.

The requirements in order to publish and operate the "Wiki-Dic" application are the following:

Figure 3. Application Interface

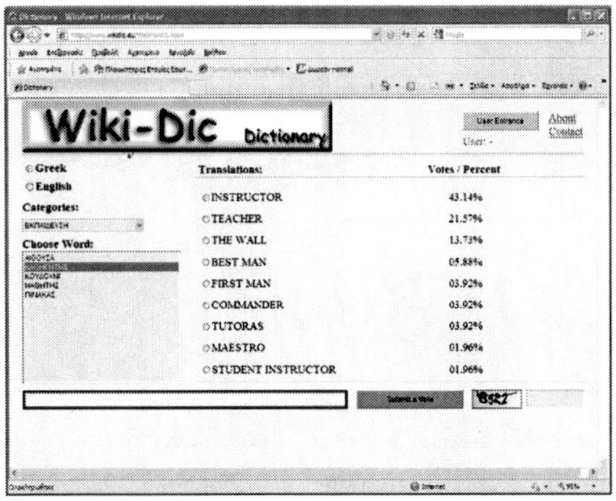

Figure 4. User login prompt on top right side of the form

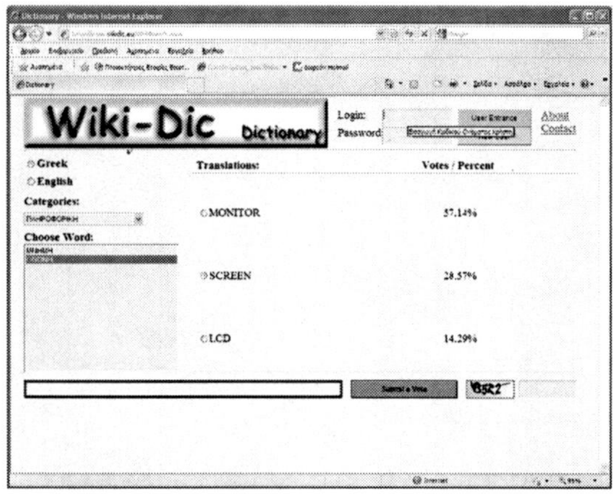

- The server side operating system should be Microsoft Windows 2003 Server. For the aspx web pages, the Microsoft Internet Information Server (IIS) and the .net v2.0 framework platform were used. All the application data are stored in a database, which operates under the Microsoft SQL Server 2005 database management system. For the time being, it is installed on a Dell Poweredge Server.
- Any browser and any operating system that supports .net technology can be used by the "Wiki-Dic" dictionary user. The application was fully tested with Internet Explorer 6.0 and above, and Mozilla Firefox.

Description and Operation

In order to use the "Wiki-Dic" application, users simply need an Internet Web browser, with security level that allows cookies and the URL address of the Web site. By typing "http://www.wikidic.eu", users enter the main page of the dictionary (Figure 3).

User has to choose a language and a category of words. In sequence, the user is able to select or search the desired word. As soon as a word is selected, a list of translations appears on the right of the page. The translation list provides as well the percentage of each translation up to that time as well, sorted by the most popular translation on the top.

User may vote about any of the translations he believes is the most appropriate by selecting the corresponding translation radio button and then pressing the "Submit vote" button. To ensure that the vote is not generated by a computer, the application uses common type of CAPTCHA that requires the typing of letters or digits from a distorted image that appears on the screen, so only humans can make the distinction.

Registered users can enter the member's area of the dictionary by typing login name and password (Figure 4).

For registered users more functionality is available. A registered user may insert, update and delete words and translations, under certain rules mentioned in the previous section.

Although the "Wiki-Dic" application is a web application accessed via a web browser, every programming effort was put for keeping the user interface as simple as possible. Implementing the most recent standard techniques of defensive programming, the application presents all the functionality components in the same web page. This way, it guides the user by making visible and invisible visual components of the web page,

Figure 5. The user selected to insert a new word translation

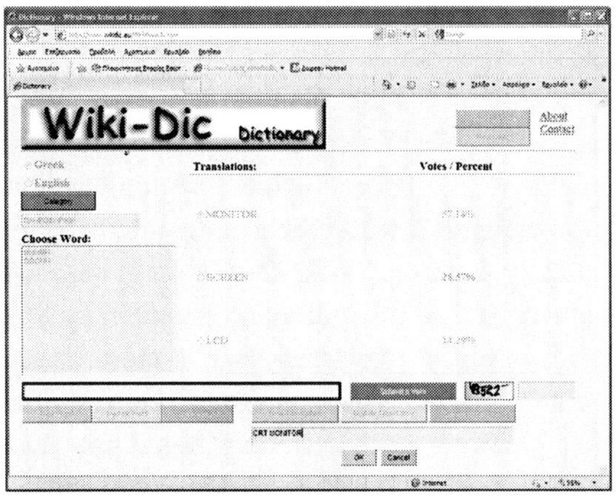

Figure 6. The message informs the user he cannot delete another users translation

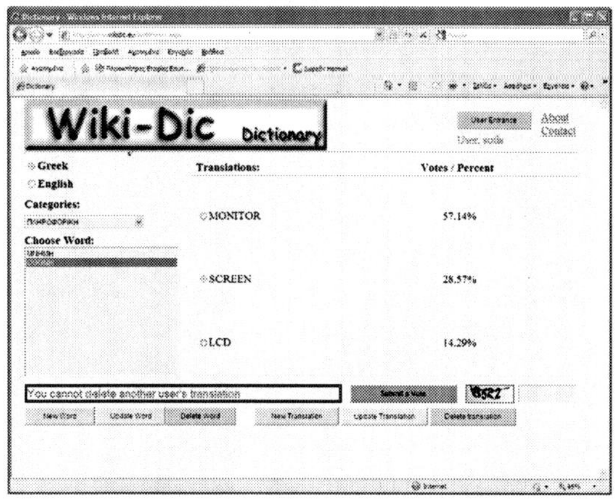

depending on the executed action (Figure 5). For example if user selects to insert a new word translation, everything in the web page is deactivated and a new text box appears under the button that was pressed. So although the user remains in the same familiar page, concentration is focused to the right position. Another advantage of that type of interface is that it makes it very difficult for any user to actually make mistakes.

The system keeps track of user actions in order to protect data between users, (e.g. a user can update only the translations he inserted and only if the specific translation was not rated yet with a vote by another user). In any case the system provides instant messages for all users' actions. For example, if a certain user tries to delete a translation belonging to someone else, he will receive a warning message (Figure 6).

The main responsible for the integrity of the dictionary information are the Administrators. When the application acknowledges a user as an Administrator, it provides full functionality (Figure 7). Administrators can make any modification they want, like deleting and/or altering words and/or translations. They are also responsible for creating the word categories (Figure 8). Moreover,

Figure 7. Administrators have full functionality

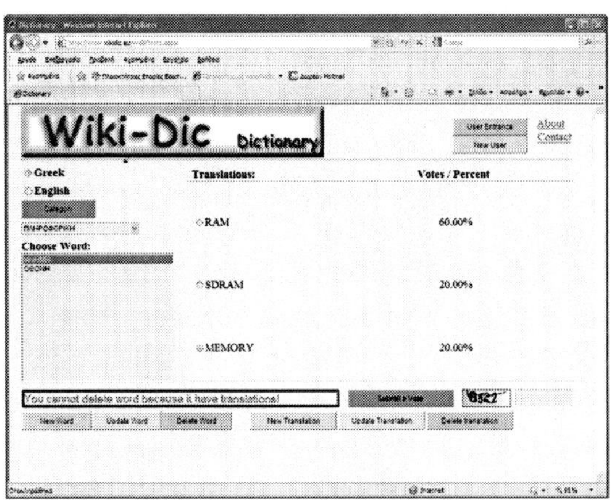

Figure 8. Insert and modify categories form

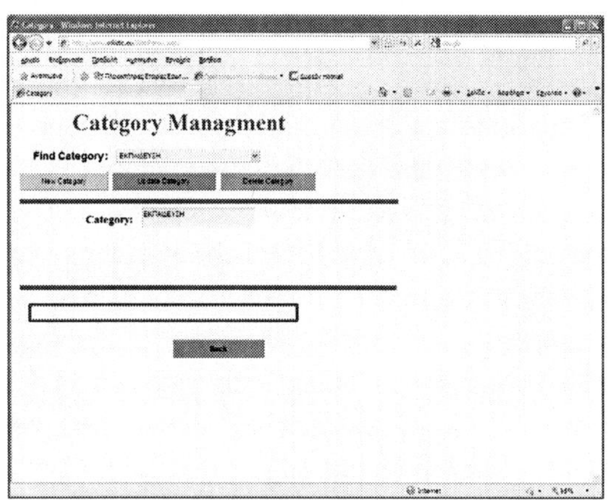

Figure 9. New user application form

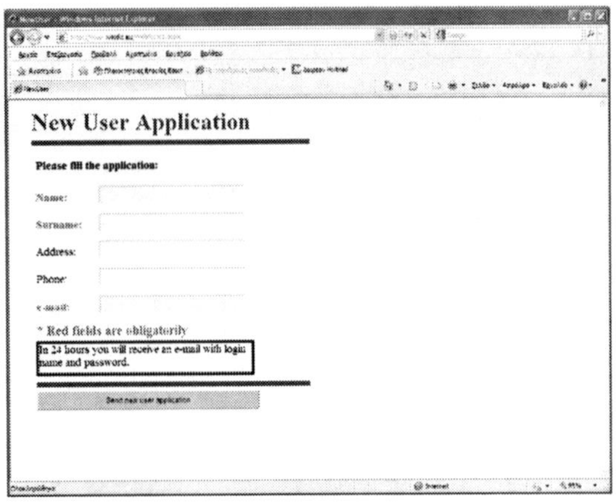

Administrators are responsible for the registered users' accounts.

Anonymous users can apply for login name and password through a web form, like the one in (Figure 9). When they submit the form, an e-mail is generated automatically and sent to admin@wikidic.eu account. Administrators do create the new users accounts and confirm the users' login names and passwords through e-mail as well.

EVALUATING E-VOTING INFORMATION OUTCOME

Another major issue of e-voting systems is the evaluation of the outcome result. Measurement and evaluation of the e-voting system extracted results is usually the aggregation of the votes and the percentage calculation for each voted subject. "Wiki-Dic" originally used that type of calculations to sort the word translations in order to present the most accepted – popular translation for each word. That first version of "Wiki-Dic" application was taking into account each vote equally. As a result the translations sorted list was based in the arithmetic average of the voted translations. But, dealing with a system that is used by -anonymous user, authorized users, and expert-users simultaneously- some votes have to be more important than others. As a result, taking into account each vote equally is a problem that is especially obvious when there were just a few votes for the translated word.

In order to handle this kind of issues, "Wiki-Dic" in the current second edition implements an intelligent algorithm which is assigning weights to the voters. Those weights are computed automatically from the "Wiki-Dic" system based on quantitative and qualitative information as well. For example, a registered user is more trusted than an anonymous user: as a result, the algorithm gives greater weight to the registered user vote. Moreover, the algorithm builds voters profile for registered users based on the votes already submitted by that user. The algorithm collects the level (position in the sorted list of translations) of each translation that the user voted for, in the past. A certain user, who voted for a word translation which appears higher in the translation list, is more likely to be a valuable voter. As a result, the algorithm gives greater weight to those users' votes. The outcome of that algorithm gives a sorted list of translations that is not simply based in the average number of the votes but also based on more complicated weighted system that aims to evaluate the votes.

FUTURE RESEARCH DIRECTIONS

The idea of using an intelligent algorithm based on quantitative and qualitative data to calculate weights in order to build a user profile, for the voting system of "Wiki-Dic" gives a whole new perspective to the system. Based on the outcomes of the algorithm, this type of implementations proposes a new way of dealing with Wikis and Web 2.0 applications in general. The idea of building user profiles graded as more trusted or valuable than others depending on their acts in comparison with other users resembles to human society behaviour. That type of intelligent e-voting evaluation algorithms can be extended to other web applications based on user collaboration, for example to automatically isolate malicious and wicked users.

Moreover, this e-voter profile evaluation can be extended to other type of e-voting systems for statistical and prediction analysis. For example, an e-voting system using user profiles to build models and compare them with other voting systems (e.g., political elections, etc.)

"Wiki-Dic" as an e-voting application, and as mentioned before, it incorporates the advantages and the disadvantages of the e-voting systems reported earlier in this chapter. For example, one of its weak points, the system's security and fraud issues is under close study those days. As repeatedly stated earlier in this chapter, this is the most important factor of e-voting. It concerns the European Committee (Remmert, 2004), the MIT (MIT, 2008), and several world conferences.

A challenging e-voting issue (that it wasn't dealt in this chapter because it is irrelative with the particular application's user requirements), is the anonymity problem. It is widely recognized however, that it is a crucial factor for a variety of applications on different domains and thus a future study is scheduled, on the use of blind signatures and cryptography mechanisms (such those in (Juels, 2004), (Yaar, Perrig, & Song, 2004), (Trechsel & Mendez, 2005), (Katsikas & Mitrou, 2004)).

Regarding usability issues, the application in this current version is not helping yet people with disabilities to vote, although it is another subject of future releases.

CONCLUSION

The "Wiki-Dic" application implements one relatively new idea of Web 2.0 that is based on participation, interaction and collaborating knowledge. The ability to allow the dictionary user to interact and participate in the dictionary knowledge base is the strongest and in the same time the weakest point of the application.

From the theoretical point of view the implementation and operation of the e-voting module of the "Wiki-Dic" application, produces feedback in order to evaluate and study e-voting systems based on weighted votes in general. The obvious inference is that systems based on participation and interaction gives a new way to manipulate difficult problems.

The "Wiki-Dic" case study could be the beginning of a number of other similar applications. New ideas could be implemented based on the power of the end-user participation and collaboration. It can also be used elsewhere with not much of a change. It can be used on a social network as part of the interactive voting system for "...the most popular person of the neighborhood", or "...the best basketball player of the year". It could be used for a travel portal for "...the hottest place to be at the summer this year in South Europe", or "...what was the best island last year in the Caribbean".

As a further use, implement it to the Web portal of a municipality of Greece, preferably a medium size one for local polls is a major future goal. This will give the opportunity to accent all the future problems and their possible solution(s). Extending its functionalities, based on user requirements is under consideration, such those that will arise when it will be placed at a university portal serving the aim it was built for: a dictionary for technical terms, for example a mechanical Greek-English dictionary.

REFERENCES

Anane, R., Freeland, R., & Theodoropoulos, G. (2007). e-Voting Requirements and Implementation. In *Proceedings of the 9th IEEE Int. Conf. on E-Commerce Technology and the 4th IEEE Int. Conf. on Enterprise Computing, E-Commerce and E-Services* (*CEC-EEE 2007*).

Bishop, M., & Wagner, D. (2007). Risks of e-Voting. *Communications of the ACM, 50*(11), 120. doi:10.1145/1297797.1297827

Council of Europe. (2004). *Electronic Governance Recommendation 15*. Strasbourg, France: Author.

Descy, E. D. (2006). The Wiki: True Web Democracy. *TechTrends, 50*(1), 4–5. doi:10.1007/s11528-006-7569-y

Juels, A. (2004). Financial Cryptography. *8th International Conference on Financial Cryptography* 2004, *Key West, FL, USA, February 9-12*, Springer LNCS 3110.

Katsikas, S., & Mitrou, L. (2004). *Electronic Voting Systems, Final Deliverable.* e-business forum, Retrieved February 23, 2008, from http:// www.ebusinessforum.gr

Kramer, M., Gregorowicz, A., & Iyer, B. (2008). Wiki Trust Metrics based on Phrasal Analysis. In *Proceedings of the 4th International Symposium on Wikis (WikiSym 2008)*, Porto, Portugal, September 8-10.

Lieshout, M. (1999, July). The Digital City of Amsterdam: between public domain and private enterprise. In *Social Learning regarding Multimedia Developments at a Local Level. The Case of Digital Cities* (pp.114). CITA-FUNDP, University of Namur.

MIT CallTech. (2008). *Voting Technology Project.* Retrieved March 11, 2008, from http://www.vote.caltech.edu

Mitrou, L., Gritzalis, D., & Katsikas, S. (2002). Revisiting legal and regulatory requirements for secure e-voting. In *Proceedings of the 16th IFIP International Information Security Conference*, Egypt.

Nov, O. (2007). What Motivates Wikipedians? *Communications of the ACM, 50*(11), 60–64. doi:10.1145/1297797.1297798

Oostveen, A., & van den Besselaar, P. (2005). Trust, Identity, and the Effects of Voting Technologies on Voting Behavior. *Social Science Computer Review, 23*(3), 304–311. doi:10.1177/0894439305275852

Remmert, M. (2004). Towards European Standards on Electronic Voting. In *Proceedings of the first International Workshop Electronic Voting in Europe –Technology, Law, Politics and Society*, Austria.

Sander, S. (2008). *Knowledge management by wikis*. Universiteit Maastricht, Switzerland: Institute for Knowledge and Agent Technology.

Tennenholtz, M. (2004). Dynamic Voting. In *Proceedings of the 5th ACM Conference on Electronic Commerce - EC'04,* New York, USA, May 2004.

Theodorou, T., Violettas, G., & Georgiadis, C. K. (2008). Wiki-Dic: Implementing an e-Voting Application to Support User-generated Content. In *Proceedings of the IADIS E-Commerce International Conference (e-commerce 2008)*, Amsterdam, The Netherlands (pp. 209-214).

Trechsel, A., & Mendez, F. (2005). *The European Union and E-voting*. London: Routledge.

Volkamer, M., & McGaley, M. (2007). Requirements and Evaluation Procedures for eVoting. In *Proceedings of the 2nd IEEE Int. Conf. on Availability, Reliability and Security* (*ARES'07*).

Wikipedia. (2008). *Web 2.0.* Retrieved March 16, 2008, from http://en.wikipedia.org/wiki/Web_2#Definition

Yaar, A., Perrig, A., & Song, D. (2004). SIFF: a stateless Internet flow filter to mitigate DDoS flooding attacks. In *Proceedings of the IEEE Security and Privacy Symposium,* Pittsburgh, USA, May 2004 (pp. 130- 143).

ADDITIONAL READING

Adida, B. (2006). *Advances in Cryptographic Voting Systems. Unpublished doctoral disertation.* Department of Electrical Engineering and Computer, Massachusetts Institute ofTechnology.

Alexander, H., Mendez, T., & Mendez, F. (2005). *The European Union and E-Voting. Addressing the European Parliament? Internet Voting Challenge.* London: Routledge.

Deloitte & Touche LLP - Canada (2008) - *Change your world or the world will change you: The future of collaborative government and Web 2.0*

Graham, P. *(2005).* Web 2.0. Retrieved 2006-08-02,*from*http://www.paulgraham.com/ web20.html

Ikonomopoulos, S., Lambrinoudakis, C., Gritzalis, D., Kokolakis, S., & Vassiliou, K. (2002). Functional Requirements for a Secure Electronic Voting System. *Proceedings of the IFIP TC11 17th International Conference on Information Security (IFIP/SEC2002), Ghonaimy M.A., El-Hadidi M., Aslan H.K. (Eds.), pp. 507-519, Kluwer Academic Publisher, Egypt, Cairo, May 2002.*

Lambrinoudakis, C., Gritzalis, D., & Katsikas, S. (2002). Building a Reliable e-Voting System: Functional Requirements and Legal Constraints. *Proceedings of the 13th International Workshop on Database and Expert Systems Applications (DEXA 2002), W07: International Workshop on Trust and Privacy in Digital Business (TrustBus), IEEE Computer Society Press, Aix-en-Provence, France, September 2002.*

Lambrinoudakis, C., Gritzalis, D., Tsoumas, V., Karyda, M., & Ikonomopoulos, S. (2003). In Gritzalis, D. (Ed.), *"Secure Electronic Voting: The Current Landscape", in the book Secure Electronic Voting* (pp. 101–122). Kluwer Academic Publishers.

Lambrinoudakis, C., Kokolakis, S., Karyda, M., Tsoumas, V., Gritzalis, D., & Katsikas, S. (2003). Electronic Voting Systems: Security Implications of the Administrative Workflow, *Proceedings of the 14th International Workshop on Database and Expert Systems Applications (DEXA 2003), W06: International Workshop on Trust and Privacy in Digital Business (TrustBus), pp. 467-471, IEEE Computer Society Press, Prague, Czech Republic, September 2003.*

Leuf, B. (2001). *The Wiki Way: Quick Collaboration on the Web.* Addison-Wesley.

Mader, S. (2007). *Wikipatterns.* John Wiley & Sons.

Manus, M., Porter R. J.(2005). *Web 2.0 for Designers.* Digital Web Magazine, May 4, 2005.

Mendez, F. (2005) The European Union and cybercrime: insights from comparative federalism? *Journal of European Public Policy Vol 12, 3: 509-527.*

Mendez, F & Trecshel, A (2005) The European Union and e-voting: upgrading Euro-elections?

Mercuri, R. (2002). Humanizing Voting Interfaces. *Usability Professionals Association Conference, Orlando, FL, July 11, 2002.*

Mitrou, L., Gritzalis, D., Katsikas, S., & Quirchmayr, G. (2003). Electronic voting: Constitutional and legal requirements and their technical implications . In Gritzalis, D. A. (Ed.), *Secure Electronic Voting* (pp. 43–60). Boston, Dordrecht, London: Kluwer Academic Publishers.

Neumann, P., Mercuri, R., & Weinstein L. (2001). *Internet and Electronic Voting, The Risks Digest.* ACM's Software Engineering Notes (SIGSOFT), Volume 26, No. 3, March 2001.

O'Reilly, T.(2005). What Is Web 2.0. *O'Reilly Network.* Deloitte & Touche LLP - Canada (2008 study) - Change your world or the world will change you: The future of collaborative government and Web 2.0

Schneier, B. (2000). *Voting and Technology*, Retrieved December 15, 2008, from http://www.counterpane.com

Tapscott, D. (2008). *Wikinomics: How Mass Collaboration Changes Everything.* Portfolio Hardcover.

Trechsel, A., Mendez, F., & Kies, R. (2003). *The European Parliament and the Challenge of Internet Voting.* Policy Paper of the European University Institute/The Robert Schuman Centre for Advanced Studies.

Vickery, G. (2007). *Wunsch S., Participative Web and User-Created Content: Web 2.0, Wikis and Social Networking.* OECD.

KEY TERMS AND DEFINITIONS

E-Voting: Electronic voting (also known as e-voting) is a term encompassing several different types of voting, embracing both electronic means of casting a vote and electronic means of counting votes.

Dictionary: A dictionary is a collection of words in a specific language, often listed alphabetically, with definitions, etymologies, phonetics, pronunciations, and other information;

Wiki: A wiki is a website that uses wiki software, allowing the easy creation and editing of any number of interlinked Web pages, using a simplified markup language or a WYSIWYG text editor, within the browser.

Wiki Application: A wiki is a type of collaborative software program that typically allows web pages to be created and collaboratively edited using a common web browser. Websites running such programs are themselves referred to as wikis. A wiki system is usually an application server that runs on one or more web servers. The content is stored in a file system, and changes to the content are stored in a relational database management system.

Web 2.0: "Web 2.0" refers to the second generation of web development and web design. It is characterized as facilitating communication, information sharing, interoperability, user-centered design[1] and collaboration on the World Wide Web.

User-Generated Content: User-generated content (UGC), also known as consumer-generated media (CGM) or user-created content (UCC), refers to various kinds of media content, publicly available, that are produced by end-users.

Chapter 12
Supporting Electronic Collaboration in Conceptual Modeling

Peter Rittgen
University of Borås, Sweden & Vlerick Leuven Gent Management School, Belgium

ABSTRACT

The authors study collaborative modeling by analyzing conversations and loud thinking during modeling sessions and the resulting models themselves. They identify the basic activities of the modeling teams on the social, pragmatic, semantic and syntactic levels and derive a schema for the pragmatic level. The authors' main conclusion is that team-based modeling is largely a negotiation process. Drawing on these results the authors derive an architecture of a system that supports the distributed development of conceptual models.

INTRODUCTION

Descriptive approaches to understanding the modeling process are scarce. Only a few deal with collaborative modeling (see section 2). The others assume a scenario where a single expert modeler creates a formal model of some part of a business (Morris, 1967; Srinivasan & Te´eni, 1995; Willemain, 1994, 1995). These studies identify sets of general heuristics for successful modeling without going down to the level of the concrete steps that are performed in creating models. Their results are hardly applicable to business modeling in general for a number of reasons. Firstly, a business model is rarely developed by an expert alone but rather by a team involving representatives of the respective stakeholders. Secondly, the problem domain of general business modeling is often less well-structured and formal languages are of limited use. Thirdly and last, the goal of providing tool support for collaborative modeling requires the identification of detailed steps.

DOI: 10.4018/978-1-61692-016-6.ch012

The objective of this paper is to discover the elementary activities and the structure of the modeling process, i.e. a meta-model of the modeling process. This is done by studying, in a descriptive way, the work performed by small groups of modelers that were assigned the same task: To develop business process models for a hospital based on a detailed description of the processes in natural language. This implied collective sense-making of a case text and conceptualizing the group's understanding of the text in the form of an analysis model. The group members were homogeneous concerning their modeling experience and their roles, i.e. there was no a-priori assignment of a group leader or modeling expert.

We then go on to interpret the results from the empirical study as requirements for a system that supports distributed modeling in groups. We develop an architecture of such a system that is in line with the empirical findings and supports the process that was observed in the study.

BACKGROUND AND ISSUES

Collaborative modelling processes have been studied from a number of different angles, e.g. the structure of the process itself, its organizational environment and techniques to support it. In (Bommel, Hoppenbrouwers, Proper, & Weide, 2006) modelling involves domain experts, modelling mediators and model builders. It is viewed as a form of information gathering dialogue where knowledge is elicited from the domain experts. This view can be challenged because modelling is a social and communicative process where much of the information is created by and through the process rather than gathered from domain experts. We have therefore studied situations where the participants, apart from the facilitator, had no a priori roles but contributed to the modelling session in the way they deemed reasonable.

(Frederiks & Weide, 2006) emphasizes the importance of natural language as the primary medium and identifies two principal activities and associated roles: the domain expert who concretizes an informal model and a system analyst who abstracts a formal model. (S. J. B. A. Hoppenbrouwers, Lindeman, & Proper, 2006) distinguishes between an elicitation and a formalization dialogue and develops a modelling procedure by generalizing existing procedures. They also acknowledge (S.J.B.A. Hoppenbrouwers, Proper, & Weide, 2005) that modelling is not only a knowledge elicitation process but also a knowledge creation and dissemination process. It is viewed as a structured conversation.

We agree that modelling is a conversation but we claim that it is a specific type of conversation, namely a negotiation. This idea is implicitly present in (S.J.B.A. Hoppenbrouwers, et al., 2005) where the dialogue structure contains negotiation elements such as propose and accept. We elaborate this point in the following sections. (S.J.B.A. Hoppenbrouwers, et al., 2005) also advocates the use of controlled language and validation. We consider the latter as problematic as it has often been observed that domain experts falsely agree with a model not being fully aware of all its implications or making assumptions that others are not aware of.

While the approaches discussed so far address the structure of the modelling process itself, (Persson, 2001) and (Araujo & Borges, 2007) look at the environment in which this process is embedded. They study the influence of situational factors on modelling. Their aim is to create an environment that facilitates and supports participative modelling in enterprise or software engineering, respectively.

Another type of work that is related to ours is that around brainstorming methods that can be considered as methods for the creation of rudimentary models in an unstructured problem area (see e.g. (Belton, Ackermann, & Shepherd, 1997; Conklin, Selvin, Buckingham Shum, & Sierhuis, 2003)). Our approach continues this work into the more structured phases of modelling.

Yet another view on collaborative modelling is related to techniques that support the modelling creation. An example of that is studied under the heading "collaborative graph editing" where the focus is on real-time collaboration on the graphical representation of a model (WYSIWIS

= What You See Is What I See). (Meire, Borges, & Araújo, 2003, 2007) suggest a technique that allows for transparent multi-person editing of a diagram by providing a mechanism to manage a hierarchy of local model versions. The approach does not offer a mechanism for the reduction of the ensuing multitude of versions to a single model, though, which is our aim. But the live character and immediate interaction of this method are strong motivational factors for engaging participants and keeping them involved.

RESEARCH METHOD

Keeping this background in mind, we set out to study a situation where groups of modelers worked on a textual description of a business case with the purpose of deriving business process models. To understand the modeling process, we assumed that two factors are important in model creation:

- The internal mental processes of each modeler, and
- The conversations between modelers and within the group.

To get access to the former we used a think-aloud process-tracing methodology (Ericsson & Simon, 1993; Srinivasan & Te´eni, 1995) where the observants speak out what they are currently thinking. The utterances were taped and then transcribed yielding the think-aloud protocols. The same was done with the conversations. In addition to that we also considered the product of the modeling process, the models themselves, to fill the gaps in the protocols and to help with interpreting ambiguous phrases in them. Open issues that could not be dealt with in this way were marked on the coding scheme and clarified by ex-post interviews with the respective groups. The latter was also done to ensure that the coding was done in the right way and that the transcripts match the participants' intentions.

To develop a preliminary coarse-grain categorization we turned to theories in the pertinent literature, particularly in organizational semiotics. We used the upper four 'rungs' of the semiotic ladder (Stamper, 1991): syntactic, semantic, pragmatic, and social. They refer to the structure of sign systems (e.g., a language), the meaning of the signs, their use, and the norms of a community, respectively. An initial coding phase within this framework revealed that the syntactic and semantic levels, which together make up the language level, are divided into the natural language domain and the modeling language domain depending on the kind of language used to describe the business.

The activities on the pragmatic level were classified as 'Understanding' and 'Organizing the Modeling Process'. The former term was then further refined into 'Understanding the language' and 'Understanding the text', the latter can be divided into 'Setting the agenda' and 'Negotiation'. The social level consists of rules for acceptance and rejection in the negotiation. A detailed discussion of these categories can be found in the respective sections. The results are summarized in (Figure 1).

We conducted 3 experiments that involved a total of 26 groups of 2-3 students in informatics over a period of 3 years. The students were provided with a textual description of four business processes in a hospital. They were asked to model these processes with the help of two different modeling languages that they could choose freely from a set of four languages: ARIS-EPC (Scheer, 1999), FMC-Petri nets (Keller & Wendt, 2003), UML (OMG, 2004, 2006), and DEMO (Dietz, 1999). Based on the results of these experiments we derived a layered meta-model of the modeling process that includes a model of the negotiation process.

The validity of student experiments is not always accepted. We think it is justified in this case because our study focuses on cognitive aspects of modeling, which are related to the individual rather than to the organizational context.

Figure 1. Levels and domains

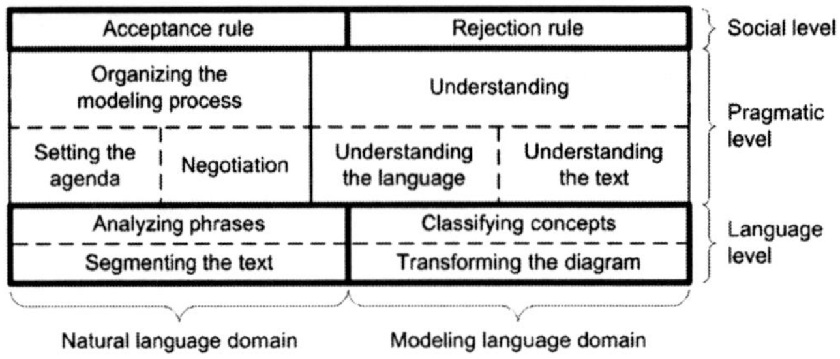

SOLUTIONS AND RECOMMENDATIONS

We carried out the main coding of the material within the framework stipulated by (Figure 1). Examples of that procedure are shown in the respective section. The activities on the pragmatic level were classified as 'Understanding' and 'Organizing the Modeling Process'. The former term was then further refined into 'Understanding the language' and 'Understanding the text', the latter can be divided into 'Setting the agenda' and 'Negotiation'. The social level consists of rules for acceptance and rejection in the negotiation. A detailed discussion of these categories can be found in (Rittgen, 2007). Here we present only the results concerning the social and pragmatic levels.

Social Level

The social norms within a modeling team are mainly made up of rules for determining whether a proposal is accepted or rejected. We observed that these rules do not have to be logical complements which allows for situations where a proposal can be neither rejected nor accepted but requires further convincing to decide one way or the other. A termination rule was applied occasionally to force a decision if a negotiation got stuck, i.e., when there were no more changes in the individuals' convictions over an extended period of time. We witnessed two types of rules:

- *Rules of majority*, where a certain number of group members had to support or oppose a proposal in order for the whole group to accept or reject it (e.g., more than half). A tie-break rule was sometimes specified (e.g., for the case of an equal number of supporters and opponents). The tie-break could involve seniority issues.
- *Rules of seniority*, where the weight of a group member's support or opposition was related to his or her status within the group. This status could be acquired (e.g., by experience) or associated with a position to which the member was appointed. A frequent example of this was the case of a more experienced modeler who was considered as the leader by the group and took decisions on their behalf. The other members filled the role of consultants in such a case.

These rules were sometimes set up explicitly before the group began their work, or in an early phase of this work. But in most cases they rather emerged as the result of each member's behavior. Individuals making regular contributions of high quality were likely to acquire seniority. In homogeneous teams majority rules were used more often.

Pragmatic Level

On the pragmatic level we discovered two distinct types of behavior, each of which can be classified

Figure 2. Negotiation pattern

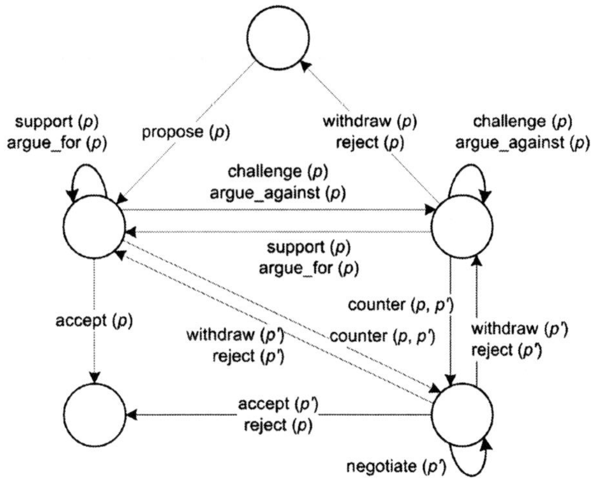

in two sub-categories (the abbreviations of the categories are used as indices of the respective coded terms later on):

- *Understanding*, which concerns the text of the case description (index UT) or the (modelling) language (index UL), and
- *Organizing the modelling process*, which involves two types of activities: *setting the agenda* (index SA) and *negotiation* (index N).

Understanding was established by questions and answers. If the respondent could not provide clarification, an assumption was made. Agendas have been used by the participants in our study as an instrument for roughly structuring the modelling session. They were introduced in the beginning and then adapted during the session if necessary. On the whole most groups started by reading the case description completely and then organized their work around the flow of the text.

The majority of the activities on the pragmatic level were associated with negotiation, though. This is surprising as modelling is typically rather pictured as an intuitive act that is largely the product of a creative brain (e.g., a consultant) that possibly receives some input from other stakeholders in the modelling process (e.g., domain experts from the respective departments).

According to our results modelling is a relatively well-structured process. It consists of a limited number of well-defined activities on all levels of the semiotic ladder. We are aware that further research will reveal more activities but from the experience of the three experiments that yielded a decreasing number of new ones, we are confident that the total number of activities will converge. The activities identified so far can therefore be assumed to be relatively stable. To a certain extent this is even true across different modelling languages, although the terminology of concepts may vary and not every concept is realized in each of the languages.

An analysis of the workflows on the pragmatic level revealed a structure that goes beyond the mere identification of generic activities. We found out that the negotiation process actually follows a certain pattern. This pattern is shown in (Figure 2).

It consists of an initial and reject state at the top, a state where acceptance is favored (upper left-hand corner), a state where rejection is favored (upper right-hand corner), a recursive sub-state for negotiating a counter-proposal (lower right-hand corner) and an accept state (lower left-hand corner). Each of the states allows for a set of certain pragmatic activities that take the negotiation to a different state. We have left out the parameters concerning the modeller who performs the activity and the argument (if present). In general any modeller can perform any activity but there are a few rules to be observed. A modeller making a proposal is implicitly assumed to support it. He is the only one who may withdraw it. A counter-argument is brought up by a different modeller but a counter-proposal can also be made by the proponent of the original proposal, e.g., to accommodate counter-arguments. With the help of the pattern of (Figure 2) we can control the negotiation component of a modelling support system. On the other levels we were not able to discover an equally strong pattern of activities. This will affect the kind of support a tool can provide at the language level.

Tool Support for the Modeling Process

Our analyses of the modeling sessions showed us that modeling is a complex process involving issues such as collective sense-making (Qu, 2007), negotiations (Mathieu & Verrons, 2002) and group decisions (Aiken, Vanjani, & Krosp, 1995). It is therefore worthwhile to consider tool support for this process. This is particularly true in an interorganizational setting where participants are often geographically distributed. The tool we envision focuses on the negotiation aspect and helps group members in understanding the modeling situation, creating and discussing modeling alternatives, and deciding on the best one, all in a shared internet-based environment. The following paragraphs elaborate on the components that such a tool should provide.

The architecture of a modeling support system, i.e., a system that supports a group in developing models, is still under investigation. Some authors have suggested groupware systems that help teams in collective sense-making (Boehm et al., 2001; Briggs et al., 2003; Conklin et al., 2003; S.J.B.A. Hoppenbrouwers et al., 2006a) which is an important part of the modeling process. (Conklin, et al., 2003) reports on an approach (Compendium) that combines three different areas: meeting facilitation, graphical hypertext and conceptual frameworks. To make them work, technical facilitation is viewed as essential to remove the cognitive overload for the group members, i.e., the necessity to develop hypertext literacy, which cannot be assumed in all participants. On the technology side, the critical elements are question-based templates, metadata and maps. They allow participants to move freely between different levels of abstraction and formalization as the need dictates. The question-based templates guide the process by supplying relevant questions, the answers to which will lead the group towards a better understanding of the problem and towards the development of appropriate solutions (e.g., models). The metadata is used to provide additional information that is also considered relevant but was not anticipated in the templates or lies at the intersection of templates. The maps have a hierarchical structure and the same concept can appear in different maps so that its use in different contexts can be understood. This feature is called transclusion.

Groupware systems for collective sense-making, as the one mentioned, address an important issue in collaborative modeling. They can therefore be used as the core of a modeling support system (MSS). So far these systems are typically tailored for specific modeling languages though (in the case of Compendium, World Modeling Framework and Issue-Based Information System). For an MSS they need to be more modular so that any modeling language can be "plugged in" (e.g., other enterprise or information systems modeling languages). In addition, there is also the need for a negotiation component that facilitates structured arguments and decisions regarding modeling choices. The model shown in (Figure 2) can function as a workflow template controlling such a negotiation component. Once instantiated

Figure 3. The model building view

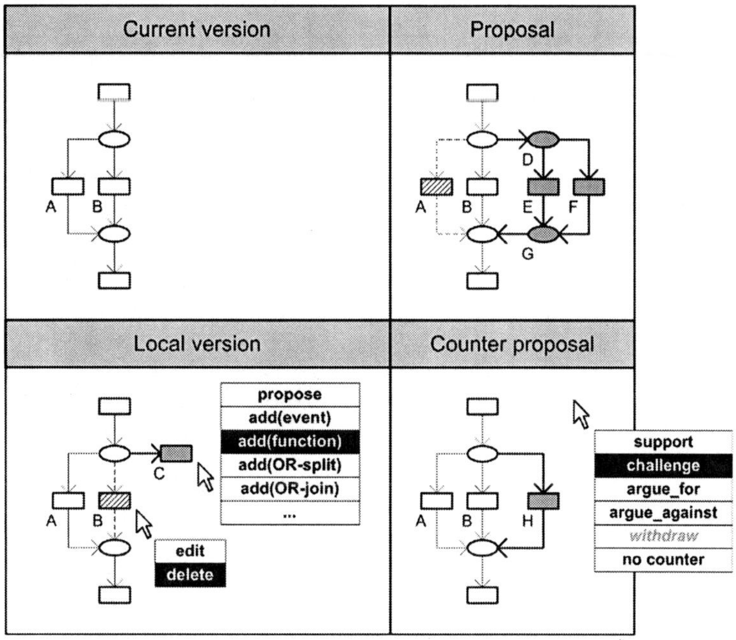

the actual workflow can then be adjusted to the concrete modeling situation.

Architecture of a Distributed Modeling Support System

A distributed modeling support system needs to coordinate the efforts of a number of modelers. To this end each modeler has to have a clear overview of the current status of the negotiation and model building processes. The latter involves the current stable version of the model as agreed upon so far, a version that includes the local changes made by the respective group member (the local model editor), a proposal suggesting changes to the current model and a counter proposal if applicable. (Figure 3) shows the screen layout of the model building view.

Regarding the status of the negotiation process the modeler needs access to the following information: What are the arguments for and against the proposal and the counter proposal? How many group members are in support of or against the proposal or counter proposal? What is the final decision regarding the (counter) proposal? This information can be presented in the form of a table. An example is given later in (Table 1).

The model building view is divided into four windows (See Figure 3). The upper left one shows the current version that has emerged from the negotiation process so far. It is used as a reference for all other temporary versions such as the proposals and the local version. This means that suggested changes are always expressed in relation to the current version, e.g. added or deleted nodes are marked in a special way.

The lower left window contains the local version, i.e. it serves as the model editor for the group member running this particular copy of the modeling support system. It offers the model creation facilities pertaining to the syntactic level such as introducing and connecting nodes. In addition to that it provides the pragmatic functions related to making proposals and counter-proposals. Making a proposal implies that the local version is put in the respective proposal queue.

Table 1. The negotiation view

Proposal	
For	**Against**
Joe: We need to differentiate between two types of prescriptions.	Harry: The different prescriptions should be handled later.
Bill: The different prescriptions must be considered in treatment planning already.	Ralph: I am missing a third alternative for patient treatment (transfer to another ward).
Frank: A ward transfer is rather part of the anamnesis phase or treatment evaluation.	
4 supporters	**5 challengers**

In the example of (Figure 3) the modeler has already made two changes to the current version. She has decided that node B is not needed and should therefore be deleted (symbolized by the hatched area). She also suggests a new node C and connects it to a node in the current version. The respective rectangle is shaded in grey and the arrow is drawn with a larger line weight. The model in this case is an Event-driven Process Chain (Scheer, 1999) of a business process. Another modeler has already made a proposal regarding the current version, which is displayed in the upper right window. He proposes to remove node A and to add the nodes D-G. This proposal is countered by yet another group member who thinks that the current version should only be augmented by the new node H.

In this situation the original modeler, the one sitting in front of the screen shown in (Figure 3), decides that the counter-proposal is not acceptable. He shows this to the others by voting against it, i.e. by triggering the *challenge* function in the counter-proposal window. If he wants to supply an argument for his rejection he chooses *argue_against* instead. He can also specify that he considers the counter-proposal not to be a counter to the original proposal and therefore be inadequate. This is treated in the same way as an *argue_against* vote with the argument being "Counter proposal does not counter the original proposal." The *challenge* serves as input to the negotiation component where the group finally accepts or rejects this counter-proposal. Observe that it is not allowed to support (or *argue_for*) both the proposal and the counter-proposal.

The negotiation view (see Table 1) shows a list of pros and cons for the proposal and the counter-proposal. These are the arguments supplied when the *argue_for* or *argue_against* function is performed on a (counter-)proposal by a modeler. This view also shows the total number of supporters and challengers of this proposal. Depending on the currently active rule on the social level this determines overall acceptance or rejection of the proposal, e.g. when a required majority has been reached. A facilitator might also force a decision if the required condition cannot be reached.

If a counter-proposal is rejected the next one in the respective queue is displayed and considered by the group. If no more counter-proposals are available, the window remains empty. A rejected proposal turns the current counter-proposal into a proposal; the counter-proposals from the queue become attached to this new proposal. The first among them becomes the new active counter-proposal (if any) and is shown in the lower right window. In the absence of counter-proposals in the queue, the next proposal from the queue is considered.

An accepted proposal makes all related counter-proposals obsolete; the next in the proposal queue becomes the new active proposal. If the counter proposal is accepted, the proposal is removed and the first among the competing counter-proposals from the queue becomes the new proposal (if any) and the second will be the

Figure 4. Update of local version following update of current version

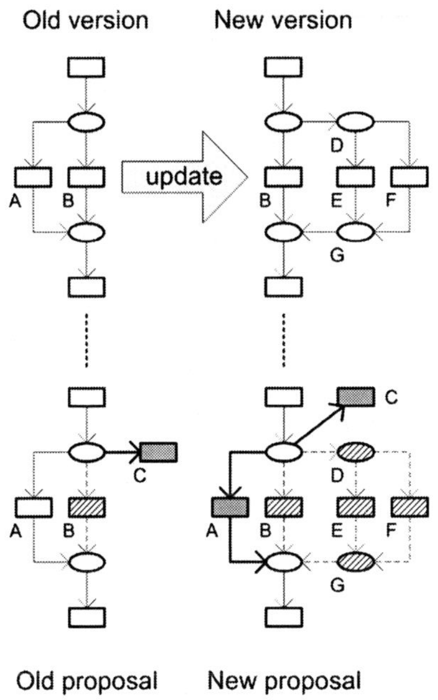

new counter-proposal (if any). The others remain counter-proposals but are now related to the new proposal. Observe that the deleted (counter-) proposals still exist as local copies so that the respective modelers can decide to post them again as proposals if applicable.

If a proposal or counter-proposal is accepted by the group it becomes the new current version, i.e. the upper left window is updated for all group members. This means that the local version has now become inconsistent as it is still related to the former version. It is therefore necessary to update the local version (as well as all the proposals and counter-proposals). (Figure 4) shows in which way this is done.

Let us assume that the proposal of (Figure 3) has been accepted and becomes the new current version now. This scenario is depicted in (Figure 4). The old proposal, i.e. the local version in relation to the former current version (old version), involved the deletion of node B (and incident arcs) and the introduction of node C (and incident arc). In the new current version (called new proposal in Figure 4) the situation concerning node B has not changed. It still exists in the new version and we still suggest removing it. But in our proposal the node A still exists whereas it has been deleted in the new accepted version. This means that our proposal in relation to the new version actually implies to reintroduce this node. It is therefore shaded in grey and the incident arcs get a larger line weight. Node C is part of neither the old nor the new version so nothing changes here. But the new version contains a number of new nodes that are not present in our local version (D-G). If we want to stick to our local version, then our "new" proposal is to remove these nodes and all incident arcs.

The architecture that we have described so far is a direct consequence of the results from the empirical study detailed in the previous sections. The architecture supports the activities on the social, pragmatic and syntactic levels. We are currently building a prototype that implements this architecture and that allows us to gain further insight into the modeling process. Such a prototype can be employed in a number of different ways: It can be used to test the suggested architecture and thereby indirectly confirm the study results in a broader empirical study. The additional tool support in this study makes it easier to perform such a study on a larger scale, e.g. with distributed team members, and it also provides additional information about the modeling process that was not available in the original study.

The existence of version histories, for example, makes it possible to analyze the modeling process in a more detailed manner regarding the development stages of a model. Another example is the negotiation log that gives us a deep insight into the arguing process and the competition between different model alternatives. A study supported by this tool can therefore also contribute to the development of new theories of the modeling process. On the practical side, the prototype can also help in detecting shortcomings and suggesting improvements. These suggestions can be related to the implementation (i.e., the tool itself) or the architecture behind it (as outlined above). Issues such as the design of the user interface and migration to other modeling languages are important considerations here.

CONCLUSION AND FUTURE RESEARCH DIRECTIONS

We studied group modeling sessions in detail, both regarding conversations between the group members and the mental processes within each individual. By doing this we derive a sub-categorization of the upper four levels of the semiotic ladder, generic activities of business process modeling at all of these levels and a negotiation pattern at the pragmatic level. On the basis of these results we suggest a tentative architecture of a system that supports group modeling. Our aim with this research is two-fold. On the one hand we want to develop a better understanding of the modeling process that has been largely neglected by researchers so far. Such an improved understanding can lead to better modeling methods and thereby ultimately to higher quality of models.

On the other hand we are also interested in providing computer support to those modelers that work in a group environment. Modeling is a highly demanding task that is further complicated by the dynamics of group work. Effective support is therefore essential, especially if some of the group members are inexperienced as is often the case in business modeling sessions, where typically a majority of the participants does not have any modeling background. But it is precisely this latter type of participant that contributes most to the actual design of the model with his or her knowledge of the relevant business domain. Both the speed and quality of the models can therefore benefit tremendously if we can manage to involve these people directly as modelers instead of relying on the bottleneck of the modeling expert for all communication within the group. The suggested tool support can accommodate this by giving the expert seniority (i.e., the right to make the final decision) and turning the domain experts into effective consultants that make proposals (thereby reversing the traditional roles in IT consulting).

A distributed modeling support system can also be seen as a special kind of group decision support system (GDSS, (Aiken, et al., 1995)) if we consider that the accept and reject decisions in the negotiation process are the key to model design. There is significant empirical support for the claim that GDSS are beneficial (Aiken, et al., 1995; Bamber, Watson, & Hill, 1996; Benbasat & Lim, 1993; Bidgoli, 1996; Burke, Chidambaram, & Lock, 1995; Cass, Heintz, & Kaiser, 1991; Chudoba, 1999; Fjermestad & Hiltz, 1998/1999; Jackson, Aiken, Mahesh, & Bassam, 1995; Townsend, Whitman, & Hendrickson, 1995), particularly for larger groups and/or complex tasks. Many of these benefits carry over to modeling support systems, e.g., reduced meeting time, higher quality of the decisions, broader involvement of all participants, higher effectiveness of decisions, etc.

Our research studied text-based modeling only. This is not a realistic scenario for practical modeling situations. We are confident though that our results are relevant for real-world modeling to some extent. The social level is fairly independent of the way in which a modeling alternative was derived (text-based or other) as the decision rule rather depends on the alternatives themselves. The same is true for the language level as we can safely assume that natural language and modeling languages will play an important role in any modeling endeavor. We therefore expect differences primarily on the pragmatic level, and here especially in the areas "setting the agenda" and "understanding". Whether modelers just interpret a text or communicate with domain experts will have considerable impact on the way the agenda is determined. Likewise the issue of understanding has to be extended to cover forms of communication other than analyzing text.

So far we have only looked at business process modeling. Other domains in the business and information systems areas remain to be explored. It should also be noted that our study has been performed in a contrived setting albeit with a realistic case. Further confirmation, and especially consolidation, is therefore required, preferably by means of a field study. The suggested architecture is only based on three of the four levels. Further research needs to address the semantic level, too. In addition to this it seems reasonable to build a prototype of a modeling support system, and to test it in a real-life modeling scenario. We assume that these measures will contribute to a better understanding of the process of modeling, both from a cognitive and a collaborative perspective, and they will eventually help us to better support modelers in their challenging task.

REFERENCES

Aiken, M., Vanjani, M., & Krosp, J. (1995). Group decision support systems. *Review of Business*, *16*(3), 38–42.

Araujo, R. M. d., & Borges, M. R. S. (2007). The Role of Collaborative Support to Promote Participation and Commitment in Software Development Teams. *Software Process Improvement and Practice*, *12*(3), 229–246. doi:10.1002/spip.314

Bamber, E. M., Watson, R. T., & Hill, M. C. (1996). The effects of group support system technology on audit group decision-making. *Auditing: A Journal of Practice & Theory*, *15*(1), 122-134.

Belton, V., Ackermann, F., & Shepherd, I. (1997). Integrated support from problem structuring through to alternative evaluation using COPE and V.I.S.A. *Journal of Multi-Criteria Decision Analysis*, *6*(3), 115–130. doi:10.1002/(SICI)1099-1360(199705)6:3<115::AID-MCDA140>3.0.CO;2-I

Benbasat, I., & Lim, L. H. (1993). The effects of group, task, context, and technology variables on the usefulness of group support systems: A meta-analysis of experimental studies. *Small Group Research*, *24*, 430–462. doi:10.1177/1046496493244002

Bidgoli, H. (1996). A new productivity tool for the 90's: Group support systems. *Journal of Systems Management*, *47*(4), 56–62.

Bommel, P. v., Hoppenbrouwers, S. J. B. A., Proper, H. A. E., & Weide, T. P. d. (2006). Exploring modelling strategies in a meta-modelling context. In R. Meersman, Z. Tari & P. Herrero (Eds.), *On the move to meaningful internet systems 2006: Proceedings of Otm 2006 workshops* (LNCS 4278, pp. 1128-1137). Berlin: Springer.

Burke, K., Chidambaram, L., & Lock, J. (1995). Evolution of relational factors over time: A study of distributed and non-distributed meetings. In *Proceedings of the Twenty-Eighth Hawaii International Conference on System Sciences* (Vol. 4, pp. 14-23).

Cass, K., Heintz, T. J., & Kaiser, K. M. (1991). Using a voice-synchronous GDSS in dispersed locations: A preliminary analysis of participant satisfaction. In *Proceedings of the Twenty-Fourth Hawaii International Conference on System Sciences* (Vol. 3, pp. 555-563).

Chudoba, K. M. (1999). Appropriations and patterns in the use of group support systems. *The Data Base for Advances in Information Systems*, *30*(3/4), 131–148.

Conklin, J., Selvin, A., Buckingham Shum, S., & Sierhuis, M. (2003). *Facilitated Hypertext for Collective Sensemaking: 15 Years on from gIBIS*. Paper presented at the Proceedings of the 8th International Working Conference on the Language-Action Perspective on Communication Modeling (LAP'03), Tilburg, The Netherlands.

Dietz, J. L. G. (1999). Understanding and modeling business processes with DEMO. In J. Akoka, M. Bouzeghoub, I. Comyn-Wattiau & E. Métais (Eds.), *Proceedings of the 18th International Conference on Conceptual Modeling ER '99* (pp. 188-202). Berlin: Springer.

Ericsson, K., & Simon, H. (1993). *Protocol Analysis: Verbal Reports as Data*. Boston: MIT Press.

Fjermestad, J., & Hiltz, S. R. (1998). An assessment of group support systems experiment research: Methodology and results. *Journal of Management Information Systems, 15*(3), 7–149.

Frederiks, P. J. M., & Weide, T. P. d. (2006). Information modelling: The process and the required competencies of its participants. *Data & Knowledge Engineering, 58*(1), 4–20. doi:10.1016/j.datak.2005.05.007

Hoppenbrouwers, S. J. B. A., Lindeman, L., & Proper, H. A. (2006). Capturing modelling processes - towards the modial modelling laboratory. In R. Meersman, Z. Tari & P. Herrero (Eds.), *On the move to meaningful internet systems 2006: Proceedings of Otm 2006 workshops* (LNCS 4278, pp. 1242-1252). Berlin: Springer.

Hoppenbrouwers, S. J. B. A., Proper, H. A., & Weide, T. P. d. (2005). Formal Modelling as a Grounded Conversation. In G. Goldkuhl, M. Lind & S. Haraldson (Eds.), *Proceedings of the 10th International Working Conference on the Language Action Perspective on Communication Modelling (LAP`05)*, Kiruna, Sweden (pp. 139-155). Linköping, Sweden: Linköpings Universitet.

Jackson, N. F., Aiken, M. W. V., Mahesh, B. H., & Bassam, S. (1995). Support group decisions via computer systems. *Quality Progress, 28*(5), 75–78.

Keller, F., & Wendt, S. (2003). *FMC: An Approach Towards Architecture-Centric System Development*. Paper presented at the 10th IEEE Symposium and Workshop on Engineering of Computer Based Systems, Pasadena, CA.

Mathieu, P., & Verrons, M.-H. (2002). *A generic model for contract negotiation*. Paper presented at the AISB'02 Symposium on Intelligent Agents in Virtual Markets, Imperial College of Science, Technology and Medicine, University of London.

Meire, A. P., Borges, M. R. S., & Araújo, R. M. d. (2003). Supporting collaborative drawing with the mask versioning mechanism. In J. Favela & D. Decouchant (Eds.), *Proceedings of CRIWG 2003, Groupware: Design, Implementation, and Use*, Autrans, France, September 28 - October 2, 2003, (LNCS 2806, pp. 208-223). Berlin: Springer.

Meire, A. P., Borges, M. R. S., & Araújo, R. M. d. (2007). Supporting multiple viewpoints in collaborative graphical editing. *Multimedia Tools and Applications, 32*(2), 185–208. doi:10.1007/s11042-006-0064-9

Morris, W. T. (1967). On the Art of Modeling. *Management Science, 13*(12), B707–B717. doi:10.1287/mnsc.13.12.B707

OMG. (2004). *UML 2.0 Superstructure Specification*. Retrieved December 20, 2005, from http://www.uml.org/

OMG. (2006). *Unified Modeling Language: Infrastructure*. Retrieved April 18, 2006, from http://www.uml.org/

Persson, A. (2001). *Enterprise Modelling in Practice: Situational Factors and their Influence on Adopting a Participative Approach*. Unpublished PhD thesis. Department of Computer and Systems Sciences, Stockholm University.

Qu, Y. (2007). *Sensemaking, Information Seeking and Retrieval: Supporting Representation Construction in Sensemaking*. Ann Arbor, MI: University of Michigan.

Rittgen, P. (2007). Negotiating Models. In J. Krogstie, A. Opdahl & G. Sindre (Eds.), *Proceedings of the 19th International Conference on Advanced Information Systems Engineering (CAiSE 2007)*, Trondheim, Norway, June 2007 (pp. 561-573). Berlin: Springer.

Scheer, A.-W. (1999). *ARIS - Business Process Modeling* (2nd ed.). Berlin: Springer.

Srinivasan, A., & Te'eni, D. (1995). Modeling as Constrained Problem Solving: An Empirical Study of the Data Modeling Process. *Management Science*, *41*(3), 419–434. doi:10.1287/mnsc.41.3.419

Stamper, R. (1991). The Semiotic Framework for Information Systems Research . In Nissen, H., Klein, H., & Hirschheim, R. (Eds.), *Information Systems Research: Contemporary Approaches and Emergent Traditions* (pp. 515–517). Amsterdam: North-Holland.

Townsend, A. M., Whitman, M. E., & Hendrickson, A. R. (1995). Computer support system adds power to group processes. *HRMagazine*, *40*(9), 87–91.

Willemain, T. R. (1994). Insights on Modeling from a Dozen Experts. *Operations Research*, *42*(2), 213–222. doi:10.1287/opre.42.2.213

Willemain, T. R. (1995). Model Formulation: What Experts Think about and When. *Operations Research*, *43*(6), 916–932. doi:10.1287/opre.43.6.916

Chapter 13
Collaborative Geospatial Web Services for Multi-Dimension: Remote Sensing Data

Chunyang Hu
Beihang University, China

Yongwang Zhao
Beihang University, China

Dianfu Ma
Beihang University, China

ABSTRACT

Satellite remote sensing imagery data is an important Geospatial data which is playing an increasingly important role in many applications such as crisis management, military activities and government decision-making. However, it will continue to be a great challenge to organize and manage these multi-dimension massive remote sensing data for collaborative visualization services in Internet environment. In this chapter the authors proposed a global hierarchical data model of massive multi-dimension remote sensing data based on tiling and pyramid technologies for the organization and management of multi-source and multi-scale remote sensing data. The authors implemented a collaborative Geospatial data visualization system based on their proposed storage structure of data model using Web Services, WSRF and Web2.0 technologies. Finally, the authors evaluated the prototype system with real data sets, which demonstrated the high performance data visualization in their system.

INTRODUCTION

Recently, remote sensing technology moves toward the paradigm of multi-sensor, high-resolution, high-spectral, and high temporal resolution. Remote sensing imagery plays an increasingly important role in many applications such as disaster, crisis management and military activities. The fast development of the Internet, especially the advent of World Wide Web, provides an infrastructure ideally suited to the widespread distribution and dissemination of remote sensing data.

Traditionally, users search remote sensing data in some pre-defined conditions (latitude and longitude, path and row, date) through an online

DOI: 10.4018/978-1-61692-016-6.ch013

metadata catalog service provided by data vendor, and order complete files that are delivered by media or over the network(P. Zhao, Yu, & Di, 2006). The process of identifying and accessing data typically takes up the most time. In addition, it is not suitable for general users without professional Geospatial domain knowledge and good technical background. They would prefer to browse data with a panoramic view way like Google Map.

Currently, remote sensing data centers store data in files that are organized in directories by time of observation rather than by physical location on the earth, and use proprietary data format for all of the data in these centers (Barkstrom et al., 2003). However, experience has shown that both the file organization and the data format do not meet the requirement of common users because users have invested large amount of time and efforts in learning to use tools that support other data formats. In addition, users need to download large amounts of unneeded data besides the desired data fields. After downloading the data files, the user must use his computing and storage resources to process these large data sets. This approach is obviously inefficient for most users. Both the file organization and the data format also make it difficult for data vendors to provide on-line data access service.

Google map provides a Web2.0 UI for the visualization of Geospatial information. Users can zoom and pan the satellite image of anyplace in the world. Nevertheless, it can neither support historic data browsing in same region nor provide collaborative visualization service that is very important for many applications.

The main objectives of this chapter are to address the above issues we put forward. We proposed a global hierarchical data Model for organization and management of massive multi-dimension remote sensing image data based on tiling and pyramid technologies. We implemented a distributed data storage system and collaborative Geospatial data visualization system including tiled WMS service based on our proposed data model storage structure using Web Services, WSRF and Web 2.0 technologies. We reported some experimental results. Our results demonstrated that our system was able to provide high performance on-line mapping service.

The remainder of this chapter is organized as follows. In the next section some OGC Web Service background are introduced. The third section we present an overview of existing work on massive remote sensing data organization and management, data visualization and Geospatial web service. The prototype system architecture is presented in the fourth section. In the fifth section we introduce our global hierarchical data model design and algorithm in support of data retrieve. The implementation of collaborative data visualization service including tiled WMS Service is presented in the sixth section. Performance evaluation of prototype system is depicted in the seventh section. Finally, in the eighth section, conclusions and future research work are presented.

BACKGROUND

The Open geospatial Consortium and the Technical Committee 211 of the international organization of Standards were established to address the interoperability issue by providing a series of standardized interface specifications. The fundamental ones include Web Map Services (WMS), Web Coverage Services (WCS), Web Feature Services (WFS), and Web Registries Services (WRS). They form the foundation for OGC web-based interoperable data access.

Web Map Service (WMS) is used for requesting and producing maps on the Internet, one of the main components of a suite of GIS interoperability standards. The WMS interaction between the client and the server is based on HTTP, with the client submitting requests in the form of Uniform Resource Locators (URLs) which contain standardized parameters specifying the details of the operation requested, using either the POST or the GET method. Three operations are defined in the current WMS standard: a request for service-level metadata GetCapabilities; the actual request for a map GetMap; and an inquiry about a point on a map GetFeatureInfo. While the implementation of the GetFeatureInfo operation is optional, the GetCapabilities and GetMap operations are mandatory for the server. If specific map characteristics such as projection and format are supported by both a client and a server, these two standard operations are sufficient for an independent mapping client application to access the map. While the WMS standard offers many other capabilities, the simplicity of achieving basic WMS functionality contributed to the rapid success and proliferation of WMS, making it one of the most common Internet services, and making interoperable Internet based GIS applications a reality.

RELATED WORK

There are some well-known projects on organizing and managing high-resolution remote sensing image data. The TerraServer project(Barclay, Gray, & Slutz, 2000) of Microsoft is the largest public repository of high-resolution satellite, aerial, and topographic data in the world. It is designed to be accessed by thousands of simultaneous users using Internet protocols via standard web browsers. TerraServer uses the so-called pyramid technique to assist the SQL Server database to manage images. With this technique, a relatively large image is extracted into different levels of detail to construct a pyramid structure. The images are transmitted only when the data of interest are requested by the user. However, TerraServer stores only one kind of remote sensing data from Russian military satellite Images SPIN-2 and does not support the management of multi-source remote sensing image data, and all tiles are stored in database as blob data type. The TerraServer treats each 160km×40km SPIN2 image as a separate scene. These scenes are not spliced together. Users can only pan and zoom within a scene, and must jump from one scene to another for browsing other parts of the Earth. Furthermore, it does not take into account the browsing of historical data.

NASA World Wind uses a multi-resolution layering technique that shows progressively more detail as a user zooms in to various locations. To do this, World Wind stores multiple copies of the same map at successively higher resolutions (Bell et al., 2007). However, World Wind is desktop software and not a web application system. The NASA JPL OnEarth(Plesea) WMS server is a high performance WMS server offering public access to very large NASA earth imagery datasets. It is a feature rich, scalable and fast implementation for WMS access to raster data. In addition to the main server binary, a tiled WMS and KML super-overlay is implemented as an apache module, offering a major boost in speed and availability to applications that can use pre-generated tiles. The main data storage format is a tiled, multi-resolution and multispectral raster data storage format that is used extensively for the production of large datasets. In this format, data is organized in tiles of uniform size, each tile being read and written as a unit. The data tiles are stored concatenated in a single file, a second index file being used to organize and keep track of the location of each tile within the whole image space. Each tile data can be compressed using either lossless or lossy compression algorithms, with raw, JPEG, abbreviated JPEG, zlib and bz2 being supported, together with a few unique optimizations for high byte count data types. A null index entry is used to symbolize non-existing data, providing explicit support for empty areas and providing efficient support for sparse datasets. Since the data and the index files can be specified separately, multiple index files can exist for a single data file, allowing different versions of a dataset to share the common areas. We used a different tile data organization method without index file for remote sensing data storage.

Google implements a distributed storage system named Bigtable for managing structured data. Many projects store data in Bigtable, including Google Earth, web indexing and Google Finance. Google Earth allows users to navigate across the world's surface: they can pan, view, and annotate satellite imagery at many different levels of resolution. This system uses one table to preprocess data, and a different set of tables for serving client data. The preprocessing pipeline uses one table to store raw imagery. During preprocessing, the imagery is cleaned and consolidated into final serving data. This table contains approximately 70 terabytes of data and therefore is served from disk. The images are efficiently compressed already, so Bigtable compression is disabled. Each row in the imagery table corresponds to a single geographic segment. Rows are named to ensure that adjacent geographic segments are stored near each other. The table contains a column family to keep track of the sources of data for each segment. This column family has a large number of columns: essentially one for each raw data image. Since each segment is only built from a few images, this column family is very sparse. The preprocessing pipeline relies heavily on Map/Reduce over Bigtable to transform data. The overall system processes over 1 MB/sec of data per tablet server during some of these Map/Reduce jobs. Bigtable has successfully provided a flexible, high-performance solution for managing satellite imagery data. However, Bigtable is built on the Google proprietary file system (GFS), GFS is more suitable for the storage and management of large raw satellite image data, not for small tile data.

A lot of work has also been concerned with providing frameworks and platforms for the integration of heterogeneous Geospatial data and the interoperability of Geospatial information service. For instance, Jim Gray and his coauthors(Barclay, Gray, Ekblad, Strand, & Richter, 2006) give technical insight into TerraService technologies through a bottom-up tour of the GIS Web service site's design and construction, as well as end-to-end descriptions of two large-scale GIS projects that use TerraService. Their proposals are mainly based on Microsoft SQL Server Database. The performance optimization of database will be a complex problem. On the contrary, our system is directly based on file system. Ahmet Sayer(Sayar, Aktas, Aydin, Fox, & Pierce, 2005)implements GIS services according to OGC standard specifications in accordance with the web service approach. However, their proposals are more focused on vector data rather than raster data.

In(Deng & Di, 2006) (Di, Zhao, Yang, Yu, & Yue, 2005) (Peisheng Zhao & Di, 2006), Liping Di proposes a framework for developing Web service based intelligent Geospatial knowledge systems based on the current advancements in Geospatial interoperability, knowledge management, and knowledge mining. The framework includes on demand information discovery, intelligent question answering, and self-evolving mechanisms. Geo-object and Geo-tree concepts are suggested to facilitate the mechanisms. Aijun Chen proposes an open, reusable, standards-compliant, and Grid-enabled Geospatial software system for archiving, managing, querying and serving NASA earth observing system data based on the Globus Toolkit(Chen, Di, Wei, Bai, & Liu, 2006). However, Liping Di and Aijun Chen more focus on the implementation of OGC Web Service specifications based on Web Services or Service Grid, and do not take into account the performance issues of the system.

A number of studies have addressed the Geospatial information system performance, Chaowei Yang proposes a set of solution to provide an improved treatment on WebGIS, including the use of pyramid and hash indices for handling large image data management and transmission problems, the use of multi-thread and cluster techniques for dealing with the problem of concurrent (C. Yang, Wong, Yang, Kafatos, & Li, 2005). We adopted some similar methods in designing our system. In(P. Yang, Cao, & Evans, 2007), Phil Yang points out existing performance problems

Figure 1. System architecture

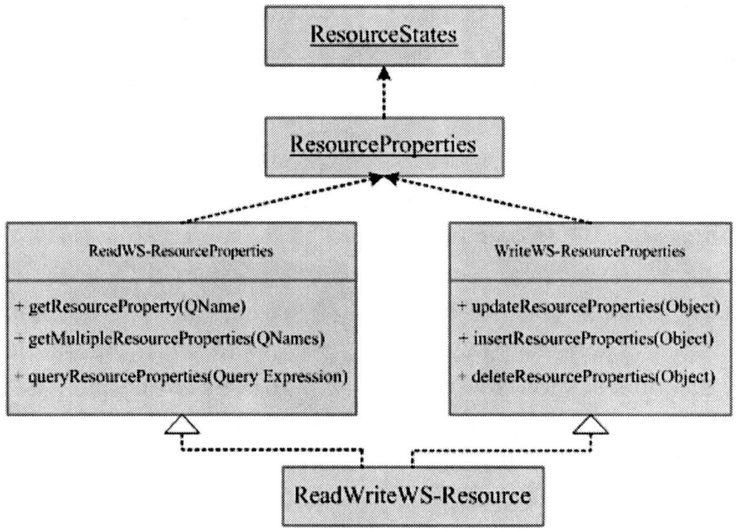

of Web Mapping servers via analyzing testing results. The response time of GetMap operation and the amount of concurrent request are primary problems. He proposes a set of principles for the design of a high-performance WMS client. Compared with Phil Yang's proposal, our system is more emphasized the comprehensive performance optimization of server and client.

SYSTEM ARCHITECTURE

The entire system architecture is depicted in (Figure 1). We adopt service-oriented architecture (SOA) for building our system. The Web Services technology provides several key benefits, including:

Interoperability: Geospatial data is easily exchanged between heterogeneous systems and incompatible data formats.

Integration: All the Geospatial applications are available as reusable services, which are combined in a loosely coupled fashion to form composite business applications.

As shown in (Figure 1), the entire system is composed of remote sensing image data distributed storage and service subsystem and Geospatial vector map service subsystem.

Remote sensing image data distributed storage and service subsystem consists of data loading pre-processing, data distribution and storage, data access and OGC web service. Data pre-processing component ensures that a new remote sensing imagery (GeoTIFF format) is distributed to appropriate file directory of storage structure for replacing old tile files through projection transformation, resolution scaling, edge expansion and image tiling. The image tiling module implemented with standard java advanced imaging libraries is responsible for shredding input imagery data into 256×256 pixels tiles stored in temporal disk space. The tile data update module updates tiles from temporal disk space to our distributed data storage system. Data distribution and storage component is primarily responsible for file system metadata management, data replication and transmission management. Data access component provides Web Services interface for data retrieval. In our implementation, the image data is not directly returned in the response, instead of a URL of the image. This allows the server to communicate in a non-blocking fashion with the client.

Geospatial vector map service subsystem consists of ArcIMS map server and gazetteer service components. ArcIMS map server provides standard OGC WMS interface for accessing vector map data with shapefile format. Gazetteer service component implements a transition service between geographic name and latitude-longitude pairs.

The Web client adopts Ajax to create customized mapping services and interactive web pages. Users drive the map updates by panning and zooming. One important aspect of Ajax is the function of XMLHttpRequest(XHR) which is the major communication mechanisms between the web servers and the client browsers. XHR can update a portion of the web page without reloading the content of the entire web page. We also implement a toolkits naming WSDL2Ajax based on IBM Web Services JavaScript library and XSLT which can generate JavaScript stub for calling web services. (Figure 2) shows the snapshot of web client.

Figure 2. The snapshot of web client

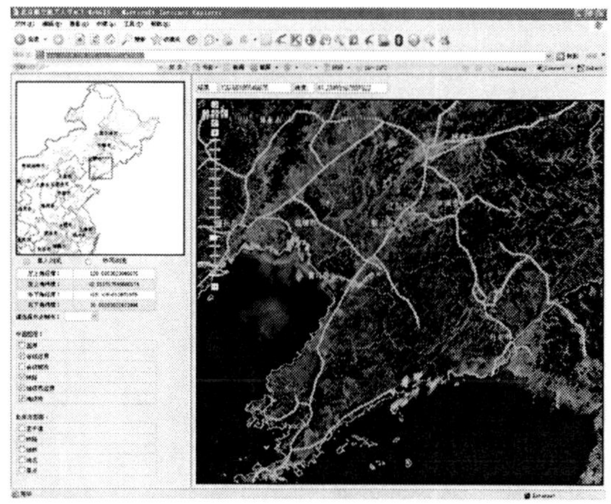

FRAMEWORK OF DISTRIBUTED DATA STORAGE AND MANAGEMENT SUBSYSTEM

The distributed data storage and management subsystem is composed of one master server and multiple storage servers, as shown in (Figure 3). Master server is used to forward the client to the right place on the storage server where they can

Figure 3. Distributed data storage and management subsystem

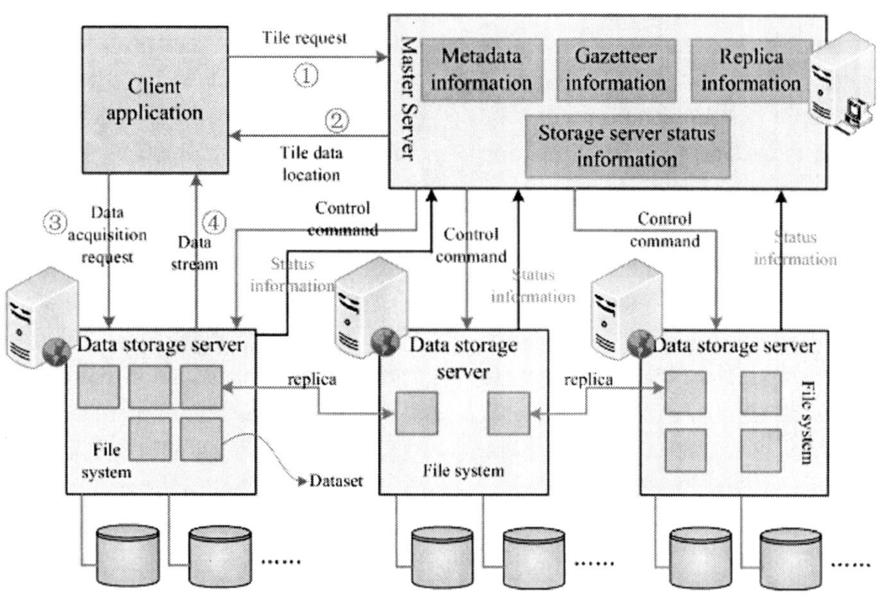

Figure 4. Global hierarchical data model

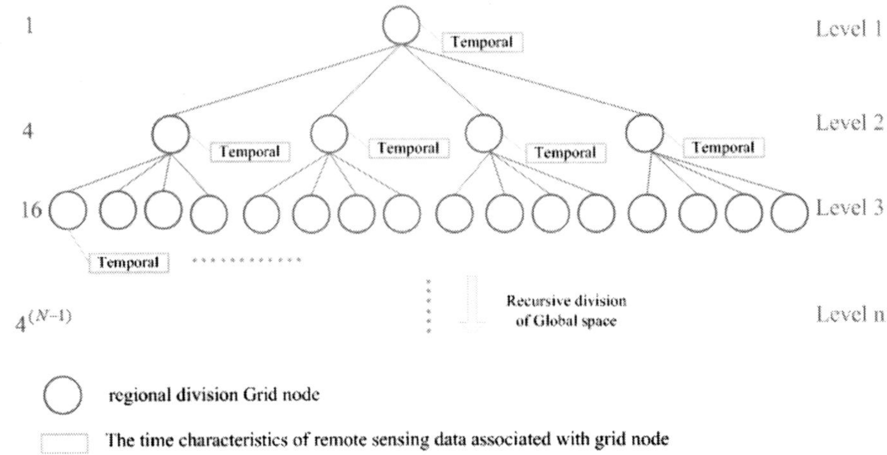

actually pick up the data they are looking for. Storage server store tile image data on disk array as file and read or write tile data specified by file name (X_i Y_j Z_k .jpg). For performance and reliability, the tile file of hot region is replicated on multiple storage servers. By default, two replicas are stored. The master server maintains all file system metadata. This includes the ID of each storage server, the create date time of data sets (the smallest unit of region partition, contain a fix number of tile), and the mapping from data sets to storage server. The master periodically communicates with each storage server in heartbeat messages to give it instructions and collect its state. Clients interact with the master for metadata operations, but all data-bearing communication goes directly to the storage servers.

The data access process of system is as follows:

Client applications send a data request; the master server accepts the data request and determine the location of data via querying the metadata information, and then sends the location of data to client; client send data acquiring request to appropriate storage server; storage server receives data requests and execute read data operation, and then directly sends data stream to client application.

ORGANIZATION OF LARGE-SCALE MULTIDIMENSIONAL REMOTE SENSING DATA

Remote sensing data has some important characteristics. Firstly, remote sensing data is collected from different satellite platform using proprietary data archiving format; Secondly, there are different spatial, temporal and spectral scales for multiple source remote sensing data; thirdly, remote sensing data is not modified or rarely modified. Finally, remote sensing data is queried according to spatial, temporal and other attribute criteria.

In order to efficiently organize and manage so complex data with the above-mentioned characteristics for data visualization, we proposed a global hierarchical data model based on image pyramid and tiling strategies. Our data model couples the physical storage and logical structure of the geospatial data, and describes the structure of quad tree by directory structure of the data storage. Our data model added temporal dimension on the basis of the traditional quad tree, as illustrated in (Figure 4). This data model has simple structure and is easy to be implemented

A nineteen level image pyramid is constructed for presenting a seamless mosaic of the earth.

Figure 5. The storage structure of Global hierarchical data model

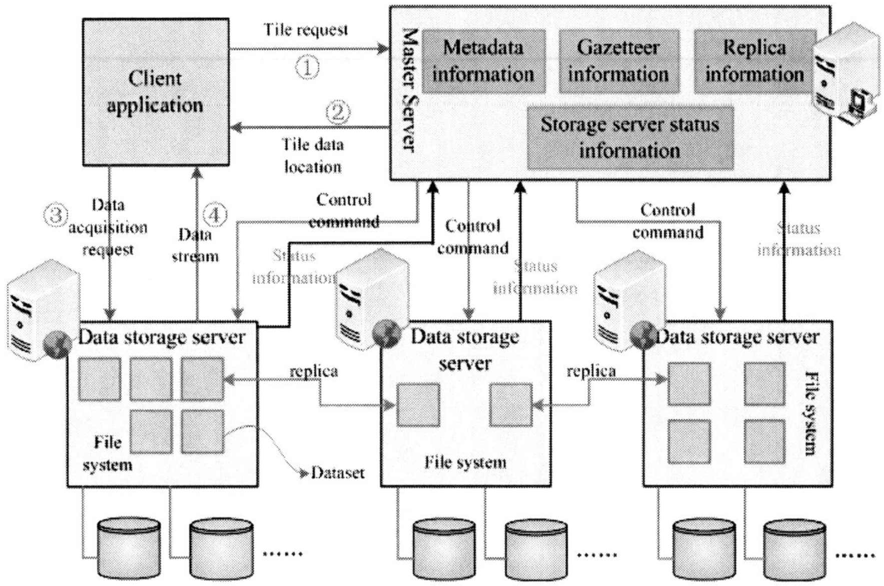

Level 1 is the top of image pyramid with the lowest spatial resolution; level 19 is the bottom of image pyramid with the highest spatial resolution. Every level divides the world into fixed number of tiles, each tiles is 256 × 256 pixel square that can be stored in JPEG image format. The whole world is covered by one tile at level 1, four tiles at level 2, each successive zoom level has 4 times as many map tiles (2x in the X direction, and 2x in the Y direction) as the previous level, so the number of tiles at level 19 is $4^{(19-1)}$.

Our image pyramid uses the 0.6-meter resolution as base resolution (the spatial resolution of level 19), and supports a powers-of-2 ladder of resolutions. The Spherical Mercator's projection is chosen by our system, this type of projections is well-suited as an interactive world map that can be panned and zoomed seamlessly to local maps, and implementations should have a latitude cut-off point (±85 degree) to avoid the infinite stretch at the poles. This requires that we transform our satellite imagery, since most of our data use UTM with datum WGS84 projection by default.

HIERARCHICAL DIRECTORY STORAGE STRUCTURE OF DATA MODEL

The hierarchical directory storage structure of our data model was shown as follows:

Considering the quantity of tile file and the characteristics of data sources vary at each pyramid level, we design several different hierarchical directory structures. As the spatial resolution of remote sensing image from level 1 to level 7 is low, it can be used for spatial navigation. In addition, the number of the tile files at each level is very small so that they can be put directly in their own directory respectively. The coordinate information is represented by the file name such as "$X_i Y_j Z_k$.jpg". The X and Y coordinates specify the location at the given zoom level. Z denotes zoom level. In (Figure 5), six master directories named from 8 to 13 are arranged in hierarchical layers using the spatial range, temporal range. Master directory represents the image pyramid zoom level. Every master directory has its own sub-directory. These subdirectories representing spatial range divide the earth plane into $4^{(S-7)}$ square regions, and are named from X_0Y_0 to $X_{2^{(S-7)}-1}Y_{2^{(S-7)}-1}$ (S denotes zoom level). In each of these spatial range subdirectories, there are further subdirectories for time of observation. The up-to-date data is stored in"Latest" folder. "Date" directory is used for storing historic data. As shown in (Figure 5), each master directory named from 14 to 19 represents zoom level. The spatial partition subdirectory divides geographic region into 4^6 partitions named from X_0Y_0 to $X_{(2^6-1)}Y_{(2^6-1)}$. Each partition is cut into $4^{(S-13)}$ small pieces by the sub-spatial partition subdirectory beneath spatial partition subdirectory (S denotes zoom level).

In summary, we fully considered the main features of remote sensing data on the hierarchical directory storage structure design. This hierarchical directory storage structure has good scalability (Time dimension can be extended) and is convenient for distributed storage (the mapping from logic storage structure to physical storage). In addition, each leaf node directory contains less than 4096 tile files which can improve file access performance. Finally, this design is more convenient for data update and historical data access.

DATA RETRIEVAL ALGORITHM

The data retrieval algorithm is based on our storage structure and grid coordinates system. The northwest (upper left) corner of Mercator projection plane is origin of our grid coordinate system, X values begin at 0, starting from the left or west side of the grid coordinate system. Y values begin at 0, starting from the top or north edge of the grid coordinate system. For example, the earth plane is consisted of 16 tiles at level 3, each tile are named as shown in (Figure 6).

The algorithm details of retrieving tile data are shown in (Algorithm 1). We also implemented a algorithm named lonlat2xy for the conversion between latitude-longitude coordinates and grid coordinates.

Algorithm 1.

Input: X and Y denote the tile's relative offset with the plane grid on the x-axis and the y-axis, Z denotes the zoom level.

Output: return a relative storage path of tile

```
{
tileDirPath ← "";
spaceDiv1 ← 0;
spaceDiv2 ← 0;
if(14 ≤ Z ≤ 19) then
  { spaceDiv1 ← 6;
    spaceDiv2 ← Z − 13;
  }
else if (Z ≥ 8) then
  spaceDiv1 ← Z − 7;
 tileDirPath ← "Scale"+ Z + "/ ";
 if (Z ≥ 8) then
 {
   xSpaceDiv1 ← X / 2^(Z−1−spaceDiv1);
   ySpaceDiv1 ← Y / 2^(Z−1−spaceDiv1);
   level2Dir ← " X "+ Math.floor(xSpaceDiv1)
+" Y "+ Math.floor(ySpaceDiv1);
   tileDirPath ← tileDirPath + level2Dir + "/ ";
 }
 if(Z ≥ 14) then
 {
   xSpaceDiv2 ← X / 2^(Z−1−spaceDiv1−spaceDiv2);
   ySpaceDiv2 ← Y / 2^(Z−1−spaceDiv1−spaceDiv2);
   level3Dir ← " X "+ Math.floor(xSpaceDiv2) +
" Y "+ Math.floor(ySpaceDiv2);
   tileDirPath ← tileDirPath + level3Dir
+"/ "+ "latest";
 } / /end
```

Algorithm 1. Algorithm of data retrieving

Algorithm 2. lonlat2xy

Input: long (longitude), lat (latitude), zoom (1~19)

Out: XY Grid coordinates

$$
\begin{array}{l}
\{ \\
\quad \mathrm{int}[]\, xy; \\
\quad width \leftarrow 2^{(zoom-1)}; \\
\quad height \leftarrow 2^{(zoom-1)}; \\
\quad tilewidth \leftarrow \dfrac{360}{width}; \\
\quad x \leftarrow \dfrac{(lon+180.0)}{tilewidth}; \\
\quad xy[0] \leftarrow x; \\
\quad yTop \leftarrow lat2y(+85.0511289); \\
\quad yBottom \leftarrow lat2y(-85.0511289); \\
\quad yTemp \leftarrow lat2y(lat); \\
\quad y \leftarrow height \times \dfrac{(yTemp - yTop)}{(yBottom - yTop)}; \\
\quad xy[1] \leftarrow y; \\
\quad return\; xy; \\
\\
\quad double\; lat2y\,(double\; \varphi) \\
\quad \{ \\
\quad\quad pi \leftarrow 3.14159265358979; \\
\quad\quad double\; sv \leftarrow \sin\dfrac{(\varphi \times pi)}{180}; \\
\quad\quad return\, \dfrac{1}{2}\ln\dfrac{(1+sv)}{(1-sv)}; \\
\} //end
\end{array}
$$

Algorithm 2. The algorithm for transform the latitude and longitude coordinates into a grid coordinate

For example, there is a latitude and longitude point (40.050737, 116.1447114), we can compute a corresponding tile file name (X215646Y99194Z19.jpg) through using (Algorithm 2), and then we can find its storage path by using (Algorithm 1), the calculating process of (Algorithm 1) was illustrated as follows:

$$
\begin{array}{l}
Because\; z = 19, then\; spaceDiv1 = 6, \\
spaceDiv2 = 6(code\; line\, 5 \sim 8) \\
tileDirPath = "Scale" + 19(code\; line\, 11) \\
Because\; z = 19 \geq 18, then \\
xSpaceDiv1 = \dfrac{215646}{2^{19-1-6}} = \dfrac{215646}{2^{12}} = 52.64 \\
ySpaceDiv1 = \dfrac{99194}{2^{19-1-6}} = 24.21 \\
tileDirPath = "Scale" + 19 + "/" + "X" + 52 \\
+ "Y" + 24; \\
Because\; z = 19 \geq 14(code\; line\, 19), then \\
xSpaceDiv2 = \dfrac{215646}{2^{19-1-6-6}} = \dfrac{215646}{2^{6}} = 3369.46 \\
ySpaceDiv2 = \dfrac{99194}{2^{6}} = 1549.90 \\
tileDirPath = "Scale" + 19 + "/" + "X" + 52 \\
+ "Y" + 24 + "/" + "X" + 3369 + "Y" + 1549 \\
+ "/" + "latest"
\end{array}
$$

WSRF-BASED COLLABORATIVE BROWSING

We have extended our Web clients and services to build a collaborative system using WSRF-compliant SOA model. The Web services Resource

Figure 6. Grid system coordinates and tile naming

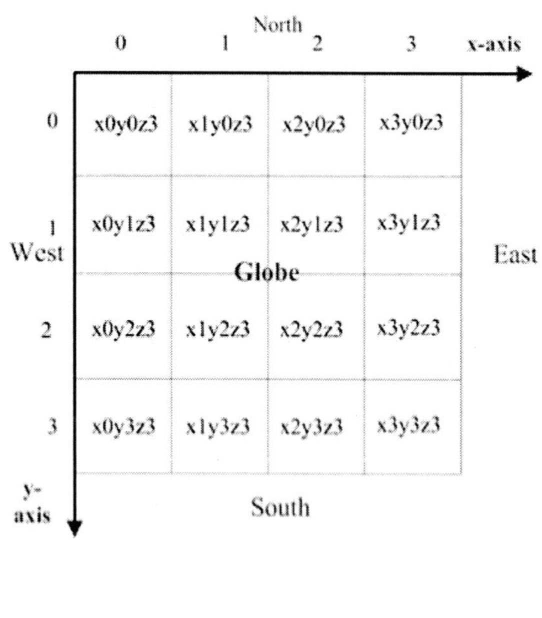

Figure 7. Co-browsing

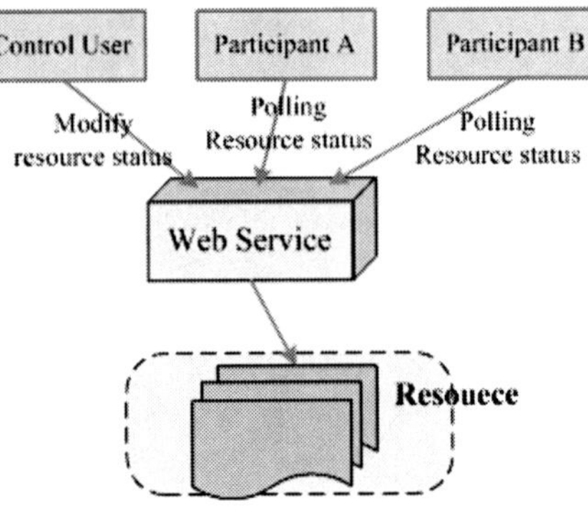

Figure 8. The tile grid

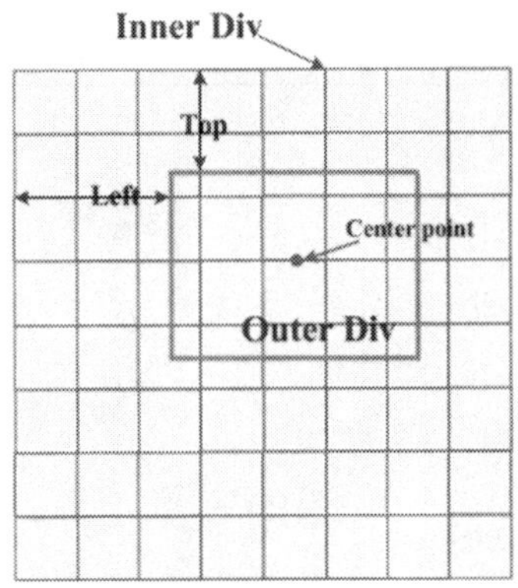

Framework(Banks, 2006) is an open framework for modeling and accessing persistent resources using web services. WSRF specifications build on existing Web Services standards to address the limitation of statelessness inherent to plain web services through the concept of WS-Resources, and also by defining conventions for the management of state.

A WS-Resource is the combination of a stateful resource and a Web Services that interacts with it, and is addressable by an Endpoint Reference (EPR) that adheres to WS-Addressing. WSRF comprise four specifications, explaining how WS-Resources can be represented, accessed, managed, and collected: WS-ResourceProperties, WSResourceLiftime, WS-ServiceGroup, and WS-BaseFaults. WSRF specifications enable the discovery of, introspection upon, and interaction with stateful resources in standard and interoperable ways.

Our system allows two or more browsers to synchronize their displays using shared resource status: if the controlling user zooms or pans the display, the other participants in the session will have their browser displays automatically updated, as shown in (Figure 7).

As shown in (Figure 8), the scrolling map effect is achieved by moving an "inner div" inside of an "outer div" (inner div and outer div are element defined in HTML, outer div represents visible windows); therefore, the tiles we need to display are calculated by determining the current position of the "inner div" relative to the "outer div" and then working out which tiles are visible in the portion of the "inner div" that are visible. We'll then add those tiles to the"inner div".

To enable "co-browsing" and synchronous collaboration of multiple clients, the current position of the "inner div" relative to the "outer div" (InnerDivPosition) is a state resource. It has three properties: top, left and zoom values. We wrap the resource properties with Web Services interfaces defined in the WSRF specifications to implement the WS-Resources. Six portTypes defined in WSResourceProperties can meet the requirements for accessing resource properties. Each of the portTypes exposes a single operation with the same name as the portType. Using these interfaces we can dynamically retrieve, query, update, insert and delete the resource properties of a WS-Resource at runtime. The details are shown in (Figure 9).

THE IMPLEMENTATION OF TILED WMS SERVICE

We have implemented a tiled web map server in accord with OGC WMS specification with the purpose of providing standard data visualization

Figure 9. WSRF operations

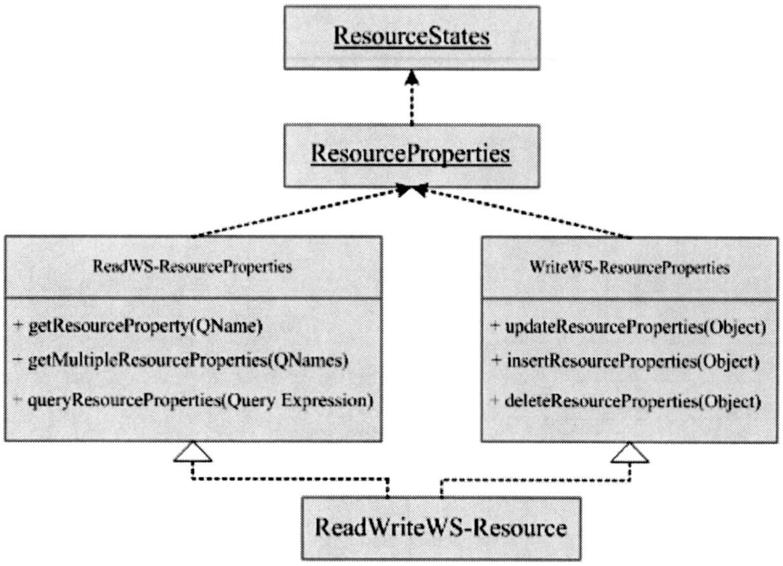

service and data access interface for other system or applications. The WMS was designed on the basis of our tile data storage structure. The process of GetMap was shown below.

Figure 10. GetMap work flow

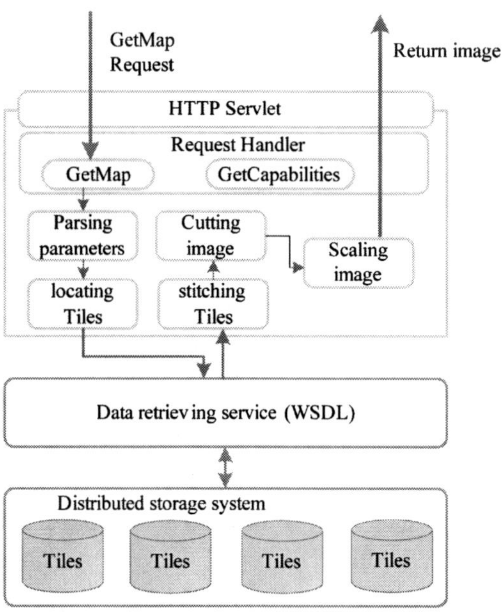

The core algorithm of implementing WMS is described as follows:

a. Accepting the user's HTTP request and parsing the relevant parameters (BBOX, Width and Height);
b. Computing the requested remote sensing image scale according to the range of longitude and latitude(BBOX), width and height($Scale_{req} = \frac{(lon_{ne} - lon_{sw})}{Width}$) (Figure 11);

Figure 11. The user's requested BBOX, width and height parameters

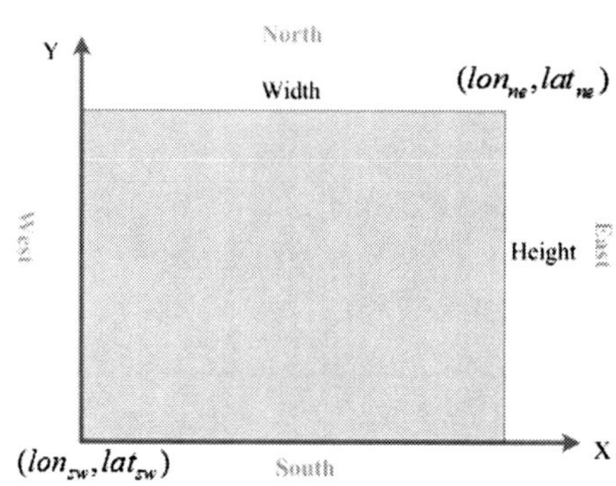

Table 1. Pre-defined scale list

Zoom level	Scale division (degree/ pixel)	Spatial resolution
19	5.364418029785156E-6	0.6 m
18	1.0728836059570312E-5	1.2 m
17	2.1457672119140625E-5	2.4 m
16	4.291534423828125E-5	4.8 m
15	8.58306884765625E-5	9.6 m
14	1.71661376953125E-4	19.2 m
13	3.4332275390625E-4	38.4 m
12	6.866455078125E-4	76.8 m
11	0.001373291015625	153.6 m
10	0.00274658203125	307.2 m
9	0.0054931640625	614.4 m
8	0.010986328125	1228.8 m
7	0.02197265625	2457.6 m
6	0.0439453125	4915.2 m
5	0.087890625	9830.4 m
4	0.17578125	19660.8 m
3	0.3515625	39321.6 m
2	0.703125	78643.2 m
1	1.40625	157286.4 m

c. Searching pre-defined scale list (Table 1) and determining the target zoom level;
d. Computing XY grid coordinate (X_iY_k) according to the upper left corner latitude and longitude and zoom level, and (X_jY_m) according to the lower right corner latitude and longitude and zoom level (Algorithm 2);
e. Finding related tiles at target zoom level by using grid coordinate information (Figure 12);
f. Stitching these related tiles to form an image, which may have a spatial extent larger than the requested area;
g. Cutting the image to match the requested width and height;
h. Scaling the image to the requested scale level, if necessary;
i. Returning the generating image to client.

Figure 12. Locating Tiles from a pyramid level

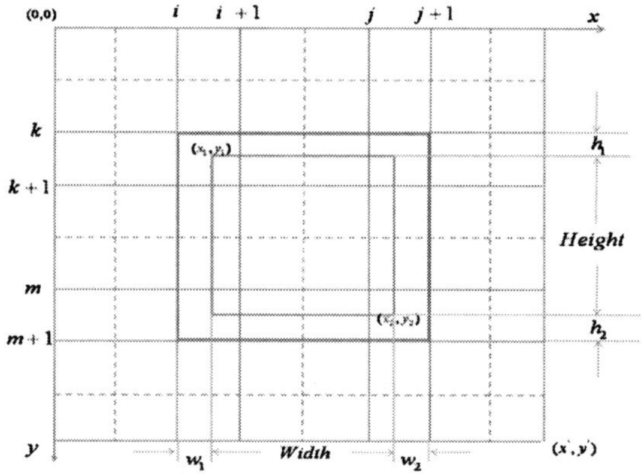

Figure 13. The snapshot of OGC WMS Web Client

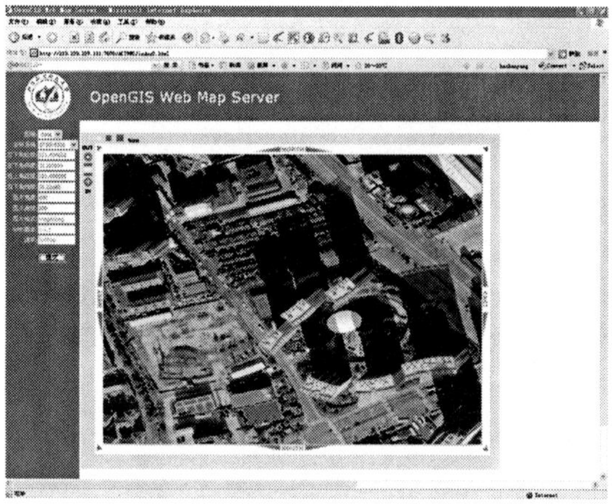

It is possible that no zoom level in pyramid has the scale of exactly $Scale_{req}$,and therefore the goal is to identify the two zoom level such that their scales are in the relation of $S_m \leq Scale_{req} < S_{m+1}$, $Zoom_{m+1} < Zoom_{req} \leq Zoom_m$. In this case, the image of $Zoom_m$ will be used to provide a better display of the data.

In order to allow users access remote sensing data provided by WMS Server via visualization style, we developed an Ajax-based OGC WMS client. The user can browse data through pan, zoom in and zoom out operations. The screenshots of client is illustrated in (Figure 13).

Table 2. Remote Sensing image data sources

Satellite sensor	*Spatial resolution*	*Temporal resolution*	*Product Type*
QuickBird(CCD)	*0.6m*	*1-3 days*	*Multi-band Synthetic image*
CBERS02B(IIR)	*2.36m*	*104 days*	*Panchromatic image*
CBERS02B(CCD)	*19m*	*26 days*	*Multi-band Synthetic image*
Landsat-7	*30/60m*	*15 days*	*Multi-band Synthetic image*
CBERS02B(WFI)	*258m*	*5 days*	*Multi-band Synthetic image*
Terra(MODIS)	*500/1000m*	*1-2 days*	*Multi-band Synthetic image*

PERFORMANCE EVALUATION

To evaluate the performance of prototype system using our file storage structure, we performed our experiments on real data sets, and compared with Deegree(Fitzke, Greve, M\üller, & Poth, 2004) WMS using the same data sources. The result indicated that our design of data organization and management structure achieved good performance on data access, especially when a large number of users are accessing the server simultaneously. In the first subsection, we start with describing the real data sets used in our experiment. We detail our experimental results in the second subsection.

Figure 14. The network topology structure

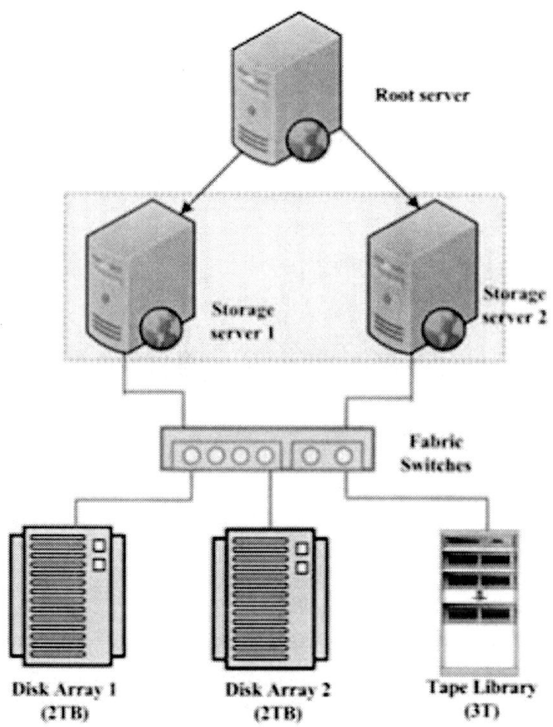

Experimental Data Sets

In this evaluation we used several types of data sets, as seen in (Table 2).

Most of these data are provided by the China Center for Resource Satellite Data and Applications (CRESDA). MODIS data are acquired from China national MODIS data center. Part of our data comes from the site of http://www.worldwinddata.com/. The total volume of all data is approximately 2TB.

Experimental implementation

There are two high-performance HP data storage servers with 16GB memory, four Intel Xeon MP Processors and 160GB disk place for providing data access service. They are connected two 2TB RAID disk arrays via fiber channel switch.

The entire hierarchical storage directory structure is created on two high capacity raid disk arrays respectively. All image tiles are distributed into these two disk arrays according to different geographic region partition. In (Figure 14), one disk array stores all recent Western China satellite image data at each zoom level, and all latest East China satellite image data at each zoom level are stored in another disk arrays. Most of historical data are stored in tape library.

Figure 15. Average response time of pan operation with 30 concurrent users (a) Deegree WMS (b) ACTGIS WMS

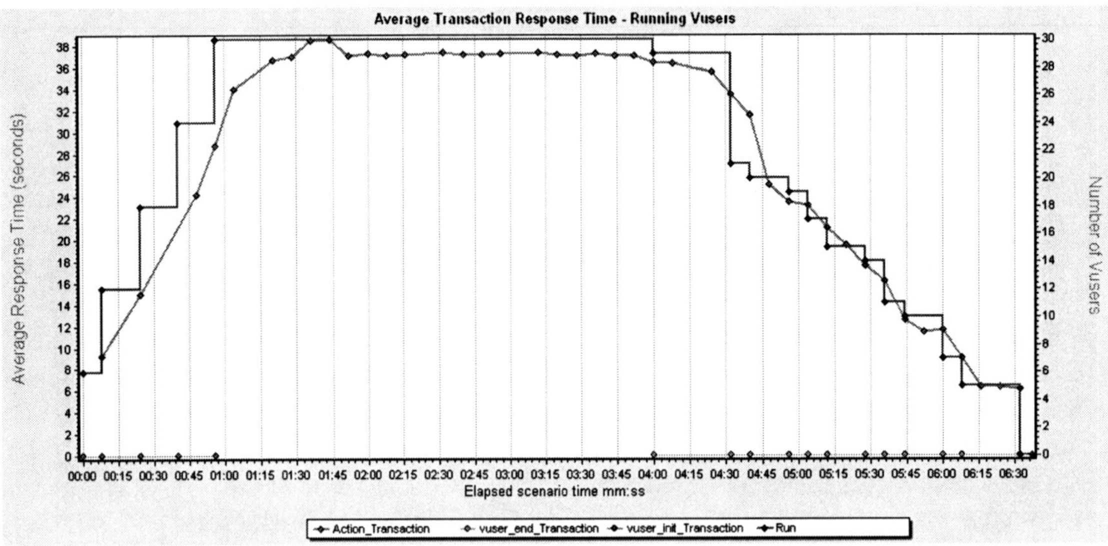

15(A)

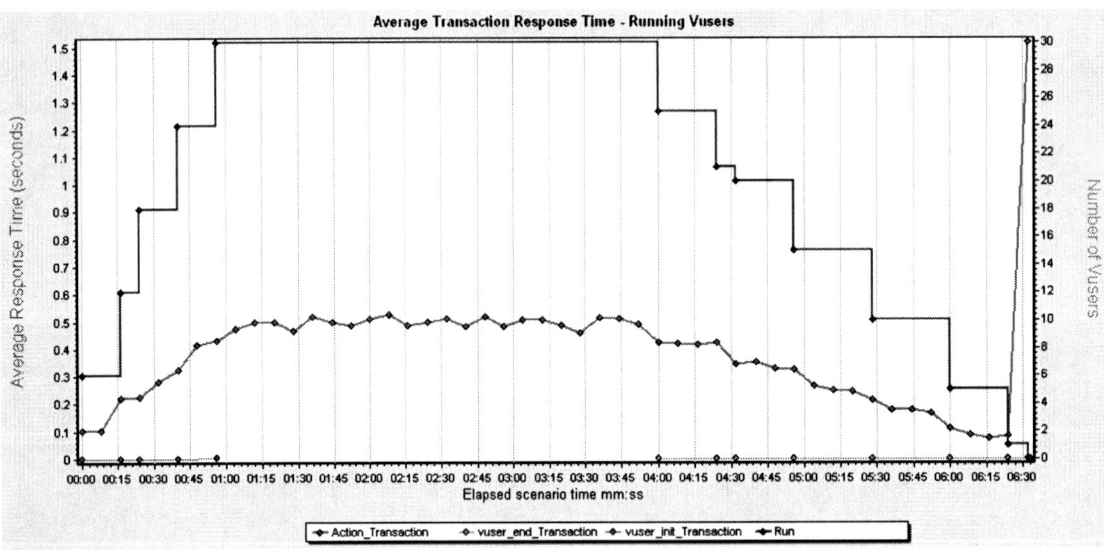

15(B)

The tests were conducted with a client running on a computer with a intranet connection, 1.8 GHz CPU, and 1GB RAM. We adopted LoadRunner 9.0 software for system performance test, and simulated 30,50 and 100 concurrent users executing pan operation(panning the same distance along

Figure 16. Average response time of pan operation with 50 concurrent users (a) Deegree WMS (b) ACTGIS WMS

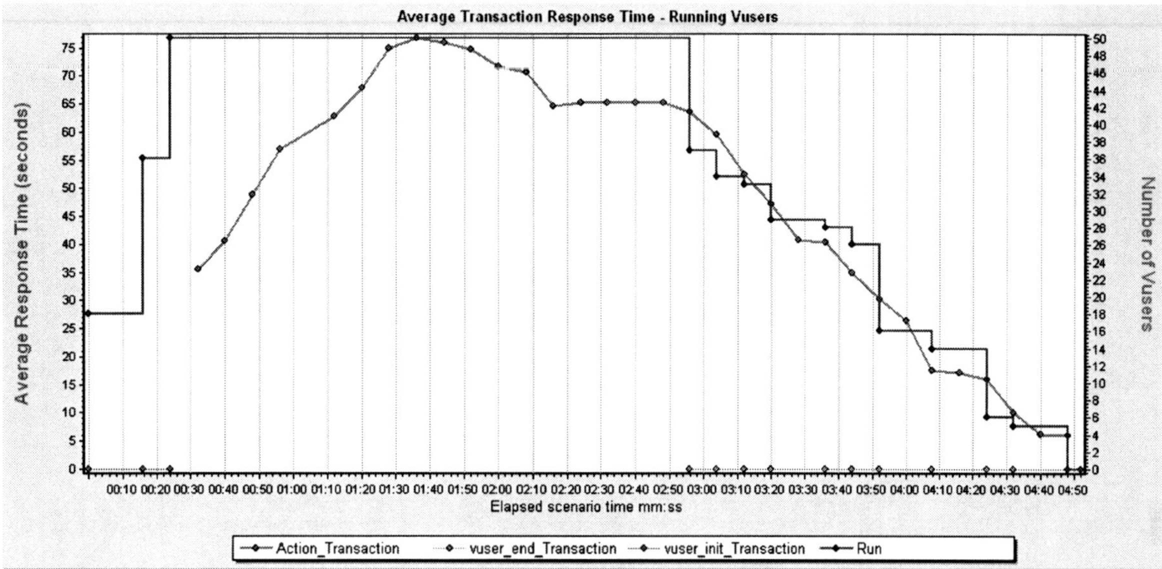

16(A)

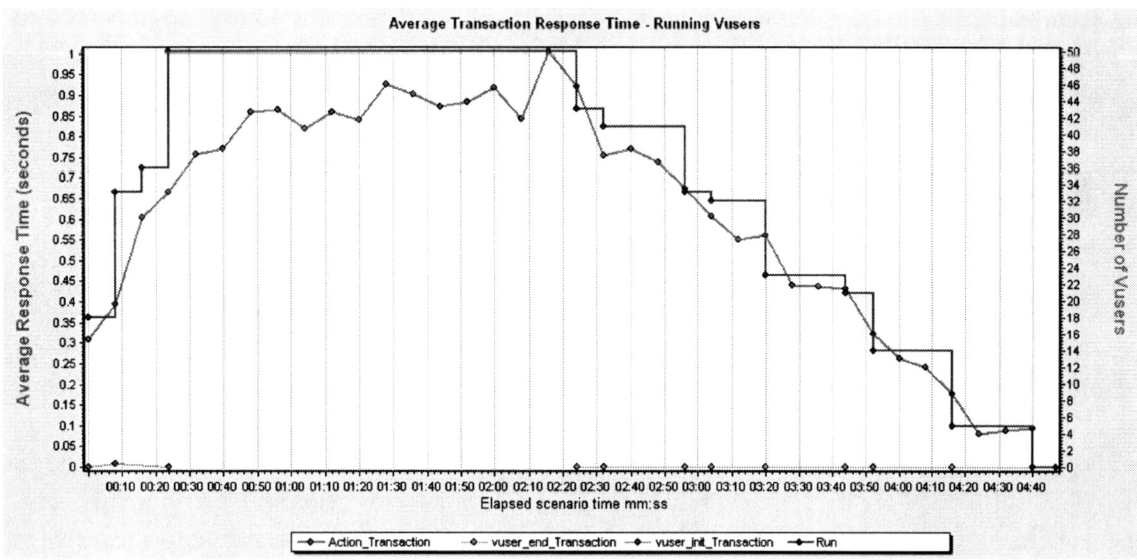

16(B)

the horizontal direction with the same viewer's windows size and region) respectively for two minutes. The test results were illustrated in (Figure 15), (Figure 16) and (Figure 17).

Figure 17. Average response time of pan operation with 100 concurrent users; ACTGIS WMS

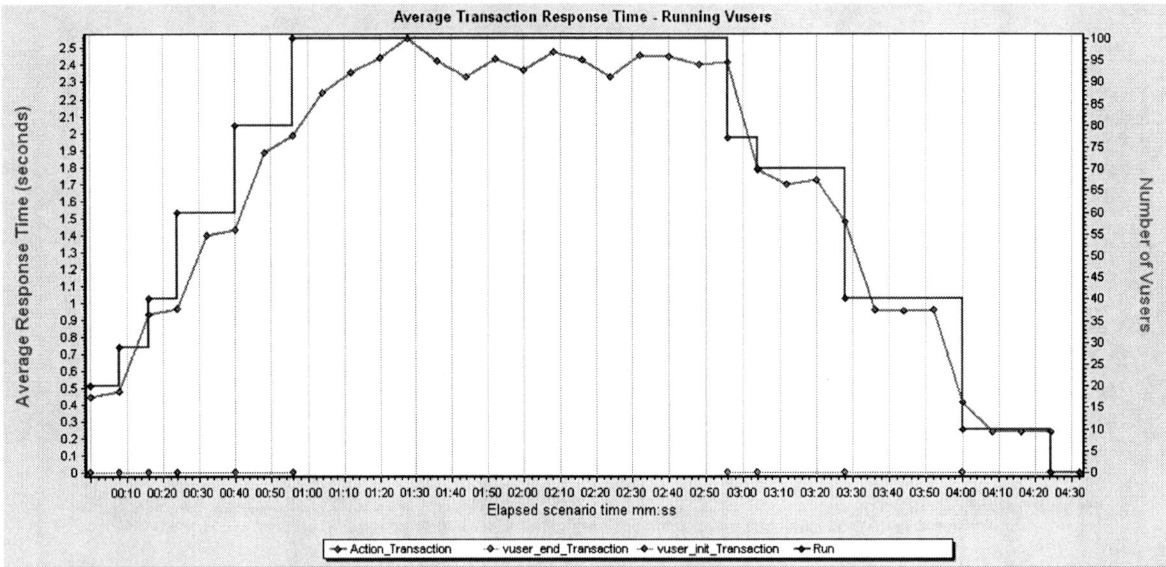

We made several observations from (Figure 15). The average response time of ACTGIS WMS was about 0.5 seconds (purple curve) with 30 concurrent requests. On the contrary, the average response time of Deegree WMS exceeded 35 seconds. In (Figure 16), the average response time of Deegree WMS reached 76 seconds with 50 concurrent requests. The performance of the Deegree WMS was significantly decreased and our system still had a good performance (1 seconds) when accessed by 50 concurrent users. As depicted in the (Figure 17), the average response time of our system was 2.5 seconds with 100 concurrent users. Deegree WMS server cannot return valid response.

In order to improve performance, Deegree WMS also uses image pyramid technology for organizing raster image data. A raster image is split into a number of small tiles and all tiles forming a layer can be stored in a shapefile with polygons representing the footprint of each file. However, the speed is still slow especially when more concurrent users access data. This is due to the size of tile index file will become bigger and bigger when the number of tile files are increasing. This greatly affects data access speed. Our data retrieve algorithm can calculate storage path of tile file according to grid coordinates information without shapefile index file. Our experimental results showed that our system can handle concurrent users' requests within a reasonable time span.

CONCLUSION

In this paper we proposed a global hierarchical data model that demonstrates how to manage multiple sources remote sensing effectively, and implemented a distributed data storage management system. It improves the efficiency of publishing large images and reduces response time for user's processing request. We also represented a web2.0-based service-oriented software paradigm for developing collaborative visualization service.

We plan to extend our work in several directions. First, we will implement role-based collaborative service on the basis of the WS-ServiceGroup specification. Second, access control service will be added in distributed data storage management system.

ACKNOWLEDGMENT

This research work was supported by grants from National High Technology Research and Development Program of China (2006AA01Z19A and 2007AA010301), China 973 Fundamental R&D Program (No.2005CB321901). The authors are grateful to Ying Wang, Min Liu and the other members of the Web Services Group for many insightful discussions during the work on the system development.

REFERENCES

Banks, T. (2006). *Web Services Resource Framework (WSRF)–Primer v1. 2*. OASIS Committee Draft.

Barclay, T., Gray, J., Ekblad, S., Strand, E., & Richter, J. (2006). Designing and Building TerraService. *IEEE Internet Computing*, *10*(5), 16–25. doi:10.1109/MIC.2006.95

Barclay, T., Gray, J., & Slutz, D. (2000). Microsoft TerraServer: a spatial data warehouse. *SIGMOD Record*, *29*(2), 307–318. doi:10.1145/335191.335424

Barkstrom, B. R., Hinke, T. H., Gavali, S., Smith, W., Seufzer, W. J., & Hu, C. (2003). Distributed Generation of NASA Earth Science Data Products. *Journal of Grid Computing*, *1*(2), 101–116. doi:10.1023/B:GRID.0000024069.33399.ee

Bell, D. G., Kuehnel, F., Maxwell, C., Kim, R., Kasraie, K., Gaskins, T., et al. (2007). *NASA world wind: Opensource GIS for mission operations*.

Chen, A., Di, L., Wei, Y., Bai, Y., & Liu, Y. (2006). *An optimized grid-based, OGC standards-compliant collaborative software system for serving NASA geospatial data*.

Deng,M., &Di,L.(2006). Utilization of latest geospatial Web service technologies for remote sensing education through GeoBrain sysem.

Di, L., Zhao, P., Yang, W., Yu, G., & Yue, P. (2005). *Intelligent geospatial Web services*.

Fitzke, J., Greve, K., M\üller, M., & Poth, A. (2004). *Building SDIs with Free Software-the deegree project*.

Plesea, L. (n.d.). The Design . *Implementation and Operation of the JPL OnEarth WMS Server*.

Sayar, A., Aktas, M. S., Aydin, G., Fox, G., & Pierce, M. (2005). *Developing a Web Service-Compatible Map Server for Geophysical Applications*. Paper presented at the Submitted to ACM-GIS Conference.

Yang, C., Wong, D. W., Yang, R., Kafatos, M., & Li, Q. (2005). Performance-improving techniques in web-based GIS. *International Journal of Geographical Information Science*, *19*(3), 319–342. doi:10.1080/13658810412331280202

Yang, P., Cao, Y., & Evans, J. (2007). Web Map Server Performance and Client Design Principles. *GIScience & Remote Sensing*, *44*(4), 320–333. doi:10.2747/1548-1603.44.4.320

Zhao, P., & Di, L. (2006). *Semantic Web service based geospatial knowledge discovery*.

Zhao, P., Yu, G., & Di, L. (2006). Geospatial Web Services. *Emerging Spatial Information Systems and Applications*, *1*(1).

KEY TERMS AND DEFINITIONS

Geospatial Web service: are applications that process geospatial data. There are many types of geospatial services, such as Web mapping services, spatial analysis services, metadata services, and visualization services. A service may be tightly coupled with a specific dataset or dataset collection, or loosely coupled, otherwise.

Pyramid model: is a type of multi-scale signal representation developed by the computer vision, image processing and signal processing communities, in which a signal or an image is subject to repeated smoothing and sub-sampling. Historically, pyramid representation is a predecessor to scale space representation and multi resolution analysis.

Web 2.0: is commonly associated with web applications which facilitate interactive information sharing, interoperability, user-centered design and collaboration on the World Wide Web. A Web 2.0 site allows its users to interact with other users or to change website content, in contrast to non-interactive websites where users are limited to the passive viewing of information that is provided to them.

WSRF: provides a set of operations that web services may implement to become stateful; web service clients communicate with resource services which allow data to be stored and retrieved. When clients talk to the web service they include the identifier of the specific resource that should be used inside the request, encapsulated within the WS-Addressing endpoint reference. This may be a simple URI address, or it may be complex XML content that helps identify or even fully describe the specific resource in question.

Section 5
Information Storage

Chapter 14
Query Performance Optimization in XML Data Warehouses

Hadj Mahboubi
Université de Lyon, France

Jérôme Darmont
Université de Lyon, France

ABSTRACT

XML data warehouses form an interesting basis for decision-support applications that exploit complex data. However, native-XML database management systems (DBMSs) currently bear limited performances and it is necessary to research for ways to optimize them. In this chapter, the authors present two such techniques. First, they propose an XML join index that is specifically adapted to the multidimensional architecture of XML warehouses. It eliminates join operations while preserving the information contained in the original warehouse. Second, the authors present a strategy for selecting XML materialized views by clustering the query workload. To validate these proposals, the authors measure the response time of a set of decision-support XQueries over an XML data warehouse, with and without using their optimization techniques. The authors' experimental results demonstrate their efficiency, even when queries are complex and data are voluminous.

INTRODUCTION

Decision-support applications aim at facilitating the decision-making process. They collect data from operational databases and various sources, transform them into information available to decision-makers in a consolidated and consistent manner (Kimball & Ross, 2002).

Furthermore, the development of the Web 2.0 and the proliferation of multimedia documents contributed to the analysis of data are not only numerical nor symbolic. Indeed, such data can be represented in various formats (databases, texts, images, sounds, videos...); diversely structured (relational databases, XML document repositories...); originating from several different sources (distributed databases, the Web...); described through several channels or points of view (x-ray photographs and audio diagnosis of a physician,

DOI: 10.4018/978-1-61692-016-6.ch014

data expressed in different scales or languages...); changing in terms of definition or value (temporal databases, periodical surveys...). We term data that fall in several of the above categories *complex data* (Darmont *et al.*, 2005).

In this context, XML proves a very interesting tool for integrating and warehousing complex data for analysis thanks to its self-description (akin to warehouse metadata) and extensibility features (Darmont et al., 2003). Moreover, XML has become a standard for representing complex business data (Beyer et al., 2005). Hence, many efforts toward XML data warehousing have been achieved in the past few years (Park et al., 2009; Pokorný, 2002).

However, decision-support queries are generally complex because they involve several join and aggregation operations, while most XML-native database management systems (DBMSs) present relatively poor performances when data volume is very large and/or queries are complex.

In classical (i.e., relational) data warehouses, these issues are customarily addressed by indexing data and materializing views (Gupta & Mumick, 2005). Indexes and materialized views are physical data structures that improve data access time. An index allows direct (vs. sequential) access to data, while a materialized view precomputes query results and avoids accessing the whole original data. Both these physical data structures require additional storage space and induce some refreshing process overhead. It is thus crucial to select them wisely.

Several solutions have been proposed for XML data indexing in the literature. However, the existing techniques support single-labeled path expressions within one single XML document (Goldman & Widom, 1997; Chung et al., 2002). Such path expressions help explore an XML document and extract a specific node (element) or sub-tree (subdocument). They cannot perform join operations over several XML documents. In the context of XML data warehouses, decision-support queries are complex and involve several path expressions. Data are also generally distributed into several XML documents due to their large volume. Hence, XML queries should use specific indexes to access these documents.

In the context of relational data warehouses, several studies address the materialized view selection problem (Agrawal et al., 2000; Aouiche et al., 2006). Views that are relevant to materialize are selected to minimize the processing time of a given workload under maintenance cost and/or storage space constraints (Kotidis & Roussopoulos, 1999). Unfortunately, no such view materialization approach exists for XML databases and XML data warehouses in particular.

In this chapter, we propose a new index structure that is specifically adapted to multidimensional XML data warehouses. This structure is able to maintain a star schema[1] of several XML documents and to preserve the information contained in these documents. It is actually a join index that ensures faster execution of decision-support XQueries by eliminating join costs.

Our second contribution consists in adapting Aouiche et al.'s (2006) query clustering-based relational view selection approach to the XML context. We cluster queries and build candidate XML views that can resolve multiple similar queries belonging to the same cluster. Our approach exploits XML-specific cost models to select XML views that are pertinent to materialize.

The remainder of this chapter is organized as follows. We first discuss previous research related to XML indexing and materialized view selection, respectively. Then, we introduce the technical context of our studies, namely the XML data warehouse model we use, before detailing our join index for XML data warehouses and our XML materialized view selection strategy. To validate our proposals, we also present some experimental results. Finally, we conclude this chapter and hint at future research issues.

RELATED WORK

In this section, we discuss the state-of-art XML related to index and materialized view selection approaches.

XML Data Indexes

In the following, we assume that an XML document is defined as a labeled graph whose nodes represent document elements or attributes, and edges represent element-subelement (or parent-child) relationships. Edges are labeled with element or attribute names.

Several studies address the issue of XML data indexing (Goldman & Widom, 1997; Milo & Suciu, 1999; Cooper et al., 2001; Chung et al., 2002). They are more particularly devoted to optimize XML path expressions. Generally, they help traverse XML document hierarchies by referencing structural information about these documents. These techniques extract structural information directly from data and create a structural summary that is a labeled, directed graph. Graph schemas can be used as indexes for path queries. In practice, an XML index is a new XML document that is accessed instead of the original document.

Dataguide is a summary structure for semi-structured and XML data (Goldman & Widom, 1997). Its structure describes by one single label all the nodes (elements) whose labels (names) are identical. Its definition is based on targeted path sets, i.e., the set of nodes that are reached by traversing a given path. 1-index clusters nodes that share the same path in the XML data graph (Milo & Suciu, 1999). This process is performed through a bi-similarity relationship. To select labels or express path expressions, a hash table or a B-tree structure is used to index graph labels.

Dataguide and 1-index code all the paths from the root node. Hence, their size may become larger than the original XML document when XML data are represented as graphs (cyclic XML document), which dramatically degrades query performance. A(k)-index, a variant of 1-index, addresses this issue (Kaushik et al., 2002). It is based on the notion of k-bisimilarity[2] and builds an approximate index that reduces index graph size. An A(k)-index can retrieve, without referring to the original data graph, path expressions of length of at most k, where k controls the resolution of the index and influences its size in a proportional manner. However, for large values of k, index size may still become very large. For small values of k, index size is substantially smaller, but the index cannot handle long path expressions.

To accommodate path expressions of various lengths, without unnecessarily increasing the size of the whole index, D(k)-index assigns different values of k to different index nodes (Qun et al., 2003). These values conform to a given set of frequently-used path expressions (FUPs). Large values of k are assigned to parts of the index corresponding to parts of the data graph targeted by long path expressions; while small values of k are assigned to parts of the index corresponding to data targeted by short path expressions. To facilitate the evaluation of path expressions with branching, a variant called UD(k, l)-index also imposes downward similarity (Wu et al., 2003).

APEX is an adaptive index that searches for a trade-off between size and effectiveness (Chang et al., 2002). Instead of indexing all the paths from the root, APEX only indexes FUPs and preserves the source data structure in a tree. However, since FUPs are stored in the index, path query processing is quite efficient. APEX is also workload-aware, i.e., it can be dynamically updated according to changes in the query workload. A data mining method is used to extract FUPs from the workload for incremental update (Agrawal & Srikant, 1995).

Unfortunately, all these indexing techniques are ill-suited to decision-support queries. Data structures such as Dataguide, 1-index and its variants, and APEX are indeed applicable only on XML data that are targeted by simple path expressions. However, in the context of XML data warehouses, queries are complex and include several path expressions that compute join operations. Moreover, these indexes operate on one XML document only, whereas in XML warehouses, data are managed in several XML documents and decision-support queries are performed over these documents.

Finally, other techniques such as extended inverted lists (Zhang et al., 2001) and Fabric (Cooper et al., 2001) process containment queries over XML data stored in relational databases. Extended inverted lists includes a text index (T-index; Milo & Suciu, 1999) that is similar to traditional indexes in information retrieval systems, and an element index (E-index) that maps elements into inverted lists. Fabric indexes several XML documents by encoding paths, from root to leaf nodes, with indicators that code path labels. These codes are then inserted in a Patricia trie (Cooper et al., 2001) that processes them like simple characters. However, Fabric is not adapted to XML data warehouses either, because it does not take into account the relationships that exist between XML documents in a warehouse (facts and dimensions). This index is thus not beneficial to decision-support queries.

Materialized View Selection

The view selection problem has received significant attention in the literature, in the relational database context. To the best of our knowledge, no such view materialization approach exists in XML databases and XML data warehouses in particular. Researches about it differ by several points:

- the way of determining candidate views;
- the frameworks used to capture relationships between candidate views;
- the use of mathematical cost models vs. calls to the query optimizer;
- the context of view selection (relational vs. multidimensional);
- the way optimization is performed (over multiple or single queries);
- the nature of solutions (theoretical or technical).

Uchiyama et al. (1999) and Kotidis et al. (1999) introduce a lattice framework that models and captures dependency (ancestor or descendent) among aggregate views in a multidimensional context. This lattice is greedily browsed with the help of cost models to select the best views to materialize. This approach has also been used in one data cube and then extended to multiple cubes (Shukla et al., 2000). Valluri et al. (2002) propose another theoretical framework, AND-OR view graphs, to capture relationships between views. Though conceptually nice, these theoretical solutions are not truly scalable.

Most recent approaches are workload-driven. They syntactically analyze the query workload to enumerate relevant candidate views. A representative workload helps predict future queries, which are likely to belong to it or be syntactically close to current queries. Thus, extracting candidate materialized views from the workload ensures that they will probably be exploited when processing future queries. By calling to the DBMS' query optimizer (Agrawal et al., 2000) or by using maintenance cost and/or storage space constraints (Kotidis et al., 1999), workload-driven approaches greedily build a configuration of the most pertinent views. Clustering algorithms are also used to select pertinent views to materialize. Aouiche et al. (2006) indeed cluster similar queries together, and then merge queries in each cluster to build a set of candidate views. A greedy algorithm guided by cost models (for data access and storage) finally helps select the final set of views to materialize. In opposition to previous proposals, this approach is scalable thanks to the low complexity of clustering.

STUDY CONTEXT

Although XML data warehouse architectures from the literature share a lot of concepts (mostly originating from classical data warehousing), they are nonetheless all different. Hence, we present in this section the XML data warehouse model that we choose and on which we base our query performance optimization techniques. We also present a sample XML decision-support query.

XML Data Warehouse Specification

When designing and building XML data warehouses, XML documents are used to manage or represent facts and/or dimensions. This allows natively storing documents and easily interrogating them with XML query languages.

Some XML warehousing approaches are user-driven. They are applied when an organization has fixed warehouse requirements. Nassis et al. (2005) propose methods to conceptually design and build an XML repository, based on object-oriented concepts and a view-driven approach, respectively. This repository represents the warehouse analysis context. Baril & Bellahsène (2003) envisage XML data warehouses as collections of views represented by XML documents. Zhang et al. (2005) propose an approach to materialize XML data warehouses based on the frequent query patterns discovered from historical queries issued by users. Finally, Vrdoljak et al. (2003) propose a design approach for Web warehouses that is based on XML schemas describing data sources. All these approaches assume that the warehouse is composed of XML documents representing facts.

Other approaches are explicitly based on classical data warehouse logical models. For instance, Pokorný (2003) models a star schema in XML by defining dimension hierarchies as sets of logically connected collections of XML data, and facts as XML data elements. Park et al. (2005) propose an XML multidimensional model in which each fact is described by a single XML document, and dimension data are grouped into a repository of XML documents. Rusu et al. (2005) build facts and dimensions from XML documents generated through XQueries. Eventually, Hümmer et al. (2003) propose a family of templates, called XCube, to describe a multidimensional structure (dimension and fact data) for integrating several data warehouses into a virtual or federated data warehouse. All these approaches assume that the warehouse is composed of XML documents that represent both facts and dimensions. They are used when dimensions are dynamic and allow the support of end-user analytical tools.

All these studies more or less converge toward a unified XML warehouse model. They mostly differ in the way dimensions are handled and the number of XML documents that are used to store facts and dimensions. In this chapter, we select the XCube specification, which is the most explicit, to model a reference XML data warehouse. However, since other models from the literature are quite similar, this is not a binding choice.

The advantage of XCube is its simple structure for representing facts and dimensions in a star schema. One XML document is used to represent dimensions and another one to represent facts. Hence, our reference data warehouse is composed of the following XML documents: *Schema.xml* specifies data warehouse metadata; *Dimensions.xml* defines all dimensions, each characterized by attributes their values; and *Facts.xml* specifies facts, i.e., sets of dimension identifiers and measure descriptions and values.

The tree structure of *Facts.xml* is described in Figure 1(a). Root node *CubeFact* has one child, *cube*, which is itself composed of *Cell* nodes defining facts, i.e., *fact* nodes (measures) and dimension references. A *fact* node has two attributes, *@id* and *@value, which* define the measure's name and value, respectively. A *dimension* node has two attributes, *@id* and *@value, which* define the dimension's name and its identifier's value, respectively.

Figure 1. Structure of dimension and fact documents

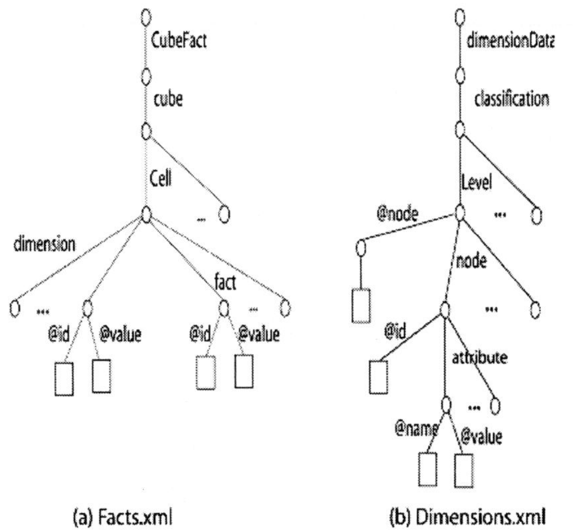

The tree structure of *Dimensions.xml* is described in Figure 1(b). Root node *dimensionData* has one child, *classification*, which is itself composed of *Level* nodes. A *Level* node is composed of *node* nodes defining dimension instances. A *node* is composed of *attribute* nodes that define a dimension's attributes (*@name*) and their values (*@value*).

XML Data Warehouse Interrogation

We select the XQuery language (Boag et al., 2004) to formulate decision-support queries because, unlike simpler languages such as XPath, it allows complex queries, including join queries over multiple XML documents, to be expressed with the FLWOR syntax.

However, XQuery does not support well the type of queries that are common in business analysis (Beyer et al., 2004). XQuery does indeed not include an explicit grouping construct comparable to the *group by* clause in SQL. Hence, several papers propose to extend XQuery to formulate decision-oriented queries (Borkar & Carey, 2004; Beyer et al., 2005). In our implementation, we acknowledge this effort by adding to FLWOR expressions explicit group by clauses. More precisely, we added two functions: *group by (attribute-list)* and *aggregation (aggregation-operations, measure-list)*, to the XQuery syntax. (Figure 2) provides an example of decision-support query with a multiple *group by* clause that exploits these functions.

Figure 2. Sample decision-support XQuery

```
for $a in //dimensionData/classification/Level
[@node='customers']/node,
$x in //CubeFacts/cube/Cell
let $q := $b/attribute[@name='cust name']/@value
let $z := $b/attribute[@name='cust zip code']/@value
where $a/attribute/@name='cust city'
and $a/attribute/@value='Lyon'
and $x/dimension /@id=$a/@id
and $x/dimension/@id='customers'
group by(cust name,@cust zip code)
return name='cust name', aggregation(sum, quantity)
```

JOIN INDEX FOR XML DATA WAREHOUSES

In this section, we present our join index structure and show how it allows indexing several related XML documents, which classical XML database indexes fail to do. We also present a theoretical study that to demonstrate our index' effectiveness.

Join Index Structure

Building actual XML indexes on an XML warehouse causes a loss of information in decision-support query resolution. Indeed, clustering (1-index) or merging (Dataguide) identical labels causes the disappearance of relationships between fact measures and dimensions. We illustrate this problem in the following example.

The *Facts.xml* document is composed of *Cell* elements, each cell being characterized by dimension identifiers and one or more measures. (Figure 3) shows the structures of *Facts.xml* and of its corresponding 1-index (which we selected as an

Figure 3. Facts.xml structure (A) and corresponding 1-index (B)

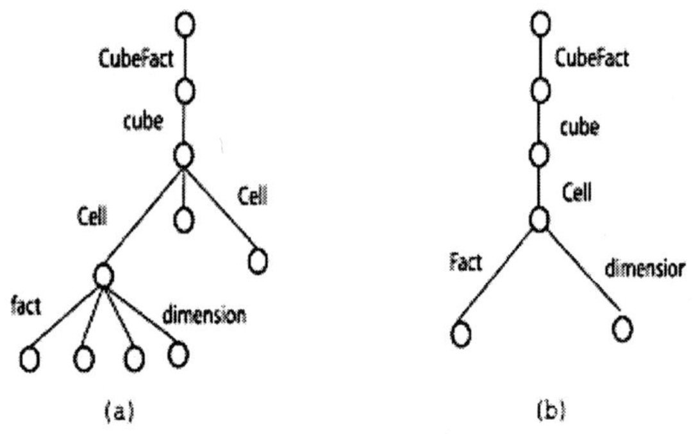

Figure 4. XML join index structure

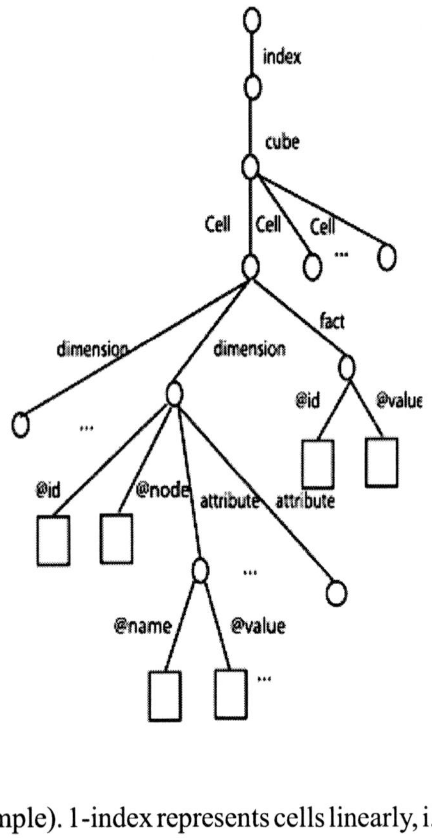

example). 1-index represents cells linearly, i.e., all labels for the same source are represented by only one label. Hence, recovering a cell characterized by its measures and their dimension identifiers is impossible.

An index should be able to preserve the relationships between dimensions and fact measures. Thus, our index' structure is similar to that of the *Facts.xml* document, except for the attribute element. Moreover, XML indexes usually summarize or reorganize the structure of the indexed XML documents into new XML documents that are then accessed instead of original data. Our index structure is similar. It is stored in an XML document named *Index.xml*, whose structure is showed in (Figure 4). Each *Cell* element is composed of dimensions and one or more facts. A *Fact* element has two attributes, *@id* and *@value*, which respectively represent measure names and values. Each *dimension* element is composed of two attributes: *@id*, which stores the dimension's name, and *@node*, which stores the dimension identifier's value. A *dimension* element also has children *attribute* elements. They are obtained from the *Dimensions.xml* document. An *attribute* element is composed of two attributes, *@name* and *@value*, which respectively store its name and value.

Data migration from *Dimensions.xml* and *Facts.xml* to *Index.xml* helps store facts, dimensions and their attributes in the same cell. This feature wholly eliminates join operations since all the information that is necessary for a join operation is stored in the same cell. Queries need to be rewritten to exploit our index, though. The rewriting process consists in preserving selection expressions and aggregation operations. We illustrate query execution by an example in (Figure 5). Further details are provided in the experiment section.

Theoretical Validation

Queries defined over an XML warehouse modeled according to the XCube specification perform several join operations between facts stored in *Facts.xml* and dimensions from *Dimensions.xml*. Thus, they must satisfy the following constraints.

```
document(Facts.xml)/CubeFact/
cube/Cell/dimension[@id =
document(Dimensions.xml)/classi-
```

Figure 5. Query executions over our join index

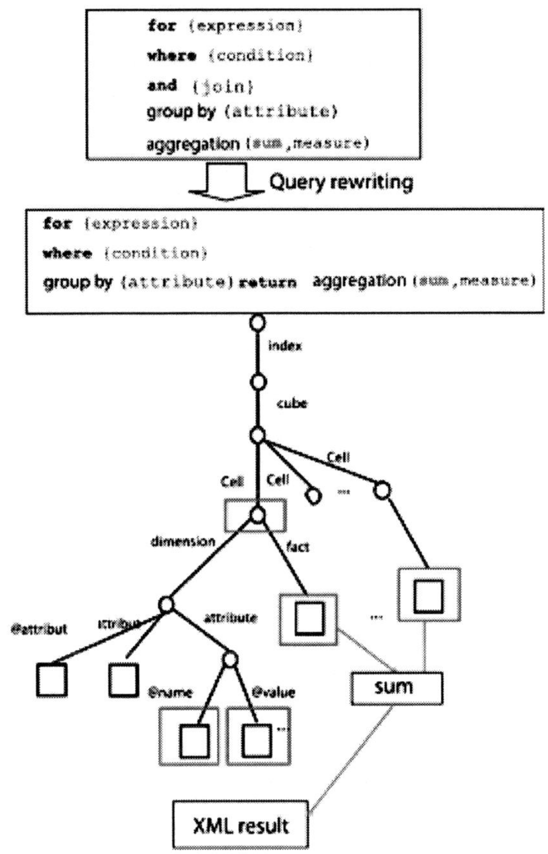


```
fication/Level/@id]
and
document(Facts.xml)/CubeFact/
cube/Cell/dimension/[@value =
document(Dimension.xml)/classi-
fication/Level/node/@id]
```

The first equality checks whether the dimension composing a cell (fact) is indeed the dimension expressed in the query. The second equality checks whether the node of a dimension (equivalent to a primary key) corresponds (can be joined) to the node, from the same dimension, defined in a cell (equivalent to a foreign key in the fact table).

Query execution without using our index may proceed as follows. For each dimension defined by *@node='name of dimension'*, identifiers *@id* verifying the *Where* clause are searched for. *Dimensions.xml* is traversed in depth first, down to the *Level* node. Child nodes of the *Level* node are then traversed in breadth first until *@node* is equal to dimension name. The cost of this traversal cost is equal to the number of *Level* nodes in *Dimensions.xml*, denoted |dimension|. If several dimensions are defined in the query, all *Level* nodes are traversed for each dimension. Each node's child is traversed in depth first, until a list of *@id* attributes verifying the conditions *@name='name of the attribute'* and *@value='value of the attribute'* is found. The cost of this traversal is equal to the number of *attribute* children. Thus, dimension cost traversal equals $|a_i| * |d_i|$, where $|a_i|$ is the number of attributes in each dimension and $|d_i|$ the number of *node* elements, i.e., the number of children in each dimension.

To join dimensions from *Dimensions.xml* and facts from *Facts.xml*, *@id* values found when processing dimensions are searched for in facts. *Facts.xml* is then traversed in depth first, down to the *Cell* level. Cells are then traversed in breadth first until dimensions whose child *@id* equals *@node* in *Dimensions.xml* and *@node* equals *@id* in *Dimensions.xml* are found. The traversal cost of *Facts.xml* is $|cell|$, where $|cell|$ is the number of cells. Finally, query execution cost without our index is defined by Formula 1.

$$E_{noindex} = \left(\left(|cell| * |dimension|\right) * \left(|dimension| + \left(|d_i| * |a_i|\right)\right)\right) \quad (1)$$

Query execution when using our index may proceed as follows. For each dimension defined by *@node='name of dimension'*, identifiers *@id* verifying the *Where* clause are searched for. *Index.xml* is traversed in depth first, down to the *Cell* level. The cost of this traversal is equal to the number of cells in *Index.xml*. Dimension child nodes are then traversed until the node whose *@id* value equals dimension name in the query is reached. The cost of this traversal is equal to the number of *dimension* nodes in *Index.xml*, i.e., the

Figure 6. Join index efficiency

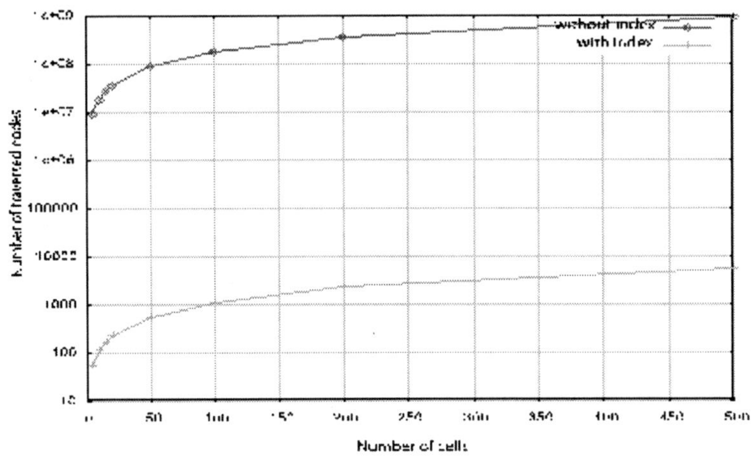

number of dimensions in the warehouse schema. This cost is denoted |*dimension*|. The children of each found node are traversed in depth first, down to the *attribute* node verifying the conditions @*name='name of the attribute'* and @*value='value of the attribute'*. The cost of this traversal is equal to the number of *attribute* children, denoted $|a_i|$.

Finally, query processing cost over our index structure is defined by (Formula 2).

$$E_{index} = |cell| * (|dimension| + |a_i|) \qquad (2)$$

(Figure 6) shows the cost variation between $E_{noindex}$ and E_{index} with respect to the number of cells (facts) from *Facts.xml*. These facts are described by five dimensions that are stored in *Dimensions.xml*. (Table 1) displays the characteristics of these dimensions. We use a logarithmic scale on the Y axis to better visualize cost differences. Using our index induces a performance gain factor of 14,000 on an average.

Table 1. Test data warehouse characteristics

Facts	**Number of cells**
Sales	16 260 336
Dimensions	**Number of occurrences**
Customers	50 000
Products	10 000
Times	1 461
Promotions	501
Channels	5
Documents	**Size (MB)**
Facts.xml	4.92
Dimensions.xml	3.77
Schema.xml	0.001

Figure 7. Materialized view selection strategy

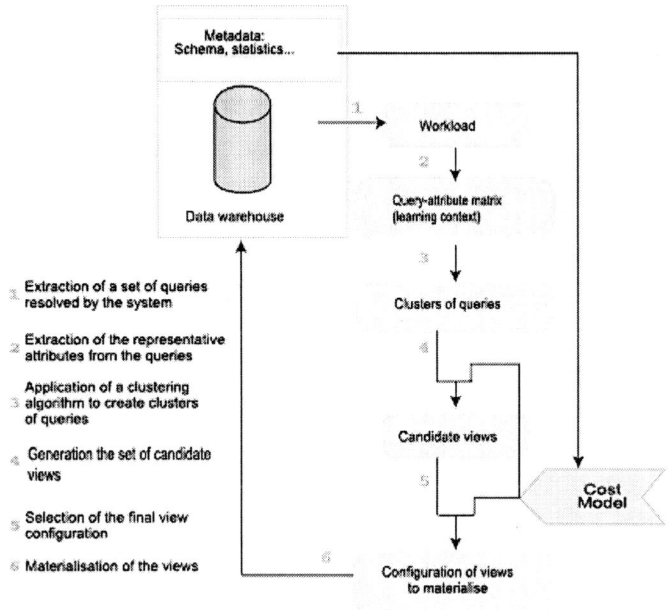

XML MATERIALIZED VIEW SELECTION STRATEGY

In this section, we present our second contribution: an XML materialized view selection strategy. This strategy only materializes pertinent views, and hence addresses both storage and maintenance cost problems. It is workload-based (i.e., based on a set of queries representing user requirements) and exploits knowledge about how views can be used to resolve a set of workload queries to cluster them together.

The principle of our materialized view selection strategy is depicted in (Figure 7). We assume that we dispose of a workload composed of representative queries (similar to the query from (Figure 2). Our objective is to select a configuration of materialized views that reduces its execution time. The first step is to build, from the workload, a clustering context. Then, we define similarity and dissimilarity measures that help cluster together similar queries. For each cluster, we build a set of candidate views. The last step exploits cost models that evaluate the cost of accessing data using views and the cost of their storage, to build a final materialized view configuration. We detail these steps in the following sections.

Query Workload Analysis

The workload we consider is a set of *selection*, *join* and *aggregation* queries. This first step consists in extracting from the workload representative attributes for each query. We mean by representative attributes those are present in *Where* (selection predicate attributes) and *Group by* clauses. We store the relationships between workload queries and the extracted attributes in a so-called "query-attribute" matrix. Matrix lines are queries and columns are extracted attributes. A query q_i is then seen as a line in the matrix that is composed of cells corresponding to representative attributes. The general term q_{ij} of this matrix is set to one if extracted attribute a_i is present in query $q_{i,}$ and to zero otherwise. This matrix represents our clustering context.

Building the Candidate View Configuration

In practice, it is hard to search all the syntactically relevant candidate views because the search space is very large (Agrawal et al., 2000). To reduce the problem's size, we propose to cluster workload queries. Hence, we group in a same cluster all the queries that are similar. Similar queries are the one having a close binary representation in the query-attribute matrix. Two similar queries can be resolved by using only one materialized view. We define similarity and dissimilarity measures that ensure that queries within a same cluster are strongly related to each other, whereas queries from different clusters are significantly different from one another.

Similarity and Dissimilarity Measures

A query is described by the attributes extracted in the query analysis phase. We thus describe a query q_i by vector $q_i = \{q_{1i}, q_{1i}, \ldots, q_{pi}\}$, where p is the number of attributes in the matrix. This description allows query comparison. We define similarity (respectively, dissimilarity) between two queries q_i and q_i with respect to attribute $a_k (k = \overline{1..p})$ in Formula 1 (respectively, Formula 2).

$$\delta_{sim}(q_{ki}, q_{kj}) = \begin{cases} 1 \text{ if } q_{ki} = q_{kj} = 1 \\ 0 \text{ otherwise} \end{cases} \quad (3)$$

$$\delta_{dissim}(q_{ki}, q_{kj}) = \begin{cases} 1 \text{ if } q_{ki} = q_{kj} \\ 0 \text{ if } q_{ki} \neq q_{kj} \end{cases} \quad (4)$$

Two queries q_i and q_j are similar with respect to attribute a_k if and only if $q_{ki} = q_{kj} = 1$, *i.e.*, a_k is present in both queries. They are dissimilar if and only if $q_{ki} \neq q_{kj}$, *i.e.*, one of the two queries does not contain attribute a_k.

These measures can be extended to a set A composed of p attributes such that we get the degree of global similarity and dissimilarity between two queries. We thus define the similarity (respectively, dissimilarity) between two queries q_i and q_j with respect to all attributes in Formula 5 (respectively, Formula 6).

$$sim(q_i, q_j) = \sum_{j=1}^{p} \delta_{sim}(q_{ki}, q_{kj}) \qquad 0 \leq sim(q_i, q_j) \leq p \quad (5)$$

$$dissim(q_i, q_j) = \sum_{j=1}^{p} \delta_{dissim}(q_{ki}, q_{kj}) \qquad 0 \leq dissim(q_i, q_j) \leq p \quad (6)$$

Thus, the closer $sim(q_i, q_j)$ (respectively, $dissim(q_i, q_j)$) is to p, the more q_i and q_j are considered similar (respectively, dissimilar). We also define similarity (respectively, dissimilarity) measures between two query sets and within a query set. These measures are defined by Formulas 7, 8, 9 and 10, respectively.

$$sim(C_a, C_b) = \sum_{q_k \in C_a, q_l \in C_b} \delta_{sim}(q_k, q_l) \qquad 0 \leq sim(C_a, C_b) \leq card(C_a) \times card(C_b) \times p \quad (7)$$

$$dissim(C_a, C_b) = \sum_{q_k \in C_a, q_l \in C_b} \delta_{dissim}(q_k, q_l) \qquad 0 \leq dissim(C_a, C_b) \leq card(C_a) \times card(C_b) \times p \quad (8)$$

$$sim(C_a) = \sum_{q_k \in C_a, q_l \in C_b, k<l} \delta_{sim}(q_k, q_l) \qquad 0 \leq sim(C_a, C_b) \leq \frac{card(C_a) \times card(C_b) \times p}{2} \quad (9)$$

$$dissim(C_a) = \sum_{q_k \in C_a, q_l \in C_b, k<l} \delta_{dissim}(q_k, q_l) \qquad 0 \leq dissim(C_a, C_b) \leq \frac{card(C_a) \times card(C_b) \times p}{2} \quad (10)$$

Figure 8. XML view structure

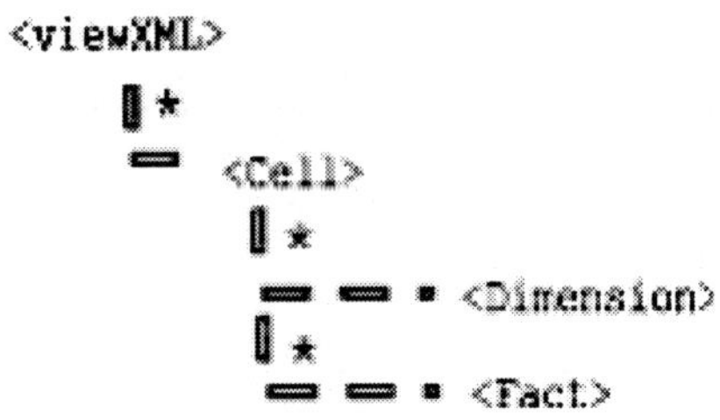

Clustering

Clustering consists in determining a so-called natural partition P_{nat} composed of objects (here, queries) that reflect the internal structure of data. This partition must be such as its clusters are composed of objects with high similarity and objects from different clusters present a high dissimilarity. Based on the previously defined functions, a clustering quality measure $Q(P_h)$ can be built (Formula 11).

$$Q(P_h) = \sum_{a=1..z,b=1..z,a<b} (sim(C_a, C_b) + \sum_{a=1}^{z} dissim(C_a)) \quad (11)$$

This measure permits to capture the natural aspect of a partition. Hence, $Q(P_h)$ measures simultaneously similarities between queries within the same cluster of partition P_h and dissimilarities between queries within different clusters. Thus, we can define $Q(P_h)$ as a homogeneity function for the same class and a heterogeneity function for different classes. Therefore, partitions presenting high intra-cluster homogeneity and a high inter-cluster disparity have a low $Q(P_h)$ value and thereby appear as the most natural.

We have selected the Kerouac clustering algorithm (Jouve & Nicoloyannis, 2003). Kerouac indeed bears several interesting properties:

1. its computational complexity is low (log linear with respect to the number of queries and linear with respect to the number of attributes);
2. it can deal with a high number of objects (queries);
3. it can deal with distributed data;
4. it allows integrating constraints within the clustering process. This last characteristic is particularly interesting, since it provides us with a way to integrate constraints concerning the view merging process.

Cost Models

The number of candidate views is generally as high as the input workload is large. Thus, it is not feasible to materialize all the proposed views because of storage space constraints. To circumvent this limitation, we propose to use cost models that retain the most pertinent views only.

(Figure 8) shows the typical structure of an XML view. In our context, it is composed of *Cell* elements. Each *Cell* is itself composed of *Dimension* elements that contain *Group by* attributes and *Fact* elements corresponding to aggregate results. We propose cost models that estimate the size and storage cost of a given XML view.

We estimate the size of a view by its number of elements. The number of *Dimension* and *Fact* elements in each *Cell* is the same. Indeed, the number of elements in a given view is estimated by the number of *Cell* elements. To compute it, we first estimate the maximum number of *Cell* elements (Formula 12).

$$ms(Cell) = \prod_{i=1}^{d} |d_i| \quad (12)$$

$|d_i|$ is the cardinality of the dimension characterizing the *Cell* element. *d* is the number of dimensions in *Dimensions.xml*. Let *ms*(*v*) be the maximum size of view *v* that is composed of dimensions $d_1 \ldots d_k$, where *k* is the number of dimensions in the view and $\left|d_i\right|$ the cardinality of dimension d_i (Formula 13).

$$ms(v) = \prod_{i=1}^{k} \left|d_i\right| \quad (13)$$

Golfarelli & Rizzi (1998) proposed to estimate the number of tuples in a given view *v* by using Yao's (1977) formula. We also use this formula to estimate the number of *Cell* elements in *v* (Formula 14).

$$\left|v\right| = ms(v) \times \left[1 - \prod_{i=1}^{Cell} \frac{ms(Cell) \times c - i + 1}{ms(Cell) - i + 1}\right] \quad (14)$$

$c = 1 - \frac{1}{ms(v)}$. If $\frac{ms(Cell)}{ms(v)}$ is large enough, this formula is well approximated by Cardenas' (1975) formula (Formula 15).

$$\left|v\right| = ms(v) \times \left(1 - \left(1 - \frac{1}{ms(v)}\right)^{Cell}\right) \quad (15)$$

Cardenas and Yao's formulas are based on the assumption that data are uniformly distributed. The size, in bytes, of a view *v* is equal to the number of *Cell* elements multiplied by the average size needed to store one element. Thus, we estimate the size of a view as shown in Formula 16.

$$size(v) = \left|v\right| \times \sum_{i=1}^{k} size(d_i) \quad (16)$$

$size(d_i)$ represents the size, in bytes, of dimension d_i from *v* and *k* the number of dimensions.

Objective Functions

We describe in this section three objective functions that help evaluate the variation of query execution cost induced by adding a new view. Query execution cost is assimilated either to the number of *Cell* elements in *Facts.xml*, if no views are used; or to the number of *Cell* elements in the views if they are exploited. Workload execution cost is obtained by adding the execution costs of each query within this workload.

The first objective function, "profit", favors views providing more profit while executing queries. The second function, "profit/space ratio", favors views providing more benefit while occupying the smallest possible storage space. The third function, "hybrid", combines the first two in order to first select all the views providing more profit and then retain only those occupying less storage space when this resource becomes critical. The profit function is useful when storage space is not limited, the profit/space ratio function is useful when storage space is small, and the hybrid function is interesting when storage space is reasonably large.

Profit Objective Function

Let $V = \left\{v_1, \ldots, v_m\right\}$ be the candidate view set, *S* the final view set and $Q = \left\{q_1, \ldots, q_n\right\}$ a query set (workload). The profit objective function, noted *P*, is defined in Formula 17.

$$P_{/S}(v_j) = C_{/S}(Q) - C_{/S \cup vj}(Q) - \beta C_{update}(v_j) \quad (17)$$
$$(v_j) \notin S$$

$C_{/S}(Q)$ is the query execution cost when all views in *S* are used. If this set is empty, $C_{/\emptyset}(Q) = \left|Q\right| \times \left|F\right|$ because all queries are resolved by accessing fact *F*. When a view v_i is added to *S*, $C_{/S \cup vj}(Q) = \sum_{k=0}^{|Q|} C(q_k, v_j)$ is the query execution cost for views in $S \cup v_i$. If query q_k exploits v_i, cost $C(q_k, v_j)$ is then equal to C_{vj} (number of instances in v_i). Otherwise, $C(q_k, v_j)$ is equal to the maximum value between F and $C(q_k, v)$ (executing cost of q_k exploiting q_k with $v \neq v_j$). Coefficient $\beta = |Q| p(v_i)$ estimates the number of updates for view v_i. The update probability $p(v_i)$ equals $p(v_i)$, where ratio $\frac{\%update}{\%query}$ represents the proportion of update vs. interrogation queries. Finally, $C_{update}(v_j)$ represents the maintenance cost of view v_j.

Profit/Space Ratio Objective Function
If view selection is achieved under a space constraint, the profit/space objective function from Formula 18 is used. This function R computes the profit provided by v_j with respect to storage space $size(v_j)$ it occupies.

$$R_{/S}(v_j) = \frac{P_{/S}(v_j)}{size(v_j)} \quad (18)$$

Hybrid Objective Function
The constraint on storage space may be relaxed if storage space in relatively large. The hybrid objective function H does not penalize space-greedy views if ratio $\frac{remaining - space}{storage - space}$ is lower or equal than a storage-space given threshold α, 0 < α ≤ 1,

where *remaining-space* and *storage-space* are respectively the remaining space after adding v_j and the allotted space needed for storing all the views. This function is computed by combining functions P and R as shown in Formula 19.

$$H_{/S}(v_j) = \begin{cases} P_{/S}(v_j) \; if \; \frac{remaining - space}{storage - space} \leq \alpha \\ R_{/S}(v_j) \; otherwise \end{cases} \quad (19)$$

View Selection Algorithm

Our view selection algorithm (Algorithm 1) is based on a greedy search within the candidate view set *V*. Objective function *F* must be one of among functions *P*, *R* or *H* described in the previous section. If *R* is used, we add to the algorithm's input the storage space *M* allotted for views. If *H* is used, we also add threshold *α* as input.

$S \leftarrow \emptyset$
repeat
  $v_{max} \leftarrow \emptyset$
  $F_{max} \leftarrow 0$
  for all $v_j \in V - D$ **do**
    if $F_{/S}(v_j) > F_{max}$ **then**
      $F_{max} \leftarrow F_{/S}(v_j)$
      $v_{max} \leftarrow v_j$
    end if
  end for
  if $F_{/S}(v_j) > 0$ **then**
    $S \leftarrow S \cup \{v_{max}\}$
  end if
until $(F_{/S}(v_j) \leq 0$ **or** $V - S = \emptyset)$

Algorithm 1. Greedy view configuration construction

In the first iteration, the values of the objective function are computed for each view within *V*. The view v_{max} that minimizes *F*, if it exists $(F_{/S}(v_{max}) > 0)$, is then added to *S*. If *R* or *H* is used, the whole storage space *M* is decreased by

Figure 9. Sample SQL-XQuery

```
Select XML-DOC.Query('for $a in //dimensionData
        /classification/Level[@node='customers']/node,
        where $a/attribute/@name="cust city"
        and $ a/attribute/@value="Lyon"
        return name="cust name"')
From DIMENSION
```

the amount of space occupied by v_{max}. Values of F are then computed for each remaining view in $V - S$, since they depend on the selected views present in S. This helps take into account the interactions that probably exist between views. This process reiterates either until there is no performance improvement $(F_{/S}(v) > 0)$ or until all the views have been selected $(F_{/S}(v) > 0)$. If functions R or H are used, the algorithm also stops when storage space is full.

VALIDATION EXPERIMENTS

Experimental conditions

In order to validate our proposals experimentally, we exploit an XML data warehouse modeled according to the XCube specifications. Actual data have been transferred from an existing, relational data warehouse derived from an Oracle example (Oracle, 2006).This classical test data warehouse is modeled as a star schema composed of *sale* facts characterized by the *amount* (of purchased products) and *quantity* (of purchased products) measures. Facts are stored in the *Facts.xml* document. They are described by five dimensions: *channels, promotions, customers, products* and *times* that are stored in the *Dimensions.xml* document. (Table 1) displays the characteristics of our test XML data warehouse.

We implemented this data warehouse within two native XML DBMSs: eXist (Meier, 2002) and X-Hive (Waldt, 2005). Both these DBMSs allow the native storage of large documents and support the XQuery language. They also provide APIs (Application Programming Interfaces) for storing, querying, retrieving, transforming and publishing XML data. We also implemented our XML data warehouse in a relational, XML-compatible DBMS: SQL Server (Rys, 2004). SQL Server 2005 handles XML data through an XML type field. It integrates XQuery queries with the help of a function called query that is embedded into SQL Select clauses (Figure 9).

Join Index Evaluation

This experiment measure the execution time of the typical decision-support query from (Figure 2) over our test data warehouse, with and without exploiting our join index, on all the DBMSs we consider (Figure 10). We also vary warehouse size. Note that, in SQL Server 2005, XML data are stored in a table field. Thus, SQL-XQuery queries must be processed for each record. This process does not allow joining XML data from different records. Hence, we only perform our experiment with our join index on SQL Server since it is not possible with the original, multi-document warehouse. We ran our tests on a Pentium 2 GHz PC with 1 GB of main memory and an IDE hard drive. Also note that we do not consider index construction time here, since an XML index is actually a new warehouse structure

Figure 10. Join index experimental results

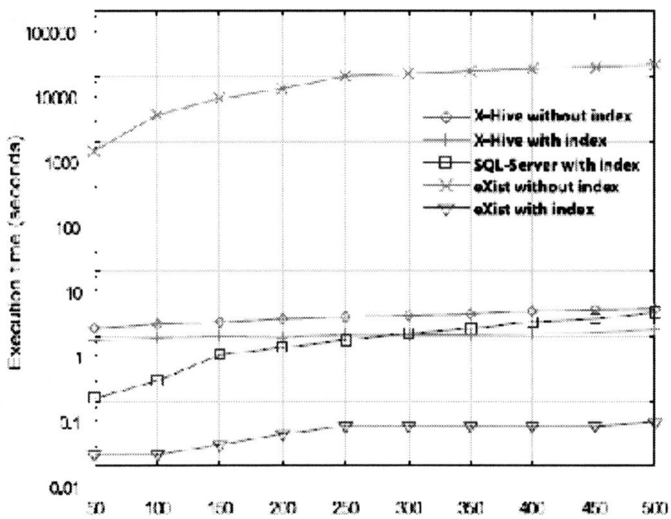

that is built once and queried thereafter. Finally, in (Figure 10), the X axis represents warehouse size and the Y axis the corresponding execution time. The Y axis is in logarithm scale to highlight the differences in execution costs.

The results we obtain show that using our index structure significantly improves response time. On an average, the gain factor is indeed 25,669for eXist and 8,411 for X-Hive. Though this is not plotted on (Figure 10), we also pushed our "with/without index" tests further on the totality of the cells from *Facts.xml*. We achieve execution times of less than two seconds with our join index. Without index, X-Hive responds in about four minutes and eXist proves unable to answer in a reasonable time. Finally, this experiment shows that, properly indexed, native XML DBMSs can compete with, and even best relational DBMSs in terms of performance when XML documents are bulky. eXist running on our join index indeed outperforms SQL-Server by a 31.5 factor, on an average. This is because relational DBMS engines combine XQuery to SQL and must convert the result from relations to XML. XML native DBMSs, on the other hand, preserve the hierarchical structure of XML data, which allows path scans to be efficiently processed by XQuery engines. Our experiment also shows that eXist's query engine performs better then X-hive when using simple path expressions. We think this is because, eXist implements a specific numbering scheme that helps easily evaluate parent/child node relationships (Meier, 2002).

Materialized View Selection Evaluation

To validate our materialized view selection strategy, we executed on our test data warehouse a workload composed of ten decision-support XQueries, with and without building materialized views. The selected views are stored in an independent collection that is targeted by rewritten queries. We plot in (Figure 11) the execution time of our query workload on the original XML documents and on the materialized views we generate. The X-axis represents the ten queries and the Y-axis the corresponding execution time. The Y-axis is represented in logarithmic scale to highlight the difference between the execution costs. On an

Figure 11. Materialized view selection experimental results

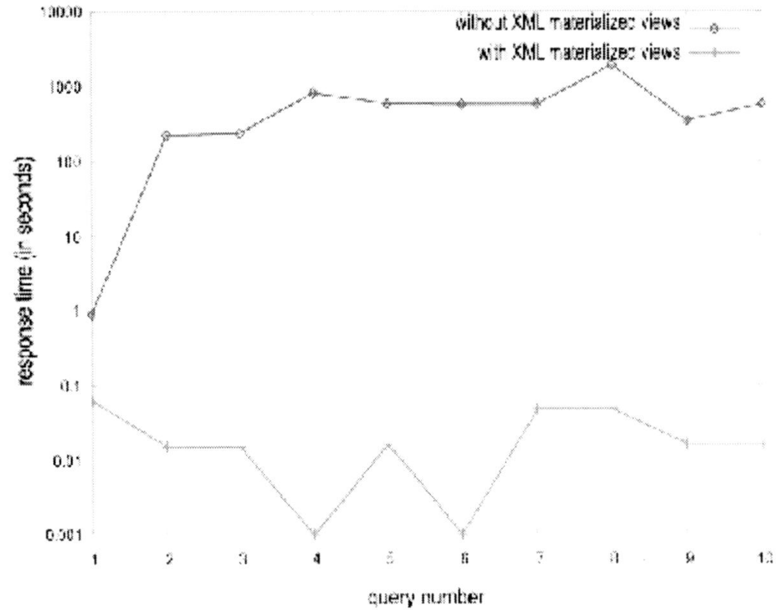

average, our XML view materializing strategy improves response time by a factor 24,700.

These results show that query response time significantly decreases using our strategy. Indeed, queries exploiting views obtained with our strategy are rewritten and join operations are avoided.

CONCLUSION AND PERSPECTIVES

In this paper, we presented both a new join index and a strategy for materializing views in XML data warehouses. Our join index allows optimizing access time to several XML documents by eliminating join costs, while preserving the information contained in the initial warehouse. Our materialized view selection strategy exploits the results of clustering applied on a given workload to build a set of syntactically relevant candidate views. With the help of cost models we specifically designed for XML warehouses, we retain only the most advantageous candidate views through a greedy process that operates under storage space constraint.

To validate our join index, we performed both a complexity study and experiments. We implemented our reference warehouse with two native XML DBMSs and one relational, XML-compatible DBMS. Our tests showed that using our index structure significantly improves the response time of a typical decision-support query expressed in XQuery. Furthermore, they also demonstrate that native XML DBMSs can compete with relational DBMSs. The experimental results we achieved to validate our materialized view selection strategy are very encouraging, and show that it guarantees a substantial gain in performance. However, our first perspective is to complement these results with other tests, on other systems than eXist, and to assert in each configuration the gain in performance vs. the overhead for generating and refreshing materialized views.

This work also opens broader axes of research perspectives. First, our indexing strategy could be better integrated into a host native XML DBMS. This would certainly help develop an incremental strategy for the maintenance of the join index data structure. Moreover, the mechanism for rewriting queries would also be more efficient if it was part of the system. XML indexes are getting more and more efficient, but there is still room for improvement (e.g., multi-document join indexes). The generalized exploitation of materialized views would also be very beneficial. Thus, a rewriting query engine and refreshing strategies should be devised.

REFERENCES

Agrawal, R., & Srikant, R. (1995). Mining Sequential Patterns. In *11th International Conference on Data Engineering (ICDE 95)*, Taipei, Taiwan, IEEE Computer Society (pp. 3–14).

Agrawal, S., Chaudhuri, S., & Narasayya, V. R. (2000). Automated selection of materialized views and indexes in SQL databases. In *26th International Conference on Very Large Data Bases (VLDB 00)*, Cairo, Egypt (pp. 496–505).

Aouiche, K., Jouve, P. E., & Darmont, J. (2006). Clustering-Based Materialized View Selection in Data Warehouses. In *10th East European Conference on Advances in Databases and Information Systems (ADBIS 06)* (LNCS 4152, pp. 81-95). Berlin: Springer.

Baril, X., & Bellahsène, Z. (2003). XML Data Management: Native XML and XML-enabled Database Systems . In *Designing and Managing an XML Warehouse* (pp. 455–473). Reading, MA: Addison Wesley.

Beyer, K. S., Chamberlin, D. D., Colby, L. S., Ozcan, F., Pirahesh, H., & Xu, Y. (2005). Extending XQuery for Analytics. In *ACM SIGMOD International Conference on Management of Data (SIGMOD '05)*, Baltimore, USA (pp. 503–514). New York: ACM.

Beyer, K. S., Cochrane, R., Colby, L. S., Ozcan, F., & Pirahesh, H. (2004). XQuery for Analytics: Challenges and Requirements. In *1st International Workshop on XQuery Implementation, Experience and Perspectives <XIME-P/>*, Paris, France (pp. 3–8).

Boag, S., Chamberlin, D., Fernandez, M., Florescu, D., Robie, J., & Siméon, J. (2004). *XQuery 1.0: An XML Query Language*. W3C Working Draft. Retrieved from http://www.w3.org/TR/xquery/

Borkar, V., & Carey, M. (2004). Extending XQuery for Grouping, Duplicate Elimination, and Outer Join. In *<XML 2004> Conference & Exhibition*, Washington, DC, USA (pp. 1–11).

Cardenas, A. F. (1975). Analysis and performance of inverted data base structures. *Communications of the ACM, 18*(5), 253–263. doi:10.1145/360762.360766

Chung, C. W., Min, J. K., & Shim, K. (2002). APEX: an adaptive path index for XML data. In *ACM SIGMOD International Conference on Management of Data (SIGMOD 02)*, Madison, Wisconsin (pp. 121–132). New York: ACM.

Chung, C. W., Park, M. J., & Shim, K. (2002). APEX: an Adaptive Path Index of XML data. In *ACM SIGMOD International Conference on Management of Data (SIGMOD 02)* (pp. 121-132).

Cooper, B. F., Sample, N., Franklin, M. J., Hjaltason, G. R., & Shadmon, M. (2001). A Fast Index for Semistructured Data. In *27th International Conference on Very Large Data Bases (VLDB 01)*, Roma, Italy (pp. 341–350). San Francisco: Morgan Kaufmann.

Darmont, J., Boussaïd, O., Bentayeb, F., Rabaseda, S., & Zellouf, Y. (2003). Web multiform data structuring for warehousing . In *Multimedia Systems and Applications* (*Vol. 22*, pp. 179–194). Amsterdam: Kluwer.

Darmont, J., Boussaïd, O., Ralaivao, J. C., & Aouiche, K. (2005). An Architecture Framework for Complex Data Warehouses. In *7th International Conference on Enterprise Information Systems (ICEIS 05)*, Miami, USA (pp. 370–373).

Goldman, R., & Widom, J. (1997). DataGuides: Enabling Query Formulation and Optimization in Semistructured Databases. In *23rd International Conference on Very Large Data Bases (VLDB 97)*, Athens, Greece (pp. 436–445). San Francisco: Morgan Kaufmann.

Golfarelli, M., & Rizzi, S. (1998). *A methodological framework for data warehouse design. In 1st ACM international workshop on Data warehousing and OLAP* (pp. 3–9). New York, USA: DOLAP.

Gupta, H., & Mumick, I. S. (2005). Selection of Views to Materialize in a Data Warehouse. *IEEE Transactions on Knowledge and Data Engineering*, *17*(1), 24–43. doi:10.1109/TKDE.2005.16

Hümmer, W., Bauer, A., & Harde, G. (2003). XCube: XML for data warehouses. In *6th International Workshop on Data Warehousing and OLAP (DOLAP 03)*, New Orleans, USA (pp. 33–40). New York: ACM.

Jouve, P., & Nicoloyannis, N. (2003). Kerouac: An algorithm for clustering categorical data sets with practical advantages. In *International Workshop on Data Mining Learning for Actionable Knowledge (DMAK 2003)*.

Kaushik, R., Shenoy, P., Bohannon, P., & Gudes, E. (2002). Exploiting Local Similarity for Indexing Paths in Graph-Structured Data. In *18th International Conference on Data Engineering (ICDE 02)*, San Jose, CA (pp. 129–140). Washington, DC: IEEE Computer Society.

Kimball, R., & Ross, M. (2002). *The Data Warehouse Toolkit: The Complete Guide To Dimensional Modeling* (2nd ed.). Hoboken, NJ: John Wiley.

Kotidis, Y., & Roussopoulos, N. (1999). Dynamat: A dynamic view management system for data warehouses. In *ACM SIGMOD International Conference on Management of Data (SIGMOD 1999)*, Philadelphia, USA (pp. 371– 382).

Meier, W. (2002). eXist: An Open Source Native XML Database. In *Web, Web-Services, and Database Systems, NODe 2002 Web and Database-Related Workshops*, Erfurt, Germany (LNCS 2593, pp. 169–183). Berlin: Springer.

Milo, T., & Suciu, D. (1999). Index Structures for Path Expressions. In 7th International Conference on Database Theory (ICDT 99), Jerusalem, Israel (LNCS 1540, pp. 277–295). Berlin: Springer.

Nassis, V., Rajugan, R., Dillon, T. S., & Rahayu, J. W. (2005). Conceptual and Systematic Design Approach for XML Document Warehouses. *International Journal of Data Warehousing and Mining*, *1*(3), 63–86.

Oracle Corporation. (2006). *Oracle9i Data Warehousing Guide Release 2* (9.2). Retrieved from http://downloadwest.oracle.com/docs/cd/B10501 01/server.920/a96520/toc.htm

Park, B. K., Han, H., & Song, I. Y. (2005). XML-OLAP: A Multidimensional Analysis Framework for XML Warehouses. In *7th International Conference on Data Warehousing and Knowledge Discovery (DaWaK 05)*, Copenhagen, Denmark (LNCS 3589, pp. 32–42). Berlin: Springer.

Pokorný, J. (2002). XML Data Warehouse: Modelling and Querying. In *5th International Baltic Conference (BalticDB&IS 02)*, Tallin, Estonia, Tallin Technical University (pp. 267–280).

Qun, C., Lim, A., & Ong, K. W. (2003). D(k)-Index: An Adaptive Structural Summary for Graph-Structured Data. In *2003 ACM SIGMOD International Conference on Management of Data (SIGMOD 03)*, San Diego, USA (pp. 134–144).

Rusu, L. I., Rahayu, J. W., & Taniar, D. (2005). A Methodology for Building XML Data Warehouse. *International Journal of Data Warehousing and Mining*, *1*(2), 67–92.

Rys, M. (2004). XQuery in Relational Database Systems. In *XML 2004 Conference and Exposition Proceedings (XML 2004)*, Washington, USA.

Shukla, A., Deshpande, P., & Naughton, J. F. (2000). Materialized view selection for multi-cube data models. In *7th International Conference on Extending DataBase Technology (EDBT 2000)*, Konstanz, Germany (pp. 269-284).

Uchiyama, H., Runapongsa, K., & Teorey, T. J. (1999). A progressive view materialization algorithm. In *2nd ACM International Workshop on Data warehousing and OLAP (DOLAP 1999)*, Kansas City, USA (pp. 36–41).

Valluri, S. R., Vadapalli, S., & Karlapalem, K. (2002). View relevance driven materialized view selection in data warehousing environment. In *30th Australasian conference on Database technologies*, Melbourne, Australia (pp. 187-196).

Vrdoljak, B., Banek, M., & Rizzi, S. (2003). Designing Web Warehouses from XML Schemas. In *5th International Conference on Data Warehousing and Knowledge Discovery (DaWaK 03)*, Prague, Czech Republic (LNCS 2737, pp. 89–98). Berlin: Springer.

Waldt, D. (2005). *Using XML and Databases: W3C Standards in Practice* [White Paper]. The Gilbane Report. Retrieved from http://www.x-hive.com

Wu, H., Wang, Q., Yu, J. X., Zhou, A., & Zhou, S. (2003). UD(k, l)-Index: An Efficient Approximate Index for XML Data. In *4th International Conference on Advances in Web-Age Information Management (WAIM 03)*, Chengdu, China (LNCS 2762, pp. 68–79). Berlin: Springer.

Yao, S. (1997). Approximating block accesses in database organizations. *Communications of the ACM*, *20*(4), 260–261. doi:10.1145/359461.359475

Zhang, C., Naughton, J. F., DeWitt, D. J., Luo, Q., & Lohman, G. M. (2001). On Supporting Containment Queries in Relational Database Management Systems. In *ACM SIGMOD International Conference on Management of Data (SIGMOD 01)*, Santa Barbara, USA (pp. 425–436). New York: ACM.

Zhang, J., Wang, W., Liu, H., & Zhang, S. (2005). X-warehouse: building query pattern driven data. In *14th International Conference on World Wide Web (WWW 05)*, Chiba, Japan (pp. 896–897). New York: ACM.

KEY TERMS AND DEFINITIONS

Database Management System (DBMS): software set that handles structuring, storage, maintenance, update and querying of data stored in a database.

XML-Native DBMS (NXD): database system in which XML data are natively stored and queried as XML documents. An NXD provides XML schema storage and implements an XML query engine (typically supporting XPath and XQuery).

XML Data Warehouse: XML database that is specifically modeled (i.e., multidimensionally, with a star-like schema) to support XML decision-support and analytic queries.

Complex Data: data that present several axes of complexity for analysis, e.g., data represented in various formats, diversely structured, from several sources, described through several points of view, and/or versioned.

Structural Summary Based-Index: labeled graph structure that summarizes XML graph structural information.

Clustering: unsupervised machine learning method that consists in assigning a set of observations into subsets (clusters) so that observations in the same cluster are similar.

XML Graph: data model representing the hierarchical nature of XML data. In a XML graph, nodes represent elements or attributes.

ENDNOTES

1 A *star schema* is the simplest data warehouse schema. It consists of a single, central *fact table* linked to peripheral *dimensions*, an analyzed fact thus being described by a combination of dimensions (or analysis axes).

2 K-bisimilarity groups nodes with respect to local structure, i.e., the incoming paths of length up to k.

Section 6

Risks and Security

Chapter 15
Towards an Elastic Risk Management Methodology by Using Business to Software Unified Process (BSUP)

Pooya Khosraviyan Dehkordi
Islamic Azad University, Iran

Farshad Kyoomarsi
Islamic Azad University, Iran

ABSTRACT

Riskit is a now a world-wide risk management methodology deployed by a number of expert software engineering communities since its first rollout by (Kontio et. al, 1994,1995,1996,1997 and 1996). Business to Software Unified Process (BSUP) has been the proprietary Business to software modeling approach introduced for the first time in 2003 (Nasiri et. al, 2004 and 2007). In this paper the goal is apply the capabilities inherent in BSUP to optimize Riskit process model. BSUP, UML 2.0 and Fuzzy Logic Concepts are widely used when ever the model is to be made.

INTRODUCTION

The Riskit method for software engineering risk management (Charette,1989) is widely in use because of its sound theoretical foundation and its major focus on qualitative cognition of risks before their possible quantification (Carr et. al, 1993), in addition to its capability to provide a defined process for conducting risk management. Today, it is being supported by various tools, techniques and also rich guidelines. But the fascinating feature may be that the use of Riskit does not preclude the use of other risk management approaches (Kontio et. al, 1994, 1995, 1996 and 1997). Since the early days of software development (Basili et. al, 1989 and 19921992), risks had been perceived inevitable because of various unanticipated problems which cause development team to go over budget, miss deadlines, or finally deliver less than satisfactory artifacts and so on.

Although risks neither could be eliminated nor might be ignored, one may strictly monitor and manage them to control and mitigate their potential

DOI: 10.4018/978-1-61692-016-6.ch015

harmful effects. Reflective and proactive methods are alternatives to achieve the Goal. There are a few shortcomings which make the risk management process so sophisticated. The shortcomings of current methods are as follows:

- Risk (MacCrimmon et. al, 1986) is very seldom a crisp straightforward concept and mostly it is perceived as a non deterministic concept which is quite close to Fuzzy Logic concepts (Harris, 2006) and measures (Ganesh, 2006). This is also true while the impression of risk on various stakeholders is measured.
- Risks may influence each others in different ways. Risks may strengthen or diminish each other. This feature may make a very complicated scenario while analyzing the potential effects of risks.
- Clarity of methods and cost effectiveness of many current risk management methods are totally in doubts since they are costly perceived as complex or too costly to use.

BACKGROUND

Riskit Methodology

The Riskit method is considered to be a suitable solution to address the issues such as those listed above. Its main characteristics can be described by the following principles.

1. The Riskit method provides precise and unambiguous definitions for risks.

The common definition of risks, either by dictionaries or every day usage, associate several different meanings to risk. It can refer to a possibility of loss (Anonymous, 1992), the actual loss that would result if the risk occurs (Anonymous, 1992), a factor or element that is associated with a threat (Anonymous, 1992), or a person that contributes to the possibility of loss (Anonymous, 1995). The dictionary definitions for risk are so broad that it is fair to define risk as anything that is related to the possibility of loss. Clearly, there is some value in having such a broad and encompassing concept to facilitate initial discussion about risk. However, we believe that this wide range of meanings associated to the word "risk" can also prevent adequate precision in more detailed analysis or risks unless this ambiguity is explicitly addressed and removed.

2. The Riskit method results in explicit definition of objectives, constraints and other.

Risk is a relative concept; its definition depends on expectations that are associated with a situation. In order to analyze risks, it is necessary to formalize the expectations as well as possible. When expectations are recognized and defined, we refer to them as *goals*. While some goals cannot be stated precisely, at least they should be identified and documented as well as the information available allows. The Riskit method contains an explicit step and supporting templates to assist in the goal definition.

3. The Riskit method is aimed at modeling and documenting risks qualitatively.

The Riskit method provides conceptual and graphical tools to model different aspects of risks qualitatively, instead of requiring quantitative estimation of risk probability and impact to take place early in the project. Given the difficulty of these estimations and the often ambiguous interpretations of risks – the margins of error in risk quantification are easily high. By emphasizing the qualitative understanding of risks, there is a better basis for understanding and communicating about risk.

4. The Riskit method can use both ratio and ordinal scale risk ranking information to prioritize risks reliably.

The estimation problem has been reduced in the Riskit approach. Instead of forcing the quantification of risks using ratio scale metrics – often an unrealistic goal – the Riskit method only attempts to accomplish the necessary quantification of risks for risk management to take place. For risk management purposes it may be enough to identify the biggest risks and propose action to control them, while the exact values of probability and loss may not be needed. The selection of the type of metrics to be used in risk analysis should be based on the objectives of the analysis and the availability of data about risks.

5. The Riskit method uses the concept of utility loss to rank the loss associated with risk.

Many current risk management approaches are based ranking of risks based on the loss they cause to some specific attributes of the project, such as cost, time delay, or quality metrics. Often a single metric is used. This can be detrimental for two reasons. First, the use of a single metric, or a small number of metrics, can create strong bias away from secondary, yet influential goals that should be considered. Second, research in economics and management science has strongly indicated that decision are made based on the changes in the expected utility (or utility loss) of alternatives. As the utility functions of stakeholders are likely to be non-linear, use of direct loss metrics can lead to wrong estimates and rankings of the risks. Therefore, the Riskit method uses the concept of utility loss to compare and rank losses of risks.

6. Different stakeholder perspectives are explicitly modeled in the Riskit method.

All projects have more than one stakeholder that is interested in its results. They may have different priorities and levels of expectations. Risk management should be based on the recognition of these stakeholder expectations and priorities. Traditional, direct project metric based approaches cannot easily support the comparison of different stakeholder views and few risk management approaches attempt to address the issue. The Riskit method supports stakeholder views by documenting their expectations explicitly and evaluating the utility loss for each separately.

7. The Riskit method has an operational definition and training support.

The Riskit method has an operational definition so that it can be applied easily and consistently. This, in fact, is the main contribution of this paper, this paper presents an operational definition of the Riskit process.

8. The Riskit Analysis graph, (Figure 1), is a graphical formalism that is used to define the different aspects of risk more formally. The Riskit analysis graph can be seen both as a conceptual template for defining risks, as well as a well-defined graphical modeling formalism (Kontio et. al, 1996).

BSUP METHODOLOGY

There were always pros and cons about the importance of business modeling in the software development process which was recently accepted and recommended as an essential stage prior to any further development by a few research communities in addition to commercial solutions such as Rational Unified Process (RUP).

Considering the new role of software in the E-business, one cannot proceed in the development process without complete and clear understanding of tight relationships between the business ele-

Figure 1. A conceptual view of the elements in the Riskit Analysis Graph

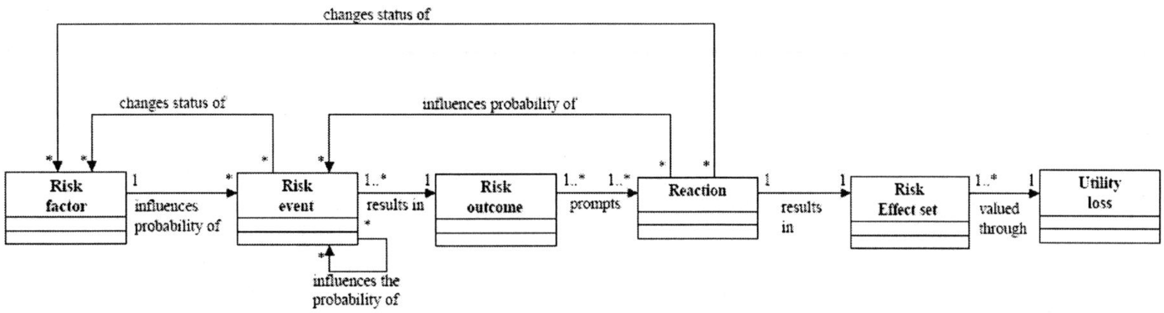

ments And software's which have mutual robust impression on each other. By modeling the business from software engineering viewpoint, one can make sure that nearly all subtle effects and side-effects from both parties being captured in a straightforward manner without any unresolved ambiguity. We already proposed a method called BSUP, stands for Business to Software Unified Process, which models a business from five orthogonal aspects to build up a complete integrated view of business. In BSUP the business model is composed of five major components including: goal, process, rule, role and resource models. (Figure 2) demonstrates the anatomy of the BSUP's business model. As one might expect, Business process model plays the major role and resides in the focal point of the whole model to integrate it. To reconcile the different nature of business model and correspondent software model(s), one may use the attractive strengths of UML to model the focused business. These approach ends to building of models which simply being perceived by software teams in addition to business experts with limited computer talent. (For details about using

Figure 2. Business Model core-Components diagram in BSUP (Nasiri et. al, 2004 and 2007)

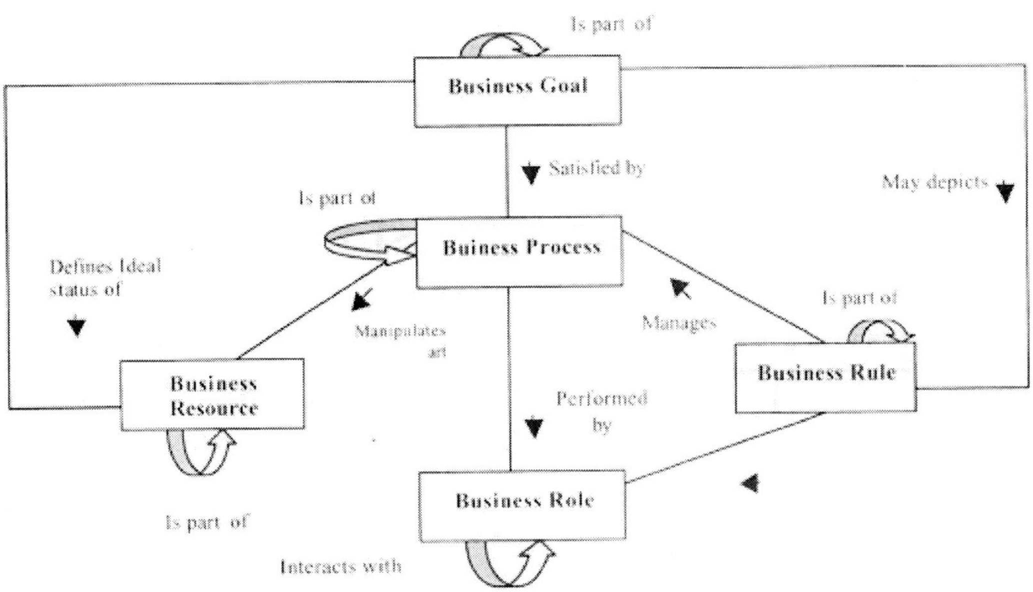

Figure 3. Business Goal Meta-Model in BSUP (Nasiri et. al, 2004 and 2007)

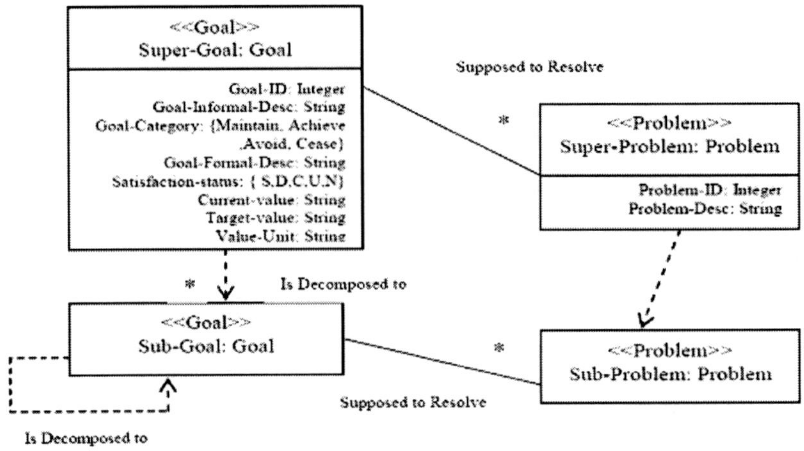

UML for business modeling, refer to (Nasiri et. al, 2004 and 2007)). Taking into account the robust capabilities provided by the UML 2.0 (Fowler, 2006), nearly all the five pillars of the model, as depicted above, may be implemented while some extension is done on it. The most significant parts of the business model reside in the Business goal and Business process models and it can be used in Riskit methodology for risk modeling. (Figure 3) and (Figure 4) represents the overall schema of these two core models.

Figure 4. Business Process Meta-model in BSUP (Nasiri et. al, 2004 and 2007)

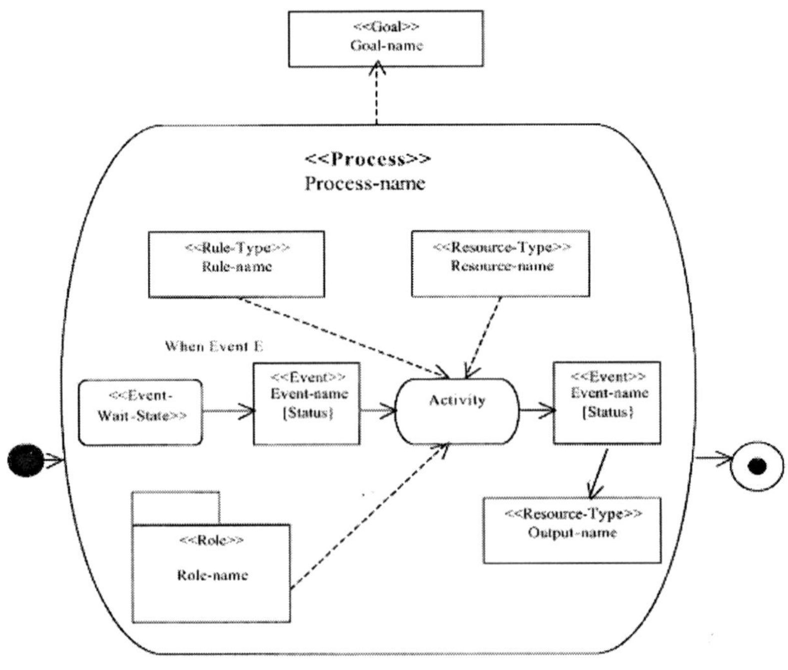

Figure 5. BSUP proposed process model for Riskit analysis graph modeling

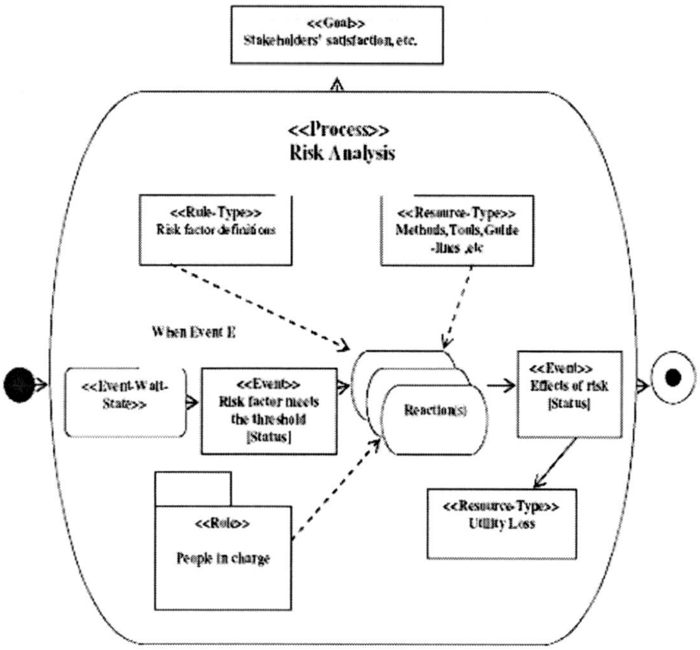

APPLYING BSUP ON RISKIT METHODOLOGY

The core of Riskit method resides in its analysis graph in addition to its definition of process that supports risk management activities throughout the project as already mentioned above.

The Riskit analysis graph, (Figure 3), is a graphical formalism that aims to define various aspects of risk in a formal way. Basically the graph brings its idea from the what first developed by (Rowe et. al, 1977) and later completed by extension done by (Knotio et. al, 1994). Considering the model proposed in BSUP (Figure 4), the Analysis graph may be extended to be a complete well formed process model (Like Figure 5 represented the new model) As it is visible in the figure, the proposed model transforms the Riskit analysis graph to be more integrated and also clustered. The new model generated a complete process encompassing all the requirements and elements of a process including goal(s), resource(s), role(s) and etc by deploying the new model any inconsistency and/or inconvenience in the model could be easily recognized and rectified. It means that the model would be something more than an informative graph. The next step toward optimization would be the process definition in Riskit. The definition in Riskit is well-designed while major characteristic may be considered as:

- Ability of risk information prioritization based on available ordinal metrics.
- Providing method to distinguish goals and stakeholders within the scope of the software project.
- Providing a method to describe the risk management mandate including scope, procedures and authorities etc.

(Figure 6) depicts process definition schema in Riskit as proposed by (Kontio, 1994). Again this design may be optimized by deploying the BSUP process model capability. The process model for Riskit may be optimized as (Figure 7).

Figure 6. Process definition for the whole Riskit process

Purpose:	Provide project and organization management with accurate and timely information of the risks in a project. Define and implement cost efficient actions to control risks.
Description:	Monitor and manage risks continuously in a project.
Entry criteria	Project planning has been initiated.
Input:	Project authorization information: goals, resources, schedule, budget. Context and history information about the organization and its process.
Output:	Continually updated information about risks. Defined and implemented risk controlling actions. Experience and data about risks and risk management process.
Methods and tools:	The Riskit process definition. Riskit documentation templates. Riskit analysis graph definition and drawing tools. Risk identification checklists. Multiple criteria decision making tools. Word-processing and spreadsheet software.
Responsibility:	Project manager.
Resources:	Technical personnel. Stakeholder representatives.
Exit criteria:	Project has been completed or terminated.

APPLYING FUZZY LOGIC CONCEPTS AND UML ON RISKIT METHODOLOGY

Revised the Riskit Analysis Graph

The underlying conceptual model – or meta-model – of the Riskit Analysis Graph components is presented in (Figure 1), using the UML (OMG, 2003). This meta-model represents the underlying, conceptual elements and their relationships. Each rectangle in the graph represents a risk element and each arrow describes the possible relationship between risk elements. The relationship arrow is read in the direction of the arrow. For example, the relationship between "risk factor" and "risk event" in (Figure 1) should be read as "[a] risk

Figure 7. BSUP proposed Process model for Riskit process definition

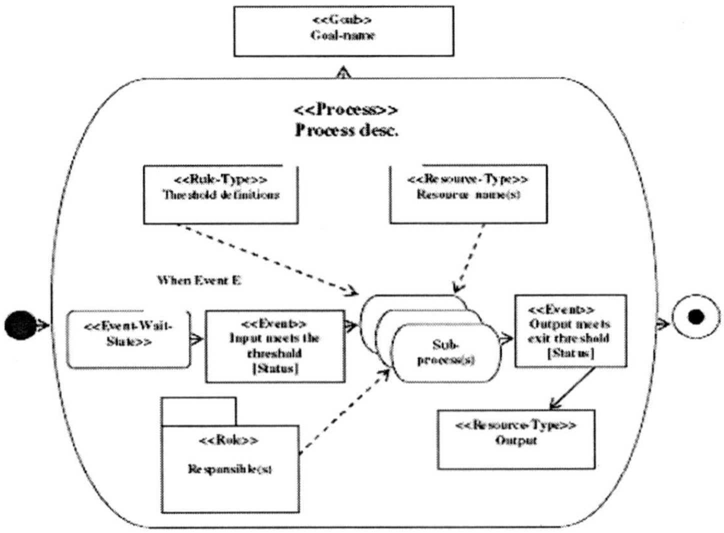

Figure 8. A Conceptual View of the Elements in the Fuzzy Riskit Analysis Graph (For example for Risk Event: RE1+RE2+RE3=1 and RE1+RF+R3=1)

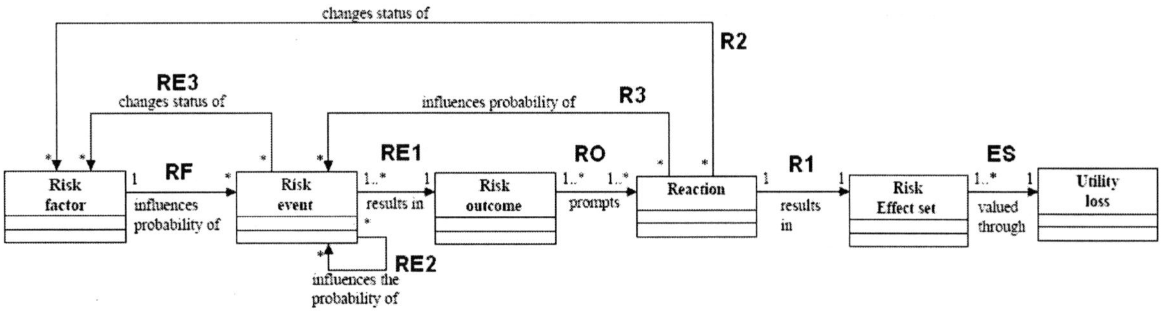

factor influences [the] probability of [a] risk event" (Kontio,1994 and 1995).

In this method relation between risk elements are deterministic but in the real world accident occurrence are probable between 0 and 1; therefore, we need fuzzy logic concepts (Harris, 2006) to modeling the Riskit analysis graph. For this purpose the design of the Fuzzy Riskit Analysis Graph must be like this:

- Each connector must have a number between 0 and 1.
- Sum of input connector number to each risk element must be equal 1.

Figure 9. The Use Case of Riskit Risk Management cycle

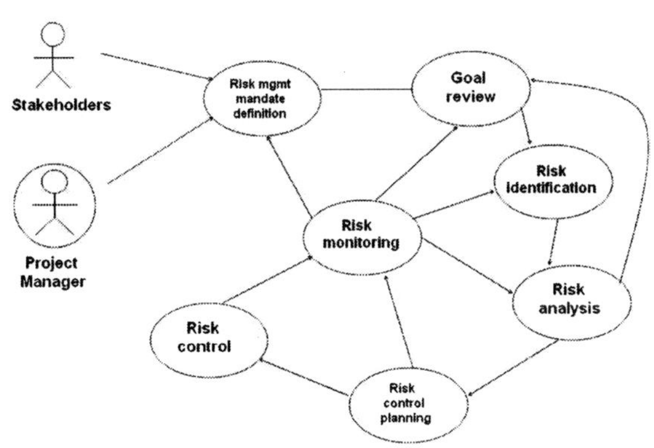

- Sum of output connector number from each risk element must be equal 1.

With these cases we can design the Fuzzy Riskit Analysis Graph like (Figure 8).

Revised Riskit Management Process

The risk management cycle (Behforooz et. al, 1996)(Fairley, 1989) in a project can be viewed as consisting of some basic activities (Boehm, 1991): defining the scope and focus of risk management; review and definition of goals; risk identification and monitoring; risk analysis; risk control planning; and controlling of risks. Main flows of information between these processes are represented in (Figure 9). Each of the processes in (Figure 9) can be instantiated several times during the project duration and they may be enacted concurrently. This behavioral aspect of the process is modeled through the input and output criteria defined for each process (Radice et. al, 1985). However, typically the most critical instances of the risk management cycle are the ones enacted in the beginning of the project.

With considering (Figure 9) symbol's and table structure for process definition (Curtis et. al, 1992), the designer become dizzy because in one section encounter with table and in other encounter with dataflow diagram therefore we use the UML diagrams to design all of diagrams

Figure 10. Goal Definition Template Class Diagram

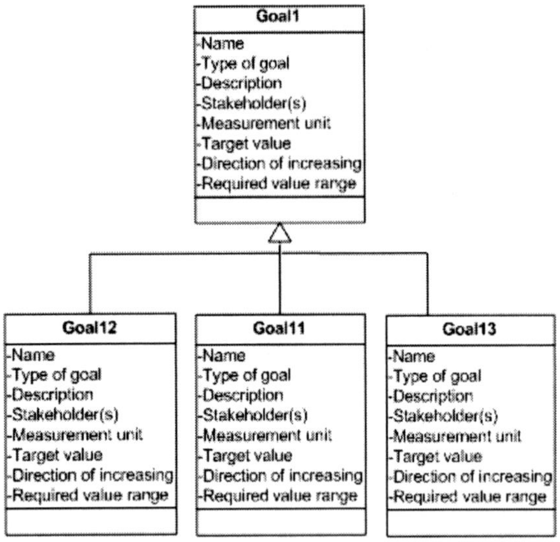

and for this purpose we apply Use Case diagram to show cycle (Fowler, 2006). Then with using Use Case diagrams we can design the Riskit risk management cycle like (Figure 9).

Revised Goals Diagram

Risks do not exist without a reference to goals, expectations or constraints that are associated with a project. If goals are not recognized, risks that may affect them may be ignored totally or, in the best case, they cannot be analyzed in any detail as the reference level is not defined.

Some of a project's goals typically have been explicitly defined but many relevant aspects that influence management decisions may be implicit. Therefore, it is necessary to begin the risk management process by a careful review, definition and refinement of goals and expectations that are associated with a project (Kontio, 1995 and 1996). We can use Class Diagram (OMG, 2003) to modeling goals diagram we can design goal class diagram like (Figure 10).

The relationships between goals and stakeholders can also be documented using a stakeholder-goal priority table presented in (Figure 11). Such a table allows approximate prioritization of goals for each stakeholder: each cell in (Figure 11) documents relative importance of goals for each stakeholder. It is important to point out that if such rankings are documented for stakeholders, each column should be read and interpreted independently (Kontio, 1997). Priority values *between* stakeholders for a given goal cannot be derived from such information. In other words, goal priority rankings should be interpreted only within a single column, not across columns in (Figure 11). As shown in (Figure 12), the relative priorities

Figure 11. Stakeholder-goal priority diagram using Sequence diagram

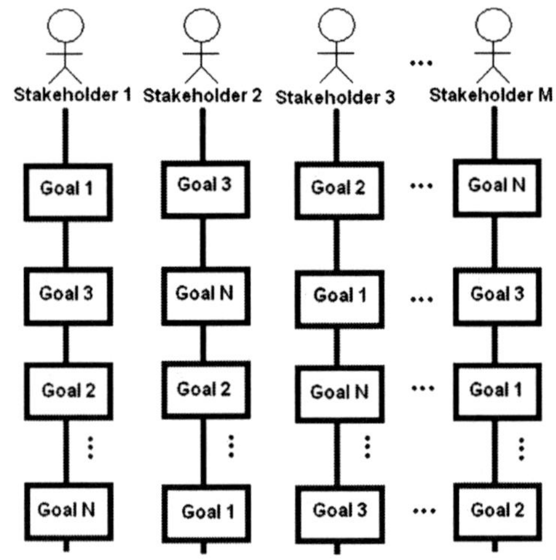

Figure 12. Risk scenario ranking diagram using Sequence diagram and Fuzzy Logic Concepts (For example X+Y=1 and Z+W=1)

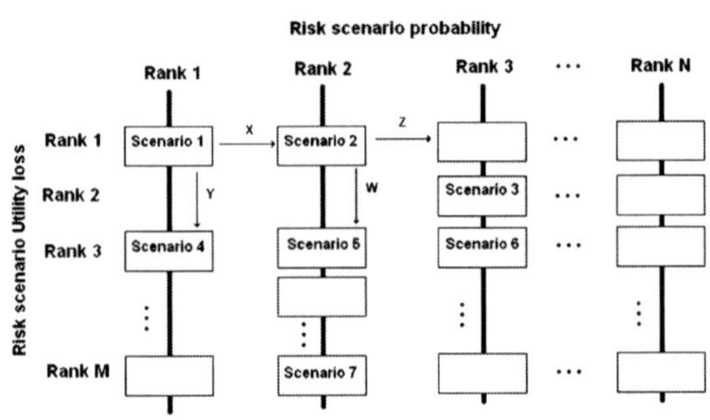

Figure 13. Risk controlling action urgency diagram using Timing diagram and vertical line for determine the time section that is shows the state of project. For example Normal state occurred when the risk controlling action was do and risk controlling action delay was not do.

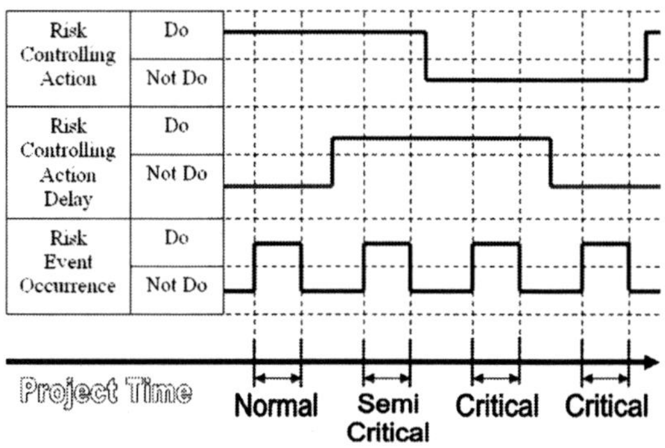

between stakeholders can also be documented in stakeholder column headings. This information is initially defined in the risk management mandate definition process (Kontio et. al, 1996).With considering above issues, (Figure 11) first must shows priority values between stakeholders and second must shows priority values of goals for each stakeholders therefore we can use Sequence diagram like (Figure 11).

Revised Risk Prioritization Diagram

As resources for risk management are limited, it may not be feasible to mitigate or analyze all risk scenarios. Instead, one should focus on most important risks and spend relatively more time and resources on their management. In order to do this, it is necessary to rank the risk scenarios. Thus, the final step in risk analysis is to prioritize risk scenarios. Using the Riskit Pareto ranking technique results in a partial ranking of risk scenarios, i.e., priorities for some scenarios can be defined but some scenarios' relative priority remains unknown. While the complete prioritization of scenarios would be desirable, the input data leading to the prioritization does not normally allow it (Kontio, 1997).

In this diagram we cannot determine to select which scenario after scenario 1 and to solving this problem, with using Sequence diagram we can design (Figure 11) and we can apply Use Case to design each scenario and we can determine probability of each scenario on its arrow like (Figure 12).

Revised Risk Control Planning Diagram

The *urgency of implementing the risk controlling action* may strongly influence on what risks to mitigate and how. The risk controlling action urgency depends both on the time of the risk event occurrence and the time delay in implementing the risk controlling action, as (Figure 13) shows. The time of risk event occurrence, naturally, influences the urgency. However, the risk controlling action impact delay is often omitted from risk timeframe analysis, although it can have a big impact on a situation as some risk controlling actions have long implementation delays. As time goes by, some risk controlling actions become infeasible if they are not considered early enough (Kontio, 1995 and 1996). For designing this diagram we can use Timing diagram and Fuzzy Logic concepts (Ganesh, 2006) like (Figure 13).

CONCLUSION

This paper presented an operational optimization of the Riskit method by using the BSUP, our proprietary methodology for business software modeling. It must be granted that the scope of optimization for Riskit is much larger than what shown in the paper. But it has been clarified the strengths of BSUP and typical areas that those strengths can be employed to enrich the Riskit models. To some degree the operational definition given here is perhaps too general for casual readers who want to read an overview of the method. So it is strongly encouraged for such readers to review relevant documents in addition to this paper. With using this method and applying these changes mentioned in this paper we can do achieve better model(s) for software risk management in a project.

REFERENCES

Anonymous, . (1992). *The American Heritage Dictionary of the English Language*. New York: Houghton Mifflin Company.

Anonymous, . (1995). *Merriam-Webster's Collegiate Dictionary*. Springfield, MA: Merriam-Webster.

Basili, V. R. (1989). Software Development: A Paradigm for the Future. In *Proceedings of the 13th Annual Computer Software and Applications Conference (COMPSAC)* (pp. 471-485). Washington, DC: IEEE Computer Society Press.

Basili, V. R., Caldiera, G., & McGarry, F. Pajerski. R., Page, G., & Waligora, S. (1992 May). The Software Engineering Laboratory - an Operational Software Experience Factory. In *Proceedings of the International Conference on Software Engineering* (pp. 370-381). Washington, DC: IEEE Computer Society Press.

Behforooz, A., & Hudson, F. J. (1996). *Software Engineering Fundamentals*. New York: Oxford University Press.

Boehm, B. W. (1991). *Software Risk Management: Principles and Practices*. Washington, DC: IEEE Software.

Carr, M. J., Konda, S. L., Monarch, I. A., Ulrich, F. C., & Walker, C. F. (1993). *Taxonomy-Based Risk Identification*. SEI Technical Report SEI-93-TR-006. Pittsburgh, PA: Software Engineering Institute.

Charette, R. N. (1989). *Software Engineering Risk Analysis and Management*. New York: McGraw-Hill.

Curtis, B., Kellner, M. I., & Over, J. (1992). Process Modeling. *Communications of the ACM, 35*, 75–90. doi:10.1145/130994.130998

Fairley, R. E. (1989). Risk Management: The Key to Successful Software Projects. In F. J. Mowle & P. F. Elzer (Eds.), *Proceedings of the 3rd IFAC/IFIP Workshop* (pp. 45-50). Oxford, UK: Pergamon.

Fowler, M. (2006). *UML 2.0 Distilled* (3rd ed.). Reading, MA: Addison Wesley.

Ganesh, M. (2006). *Introduction to Fuzzy Sets and Fuzzy Logic*. Upper Saddle River, NJ: Prentice Hall of India.

Harris, J. (2006). *Fuzzy Logic Applications in Engineering Science*. Berlin: Springer.

Kontio, J. (1994). *Software Engineering Risk Management: A Technology Review Report PI_4.1, A proprietary Nokia Research Center project deliverable*. Helsinki, Finland: Nokia Research Center.

Kontio, J. (1995). *Promises: A Framework for Utilizing Process Models in Process Asset Management*. Licentiate thesis at Helsinki University of Technology.

Kontio, J., & Basili, V. R. (1996). Risk Knowledge Capture in the Riskit Method. In *Proceedings of the 21st Software Engineering Workshop*. Greenbelt, MD: NASA.

Kontio, J., & Basili, V. R. (1997). Empirical Evaluation of a Risk Management Method. In *Proceedings of the SEI Conference on Risk Management*. Pittsburgh, PA: Software Engineering Institute.

Kontio, J., Englund, H., & Basili, V. R. (1996). *Experiences from an Exploratory Case Study with a Software Risk Management Method. CS-TR-3705, Computer Science Technical Reports*. College Park, MD: University of Maryland.

MacCrimmon, K. R., & Wehrung, D. A. (1986). *Taking Risks*. New York: Free Press.

Nasiri, R., Moeini, A., & Abdollahzadeh, A. (2004). A New Approach Towards Procurement of Software Models Via Distributed Business Models. *The Journal of Supercomputing*.

Nassiri, R., & Moeini, A. (2007). The Essential of Business Software modeling in Successful ERP implementation. In *Proceedings of the 2007 Int'l conference on Software Engineering Research & practices (SERP 2007)*, USA.

OMG. (2003 September). *UML 2.0 Diagram Interchange Specification*.

Radice, R. A., Roth, N. K., O'Hara, A. C., & Ciarfella, W. A. (1985). A Programming Process Architecture. *IBM Systems Journal*, *24*, 79–90. doi:10.1147/sj.242.0079

Rowe, W. D. (1977). *An Anatomy of Risk*. New York: John Wiley & Sons.

KEY TERMS AND DEFINITIONS

BSUP: Business to Software Unified Process

UML: Unified Modeling Language

RUP: Rational Unified Process

Fuzzy Logic: A Problem-Solving Control System Methodology

Riskit: An Elastic Method for Software Engineering Risk Management

Chapter 16
Knowledge for Managing Information Systems Security:
Review and Future Research Directions

Ken H. Guo
McMaster University, Canada

ABSTRACT

Knowledge is one of the critical factors that organizations need to consider when managing the security of resource management systems or information systems in general. This is because knowledge is not only the subject but also a tool of IS security management. On the one hand, IS security is about the security of knowledge (including data and information). On the other hand, IS security management is a knowledge-intensive activity that depends heavily on IS professionals' expertise and skills and end user awareness. Given the important role of knowledge, this chapter aims to review current security research by applying knowledge management concepts and frameworks as a tool and lens. Based on the systemic review, this chapter identifies gaps in the current information systems security literature and provides some guidelines for future research and security practices.

INTRODUCTION

Resource management systems enable organizations to track, control, and utilize their assets. Managers rely on such systems to obtain useful information about organizational resources and make the right business decisions. However, in order to fully utilize resource management systems for improving operational efficiency and building competitive advantage in the market place, organizations must ensure that the systems are secure. Indeed, security may be seen as the necessary condition for the successful implementation of not only resource management systems but also other types of information systems (IS) in general.

The implication of security (or lack of it) on organizations' business operations is profound. Without sufficient security, organizations may risk losing critical information, being distracted from normal business activities, or incurring unforeseeable financial costs. For example, the network of the TJX Companies, Inc. (TJX) was compromised

DOI: 10.4018/978-1-61692-016-6.ch016

and customer records (which are a very important resource for the company) such as payment card information were believed to be stolen in 2005 and 2006. According to the company's published reports (TJX, 2007a, 2007b), a number of class actions have been filed against the company. As a result of these lawsuits, TJX has accrued costs of more than 25 million dollars (US) and expected to continue to incur such costs.

Given the significant impact on businesses, it is important that we can learn from these incidents and understand what the causes are in order to prevent such security breaches in the future. There is little theoretical guide, however, for such endeavor. The majority of the information systems (IS) security literature is based on expert opinion, anecdotal evidence, or experience (Kotulic & Clark, 2004). Until recent years, research has emphasized mostly on technical issues such as advanced encryption algorithms, authentication technologies, anti-virus, firewalls, and so on. Technical solutions alone, however, do not necessarily guarantee security. Scholars have called for more research efforts on organizational problems, management issues and human behavior issues (Dhillon & Backhouse, 2000; Dutta & McCrohan, 2002; Hitchings, 1995).

This chapter aims to review extant IS security research from a knowledge management perspective. Knowledge management (KM) is a mature research area and we can have a systemic view of the current status of IS security research by applying KM theories and frameworks. More importantly, based on this systemic view, we expect to identify gaps in current IS security research and provide some guidelines for practices.

This chapter proceeds as follows. First, it gives a brief review of IS security in order to provide some background information on traditional and modern security concepts. It also discusses the relationship between IS security and KM. The chapter then proceeds with a review of relevant concepts the KM literature. The subsequent section gives a review of knowledge in IS security management. This section focuses on the classification and taxonomy of IS security knowledge, as well as approaches of processing and manipulating such knowledge for security planning and management. Lastly, the chapter discusses some critical issues that warrant further research and implications for IS security management practices.

A BRIEF BACKGROUND OF INFORMATION SYSTEMS SECURITY

In the IS literature, there are many seemingly similar terms used for the concept of security, e.g. computer security, information security, and information systems security, to name a few. The term of computer security is often technical-oriented and encompasses technologies such as encryption algorithm. It may also refer to the security of a single computer. Information security, according to International Standards Organization, is "the protection of information from a wide range of threats"(ISO/IEC, 2005). Information systems security differs from information security in that the former concept encompass not only data or information itself but also those systems that process and store such data and information (Theoharidou, Kokolakis, Karyda, & Kiountouzis, 2005). Despite the subtle differences, researchers and practitioners by and large use these terms interchangeably (this approach is adopted in this chapter). For example, the term of information security is also defined as the protection of both information and the systems and hardware that use, store, and transmit that information (Whitman & Mattord, 2003, p. 9).

For the purpose of providing concise background information, this section limits the discussion on two aspects of IS security: security principles and components of security management.

Security Principles

Traditional IS security principles include confidentiality, integrity, and availability – the CIA Triangle (Whitman & Mattord, 2003). Confidentiality refers the prevention of disclosure to unauthorized parties; integrity is the quality of being complete and uncorrupted; and availability refers to the state where authorized legitimate users can access the information without interference.

While the CIA Triangle principles are still valid today, they are not sufficient in the context of rapid-changing information technologies. Researchers have called for additional principles for IS security. One proposed set of principles include responsibility, integrity, trust, and ethicality (Dhillon & Backhouse, 2000). The responsibility principle requires that organizational members have a clear understanding of their respective roles and responsibilities in using organizational information systems; integrity principle here refers to the integrity of organizational members, who should not leak or reveal sensitive business information to third parties; trust principle refers to the trust on information users who are supposed to act in accordance with organizational norms and policies; and finally, ethicality principle is the expectation of information users to act in accordance with ethical practices, particularly in situations where formal policies and rules are not available.

Another principle is privacy (e.g. Head & Yuan, 2001; Whitman & Mattord, 2003). This is particularly important in electronic commerce settings where personal information of individual customers is at stake. A growing number of laws and regulations require that individuals' privacy be protected. Privacy and confidentiality are related but not the same. Confidentiality is about the owner of the information (i.e. the organization), while privacy is about the subject of the information (i.e. individuals).

Components of Security Management

Information systems security management is a complex task. There are many ways to decompose it into smaller components for facilitating efficient and effective management. For example, it can be decomposed into four layers: organizational, workflow, information, and infrastructure level (Weippl & Klemen, 2006). Infrastructure level security refers to traditional security aspects such as secure network and hardware; information level encompasses access control and user rights; workflow level refers to secure business processes; and at organizational level, IS security encompasses security strategy, corporate security culture, and risk management. A similar viewpoint is that IS security is an integral part of 3D "enterprise security" pyramid, which encompasses technology, process, people, and organization design/strategy (Kiely & Benzel, 2006). Technology involves the development and implementation of technological approaches for protecting information systems; processes refer to explicit means by which things are done; people refer to human resources of an organization; and organizational design/strategy refers to organizational structures and strategies that enable an enterprise to compete effectively in the marketplace.

There are some emerging concepts in IS security management as well. Examples of such emerging concepts include trust management and identity management, among others. Trust management is about how trust is established or negotiated and how it is managed (Bertino & Sandhu, 2005). As discussed above, trust is one principle of security. Trust management plays an important role in situations where information is shared among individual users or across organizations. Identity management is the process of creation, maintenance, and termination of a digital identity for people or systems (Pato, 2003).

The two security principles trust and privacy are closely related to identity management, as these two principles are directly or indirectly involved when managing identity information (Casassa Mont, Bramhall, & Pato, 2003).

Knowledge in Security Management

Knowledge is one of the critical factors that organizations need to consider when managing IS security. This is because knowledge is not only the *subject* but also a *tool* of IS security management. On the one hand, IS security is about the security of knowledge. Although traditionally IS security research and management focused on the confidentiality, integrity, and accessibility of data and information, it is the knowledge (derived from data and information) that matters most to organizations. Thus, it is not surprising that KM and IS security management have some striking similarities (Glaser & Pallas, 2007).

One the other hand, IS security management is a knowledge-intensive activity that depends heavily on IS professionals' expertise and skills (Belsis, Kokolakis, & Kiountouzis, 2005). An organization's IS security is also dependent on user awareness of security issues. There has been some research that focuses on this aspect. For example, a knowledge architecture for IT security was proposed for organizations to assess their security knowledge needs by determining the current and future knowledge architecture (Kesh & Ratnasingam, 2007). Some other research focused on formalizing security knowledge with a security ontology (Fenz & Ekelhart, 2009; Tsoumas & Gritzalis, 2006).

It is for these reasons that in this chapter we try to identify gaps in IS security research and provide some insights for security practices by applying relevant concepts in the KM literature.

RELEVANT CONCEPTS OF KNOWLEDGE MANAGEMENT

The concepts of knowledge and knowledge management are complex and multi-faceted (Alavi & Leidner, 2001). While a comprehensive review of knowledge literature is beyond the scope of this chapter, this section synthesizes some of the concepts that may be applied to organizational information systems security management.

Knowledge Management Ontology

An ontology is a simplified and explicit specification of a phenomenon (Gruber, 1995). A general-purpose ontology is proposed by Holsapple and Joshi (2004) as a foundation for KM research, study, and practice. The KM ontology is presented in terms of primitives, definitions, and axioms and consists of four components: KM conduct, knowledge manipulation activities, knowledge resources, and KM influences.

According to Holsapple and Joshi (2004), KM is "an entity's systematic and deliberate efforts to expand, cultivate, and apply available knowledge". KM is not limited to organizations. Rather, it can be applied to personal, trans-organizational, and national levels. An entity's KM work can be seen as composed of "episodes". KM episode is defined as the entity's execution of some configuration of knowledge management activities (KMA). Such activities are carried by some processors (human or computer systems) that operate on available knowledge resources to satisfy a knowledge need or opportunity. The activities may further result in learning and/or projections of knowledge. These components of Holsapple and Joshi's KM ontology are further elaborated below.

KM Influences

KM influences are factors that determine how knowledge is manipulated within and across each

Table 1. Classification of Organizational Knowledge

Classes	Subclasses	Examples
Schematic Knowledge	Culture	Shared assumptions; Norm; and Beliefs
	Infrastructure	Roles; Responsibilities; and Regulations
	Strategy	Path; Direction
	Purpose	Vision; Mission
Content Knowledge	Artifacts	Books; Reports; Documents; Facilities; Tangible Products
	Participants' Knowledge	Core participants; Ancillary participants

episode. There are three categories of KM influences: management, resources, and environment. Management influences refer to an organization's administrative efforts on managing knowledge. Such influences include leadership, coordination (e.g. the coordination among knowledge processors), control, and measurement. Resource influences refer to various resources that are available to the entity, including human resources, financial resources, and knowledge resources. Environment influences are factors external to the entity, including technology, completion, climate (social, political, etc), and so on.

Knowledge Resources

Knowledge resource is defined as the knowledge that an entity can manipulate in ways to yield value. Knowledge resources are one of the four classes of organizational resources (the other three are financial, human resources, and material resources) and can be further analyzed in detailed components as shown in (Table 1). There are two classes of knowledge resources: schematic knowledge and content knowledge. Schematic knowledge, which depends on the existence of the entity, has four components: culture, infrastructure, strategy, and purpose; content knowledge, which on the other hand exists independently of the entity to which it belongs, has two components: artifacts and participant knowledge. Each of the components is defined as follows:

1. Culture. An organization's culture refers to the basic assumptions and beliefs that are shared by its members. It includes the organization's values, principles, norms, traditions, unwritten rules, and informal procedures.
2. Infrastructure. An organization's infrastructure refers to the kind of knowledge that defines the organization's roles, the interrelationships, and the regulations that govern the use of these roles and relationship. It can be viewed as the counterpart of the culture component.
3. Strategy. An organization's strategy defines what it does in order to accomplish its purposes. A strategy may consist of plans for using organizational resources, which include other knowledge resource components.
4. Purpose. An organization's purposes define its reasons for existence. It includes mission, vision, objectives, and goals. Purposes are directional knowledge with which other schematic knowledge components are to be aligned.
5. Knowledge artifact. A knowledge artifact is an object that is the representation of knowledge that may be usable to knowledge processors in an organization. Artifacts are a type of knowledge content that can exist independent of the organization that holds it. Examples of knowledge artifacts include

books, reports, documents, videos, among others.

6. Participant knowledge. This refers the kind of knowledge that is possessed by employees and others who participate in the organization's business activities. In addition to employees, participants may also include customers, partners, suppliers, as well as computer systems.

Learning and Projection

Learning is defined as a process where knowledge resources are modified. It is an outcome of a knowledge management episode that involves the change of the state of the entity's knowledge. Learning can be functional or dysfunctional. The former indicates a positive change while the latter involves negative change of the state of the entity's knowledge. Learning also occurs whenever knowledge processors detect and correct errors (Argyris, 1995).

The learning process can be better explained with a theory-in-use model (Argyris, Putnam, & Smith, 1985). The model depicts the relationships among three concepts: governing variables, action strategies, and consequences. According to this model, people's action strategies are decided by governing variables, which are the values that people seek to satisfy; action strategies have intended consequences, with which people expect to satisfy the global variables. Consequences give feedback to action strategies and governing variables. There are two forms of learning when the consequences are unintended: single-loop learning and double-loop learning. In single-loop learning, people try to change their actions while in double-loop learning it is the governing variables that are to be changed.

As opposite to learning, projection is the process in which resources are emitted into the environment (rather than the entity itself) as an outcome of a KM episode. The resources that are emitted can be either knowledge or other types of resources such as financial and human resources.

The above ontology proposed by Holsapple and Joshi gives a fairly complete picture of knowledge management by identifying its major components and the interplays among these components. The ontology provides some guidelines for using knowledge management approaches as tools to investigate issues related to knowledge-intensive activities.

Knowledge Attributes

While the focus of the KM ontology reviewed above is on the structure and processes of knowledge management, it is useful to examine the characteristics or attributes of knowledge. As Holsapple (2003) pointed out, an appreciation of multiple attributes helps one get a better understanding of knowledge resources and their processing. A brief review of concepts relevant to IS security management is given below. More detailed review can be found elsewhere in the literature. Two good examples are Alavi & Leidner (2001) and Holsapple (2003).

An attribute is a dimension along which different knowledge can vary (Holsapple, 2003). It may comprise a range of values, which can be categorical. In this chapter, we consider the following dimensions: type, domain, and mode.

1. Knowledge type. There are three primary types of knowledge: descriptive, procedural, and reasoning (Holsapple & Whinston, 1996). Each of them describes a different aspect of a knowledge object. Descriptive knowledge is about the "state of some world", which includes descriptions of past, present, future, and hypothetical situations. It is about "know what". Procedural knowledge is about the detailed procedures of doing something. It is about "know how". Reasoning knowledge, however, specifies the conclusions that can be drawn from certain pre-conditions. It is about "know

why". This is similar to the classification of declarative knowledge (know-what), procedural knowledge (know-how), and conceptual knowledge (know-why) (Agarwal, Krudys, & Tanniru, 1997).

2. Knowledge domain. This is the subject area where the knowledge is used (van der Spek & Spijkervet, 1997). Examples of such knowledge domain include accounting, marketing, and so on.
3. Knowledge mode. This dimension distinguishes between "tacit" and "explicit" knowledge (Nonaka, 1994; Polanyi, 1962). Explicit knowledge is often codified and can be transmitted in formal and systematic languages; tacit knowledge, on the other hand, involves personal quality and is difficult to be formalized and transmitted. From this perspective, the "artifacts" in the KM ontology can be seen as explicit knowledge, while the knowledge of participants is essentially tacit.

SECURITY FROM A KNOWLEDGE MANAGEMENT PERSPECTIVE

The previous section gave an overview of relevant concepts in the KM literature, particularly the KM ontology proposed by Holsapple and Joshi (2004) and some attributes of knowledge. These KM concepts can provide a useful guide for understanding other knowledge-related organizational issues. In this section we use the KM ontology as a tool and apply relevant concepts to investigate the issues that have been addressed and how these issues have been addressed in the IS security literature. We then identify possible directions for future research and discuss the implications for organizational IS security practices.

Influences

Similar to knowledge management, there are a number of critical factors that affect organizational IS security management. In this review we focus on managerial influences and environmental influences.

Managerial Influences

As discussed in previous section, managerial influences include leadership, coordination, control, and measurement. In general, the importance of management influences has been recognized in the IS security literature. For example, Withman (2004) advocates the implementation of security policy and deterrence measures to prevent computer abuses. Policy and deterrence measure can be classified as "control" based on the KM ontology. From the leadership perspective, prior research suggested that top management support has a significant impact on an organization's security culture and the level of security policy enforcement (Knapp, Marshall, Rainer, & Ford, 2006).

One particular organizational control is security policy. A security policy prescribes how an organization manages its IS security. More specifically, it consists of a set of rules and practices that regulate how the organization manages, protects, and distributes its key information assets (Walker, 1985). Prior studies have investigated two issues of security policies: the content or design and the effectiveness of a policy. For example, Whitman (2008) examined the requirements and development of effective policies; Verdon (2006) provides a useful classification scheme based on functioning scopes, such as corporate security policy (which is a high-level corporate policy that serves as a legal protection against negligence), acceptance-use policy (which regulates what users can and can't do), among others. Another way of classifying security policies is based on the underlying design theory and focuses on how exceptional situations are handled (Siponen & Iivari, 2006). Recognizing the limitations of existing security policy approaches, Baskerville and Siponen (2002) proposed a meta-policy as a guide to establish how policies should be created, implemented, and enforced. Some of the policy features include: 1) policy requirements, which include identification and classification of security subjects and objects, as well as the elaboration of the process by which the organization will determine who need to access what information; 2) How policies is designed, e.g. the creation of policy and sub-policies hierarchy and when the adjustment of the level of abstraction and enforcement is needed; and 3) How policies are to be implemented, and if necessary how they should be tested in order to determine whether the goals of policies are met. Marchinkowski and Stanton (2003) analyzed IS security policies from a number of organizations to ascertain the motivational assumption. The study found that motivation factors do not receive enough attention in the research or practitioner literatures. It also raised questions of how IS security figures into employee performance evaluations. Some other studies examined the effectiveness (or ineffectiveness) of security policies in terms of deterrence measures (D'Arcy, Hovav, & Galletta, 2009; Kankanhalli, Teo, Tan, & Wei, 2003; Lee, Lee, & Yoo, 2004; Siponen & Vance, 2010; Straub, 1990), code of ethics (Banerjee, Cronan, & Jones, 1998; Harrington, 1996), or policies in a general sense (Chan, Woon, & Kankanhalli, 2005; Pahnila, Siponen, & Mahmood, 2007).

Research on the coordination aspect of KM influences is somewhat limited. Future research may be conducted on the inter-dependencies among various parties, including top management, IT department, and end users. An example of the unanswered questions is how the relationship between IT department and end users impacts organizational IS security management. One study in this direction is the investigation of security practitioners' interactions with other stakeholders in an organization (Werlinger, Hawkey, Botta, & Beznosov, 2009).

Security measurement is one of the key issues in IS security management. Generally speaking, there are two levels of measurement: technical and organizational. Technical measurement focuses on how information systems perform (e.g. detecting intrusions). Organizational level measurement, on the other hand, focuses on the effectiveness of security management activities. This type of measurement is also termed as management measurement (Brotby, 2009) and program measurement (Jaquith, 2007). Many measurement techniques fall into two general categories: checklist and scorecard (Johnson & Goetz, 2007). The checklist approach generally answers yes-or-no questions, e.g. whether users training program has been implemented; the scorecard approach usually provides some numbers in percentage, e.g. viruses detected in email messages. While they may be relatively easy to implement, these approaches suffer some problems. It is hard to prove their validity (Johnson & Goetz, 2007) and they focus on quantity or existence rather than quality of measures (Chapin & Akridge, 2005).

Environmental Influences

In the context of IS security, two environmental influences have been investigated: climate (particularly the legal environment) and technology.

From a legal standpoint, many organizations are required to meet certain laws and regulations related to information security. Two notable laws in the U.S. are Sarbanes-Oxley Act of 2002 (SOX) and Health Insurance Portability and Accountability Act of 1996 (HIPAA). SOX mainly concerns corporate financial records while HIPAA deals with medical record security and privacy issues. Internationally, there are also many laws, regulations, and non-binding guidelines. Notable examples include OECD Guidelines for the Security of Information Systems and Networks, the Council of Europe Convention on Cybercrime, and the Privacy Act of Canada, among others.

Although these laws and regulations may force organizations to invest more in information security and change certain business practices, e.g. disclosing more about security activities (Gordon, Loeb, Lucyshyn, & Sohail, 2006), whether they have any positive impact on security is still an unanswered question. Organizations may take compliance to these regulations as an objective in itself rather than as a means to achieve overall security.

The second environmental influence is technology. New information technologies virtually come into marketplace every day with higher processing and storage capacities. Many of them can pose threats to information security if not properly managed. For example, high-speed and high-capacity USB keys may help employees carry and move data, but on the other hand may cause loss of sensitive data or spread viruses if they are not properly used; peer-to-peer (P2P) file-sharing applications may contribute to inadvertent disclosure of organizational information (Johnson, 2008). Future research may be conducted on how organizations can effectively manage such new technologies without negatively affecting business operations and employee productivity.

Knowledge Resources

The second aspect is knowledge resources for IS security. Based on the KM ontology (Holsapple & Joshi, 2004), there are six categories of knowledge: culture, infrastructure, purpose, strategy, artifacts, and participants' knowledge.

Purpose and Strategy

While it is generally understood that the purpose of security is to achieve confidentiality, availability, and integrity of business information, there have not been many studies on what kind of strategy that organizations should take to accomplish this purpose, although there is no shortage of studies to seek innovative and robust technological solutions such as encryption and access control.

One exception is the discussion by Parker (1997). In terms of the purpose of IS security, Parker argued that the need of confidentiality was decreasing, i.e. fewer kinds of information require confidentiality. On the other hand, the importance of ownership, control, integrity, and authenticity of information was increasing. As such, organizations may need to reconsider the military-origin "draconian confidentiality model" of information classification (unclassified, confidential, secret, and top secret). Further simplification of information classification is much needed. Parker further argued that the strategy to achieve confidentiality may also need to change. Instead of the traditional military-origin "need-to-know" principle, a new discretionary "need-to-withhold" principle should be adopted. The latter principle suggests that an organization is better off giving everyone in the organization its information except for a small amount that must be withheld. Another strategy is to rely on the rapid obsolescence of secret information rather than trying to protect it. For example, by the time competitors obtain some trade secret information, it is already obsolete and useless.

Culture

In the KM ontology, culture refers to norms, beliefs, and basic assumptions shared by the members of an organization. In the IS security literature, the importance of organizational culture has been recognized. Information systems security is not only a technical problem, but more importantly a social and organizational one that involves people (Dhillon & Backhouse, 2000). An organizational subculture and a common belief system are needed to make members of the organization committed to their activities that might have impacts on IS security (Dhillon, 1999). Such culture should also promote responsibility, integrity of people, trustworthiness, and ethicality (Dhillon & Backhouse, 2000).

Dhillon and Torkzadeh (2006) took a step further to investigate IS security issues in terms of the values of people from an organizational perspective. By using the value-focused thinking to identify fundamental objectives of IS security and the means to achieve them, their study suggests that organizationally grounded principles and values are necessary for maintaining security of information systems in organizations. More specifically, Dhillon and Torkzadeh identified 25 clusters of objectives hold by organizational members for IS security. There are nine fundamental objectives and 16 means objectives. An objective is classified as "fundamental" if it is one of the essential reasons for interest in the IS security context, and as "means" if it has some implications for the accomplishment of other objectives. Examples of fundamental objectives include enhancing management development practices, maximizing integrity of business processes, and maximizing organizational integrity; examples of means objectives include increasing trust, providing open communication, and maximizing awareness.

Smith and Hasnas (1999) investigated ethical issues in information systems in general. While raising an important issue of ethics in IS, their study identifies some challenges facing organizations when they deal with ethical dilemmas. One of the challenges is that applying different ethical theories on the same ethical situation may have conflicting conclusions. Thus, it is important for organizations to pay attention to this issue and have a clear communication with employees in terms of what kinds of behavior are considered ethical and acceptable.

Infrastructure

In the KM ontology, infrastructure refers to roles, their relationships, and the regulations that govern them. In the context of IS security, policy is one type of such organizational regulations. Much research has been done on the content and effectiveness of policies (see the discussion in previous section). There is, however, insufficient research on the design of roles and relationships. It is still an unanswered question in terms of what constitutes a good organizational infrastructure for effective IS security management. Some specific questions include but not limited to: 1) what are the roles of top management, IT department, and business people (end users)? 2) who should make decisions on security? and 3) who should be held accountable for security? Ultimately, answers to these questions (and the design of organizational infrastructure in general) will have an impact on the coordination among various parties and the enforcement of security policies (see discussion in previous section).

Artifacts

An artifact in the KM ontology refers to an object is (or holds) a representation of knowledge that may be useful for a knowledge processor in the organization. Examples of such artifact include documents and reports.

In the IS security context, Belsis et al (2005) conducted a field research and identified a number of security-related knowledge artifacts ("sources"). These artifacts can be classified into three levels of abstraction: strategic, tactical, and operations. Strategic artifacts include security policy documents, which deal with the design and dissemination of security policies. At tactical level, artifacts include risk analysis documents, documented countermeasures, audit trail reports, automatic logs, and audit documentation. At the operations level, knowledge artifacts include network alerts and logs.

Two types of artifacts that are widely used in IS security management are checklists and standards. Checklists are based on the assumption that solutions and procedures can be observed and turned into a list, hence "checklist", for solving security problems (Siponen, 2005). Examples of IS security checklists include the risk checklist proposed by Moulton & Moulton (1996) and the control checklist proposed by Wood et al (1987). IS security standards are usually the best practices for managing security in organizations. One example of such standards is ISO/IEC 27002. The standard "establishes guidelines and general principles for initiating, implementing, maintaining, and improving information security management in an organization" (ISO/IEC, 2005). It contains best practices of control objectives and controls in areas of information security management such as security policy, physical and environmental security, and access control, among others.

Participant Knowledge

In the KM ontology, participant knowledge refers the knowledge that is possessed by a knowledge processor who participates in the organization's business activities. Participants can be employees, customers, or suppliers, among others. In the IS security context, however, research seemed to have been focusing on employees who use the organization's information systems to carry out their routine business activities.

From a domain perspective, employees' knowledge can be classified as business knowledge and information technology (IT) knowledge. IS security knowledge can be viewed as a sub-category of IT knowledge. Understandably, as a common sense, IT and IS security people have necessary IT knowledge to manage organizational information systems; and end-users (or business people) have necessary business knowledge to carry business activities and make critical business decisions.

In order to managing IS security effectively, however, IT people should also have necessary business knowledge. Such business knowledge is critical for IT people to understand how IT risks impact the organization's business performance and to manage security in a cost-effective manner. It will also enable IT people to have better communications with end-users and business people. Such knowledge is also defined as "business competence of IT professionals" (Bassellier & Benbasat, 2004), which includes organization-specific knowledge and interpersonal and management knowledge. The former can be further broken down to more specific areas of knowledge: organizational overview, organizational unit, organizational responsibility, and IT-business integration; and the latter can be broken down to areas of knowledge networking, interpersonal communication, and leadership.

IT knowledge of end users is equally important for effective security management. Lack of necessary IT knowledge and skills causes human errors, which are a significant issue for IS security (Im & Baskerville, 2005). Such IT knowledge and skills are also defined as "IT competence" (Bassellier, Reich, & Benbasat, 2001).

Based on its mode, IT competence can be classified as explicit knowledge and tacit knowledge. Based on Bassellier et al's classification, end users' explicit IT knowledge include knowledge in areas of technology, applications, systems development, management of IT, and access to IT knowledge (e.g. knowing who to contact for more information on IT); tacit knowledge includes end users' experience in IT projects and experience in the management of IT.

Based on its primary type, IT knowledge of end users can be classified into descriptive knowledge ("know what"), procedural knowledge ("know how"), and reasoning knowledge ("know why"). It can be argued that this classification scheme loosely reflects the "depth" of knowledge. Descriptive knowledge is the least in-depth while reasoning knowledge is the most in-depth understanding of a subject matter. According to this classification, the explicit IT knowledge (Bassellier et al., 2001) falls into the category of descriptive knowledge, because it focuses on "the understanding of benefits of different IT, not on their specific features".

In the IS security context, some studies focused on the end user awareness of security problems. Such awareness can also be classified as a descriptive knowledge in terms of general understanding of security issues but without in-depth "know-how" and "know-why". Siponen (2000; 2001) investigated IS security awareness from a human behavioral perspective and argued that more efforts should be put on normative and prescriptive awareness.

Learning

Scholars in IS field have long been advocating more research efforts on organizational problems, management issues and human behavior issues (Dhillon & Backhouse, 2000; Dutta & McCrohan, 2002; Hitchings, 1995). Indeed, many security problems can be attributed to these issues. Prior research has found that human error is a significant issue for IS security (Im & Baskerville, 2005). Im and Baskerville classified three levels of human error that pose as threats to IS security: 1) skill-based errors, which attribute to mainly monitoring failures; 2) rule-based errors, which arise if good rules are misapplied or bad rules are applied; and 3) knowledge-based errors, which are caused by the fact that related knowledge is nearly always incomplete and often inaccurate. These types of errors are from a rational viewpoint, which define errors simply as deviation from expected behavior (Neumann, 1995).

Another view regards human error as complex and socially constructed behavior. According to the action theory (Argyris, 1986; Argyris, Putnam, & Smith, 1985), such errors or misunderstandings are created by individuals who unconsciously follow their theories-in-use, a form of "skilled incompetence". Argyris et al (1985) distinguish two kinds of theories of action. Espoused theory is what individuals claim to follow; theories-in-use on the other hand are those that can be inferred from their actions. It is argued that IS security problems happen when end users' espoused theory and their theory-in-use are contradictory (Mattia & Dhillon, 2003). An organization's espoused-theories may be embedded in its goals, mission, and formal documents. Based on this argument, Mattia and Dhillon suggested that the double-loop learning proposed by Argyris et al (1985) can be used as a strategy for designing and implementing security actions.

More specifically, Mattia and Dhillon argued that operational and technical controls, which are used for routine security activities or emergency situations are types of "single-loop learning" in Argyris et al's terms. In other words, such controls focus on the "means" that reach the end result. In a double-loop learning situation, on the other hand, security practices should not only focus on the means but also pay attention to the frame or conceptualization of the problems. In other words, in double-loop security, assumptions underlying management controls should be questioned and changed. A double-loop security design is proposed by Mattia and Dhillon to include learning that leads to new security solutions, which could be either new actions or new problem-solving. The design has four basic steps: 1) discovering espoused and theories in use; 2) bringing the two into congruence and identifying new governing variables; 3) generating new actions; and 4) generalizing consequences into an organizational match.

Knowledge Manipulation Activity

In the KM ontology, knowledge manipulation activity refers to the acquisition, selection, generation, assimilation, and emission of knowledge, which occur in the "conduct of knowledge management" (Holsapple & Joshi, 2004).

In the IS security context, organizational security planning is a type of knowledge manipulation activity. Straub and Welke (1998) proposed a security planning model for management decision-making on security issues. The model includes four phases: 1) recognition of security problems or needs; 2) risk analysis; 3) alternatives generation; and 4) planning decisions. Each phase involves the processing of some knowledge resources. For example, risk analysis may involve an understanding of organizational strategy, end users general level of IT knowledge and skills, and the design documentation of an information system, among others. Such analysis may generate a list of risks and their priorities. Taking this knowledge of risk as an input, the next phase may generate a list of alternatives that might alleviate the risks. This kind of knowledge activities may

Table 2. Summary of Literature Review

KM ontology	Current Security Literature	Future Research
Influences:		
Management & Control	• Top management support; • Policy: design and behavioral issues	• Antecedents of top management support; • Policy enforcement (particularly the compliance of top management and IT professionals)
Environment	• Regulatory (HIPAA, SOX, etc); • Technology	• Organizations' adaptation to new technologies; • Impacts of relevant laws and regulations on security management; • Evolution of laws and regulations
Coordination	• Interaction between security practitioners and other stakeholders	• Coordination among top management, IT department, and end-users;
Measurement	• Checklist-style measures; • Scorecard	• Improvement of security measurement (organizational level)
Resources:		
Purpose & Strategy	• Security principles	• Comparison of different strategies (e.g. need-to-know vs. need-to-withhold)
Culture	• Value-focused assessment; • Ethical dilemmas	• Definition, scope, and measurement of "security culture"; • Antecedents of security culture
Infrastructure	• Security policies	• Roles of IT department and business people (end-users); • Allocation of security costs; • Impact of IT organizational structure on security culture
Artifacts	• Security-related knowledge artifacts; • Checklist; Standards	• Antecedents of the adoption of standards; • The creation and evolution of international security standards
Participants' Knowledge	• Business knowledge vs. IT knowledge; • Security awareness	• Knowledge requirements (business, IT, and security) for different roles (end-user, IT professionals, business managers, IT auditors, etc)
Learning & Projection	• Human errors; • Double-loop vs. single-loop learning	• Security knowledge sharing among organizations
Knowledge manipulation activity	• Security planning model; • Risk evaluation framework	• The impact of IT professionals' behaviors (in using and managing IT) impact security

go on until a decision is made. The output could be a documented IS security strategy, which is also a knowledge resource according to the KM ontology (Holsapple & Joshi, 2004).

A similar approach is the Operationally Critical Threat, Asset, and Vulnerability Evaluation (OCTAVE) Framework (Alberts, Behrens, Pethia, & Wilson, 1999). The OCTAVE framework has three phases: 1) building enterprise-wide security requirement; 2) identifying infrastructure vulnerabilities; and 3) demining security risk management strategy. Similar to that of previous approach, each phase in this OCTAVE framework involves the knowledge manipulation activities. For example, in the first phase of assessment, several types of knowledge need to be analyzed: enterprise knowledge, operational area knowledge, and staff knowledge.

SUMMARY AND DISCUSSION

In this chapter we review the IS security literature based on the knowledge management ontology and other relevant knowledge concepts. A summary of the findings is shown in (Table 2). In this section, we discuss the implications for security practices and research.

Implications for Research

The review indicates that the current security literature covers most components of the KM ontology. There are, however, some gaps in the IS security literature. Some questions remain unanswered and warrant future research (as shown in Table 2).

1. Management influences. Prior research suggests that top management support has a significant impact on IS security. Future research may investigate the antecedents of top management support. For example, other than the often-cited factor of return on investment, do senior managers act on fear, uncertainty, and doubt (FUD)? Another area for future research is security policy enforcement. Some studies focused on policy enforcement on end users. An unanswered question is whether top management and IT professionals comply with those policies that IT professionals themselves try to enforce? If not, what are the reasons and what is the impact of their incompliance on overall IS security management?
2. Environmental influences. Laws and ever-changing technological landscape are among the major external factors that influence organizational IS security management. Two areas may require further research. One is the impact of new technologies. How should organizations deal with new technologies that may have security impact, e.g. P2P file sharing, social networking, mobile storage devices, etc? What are the best strategies, to embrace or to resist? The second area for future research is the impact of laws and regulations. Organizations may put efforts to comply with those laws and regulations, such as the SOX act. But the question is, does compliance really improve security?
3. Coordination. As discussed previously, there is a lack of research on coordination in the IS security literature. Future research may be conducted on the interdependencies among various parties, including top management, IT department, and end users, and the impact of such relationships on organizational IS security management.
4. Measurement. Organizational security measurement is another area that requires more research. Current measurement techniques are mostly checklist-style and scorecards, which focus on quantity or mere existence rather than quality. Better measurement at organizational level can help organizations to make better decisions on IS security-related investment.
5. Strategy. What kinds of strategy can best manage IS security? Parker (1997) contrasted two different strategies: need-to-know approach and need-to-withhold approach. The question is, can the latter approach perform better than the former? What are the conditions, environmental or organizational, should be met in order for this to happen?
6. Culture. Culture is an important factor in IS security management. Prior studies have investigated values and ethics. Future research may be conducted to provide a clear definition of "security culture" as well as its scope and measurement. Subsequently, it would be worthwhile to investigate the antecedents of IS security culture.
7. Infrastructure. In terms of infrastructure, future research may investigate what constitutes a good organizational infrastructure for effective IS security management. Warkentin and Dhillon's study (2008) on organizational structure in the IS security context may serve as a good starting point. As discussed previously, some specific research questions include but not limited to: 1) what are the roles of top management, IT department, and business people (end users)? 2) who make decisions on security? and 3) who are accountable for IS security? This line

of research may also help address the issue of security policy enforcement.

8. Artifacts. One of the key security artifacts is international security standards. Although such standards may be viewed as collective best practices, their impact on organizational IS security is still unknown. Two other areas also warrant further research. One is the antecedents of organizations' adoption of security standards. In addition to the perception of best practices, are there any other factors influencing organizations' decision to implement those standards? The other area is the creation and evolution of such standards. What factors influence the standard-setting process, particularly in the ever-changing technological context?
9. Participant knowledge. Most researchers and practitioners agree that end user awareness is a key factor in IS security management. However, some questions remain unanswered. What level of knowledge should end users have? Furthermore, what level of business knowledge is needed for IT professionals? Although prior research suggested that both types of knowledge are important for the two groups of people, it is still unclear what level of knowledge is optimal.
10. Learning & projection. Future research could be conducted on IS security knowledge projection. One specific area is security knowledge sharing among organizations such as businesses, software vendors, and security solution providers. Possible research questions include how and why organizations share security knowledge such as virus information and software vulnerabilities, what benefits organizations can achieve by sharing such knowledge, and what factors encourage or discourage organizations to share their security knowledge.
11. Knowledge manipulation activity. The activities carried out by IT professionals (and security professionals) during the course of IT management and security management have not drawn much attention in the IS security literature. Future research may be done to investigate the criteria for evaluating the effectiveness of security management activities. While much research has been devoted to the impact of end user behaviors on IS security, it would be worthwhile to investigate how IT professionals' behaviors (in both using and managing IT) impact on information security.

Given the importance of knowledge, we may revisit IS security management from a different angle. One particular issue is security measurement. Security, according to Merriam-Webster Dictionary, means "the quality or state of being secure". By definition, IS security is the "current" state of an organization's information systems. However, most existent security metrics measure neither quality nor state. As discussed previously, some techniques focus on quantity or existence of certain activities (e.g. number of user training sessions); others measure "past" performance (e.g. number of virus detected).

So instead of measuring past performance, we should focus on what will happen now and in the future. After all, security is not about what happened to organizational information systems in the past. It is *now and future* that matters. Knowledge (e.g. IT professional's security knowledge) in this case would be a potential candidate indicator for measuring how well an organization could do to secure its information systems. But knowledge only is probably not sufficient. Knowledge is often seen as static. Effective IS security management also depends on how well the organization as a whole apply its collective knowledge to solve real problems. This capability is referred as *organizational security competence*. More specifically, organizational security competence (OSC) is defined here as *an organization's collective knowledge and the capability to acquire and apply such knowledge to secure its information systems*. It would be reasonable to expect that a more competent organization have better security than a less competent one does.

Based on the knowledge management ontology, OSC may be analyzed from different perspectives. For example, from participants' perspective, it can be decomposed into IT professional competence, top management competence, and end user competence; from knowledge manipulation perspective, it can be decomposed into prevention competence, detection competence, and recovery competence. While these lower level competences and the OSC in general would be a better indicator for measuring (or predicting, strictly speaking) IS security, further extensive research is needed for its nature, development, and measurement.

Implications for Practices

Based on the literature review, we offer some guidelines that practitioners may consider for improving overall IS security management.

1. Culture. From the cultural perspective, IS security practitioners should try to have a better understanding of what values most to other stakeholders, particularly top management and end users. What are their attitudes toward IS security? What does IS security mean to them? With a better understanding of these issues, security practitioners would be able to implement security policies or measures that best meet these stakeholders' needs.
2. Participant knowledge. One of the key issues in IS security management is end user awareness. Practitioners should focus on the quality rather than quantity of user security training. Practitioners may also need to rethink about the methods of providing user training. The traditional classroom training is a push method. It is passive and is isolated from end user business practices. A better approach is to "embed" security training in end users' daily business activities. For example, IT professionals may work inside end user workgroups. Thus IT professionals could act as a role model of security behaviors. They would be able to provide on-site help to users. More importantly, IT professionals would be able to have a better understanding of the security situation in the field. This approach would also improve the coordination and communication between the IT group and end user groups.
3. Security practitioners' knowledge. When speaking about security awareness and training, security practitioners often neglect their own awareness and training about business. It would be necessary for end-user to know more about security, but at the same time, security practitioners should know more about business requirements, i.e. top management and end users' needs.

LIMITATION AND CONCLUSION

One limitation of the review presented in this chapter should be noted. Those studies reviewed in this chapter are very selective. It is by no means comprehensive and exhaustive. Although we looked through major IS journals, some relevant research could have been unintentionally excluded.

Despite the above limitation, this chapter presented a fairly good picture of current research in information systems security literature from a knowledge management perspective. More specifically, it applied the knowledge management ontology to investigate knowledge and knowledge activities associated with IS security. Some gaps in current IS security literature were identified and discussed for future research.

ACKNOWLEDGMENT

I thank Dr. Eshaa M. Alkhalifa (Editor) and three anonymous reviewers for their insightful comments and suggestions. An earlier version of this chapter appeared in the proceedings of the International Conference on Information Resources Management (Conf-IRM 2008).

REFERENCES

Agarwal, R., Krudys, G., & Tanniru, M. (1997). Infusing learning into the information systems organization. *European Journal of Information Systems*, *6*(1), 25–40. doi:10.1057/palgrave.ejis.3000257

Alavi, M., & Leidner, D. E. (2001). Knowledge management and knowledge management systems: Conceptual foundations and research issues. *Management Information Systems Quarterly*, *25*(1), 107–136. doi:10.2307/3250961

Alberts, C. J., Behrens, S. G., Pethia, R. D., & Wilson, W. R. (1999). *Operationally Critical Threat, Asset, and Vulnerability Valuation (OCTAVE) Framework*. Pittsburgh, PA: Carnegie Mellon Software Engineering Institute.

Argyris, C. (1986). Skilled incompetence. *Harvard Business Review*, *64*(5), 74–79.

Argyris, C. (1995). Action science and organizational learning. *Journal of Managerial Psychology*, *10*(6), 20–26. doi:10.1108/02683949510093849

Argyris, C., Putnam, R., & Smith, D. M. (1985). *Action science* (1st ed.). San Francisco: Jossey-Bass.

Banerjee, D., Cronan, T. P., & Jones, T. W. (1998). Modeling IT ethics: A study in situational ethics. *Management Information Systems Quarterly*, *22*(1), 31–60. doi:10.2307/249677

Baskerville, R. L., & Siponen, M. T. (2002). An information security meta-policy for emergent organizations. *Logistics Information Management*, *15*, 337–346. doi:10.1108/09576050210447019

Bassellier, G., & Benbasat, I. (2004). Business Competence of Information Technology Professionals: Conceptual Development and Influence on It-Business Partnerships. *Management Information Systems Quarterly*, *28*(4), 673–694.

Bassellier, G., Reich, B. H., & Benbasat, I. (2001). Information Technology Competence of Business Managers: A Definition and Research Model. *Journal of Management Information Systems*, *17*(4), 159–182.

Belsis, P., Kokolakis, S., & Kiountouzis, E. (2005). Information systems security from a knowledge management perspective. *Information Management & Computer Security*, *13*(3), 189–202. doi:10.1108/09685220510602013

Bertino, E., & Sandhu, R. (2005). Database security - concepts, approaches, and challenges. *IEEE Transactions on Dependable and Secure Computing*, *2*(1), 2–19. doi:10.1109/TDSC.2005.9

Brotby, W. K. (2009). *Information Security Management Metrics: A Definitive Guide to Effective Security Monitoring and Measurement*. Boca Raton, FL: Auerbach Publications. doi:10.1201/9781420052862

Casassa Mont, M., Bramhall, P., & Pato, J. (2003). *On Adaptive Identity Management: The Next Generation of Identity Management Technologies*. Retrieved October 30, 2009, from http://www.hpl.hp.com/techreports/2003/HPL-2003-149.pdf

Chan, M., Woon, I., & Kankanhalli, A. (2005). Perceptions of information security at the workplace: Linking information security climate to compliant behavior. *Journal of Information Privacy and Security*, *1*(3), 18–41.

Chapin, D. A., & Akridge, S. (2005). How can security be measured? *Information Systems Audit and Control, 2*.

D'Arcy, J., Hovav, A., & Galletta, D. (2009). User awareness of security countermeasures and its impact on information systems misuse: A deterrence approach. *Information Systems Research*, *20*(1). doi:10.1287/isre.1070.0160

Dhillon, G. (1999). Managing and controlling computer abuse. *Information Management & Computer Security*, *7*(4), 171–175. doi:10.1108/09685229910292664

Dhillon, G., & Backhouse, J. (2000). Information systems security management in the new millennium. *Communications of the ACM*, *43*(7), 125–128. doi:10.1145/341852.341877

Dhillon, G., & Torkzadeh, G. (2006). Value-focused assessment of information system security in organizations. *Information Systems Journal*, *16*, 293–314. doi:10.1111/j.1365-2575.2006.00219.x

Dutta, A., & McCrohan, K. (2002). Management's role in information security in a cyber economy. *California Management Review*, *45*(1), 67–87.

Fenz, S., & Ekelhart, A. (2009). *Formalizing information security knowledge.* Paper presented at the The 4th International Symposium on Information, Computer, and Communications Security, Sydney, Australia.

Glaser, T., & Pallas, F. (2007). *Information security and knowledge management: Solutions through analogies?* Retrieved October 30, 2009, from http://iv.tu-berlin.de/TechnBerichte/2007/2007-18.pdf

Gordon, L. A., Loeb, M. P., Lucyshyn, W., & Sohail, T. (2006). The impact of the Sarbanes-Oxley Act on the corporate disclosures of information security activities. *Journal of Accounting and Public Policy*, *25*(5), 503–530. doi:10.1016/j.jaccpubpol.2006.07.005

Gruber, T. R. (1995). Toward principles for the design of ontologies used for knowledge sharing. *International Journal of Human-Computer Studies*, *43*(5/6), 907–928. doi:10.1006/ijhc.1995.1081

Harrington, S. J. (1996). The effects of codes of ethics and personal denial of responsibility on computer abuse judgments and intentions. *Management Information Systems Quarterly*, *20*(3), 257–278. doi:10.2307/249656

Head, M., & Yuan, Y. (2001). Privacy protection in electronic commerce - a theoretical framework. *Human Systems Management*, *20*, 149–160.

Hitchings, J. (1995). Deficiencies of the traditional approach to information security and the requirements for a new methodology. *Computers & Security*, *14*, 377–383. doi:10.1016/0167-4048(95)97088-R

Holsapple, C. W. (2003). Knowledge and its attributes . In Holsapple, C. W. (Ed.), *Handbook on Knowledge Management* (*Vol. 1*, pp. 165–188). Berlin: Springer.

Holsapple, C. W., & Joshi, K. D. (2004). A formal knowledge management ontology: Conduct, activities, resources, and influences. *Journal of the American Society for Information Science and Technology*, *55*(7), 593–612. doi:10.1002/asi.20007

Holsapple, C. W., & Whinston, A. B. (1996). *Decision Support Systems: A Knowledge-Based Approach*. Minneapolis, MN: West Pub. Co.

Im, G. P., & Baskerville, R. L. (2005). A longitudinal study of information system threat categories: The enduring problem of human error. *The Data Base for Advances in Information Systems*, *36*(4), 68–79.

ISO/IEC. (2005). *Information Technology - Security Techniques - Code of Practice for Information Security Management (ISO/IEC 27002)*. Geneva, Switzerland: International Organization for Standardization.

Jaquith, A. (2007). *Security Metrics: Replacing Fear, Uncertainty, and Doubt*. Upper Saddle River, NJ: Addison-Wesley.

Johnson, M. E. (2008). Information risk of inadvertent disclosure: An analysis of file-sharing risk in the financial supply chain. *Journal of Management Information Systems, 25*(2), 97–123. doi:10.2753/MIS0742-1222250205

Johnson, M. E., & Goetz, E. (2007). Embedding information security into the organization. *IEEE Security & Privacy, 5*(3), 16–24. doi:10.1109/MSP.2007.59

Kankanhalli, A., Teo, H. H., Tan, B. C. Y., & Wei, K. K. (2003). An integrative study of information systems security effectiveness. *International Journal of Information Management, 23*, 139–154. doi:10.1016/S0268-4012(02)00105-6

Kesh, S., & Ratnasingam, P. (2007). A knowledge architecture for IT security. *Communications of the ACM, 50*(7), 103–108. doi:10.1145/1272516.1272521

Kiely, L., & Benzel, T. V. (2006). Systemic security management. *IEEE Security & Privacy, 4*(6), 74–77. doi:10.1109/MSP.2006.167

Knapp, K. J., Marshall, T. E., Rainer, R. K., & Ford, F. N. (2006). Information security: Management's effect on culture and policy. *Information Management & Computer Security, 14*(1), 24–36. doi:10.1108/09685220610648355

Kotulic, A. G., & Clark, J. G. (2004). Why there aren't more information security research studies. *Information & Management, 41*, 597–607. doi:10.1016/j.im.2003.08.001

Lee, S. M., Lee, S. G., & Yoo, S. (2004). An integrative model of computer abuse based on social control and general deterrence theories. *Information & Management, 41*, 707–718. doi:10.1016/j.im.2003.08.008

Marcinkowski, S., & Stanton, J. M. (2003). *Motivational aspects of information security policies.* Paper presented at the IEEE International Conference on Systems, Man and Cybernetics.

Mattia, A., & Dhillon, G. (2003). Applying double loop learning to interpret implications for information systems security design, *IEEE International Conference on Systems, Man and Cybernetics* (Vol. 3, pp. 2521-2526).

Moulton, R. T., & Moulton, M. E. (1996). Electronic communication risk management: A checklist for business managers. *Computers & Security, 15*(5), 377–386. doi:10.1016/0167-4048(96)82560-0

Neumann, P. G. (1995). *Computer-Related Risks*. New York: ACM Press.

Nonaka, I. (1994). A dynamic theory of organizational knowledge creation. *Organization Science, 5*(1), 14. doi:10.1287/orsc.5.1.14

Pahnila, S., Siponen, M. T., & Mahmood, A. (2007). *Employees' behavior towards IS security policy compliance.* Paper presented at the 40th Annual Hawaii International Conference on System Sciences, Hawaii.

Parker, D. B. (1997). The strategic values of information security in business. *Computers & Security, 16*, 572–582. doi:10.1016/S0167-4048(97)80793-6

Pato, J. (2003). Identity Management: Setting Context. Retrieved October 30, 2009, from http://www.hpl.hp.com/techreports/2003/HPL-2003-72.pdf

Polanyi, M. (1962). *Personal Knowledge: Towards a Post-Critical Philosophy*. New York: Harper Torchbooks.

Siponen, M. T. (2000). A conceptual foundation for organizational information security awareness. *Information Management & Computer Security, 8*(1), 31–41. doi:10.1108/09685220010371394

Siponen, M. T. (2001). Five dimensions of information security awareness. *ACM SIGCAS Computers and Society*, *31*(2), 24–29. doi:10.1145/503345.503348

Siponen, M. T. (2005). An analysis of the traditional IS security approaches: Implications for research and practices. *European Journal of Information Systems*, *14*, 303–315. doi:10.1057/palgrave.ejis.3000537

Siponen, M. T., & Iivari, J. (2006). Six design theories for IS security policies and guidelines. *Journal of the Association for Information Systems*, *7*(7), 445–472.

Siponen, M. T., & Vance, A. (2010). (forthcoming). Neutralization: New insight into the problem of employee information systems security policy violation. *Management Information Systems Quarterly*.

Smith, H. J., & Hasnas, J. (1999). Ethics and information systems: The corporate domain. *Management Information Systems Quarterly*, *23*(1), 109–127. doi:10.2307/249412

Straub, D. W. (1990). Effective IS security: An empirical study. *Information Systems Research*, *1*(3), 255–276. doi:10.1287/isre.1.3.255

Straub, D. W., & Welke, R. J. (1998). Coping with systems risk: Security planning models for management decision-making. *Management Information Systems Quarterly*, *22*(4), 441–469. doi:10.2307/249551

Theoharidou, M., Kokolakis, S., Karyda, M., & Kiountouzis, E. (2005). The insider threat to information systems and the effectiveness of ISO17799. *Computers & Security*, *24*, 472–481. doi:10.1016/j.cose.2005.05.002

TJX. (2007a). *Annual Report of 2006: The TJX Companies, Inc.*

TJX. (2007b, April 28). *Quarterly Report of The TJX Companies, Inc.* SEC Form 10-Q, for the Quarterly Period.

Tsoumas, B., & Gritzalis, D. (2006). *Towards an ontology-based security management.* Paper presented at the The 20th International Conference on Advanced Information Networking and Applications (AINA'06), Vienna.

van der Spek, R., & Spijkervet, A. (1997). Knowledge management: Dealing intelligently with knowledge . In Liebowitz, J., & Wilcox, L. (Eds.), *Knowledge Management and Its Elements*. New York: CRC Press.

Verdon, D. (2006). Security policies and the software developer. *IEEE Security & Privacy*, *4*(4), 42–49. doi:10.1109/MSP.2006.103

Walker, S. T. (1985). *Network security overview.* Paper presented at the IEEE Symposium on Security and Privacy.

Warkentin, M., & Johnston, A. C. (2008). IT governance and organizational design for security management . In Straub, D. W., Goodman, S., & Baskerville, R. L. (Eds.), *Information Security: Policy, Processes, and Practices* (pp. 46–68). Armonk, NY: M.E. Sharpe.

Weippl, E. R., & Klemen, M. (2006). Implementing IT security for small and medium enterprises . In Warkentin, M. E. (Ed.), *Enterprise Information Systems Assurance and Systems Security*. Hershey, PA: Idea Group Publishing.

Werlinger, R., Hawkey, K., Botta, D., & Beznosov, K. (2009). Security practitioners in context: Their activities and interactions with other stakeholders within organizations. *International Journal of Human-Computer Studies*, *67*(7), 584–606. doi:10.1016/j.ijhcs.2009.03.002

Whitman, M. E. (2004). In defense of the realm: Understanding the threats to information security. *International Journal of Information Management*, *24*, 43–57. doi:10.1016/j.ijinfomgt.2003.12.003

Whitman, M. E. (2008). Security policy: From design to maintenance . In Straub, D. W., Goodman, S., & Baskerville, R. L. (Eds.), *Information Security: Policy, Processes, and Practices* (pp. 123–151). Armonk, NY: M.E. Sharpe.

Whitman, M. E., & Mattord, H. J. (2003). *Principles of Information Security*. Boston: Thomson.

Wood, C. C., Banks, W. W., Guarro, S. B., Garcia, A. A., Hampel, V. E., & Sartorio, H. P. (1987). *Computer Security: A Comprehensive Controls Checklist*. New York: John Wiley & Sons.

Section 7
Project Supervision and Issues

Chapter 17
COTS Software Procurement Methodology

Seema Al-Mahmood
Ahlia University, Kingdom of Bahrain

Mansoor Al A'ali
Ahlia University, Kingdom of Bahrain

ABSTRACT

Two of the most important COTS software acquisition processes are the COTS software solution evaluation and selection process and the COTS software solution contract management process. This chapter presents a new methodology to deal with these two phases in detail. The evaluation and selection part consists of 12 steps divided over four phases. The contract management part consists of nine steps divided over four phases. The authors explain each of the two parts of the methodology by describing each of the 21 steps. This research presents a solution to the difficult problems facing the vendors, users, and experts involved in COTS software evaluation, selection, and acquisition and guides them systematically to make the best educated decision. To the authors' knowledge, this work presents the first integrated solution to the software evaluation, selection, and acquisition processes of COTS software. The research is based on real experience obtained from the analysis of three case studies of major COTS software acquisition projects in Bahrain. This chapter is a step forward in the continuous research of COTS software acquisition and procurement processes.

INTRODUCTION

Commercial off-the-shelf (COTS) software has been widely used by organizations to develop information systems (IS) instead of traditional in-house development (Al-A'ali, Al-Mahmood, & Al-Zobaidie, 2006). COTS software is supposed to contribute to the development of IS in a shorter period with lower costs and lower risks and is supposed to take advantage of the best technologies available in the market that enhance the functionalities and capabilities of the system. COTS can be made available in multiple identical copies and used without internal modification by the consumer (Meyers & Oberndorf, 2001).

DOI: 10.4018/978-1-61692-016-6.ch017

The process of COTS software acquisition using a defined formal supplier management process has been a major research issue (Tayntor, 2006). Heckman (1999) studied how organizations manage and organize their relationships with IT suppliers. Heckman (1999) discussed three issues: the degree of formalization of IT supplier-management practices, the extent of discretionary collaborative behavior (DCB) on the part of information technology customers, and the relationship between formalization, DCB, and perceived effectiveness in influencing supplier performance. In addition, Yardley (2002) described the process of COTS procurement and contracting in three stages: precontract, invocation (signature), and during the contract. The precontract stage is the process of inviting IT suppliers or service providers to bid for work through mechanisms such as an invitation to tender (ITT) or a request for proposal (RFP). The contracting process is vital in dealing with external suppliers, and its content is the key to monitoring the suppliers' work (Meyers & Oberndorf, 2001). The software selection process is another critical area covered by Assmann and Punter (2004); they presented a method for assessing software subcontractor process (MASS), which consists of preselect, prepare RFP, prepare response, and evaluate proposals.

Another aspect in COTS software acquisition is the participation of an external party (Rawashdeh & Matalkah, 2006). Yardley (2002) discussed the supplier-customer relationship communication methods between the two parties in the case where the customers are dissatisfied with the suppliers' performance. Lander, Purvis, McCray, and Leigh (2003) explored the mechanisms and strategies for building trust between project team members, users, and outsourcers in outsourced IS development projects. Although these areas are not directly related to this research, they are considered critical in the COTS software acquisition field.

The COTS software life cycle is different from the traditional software life cycle, in which the COTS life cycle introduces new processes that do not exist in the traditional life cycle, but at the same time both share some common processes. The communication phase, the project initiation phase, the requirements gathering phase, the planning phase, and the deployment phase are common in both life cycles. However, the differences are clear in the modeling and construction phases as the developer need not perform analysis, design, and coding activities (Pressman, 2005).

Software requirements are the first order of business and take place before design, cost estimation, planning, or programming. Certain straightforward criteria require satisfaction: completeness, consistency, traceability, and testability (Boehm, 2000; Boehm, Maiden, & Moore, 2004). The most significant problem with the airtight-requirements approach was its attempt to be a one-size-fits-all solution. Although this tactic fails most COTS and rapid change situations, the airtight-requirements approach proves valuable in many situations (Boehm, 2000).

The objectives of this chapter are as follows:

1. Investigate the literature for issues pertaining to the COTS software evaluation and selection process.
2. Investigate the literature for the COTS procurement and contract management process.
3. Present a new integrated methodology to deal with these two major processes in detail.
4. Develop a methodology to present a solution to the difficult problems facing the vendors, users, and experts involved in COTS software evaluation, selection, and acquisition and guide them systematically to make the best educated decision.

BACKGROUND

The critical elements of software development projects and the agreements that underpin them is a major issue (Comela-Dorda, 2002; Murphy,

2004; Pressman, 2005). The starting point for a software development project is the definition of requirements, which is usually triggered by the need for a new business product or the implementation of new or upgraded business support systems, such as inventory management or e-procurement. Once the high-level business requirements have been agreed on, they are expanded into a detailed specification, akin to architectural drawings and materials specifications for building a house.

The importance of the relationship between customers and suppliers of goods and services has long been recognized (Brereton, 2004; Lander et al., 2003). The management of customer/supplier relationships encompasses all the activities associated with the flow of goods and services from suppliers to end users. A number of organizations may be involved in such supply chains, and the relationships established between partner organizations play a vital role in the success of a particular supply chain. The characteristics of software supply chains across a range of development/procurement paradigms depend primarily on the nature of the relationship between software customers and software suppliers, with insights into the changing role of the customer. The procurement paradigms include COTS products, component-based software engineering, and software service engineering.

Companies have not taken advantage of the benefits reaped from having procurement professionals involved in purchasing software (Atkinson, 2003; Thoren, 2004). Benefits include objective supplier evaluation, fair bidding opportunities, negotiation experience, and long-term software provider relationship management.

The purchasing process coordinates all the different players involved in the process to secure, implement, and manage the contract. Purchasing takes on such a leadership position because of its expertise at negotiation and contract management (Avery, 2003). The benefits of purchasing involvement in the software purchase include cost savings resulting from successful negotiation. Purchasing professionals involved in the software purchase have an understanding of terminology and components of the agreement. Software buyers should follow the best practices and know the type of software needed. A standard approach for the contracting process helps to reduce the time it takes to go through the contracting process. To manage the agreement, software buyers may use contract management software or a simple access database.

Contemporary software is increasingly developed using an agile development approach, yet the supplier is generally selected as a result of a waterfall-style competitive tendering and contracting process (Jamieson, Vinsen, & Callender, 2005). The procurement activity may be incompatible with an agile development of functionality and lead to suboptimal outcomes. The interaction of the procurement and software development life cycles and the potential causes of project or system failures must be explored.

Recently, researchers have begun investigating an emerging, technology-enabled innovation that involves the use of intelligent software agents in enterprise supply chains (Nissen, & Sengupta, 2006). Software agents combine and integrate the capabilities of several information technology classes in a novel manner that enables supply chain management and decision making in modes not supported previously by IT and not reported previously in the information systems literature. Indeed, federations and swarms of software agents today are moving the boundaries of computer-aided decision making more generally. Such moving boundaries highlight promising new opportunities for competitive advantage in business, in addition to novel theoretical insights. However, they also call for shifting research thrusts in information systems. The stream of research is taking some first steps to address such issues by examining experimentally the capabilities, limitations, and boundaries of agent technology for computer-based decision support and automation in the procurement domain (Moynihan, Saxena, & Fonseca, 2006).

Procurement represents an area of particular potential for agent-based process innovation, as well as reflecting some of the greatest technological advances in terms of agents emerging from the laboratory (Nissen et al., 2006). Procurement is imbued with considerable ambiguity in its task environment, ambiguity that presents a fundamental limitation to IT-based automation of decision making and knowledge work. By investigating the comparative performance of human and software agents across varying levels of ambiguity in the procurement domain, the experimentation helps to elucidate some new boundaries of computer-based decision making quite broadly. The techniques should be thought of as aids to decision making and not substitutes for it. Numerous decision-making techniques have been proposed as effective methods of ranking software products for selection for use as components in large-scale systems. Many of these techniques have been developed and successfully applied in other arenas and have been either used directly or adapted to be applied to COTS product evaluation and selection.

Component-based software engineering is typically perceived as application development in which existing individual software components are assembled and integrated in order to make up the final product (Gross, Melideo, & Sillitti, 2005). The main recent technological advances in this field therefore mainly focus on the integration step. This encompasses the syntactic and semantic mapping between components, the development of component wrappers and adapters, and the validation of all pairwise component interactions. Additionally, before integration, components have to be located on a component market place, evaluated for their fitness for the purpose, and selected according to nonfunctional requirements. These activities are typically referred to as component procurement. Component brokerage platforms provide support for these early phases of component assembly and are indispensable for strengthening the software component market. Although such platforms are good at the provision of components, these platforms are not as good at their certification. A combination of two contrasting technologies and component brokerage at one end of the component technology spectrum is required. Built-in contract testing may alleviate the efforts involved in component certification.

COTS software have been widely used by many organizations as a means of developing IS with lower risks, lower costs, and a shorter development schedule while increasing functionalities and the capabilities of the system. The management expectation is that COTS system components are easy to implement to work in different environments and to customize to the organization's local requirements. This is not entirely true in all situations. Project managers find that managing this type of software acquisition project is a challenge and carries many risks. Project managers face many problems during the life cycle of the project, and some of these problems may cause the project to fail, to increase the project costs significantly (due to unexpected costs), and to not meet any special requirements.

Investigating the problems that project managers face in managing software acquisition projects represents a substantial issue for study and research. The move to COTS products caused fundamental changes in the way that organizations do business. This change can be described as a paradigm shift. The essence of the paradigm shift is that organizations will change from a producer to a consumer. In a producer case, developers create the components or implement the system. Therefore, the system will be viewed from every aspect because developers have control over all its features and functions. In a consumer case, the organization purchases a COTS product after viewing only the product's interfaces instead of defining unique interface specifications; consumers adopt standard interface specifications. The specifications are selected as a result of market research. Instead of developing implementations, the consumer procures implementations that are based on standard interfaces.

These implementations will be standard-based COTS products. The integration of the product is different and possibly more difficult, because the consumer has less insight into the product. In some cases, a vendor may not want its products to integrate with others. The COTS process as presented by Maurizio et al. (2002) lists the stages of the COTS software acquisition process as follows: requirements analysis, system requirement review, package identification evaluation/selection, glueware and integration requirements, system design review, non-COTS development (glueware and interfaces), integration and testing, target system installation and acceptance test, discrepancy resolution, and sustaining engineering. With regard to IS procurement formalization, Heckman (1999) studied the formalization of IT procurement function, and his findings show that most companies have a formal defined supplier management process and assigned staff full-time to manage supplier relationship. Meyers and Oberndorf (2001) emphasized that training is required in COTS products for the contractor team.

Meyers and Oberndorf (2001) discussed the importance of the contract and defined the basic contract types used in software acquisition projects. A fixed-price contract provides a price that is not subject to any adjustment based on the contractor's cost experience in performing the contract. Another type is the "cost-reimbursement contract," This type promises payment to the contractor of allowable costs incurred during the contract process development that will be included in the contract itself. It establishes an estimate of the total cost for the purposes of obligation of funds and establishes a ceiling that the contractor may not exceed, except at its own risk, without prior approval or subsequent ratification of the contracting offices. The third type is "time and material contract," which promises an hourly rate for labor and a fixed price for materials owed to the contractor for the entire transaction described in the contract.

Another aspect discussed by Meyers and Oberndorf (Meyers, 2001) when acquiring a system is the contracting strategies; the authors defined five basic strategies as follows:

1. Control strategy: The client specifies the system requirements, standards, profile, and standards-based implementations and conducts conformance qualifications. The vendor integrates the system.
2. Direct strategy: The client collects and specifies requirements, standards, and a profile. The vendor conducts the conformance qualifications, selects the standards-based implementations, and integrates the system.
3. Guide strategy: The client specifies requirements and set standards to be used. The vendor creates the standards profiles, conducts the conformance qualifications, selects the standards-based implementations, and integrates the system.
4. Initiate strategy: The client specifies the requirements, and the vendor performs the rest.
5. Joint strategy: Both the client and the vendor share the decision-making responsibility through one or more integrated product teams.

The authors also mentioned the key difference among the five strategies is in how they spread the risks and responsibilities among various participants. Strategy 1 places a heavy burden on the acquirer with respect to both risk and responsibility, whereas strategy 4 shifts a large share of that burden to the contractor, and strategy 5 shares the risk and responsibility more equitably.

Regarding the content of the contract, the four key aspects of contract documentation as defined by Meyers and Oberndorf (Meyers, 2001) are request for proposal (RFP), statements of work, and instructions to vendor and evaluation factors. Yardley (2002) described the supplier management process in three stages: precontract, invocation (signature), and during the contract. The precontract stage is the process of inviting IT suppliers or service providers to bid for work through mechanisms such as an invitation to tender (ITT) or a request for proposal (RFP). One of the key points discussed here that the information sent to suppliers should indicate the schedule for the selection process but should not disclose any details about the selection process itself. In the invocation stage, the basis of the contract must be a signed agreement between both parties, in which the details are clearly defined. In this stage, he focused on the importance that the individual who will negotiate the contract with supplier is not the same individual who will manage the project of which the contract forms a part; this is to avoid the strain that may happen in the relationship between the customer and supplier. The final stage is during the contract, which he pointed that once the contract is signed it should not be referred to unless if there are problems with the supplier. In addition, he mentioned that one of the causes of IS project failure is not having a contract with the supplier, which means that the project is based on an informal understanding of work.

The subject of COTS software selection has been addressed by multiple researchers from different angles in relation to requirements engineering such as Mohamed, Ruhe, and Eberlein (2007), Cortellessa, Crnkovic, Marinelli, and Potena (2007), and Carvallo, Franch, and Quer (2008). Mohamed et al. (2007) discussed the issue of mismatches between COTS products and system requirements. The study proposed a decision support approach called MiHOS (mismatch handling for COTS selection) that aims at resolving the COTS mismatches at two stages in the selection process. First, when the best COTS candidates are evaluated, the MiHOS estimates the expected fitness if the right mismatches are resolved for each candidate. Second, MiHOS is applied after a COTS product is selected in order to help planning the resolution of the right mismatches using the right resolution-actions. MiHOS accounts for important factors such as the impact of a mismatch on COTS fitness, the cost, effort, and risk of resolution actions. A case study was presented to show the benefit of implementing MiHOS. Using this approach would assist in achieving successful COTS software selection but does not consider important evaluation criteria such as the user requirements or type of requirement (nonfunctional) or criteria to be inputted in the proposed method.

Another recent study in the same field was conducted by Cortellessa et al. (2007), who proposed a framework called DEcision support for componEnt-based software (DEER). The framework supports the selection of COTS products in the requirements phase of a component-based development process. The core of the DEER framework is a tool that builds and solves an optimization model that provides the best COTS product selection. The model bases its selection of the best COTS products in balancing between two important factors such as cost minimization and system requirements satisfaction. The framework presents an important support tool that can be useful during the COTS software selection phase but has limited cost minimization selection criteria and does not consider other important criteria that may affect the selection decision.

These researchers have greatly contributed to the COTS software selection subject by developing sophisticated frameworks, but none of the studies referred to or discussed the underlying selection and procurement processes that definitely would add a lot to the proposed selection frameworks.

MAIN FOCUS OF THE CHAPTER

Case Studies of Real COTS Software Products

Case Studies Projects

We selected for our research three major multimillion-dollar COTS software acquisition projects for analysis in terms of the contracting and procurements procedures and issues adopted. The three case studies were selected based on the following factors: the size and type of the projects, the environment in which these projects were running, and access to information resources related to these projects. These factors contributed positively in formulating detailed case studies about the three projects that we believe represent the ideal examples of our study. A summary of these three COTS projects is given below.

Project 1. Human Resources Management Systems

The Human Resources Management Systems HRMS project (P1) was initiated in September 2000 to replace the old HR system with an authorized budget of $1.8m and the expectation of a project completion of 9 months. The project was divided into two phases: Phase 1 (Oracle HRMS Implementation [5 months] to cover the delivery of the core HRMS product, i.e., HR, Payroll, and Training modules) and Phase 2 ([4 months] to cover Employee Self-Service and HR intelligence). This solution was selected due to its superior functionality and best fit for the company HR requirements. Phase 1 of the project was completed 12 months behind schedule. Due to major problems with the vendor, the contract was terminated, and the project was stopped at that stage. The project was restarted 8 months after it was first stopped, and another vendor was selected to complete the project. The new vendor reimplemented Phase 1, upgraded the applications, and completed Phase 2 of the project. The system was launched 6 months after the start date, serving around 1,176 users.

Project 2. Corporate Financial Systems (CFS)

The CFS project (P2) was initiated in September 2000 with a budget of $8.5m and the expectation of a project completion in February 2002 (a time frame of 18 months). A vendor was selected to implement SAP R/3 computer applications that replaced the old systems in areas of finance and logistics. Five SAP modules were implemented. The system was launched in January 2002, and the project was marked as a success with comparison to other major IS projects as it was implemented on time and under budget.

Project 3. Call Centre Automation (CCA)

The CCA project (P3) was initiated in November 2002 with an authorized budget of $2.7m and the expectation of project completion in July 2003 (a time frame of 9 months). Vendor D was selected to implement an integrated interactive voice response system (IVR), a call routing system, and a computer telephony integration (CTI) that replaced the old systems on the company call centers. The system was launched in November 2003 after a delay of 4 months.

The major contribution for this study is the proposal of the listed set of guidelines for the evaluation, selection, and contract management of major COTS software system as shown. When project P1 was started, there was a newly formulated Information Systems (IS) procurement group that was not available when projects P2 and P3 started up. Although a job description was created especially for the procurement job, none of the procurement staff had IS background, and they did not report to IS management but to the finance management.

In the case of P1 and P2, a procurement manager was assigned to handle the contract preparation; he was specialized in preparing IS contracts but did not have an IS background. In the case of P3, a new procurement employee was assigned to participate in the contract preparation. She was new to the job, did not have experience in contract preparation, and did not have an IS background either.

IS Procurement Strategies

The three project managers agreed that no procurement strategy was defined for software acquisition projects, but the most appropriate and applied strategy was the "control strategy."

Contract Issues

In P1 and P2, a very detailed legal contract was prepared and signed with the vendor; it was prepared by the procurement manager, but some contract parts related to hardware and software were developed jointly by IS managers, IS specialists, and procurement manager. This was considered a template to be used for future IS projects. The project P1 contract supported IS project manager to terminate the contract with the first vendor when major problems arose during the project. In the case of P3, no final contract was prepared or signed with the vendor; instead, only a letter of intent (LOI) was signed with the vendor.

P1 and P2 Contracts

The contracts covered technical fit, functional fit, and commercial fit, which met almost all the project expectations; the contracts covered the following areas in detail:

1. Request for proposal (RFP)
2. Statement of work (SOW)
3. Instructions to vendor
4. Terms and conditions
5. Cost schedule
6. Project plan
7. Non-disclosure agreement (NDA)
8. Vendor responses to RFP
9. All correspondence with the vendor, from the RFP until the final agreement. This was important for future reference and to keep track of clarification of some critical issues.

The contract type for P1 and P3 was a fixed price contract, which provided a price that is not subject to any adjustment based on the vendor's cost experience in performing the contract. However, the project manager of P1 emphasized that this type of contract was good because it put a time frame and budget limits for the vendor but at the same time needed a well-defined project scope and requirements. Moreover, additional requirements that were added later during the project incurred more cost on the project. In the P3 case, due to the lack of a finalized contract, the company lost BD 660,000, due to cancellation of one of the requirements. The vendor had to refund the amount of this requirement, which was BD 670,000, but they refunded only BD 10,000.

The P2 contract type was time and material with ceiling contract. The P2 project manager said regarding this issue:

The contract type overcame the problems of fixed price contract, as it was difficult to get an accurate project scope and requirements at the beginning of the project. This type made the project more flexible in accommodating new or changes in business requirements and in time too. It also made us better control the cost of the project.

Contract Negotiation Process

Regarding the contract negotiation process with the vendor, P1 and P2 described the negotiation process as long and consisting of the following steps:

Figure 1. COTS Software Solution Evaluation and Selection Processes

Phase 1: Formation of Evaluation and Selection Team & User Requirements Review	**Phase 2: Market Research & RFI Issuance**	**Phase 3: Evaluation of COTS Software Solutions and Vendors**	**Phase 4: Selection of COTS Software Solution**
1.1. Form Evaluation and Selection (ES) team 1.2. Review and understand users' requirements and business objectives	2.1. Conduct research on available COTS software solutions and vendors 2.2. Issue a request for information (RFI) 2.3. Identify 1st list of qualified COTS software solutions and vendors	3.1. Define COTS software solution and vendor evaluation criteria 3.2. Prepare and send RFP 3.3. Evaluate RFP responses 3.4. Conduct COTS software solutions presentations	4.1. Analyze and review RFP responses and presentations outcomes 4.2. Make COTS software solution selection 4.3. Issue a letter of intent (LOI)

1. Prepared first draft of the contract
2. Discussed each clause of the contract in detail with the selected vendor
3. Updated the contract and continued negotiating until a final contract was prepared and signed

The P3 negotiation process was done late in the project and was very weak because the vendor knew earlier the budget allocated by the company to the project so the vendor insisted on charging high costs. Another factor that affected the negotiation process negatively was the fact that the procurement staff assigned to the job was new and inexperienced.

IS Procurement Staff

The findings support Heckman's (1999) study in that the company had a formal IS procurement strategy. In line with Meyers and Oberndorf (2001), the strategy used in all three projects was the "control" contracting strategy; using this strategy placed a heavy burden on the IS project team in terms of risk and responsibility.

COTS Software Procurement Methodology Overview

The methodology has been divided into two phases: the evaluation and selection phase and contract management phase. Each part presents subprocesses that are related to each other rather than their sequence. The evaluation and selection part consists of four phases and 12 subprocesses; it focuses on market research and analysis, COTS software, and vendor qualification and final selection. The contract management part consists of four phases and consists of nine subprocesses; it focuses on contract strategy formulation, contract formulation, and contract signature and monitoring. Refer to Figures 1 and 2.

Proposed COTS Software Procurement Methodology

This section explains the methodology in detail, stating the outcomes and outputs of each phase that will be used as an input for other phases. The outcome refers to a conclusion reached through each phase process; while the output refers to information documented in any file format.

Figure 2. COTS Software Solution Contract Management Processes

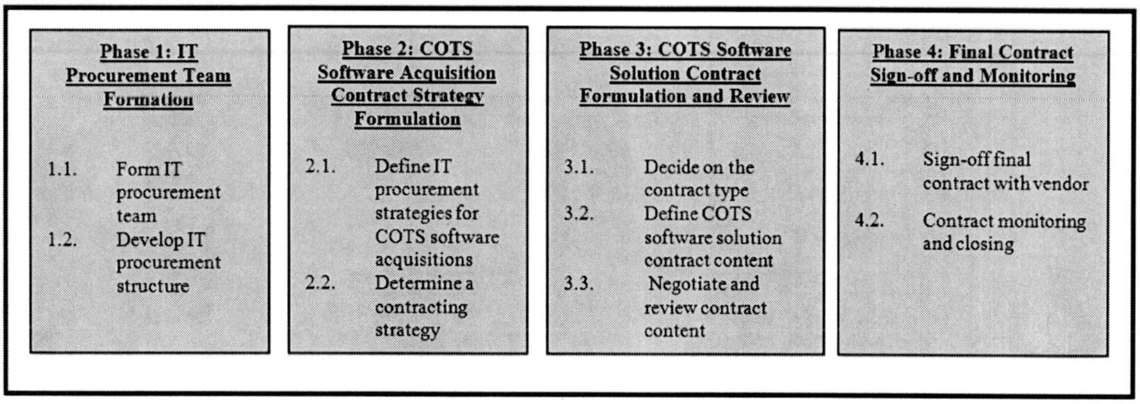

Part 1. Evaluation and Selection Processes

Phase 1. Formation of Evaluation and Selection Team and User Requirements Review

<u>Form evaluation and selection (ES) team</u>

This phase starts with forming an ES team that will perform the sub processes described in the evaluation and selection part of the methodology. The ES team should include the following members: IT procurement staff, COTS software specialist, key business users, and IT technical staff. It is important that members of this team have a background in COTS software solutions and an IT technical background to achieve the best COTS software and vendor selection. The team must be made aware of their individual and collaborative roles throughout the COTS process.

Review and understand users' requirements and business objectives:

The ES team should review and understand users' requirements and business objectives. This is a critical activity because it will provide the members with the basis of their evaluation and selection decisions. The requirements document will clarify which requirements are considered mandatory and which ones are not, and will define any special requirements the users are looking for. The business objectives will provide a broader understanding of business users' direction and

Figure 3. (Phase 1) Evaluation and Selection Team Formulation

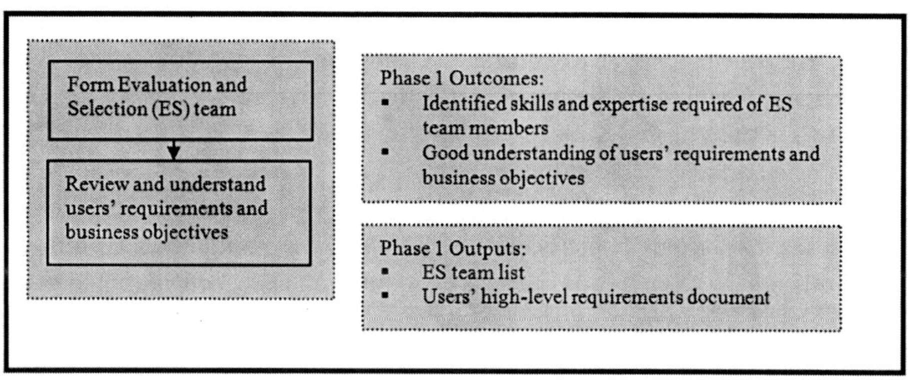

Figure 4. (Phase 2) Market Research

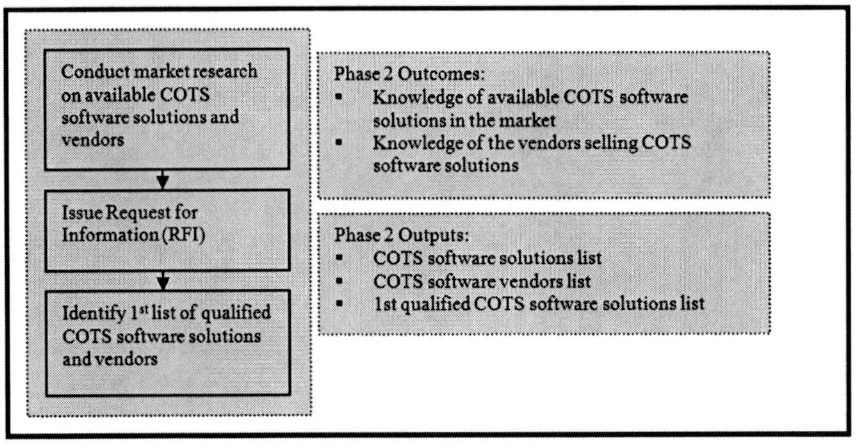

how the COTS software will assist in achieving them. This document can be seen as the foundation upon which COTS software will be measured.

Phase 2. Market Research

Conduct market research on available COTS software solutions and vendors:

Based on the user requirements document, the ES team will conduct market research to identify available COTS software solutions and the best vendors in the market. Unbiased information technology research organizations can be referenced to obtain COTS software solutions and vendors comparison studies. The reference sites of users of these software products could be contacted to identify these products.

Issue request for information (RFI):

Another way to research the market is to issue a request for information (RFI) that includes high-level requirements. The aim of issuing an RFI is to collect information about existing COTS software solutions and vendors in the market.

Identify 1st list of qualified COTS software solutions and vendors:

By analyzing the market research results or the RFI process outcomes, the ES team will produce the first list of qualified COTS software solutions and vendors in the market. At this stage, the team will list the possible best COTS software solutions without going into detail.

Phase 3. Evaluation of COTS Software Solutions and Vendors

Define COTS software and vendor evaluation criteria:

The ES team at this stage is ready to define two groups of evaluation criteria: first, the COTS software solution evaluation criteria that will be mainly based on users requirements. The ES team should utilize users' functional and nonfunctional users' requirements to develop the criteria that will identify which COTS software solution is best to meet the user requirements.

The second evaluation criteria group is developed to evaluate which vendors are considered the best in the market. Criteria may include vendors' profile, vendors' market stability, cost, time frame of implementation, conformance to standards, and support services.

Prepare RFP:

The Request for Proposal (RFP) document includes the evaluation criteria groups developed above, some background information about the company, COTS software solution requirements, technical detail, and financial information. The

Figure 5. (Phase 3) COTS Software Solution and Vendor Evaluation

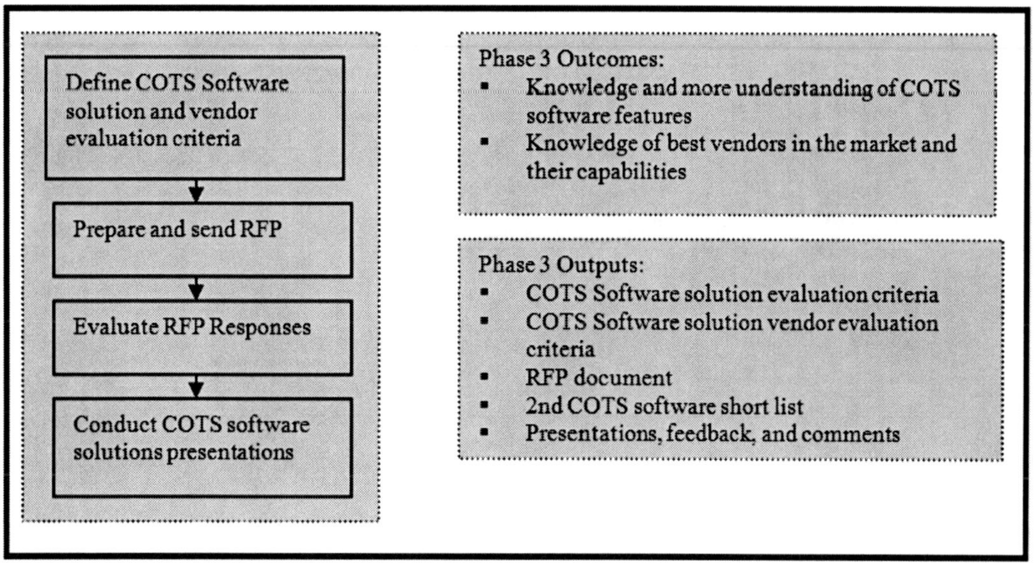

RFP will be sent to vendors listed in the second short list.

Evaluate RFP responses:

The ES team will convert RFP responses into measurable evaluation criteria that will enable the team to evaluate the COTS software solutions and vendors and select the best COTS software solution and vendor.

Conduct COTS software solutions presentations:

The vendors will conduct multiple presentations to ES team to ensure the vendor's understanding of the users' requirements. These sessions will enable both parties (the ES team and the vendor) to clarify unclear issues and answer questions raised by both parties. Different sessions can be conducted for different groups if required. A special session for COTS software solution specialists and IT technical teams, and sessions for IT procurement teams and ES teams too.

Phase 4. Selection of COTS software solution

Analyze and review RFP responses and presentations results:

The ES team can now further analyze the evaluation results and RFP responses in light of the presentations' outcomes and information collected in the market research stage to decide which COTS software solution best meets the users' requirements and which vendor is the most capable and experienced in the field to implement the solution.

Make final selection:

The results are available to the ES team to make a final selection of COTS software solution and best vendor.

Issue and sign the letter of intent (LOI):

The IT procurement team will inform the selected vendor of acceptance through issuing and signing the LOI document. The aim of this document is to formally inform the vendor of the selection results as well as to immediately start working on the COTS software acquisition project until a final contract is signed. Careful attention should be given during this period (the precontract signature period) as the LOI is only a temporary legal agreement between the vendor and customer, and there should be a time limit.

Figure 6. (Phase 4) COTS Software Solutions Selection

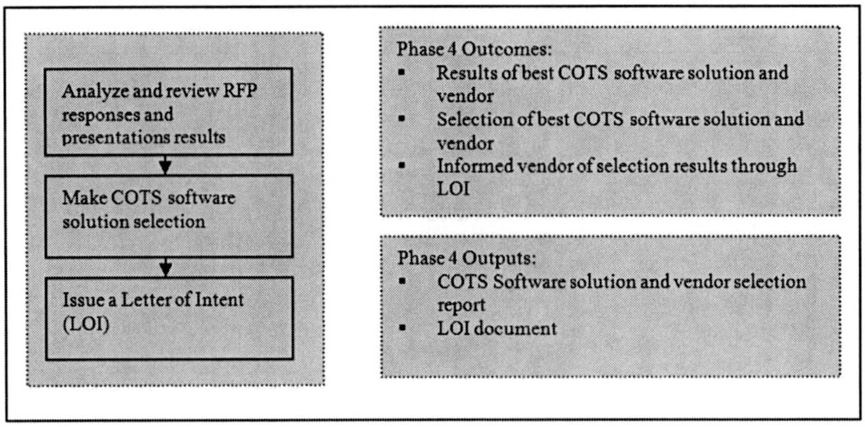

Part 2. Contract Management Processes

Phase 1. IT Procurement Team Formation

Establish the IT procurement team:

The team should be formed to include an IT procurement manager, IT procurement specialists, and a contract manager specialized in developing IT contracts. It is important that the team has an IT background and acceptable knowledge and experience in COTS software solutions.

Develop IT procurement structure:

The team should establish a decision-making hierarchy or procedure whereby IT procurement team should apply a cross-functional reporting method to IT function and procurement function to make decision making a well-studied process and taken without being affected by decisions in other functions.

Phase 2. COTS Software Acquisition Contract Strategy Formulation

Define IT procurement strategies for COTS software acquisitions contracts:

The IT procurement team should develop a special contracting strategy when dealing with COTS software acquisition projects. There are four contracting strategies: control strategy, Direct strategy, guide strategy, initiate strategy, and joint strategy (Meyers & Oberndorf, 2001). The

Figure 7. (Phase 1) IT Procurement Team Formulation

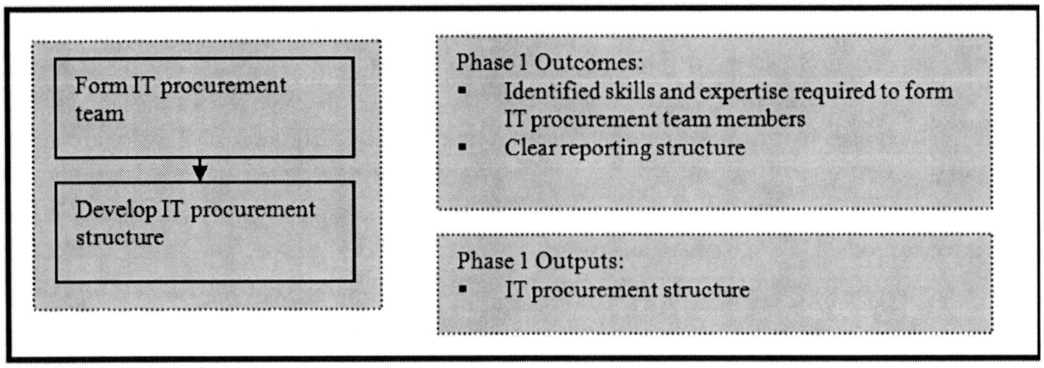

Figure 8. (Phase 2) COTS Software Acquisition Contract Strategy Formulation

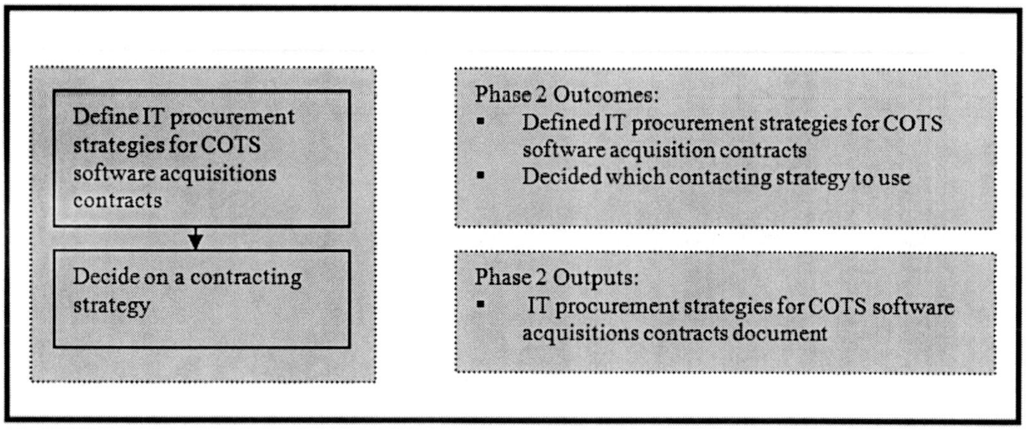

team should work on the details of each type and define the obligations of both parties; vendor and customer. The difference between these strategies is how the responsibilities and risks are distributed between the two parties.

Decide a contracting strategy:

The ES team at this stage needs to decide which contracting strategy to use. This decision is based on the specific COTS software acquisition project and how the project requirements are defined and clear. For example, if the customer requirements are vague due to the nature of the system the team acquiring (a totally new one), guide or initiate strategies may best fit the project conditions. The ES team has to be aware that each strategy defines a control limit for each party, and caution has to be taken by the customer if using the initiate strategy because the customer will have limited control over the project.

Phase 3. COTS Software Solution Contract Formulation and Review

Decide on the contract type:

The IT procurement team and the IT project manager should identify which contract type is suitable to be used with the specific COTS software acquisition project. They should identify the advantages and disadvantages of each contract type and its effect on the project cost and what limitations the contract could impose later on in the project. The contracts types may include fixed price contract, cost reimbursement contract (cost plus fixed fee, cost plus incentive fee), and time and material contract (Meyers & Oberndorf, 2001). Defining new contract types is beyond the scope of this paper.

Define contract content:

Each organization has standard contract content, but for COTS software acquisition projects, the content may differ from the standard ones. The contract may include and not be limited to the following:

1. Statement of work (SOW)
2. Instructions to vendors
3. RFP
4. Vendor response to RFP
5. Evaluation and selection results
6. Terms and conditions
7. Penalties clauses
8. Service level agreements (SLA) if applicable
9. Non-disclosure agreement (NDA)
10. Project cost and plan
11. Vendor team members detail and CVs to ensure resources withdrawal from the project
12. Project detailed requirements including all types of requirements (users functional, non-functional, customization, etc.)

Figure 9. (Phase 3) COTS Software Solution Contract Formulation and Review

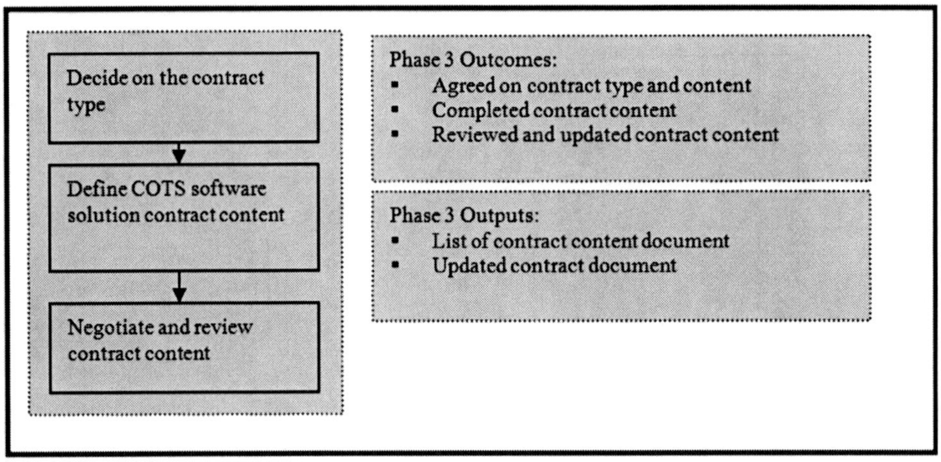

13. Correspondence between vendor and customers

Negotiate and review contract content:

This process is the most time-consuming as the vendor and IT procurement team need to meet to discuss, review, and update the contract content, especially the terms and conditions and penalties clauses, until both parties are satisfied and agreed. Until this process is complete, an LOI may be used as a temporary agreement with the vendor to avoid delays in project startup. Once the contract is finalized, a final copy is formulated and ready for sign-off.

Phase 4. Final Contract Sign-off and Monitoring

Sign final contract with vendor:

Once the contract has been finalized and reviewed by vendor and customer, it must be signed-off, and a copy of the contract is maintained by both parties for future reference.

Contract monitoring and closing:

As the project progresses, the IT project team must update the IT procurement team about the project's progress to ensure that the contract has not been breached by the vendor. Regular monitoring also tells the IT procurement team when to process vendor payments on time. Once the project is completed, the IT procurement team must ensure that there are no pending issues or work related to the project. At that stage, once the project is closed, the contract is closed and saved in the archive for future reference.

Benefits of Applying the Methodology

The proposed methodology will provide the following benefits to any organization welling to apply it because it will:

- Ensure that the right team members with the necessary background and skills are identified from the beginning to conduct the process activities both in the evaluation and selection and contract management processes
- Provide details on what to consider when conducting market research and its benefit to the selection process
- Assist in identifying best-fit COTS software solutions and vendors and how to filter them based on the evaluation and selection criteria before and after conducting COTS software solutions presentations

Figure 10. (Phase 4) Final Contract Sign-off and Monitoring

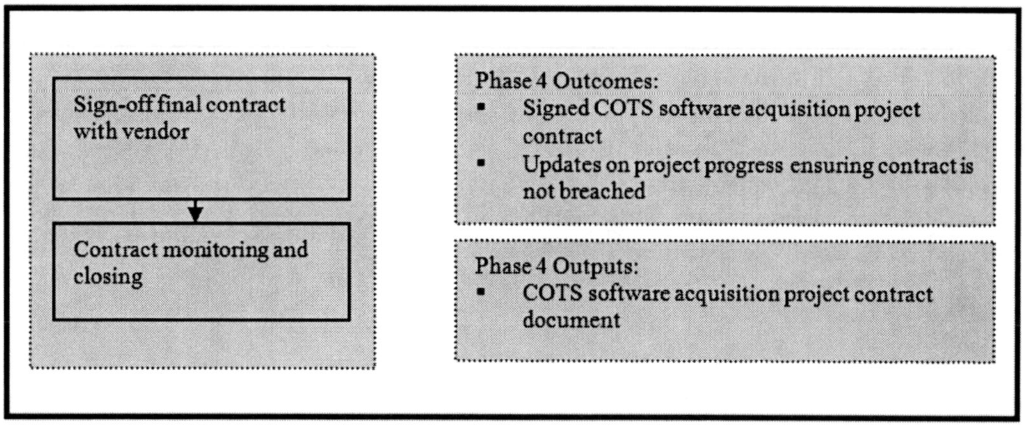

- Provide confidence on the selection decision of the best-fit COTS software solution as the methodology ensures that all important factors are studied, analyzed, and evaluated
- Provide guidelines on how to establish IT procurement team and strategy if some organizations have not yet valued the importance of this role
- Focus on the importance of reviewing and signing-off the contract before the project starts up, and monitoring and referencing the contract while the project is running

FUTURE RESEARCH DIRECTIONS

The methodology presented in this chapter focused on two major issues of COTS software acquisition. These are the evaluation and selection process and the contract and procurement process. The chapter presented a methodology divided into two major parts and divided over eight phases and 21 steps. This methodology needs to be tested on real-life scenarios involving real-life projects such that the COTS software acquisition project team put this methodology to the test over the entire life cycle of the processes listed in the methodology. Research on issues relating to the formation of COTS team, flow of the phases and steps, and the real benefit of the methodology are but a few future research directions. One more future research direction is to quantitatively measure the real benefits of the methodology in terms of avoiding mistakes, making the wrong selection, satisfying users, controlling the vendors, time scales, etc. The whole topic of COTS evaluation, selection, contract, and procurement requires research in order to fine-tune these processes.

CONCLUSION

This chapter presented the first integrated solution to the software evaluation, selection and acquisition processes of COTS software solutions. We presented a new methodology for dealing with the two most important COTS software phases, which are the COTS Software Solution Evaluation and Selection Processes and the COTS Software Solution Contract Management Processes. The methodology is divided into two major parts, a total of eight phases and 21 steps divided over the eight phases. This research presented, based on three case studies, a solution to the difficult problems facing the vendors, users, and experts involved in COTS software evaluation, selection, and acquisition and guides them systematically to make the best educated decision. Finally, the benefits of applying the methodology were also highlighted for any organization willing to implement the methodology in areas such as member skills and background, market research, evaluation and selection criteria, and contract formulation and monitoring.

REFERENCES

Al-A'ali, M., Al-Mahmood, S., & Al-Zobaidie, A. (2006). A study of user requirements for COTS - Computer off the shelf software solutions. *Software Quality Professional*, *9*(1), 32–39.

Al-Mahmood, S. (2004). *Managing software acquisition projects: Challenges and lessons. Unpublished master's project*. University of Bahrain, Kingdom of Bahrain.

Assmann, D., & Punter, T. (2004). Towards partnership in software subcontracting. *Computers in Industry Journal*, *54*(2), 137–150. doi:10.1016/j.compind.2003.09.005

Atkinson, W. (2003). Buying software: Why you need to be involved. *Purchasing Journal, 132*, 22-23. Retrieved December 1, 2006, from http://www.purchasing.com

Avery, S. (2003). Sourcing software? An expert offers how-to tips. *Purchasing Journal, 132*(26), 28-29. Retrieved December 1, 2006, from http://www.purchasing.com

Boehm, B. (2000). Requirements that handle IKIWISI, COTS, and rapid change. *IEEE Computer*, *33*(7), 99–102.

Boehm, B., Maiden, N., & Moore, M. (2004). Do we need requirements in COTS-based software development. In R. Kazman & D. Port (Eds.), *COTS-Based Software Systems: Third International Conference, ICCBSS 2004, Redondo Beach, CA, USA, February 1-4, 2004, Proceedings* (pp. 11-12). New York: Springer-Verlag.

Brereton, P. (2004). The software customer/supplier relationship. *Communications of the ACM*, *47*, 77–81. doi:10.1145/966389.966394

Carvallo, J., Franch, X., & Quer, C. (2008). Requirements engineering for COTS-based software systems. In *Proceedings of the 2008 ACM symposium on Applied Computing* (pp. 638-644). Ceará, Brazil: ACM.

Comela-Dorda, S., Dean, J., Morris, E., & Oberndorf, P. (2002). A process for COTS software product evaluation. In *Proceedings of the First International Conference on COTS-Based Software Systems* (pp. 86-96). New York: Springer-Verlag.

Cortellessa, V., Crnkovic, I., Marinelli, F., & Potena, P. (2007). Driving the selection of COTS components on the basis of system requirements. In *Proceedings of the Twenty-second IEEE/ACM International Conference on Automated Software Engineering* (pp. 413-416). New York: ACM.

Gross, H.-G., Melideo, M., & Sillitti, A. (2005). Self-certification and trust in component procurement. *Science of Computer Programming*, *56*, 141–156. doi:10.1016/j.scico.2004.11.009

Heckman, R. (1999). Organizing and managing supplier relationships in information technology procurement. *International Journal of Information Management*, *19*, 141–155. doi:10.1016/S0268-4012(99)00005-5

Jamieson, D., Vinsen, K., & Callender, G. (2005). Agile procurement to support agile software development. In *3rd IEEE Intl. Conf. Industrial Informatics* (pp. 419-424). Perth: IEEE.

Lander, M., Purvis, R., McCray, G., & Leigh, W. (2003). Trust-building mechanisms utilized in outsourced IS development projects: A case study. *Journal of International Management, 41*, 509–528.

Maurizio, M., Seaman, C. B., Basili, V. R., Parra, A. T., Kraft, S. E., & Condon, S. E. (2002). COTS based software development: Processes and open issues. *Journal of Systems and Software, 61*, 189–199. doi:10.1016/S0164-1212(01)00147-9

Mohamed, A., Ruhe, G., & Eberlein, A. (2007). Decision support for handling mismatches between COTS products and system requirements. In *Proceedings of the Sixth International IEEE Conference on Commercial-off-the-Shelf (COTS)-Based Software Systems* (pp. 63-72). Washington, DC: IEEE Computer Society.

Moynihan, G. P., Saxena, P., & Fonseca, D. J. (2006). Development of a decision support system for procurement operations. *International Journal of Logistical Systems Management, 2*, 1–18. doi:10.1504/IJLSM.2006.008214

Murphy, R. (2004). Creating the contract - software sourcing. *Supply Management Journal, volume number unknown*, 30-31.

Myers, B., & Oberndorf, P. (2001). *Managing software acquisition: Open systems and COTS products*. Reading, MA: Addison Wesley.

Nissen, M. E., & Sengupta, K. (2006). Incorporating software agents into supply chains: Experimental investigation with a procurement task. *Management Information Systems Quarterly, 30*, 145–166.

Pressman, R. (2005). *Software engineering: A practitioner's approach*. Singapore: McGraw-Hill.

Rawashdeh, A., & Matalkah, B. (2006). A new software quality model for evaluating COTS. *Journal of Computer Science, 2*(4), 2006.

Tayntor, B. C. (2006). *Successful packaged software implementation*. Boca Raton, FL: Auerbach.

Thoren, C. (2004). The procurement of usable and accessible software. *Universal Access in the Information Society, 3*, 102–106. doi:10.1007/s10209-003-0077-3

Yardley, D. (2002). *Successful IT project delivery: Learning the lessons of project failure*. London: Addison Wesley.

Chapter 18
Making Decisions in IS/IT Outsourcing: A Dynamic Perspective

Cheng-Chieh Huang
National Taiwan University, Taiwan (R.O.C.)

Ching-Cha Hsieh
National Taiwan University, Taiwan (R.O.C.)

ABSTRACT

Making decisions in an IS/IT outsourcing project is complex and the outcome is unpredictable. Prior research on IS/IT outsourcing decisions simply assumed the decision-making process is rational, comprehensive and independent that is not descriptively accurate, and thus, cannot be prescriptively useful in such a complex environment. In order to gain a deeper understanding of decision-making in IS/IT outsourcing processes, this chapter creates an outsourcing decision framework, derived from a dynamic perspective, to illustrate the decision-making process and how the decisions impact outsourcing results. An in-depth case study methodology is used to interpret an e-strategy transformation outsourced project. The analysis indicates interwoven decisions, knowledge as power, decision-makers' cognition, and ideologies should be the focus of future studies on IS/IT outsourcing.

INTRODUCTION

Beginning in 1990, outsourcing became a key approach to manage IS/IT. The Gartner Group has estimated that the market for outsourced IS/IT services reached $280 billion in 2005, and would expand to $410 billion by 2007. However, there are considerable intractable and unforeseen risks in outsourced IS/IT projects (Taylor, 2006), and making decisions therein is complex and unpredictable.

Much of the research on IS/IT outsourcing decision-making are based on economic theories (i.e., transaction costs, resource dependency, and agency theories) or critical success factors to solve outsourcing motivation, scope, performance, or insourcing/outsourcing "problems" (Lacity & Willocks 1995; Watjatrakul, 2005). These studies have derived largely from economists' view of "rational" decision-making. They assume the

DOI: 10.4018/978-1-61692-016-6.ch018

decision maker is a rational economic man (Simon, 1947) who can plan comprehensively, decide independently, and make the value-maximizing choice.

Most of all, they illustrate a single perspective from outsourcing clients, while excluding the vendors' views. Ironically, more and more research shows that outsourcing activities are influenced by institutional, social-political environment, or organizational structure constraints (Allen et al., 2002; Ang & Cummings, 1997; Loh & Venkatraman, 1992). Moreover, more studies have suggested that the relationships between outsourcing companies and vendors impact outsourcing decisions and results (Kern & Willcocks, 2002; Sabherwal, 1999; Levina & Ross, 2003). Thus, the concepts which portray the IS/IT outsourcing decision-making process as rational, comprehensive, independent are not descriptively accurate, and perhaps not even prescriptively useful in such a complex environment. A more dynamic view of decision-making is required to illustrate real situations (Pettigrew, 1990).

To obtain a deeper understanding of IS/IT outsourcing decision-making, this chapter adopts the dynamic perspective of strategic choice domain, links to IS/IT outsourcing literature, then creates an IS/IT outsourcing decision framework. Through this framework, this study analyzed an e-strategy transformation outsourced project, and determined additional managerial insights and theoretical directions for IS/IT outsourcing.

The remainder of this chapter is organized as follows. Section 2 reviews IS/IT outsourcing decision-making literature, and identifies the gaps. Section 3 explores the dynamic perspective concepts of choice strategic literature, and then creates an IS/IT outsourcing decision framework. Section 4 discusses the research approach and methodology, and presents the case study for analysis with the developed framework. Finally, conclusions and discussions are given in Section 5.

LITERARURE REVIEW

In this section, this chapter reviews three perspectives from the IS literature on outsourcing. It describes their differences on assumptions, their considerations to how decision makers make decisions and how decisions impact outsourcing results (See Table 1). Through this review, we indicate the theoretical gaps to explain current complex IS/IT outsourcing decisions phenomenon.

Prescriptive Perspective

Prescriptive perspective assumes that management can clearly define all issues, analyze all types of outsourcing, and make decisions that result in maximum benefits for the organization. In literature related to IT outsourcing decisions, researchers have a tendency to evaluate special assets and transaction frequencies according to the theory of transaction costs in order to define IT outsourcing strategies and scopes. They define lower cost and higher efficiency issues of outsourcing firms by neoclassical economic and resource dependency theories, they decide the scope of outsourcing by core competition, resource-based, management innovation theories, and strategic intentions; they evaluate the firms' agency costs and risks according to agency costs; and elaborate contract contents according to contract theories to avoid any opportunism of the firm (Aubert et al. 2004; DiRomualdo et al. 1998; Lacity et al.1995; Lacity et al. 1996; Watijatrakul 2005).

These researches assume management outsourcing decisions, when made according to the rules, will result in maximum benefits and successful outsourcing projects; however, different studies have led to contradictory findings. For instance, the research of Aubert et al. (1996) on 10 large-scale firms in different industries found that the uniqueness of assets could define outsourcing decisions; Ang and Straub (1998) studied outsourcing decisions in several banks and showed that

Table 1. IS/IT Outsourcing Decision Literature Review

Perspective	Assumptions	How to make decisions	How decisions impact outsourcing results	Literature
Prescriptive Perspective	1. Decision makers can judge outsourcing decisions, which result in maximum economic benefits by the prescriptive managerial principle. 2. Decision makers make outsourcing decisions rationally and independently.	1. Outsourcing firms (buyers) make the decisions alone. 2. Analysis of single decision.	Based up certain principles, decisions will result in expected successful outsourcing results.	Ang & Straub, 1998; Aubert et al., 2004; Aubert et al., 2006; Di-Romualdo et al., 1998; Lacity & Willocks, 1995; Lacity & Willocks, 1998; Loh & Venkatraman, 1992; Miranda & Kim, 2006; Rao & Chaudhury, 1996; Watjatrakul, 2005
Configurational Perspective	1. Outsourcing is a series of selections, details of which management considers according to different kinds of outsourcing. 2. Each decision is based on managerial principles.	1. Outsourcing firms (buyers) make suitable decisions alone. 2. Analysis of multiple decisions.	Decisions will result in expected and successful outsourcing choices, by selecting suitable decision combinations.	Cullen et al., 2005; Lee, Miranda & Kim, 2004
Structural Perspective	1. Outsourcing decisions are influenced by society, politics, institutions, culture, internal structure of organizations, etc.	1. Outsourcing firms (buyers) make decisions alone. 2. Analysis of single decision.	Outsourcing results will be varied, according to different environmental factors.	Ang & Cummings, 1997; Barthelemy & Geyer, 2005; Khalfan & Alshawaf, 2003; Loh & Venkatraman, 1992

the explanatory power of the theory of transaction costs on outsourcing decisions was insignificant.

In addition, prescriptive perspective tends to be argued whether decision makers are rational regarding maximum benefits for the organization. For example, when analyzing IT outsourcing decisions of 61 companies, Lacity and Willcocks (1995) suggested that many decisions are influenced by political issues instead of economic efficiency, and organizational goals involve individual objectives. In research on financial business factors and large-scale IT outsourcing decisions, Hall and Liedtka (2005), indicated that there is significant correlation between the CEO's stock options, annual returns, and outsourcing decisions. Thus, CEO's and shareholders' individual benefits might affect IT outsourcing decisions.

Third, some literature indicate the institutional police, political benefits, organizational structures, and cultures, both within and outside the organization, would likely influence IT outsourcing decisions (Allen et al., 2002; Ang & Cummings, 1997; Loh & Venkatraman, 1992).

Thus, prescriptive perspective seems to propose an easy answer to the complex outsourcing phenomenon.

Configurational Perspective

Configurational Perspective of IT outsourcing was proposed by Lee, Miranda, and Kim (2004). Lee et al. (2004) indicated that past studies defined successful IT outsourcing only by a single strategy or decision, and thus, were restricted. They suggested that complete considerations, in the scope of decisions, the forms of contracts, and the duration of the contracts should define successful outsourcing. Cullen et al. (2005) further designed the factors and risks of IT outsourcing decision portfolios, including the scope of outsourcing, selection of suppliers, prices, duration of contracts, and forms of contracts, for management to make outsourcing decisions.

Configurational Perspectives could enhance past studies, which only probe into single decision questions (i.e. sourcing decision, outsourc-

Figure 1. The IS/IT decision-making process and result, from three perspectives

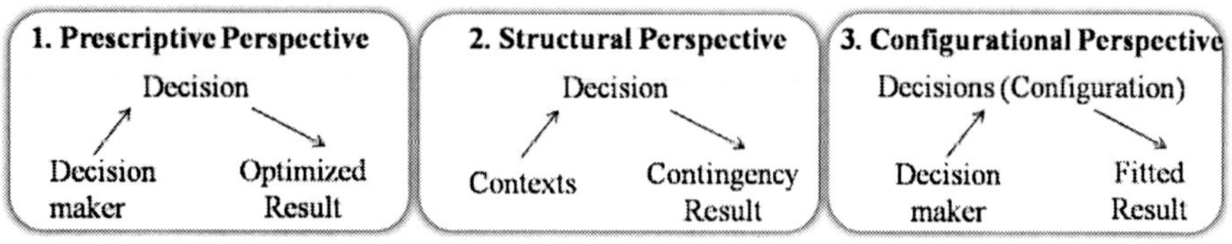

ing scope or contract design), and indicate that decision makers should select suitable portfolios for their decisions environment(Lee et al. 2004). However, this perspective still assumes that decision makers decide rationally and independently, neglect considering the social impacts (Cullen et al., 2005).

Structural Perspective

As to structural perspective, scholars have suggested that outsourcing decisions are influenced by internal and external factors of organizations. Loh and Venkatraman (1992) indicated that the Kodak Effect, upon which Kodak outsourced IT to IBM, would influence outsourcing decisions of other companies; it implied that institutional isomorphism is caused by other companies in the same industry mimic the outsourcing decisions. The research of Barthelemy and Geyer (2005) on IT department outsourcing of firms in France and Germany indicated that IT outsourcing decisions are influenced by different types of national industrial organizations and the environment. Ang and Cummings (1997) studied IT system outsourcing of banks in U.S., and found the influence of colleague pressures and governmental regulations. The literatures mentioned above demonstrate that IT department outsourcing, IT operational outsourcing, and information system outsourcing are influenced by industrial institutional environment. Research on IT outsourcing of national hospitals in Kuwait, Khalfan, and Alshawaf (2003), analyzed the influences of technology, laws, economic environments, culture, religion, contract forms, motivation, and risk on outsourcing by a contingency approach.

Although structural perspective enhances the disadvantages of the above two perspectives, which indicated that decision makers are not influenced by external environments, but it neglects the influence of the decision makers on the decisions, and suggests that organizational structure would arbitrarily determine the decisions (Lee et al., 2004; Miranda & Kim, 2006).

Summary

According to literature and discussion on the three perspectives, the disadvantages of each are summarized as follows. The prescriptive perspective values the optimized principles of singe decision, and neglects complete considerations of multiple decision factors, and external and internal environments impact. The configurational perspective neglects the influence of internal and external environments, and still considers decision makers can decide independently and get contingency result suitable for their selective portfolios. Although structural perspective focuses the effects of internal and external environments on decisions, but less considers the role of the decision makers in the decision-making process. Figure 1 shows three perspectives on outsourcing decision-making process and outsourcing result.

In addition, regarding the limitations of respective views, the three perspectives only value the decisions of outsourcing firms (buyers) and neglect the influence of outsourcing vendors (sellers). In fact, in recent years, studies on outsourcing have demonstrated the importance of vendors for outsourcing, and emphasize the social reciprocity, trust, long-term relationships, and interactions with vendors (Kern & Willcocks 2000; Kern & Willcocks, 2002; Sabherwal, 1999; Willcocks & Choi, 1995). Thus, when studying outsourcing decisions, the influences of outsourcing vendors should be concerned.

Following section, this study constructs an IS/IT outsourcing decision framework derived from dynamic perspective of strategic choice to fulfill the gaps mentioned above.

BUILDING A FRAMEWORK FROM A DYNAMIC PERSPECTIVE

Most strategic choice literature focuses on **rational choice** modes, and they have been the target of sustained criticism for over four decades. Neoclassical economic assumptions lie at the heart of rational choice models, which are predicated on the supposition that individuals normally act as maximizing enterprises, and decisions are thought to be arrived at by a step-by-step process, which is both logical and linear. These models also assume that if individual managers make rational decisions, the decisions made by groups within organizations will be equally rational, and if they behave in accordance with rationality, then little or no interference is required. Simon (1945) was an early author that provided a comprehensive critique of the limitations of rational choice models, by asserting that decision makers' limited cognitive capacities rendered them unable to make rational decisions. Simon's work focused on 'limited rationality', and since, more studies have moved from 'rationality' to more practical and dynamic views. In response, this paper summarizes the three dynamic perspective concepts, taken from strategic choice literature, and then creates a framework to enhance the understanding of decision-making processes in IS/IT outsourcing.

Many researchers have pointed out that decision-making may be seen more accurately as a game of power, in which the decisions are negotiated outcomes (Murray, 1978; Wilson, 1982). Murray (1978) argued that decision makers rarely have the power to make major decisions that are totally independent of others, and that organizations experience a variety of pressures stemming from coalitions of interest groups with different goals. The study showed that the management teams of government-regulated electric utility companies, though intending to be rational, were subject to resistance and revision through a protracted process of negotiation and bargaining with numerous external parties. Wilson (1982) described a chemical organization's generation of electricity, in which the focus shifts from economic criteria to the decisions makers' career aspirations. The author defined decision making as resulting from power exertion that serves localized interests, often at the expense of other conflicting interests. These studies indicate that decisions are negotiated by internal or external interest groups.

Few studies of IS/IT outsourcing decisions discuss the negotiated outcome of decisions; however, some have implied possibilities. Lacity and Willcocks (1995) analyzed 61 sourcing decisions and found that the participants, in part, based decisions on personal political agendas rather than on economic efficiency, but they did not describe how the political concerns influenced the outcomes. More recent literatures have focused on social reciprocity, trust, long-term relationships, and interactions between outsourcing clients and vendors (Kern & Willcocks, 2002; Sabherwal, 1999; Willcocks & Choi, 1995), but neglected the impact of conflicting interests. According to the mentioned literatures on strategic choice, and their implications, it is suggested that negotiated outcomes are relevant themes for interpreting IS/IT outsourcing decision-making.

Some literatures argue that decision-making is context-dependent, and decision makers operate in shared organizational contexts of deeply rooted cultures, ideologies, convictions, or social-political environments, which influence their decisions (Langley et al., 1995; Pettigrew, 1990). Mintzberg et al. (1976) noted that environmental events strongly influence the pace or direction of decisions. For example, a decision on a retirement policy is influenced by a recession, and the acceptance of a new form of medical treatment is influenced by an accusation of malpractice. Miller et al. (1996) further pointed out that decision-making models are influenced by societal culture or ideologies. For example, decision making in Asia tends to be centralized because of higher regard for status-based authority or family position. In summary, the contextual dependence perspective places the decision-making process in a context that includes internal contexts, as well as external contexts of the organization (Pettigrew, 1990).

Past literature on IS/IT outsourcing also show that institutional environments (i.e., 'Kodak Effect', sector IT intensity), social-political environments, peers, federal regulators, or internal structures influence outsourcing adaptations or successful implementation (Ang & Cummings, 1997; Barthelemy & Geyer, 2005; Loh & Venkatraman, 1992). Linking the strategic choice and the IS/IT outsourcing literature, it can be concluded that making a decision in IS/IT outsourcing is dependent on its specific internal and external contexts.

Langley et al. (1995) argued that decisions in real organizations are not seen in isolation, but interlinked with other decisions into "issue streams" that dynamically evolve over time, meaning that previous decisions may become the 'rules of game' that impact subsequent decisions, and these decisions are all intertwined. Butler (1990, p. 14) described a similar idea, "Decisions are made within a context and help to influence the context for future decisions. The output from decision 1 forms part of the input for decision 2". This concept is referred to as "interwoven decisions" that describe how different decisions are interlinked and impact each other.

The "interwoven decisions" concept considers multiple outsourcing decisions is similar to configurational perspective, but more situated and dynamic. It argues that some decisions are impact by previous decisions having made rather than decision makers accurately planning prior to making any decisions and getting fitted outsourcing results of configurational perspective claims.

Based on the above, this study creates an IS/IT outsourcing decision framework, derived from a dynamic perspective (Figure 1 & key concepts in Table 1). This framework describes that the outsourcing decision-making is impacted by inner and outer contexts, and are negotiated by internal and external interest groups. In addition, the decisions are intertwined and the outsourcing result is impacted by multiple decisions made in an outsourcing process. This framework can be used to interpret and understand the complex and dynamic decision-making in an IS/IT outsourcing process.

RESEARCH METHODOLOGY

To understand complex decision-making in IS/IT outsourcing, the authors adopt the in-depth case study methodology. The case study is an exploration of a "bounded system" or a case over time through detailed, in-depth data collection involving multiple sources of information rich in context. The bounded system is bounded by time and place, which in this study, we analyze decisions of an information system outsourcing project. The objective of a single in-depth case study is not to generalize, but rather to gain deeper understandings of specific phenomenon (Yin, 2003). This methodology is expected to result in insights into IS/IT outsourcing decision-making.

The case methodology adopts the purposeful sampling strategies, which selecting cases that show different perspectives on the problem,

Figure 2. The IS/IT outsourcing decision framework

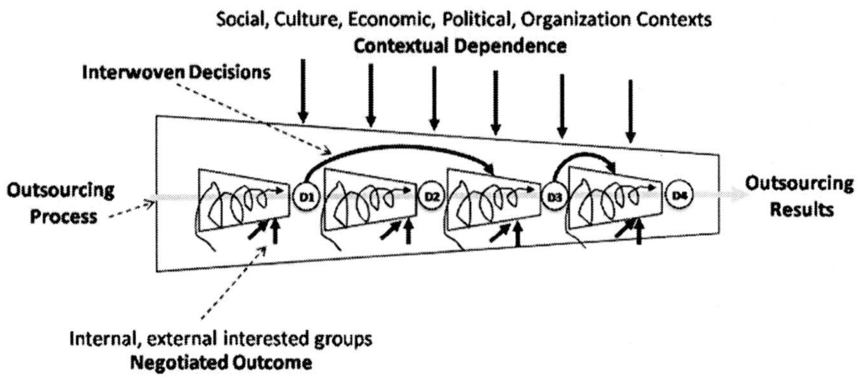

process, or event that researchers want to portray (Creswell, 2005).

This study selected a company that had struggled to close a government-subsidized outsourced project for case study for two reasons: 1) it was subsidized by the government, which meant it was exposed to influences from policies, interest groups, participants, and other social-political factors; 2) it was a strategic transformation project, which involved every department's future business model, and had aroused their concerns.

To collect the data, semi-structured questions were addressed to participants, including project managers, programmers, and vendors' representatives, who asked questions that allowed them to provide their interpretations of their decisions, decision considerations, and interactions with other participants. Moreover, this study gathered requests for proposals (RFP), the proposal, function specifications, meeting minutes, taped records, and emails as the triangulation data (Yin, 2003). These data can be a holistic and contextual analysis of the entire case (Creswell, 2005; Klein & Myers, 1999).

There are many methods or approaches to analyze the case data. In this study, we choose the interpretive analysis method and process-oriented approach. The interpretive analysis method allowed this chapter to interpret decision makers' meanings, intentions, interactions, and decisions within a specific context (Klein & Myers, 1999). By adopting the process-oriented approach, this study examined how one decision could lead to changes in context, which could affect decisions in subsequent periods (Langley, 1999). Thus the following steps are conducted:

- Construction of a framework, based on a dynamic perspective, with key concepts forming the theme, obtained from strategic choice literature (Figure 2 and Table 2).
- Analysis of interview transcripts and identification of decision episodes (Table 3).
- Triangulation of sources.
- Interpretation and mapping of themes and decision episodes.
- Discussions, challenges, clarifications, and modifications of categories (Table 2) until the two authors achieved consensus.

Following Langley's "Temporal Bracketing Strategy" of process-oriented analysis approach (Langley, 1999), this study categorized seven decisions into different outsourcing phases, as mentioned by Mahnke, Overby & Vang (2005) (Table 3), and illustrated the decision categories, defined the decision makers' interpretations, interactions, and contexts. Then, it applied the three concepts of the framework as themes to analyze the outsourcing decision-making phenomenon.

Table 2. Three concepts in the IS/IT outsourcing decisions framework

Concepts	Key Points	Literature
Negotiated Outcome	1. Decision makers do not make decisions independently, or achieve value-maximizing objectives. 2. Decisions are negotiated via internal or external interest groups.	Miller et al., 1996 Murray, 1978 Wilson, 1982
Contextual Dependence	1. 1. Decision makers are influenced by environmental factors or organizational structures. 2. 2. Decisions are situated in specific internal or external contexts.	Langley et al., 1995 Mintzberg et al., 1976 Miller et al., 1996 Pettigrew, 1990
Interwoven Decisions	1. Decisions are not isolated, but are interlinked with earlier decisions. 2. Previous decisions may become the 'rules of game' that impact subsequent decisions.	Butler, 1990 Langley et al., 1995 Pettigrew, 1990

CASE STUDY

Case Background

Company A has been positioned as an integrated platform to promote creative design. Its main mission is to upgrade original creativity of Taiwanese designers, promote international design exchanges, help enterprises build up their own brand, raise value-added of the industries. The company earns the profits through the industry design consulting projects, creative design product promotion or journal publication. For company A, if their business could be operated on the internet, an e-platform, it will create more opportunities to contact more designers and exchange more information and ideas.

Company A then get a Taiwan government-supported project, which subsidized Company A to implement an e-commerce platform. Company A further outsourced the development work to Vendor B as the main contract vendor, as well as to four other subcontractors. Company A also hired an information systems consulting company, Company C, as a quality assurance unit to ensure the project's success.

There were two subsystems in the project; Company A assigned three project managers from its IT department, two were in charge of the two subsystems, which were run separately, and the other was named an integration project manager to coordinate the two subsystems' development. The two subsystems addressed different functions: one was knowledge management, which duties included subscriptions to publication databases within the industry, search and gather activities, job matches, online forums, advertising, etc; the other provided project management for outsourced

Table 3. Seven case decisions and outsourcing phases

Outsourcing phases (Mahnke et al., 2005)	Critical decisions derived from the case
Outsourcing decision	Decision 1: decision to outsource Decision 2: deciding the scope of the project
Vendor selection	Decision 3: deciding the main contractor Decision 4: deciding on a quality assurance company
Contract design & Relationship management	Decision 5: deciding the requirements Decision 6: deciding the project's acceptance criteria
Performance evaluation	Decision 7: decision to close the project

clients and upstream companies, which duties included registration of the project, discussions on the project, co-development of designs, communications, sharing project documents, processes, progress control, etc.

After ten months of implementation, from November 2005 to August 2006, the project was closed, on schedule and with high quality documentation, thus, this project was viewed as a good pattern example of government-supported projects. However, for Company A, it proved a failure, as the e-commerce platform remained inoperable six months after closing the project.

The following section illustrates the seven decisions made during the outsourcing processes, followed by a dynamic view analysis of the seven decisions.

Making Decisions in the Outsourcing Process

Decision 1. Decision to Outsource

"The decision to make or buy" is the first decision episode in the outsourcing process. In the case study, the decision to initialize the project was based on the context of historical, social relations. Company A was a government unit, which had been detached four years prior to this project, however, most of its business depended on government projects. Due to budget limitations of the government, Company A wanted to earn profits from other sources, and one member of the board of directors for Company A was a government officer; who suggested that a transformation to an e-commerce business model would be an innovative method to gain profits, and promote design industry development. He asked Company C to prepare a proposal, and then convinced the government to subsidize the project.

For helping Company A to prepare the proposal and acquire the subsidy, Company C played a significant role in this project. For the officials of the government department, they felt they had accomplished their goal, which was to facilitate an industry through subsidy, which could stimulate company in the specific industry to use e-commerce platform to improve their business operation.

The project manager for contractor B, the major bidder in this project, suggested that,

The project benefits both Company C and the government! Company C can play a certain role in future system implementation, and the government department officer could display his performance because of this project.

The outsourcing project was thus subsidized by the government, as presented from the cooperation between Company A and Company C.

Decision 2. Defining the Scope of the Project

After deciding to outsource, the next important decision is to define the scope of the project. In general, outsourcing projects use a Request For Proposal (RFP) form to define the scope of an outsourced project. Past research suggests that a detailed RFP and a timely contract can reduce coordination costs and prevent vendor opportunism from occurring (Beulen & Ribbers, 2003; Byson & Sullivan, 2003), however, the studies neglected the impact of political conflicts within companies, and other pressures, such as company stakeholders, when determining the RFP scope.

In this case, more than one year was spent on discussions of the project scope, however, a company-wide consensus was not achieved because the e-commerce business model impacted the company's existing operational model and their profit distribution. Moreover, they debated over whether the e-platform operational model would be a commercial or a non-profit pursuit. A project manager from Company A described the controversy:

The operational model of this project involves a dilemma: profits for company and the promotion of public welfare. The government intends to avoid commercial purposes as the project is subsidized by their authority! However, our company wants to make profits from this platform, otherwise, it will not be worth it!

However, all allocated government budget monies must be executed within a specified time frame. Finally, Company A chose the government version, as proposed by Company C for the RFP scope, as there was no time to create a version based on their consensus, and still meet the budget's execution deadline. Nevertheless, the version was rough, and significantly different from the actual business proposal of Company A. One of the project managers in Company A suggested,

Company C only provided a version of a system framework, instead of firm suggestions for operation. With only descriptions of system functions, and no operational framework for reference, it was difficult to develop and practice overall processes to construct the system!

Decision 3. Deciding on the Main Contractors

After deciding the RFP content, the outsourcing company opened bids for candidate vendors. Vendors' proposals detailed how they would manage technological details, human resources, budget disbursements, schedules, etc. Finally, Company A decided on Vendor B as its main outsourcing vendor based on their integration capabilities and detailed functions illustrations, as presented in their proposal. The project manager of Company A described their decisions,

The reason for choosing Contractor B as the outsourcing company was that many functions in the proposal were new to me, and besides, Contractor B already had the model, and the system could be developed immediately.

However, economic efficiency was not achieved, given the pressures of government projects and a policy requiring three or more vendors for open bids, the bidding vendors exaggerated their abilities by amplifying the functions and scope promised in their proposals of their e-commerce business model. Winning was the first priority, and their proposals were far beyond both the RFP scope and their capabilities to deliver. The director of Vendor B, the author or their proposal, said:

In the bidding of projects subsidized by the government, it is normal to promote the system, techniques, and functions of the companies. "Winning the bid" is the priority of bidding. Since the amount and time of the projects subsidized are fixed, after winning the bid, the bidders can negotiate with outsourcing firms regarding the scope and details of the project.

Decision 4. Deciding on a Quality Assurance Company

In this case, a quality assurance company was another important partner to be selected. From a financial perspective, a quality assurance company can help an outsourcing company to manage the outsourced project. Moreover, government project policy recommends engaging such a company to ensure a project's success. However, the decision to engage Company C involved more than the above two factors, as the integration project manager of outsourcing Company A noted:

Why did we select Company C as a quality assurance unit? Because I hope Company C could share our responsibility to the government. That

is, if the project failed, our responsibility would be diminished.

In addition, one of the Company A's project managers indicated that some decisions regarding specific subcontract vendors resulted from pressures and canvassing of special interest groups.

Decision 5. Deciding the Requirements

There are many decisions during the implementation phase. This section will describe two decisions that significantly influenced this project.

First, the RFP decision impacted the original system requirements, and government policy states that the contents of the government's version of the RFP must be the acceptance criteria to close project bidding. Since the government's e-commerce profit model platform was inconsistent with Company A's non-profit culture, it was difficult for the intended users to visualize system requirements. In addition, Company A's project management was not authorized to select users, for system discussions, from appropriate departments, as they deliberately assign persons unfamiliar with system requirements in order to force senior department management and members to focus on their own regular operations, rather than innovative projects. Finally, the resulted user requirements that emerged differed greatly from the original RFP version.

Operating under such conditions, Company A and Vendor B project management settled on a solution, to create two different versions: the "RFP requirements" and the "real requirements". Vendor B developed the system according to the original "RFP requirements" that met the government's acceptance criteria for closing the project. After closing, in the maintenance phase, Vendor B was to modify the system to fulfill the "real requirements". However, the gaps in the maintenance phase were huge, and they were unable to modify the system to meet the "real requirements".

Decision 6. Deciding a Project's Acceptance Criteria

The second important decision in the implementation phase is deciding the rigorous standards of quality systems documents as acceptance criteria. Although good quality documents assist in the management of a project, this does not provide a sufficient explanation for why Company A, the outsourcing company, was so insistent on quality documents that it eventually impacted the entire project schedule. The situation context explains this decision.

Company C, as the quality assurance unit, needed to prove their contribution to the project. However, due to the difficulty of evaluating the quality of the information system, Company A project managers and Company C consultants decided that quality system documents would provide proof of Company C's performance measurement. Thus, Company C assigned Vendor B rigorous document standards, which seriously impacted Vendor B's development schedule. The integration project manager of Company A described the situation:

Originally, I intended to control project quality through the documents, but now it has severely impacted the project schedule. Even when I became aware of this situation, I could not request Company C's consultants to lower their quality evaluation standards, I had to respect their professional judgment.

Decision 7. Decision to Close the Project

Although the development work was not yet complete, the project deadline loomed. To finish the project on time, Company A project management decided to approve the acceptance test results, and closed the project before the project deadline, even though the system was not operating smoothly. The integration manager said:

Although the users test group attended the final acceptance test meeting, Vendor B's programming leader did not prove the system's functionality by demonstrating the users' daily operational processes. This confused the users, but based on my intuition, I knew that the process was not very smooth, and some systems issues still existed. However, my first priority was to close the project on time; so we approved the test results, and closed it.

ANALYSIS AND FINDINGS

Negotiated Outcome

Murray (1978) argued that decision makers rarely have the power to make major decisions totally independent of others; and that decisions are negotiated from the participants' own "local rationalities". In this case, at least three decisions (decisions 2, 5, and 6) are shown to have emerged from negotiations. The decisions of project scope, or RFP (decision 2), and requirements (decision 5) were derived from conflicting interests among different departments. Although the project managers wished to achieve a consensus on a rational objective, in the end, they could not, and thus, adopted the government's rough version of the RFP to resolve the conflicts, however, this made the project very difficult to implement. The final decision for the requirements was the "two versions of requirements", which also had severe impact on the project schedule.

Coalitions of various interests existed within both the organization and among the partners of the outsourcing processes, and in spite of a trusting, long-term relationship between the outsourcing company and vendors, the participants continued to seek self interests. With regard to rigor for quality documents (decision 6), for example; the integration project manager from Company A hoped to control project risks, whereas, the consultants of Company C pursued their need to demonstrate their contribution. The two parties agreed to approve the acceptance criteria without conflict, which ultimately influenced the whole project schedule. The decisions regarding IS/IT outsourcing were seldom value-maximizing for the outscoring company, as a rational choice would assume, but rather catered to various coalitions of participants' interests.

Contextual Dependence

The contextual dependence view argues that decisions are impacted by socio-political and organizational contexts. Table 4 shows that six of the seven decisions were influenced by context, including external context and internal contexts.

The decision to initialize the project (Decision 1) was triggered by government budget cuts, which impacted Company A's profits. Then, because of social relations with the government, Company A was awarded a government-supported project that provided an opportunity to transform Company A to an e-commerce business model, which served an industry that the government wanted to support. Herein, historical, economic, and social relations contexts influenced Decision 1.

Meanwhile, the regulations for government-supported projects, formed the institutionalized environment that originally constrained the decisions. In this case, the decisions on project scope (Decision 2), requirements (Decision 5), and closing (Decision 7) were deeply circumscribed by institutional regulations (project start time, deadline, and unalterable RFP as acceptance criteria). These institutional regulations were originally designed to prevent opportunism and ensure project success, however, in the end, they became institutionalized ceremonies that

Table 4. Illustrations of the case using a dynamic perspective framework

Themes	Analyzed Decisions	Findings
Negotiated Outcome	D2: negotiated between different departments within an organization D5: negotiated with different departments of Company B D6: negotiated with Company C	1. The IS/IT outsourcing decisions are negotiated with the participants. 2. Every participant seeks local rationalities, and sometimes negotiated outcomes are unexpected. 3. The negotiated decisions are also context dependent.
Contextual Dependence	D1: historical context, economic context, social relations context D2: institutional regulation (project start time) D3: institutionalization myth D4: 'share responsibility' ideology D5: culture, authorization, institutional regulation (RFP as acceptance criteria) D7: institutional regulation (project deadline)	1. The IS/IT outsourcing decisions are influenced by internal and external contexts. 2. The contexts could enable or constraint the decisions. 3. The contexts could become institutionalization myths or ceremonies. 4. The decision makers conform and decouple decisions to respond to ceremonial rules.
Interwoven Decisions	1. Rules of game: D2 → D5; D4→D6 2. Compete for same resources: D5 and D6	1. These decisions are intertwined; they limit subsequent decisions, and compete for the same resources.

* D stands for Decisions

led to inefficiency. Moreover, decision makers employed conformity or decoupling strategies to response the institutional pressures. For example, the decision makers in this case came up with "real requirements" and "RFP requirements" to decouple the "RFP as unchanged acceptance criteria" ceremonial rule (Decision 5). On Decision 7, project management conformed to the rule regarding the project deadline, and neglected or ignored the system's inability to operate smoothly.

Additionally, the contexts within the organizations also circumscribe outsourcing decisions. This case shows how authorization structure (Decision 5) or the "shared responsibility" ideology (Decision 4) impacted decision-making for outsourcing.

Interwoven Decisions

Pettigrew (1990) suggested that past decisions will become antecedent conditions that shape present and emerging decisions. Butler (1990) also mentioned that decisions made within a context influence the context of future decisions. The case data of this project show how the antecedent decisions became the 'rules of the game' for subsequent decisions (Table 4).

For example, decisions makers of Company A decided on the government's rough proposal as the final RFP (Decision 2). The rough RFP could not fulfill users' requirements, because an unchangeable institutional rule limited their decisions of requirements. Finally, they decided that two versions of requirements were necessary to manage the situation (Decision 5). Moreover, the decision to engage a quality assurance company (Decision 4) generated a situation, where Company C had to show its contributions to the project, which was jointly determined by the integration project manager and Company C consultants to be high quality documentation of Company C's performance measurement (Decision 6).

In addition, decisions can cause competition for the same resources (Langley et al., 1995). In this case, the decision to use two versions of requirements and th decision for rigorous documentation acceptance criteria (Decisions 5 and 6), placed the companies in competition for the energy of the development team and the project time.

In summary, some decisions in this case are intertwined, the antecedent decisions limit the subsequent decisions, and they compete for the same resources.

CONCLUSION AND IMPLICATIONS

Unlike the past studies on IT outsourcing decisions, which take rational decisions as assumptions, economic models as a base, outsourcing firms as subjects, cross sectional decisions as unit of analysis, this study attempts to illustrate how decisions are made in outsourcing processes, and how outsourcing results are influenced by the dynamic decisions assumptions, situational perspectives, co-construction of outsourcing firms and contractors, and process-oriented research approaches. Through the dynamic framework of IT outsourcing decisions constructed in this study, including "negotiated outcome", "context dependency", "interwoven decisions", this study probes into complicated IT outsourcing decisions and get more insights. Further discussions on the theoretic and practical implications of IT outsourcing are made as follows.

Theoretical Implications

First, according to the case, this study realizes that decisions are made upon negotiations and profit conflicts between internal and external participants of organizations; the results usually do not achieve the maximum economic benefits of the organizations. For instance, in Decision 5 (decision for system function), in order to meet regulations of government, a final decision is to accept two versions of system functions. For outsourcing firms, although they can successfully pass government acceptance test, they cannot implement the proper functions, due to a lack of maintenance hours. For the contractors, they must develop an information system that will be significantly revised by increased working hours, which is wasting time and labor-force. For the government, although the project is closed on time, it does not actually construct an e-commerce platform able to facilitate the cooperation of companies in the industry. It is a waste of budget monies, and shows an incredible lack of efficiency. Another example is Decision 6, in order to allow Company C to introduce its works to the government, outsourcing firms and Company C set up precise document as acceptance criteria, which significantly influence the schedule of the project. Thus, the project is finally roughly closed, even though the complete documents are highly praised by the government.

Thus, in outsourcing decisions, due to negotiations among various interest groups and participants, the results sometimes do not involve economic profits and are outside the realm of expectations, which contradict the economic rational decision model that assumes the decision makers can fully predict or control the outsourcing results. Currently, IT outsourcing relationships are extremely complicated, including multi-level outsourcing, international, and cross-cultural outsourcing (Ollson, Conchuir, Agerfalk & Fitzgerald, 2008; Mahnke, Wareham & Bjorn-Andersen, 2008). Thus, there will be more participants and the negotiation results will be more unexpected. We suggest probing into such complicated decisions to determine how to assist management in future negotiation.

In-depth studies revealed that the power in decisions is not necessarily attached with positions in the organizations; instead, it derives from knowledge or technique (Miller & Wilson, 2006). The power attached with organizational positions is illustrated by the interest conflict between two departments in Decision 2. Allen et al. (2002) also mentioned the conflict between a school IT department and an organizational department; besides, an outsourcing project manager could not execute without a high-ranking authority (Decision 5). But power derives from knowledge is more situated. For examples, in Decision 6, to decide the acceptance conditions, project managers of outsourcing firms must respect the "professionalism" of Company C, and they "cannot" require the reduction of the demands in document quality. Finally, the precise document writing work affects the schedule of the project. The knowledge capital in outsourcing processes becomes a source of power and status, and affects outsourcing (Levina & Vasst, 2008). Large-scale outsourcing projects involve cooperation and conflict among different knowledge workers or roles (such as business consultant, IT consultant, program designer, and system manager). The past literatures on IT outsourcing or strategic selection rarely probe into the influence of **knowledge power** on decision negotiation, and it relies on future studies.

Secondly, this study elaborated on the "rules of game" of IT outsourcing decisions, which suggests the influence of the past decisions on future ones and "interwoven decision", upon which the past and future decisions "compete for the resources". This case not only demonstrates mutual effects among the decisions, as indicated by Langley et al. (1995) and Butler (1990). But also become the special contexts of decisions will dynamically influence the decisions indicated by Pinfield (1986). Thus, the complicated outsourcing decisions are not only affected by the "static" environments, such as culture, institutions, and organizational structure. In addition, dynamic situations of different decisions and behaviors have influence on the direction or limitation of the subsequent decisions; contexts are not only static, but also situated, decisions become dynamic and unpredictable. Further studies are needed to explore how decision makers make sense the situated and dynamic contexts, and how to make decisions upon the complicated contexts.

Thirdly, in the section of case analysis and findings, this study demonstrated that outsourcing decisions are influenced by the institutional environments (such as Decisions 7 and 5). The decision makers conform the limited time of projects (Decision 7), or decouple the "RFP as acceptance criteria" rituals to decide two versions of systems (Decision 5). Moreover, it becomes a "exaggerating the function" myth in the outsourcing vendors' cognition (Decision 3) or project managers' "responsibility sharing" ideology (Decision 7). Thus, decision makers can also become the carriers of this kind of ritual system (Langley et al., 1995), and interpret the "rationality" of decisions (Miller & Wilson, 2006). In other words, these institutionalization ceremonies become the decision makers' ideologies, and their decisions are legitimated upon their cognition. For instance, in Decision 3, because of the on-time and unchanged payment of projects subsidized by the government, the bidders tend to prepare a proposal, which "exaggerates the system functions" without considering their costs and time. Project managers in outsourcing firms have the ideology that "sharing the responsibility" is more important than the online operations of a system, which will result in subsequent decisions and results. Miranda and Kim (2006) studied city governments in the U.S., and found that professional or bureaucratic systems limited the city government decision makers' logic with regard to outsourcing decisions of transaction costs. Miranda and Kim (2006) indicated that, "rather than viewing decision making as strategic interventions into an institutional context, this research takes the more basic position of institutions circumscribing decision making" (p. 731). For the case in this study, not only the economic logic; but, decision makers' definitions on cost, time, efficiency, and even definitions of successful projects, are is circumscribed to their institutionalized cognition framework. Future studies can target more on the decision makers' cognition and impacts on the outsourcing decision-making process and results.

Managerial Implications

According to the case, this study realizes that IT outsourcing decisions are significantly influenced by institutions and policy; although the design of the original system aims to avoid the risk of management (for instance, in this study, the case treats RFP as the criterion of examination), finally it restricts decisions, and even turns into an inefficient ceremony. The designs of institutions should be flexible in order to meet more and more complicated IT outsourcing.

In addition, with regard to the construction of RFP, proposals, or contracts, besides the "psychological contract" between outsourcing firms and the contractors, as indicated by Koh, Ang, and Straub (2004), there should also be common consensus within organization members. The proposals of information systems are not simply the regulations of system functions; it should consider the operation process from the users' perspective.

More importantly, IT outsourcing decision makers in organizations should treat outsourcing decisions as an integrated and continuous process, instead of dispersed, single decisions of the past. In complicated outsourcing processes, the decisions are influenced by both the internal and external environments of the organizations, and negotiations among internal, external, and situated situations upon "IT outsourcing dynamic decision framework", as proposed by this study, decision makers could consider in each decision-making, "How to negotiate with the related stakeholders?" and "What kind of internal and external environments will influence the construction and practice of decisions?" "Will this decision turn into an obstacle for future decisions?" "Will this decision complete the same resource with the previous decision?" For decision makers, being flexible, adaptive, and innovative would be the best strategy in the complicated outsourcing environments.

REFERENCES

Allen, D., Kern, T., & Mattison, D. (2002). Culture, power, and politics in ICT outsourcing in high education institutions. *European Journal of Information Systems*, *11*(2), 159–173. doi:10.1057/palgrave/ejis/3000425

Ang, S., & Cummings, L. L. (1997). Strategic response to institutional influence on information systems outsourcing. *Organization Science*, *8*(3), 235–256. doi:10.1287/orsc.8.3.235

Ang, S., & Straub, D. W. (1998). Production and transaction economies and IS outsourcing: A study of the U.S. banking industry . *Management Information Systems Quarterly*, *22*(4), 535–552. doi:10.2307/249554

Aubert, B. A., Rivad, S., & Patry, M. (1996). A transaction cost approach to outsourcing behavior. *Information & Management*, *30*(2), 51–64. doi:10.1016/0378-7206(95)00045-3

Aubert, B. A., Rivad, S., & Patry, M. (2004). A transaction cost model of IT outsourcing. *Information & Management*, *41*(7), 921–932. doi:10.1016/j.im.2003.09.001

Barthelemy, J., & Geyer, D. (2005). An empirical investigation of IT outsourcing versus quasi-outsourcing in France and Germany. *Information & Management*, *42*(4), 533–542. doi:10.1016/j.im.2004.02.005

Beulen, E., & Ribbers, P. (2003). IT outsourcing contracts: Practical implications of the incomplete contract theory. In *Proceedings of the 36th Hawaii International Conference on System Sciences*.

Butler, R. (1990). Decision-making research: Its uses and misuses. A comment on Mintzberg and Waters: 'Does decision get in the way.' . *Organization Studies*, *11*(1), 11–16. doi:10.1177/017084069001100103

Creswell, J. W. (1997). *Qualitative Inquiry and Research Design: Choosing among five Traditions*. Thousand Oaks, CA: Sage Publications.

Cullen, S., Seddon, P., & Willcocks, L. (2005). IT outsourcing configuration: Research into defining and designing outsourcing arrangements. *Strategic Information Systems*, *14*(4), 357–387. doi:10.1016/j.jsis.2005.07.001

DiRomualdo, A., & Gurbaxani, V. (1998). Strategic intent for IT outsourcing. *Sloan Management Review*, *39*(4), 67–80.

Kern, T., & Willcocks, L. (2002). Exploring relationships in information technology outsourcing: The interaction approach. *European Journal of Information Systems*, *11*(1), 3–19. doi:10.1057/palgrave/ejis/3000415

Khalfan, A. M., & Alshawaf, A. (2003). IS/IT outsourcing practices in the public health sector of Kuwait: A contingency approach. *Logistics Information Management*, *16*(3/4), 215–228. doi:10.1108/09576050310483817

Klein, H. K., & Myers, M. D. (1999). A set of principles for conducting and evaluating interpretive field studies in information systems. *Management Information Systems Quarterly*, *23*(1), 67–94. doi:10.2307/249410

Koh, C., Ang, S., & Straub, D. W. (2004). IT outsourcing success: A psychological contract perspective. *Information Systems Research*, *15*(4), 356–373. doi:10.1287/isre.1040.0035

Lacity, M. C., & Willocks, L. P. (1995). Interpreting information technology sourcing decisions from a transaction cost perspective: findings and critique. *Accounting Management and Information Technology*, *5*(3/4), 203–244. doi:10.1016/0959-8022(96)00005-7

Lacity, M. C., & Willocks, L. P. (1998). An empirical investigation of information technology sourcing practices: Lessons from experience. *Management Information Systems Quarterly*, *22*(3), 363–408. doi:10.2307/249670

Langley, A. (1999). Strategies for theorizing from process data. *Academy of Management Review*, *24*(4), 691–710. doi:10.2307/259349

Langley, A., Mintzberg, H., Pitcher, P., Posada, E., & Saint-Macary, J. (1995). Opening up decision making: The view from the black stool. *Organization Science*, *6*(3), 260–279. doi:10.1287/orsc.6.3.260

Levina, N., & Ross, J. W. (2003). From the vendor's perspective: Exploring the value proposition in information technology outsourcing. *Management Information Systems Quarterly*, *27*(3), 331–364.

Levina, N., & Vasst, E. (2008). Innovating or doing as told? Status differences and overlapping boundaries in offshore collaboration. *Management Information Systems Quarterly*, *32*(2), 307–322.

Loh, L., & Venkatraman, N. (1992). Diffusion of information technology outsourcing: Influence sources and the Kodak Effect. *Information Systems Research*, *3*(4), 334–358. doi:10.1287/isre.3.4.334

Mahnke, V., Overby, M. L., & Vang, J. (2005). Strategic outsourcing of IT services: Theoretical stocktaking and empirical challenges. *Industry and Innovation*, *12*(2), 205–253. doi:10.1080/13662710500087958

Mahnke, V., Wareham, J., & Bjorn-Andersen, N. (2008). Offshore middleman: transnational intermediation in technology sourcing. *Journal of Information Technology*, *23*(1), 18–30. doi:10.1057/palgrave.jit.2000124

Miller, S. J., Hickson, D. J., & Wilson, D. C. (1996). Decision-making in organizations . In Clegg, S. R., Hardy, C., & Nord, W. R. (Eds.), *Handbook of Organization Studies* (pp. 293–312). London: Sage Publications.

Mintzberg, H., Raisinghani, D., & Theoret, A. (1976). The structure of 'unstructured' decision process. *Administrative Science Quarterly*, *21*(2), 246–275. doi:10.2307/2392045

Miranda, S. M., & Kim, Y. M. (2006). Professional versus political contexts: Institutional mitigation and the transaction cost heuristic in information systems outsourcing. *Management Information Systems Quarterly*, *30*(3), 725–753.

Murray, E. A. (1978). Strategic choice as a negotiated outcome. *Management Science*, *24*(9), 960–972. doi:10.1287/mnsc.24.9.960

Ollson, II. II., Conchuir, E. O., Agerfalk, P. J., & Fitzgerald, B. (2008). Two-stage offshoring: A investigation of the Irish bridge. *Management Information Systems Quarterly*, *32*(2), 257–279.

Pettigrew, A. M. (1990). Studying strategic choice and strategic change. A comment on Mintzberg and Waters: 'Does decision get in the way?' . *Organization Studies*, *11*(1), 6–11. doi:10.1177/017084069001100102

Rao, H. R., & Chaudhury, A. (1996). A two-level investigation of information systems outsourcing. *Communications of the ACM*, *30*(7), 36–44.

Sabherwal, R. (1999). The role of trust in outsourced IS development projects. *Communications of the ACM*, *43*(2), 80–87. doi:10.1145/293411.293485

Simon, H. A. (1976). *Administrative Behaviour* (3rd ed.). New York: Free Press.

Taylor, H. (2006). Critical risks in outsourced IT projects: The intractable and the unforeseen. *Communications of the ACM*, *49*(11), 75–79. doi:10.1145/1167838.1167840

Watjatrakul, B. (2005). Determinants of IS sourcing decisions: A comparative study of transaction cost theory versus the resource-based view. *The Journal of Strategic Information Systems*, *14*(4), 289–415. doi:10.1016/j.jsis.2005.05.001

Willcocks, L., & Choi, C. J. (1995). Co-operative partnership and 'total' IT outsourcing: From contractual obligation to strategic alliance. *European Management Journal*, *13*(1), 67–78. doi:10.1016/0263-2373(94)00059-G

Wilson, D. C. (1982). Electricity and resistance: A case study of innovation and politics. *Organization Studies*, *3*(2), 119–140. doi:10.1177/017084068200300203

Yin, R. K. (2003). *Case study research, design and methods* (3rd ed.). Thousand Oaks, CA: Sage Publications.

ADDITIONAL READING

Bell, G., Bromley, P., & Bryson, J. (1998). Spinning a complex web: links between strategic decision making context, content, process, and outcome . In Papadakis, V., & Barwise, P. (Eds.), *Strategic Decisions* (pp. 163–178). Boston, MA: Kluwer.

Cheon, M. J., & Teng, J. T. C. (1995). Theoretical perspectives on the outsourcing of information systems. *Journal of Information Technology*, *10*, 209–219. doi:10.1057/jit.1995.25

Dibbern, J., Goles, T., Hirschheim, R., & Jayatilaka, B. (2004). Information systems outsourcing: a survey and analysis of the literature. *The Data Base for Advances in Information Systems*, *35*(4), 6–102.

Garvin, D. A., & Roberto, M. A. (2001, September). What you don't know about making decisions. *Harvard Business Review*, ▪▪▪, 108–116.

Lacity, M. C., & Hirschheim, R. (1993). *Information systems outsourcing: myths, metaphors, and realities.* New York: Chichester.

Lee, Jale-Nam, Huynh, M. Q., Kwok, Chi-Wai, & Pi Shih-Ming. (2003). IT outsourcing evolution-past, present, and future. *Communications of the ACM*, *46*(5), 84–89. doi:10.1145/769800.769807

Nutt, P. C. (2008). Investigating the success of decision making processes. *Journal of Management Studies*, *45*(2), 425–455.

KEY TERM AND DEFINITIONS

RFP: Request For Proposal. The outsourcing company provides a document about project scope that requests the vendors to submit detail plan/proposal to implement the information systems project. This document usually includes objective, system architecture, rough system functions, and estimated budget and timeline.

Proposal: The vendor responses the RFP and propose the a plan about project schedule, human resources, project schedule, deliverables, solutions to response the rough system functions, project management and change management plan.

Section 8
SME Research and Issues

Chapter 19
An Investigation into the Adoption and Implementation of Electronic Commerce in Saudi Arabian Small and Medium Enterprises

Sabah A. Al-Somali
Aston University, UK

Ben Clegg
Aston University, UK

Roya Gholami
Aston University, UK

ABSTRACT

Saudi Arabian Small and Medium Enterprises (SMEs) will face fierce competition from new entrants to local markets as a result of their accession to the Word Trade Organisation (WTO), and electronic commerce (e-commerce) technologies can reinforce SME's competitive edge. This study investigates the state of e-commerce adoption and analyses the factors that determine the extent to which SMEs in Saudi Arabia are inclined towards deploying e-commerce technologies. This could assist future firms in designing effective implementation projects. Seven SMEs' e-commerce adoption levels are studied as a case. The Technology-Organization-Environment (TOE) framework was used as the major source of inspiration in our analysis of e-commerce adoption amongst Saudi SMEs. In addition to advancing research on e-commerce in Saudi Arabia, this chapter also highlights several directions for future inquiry and implications for managers and policymakers.

DOI: 10.4018/978-1-61692-016-6.ch019

INTRODUCTION

The rapid increase in the number of Internet users has fueled a phenomenal growth in electronic commerce (e-commerce). The Internet provides an excellent opportunity to increase sales while resulting in lower operating costs. Indeed, firms that pass up this tremendous opportunity will possibly not survive in the 21st century (Saunders, 2007). E-commerce involves the use of Internet technologies such as Electronic Data Interchange (EDI), electronic e-mail and Electronic Fund Transfer (EFT) to support financial transactions and purchases online.

E-commerce enables consumers and companies to gain access to worldwide markets, to expand access from regional to national or national to international markets (Iacovou *et al.* 1995; Rama Rao, 2001; Andam, 2003). Because of its potential, enterprises throughout the globe have either created or are in the process of creating e-commerce 'front-ends' (i.e., online shops) to complement their traditional business channels.

A leading market analysis firm, Forrester Research (Mulpuru et al., 2008) has indicated that online retail sales alone in the United States (US) reached $175 billion in 2007 (an increase of 19% from 2006) and this is projected to grow to $335 billion by 2012. Moreover, business-to-consumer (B2C) e-commerce sales totaled 106 billion Euros ($133 billion) in 2006 and this is set to triple over the next 5 years to reach nearly 323 billion Euros ($407 billion) by 2011 (eMarketer, 2007). It would nevertheless seem that there is a sizable gap between the developed and developing countries in which e-commerce successes occur more in the former than the latter (Licker and Motts, 2000; Johnston and Acquaah-Gaisie, 2001).

Recently, many studies have been conducted to explore the factors that influence the use of e-commerce in different countries and unfortunately, the majority of these studies were conducted in the United States (e.g. Grandon and Pearson, 2004), United Kingdom (e.g. Matlay and Addis, 2003), Canada (e.g Sparling *et al.*, 2007) and few have focused on countries in developing countries such as Brazil (i.e., Tigre, 2003), South Africa (i.e., Molla and Licker, 2005) and India (i.e., Tarafdar and Vaidya, 2004). Yet, there is a shortage of data coming from countries in the Middle East and Arab World (Parker and Castleman, 2006) and in general this region has not yet received enough attention from social scientists and organizational analysts (Al-Yahya, 2009).

It is believed that using the findings of innovation studies in advanced countries to explain the innovative behaviour in less developed countries is likely to be inappropriate (Hofstede, 1991). Indeed, Western management theories and practices might not apply abroad and this same thought applies to the transferability of innovation theories and practices from the West to the Arabs (Hofstede, 1980).

Thus, the present study attempts to address this gap in the extant literature and sheds some light on e-commerce adoption by Small and Medium Enterprises (SMEs) in Saudi Arabia. Saudi Arabia is a unique place in which to conduct the study to test the findings derived from innovation adoption literature in SMEs. First, Saudi Arabia covers a very large area of the Arabian peninsula with a diverse immigrant population and a developing economy. Moreover, the region has been frequently cited for the lack of real involvement in ICT and e-business progress in achieving good work environment and organizational performance (UNCTAD, 2004; Nour, 2002).

This remainder of this chapter consists of seven sections. *Section 2* will briefly discusses the research national context and gives a picture about Saudi Arabia including its economy, the state of Internet usage and some cultural background. *Section 3* discusses the different definitions and characteristics concerning SMEs. *Section 4* then discusses the theoretical foundation for studying e-commerce adoption in organisations. The main method employed in our research will be briefly described in *Sections 5*. Research findings

Figure 1.

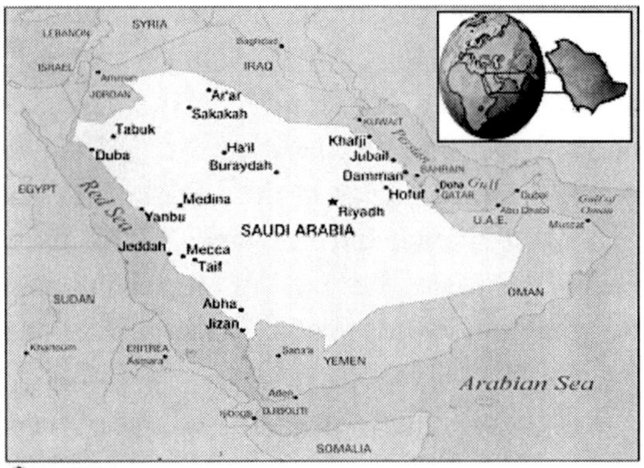

*The Capital

are outlined in *Section 6,* and finally *Section 7* will provide a series of conclusions in light of the findings, put forward directions for future research, address research limitations as well as implications for managers, government bodies and policy makers.

THE RESEARCH NATIONAL CONTEXT

This empirical study is conducted in the Saudi Arabian business context. In fact, over the last ten years, Saudi Arabia has made remarkable progress in different fields of Information and Communications Technology (ICT) including connectivity and access, national IT initiatives and e-services. In fact, Saudi Arabia's ICT market is the largest in the Middle East and will remain so through 2012 (Rosenthal, 2008). This section presents a brief country profile including geography, population, economy and some cultural background to give a picture about this country.

Geography

The Kingdom of Saudi Arabia is located in the heart of the Arabian Peninsula in the Middle East and it is geographically, the largest country of the Arabian Peninsula (see figure 1). It extends from the Gulf in the east to the Red Sea in the west, and from the Jordanian-Iraqi border in the north to Oman and Yemen in the south. Arabic is the main language in the country and Islam's two holiest sites, Mecca and Medina, are located in the country (Technology integration division, 2007)

Population

In 2008 Saudi Arabia had a population of 28 million, up from 26.4 million in 2005 and 11.2 million in 1985. The annual growth rate for 2008 was is 1.9%. The population includes 22.6 million Saudis, 5.6 million foreign nationals (CIA World Factbook, 2009).The literacy rate among youth has been improving and they are becoming more Internet savvy and prefer to own sophisticated electronic gadgets like mobile phones, laptops etc (Rao, 2006).

Economy

Saudi Arabia has a stable political, economic and social system. It is the world's largest oil producer and exporter. It plays a leading role in the Organization of Petroleum Exporting Countries (OPEC). On December 2005, Saudi Arabia became the 149th Member of the World Trade Organization (WTO).

The membership of WTO means that Saudi Arabia is required to adapt its trade laws and practices with WTO obligations and open up its financial and other service areas on a level playing field basis to the institutions and companies of other WTO members (World Trade Organization, 2005). However, accession to WTO provides the domestic companies with challenges such as modernization of production technologies, better quality systems, improving productivity, training and development of workforce (Rao, 2006).

It is worth mentioning here that, the economic progress which in some societies has taken a century or more, has been accomplished in Saudi Arabia in only a decade (Al-Farsy, 1986; Al-

Figure 2.

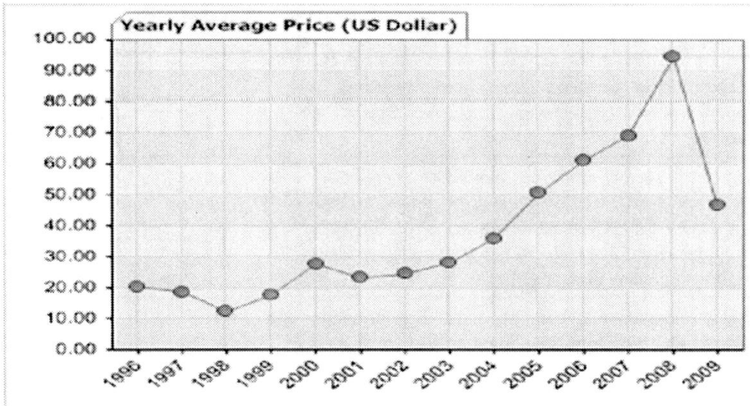

Year	Price
1996	20.29
1997	18.68
1998	12.28
1999	17.48
2000	27.6
2001	23.12
2002	24.36
2003	28.1
2004	36.05
2005	50.64
2006	61.08
2007	69.08
2008	94.45
2009	46.55

But'hie and Eben Saleh, 2002). In fact, this has been best described in the words of Rao (2006), who asserts that 'going by the current developments on the economic front in Saudi Arabia, it is no exaggeration to say that Saudi Arabia is the "Emerging Economic Tiger of the Middle East"' (Rao, 2006, p.1). Moreover, the government announced plans to establish six new 'economic cities' scheduled for completion by 2020, in its bid to diversify the economy, increase employment opportunities and encourage growth in the non-oil industrial sector (Martin, 2009).

Saudi Arabia has been recording surplus budget through mid-2008 driven by high oil prices which have increased government revenues and Saudi ownership of foreign assets. (Figure 2) presents the oil prices from 1996 to 2009.

The economic growth averaged over 3.2% in 2006 and reached 4.2% in 2008. Unemployment was around 8.8% in 2008 and the industrial annual production growth rate was 4.5% in 2008 (CIA World Factbook, 2009a). It is noteworthy that, the global downturn, falling oil prices and limited international credit are expected to affect Saudi economic growth (CIA World Factbook, 2009a). (Table 1) provides a summary for the Saudi Arabian's economy from 2006-2008.

Culture

Hofstede identified four dimensions of cultural variability which provide broad explanatory concepts for differences between cultures. The Geert Hofstede analysis for Saudi Arabia is

Table1. Saudi Economy at glance (Source: CIA World Factbook, 2009a)

	2008	2007	2006
GDP (purchasing power parity)	$582.8 billion	$553.5 billion	$535.3 billion
GDP - real growth rate:	4.2%	3.4%	3.2%
Exchange rates: Saudi Riyals (SAR) per US dollar	3.75 (2008 est.)	3.745 (2007)	3.745 (2006)
Unemployment rate (2008): 8.8%			
Industrial production growth rate (2008): 4.5%			
Note: data are in US dollars			

Table 2. Scores for Saudi Arabia for the four dimensions of cultural values of Hofstede (Hofstede, 1980)

Dimension	Definition	Scores for Saudi Arabia
Power distance	Refers to the degree of equality, or inequality, between people in the country's society. High Power distance indicates that inequalities of power and wealth are accepted practices and have been allowed to grow within the society.	80
Individualism	Focuses on the degree the society reinforces individual or collective achievement and interpersonal relationships. Low iindividualism typifies societies of a more collectivist nature with close ties between individuals. These cultures reinforce collectives where everyone takes responsibility for fellow members of their group	38
Uncertanty avoidance	Focuses on the level of tolerance for uncertainty and ambiguity within the society. High uncertainty indicates a structured, rule-oriented society that institutes rules, regulations, and controls in order to reduce the amount of uncertainty	68
Masculinity	Masculinity measures the degree to which "masculine" values like assertiveness, performance, success and competition prevail over "feminine" values like the quality of life, maintaining warm personal relationships, service, caring, and solidarity	52

almost identical to other Middle East countries (Hofstede, 1980) where Islam plays a large role in the people's lives.

Hofstede (1980) found that the Middle Eastern countries exhibited cultural characteristics of a considerably high power distance, high collectivism orientations and high uncertainty avoidance. High power distance index indicates a high level of inequalities of power and wealth in Saudi society (Al-Gahtani et al., 2007). Bjerke and Al-Meer (1993) note that, the high power distance orientation could be attributed to the Moslem belief about authority in Islamic societies.

It is worth mentioning that, cultures that exhibit high collectivism often have very clear norms for proper behavior in social situations and avoid new situations with no clear norms (Hofstede, 1980). Furthermore, a high uncertainty avoidance deals with tolerance for uncertainty and as a result of this characteristic, the society does not readily accept change and is very risk adverse. Definitions for the four dimensions of cultural values of Hofstede and scores for Saudi Arabia are illustrated in (Table 2).

In summary, the Saudi culture is best described in the words of Al-Ghamdi (2008) who asserts that, the Saudi culture relies heavily on non-direct communication cues such as body language and eye-contact, tone of voice, facial cues, and the use of silence. Establishing trust is an essential part of Saudi business culture and favors based on mutual benefit trust are ways of enhancing these cultural values.

Internet Development in Saudi Arabia

It is worth mentioning that Saudi Arabian Internet service was launched (as per ministerial decree No. 163) in March 1998 and the Internet in Saudi Arabia is supervised by King Abdulaziz City for Science and Technology (KACST). Moreover, KACT formulates the rules and regulations that govern the use of the Internet in the country and took care of the Saudi domain name system (CITC, 2007). (Figure 3) illustrates the Internet structure in Saudi Arabia.

In fact, Saudi Arabia is one of the fastest growing Internet markets in the Middle East. According to the communications and information technology commission's (CICT) annual report (2008), Internet users in Saudi Arabia grew from around

Figure 3.

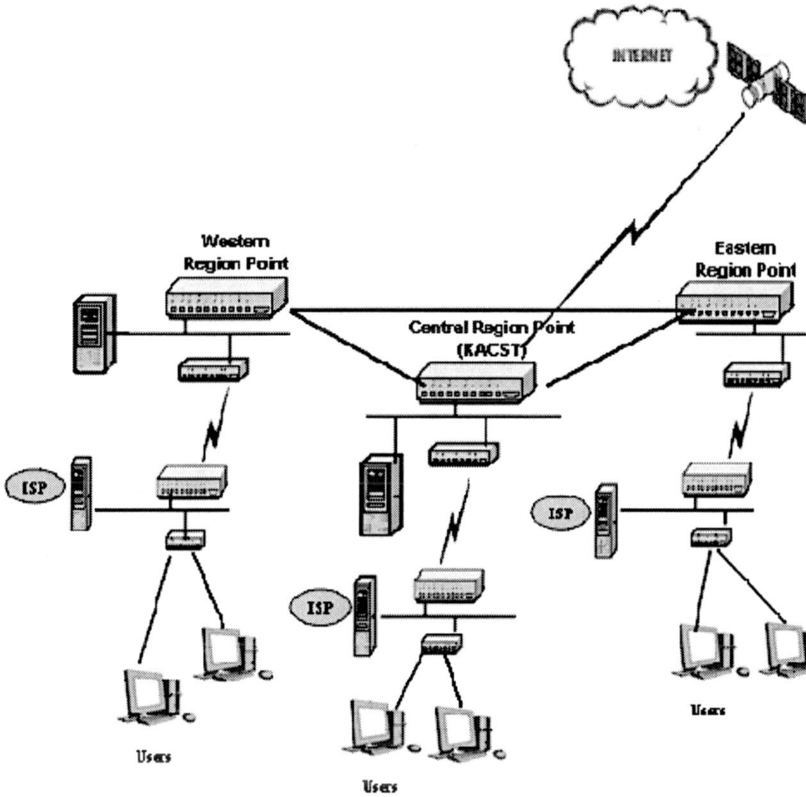

1 million in 2001 to an estimated 7.7 million at the end of 2008, as shown in (Figure 4). It can be seen from (Figure 4) that the Internet penetration increased to 31% of the population in 2008.

Internet usage will continue to grow rapidly and one reason for this growth is that 60% of the Saudi population consists of teenagers and young adults aged less than 25 years old who are adapting faster than expected to new technologies (Central Department of Statistics, 2005). According to the World Economic forum (2009), Saudi Arabia is ranked (40) and recognised as one of the ICT leaders in the Middle East and North Africa (MENA) region, moving well ahead of its highly touted Asian neighbours China (46), and India (54).

Over the last few years, Saudi Arabia has made remarkable progress in different ICT fields including connectivity and access, national IT initiatives and e-services (ITU, 2005).The Saudi Arabian Ministry of Commerce established an e-commerce committee to facilitate Internet buying and selling operations and to provide a supportive environment for effective e-commerce adoption targeted towards businesses and residential customers (Al-Sudairy and Tang, 2000).

SMALL AND MEDIUM ENTERPRISES (SMES) DEFINITIONS

SME definitions vary from country to country and according to different parameters. Some of these definitions are based on quantitative measures such as number of employees, amount of assets or annual sales turnovers, while others employ qualitative features. Some researchers suggest

Figure 4.

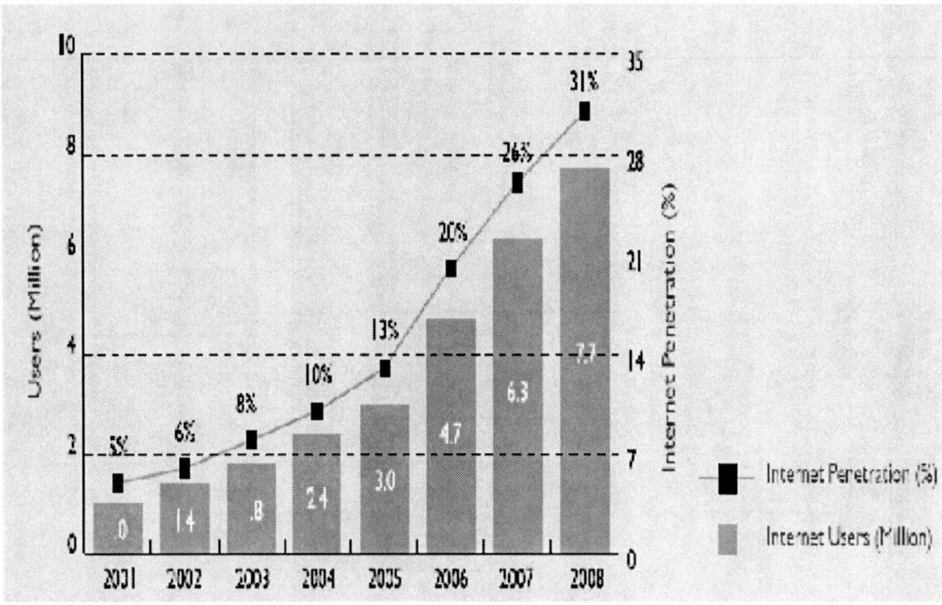

that any description or definition must include a quantitative component that takes into account number of employees, turnover and assets, but the description must also include a qualitative component that reflects how the business is organised and how it operates (MacGregor and Vrazalic, 2004 r. Macgregor and L. Vrazalic, Electronic Commerece Adoption in Small to Medium Enterprises (SMEs), A Comparative study of SMEs in Wollongong (Australia) and Karlstad (Sweden), University of Wollongong (2004). MacGregor and Vrazalic, 2004). For example, the North American Industry uses measures such as number of employees and total turnover. On the other hand, the European Union (EU) has proposed a uniform definition that views SMEs as independent companies with fewer than 250 employees and with turnovers of less than 50 million Euros (European Commission, 2004). These enterprises are also characterised by an ownership structure where independents have 25% or more of the capital or voting rights.

In the case of Saudi Arabia, small enterprises are those which employ between 10 and 25 workers. Moreover these enterprises operate with capital between 200,000 SR and 1 million SR [1] whereas medium-sized enterprises employ between 26 and 100 workers with capital between 1 million SR and 5 million SR (Radwan, 2001).

SMEs are characterised by small management teams, limited resources, lack of specialist staff, limited market share, and low employee turnover (MacGregor *et al.*, 1998; Yap *et al.*, 1992). As one of the most dynamic features of a growing economy, SMEs are important contributors to national economies and play a critical role in creating employment opportunities. For instance, in the U.S., small businesses generate two-thirds of new jobs; produce 39 percent of the gross national product (GNP). In Europe, 99.8% of the firms are SMEs, responsible for two-thirds of the turnover and business employment (Bruque and Moyano, 2007). Similarly, in New Zealand (NZ), SMEs account for approximately 35% of the economy's output, employ 41% of the workforce, and represent 96% of NZ firms (Al-Qirim, 2007).

In Saudi Arabia, the majority of Saudi firms (93 percent) are SMEs (Sajini, 2004) and they employ approximately 50 percent of the Kingdom's labour force (Otsuki, 2002). Nearly half (47%) of SMEs are engaged in commercial and hotel businesses, 27% in construction, 12% in industrial manufacturing, 6% in social services and 8% in other different businesses (Otsuki, 2002).

According to a recent survey, Saudi Arabian SMEs encounter a range of challenges namely, lack of funds and difficulty of obtaining funds from financial institutions. Other constraints are of a technical and administrative nature such as lack of skilled workers and qualified human resources, lack of skilled managers and administrators, lack of marketing expertise and modern technology. However, despite these challenges, the development of Saudi SMEs has been shown to have a strong impact on job creation, poverty alleviation, and hence quality of life (Ministry of Economy and Planning, 2008).

Finally, the membership of WTO means that Saudi Arabia fully opened its domestic market and this in turn led to fierce competition between domestic SMEs and foreign companies entering the local market. Some words on our theoretical influences are now discussed below.

THEORETICAL BACKGROUND

It is important for business transforming to e-commerce to assess all aspects of their business processes and performance. The business needs to identify the critical factors that will establish successful transformation, and then direct strategy and resources towards those factors (Molla and Licker, 2005).

Generally speaking, enterprise e-commerce adoption has been a topic of interest to researchers (Kowtha and Choon, 2001; Love *et al.*, 2001; MacGregor and Vrazalic, 2004; Molla, 2005; Molla and Licker, 2005; Kartiwi, 2006; Al-Qirim, 2007; Chong, 2008) and the literature suggests that most research is based on four theoretical frameworks:

- The Innovation Diffusion Theory (Rogers, 1995; Beatty et al., 2001; Mehrtens *et al*, 2001; Zhu and Kraemer, 2005)
- Organizational Innovation Theory (Technology-Organization-Environment Model) (Tornatzky and Klein, 1982; Tornatzky and Fleischer,1990; Depietro *et al.*, 1990; Damanpour, 1991; Kuan and Chau, 2001; Xu *et al.*, 2004; Zhu *et al.*, 2003; Zhu and Kraemer, 2005),
- Perceived E-commerce Readiness Model (PERM) (Molla, 2005; Molla and Licker, 2005; Tan *et al.*, 2007)
- Technology Acceptance theories (Davis *et al.*,1989; Igabria *et al.*,1997; Venkatesh & Davis, 2000)

The following sections discuss the four research approaches in further detail.

Innovation Diffusion Theory

Rogers (1995) introduced the Innovation Diffusion[2] Theory (IDT) and it represents an approach to technology acceptance and use. Moreover, it has been the basis of many studies to explain the adoption and diffusion of ICT. It is generally used in the study of how, why, and at what rate innovations are accepted by individuals or other units of adoption (Roger, 1995). Generally, IDT explains the innovation decision process, the determining factors of rate of adoption and different categories of adopters.

There are five important innovation attributes that explain the different rates of adoption by users, namely relative advantage, compatibility, complexity, trialability, and observability. Further, Rogers (1995) defines relative advantage as "the degree to which an innovation is perceived as being better than existing one"; compatibility as "its consistency with existing social norms or values, past experiences and needs"; complexity as "the degree to which the new technology is easy to use and learn"; trialability as "the degree to which an innovation may be experimented with prior to actually using it on a limited basis"; and observability as " the extent to which a new technology's outcomes are clear and visible to others".

Technology-Organization-Environment framework (TOE)

Tornatzky and Fleischer (1990) identify three elements of a firm's context that influence the process by which it adopts and implements technological innovations and those are:

- **Technological context:** In which it describes both the internal and external technologies relevant to the business.
- **The organisational context:** It is defined in terms of several descriptive measures such as business size, nature of the business, the managerial structure, the quality of its human resources, and the amount of slack resources available internally.
- **The environmental context:** It is the arena that a business conducts its operations: its industry, competitors, access to resources supplied by others and dealings with government.

The Technology-Organization-Environment framework has been applied to Information systems (IS) innovation domains and it showed consistent empirical support (Iacovou *et al.*, 1995; Thong, 1999; Kuan and Chau, 2001; Zhu *et al.*, 2003).

Perceived E-Readiness Model (PERM)

Molla and Licker (2005) discussed e-commerce adoption amongst businesses in developing countries. They empirically tested the Perceived eReadiness Model (PERM) and they identified relevant e-commerce, managerial, organisational, and contextual factors that could explain e-commerce adoption amongst South African firms.

The model includes two major constructs which measures both perceived organizational eReadiness and perceived external eReadiness (Molla and Licker, 2005). Perceived organizational eReadiness is defined as managers' perception and evaluation of the degree to which they believe that the organization has the awareness, resources, commitment, and governance to adopt ecommerce (Molla and Licker, 2005). Perceived external eReadiness is the degree to which managers believe that market force, government, and other supporting industries are ready to aid in their organisation's e-commerce implementation (Molla and Licker, 2005).

Technology Acceptance Theories

The Technology Acceptance Model (TAM) is one of the better known models for explaining intention to use a technological innovation (Davis *et al*, 1989). TAM assumes that the intention to use a technology is influenced by the adopter's perceived usefulness as well as the perceived ease of use of the technology. Hence the intention to use motivates the actual use. TAM Davis (1989) was extended to TAM2 by Venkatesh and Davis (2000) to include subjective norms and voluntariness. Unified Theory of Acceptance and Use of Technology (UTAUT) (Venkatesh *et al.*, 2003) is the latest development. UTAUT integrates eight previously established models on individual acceptance of information technology.

In what follows we attempt to cluster the emerging themes into the three contexts in the Technology-Organization-Environment (TOE) framework. In fact, it is believed that e-commerce is enabled by technological development of the internet, driven by organisational factors and finally influenced by environmental factors related to customers, business partners, as well as competitors (Zhu *et al.*, 2002; Zhu *et al.*, 2003; Kurnia, 2008). Therefore, the TOE framework was used as the major source of inspiration in our analysis of e-commerce adoption amongst Saudi SMEs.

(Figure 5) ties together various factors which are believed to be relevant to the context of this study. It is a new and unique model. The following section discusses the research methodology.

RESEARCH METHODOLOGY

Given the exploratory nature of the study, and the limited empirical research on e-commerce and SMEs in Saudi Arabia to guide this study, a qualitative approach was considered appropriate to describe and explain the phenomenon of e-commerce.

Setting and Participants

This study was conducted in the city of Jeddah. Jeddah is Saudi Arabia's greatest commercial centre and its second largest city. It is also the largest seaport in the country. It is located in the west of Saudi Arabia in an area known as the Hizaj region which contains the two holy cities of Makkah (Mecca) and Madena (Medina). Jeddah is a cosmopolitan city with a rich cultural heritage and many of its residents are pilgrims who settled in the Arabian Peninsula hundreds of years before the formation of the Saudi Arabian Kingdom. Moreover, Jeddah is seen as Saudi Arabia's most liberal city (Technology integration division, 2007).

Interviews were conducted with seven Saudi SMEs from various industries, with associated representative having different IT experiences and e-commerce adoption levels. The companies were selected on the basis of the following criteria:

- They should be registered local companies and classified as SMEs according to the Saudi definition of firms ranging from 10 to a maximum of 100 employees.
- This study did not include any multinational or transnational organisations, as our intent was to study 'local' business firms operating in Saudi Arabia.

Data Collection Methods and Analysis

The unit of analysis is the individual SMEs. Semi structured interviews were used as the data collection technique. The interview questions focused on the three theoretical contexts shown in (Figure 5).

The first set of questions focused on the technological context and included questions on the perceived benefits and impediments of e-commerce. The next set of questions focused on the organizational context and included questions about firms' size, sector, management support for e-Commerce and more importantly current IT usage, infrastructure, capabilities and e-Commerce understanding. Finally, the third set of questions shed light on the macro arena or environmental context by enquiring about the customer and trading partner readiness, IT Vendor support and more importantly regulatory environment and government support. The interviews for this study took place during April 2007.

The in-depth interview was used and formed the primary source of data. We consider this technique to be flexible, unstructured and suitable for collecting the required information. Moreover, use of the in-depth interview method enabled us to identify the underlying factors influencing e-commerce adoption and to consider relations between the identified factors (Pettigrew, 1985; Yin, 1984; Bruque and Moyanob, 2007).

The first author undertook all of the interviews. Face-to-face Interviews were conducted with SME owners and were audio recorded. No other person was present during the interviews. Each interview lasted between one and two hours. Interviewees were not given the questions in advance in order to avoid prejudging the interview. Interviewees were assured of data confidentiality before the

Figure 5.

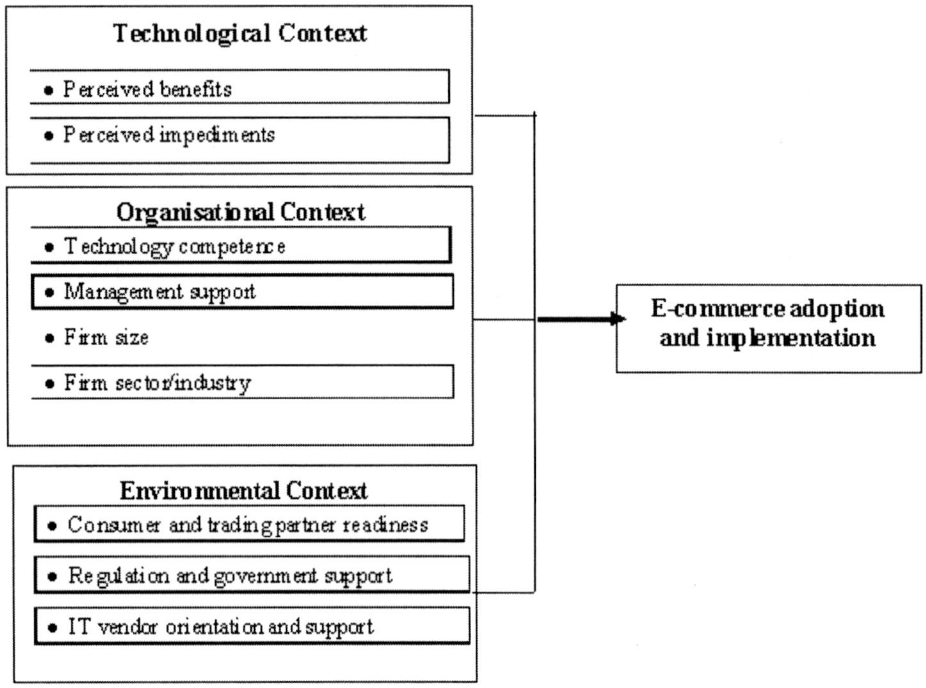

interview began, and their permission to record the interview was requested and granted by the respondents.

The Qualitative data analysis technique was used to identify and categorise themes/concepts of interest through close examination of data in the field notes (Kurnia, 2008). Moreover, due to the non-disclosure agreements with these firms, pseudonyms will be used to protect anonymity of the interviewee's identities.

RESEARCH RESULTS

We classified companies according to the level of e-commerce adoption and implementation (Figure 6). SMEs in *Level 1* are those with very basic or no online capabilities, while *Level 2* represents SMEs that use e-mail for internal and external communication, but with no advanced capabilities. *Level 3* includes SMEs that have a static website that does not enable online business transactions. Finally, *Level 4* constitutes firms that can take orders, make complete transactions and receive payments on their website (PriceWaterhouseCoopers, 1999; Sergeant, 2000; Martin and Matlay, 2001).

In the following sections, we describe the findings from the study. We first describe briefly the data from each of the seven SMEs and we next present different factors that influence SMEs' tendency to deploying e-commerce technologies.

Company Description

(Table 3) summarises the profile of the SMEs that participated in this study. SMEs were selected from the directory of companies distributed by the Council of Saudi Chambers of Commerce and Industry (CSCCI). The companies were taken from different business sectors such as retailers, manufacturers and services because it was reasoned that investigating firms from different sectors would

Figure 6.

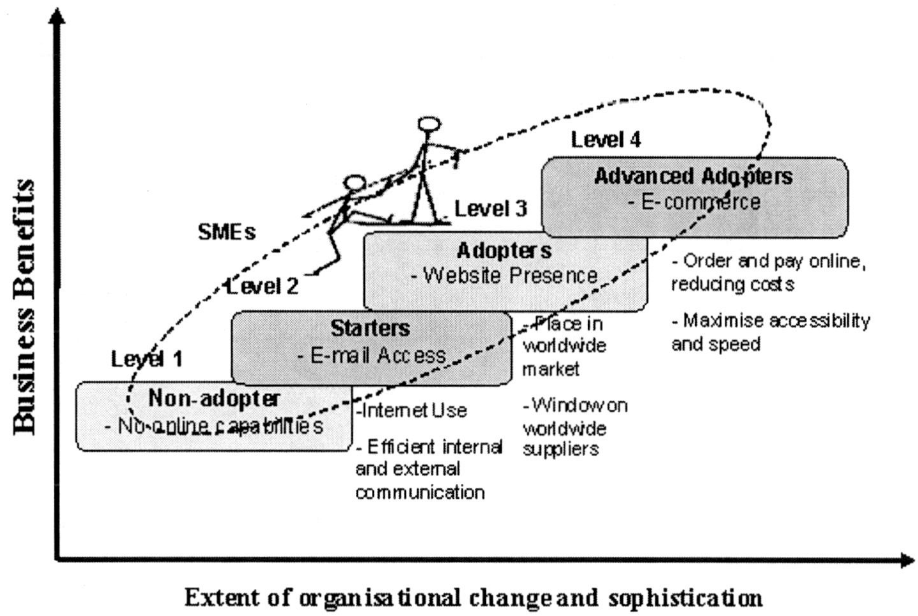

lead to a richer data set than companies belonging to the same sectors (Scupola, 2003).

It can be seen that three firms (S1, S2 and S6) are small (fewer than 25 employees) and four (S3, 4, S5 and S7) are medium-sized firms (25-100 employees). Four firms (S4, S5, S6, and S7) have websites and most offer online brochures, providing limited information about the firms and their products or services. Only S4 uses a website as part of its strategy to develop its e-business markets, but customers do not use it, primarily because of security concerns. Internet access and e-mail were found to occur together as in Saudi Arabia most of the Internet Service Providers (ISPs) provide Internet e-mail accounts to users for free.

Company S1

The first company (S1) is a coffee shop and restaurant. It is a family-owned firm established in 2007. S1 has 12 employees and the firm has a computer network with direct access to the Internet. S1 provides a wireless Internet connection for its customers. The firm has access to e-mail and it is used within the firm to circulate documents to employees. Moreover, e-mail is also used to contact customers, place orders and negotiate with suppliers. S1 is planning to have a website which will be mainly used as a promotional and advertisement tool. S1 capability level is 2 (i.e. starter).

Company S2

The second company (S2) is a retail clothing store offering a wide range of casual, informal and formal women's clothing apparel. It has been operating for six years. S2 has ten employees and there are only two staff members with the appropriate PC usage and email application skills. An outsourced IT consultant supports the firm in its computing networks and systems. The Internet is not used extensively and is mostly used for basic purposes such as e-mail to communicate with their overseas clothing suppliers. S2 is in the process of designing a static website as the firm believes that it is important to prepare for the future where

Table 3. Participants' profile

Firm	Business Type	Years in business	Ownership	Employees	E-commerce Platforms & capabilities
S1	Coffee Shop and Restaurant	Two years	Family-Owned	12	Internet connection, e-mail, no website (Level 2- Starter)
S2	Retail Clothing Store	Six years	Family-Owned	10	Homepage (under construction). Internet connection, e-mail, no website (Level 2-Starter)
S3	Women's Clothing Manufacturer	Five years	Owned by CEO	33	No online capabilities: no Internet connection and no webpage (Level 1-Non Adopter)
S4	Architecture & Engineering Design Specialists	Five years	Owned by CEO	30	Homepage, e-mail, and online selling and online catalogue (Level 4-Advanced Adopter)
S5	IT Support Services: Computer Sales & maintenance	Five years	Owned by CEO	27	Basic homepage, e-mail and Internet connection using DSL (Level 3-Adopter)
S6	Service Company: IT/IS training & ICT solutions	Six years	Family-Owned	10	Homepage, e-mail and permanent Internet connection (Level 3- Adopter- moving towards Level 4)
S7	Advertising, Graphic Design & Printing Services	Eighteen years	Owned by CEO	65	Basic homepage, e-mail and Internet connection using DSL (Level 3- Adopter)

Internet usage will continue to expand. S2 is at capability level 2.

Company S3

The third company (S3) is a women's clothing manufacturer. It is a family owned enterprise. S3 imports the raw materials from France and the United States. The SME employs 33 people and it has two branches to show product samples to clients. S3 uses personal contacts and word of mouth to attract customers. Moreover, phone and fax are used mainly for receiving and placing orders, and to contact customers. S3 is not willing to have an online catalogue because the CEO thinks that this will decrease competitive advantage by passing useful sensitive product information to competitors, who will be able to copy designs and styles. S3 has standalone PCs which have Microsoft applications and an inventory system. The firm outsources its IT services but it is considering hiring skilled IT employees to support their computing systems. S3 is at capability level 1 (i.e. non-adopter).

Company S4

The fourth company (S4) is an architecture and engineering design specialist. It has been operating for four years. The firm achieved 30% growth in 2008. Although S4 provides online shopping service on their website, customers do not use it, primarily because of security concerns. The company has an online catalogue that provides useful information about its product lines. Moreover, the company has open Internet access all the time and it has started introducing online order processing. S5 has an IT department comprised of two full time engineers and does not believe in outsourcing if the Internet is to be used to achieve competitive advantage. S4 uses e-mail extensively to contact overseas suppliers. The firm checks e-mail on a daily basis and internal e-mail is used to transfer data between employees such as electronic forms and images. S4 is at capability level 4.

Company S5

The fifth company (S5) was founded in 2004 and it provides IT Support Services such as computer sales and maintenance. It currently employs 27 people and the firm is considering hiring more employees. Technology staff turnover is high and considerable energy is involved in recruiting and retaining skilled technology workers. Not surprisingly, there is a local area network (LAN) and Internet connection used by all staff. The company has a customer database and a timesheet reporting system. S5 has a marketing website that is updated regularly on a weekly basis. However, there is no plan to offer online selling for computer hardware and software as a result of the economic downturn. The company believes in focusing on improving the quality of current IT services as opposed to introducing new services. S5 is at capability level 3.

Company S6

Company number six (S6) is a service firm that offers IT/IS training and also ICT solutions including software development and website design for local SMEs. S6 is a family-owned firm comprised of ten employees. The company has a PC network and all employees have computers. The systems have been set up and maintained by staff. S6 has a permanent Internet connection using a Digital Subscriber Line (DSL), a static website; both internal and external e-mails are extensively used. In terms of future development, there is recognition of the need to develop an e-business system to host a portal to sell local SME products online. S6 capability is at level 3, but moving towards Level 4.

Company S7

Company number seven (S7) was established by the CEO in 1991 to provide advertising, graphic design and printing services. The owner believes that the market is competitive, with the Internet seen as a means of offering added value to customers. Therefore, S7 recently developed its website for advertising and marketing their services to generate future profits. The firm uses e-mail to contact their suppliers and the company sees this communication channel as a positive way to offer better customer service. Moreover, the company believes that it is important to always remember that customers today expect excellent customer service and will go where they can find it. Indeed, companies lose customers over bad service. S7 has continuous open Internet access and it is used to download clipart images and to access commercial databases. S7 is planning to implement a local area network that enables all departments to communicate with each other to minimise duplication of resources and improve efficiency. S7 capability is at level 3. (Figure 7) presents participants' level of e-commerce and Internet-based technologies adoption.

The Interviews with SME Owners and Manager Revealed Some Important Considerations Related To E-Commerce Adoption and Use. They are Discussed in the Following Section.

Technological Factors that Affect E-commerce Adoption

Perceived Benefits and Impediments of E-commerce Adoption

Firms realised benefits by being able to reach out to customer groups in diverse geographical areas. Moreover, most of the interviewed representatives note that e-commerce adoption can result in easier market access.

Conversely, some interviewees (from S3 and S1) believed that the cost of implementing e-

Figure 7.

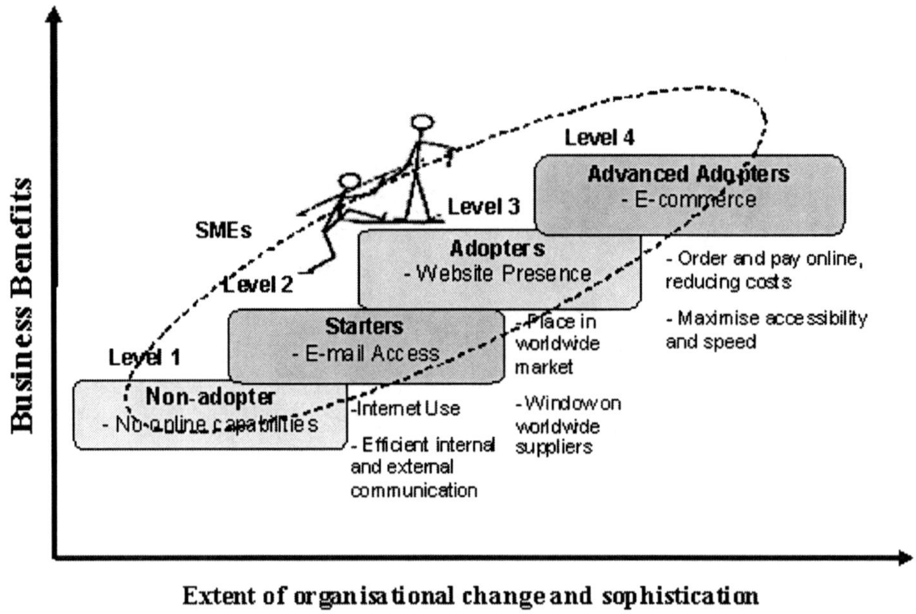

commerce is too high and that the money can be used for other purposes that would generate greater benefits than those derived from e-commerce. Furthermore, most of the interviewees were concerned about cybercrime such as hacking, and they noted that e-commerce is associated with insufficient security safeguards and authentication issues.

Another challenge that was identified was the technical barrier that pertained to issues such as identifying the type of technologies that would match the organisation's business requirements, the types of software, lack of education and knowledge about system requirements. In addition, one SME representative (from S6) observed that if a firm's information system is not aligned with the new technologies adopted (i.e. e-commerce) then this could result in loss of business and added costs. S6 asserted that their firm appointed an external consultant to ensure that e-commerce applications were aligned with the existing computer systems and technologies. This can be a costly endeavour, and may lead the organisation to ongoing costs, which small and medium firms may not be able to afford.

It is noteworthy that, language problems caused by the preferences for Arabic, or unfamiliarity with other languages were found to reduce the maximum perceived benefit to be gained from the Internet. S2 asserts that "using e-commerce and Internet technologies requires a good knowledge in English language as most website address or e-mails are in English". (Table 4) illustrates the benefits and barriers of e-commerce adoption as perceived by the SME interviewees.

Organisational Factors that Affect E-commerce Adoption

Technology Competence

With the exception of S3, all SME representatives confirmed having established some basic online and ICT infrastructures. Company S4 has sophisticated computer networks and also an interactive and transactional website for conducting B2C

Table 4. Perceived benefits and barriers of e-commerce adoption

Perceived benefits of e-commerce	Perceived barriers of e-commerce
E-commerce use will increased business profitability	The cost of e-commerce applications and systems is high and E-commerce requires a substantial investment in training for employees to maintain a multi-skilled workforce
E-commerce is useful to expand market share for existing products/ services	E-commerce is associated with insufficient security safeguards and authentication processes
E-commerce is useful to improve coordination with suppliers and trading partners	There are insufficient individual(s) with 'expert' knowledge of IT and e-commerce technologies in the labour market
E-commerce is useful to improve internal communications and processes	The postal service is reliable to support e-commerce and e-business practices
E-commerce is useful to communicate better with customers	Difficulties in accessing English content websites
E-commerce is useful to increase customer satisfaction	The implementation of e-commerce is incompatible with the firm's IT infrastructure and software and applications

transactions and B2B to attract business partners. S5, S6, and S7 all confirmed having DSL connections, and recognised that this made Internet use and adoption simpler. This evidence supports the view in the literature that organisations that have high levels of IT are more likely to adopt the Internet (Mehrtens *et al.,* 2001). Other SMEs (S1 and S2) used basic IT infrastructures, and mainly consisting of networked computers with direct access to the Internet and various other software applications such as word processing, spread sheets and database.

On the other hand, all interviewees responded very positively when asked about the IT infrastructure in their immediate market. The national telecommunication infrastructure, in particular, was believed to be reliable and effective. However, many interviewees observed that the cost of Internet access in Saudi Arabia was still high compared to other nations, and this may discourage businesses and customers from enjoying the potential benefits of e-commerce.

When asked about the existence of employees with 'expert' knowledge of information technology (IT) and e-commerce technologies within the firm to support future advancement of e-commerce, only interviewees S4, S5 and S6 provided an affirmative answer. Other interviewees believed that their workers were not skilled enough to deal with technical issues such as wired and wireless network setup and that this could stall their business growth. Three companies (S4, S5 and S6) handled IT on their own and had staff members dedicated to IT to support the firm in their e-commerce adoption, without the need to outsource. S2 outsourced IT and computing services.

Management Support

In general, companies that adopt and use e-commerce had greater support from top management and this support was found to be a strong driver in the initial move towards participation, which may begin with using e-mail or developing a website (level 2 or level 3) move towards a higher level of e-commerce adoption (level 4: order and pay online). Although S2 had limited financial resources, senior management asserted that they strived to ensure that e-commerce adoption projects always received the required resources and support.

Firm's Size

As discussed in section 3, in the case of Saudi Arabia, small enterprises are those which employ between 10 and 25 workers whereas medium-sized enterprises employ between 26 and 100 workers. Despite of its small size (10 employees), S6 is in the process of moving towards level 4 (advanced adopter) while S3 is a medium sized firm with 33 employees that is still a non-adopter of e-commerce technologies.

Smaller firms (S1 and S2) were less likely to adopt advanced e-commerce technologies as a result of their limited financial resources and lack of specialist staff (see (Table 1) for Participants' profile).

Firm Industry/Sector

ICT-related companies (S5 and S6) were leaders in e-commerce adoption in which S6 was moving to fully adopt e-commerce (level 4- advanced adopter). They have the required resources for e-commerce adoption and are the most optimistic about its potential in enhancing their performance. Others that were moving up the scale were those operating in the architecture and engineering industries (S4, S7); all seem to greatly influence the decision to participate in e-commerce activities and they are also willing to invest in adopting e-commerce.

Retailers (S2), restaurant and food services (S1), although small in size and with limited resources (financial and IT expertise), nevertheless have a positive attitude towards e-commerce adoption. Moreover, they are willing to use e-commerce in their business activities to contact their suppliers, customers and for the purposes of online marketing. Finally, manufacturers (S3), although large in size (33 employees), lack the scope to make e-commerce appealing. This was reflected by their reticence to undertake advancement in e-commerce as they believe that having a website and online catalogue will pass useful product information to competitors.

The results revealed that, the service-oriented SMEs (S4, S5, S6, and S7) tended to adopt e-commerce far more than their manufacturing counterparts (S3). On the other hand, SMEs in the food industry and retailer (S1 and S2) tended to adopt basic e-commerce technologies such as e-mail and use the Internet.

Environmental Factors that Affect E-commerce Adoption

Consumer and Trading Partner Readiness

Apart from S4, the pressure from suppliers and trading partners to use the Internet had no effect on the decision to adopt e-commerce. S4 believed that the Internet allows for more effective and efficient interactions with suppliers and makes ordering faster and cheaper. Moreover, S4 asserted that "our [overseas] suppliers and trading partners prefer to use the Internet as the only means for getting support, accessing product information, placing orders and for other business activities".

Although, other firms (S1 and S6) use e-commerce to contact their suppliers and business partners, they have not experienced any pressure to adopt this technology. Furthermore, customer pressure does not have a big influence on companies to adopt e-commerce. All companies (adopters and non-adopters) confirmed that customers generally prefer to come in person to have services and products or call for any inquiry instead of sending an e-mail or accessing a website. Importantly, although S4 has online shopping services on their website as part of its strategy to develop its e-business markets; customers tend not use it, primarily because of security concerns. Moreover, S4 highlighted that "a possible reason for the lack of external pressure from customers to adopt e-commerce is that Saudi Arabian consumers prefer shopping in person as a recreation activity, and also customers want to negotiate prices with sellers".

S3 (a non-adopting company) indicated lack of external pressure from customers and suppliers, stating: "We haven't encountered any pressure from our customers or suppliers to use e-mail or to put an online catalogue so that customers would order from there, to make it worthwhile".

Technology Vendor Support

Support from technology vendors seemed to impede the adoption decision of e-commerce in Saudi Arabian SMEs. Most of the interviewees noted that technology vendors do not offer good after-sales support, nor sufficient information to assist in decision making. In addition, they often fail to provide guaranteed delivery dates for products and services. Indeed, the negative effect of technology vendors on e-commerce adoption needs to be resolved in order for e-commerce adoption to succeed. However, S6 note that the get efficient support from technology vendor (IT consultant) to support their move on the Internet.

In fact, the role of technology vendors is an important element in selection and resourcing for an e-commerce project. The greater the availability of external support from technology vendors, the more likely e-commerce technologies will be adopted by SMEs. Most of the interviewed SME representatives note that technology vendors were seen as too expensive, unhelpful and undependable.

Regulation and Government Support

All SMEs identified 'regulative uncertainty and the lack of e-commerce legal framework' as strong barriers to organisations' adoption of e-commerce. Moreover, all SME representatives believed that there is a significant lack of clear regulation and laws that can effectively make e-commerce a trustworthy business platform and, hence in this respect, Saudi Arabia is considered poorly prepared for e-commerce. Moreover, a perceived lack of support from government in terms of high Internet fees, negative experiences with connectivity and lack of common standards discourage SMEs from establishing any initial e-commerce adoption initiatives. Government policies and regulations are important factors that are practical reasons to drive firms to adopt and achieve benefits of e-commerce technologies.

DISCUSSION

Previous studies on innovation adoption and diffusion have rarely been applied to developing countries in the Arab nations. The study aims to determine the factors that influence the extent to which SMEs in Saudi Arabia are inclined towards deploying e-commerce technologies. The results presented in this study indicate that the level of e-commerce implementation has yet to mature amongst the sampled SMEs. Many SMEs possess only standalone internal computer networks, word processing and informational websites and few have progressed further into e-commerce adoption by introducing transactional and interactive websites to facilitate B2C and B2B e-commerce. It is worth mentioning that service-oriented SMEs had the greatest absolute (and relative) number of adopters and were the most advanced in terms of e-commerce adoption.

The chapter has identified that there are substantial barriers to implementing e-commerce, which can affect organisational performance. The lack of IT expertise in the market and the lack of trust towards ICT technology vendors and consultants remain major barriers to e-commerce adoption.

Security issues such as hacking and language barriers were identified as the underlying factors that acted as constraints to the introduction of e-commerce technologies. In fact, none of the interviewees confirmed embracing business-to-business e-commerce. An increased fear and risk of viruses and hackers accessing confidential information and tampering with network messages is underpinned by lack of IT expertise (Ellis, 2008).

Language problems caused by the preferences for Arabic, or unfamiliarity with other languages were found to reduce the maximum perceived benefit to be gained from the Internet. Indeed, more Arabic language websites would encourage firms and customers to adopt e-commerce.

Subsequently, customers were not ready to conduct any online transactions with SMEs because they did not trust the security of electronic transactions. Moreover, payment methods on the Internet, is an additional deterrent for SME's use of Internet technologies in Saudi Arabia.

Implications for Managers, Government Bodies and Policy Makers

To facilitate adoption of e-commerce, laws and regulations need to be put into place to protect vulnerable parties and foster trust. Stronger legal frameworks will also help facilitate online activities and reassure organisations when conducting e-commerce. Supportive regulations can be established in three ways (1) developing supportive e-commerce legislation on key issues such as digital signatures and intellectual property (2) regulating the Internet to make it a trustworthy business platform by establishing privacy and consumer protection laws and dealing with fraud and credit card misuse and (3) providing incentives for using e-commerce such as offering technical support, training, and funding for e-commerce use.

Government support to develop e-commerce and the existence of legal frameworks are critical factors in fostering e-commerce and have an important role to overcome associated challenges. Government strategies should thus focus on knowledge building, regulation setting, conducting informational campaigns to increase awareness and provide financial subsidies.

The authors suggest that the government needs to provide specialised courses; seminars and workshops aimed at helping SMEs understand the prerequisites for launching their online presence. Moreover, the Council of Saudi Chambers of Commerce and Industry (CSCCI) should have a role in providing technical support and training for professional manpower to meet the labour requirements of SMEs as well as the role of the Saudi commercial banks in providing loans to such enterprises to support their development (Pillai, 2006). Indeed, this will protect SMEs against any adverse developments, and will provide a supportive business environment.

The study findings also suggest that the government must increase public awareness for both people and businesses about the potential benefits of IT and Internet technologies such as e-commerce. A lack of awareness of the use and potential benefits of Internet technologies and IT can hinder the growth of e-commerce. Some SMEs were only aware of limited e-commerce applications such as email and browsing websites.

Senior management support has emerged as a key element for the successful adoption and implementation of e-commerce. In terms of security issues, organisations must develop sophisticated security measures that provide secure communications on the Internet such as secure socket layers (SSL) so that credit card numbers cannot be accessed by hackers. Moreover, organisations must organise open lectures on television and radio stations to assure people that they are free of threats to privacy and security.

Interacting via the Internet is found to enhance relationships with suppliers. This includes accessing product information, product support and online ordering. In fact, using e-commerce and Internet technologies to manage suppliers and business partners will enable SMEs to decrease operational costs and an increase in flexibility of supply as well as more effective and efficient relationships with suppliers.

Limitations and Scope for Further Research

Firstly, it is worth noting that, the current study adopted the case study approach to give an in-depth qualitative analysis and provide a general picture of e-commerce readiness and use among Saudi SMEs. However, the current study suffers from the problems of qualitative work and gives very limited scope for generalisation of facts due to the limited number of cases.

Second, although the study was conducted in the city of Jeddah - the most cosmopolitan city in the western region of Saudi Arabia, opportunities for substantial cultural variations may exist. Moreover, information about e-commerce adoption in other parts of the country especially in rural areas may vary. In fact, comparative research could target other regions and cities to gain comparative national results.

Based on the analysis of e-commerce adoption and implementation among SMEs in Saudi Arabia, some useful suggestions have been offered and could serve as starting points for further research directed at identifying more factors such as organizational learning capabilities, strategic posture, receptivity to change and receptivity to market pressure that can influence e-commerce adoption at differing levels of SME's e-readiness and adoption level. Moreover, it would be advisable to combine qualitative and quantitative approaches, as this would potentially overcome the generalisation problems mentioned above.

Finally, the study findings will thus provide points of reference for policy makers or government organisations, practitioners and officials from the private sector engaged in promoting SME e-commerce adoption. Other nations, especially those in the Gulf States and Middle East who share some common characteristics can also learn from the cases reported in this study to better understand the potential for e-commerce, assess their readiness and formulate appropriate strategies for e-commerce adoption and use.

REFERENCES

Al-But'hie, I. M., & Eben Saleh, M. A. (2002). Urban and industrial development planning as an approach for Saudi Arabia: the case study of Jubail and Yanbu. *Habitat International*, *26*(1), 1–20. doi:10.1016/S0197-3975(01)00026-1

Al-Farsy, F. (1986). *Saudi Arabia: A case study in development*. London: Keegan Paul International Limited.

Al-Gahtani, S. S., & Hubona, G., S., & Wang, J. (2007). Information technology (IT) in Saudi Arabia: Culture and the acceptance and use of IT. *Information & Management*, *44*, 681–691. doi:10.1016/j.im.2007.09.002

Al-Ghamdi, S. M. (2008). *International Business Practices in Saudi Arabia: Cultural effect*. King Fahd University of Petroleum & Minerals. Retrieved October 18, 2009, from http://faculty.kfupm.edu.sa/MGM/sghamdi/Dr_Salem_Al-Ghamdi/home.html

Al-Hawari, M. AL–Yamani, H., & Izwawa, B. (2008 February). Small Businesses' Decision to have a Website: Saudi Arabia Case Study. In *Proceedings of World Academy of Science, Engineering and Technology*, 27.

Al-Qirim, N. (2005). An Empirical Investigation of an e-commerce Adoption-Capability Model in Small Businesses in New Zealand. *Electronic Markets*, *15*(4), 418–437. doi:10.1080/10196780500303136

Al-Qirim, N. (2007). The adoption of eCommerce communications and applications technologies in small businesses in New Zealand. *Electronic Commerce Research and Applications*, *6*(4), 462–473. doi:10.1016/j.elerap.2007.02.012

Al-Qirim, N. (2007). A research trilogy into e-commerce adoption in small businesses in New Zealand. *Electronic Markets*, *17*(4), 263–285. doi:10.1080/10196780701635872

Al-Sudairy, M. A., & Tang, N. K. H. (2000). Information technology in Saudi Arabia's supermarket chains. *International Journal of Retail & Distribution Management*, *28*(8), 341–356. doi:10.1108/09590550010337292

Al-Yahya, K. (2009). Power-Influence in Decision Making, Competence Utilization, and Organizational Culture in Public Organizations: The Arab World in Comparative. *Journal of Public Administration: Research and Theory*, *19*(2), 385–407. doi:10.1093/jopart/mun005

AME Info - The ultimate Middle East business resource. (2005). *E-Commerce reaches new highs in Saudi Arabia*. Retrieved November 11, 2008, from http://www.ameinfo.com/61990.html

Andam, Z. R. (2003). E-commerce and e-business. *Asia-Pacific e-primers*. Retrieved May 11, 2008, from http://www.apdip.net/publications/iespprimers/eprimer-ecom.pdf

Beatty, R. C., Shim, J. P., & Jones, M. C. (2001). Factors influencing corporate web site adoption: a time-based assessment. *Information & Management*, *38*, 337–354. doi:10.1016/S0378-7206(00)00064-1

Bjerke, B., & Al-Meer, A. R. (1993). Culture's consequences: management in Saudi Arabia. *Leadership and Organization Development Journal*, *14*(2), 30–35. doi:10.1108/01437739310032700

Bruque, S., & Moyanob, J. (2007). Organisational determinants of information technology adoption and implementation in SMEs: The case of family and cooperative firms. *Technovation*, *27*, 241–253. doi:10.1016/j.technovation.2006.12.003

Central Department of Statistics. (2005). *General Population Census and Housing*. Retrieved June 25, 2009, from http://www.cds.gov.sa/english/enewsectiondetail.aspx?id=63

Chong, S. (2008). Success in electronic commerce implementation: A cross-country study of small and medium-sized enterprises. *Journal of Enterprise Information Management*, *21*(5), 468–492. doi:10.1108/17410390810904247

CITC - Communications and Information Technology Commission. (2007). *Internet in Saudi Arabia*. Retrieved October 14, 2009, from http://www.internet.gov.sa/learn-the-web/guides/internet-in-saudi-arabia

CITC - Communications and Information Technology Commission. (2008). *Internet Usage in the Kingdom of Saudi Arabia - Business establishments*. Retrieved November 4, 2008, from http://www.citc.gov.sa/

Damanpour, F. (1991). Organisational Innovation: A Meta-Analysis of Effects of Determinants and Moderators. *Academy of Management Journal*, *34*(3), 555–590. doi:10.2307/256406

Davis, F., Bangozzi, R., & Warshaw, P. (1989). User Acceptance of Computer Technology: A Comparison of Two Theoretical Models. *Journal of Management science, 35*(8), 982-4.

Depietro, R., Wiarda, E., & Fleischer, M. (1990). The Context for Change: Organisation, Technology, and Environment . In Tornatzky, L. G., & Fleischer, M. (Eds.), *The Processes of Technological Innovation* (pp. 151–175). Lexington, MA: Lexington Books.

Ellis, S. (2008). The status of e-commerce in New Zealand. *Otago Marketing Review*, 1. University of Otago, New Zealand. Retrieved February 1, 2009 from, http://marketing.otago.ac.nz/OMR/img/Samuel%20Ellis%20June%202008.pdf

Emarketer. (2007). *European E-Commerce on Pace to Reach €323 Billion in 2011*. Retrieved February 1, 2009, from http://www.emarketer.com/Article.aspx?id=1005231

European Commission. (2004). *SME definitions*. Retrieved May 14, 2009, from http://europa.eu.int/comm/enterprise/enterprise_policy/sme_definition/index_en.htm.

Hofstede, G. (1980). *Culture's consequences: International differences in work-related values*. Beverly Hills, CA: Sage.

Hofstede, G. (1991). *Cultures and Organizations: Software of the Mind: Intercultural Cooperation and its Importance for Survival*. Cambridge, UK: McGraw-Hill.

Iacovou, C. L., Benbasat, I., & Dexter, A. S. (1995). Electronic data interchange and small organizations: Adoption and Impact of Technology. *Management Information Systems Quarterly*, *19*(4), 465–485. doi:10.2307/249629

Igabria, M., Zinatelli, N., Cragg, P., & Cavaye, A. L. M. (1997). Personal computing acceptance factors in small firms: a structural equation model. *Management Information Systems Quarterly*, *21*, 279–305. doi:10.2307/249498

Johnston, S., & Acquaah-Gaisie, G. (2001). Development via the Net in Oceania. In *Proceedings of the 3rd world conference of the Global IT Management*, Dallas, USA.

Kartiwi, M. (2006). Case Studies of E-Commerce Adoption in Indonesian SMEs: The Evaluation of Strategic Use. *Australasian Journal of Information Systems, 14*(11).

Kowtha, N. R., & Choon, T. M. I. (2001). Determinants of website development: a study of electronic commerce in Singapore. *Information & Management*, *39*(3), 227–242. doi:10.1016/S0378-7206(01)00092-1

Kuan, K. K. Y., & Chau, P. Y. K. (2001). A perception-based model for EDI adoption in small businesses using a technology-organisation-environment framework. *Information & Management*, *38*(8), 507–521. doi:10.1016/S0378-7206(01)00073-8

Kurnia, S. (2008). Exploring e-Commerce Readiness in China: The Case of the Grocery Industry. In *Proceedings of the 41st Hawaii International Conference on System Sciences,* January 7-10, 2008.

Licker, P., & Motts, N. (2000). Extending the benefits of e-commerce in Africa: Exploratory phase. In *Proceedings, First Annual Global Information Technology Management World Conference*, Memphis, 11-13 June (pp. 115-118).

Love, P. E. D., Irani, Z., Li, H., Cheng, E. W. L., & Tse, R. Y. C. (2001). An empirical analysis of the barriers to implementing e-commerce in small-medium sized construction contractors in the state of Victoria, Australia. *Construction Innovation*, *1*, 31–41.

MacGregor, R., & Vrazalic, L. (2004). *Electronic Commerce Adoption in Small to Medium Enterprises (SMEs), A Comparative study of SMEs in Wollongong (Australia) and Karlstad (Sweden)*. Australia: University of Wollongong.

MacGregor, R. C., Bunker, D. J., & Waugh, P. (1998). Electronic Commerce and Small/Medium Enterprises (SMEs) in Australia: An Electronic Data Interchange (EDI) Pilot Study. In *Proceedings of the 11th International Bled Electronic Commerce Conference*, Slovenia, June

Martin, L., & Matlay, H. (2001). Blanket approaches to promoting ICT in small firms: some lessons from the DTI ladder adoption model in the UK. *Internet Research: Electronic Networking Applications and Policy*, *11*(5), 399–410. doi:10.1108/EUM0000000006118

Martin, P. (2009). *The Recession and Migration: Alternative Scenarios*. Working Papers. International Migration Institute. James Martin 21st Century School. University of Oxford, UK. Retrieved October 17, 2009, from http://www.unitar.org

Martyr, J. W. (1985). *Cultural discontinuities and the transfer of management philosophies and practices With particular reference to Great Britain, and the Arab countries of the Arabian Gulf and Saudi Arabia.* Unpublished PhD Thesis. Uxbridge, UK: Brunel University.

Matlay, H., & Addis, M. (2003). Adoption of ICT and e-commerce in small businesses: an HEI-based consultancy perspective. *Journal of Small Business and Enterprise Development, 10*(3), 321–335. doi:10.1108/14626000310489790

Mcdonagh, P., & Prothero, A. (2000). Euroclicking and the Irish SME: prepared for e-commerce and the single currency. *Irish Marketing Review, 13*(1), 21–33.

Mehrtens, J., Cragg, P., & Mills, A. (2001). A model of Internet adoption by SMEs. *Information & Management, 39*, 165–176. doi:10.1016/S0378-7206(01)00086-6

Ministry of Economy and Planning. (2008). *Saudi Arabia: Long-Term Strategy 2025.* Retrieved June 24, 2009, from http://www.mep.gov.sa/

Molla, A. (2005). E-Readiness and Successful E-Commerce Diffusion in Developing Countries: Results from a Cluster Analysis . In Kamel, S. (Ed.), *Electronic Business in Developing Countries: Opportunities and Challenges* (pp. 214–233). Hershey, PA, USA: Idea Group Publishing.

Molla, A., & Licker, P. S. (2005). Ecommerce adoption in developing countries: a model and instrument. *Information & Management, 42*, 877–899. doi:10.1016/j.im.2004.09.002

Mulpuru, S., Johnson, C., McGowan, B., & Wright, S. (2008). US eCommerce Forecast: 2008 To 2012. B2C eCommerce Expected To Top $300B In Five Years. *Forrester Research, Inc.* Retrieved February 1, 2009, from http://www.forrester.com/Research/Document/Excerpt/0,7211,41592,00.html

Nachira, F., Chiozza, E., Ihonen, H., Manzoni, M., & Cunningham, F. (2002). *Towards a network of digital business ecosystems fostering the local development.* Retrieved May 26, 2008, from http://www.digital-ecosystems.org/doc/discussionpaper.pdf

Nour, S. S. O. M. (2002). *ICT Opportunities and Challenges for Development in the Arab World.* WIDER Discussion Paper 2002/83. United Nations University/World Institute for Development Economics Research. Retrieved October 10, 2009, from http://www.wider.unu.edu/publications/publications.htm

Otsuki, M. (2002). *SMEs Supporting Systems in Saudi Arabia.* Retrieved February 1, 2009, from http://www.ssic2008.com/assets/files/

Parker, M. C., & Castleman, T. (2006). A preliminary Meta-Analysis of SME –eBusiness Journal Publications: Current Trends and Future Research Opportunities Moving Beyond Adoption Factor Studies. Retrieved May, 1 2008, From, http://www.collecter2006.unisa.edu.au/

Pettigrew, A. M. (1985). Contextualist research and the study of organizational change processes. In Mumford, E. (Ed.), *Research Methods in Information Systems* (pp. 53–78). Amsterdam: North-Holland.

Pillai, P. K. (2006). Saudi Arabia: 8th Five-year Plan (2005-2009). *Saudi Commerce and Economic Review.* Retrieved February. 1, 2009 from, http://zawya.com/story.cfm/

PriceWaterhouseCoopers. (1999, September 24). SME E-commerce Study (Final Report). *Asia Pacific Economic Cooperation (APEC).*

Radwan, I. (2001). *Small and medium enterprise development: a vision for action in Saudi Arabia.* Paper prepared for the Economic Vision Conference Riyadh, Saudi Arabia. Retrieved January 28, 2007, from http://www.planning.gov.sa/

Rama Rao, T. P. (2001). E-Commerce and Digital Divide: Impact on Consumers. In *The Asia-Pacific: New Dimensions of Consumer Protection in the Era of Globalisation*, Goa, India. Retrieved October 3, 2008 from, http://www.iimahd.ernet.in/egov/documents

Rao, D. N. (2006). *Saudi Arabia: The Emerging Economic Tiger of the Middle East*. Retrieved October 17, 2009 from, http://ssrn.com/abstract=935080

Rogers, E. M. (1995). *Diffusion of innovations* (4th ed.). New York: The Free Press.

Rosenthal, R. (2008). Saudi Arabia Vertical Markets 2008-2012 Forecast. *IDC Middle East and Africa*. Retrieved June 14, 2009, from http://www.idc-cema.com

Sajini, I. I. (2004). Effects of WTO on Small & Medium Enterprises. *Arab News*. Retrieved April 4, 2008, from http://www.arabnews.com/?page=1&section=0&article=38268&d=19&m=1&y=2004

Sanders, N. R. (2007). An empirical study of the impact of e-business technologies on organizational collaboration and performance. *Journal of Operations Management*, *25*, 1332–1347. doi:10.1016/j.jom.2007.01.008

Scupola, A. (2003). The Adoption of Internet Commerce by SMEs in the South of Italy: An Environmental, Technological and Organizational Perspective. *Journal of Global Information Technology Management*, *1*(6), 52–71.

Sergeant, J. (2000). *Presentation by the e-envoy of UK Online*. British Academy of Management Conference. Birmingham, UK: Aston University Business School.

Sparling, L., Cater-Steel, A., & Toleman, M. (2007). SME adoption of e-Commerce in the Central Okanagan region of Canada. In *18th Australasian Conference on Information Systems (ACIS 2007): The 3 Rs: Research, Relevance and Rigour - Coming of Age*, Toowoomba, Australia.

Tan, J., Tyler, K., & Manica, A. (2007). Business-to – business adoption of ecommerce in China. *Information & Management*, *44*, 3321–3351. doi:10.1016/j.im.2007.04.001

Tarafdar, M., & Vaidya, S. D. (2004). Adoption of electronic commerce by organizations in India: Strategic and environmental imperatives. *Electronic Journal of Information Systems in Developing Countries*, *17*(2), 1–25.

Technology integration division. (2007). *Saudi Arabia in perspective: an orientation guide*. Defense Language Institute Foreign Language Center. Retrieved October 16, 2009, from ttp://fieldsupport.dliflc.edu/products/cip/saudi/

Thong, J. (1999). An integrated model of information systems adoption in small business. *Journal of Management Information Systems*, *15*(4), 187–214.

Tigre, P. B. (2003). Brazil in the age of electronic commerce. *The Information Society*, *19*(1), 33–43. doi:10.1080/01972240309476

Tornatzky, L. G., & Fleischer, M. (1990). *The Processes of Technological Innovation*. Lexington, MA: Lexington Books.

Tornatzky, L. G., & Klein, K. J. (1982). Innovation characteristics and innovation adoption–implementation: a meta analysis of findings. *IEEE Transactions on Engineering Management*, *29*(11), 28–45.

UNCTAD. (2004). *E-commerce and Development Report (2004)*. Retrieved October 18, 2009, from http://www.unctad.org/

Venkatesh, V., & Davis, F. D. (2000). A theoretical extension of the technology acceptance model: four longitudinal field studies. *Management Science*, *46*(2), 186–204. doi:10.1287/mnsc.46.2.186.11926

Venkatesh, V., Morris, M. G., Davis, G. B., & Davis, F. D. (2003). User acceptance of information technology: towards a unified view. *Management Information Systems Quarterly*, *27*(3), 425–478.

World economic forum. (2009). *Global Information Technology Report 2008-2009*. Retrieved June 12, 2008, from http://www.weforum.org

World Factbook, C. I. A. (2009). *Saudi Arabia*. Retrieved May 25, 2009, from https://www.cia.gov/library/publications/the-world-factbook/geos/sa.html

World Factbook, C. I. A. (2009a). *Saudi Arabia Economy 2009*. Retrieved October 14, 2009, from http://www.theodora.com/wfbcurrent/saudi_arabia/saudi_arabia_economy.html

World Trade Organization (WTO). (2005). *WTO General Council successfully adopts Saudi Arabia's terms of Accession*. WTO press releases. Retrieved November 5, 2008, from http://www.wto.org/english/news_e/pres05_e/pr420_e.htm

Xu, S., Zhu, K., & Gibbs, J. (2004). Global technology, local adoption: a cross-country investigation of Internet adoption by companies in the United States and China. *Electronic Markets*, *14*(1), 13–24. doi:10.1080/1019678042000175261

Yap, C. S., Soh, C. P. P., & Raman, K. S. (1992). Information systems success factors in small businesses. *Omega . International Journal of Management Science*, *20*(5), 597–609.

Yin, R. K. (1984). *Case Study Research: Design and Methods*. Newbury Park, CA: Sage Publications.

Zhu, K., Kraemer, K., & Xu, S. (2002). A cross-country study of e-business adoption using the technology-organisation-environment framework. In *Proceedings of International Conference on Information Systems*, Barcelona, Spain.

Zhu, K., Kraemer, K., & Xu, S. (2003). Electronic business adoption by European firms: a cross-country assessment of the facilitators and inhibitors. *European Journal of Information Systems*, *12*(4), 251–268. doi:10.1057/palgrave.ejis.3000475

Zhu, K., & Kraemer, K. L. (2005). Post-Adoption Variations in Usage and Value of E-Business by Organizations: Cross-Country Evidence from the Retail Industry. *Information Systems Research*, *16*(1), 61–84. doi:10.1287/isre.1050.0045

ENDNOTES

1. 1USD$ = 3.75 Saudi Arabian Riyals (SAR)
2. It should be noted that the adoption refers to the decision of any individual or organization to make use of an innovation, whereas diffusion refers to the process by which an innovation is communicated through certain channel over time (Rogers, 1995).

Chapter 20
ICT Adoption in SME in an Arab GCC Country: Oman

Rafi Ashrafi
Sultan Qaboos University, Oman

Muhammad Murtaza
Industrial Management Technology & Contracting LLC, Oman

ABSTRACT

It has been widely recognized that Small and Medium size Enterprises(SMEs) not only play an important role in the economy of a country, but are crucial to the country's economic stability. This article reviews UN and World Economic Forum ICT indicators for assessing the adoption of Information and Communication Technologies (ICT) in Gulf Cooperation Countries (GCC). Also, it presents the results of an exploratory study carried out to learn about the adoption of ICT in SMEs in Oman. The study investigates infrastructure, software used, driver for ICT investment, perceptions about business benefits of ICT and outsourcing trends of SMEs. The study provides an insight on the barriers for the adoption of ICT. Data on these aspects of ICT was collected from 51 SMEs through a survey questionnaire. The results of the study show that only a small number of SMEs in Oman are aware of the benefits of ICT adoption. The main driving forces for ICT investment are to provide better and faster customer service and to stay ahead of the competition. A majority of surveyed SMEs have reported a positive performance and other benefits by utilizing ICT in their businesses. A number of SMEs outsource most of their ICT activities. Lack of internal capabilities, high cost of ICT and lack of information about suitable ICT solutions and implementation were some of the major barriers in adopting ICT. These findings are consistent with other studies. There is a need for more focus and concerted efforts on increasing awareness among SMEs on the benefits of ICT adoption. The results of the study recognize the need for more training facilities in ICT for SMEs, measures to provide ICT products and services at an affordable cost, availability of free professional advice and/or consulting services at reasonable cost to SMEs. Our findings can help policy makers focusing on ICT adoption by SMEs. Also, the findings of this research will provide a foundation for future research and will help policy makers in understanding the current state of affairs of the usage and impact of ICT on SMEs in Oman and other GCC countries.

DOI: 10.4018/978-1-61692-016-6.ch020

INTRODUCTION

Today organizations of all types are utilizing Information and Communication Technologies (ICT) around the globe, not only for cutting costs and improving efficiency, but also for providing better customer service. Governments, too, around the world are adopting ICT to provide better services to their citizens. The adoption of ICT by organizations requires a business environment encouraging open competition, trust and security, interoperability and standardization and the availability of finance for ICT (UNCTAD, 2004).

Most of the large and international organizations in GCC countries have effective computer systems to efficiently conduct business. A number of large organizations have spent huge amounts of money on installing computer systems to support their business processes. However, the situation has not been the same with SMEs - similar to other parts of the world for various reasons (Shiels et al., 2003, Fink and Disterer, 2006; Parker and Castelman, 2007). SME's do not have monetary and human resources to acquire, maintain and utilize sophisticated ICTs.

Sultanate of Oman, with an area of 309,500 square kilometers and a population density of 9.3 per square kilometer, like other Arab GCC (Gulf Cooperation Council) countries is an emerging economy with a young population that heavily depends on its most abundant natural resource; crude oil and gas. Oman's capital, Muscat, has an area of 3,900 square kilometers and a density of 214 per square kilometer, which is the most densely populated area among governorates and regions in the country. It is also the most developed city in terms of infrastructure and services. Along with Saudi Arabia, Oman is the only Arab GCC country with number of nationals significantly higher than expatriates. Oman has a population of three million with two million Omanis and one million expatriates. In Muscat, however, the population of 0.84 million is almost equally divided between Omanis and expatriates.

The government is the biggest employer in Oman and has the highest rate of Omanization (employment of Omani nationals). This is followed by the financial institutions, especially the banking sector. The ICT infrastructure in Oman has seen significant growth, encouraging many organizations to adopt technology. Through government legislation, Omanization of various jobs has been forced, after 2000, in order to tackle, back then, relatively high unemployment rate among Omani nationals. This included low paid jobs and many business types within the retail sector. The government is also, through various programs, encouraging entrepreneurship (Ministry of National Economy, 2008).

The government of Oman has taken various measures to diversify the economy for sustainable development of the country and one of the major steps is to transform Oman into a digital society. The adoption of ICT will have significant positive consequences on SMEs and consequently on the economy of Oman. There is a dearth of data and research about the size and contribution of SMEs towards Oman's economy. Therefore, through this research, we would like to shed light on the effects and usages of ICT on SMEs in Oman and their current and future perceptions towards ICT. This study is based on the Net Impact Canada 2006 (Illuminas, 2006). The findings of this research will provide a foundation for future researchers and will help policy makers in understanding the current state of affairs of the usage and impact of ICT on SMEs in Oman. We collected the data through a survey of fifty one randomly selected SMEs in Muscat, the Capital of Oman. We will also take a comparative look at other GCC countries and how they are progressing at an international level in regards to ICT adoption.

Definitions: It is important to note that the term "ICT" in context of this research refers to the wide range of information and communication technologies. These technologies include products and services such as desktop computers, laptops, handheld devices, wired or wireless intranet, business productivity software such as text editor and spreadsheet, enterprise software, data storage and security, network security and others.

SME: There is no official definition of SMEs available in Oman. Different countries, based on different factors such as size of economy, define SME as suitable. In this research, we have adopted the following definitions of SMEs, which we find to be suitable for a country like Oman. Businesses with less than ten employees as a Micro Enterprise, between ten and fifty as Small Enterprises, and between fifty to two hundred and fifty employees as Medium sized enterprises. This criterion is consistent with other similar studies (Kapurubandara et al., 2006) and was used to identify and qualify SMEs for the purpose of this research.

In the next section we review selected literature on the areas related to the topic, followed by diffusion of ICT in GCC countries and Oman, objectives of the study and research design of the study. In the later sections we present findings of our study with conclusions, limitations and directions for future research. An earlier version of this study was presented at 2008 International Conference on Information Resource Management (Conf-IRM) in Canada and was published in the Electronic Journal Information Systems Evaluation (Ashrafi and Murtaza, 2008).

ICT ADOPTION IN SMES LITERATURE REVIEW

Importance of SMEs: It has been widely recognized that small and medium enterprises (SMEs) not only play an important role in the economy of a country, but are crucial to the country's economic stability. In New Zealand SMEs make up more than 99% of all businesses and account for about 60% of employment. In the USA more than half of all the employment comes from firms with fewer than 500 employees (Baldwin et al., 2001). In the UK, SMEs employ 67% of the workforce (Lange et al., 2000). In most EU member states SMEs make up over 99% of enterprises, 67% of jobs and 59% of GDP. In most countries SMEs generate a substantial share of GDP and a key source of new jobs as well as a breeding ground for entrepreneurship and new business ideas. That is why most countries have begun paying special attention to SMEs. The United States of America, UK, Japan, Australia, New Zealand, Canada and other developed, as well as developing, countries are making policies to facilitate the growth of SMEs. Realizing the importance of ICT New Zealand spend about 10% of its GDP on ICT, making it the top ranking country in the world (Clarke, 2004). Estimates from the World Bank indicate that SMEs have contributed over 55 percent of GDP in Organization for Economic Co-operation and Development (OECD) countries and between 60 to 70 percent of GDP in middle-income and low income countries, generating 60 to 70 percent employment (Oman Economic Review, 2008). The above facts show that SMEs play a very important role in the growth of economy of a country and GCC countries are no exception.

ICT Diffusion in SMEs: In a recent study about European service SMEs, it was stated that about 25% of them are capable of receiving orders online in comparison to 45% of large organizations. In general, around 26% of service SMEs depend on e-business to a substantial extent compared to 40% of large organizations (eBusiness in Europe, 2008). There are a number of studies that discuss adoption of Internet and e-business in SMEs in developed countries (Doczi, 2000; Stroeken, 2001; Caldeira and Ward, 2002; Morikawa, 2002; Gregor et al., 2004; Love, et al., 2004; Lucchetti and Sterlacchini, 2004; Koellinger, 2006; Schubert and Leimstoll, 2006 and 2007).

Premkumar (2003), in a study of 207 organizations, investigated six factors that impact the adoption of computer-mediated communication technologies in small organizations. These factors were identified as perceived usefulness, compatibility, top management support, cost, competitive advantage, and finally the size. The results of the research revealed that top management support, competitive advantage, and size are significant factors for the adoption of computer-mediated communication technologies. Bruque and Moyano (2007) have used a qualitative approach to investigate the opinions of SMEs managers and entrepreneurs to identify the factors behind the intensity and speed for adopting information technology in these organizations. Their findings indicated that internal factors like systems used for the rotation of personnel, the socialization of the workers, the implementation of information technology and quality systems, and professionalization are adopting factors. On the other hand, inhibiting factors were identified like the modification of the organization's power structures and hierarchy, and the lack of qualified personnel.

Riemenschneider et al. (2003) combining both the Theory of Planned Behavior (TPB) and Technology of Accepted Model (TAM), identified that the driving force for website adoption is the improved social contact with the stakeholders online. Grandon and Pearson (2004) examined the strategic value and adoption factors of electronic commerce for SMEs in the Midwest region of the US by top managers. Proposing a model based on previous studies, factors like operational support, managerial productivity, strategic decision aids were identified as determinants of the perceived strategic value of e-commerce. In addition, organizational readiness, external pressure, perceived ease of use, and perceived usefulness were identified as determinant factors for e-commerce adoption in SMEs. The findings identified a significant relationship between the two streams. In other words, top level managers who perceived e-commerce as adding strategic value to their organization have a positive attitude toward adopting it.

Governments around the globe recognize the importance of adoption of ICT by SMEs and they have created special groups to study various aspects of ICT adoption in SMEs. Despite the importance of ICT and emphasis by various governments to encourage SMEs to adopt ICT, it has been reported that SMEs have been slow in adopting ICT for various reasons (Smallbone et al., 2001; Dawn et al., 2002, Lawson et al., 2003; Houghton and Winklhofer, 2004). We wanted to find out reasons for the apparently slow adoption of ICT in Oman.

Barriers to ICT Adoption: Large organizations have enough resources to adopt ICT while, on the other hand, SMEs have limited financial and human resources to adopt ICT. Duan et al. (2002) identified lack of ICT skills and knowledge in SMEs as one of the major challenges faced by all European countries, particularly in the UK, Poland and Portugal, in their study. Houghton and Winklhofer (2004) have reported a slow response of SMEs relating to adoption of ICT. Shiels et al. (2003) found that characteristics of the firm and industry sector are contributory factors to the adoption and exploitation of ICTs by SMEs. Kapurubandara et al. (2006) have categorized internal and external barriers that impede adoption of ICT by SMEs in a developing country. The internal barriers include owner-manager characteristics, firm characteristics, cost and return on investment, and external barriers include: infrastructural, social, cultural, political, legal and regulatory.

ICT Diffusionin Developing Countries: There are very few studies about ICT adoption in developing countries (Temtime et al., 2003; Kapurubandara et al., 2006; Mutula et al., 2006; Ssewanyana et al., 2007; Yeh et al., 2007). Lal (2007) investigating adoption of ICT in Nigerian SMEs, found that one of the major factors inhibiting ICT diffusion and intensive utilization is poor physical infrastructure. In developing countries some of the ICT adoption challenges include legal and regulatory issues, weak ICT strategies, lack of research and design, excessive reliance on foreign technology and ongoing weaknesses in ICT implementation (Dutta et al., 2003).

Benefits of ICT Adoption:Antlova (2009) identified that ICT can help SMEs to enter new markets, supply new products and services, in-

(Table 1). Human Capital – GCC countries (Source: UN E-Government Survey, 2008)

Country	Adult Literacy	Gross Enrolment	Education Index
Oman	81.4	67.052	0.7659
Kuwait	93.3	74.870	0.8714
Saudi Arabia	82.9	75.966	0.8056
UAE	88.7	59.895	0.7908
Qatar	89.0	77.692	0.8521
Bahrain	86.5	86.091	0.8640

crease its added value, change business processes, increase performance and productivity of the organization, employ new business channels, and in providing rapid response to competitors activities.

ICT DIFFUSION IN ARAB AND GULF COOPERATION COUNCIL (GCC) COUNTRIES

While the Arab region is home to five percent of the world's population, it represents less than one percent of world's Internet users (Sabbagh, 2003). The ICT implementation in the Arab world is not going smoothly. The major problems negatively affecting the adoption of ICT in most Arab countries can be attributed to the lack of basic infrastructure and to problems related to their government's policies and regulations (Hamade, 2009).

A recent market survey shows that Middle East will be spending approximately $50 billion in 2009 in IT, with the Gulf region spending about $12 billion. ICT spending in the Middle East in 2008 was almost $50 billion, the highest in recent years, and up from around $30 billion in 2007 (MENAFN, 2009). The average ICT spending in the region is 4% of the GDP, compared to an average of 8% in developed countries. Also, PC penetration is below the world average. The region spent less than 0.5% on research, development and innovation in comparison to developed countries, who average 2.5% of their GDP. The highest growth rate of internet usage access over the past six years is an encouraging sign in the Middle East (Patel, 2007). Most of the ICT activities in these countries, like in other developing countries, are based on government initiatives and policies. Since there is lack of available data about ICT usage in GCC countries, we have extracted data from the UN e-Government Readiness Report and World Economic Forum Reports. The UN e-Government Readiness Report (UN, 2008) provides an overview of the current state of the various elements (e.g. Human capital, PC index, Internet users, Broadband, Infrastructure, Web Measure Index, E-readiness and E-participation indices) that contribute to the ICT adoption in countries around the globe. World Economic Forum (2009) provides ICT indicators that measure the Network Readiness Index, Environment Index, Readiness Index, and ICT Usage Index. Following paragraphs provide a summary of these indicators in GCC countries.

Human Capital: The human capital index shows the adult literacy rate which consists of a combination of primary, secondary and tertiary gross enrolment ratios. (Table 1) shows that the adult literacy index and education index for GCC countries are quite high. These countries are taking various measures to increase literacy and, in particular, ICT education and training.

Telecommunication Infrastructure: The telecommunication infrastructure index is composed of five primary indices to a country's infrastructure capacity as they relate to the delivery of e-government services. These are:

Table 2. Telecommunication Infrastructure in GCC countries (Source: UN E-Government Survey, 2008)

Country	Internet per 100 Users	PC per 100 Users	Cellular Subscribers per 100 Users	Main Telephone Lines per 100 Users	Broadband per 100 Users
Oman	12.22	5.06	69.59	10.65	0.58
Qatar	34.55	18.64	109.60	27.21	5.57
Saudi Arabia	18.66	12.82	78.05	15.68	0.87
Kuwait	29.53	22.33	88.57	18.99	0.93
UAE	36.69	23.35	118.51	28.11	5.17
Bahrain	21.30	17.62	121.71	26.18	5.23

- Internet users/100 persons
- PCs/per 100 persons
- Main telephone lines/100 persons
- Cellular telephones/100
- Broad banding/100 persons.

Each index represents 20 percent of the overall telecommunication infrastructure index. (Table 2) shows the data for telecommunication infrastructure, including: PC penetration, internet users and main line telephone users rates, which are much lower than world averages. However, there has been increase in cellular subscribers in the region.

Web Assessment: (Table 3) provides data on web assessment. The web measurement assessment looks at how governments are providing e-government policies, applications and tools to meet the growing needs of their citizens for more e-information, e-services and e-tools. It measures the online presence of national websites, along with those of the ministries of health, education, welfare, labor and finance of each member state. UAE was ranked 12th (with 0.7157 index) among the top 35 countries of the world and has the highest Web Index in the region. Other GCC countries have low rankings in Web Index.

E-government Readiness: The average of e-government index continues to increase as more countries invest resources in developing websites that are informative. Most countries have e-information on policies, laws and an archive section on their portals/websites. The gap between e-information, e-consultation and e-decision-making is still wide between developing and developed countries. UAE ranked 32 out of the top 35 counties of the world in e-Government Readiness.

E-Participation Index: E-participation Index is based on questions that were grouped under three categories: e-information, e-consultation and e-decision-making. Each country was assessed on a scale of 0 to 4.35. The index was constructed by standardizing the scores. Table 5 shows that

Table 3. Web Measurement Assessment (Source: UN E-Government Survey, 2008)

Country	Web Index	Rank
Oman	0.4849	52
Kuwait	0.4147	n/a
Saudi Arabia	0.4649	60
UAE	0.7157	12
Qatar	0.3913	n/a
Bahrain	0.5201	44

Table 4. E-Government Readiness Data 2008 (Source: UN E-Government Survey, 2008)

Country	Web Measure Index		Infrastructure Index		Human Capital index		E-Government Readiness Index	
	Index	Rank	Index	Rank	Index	Rank	Index	Rank
Oman	0.4849	52	0.1559	n/a	0.7659	n/a	0.4691	84
Kuwait	0.4147	n/a	0.2777	n/a	0.8714	n/a	0.5202	57
Saudi Arabia	0.4649	60	0.2113	n/a	0.8056	n/a	0.4935	70
UAE	0.7157	12	0.3813	n/a	0.7908	n/a	0.6301	32
Qatar	0.3913	n/a	0.3549	n/a	0.8521	n/a	0.5314	53
Bahrain	0.5201	44	0.3346	n/a	0.8640	n/a	0.5723	42

Bahrain and Saudi Arabia are ranked 36th and 38th in the E-participation Index.

World Economic Forum and INSEAD's (2009) key indicators of ICT adoption in a country are reflected by their Networked Readiness Index (NRI) that measure the existence of an ICT-conducive environment in a country. The NRI is divided into three dimensions: the Environment Component Sub-index, the Readiness Component Sub-index, and the Usage Component Sub-index. These indicators included data from 134 worldwide countries (from both developed and developing worlds) in which these countries are ranked and scored. (Tables 6 to 9) summarize theses indicators for GCC countries.

The above data show that there are marked variations among the GCC countries in their efforts to adopt ICT. As suggested by Sabbagh (2003) Arab countries can build on each other's experiences to develop and implement their individual ICT agendas and integrate regional ICT markets. By working together to position themselves on a common competitive platform they can improve their combined standing in the world ICT market. These tables show that GCC countries have made large strides in advancing the development of their ICT sector, yet they have a long way to go before they reach developed world averages.

Use of ICT in Oman

Realizing the importance of ICT for the economic development of the country, Oman's government has placed a great emphasis on creating a digital economy as a key driver for the sustainable growth of the country. Oman is heavily investing in ICT as one of the building blocks to diversify the economy. In September 2003 Oman established Knowledge Oasis Muscat (KOM), a technology park as one of the initiatives taken to help develop a knowledge-driven economy, attract investment, and to serve as an incubator for local startup

Table 5. E-Participation Index (Source: UN E-Government Survey, 2008)

Country	E-Participation index	Ranking
Oman	0.2045	60
Kuwait	0.0682	116
Saudi Arabia	0.3182	38
UAE	0.2955	41
Qatar	001818	71
Bahrain	0.3409	36

Table 6. The Networked Readiness Index (Source: World Economic Forum and INSEAD, 2009)

Country	2008-2009		2007-2008	
	Rank	Score	Rank	Score
Oman	50	4.08	53	3.97
UAE	27	4.76	29	4.55
Qatar	29	4.68	32	4.42
KSA	40	4.28	48	4.07
Bahrain	37	4.38	45	4.13
Kuwait	57	3.98	52	4.01

(Table 6) shows that UAE has the highest rank among the GCC countries, ranking 29th, followed by Qatar placing 32nd in the Network Readiness Index.

Table 7. Environment component sub index for 2008-2009 (Source: World Economic Forum and INSEAD, 2009)

Country	Market Environment		Political and Regulatory Environment		Infrastructure Environment		Overall	
	Rank	Score	Rank	Score	Rank	Score	Rank	Score
Oman	42	4.31	44	4.52	78	2.69	51	3.84
UAE	24	4.74	39	4.62	40	3.52	32	4.29
Qatar	26	4.72	33	4.74	35	3.76	29	4.41
KSA	38	4.35	42	4.55	44	3.44	38	4.11
Bahrain	27	4.71	49	4.37	49	3.28	37	4.12
Kuwait	34	4.44	58	4.19	45	3.44	44	4.02

(Table 7) shows that Qatar leads the GCC countries in the overall environment index, ranked 29th, followed by UAE at 32.

Table 8. Readiness Component Sub index for 2008-2009(Source: World Economic Forum and INSEAD, 2009)

Country	Individual readiness		Business readiness		Government readiness		Overall	
	rank	score	rank	score	rank	score	rank	score
Oman	49	5.54	48	4.60	39	4.47	42	4.87
UAE	32	5.89	33	4.94	9	5.33	25	5.39
Qatar	20	6.05	30	5.01	22	4.99	26	5.35
KSA	79	5.06	28	5.04	36	4.55	41	4.88
Bahrain	35	5.70	62	4.32	28	4.75	38	4.93
Kuwait	62	5.37	64	4.30	80	3.80	66	4.49

(Table 8) shows that UAE and Qatar lead the GCC countries in Readiness Sub index by placing respectively 25th and 26th.

Table 9. Usage Component Sub index for 2008-2009(Source: World Economic Forum and INSEAD, 2009)

Country	Individual usage		Business usage		Government usage		Overall	
	rank	score	rank	Score	rank	score	rank	score
Oman	70	1.97	66	4.44	45	4.21	55	3.54
UAE	31	3.57	27	5.18	16	5.06	25	4.60
Qatar	38	3.26	41	4.86	25	4.73	31	4.28
KSA	53	2.38	39	4.87	42	4.30	44	3.85
Bahrain	44	2.90	45	4.77	29	4.58	35	4.08
Kuwait	51	2.41	54	4.63	97	3.23	65	3.42

(Table 9) shows that UAE leads the GCC countries ranking 25th followed by Qatar at 31 in the Usage Component Sub index.

companies in the ICT sector (Knowledge Oasis Muscat, 2008). Also, in 2006 the government of Oman created an Information Technology Authority (ITA) for developing a national IT strategy, help facilitating and implementing an ICT infrastructure and overseeing the implementation of Oman's digital strategy (Information Technology Authority, 2008). The government has encouraged private sector to open universities and technical colleges in order to increase ICT literacy in the country. Government of Oman has established a Sanad program to encourage entrepreneurship and develop SMEs by providing them necessary finance, guidance and training. From the private sector, a number of organizations are contributing in the growth of SMEs. For example, Shell has established a $10 million Intilaaqah Enterprise Fund to provide capital and on-going support for SMEs in Oman. Microsoft has signed a Memorandum of understanding with Ministry of Education to provide training in schools. Also, there are a number of other initiatives in place in order to transform Oman into a digital society.

According to an estimate of HSBC Middle East Bank, there are only 15,000 to 20,000 SMEs in Oman generating only 10-20% employment (Oman Economic Review, 2008). These estimates show that there is a significant potential for the SMEs in Oman to grow in terms of contribution to GDP and employment, and to be competitive at regional and international levels. This study discusses the impact of ICT as it relates to financial performance and productivity improvement of SMEs in Oman.

OBJECTIVES OF THE STUDY

Realizing the importance of SMEs for the economy of Oman and the impact of ICT on improving the performance of SMEs, data was collected on various aspects of ICT usage and utilization. The investigation took place during January and April 2008 and is the first step towards an exploratory study on learning more about the use and impact of ICT on SMEs in Oman. Through this study we aim to find answers to the following questions:

- What is the level of usage of ICT in terms of ICT infrastructure, internet connection, IT staff and types of website used in SMEs?
- What Enterprise software SMEs used?
- What are the drivers for ICT Investment?
- What percentage of budget is allocated to ICT?
- What are long term business goals for investment in ICT?
- How is competition among SMEs?
- What are the barriers towards to ICT Investment?
- What approach SMEs use to differentiate their business from competitors?

- What are realities and perceptions about business benefits of ICT implementation?
- What are out-sourcing trends?
- What internal capabilities and processes SMEs have in place for managing ICT?

RESEARCH DESIGN

We performed the following tasks to conduct the research and determine the usages and effects of information and communication technologies in SMEs in Oman:

1. A questionnaire was prepared based on the Net Impact Canada 2006 study (Illumines, 2006) to determine the usages, effects and perceptions of Omani SMEs towards ICT. Specifically, to know about the present technological infrastructure, the reasons behind ICT investment, the restrictions and barriers for adoption of ICT, and the implementation methods and benefits of ICT investments. These aspects essentially formed the basis of our research.
2. The questionnaire was distributed to 51 SMEs in Oman that utilized some sort of ICT. The questionnaires were filled by the founder, general manager or accounts manager because of their ability and understanding of the issues investigated in the questionnaire. In very few cases, more than one individual representing the enterprise filled out the questionnaire - this actually ensured preciseness.
3. Based on the collected data through questionnaires, simple statistics were carried and logical inferences were made to determine the general usages and effects of ICT on SMEs in Oman. The general conditions and perceptions of the business people thriving in the Omani market were also uncovered with regards to information and communication technologies. It helped us understand some of the major barriers and stimuli for ICT investment in these firms.

The Sample Population

It is important to note that no data on the total number of SMEs in Oman is available. However, the number of large organizations in Oman, with more than 250 employees (using the definition above), are a handful. Most of them are either government companies or corporations in the petroleum (oil) or banking sectors. This means that the vast majority of enterprises in Oman are SMEs.

Bouma and Ling (2004) had mentioned that a sample size of 30 or more subjects is considered as significant for statistical analysis. We surveyed 51 randomly selected enterprises in Muscat, which is the capital city, the commercial hub and most developed technological infrastructure wise in Oman. These businesses were of different type, including retail stores, trading companies and special service providers and we believe that these organizations represent a general composition of SME's in Oman.

Our main purpose was to capture new trends and mindsets of people towards ICT in this majority group, especially now that the government has started to invest in ICT through improvement of telecom infrastructure and market, introduction of electronic services and mass education programs. It would be interesting to compare these results with the results of a similar study after a few years of such an initiative from the government.

RESEARCH FINDINGS

In this section we present the findings of our research based on the simple statistical analysis of the collected data through a survey of 51 SMEs in the Muscat governorate in Oman in 2008. Based on our definition of SMEs, 41% can be classified as Micro Enterprises (less than 10 employees),

Figure 1. Size of SMEs in Terms of Employees (workforce)

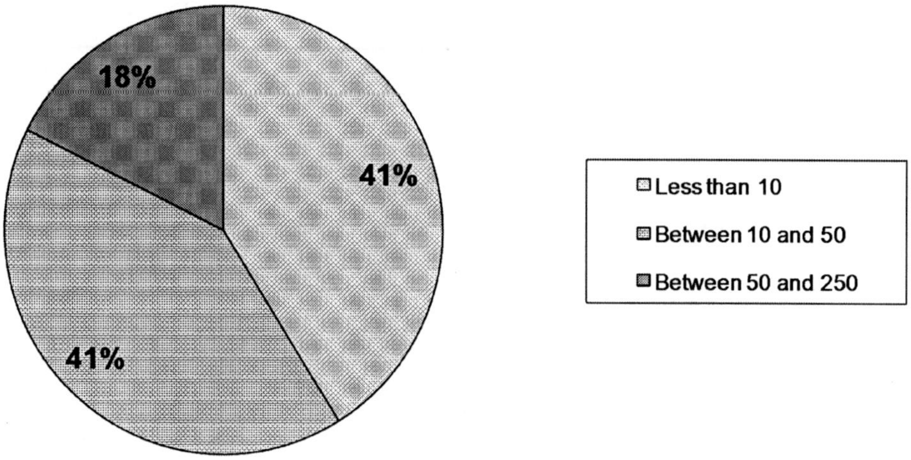

41% as Small Enterprises (between ten and fifty employees) and 18% Medium sized Enterprises (between fifty and two hundred fifty employees) as shown in (Figure 1).

ICT Usage

We investigated IT infrastructure, Internet connection type, IT staff, usage of enterprise software, and type of website used as a measure for ICT usage.

ICT Infrastructure

It seems that the ICT infrastructure in most of the large organizations in Oman is not very different from large organizations elsewhere. As opposed to the ICT infrastructure of large and international organizations in Oman, which include networking hardware and software, network and data security solutions and enterprise software solutions, the situation in most SMEs in Oman was found to be little different from SMEs in developed countries but very similar to SMEs in the GCC countries.

Analysis of the collected data (Figure 2) reveals that desktop, laptop or handheld computers are universally used by 100% of the SMEs surveyed. Business productivity software, such as Microsoft Word, Excel and PowerPoint were used in more than four fifths (82%) of the surveyed firms. About 67% of the firms use enterprise software such as CRM, Inventory Management, E-Commerce or ERP. Wired computer network solutions such as servers, routers and firewall were utilized in 45% of the SMEs. Data storage and security solutions (such as file servers, storage area network or web-based storage) were used by 25% of the surveyed firms, and wireless networking technologies (such as access points and wireless routers) and network security solutions by only 14% of the organizations surveyed.

This shows that ICT usage within SMEs in Oman is relatively high in common technologies (such as desktop, laptop, productivity software etc), but limited in the more sophisticated technologies such as wireless, data storage and network security solutions. The pattern seems to be very similar to SMEs in Canada (Illuminas, 2006).

Internet Connection Type

The type of internet connection in organizations largely indicates the required bandwidth and frequency or purpose of usage. In Oman, the SMEs have shown no reluctance in subscribing to high-speed broadband internet connection. This might be because of the relatively lower costs

Figure 2. ICT Infrastructure

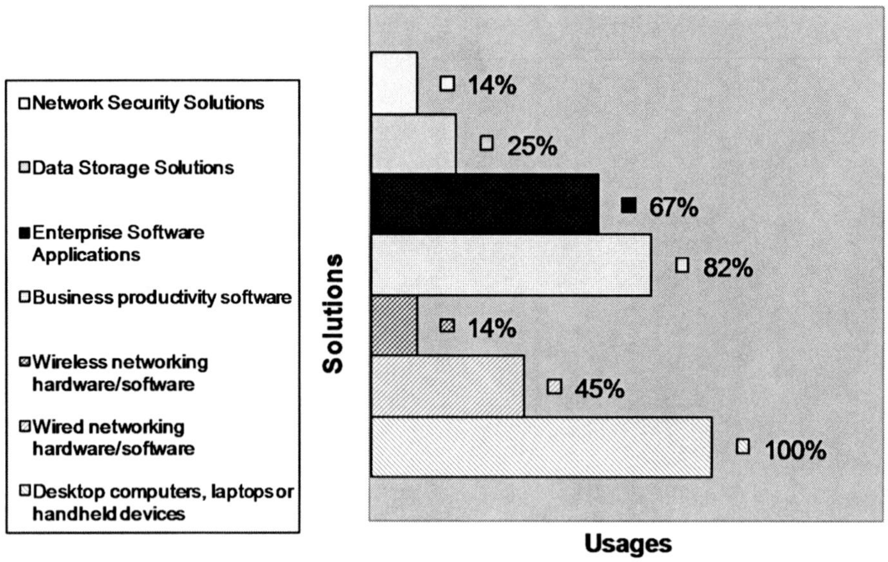

and higher speeds as compared to the dial-up, nevertheless, businesses heavily used internet as indicated by the surveyed enterprises. (Figure 3) shows that 49% of the respondents use high speed broadband (ISDN, ADSL, DSL), 35% use dial up connection, 2% use Satellite and 16% have no internet connection.

IT Staff

One may assume that small and medium sized enterprises often lack the supporting workforce needed, such as IT staff, for the quality and quantity of the required support; the expertise of such staff are too little and basic. However some do have a special IT department with multiple support-

Figure 3. Type of Internet Connection

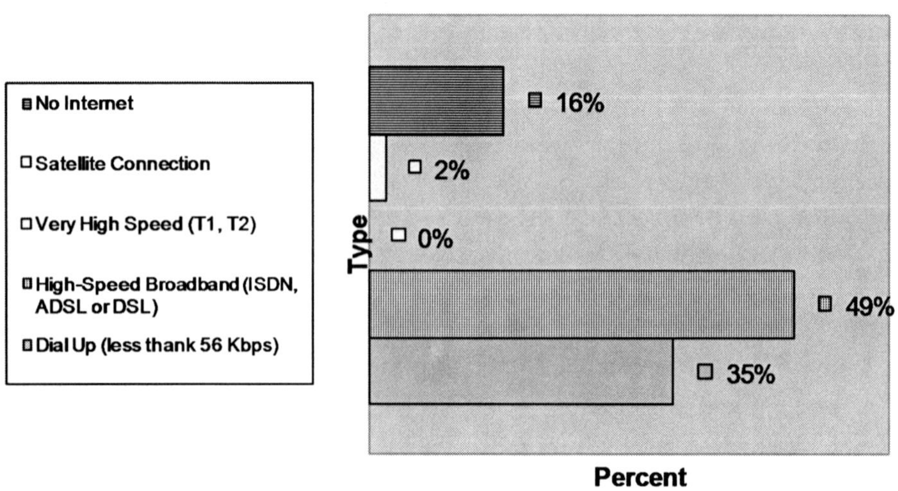

Figure 4. IT Staff

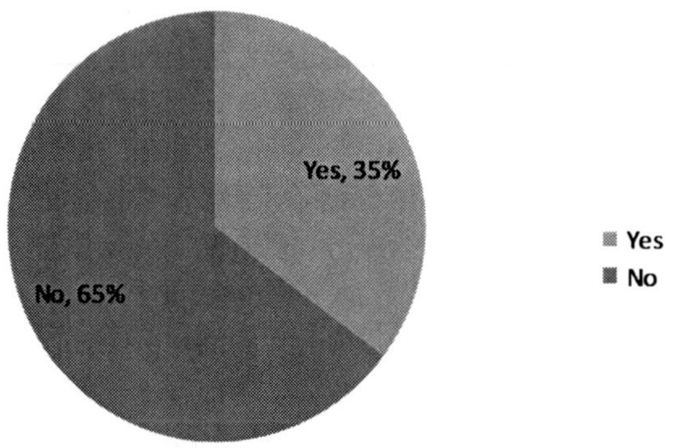

ing staff. The decisive factors that determine the existence of such staff in SMEs around the world are the size of the firm and more importantly the relative complexity of the adapted ICT solutions. The same is the case with SMEs in Oman as around 65% of the surveyed firms do not have full-time IT staff (compared to 63% SMEs in Canada), and 35% of the firms have IT/IS departments with full-time IT staff as shown in (Figure 4).

Usage of Enterprise Software

Investment in ICT infrastructure enables businesses to take advantage of the large number of different technologies available in the market. No matter how small the business and how basic the infrastructure, businesses always look to automate and computerize the essential business functions to save costs and time and to eliminate the need for support staff. Almost 84% of the surveyed firms use finance and accounting enterprise software such as Tally and Peachtree. It was found that even some of the smallest family run businesses used such software. Inventory management software is being used by 69% of the firms and 31% of the enterprises use customer relationship management (CRM) software as illustrated by (Figure 5).

It was observed that organizations that invested in enterprise software are of medium size, in terms of the size of workforce or annual turnover within the SME category, or they are micro enterprises with high inventory turnover. For example, one small retail business run by a single person (owner) used enterprise software for automating accounting, inventory and customer related business processes. (Figure 5) shows that a majority of SMEs in Oman are utilizing basic Enterprise software such as finance/accounting and inventory management in their businesses.

Figure 5. Use of Enterprise Software

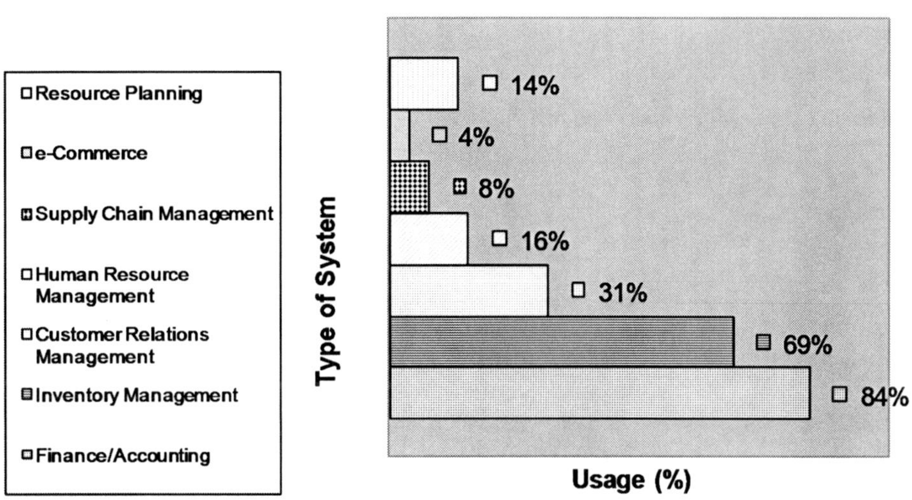

Figure 6. Types of Website

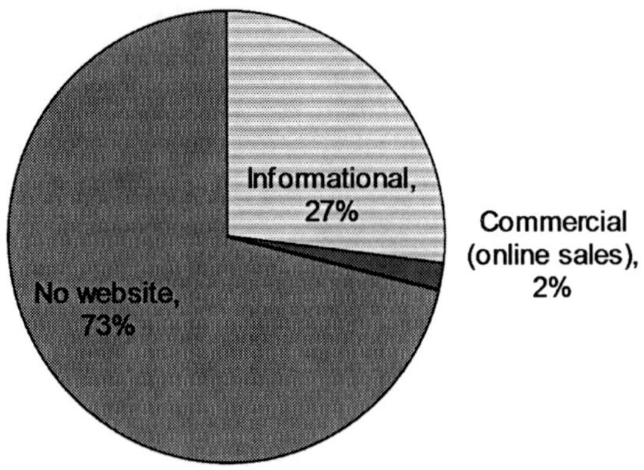

Types of Website Used

Unlike SMEs in developed countries, the SMEs in Oman have not managed to utilize and use commercial websites. (Figure 6) shows that only 2% of the firms have commercial websites which helps them reach new customers. As for informational websites, 27% of the surveyed enterprises run websites which simply introduce the business and publish their contact information. About 73% of the businesses had no website, the main reason was lack of internal staff and high maintenance costs in the long term.

The data on IT infrastructure, Internet connection type, IT staff, usage of enterprise software and types of website used show that penetration of key technologies within Omani SMEs is reasonably moderate.

Investments in ICT

Many of the decision makers in small and medium firms are not always aware of relevant ICT that could revolutionize their business. This in itself is a barrier to ICT investment. As for those enterprises that have already invested and are willing to continue, what really encourages them to do so? And what is the proportion of their investment? Also, what is the nature and true reason behind their investments? We have used amount of budget dedicated to ICT, drivers for ICT Investment, number of competitors, long term ICT investment goals and organization's strategy for competitive advantage as key elements to learn about reasons for ICT investment.

IT Budget

(Figure 7) shows that 70% of the SMEs assign less than 10% of their annual budget to ICT investment, 2% of the firms invest between 10% and 20%, and only 8% of the surveyed firms assign greater than 40% of their budgets to ICT. These results are logical as the size and resources of small and medium businesses around the world are restricted. Because of this, enhancement and development of business processes is slow and gradual.

ICT Investment Drivers Regardless of the relative proportion of budget invested in ICT certain stimuli exist that encourage and push deci-

Figure 7. Proportion of Budget Assigned to ICT

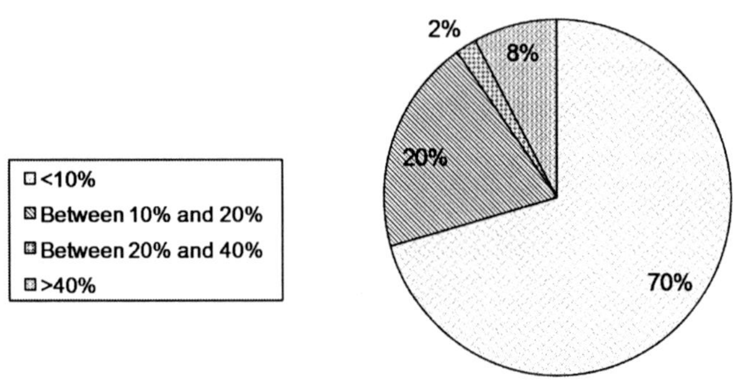

Figure 8. ICT Investment Drivers

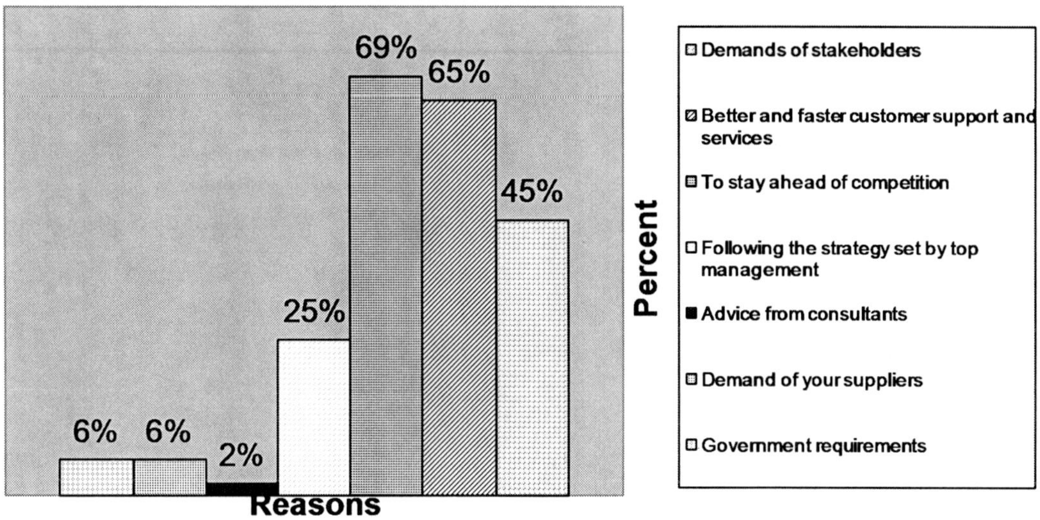

sion makers in SMEs to invest in ICT. The main driving forces for ICT Investment are to provide better and faster customer service (65%), and to stay ahead of competition (69%). Then, demands of stakeholders (45%) and following the strategy set by top management (25%) follow. (Figure 8) shows stimuli for ICT investments in SMEs.

Number of Competitors

Most of the business decisions are based on the competition in the market. (Figure 9) shows that 51% of the enterprises (as compared to 26% enterprises in Canada) have more than twenty direct competitors. About 16% of SMEs have between ten and nineteen competitors, 15% between five to nine competitors and 14% have between one to four competitors. This shows that there is reasonably strong competition among SMEs in Oman, and perhaps that is one of the main reason that SMEs would like to be more competitive by adopting ICT.

Figure 9. Number of Direct Competitors

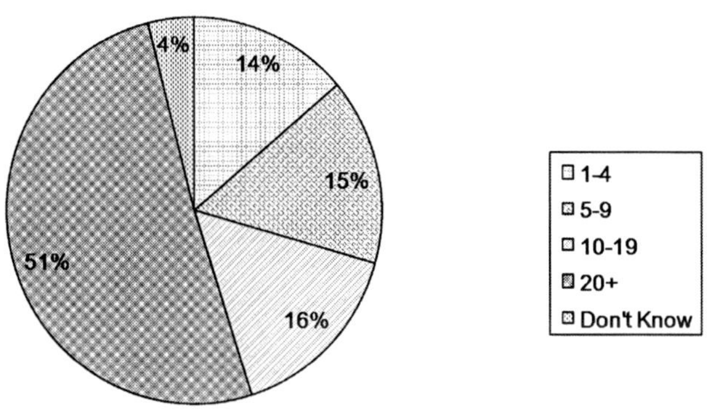

Figure 10. Long term plans

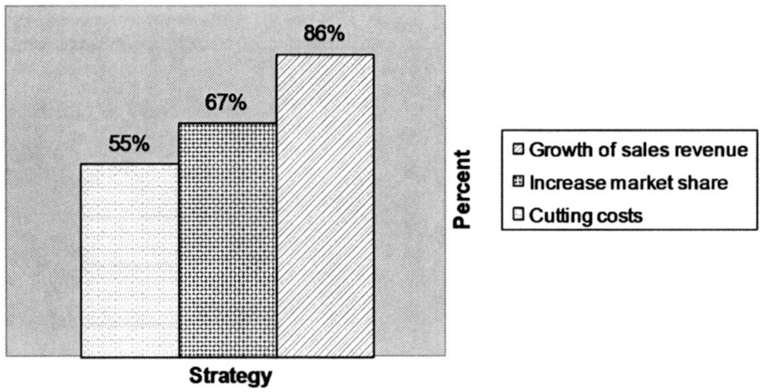

Long Term Goals for ICT Investment

Most of the surveyed firms' long-term plan with regards to their ICT investment was to increase their market share, grow their sales revenue and cut costs and expenses. About 86% of the firms expect to increase sales revenue, 67% expect to increase their market share and about 55% expect to cut costs as shown in (Figure 10).

Approaches to Achieve Competitive Differentiation

A common way of achieving business goals is to differentiate one's business from the competition. The surveyed SMEs have chosen the approach of providing the highest quality products and services (80%) to their customers as the principal method for differentiating as well as establishing long-term relationships with customers (47%), as illustrated in (Figure 11).

The above results show that Omani SMEs have strong competition and are devoting a reasonable

Figure 11. Approaches to Achieve Competitive Advantage

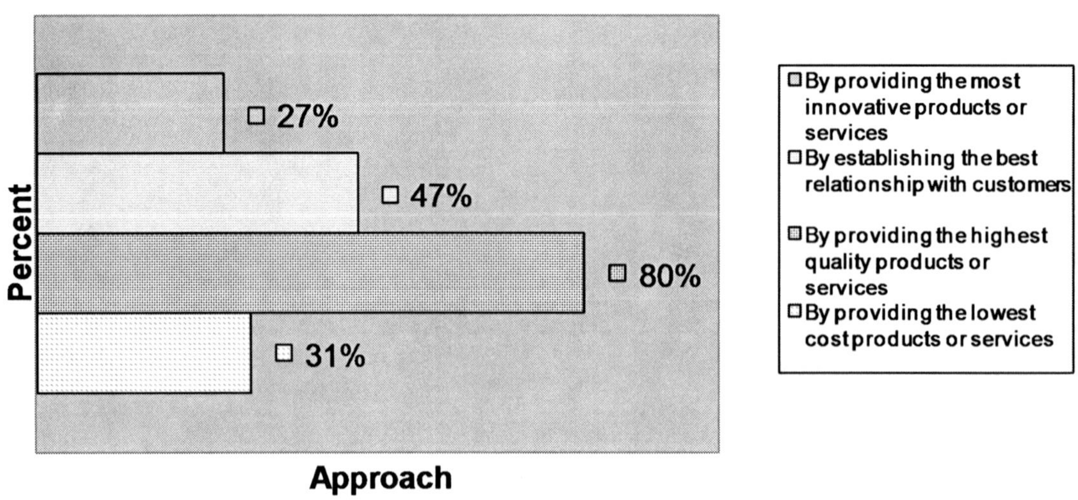

Figure 12. Barriers to ICT Investment

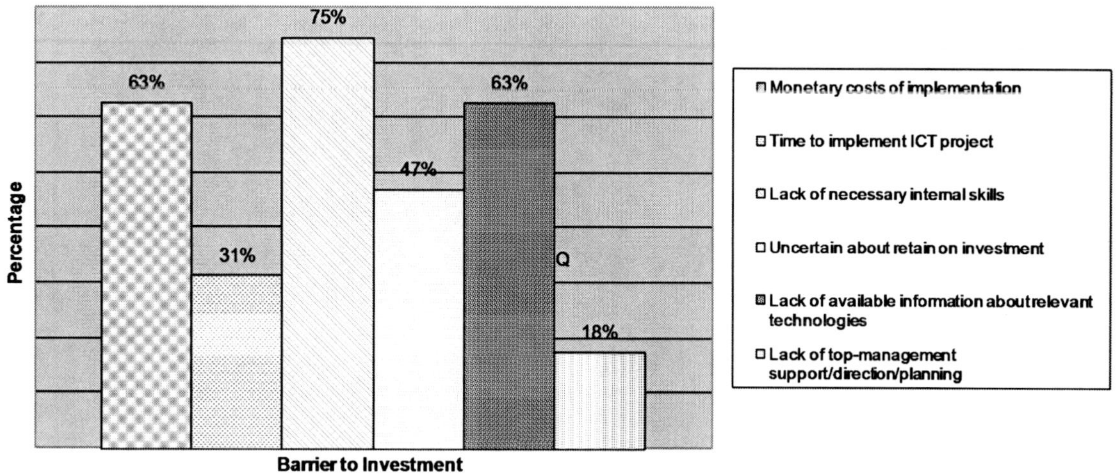

amount, considering their size and business type, of their budget to ICT in order to provide better and faster customer service. Also to realize benefits of ICT investment, SMEs expect to increase sales revenue and market share as well to reduce costs. Most of the SMEs aim to provide highest quality products and services to their customers as well as establishing long term relationships with customers.

Barriers to ICT Investment

While SMEs in Oman are clearly aware of ICT and its benefits, there exist certain restrictions and barriers to ICT investment. (Figure 12) show that 75% of the firms feel that a lack of necessary internal skills is a major barrier. This is consistent with other studies as SMEs do not have enough human resources. There has been a recent increase in technological colleges and the general investment by the Omani government in the ICT industry to overcome shortage of IT staff. About 63% feel that the monetary costs of implementation are too high. The reasons could be high cost of ICT solutions or shortage of available funds to SMEs. Almost 63% of the decision-makers within the surveyed firms feel that there is not enough information available at their disposal about relevant and effective technologies. This shows that there is a need for free advice and relevant information for SMEs. And 31% feel they simply have no time to implement the projects. About 47% of the firms are uncertain about retaining their ICT investment and 18% of the managers feel there is not enough support from the top-management in the firms. Other barriers identified include: government regulations and requirements (6%), and bad experiences in the past (8%). A few of the firms also complained about lack of infrastructure in certain areas in the country. One business specifically complained about the unavailability of internet access in some of the areas far away from Muscat, the capital of Oman. (Figure 12) shows some of the main barriers to ICT adoption of SMEs in Oman.

Realization of Business Performance Improvements

We solicited opinions about the actual and expected benefits of ICT investment in improving the business in a series of questions.

Figure 13. Impact of ICT Investment to Reach Beyond Their Area

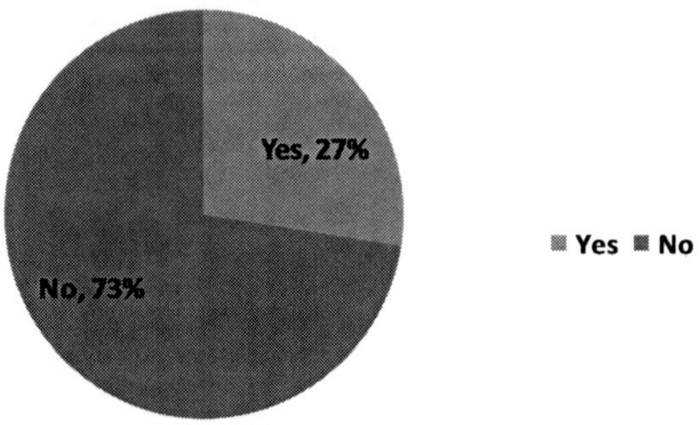

Figure 14. ICT investment impact on cutting costs

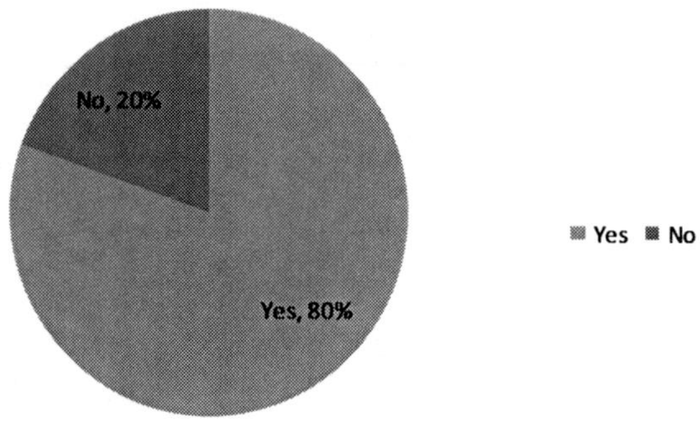

Actual Business Performance Improvements

Actual impact of ICT investment to reach beyond their area: We asked the respondents if their ICT investment helped reach customers beyond their physical geographical area. Only 27% of the respondents said yes, while the remaining 73% do not seem to have reached beyond their area as shown in (Figure 13):

However, this is obvious as the (Figure 6) shows that 73% of the respondents had no website whatsoever.

Actual impact of ICT investment in cutting costs: We asked the respondents if their ICT investment resulted in cutting costs, 80% of respondents said ICT investment has resulted in cutting costs, where as 20% did not receive benefits of cutting costs as shown in (Figure 14):

Actual impact of ICT investment on revenue: We asked the respondents if their ICT investment resulted in growth and increase in revenue, 53% of respondents said ICT investment has increased their revenue; where as 47% did not receive notice any growth in revenue as shown in (Figure 15):

Actual impact of ICT investment on customers: We asked the respondents if their ICT investment helped build better relationships with customers through providing better and faster services, 57% of respondents believed it did, where as 43% believed otherwise as shown in (Figure 16):

Expected Business Performance Improvement

Expected impact of ICT investment to reach beyond their area: We asked the respondents if they expected their ICT investment to help them

Figure 15. ICT Investment Impact on Revenue

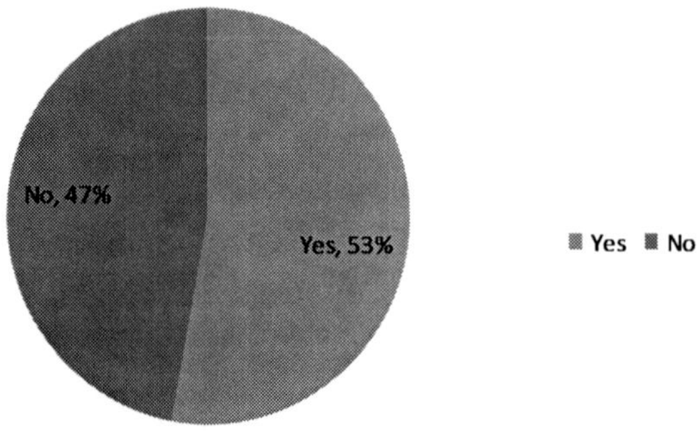

Figure 16. ICT Investment Impact on Customer Relationship

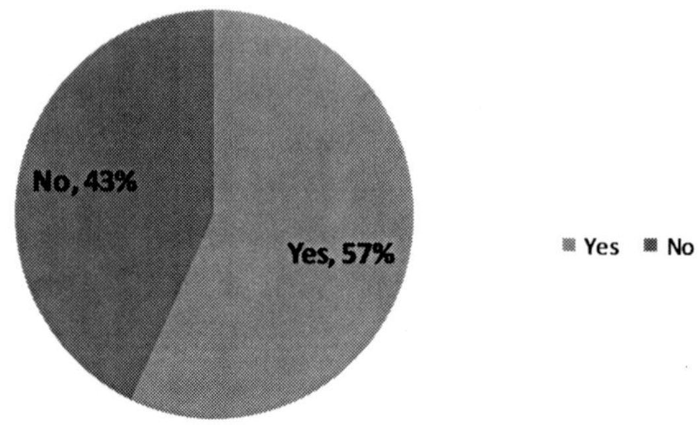

Figure 17. Expected Impact of ICT Investment to Reach Beyond Their Area

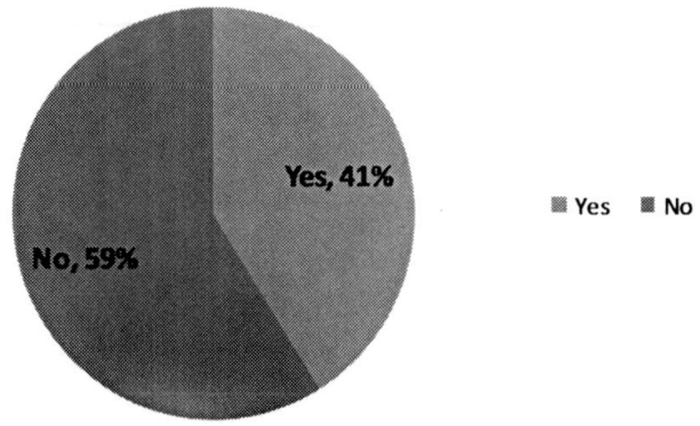

reach customers beyond their physical geographical area in the future. As (Figure 17) shows, 41% said yes, which indicates optimistic expectations as only 27% had actually realized such benefits. As for the remaining 59%, they do not expect to reach beyond their geographical area and this demands additional work and activity from the government.

Expected impact of ICT investment in cutting costs: We asked the respondents if they expected their ICT investment to help reduce costs in the future, 84% of respondents responded positively, where as 16% did not expect any reduction costs as shown in (Figure 18):

Figure 18. Expected impact of ICT on cutting costs

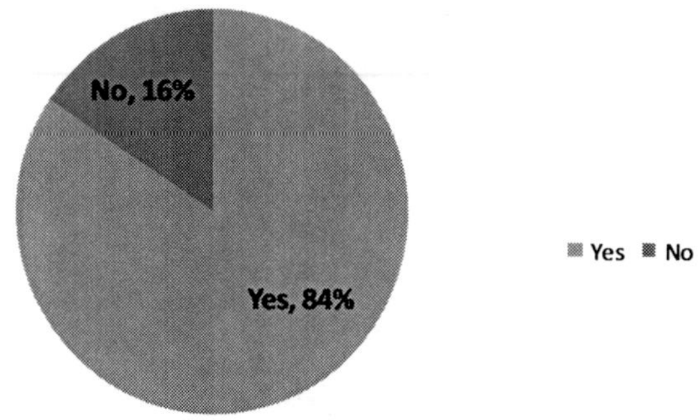

Expected impact of ICT investment on revenue: We asked the respondents if they expect increase of future revenue due to their ICT investment, and as (Figure 19) shows, 55% of respondents replied positively, where as 45% did not expect any growth in sales:

Figure 19. Expected Impact of ICT on Revenue

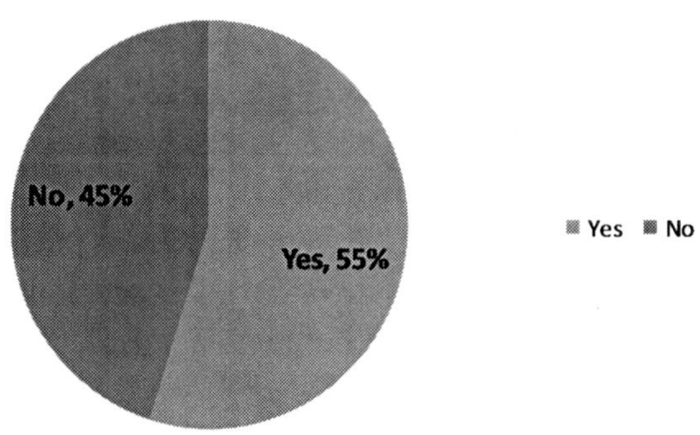

Expected impact of ICT investment on customers: We asked the respondents if they expected to build better relationship with customers in the future and 67% of respondents expected to do so as a result of better and faster customer service, where as 33% believed otherwise as shown in (Figure 20):

Figure 20. Expected Impact of ICT on Customer Relationship

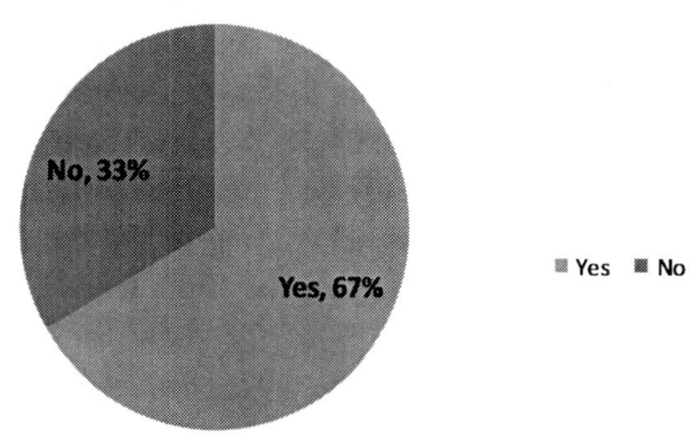

ICT Implementation and Outsourcing

One of the solutions to solve the problem of unavailability of internal skills many organizations have the option of "outsourcing" their ICT related work. Therefore, what we know as outsourcing has become one of the most common practices performed by almost all organizations, both private

Figure 21. Proportion of ICT Activities Outsourced

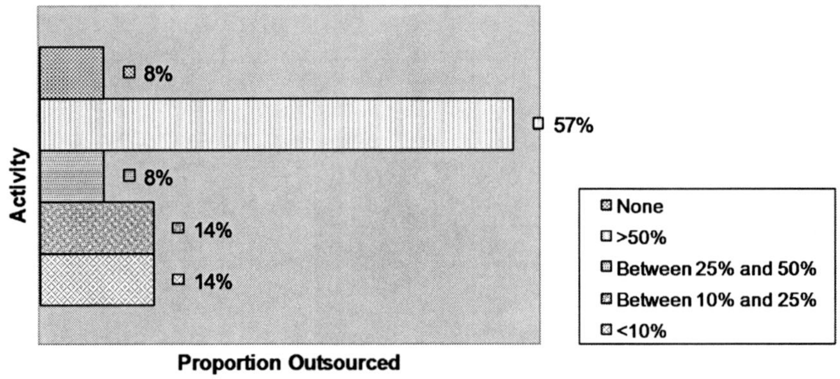

and public, small and large, in order to remain competent within their fields of business or work.

Proportion of Activities Outsourced

Majority of the SMEs that participated in this research outsourced a portion of their ICT activities and work. (Figure 21) shows that 57% of SMEs outsourced more than 50% of their activities, 14% outsourced between 10 and 25 percent of their activities, and 14% outsourced less than 10% of their ICT activities.

Resources Used for ICT Implementation

It is important to know what ICTs were adopted and used within SMEs, but it is also important to know which internal or external resources were used to implement these technologies. Most of the enterprises surveyed used internal resources to implement basic technologies such as the installation and setup of desktop or laptop computers, data storage hardware or business productivity software. As the technologies become more sophisticated, like the use of enterprise software applications, wireless networking or the use of mobile phone applications, the firms tended to use external resources. (Figure 22) show that 33% organizations use internal resources for Desktop or laptops, as well as 24% for data storage solutions and 24% for business productivity software. About 59% of the SMEs outsourced more sophisticated technologies such as enterprise software applications. Also, it seems that some of the organizations lack internal capacity for basic technologies such as Desktop or laptops (47%), business productivity software (41%) and data storage (35%), as they used outsourcing for these activities

A number of firms use both internal and external resources to implement some of the technologies. It was observed that SMEs often use external resources to initially implement the technology, and then tend to use internal resources to maintain and upgrade the implemented technologies.

CONCLUSION

GCC countries have made significant progress during the past few years in adopting ICT. Bahrain and Saudi Arabia ranked 36th and 38th respectively in the E-Participation Index in the recent World Economic Forum survey. UAE ranked 27th and Qatar ranked 29th in the Network Readiness Index. Qatar ranked 29th in Environment index. UAE and Qatar ranked 25th and 26th in the Readiness Index, and 25th and 31st respectively in the Usage Index of the World Economic Forum.

Figure 22. Resourcing Trends Internal vs. External

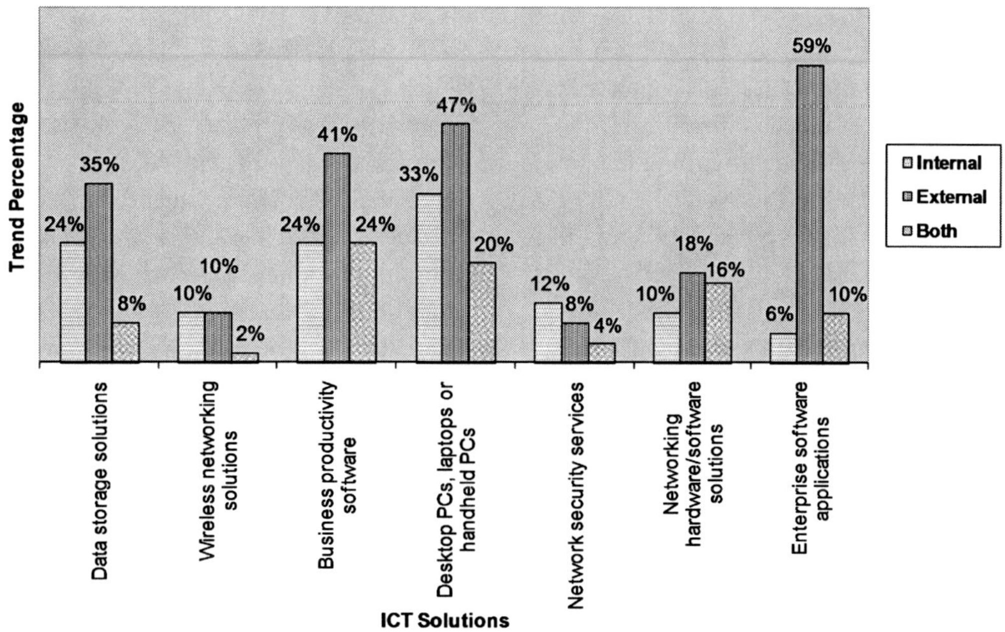

While the GCC countries are making large strides, they still have a long way to go before reaching level of developed countries. It is worthy to note that all ICT adoption in the GCC has taken place at a general level and has not yet focused on ICT adoption in SMEs. We do not find any specific policies that address ICT adoption in SMEs.

We found that ICT usage within SMEs in Oman is reasonable in common technologies, but limited in the more sophisticated technologies such as wireless, data storage and network security solutions. The pattern seems to be very similar to SMEs in Canada (Illuminas, 2006). It was noticed that Omani SMEs are taking a comprehensive approach to their ICT investment. The results of our study show that Omani SMEs are making significant investment in ICT. About 8% of SMEs assign more than 40% of their budget to ICT, About 20% of organizations invest between 10% and 20% of their budget and more than half respondents spend less than 10% of their budget to ICT. This is quite common considering the heterogeneity of SMEs surveyed. Furthermore, nearly half of the SMEs have more than twenty direct competitors; this may be one of the major reasons for increased ICT adoption for those SMEs. The main driving forces for ICT investment was to provide better and faster customer service, to stay ahead of competition and following top management strategy. The differentiation strategy for the majority of SMEs was to provide high quality products and services to their customers and to establish long term relationships with customers. Nearly half of the respondents have realized business benefits of ICT adoption such as better customer relationships, increase in revenue and in reducing costs. Two thirds of the respondents are very positive about increasing their business performance in the future.

With regard to barriers to ICT investment, three fourths of the firms feel that a lack of necessary internal skills is a major barrier. This is consistent with other studies. More than half of the respondents feel that the costs of implementation are too high and there is not enough information available about relevant and effective technologies. Other barriers include SMEs having no time to implement ICT projects, lack of top management support, bad experience in the past and government regulations and requirements. This emphasizes the need for more training facilities in ICT for SMEs, measures to provide ICT products and services at an affordable cost, and availability of free professional advice and consulting at reasonable cost to SMEs.

A number of organizations around the globe are using outsourcing as a means to reduce costs of ICT implementation. More than half of the participants outsourced over 50% of their activities and 14% of respondents outsourced between 10 and 25% of their activities, and another 14% outsourced less than 10% of their ICT activities. Also more than half of the participants used outsourcing for ERP implementation, whereas nearly half used outsourcing for desktop and laptops, and one third outsourced data storage solutions. About one third of the SMEs have in-house capability for PCs and laptops management, and more than 40% for business productivity software installation and maintenance.

Overall, it seems that a small number of SMEs in Oman are aware of the benefits of ICT adoption and are using it for the benefit of their businesses. However, there is a need for more focus and concerted efforts on increasing awareness among SMEs on the benefits of ICT adoption in order SMEs to be more productive and competitive. Also, there is a need for providing affordable ICT products, services, solutions and relevant professional advice for SMEs. The findings of this research will provide a foundation for future research and will help policy makers in understanding the current state of affairs of the usage and impact of ICT on SMEs in Oman.

LIMITATIONS OF THE RESEARCH AND DIRECTIONS FOR FUTURE RESEARCH

This study was a preliminary exploratory study to learn about a few selected aspects of ICT adoption in a GCC country, Oman. There are number of issues such as legal, regulatory, interventions from the government, just to name a few, in the adoption of ICT that needs further investigation. A detailed study should take a more comprehensive approach considering a wide range of areas of ICT adoption. These results are based on a small sample of 51 SMEs, out of that 80% belongs to Micro and Small enterprises. Data was collected from SMEs who use some form of ICT in their business. Those organizations that do not use computers were excluded from the study. Our conservative estimate is that currently, more than 80% of Micro businesses do not use any form of ICT for reasons mentioned earlier in the paper. The results show a general trend and practices of the use and impact of ICT on SMEs in Muscat, the Capital of Oman. The results should be interpreted or used with these perspectives in consideration. A larger sample is needed to further validate these trends. There is a need to carry out similar studies to investigate reasons for the slow adoption of ICT in SMEs in other GCC countries.

REFERENCES

Antlova, K. (2009). Motivation and barriers of ICT adoption in small and medium sized enterprises. *E+M Ekonomie a Management*, 2, 140-155.

Ashrafi. R., & Murtaza, M. (2008). Use and impact of ICT on SMEs in Oman. *The Electronic Journal Information Systems Evaluation, 11*(3), 125-138. Retrieved from http://www.ejise.com

Baldwin, J. R., Jarmin, R. S., & Tang, J. (2001). The Trend to Smaller Producers in Manufacturing in Canada and the US. *Statistics Canada Working paper*.

Bouma, G. D., & Ling, R. (2004). *The Research Process* (5th ed.). Victoria, Australia: Oxford University Press.

Brindley, C., & Ritchie, B. (2005). ICT Adoption by SMEs: Implications for Relationships and Management. *New Technology, Work and Employment, 20*(3), 205–217. doi:10.1111/j.1468-005X.2005.00154.x

British Computer Society. (2007 October). *Growing SMEs need IT*. Retrieved March 11, 2008, from http://www.bcs.org/server.php?show=ConWebDoc.15442

Bruque, S., & Moyano, J. (2007). Organizational determinants of information technology adoption and implementation in SMEs: The case of family and cooperative firms. *Technovation, 27*(5), 241–253. doi:10.1016/j.technovation.2006.12.003

Caldeira, M. M., & Ward, J. M. (2002). Understanding the Successful Adoption and Use of IS/IT in SMEs: an Explanation from Portuguese Manufacturing Industries. *Information Systems Journal, 12*, 121–152. doi:10.1046/j.1365-2575.2002.00119.x

Clarke, J. (2004). Information Systems Strategy and Knowledge-based SMEs in the Australian Biotechnology Industry: Does IS need to reorient its thinking? In *15th Australian Conference on Information Systems*, Hobart, Australia.

Dawn, J., Podonik, P., & Dhaliwal, J. (2002). Supporting the E-business Readiness of Small and Medium-Sized Enterprises: Approaches and Metrics. *Internet Research, 12*(2), 139–195. doi:10.1108/10662240210422512

Doczi, M. (2002). Information and Communication Technologies and Social and Economic Inclusion. In *Information technology Policy Group, Ministry of Economic Development*, Manatu, Ohanga, NZ.

Duan, Y., Mullins, R., Hamblin, D., Stanek, S., Sroka, H., Mavhado, V., & Araujo, J. (2002). Addressing ICTs Skill Challenges in SMEs: Insights from three country investigations. *Journal of European Industrial Training, 26*(9), 430–441. doi:10.1108/03090590210451524

Dutta, S., & Coury, M. E. (2003). ICT Challenges for the Arab World. In *The Global Information Technology Report 2002-2003: Readiness for the Networked World* (pp. 116-131). New York: World Economic Forum/Oxford University Press.

eBusiness in Europe. (2008). *eBusiness Watch*. Retrieved from http://www.ebusiness-watch.org

Falk, M. (2001). Diffusion of Information Technology, Internet Use and the Demand for Heterogeneous Labor . In *European Association of Labour Economists*. Jyväskylä, Finland: EALE.

Fink, D., & Disterer, G. (2006). International Case Studies: To what extent is ICT infused into the Operations of SMEs? *Journal of Enterprise Information Management, 19*(6), 608–624. doi:10.1108/17410390610708490

Grandon, E. E., & Pearson, J. M. (2004). Electronic commerce adoption: an empirical study of small and medium US businesses. *Information & Management, 42*(1), 197–216.

Gregor, S., Fernandez, W., Holtham, D., Martin, S., Vitale, M., & Pratt, G. (2004). *Achieving Value from ICT: Key Management Strategies*. Canberra, Australia: ICT Research Study, Department of Communications, Information Technology and the Arts.

Hamade, S. N. (2009). Information and Communication Technology in Arab Countries: Problems and Solutions. In *Sixth International Conference on Information Technology: New Generations* (pp. 1498-1503).

Houghton, K. A., & Winklhofer, H. (2004). The Effect of Website and E-commerce Adoption on the Relationship between SMEs and Their Export Intermediaries. *International Small Business Journal*, *22*(4), 369–388. doi:10.1177/0266242604044305

Illuminas. (2006). *Net Impact Canada 2006*. Retrieved March 20, 2008, from http://www.netimpactstudy.com/ca/

Information Technology Authority. (2008). *About ITA*. Retrieved March 15, 2008, from http://www.ittf.gov.om/english/about_ita.html

InnoVest Group. (n.d.). *The Technology Small and Medium-Sized Enterprises (SMEs) in Middle East Region*. Retrieved march 12, 2008, from http://www.theinnovestgroup.com/43.html

Johnston, D. A., Wade, M., & McClean, R. (2007, July). Does e-business matter to SMEs? A Comparison of the Financial Impacts of Internet Business Solutions on European and North American SMEs. *Journal of Small Business Management*, *45*(3), 354–361. doi:10.1111/j.1540-627X.2007.00217.x

Kapurubandara, M., & Lawson, R. (2006). *Barriers Adopting ICT and E-commerce with SMEs in Developing Countries: An Exploratory Study in Sri Lanka*. Retrieved March 13, 2008, from http://www.collecter.org/archives/2006_December/07.pdf

Knowledge Oasis Muscat. (2008). *About KOM*. Retrieved March 12, 2008, from http://www.kom.om/ev.htm

Koellinger, P. (2006). *Impact of ICT on Corporate Performance, Productivity and Employment Dynamics*. Berlin: European Commission Enterprise & Industry Directorate General.

Lal, K. (2007). Globalization and Adoption of ICTs in Nigerian SMEs. *Science, Technology & Society*, *12*(2), 217–244. doi:10.1177/097172180701200203

Lange, T., Ottens, M., & Taylor, A. (2000). SMEs and Barriers to skills development: A Scottish Perspective. *Journal of European Industrial Training*, *24*(1), 5–11. doi:10.1108/03090590010308219

Lawson, R., Alcock, C., Cooper, J., & Burgess, L. (2003). Factors Affecting the Adoption of Electronic Commerce Technologies by SMEs: An Australian Study. *Journal of Small Business and Enterprise Development*, *10*(3), 265–276. doi:10.1108/14626000310489727

Love, E. D., Irani, Z., & Edwards, D. J. (2004). Industry-centric Benchmarking of Information Technology Benefits, Costs and Risks for Small-to-Medium Sized Enterprises in Construction. *Automation in Construction*, *13*, 507–524. doi:10.1016/j.autcon.2004.02.002

Lucchetti, R., & Sterlacchini, A. (2004). The Adoption of UCT among SMEs: Evidence from an Italian Survey. *Small Business Economics*, *23*, 151–168. doi:10.1023/B:SBEJ.0000027667.55821.53

MENAFN. (2009). Middle East North Africa Financial Network – Mideast IT spend to Hit $50 b in 2009. *Khalij Times*. Retrieved March 6, 2009, from http://www.menafn.co

Morikawa, M. (2004). Information Technology and the Performance of Japanese SMEs. *Small Business Economics*, *23*, 171–177. doi:10.1023/B:SBEJ.0000032023.11566.4b

Mutula, S. M., & Brakel, P. (2006). E-readiness of SMEs in the ICT Sectors in Botswana with Respect to Information Access. *The Electronic Library*, *24*(3), 402–417. doi:10.1108/02640470610671240

Oman Economic Review. (2007). *SME Forum –Making Life Easy*. Retrieved August 3, 2008, from http://www.oeronline.com/php/2007_dec/sme_forum.php

Parker, C. M., & Castelman, T. (2007). New Directions for Research on SME-eBusiness: Insights from an Analysis of Journal Articles from 2003 to 2006. *Journal of Information Systems and Small Business*, *1*(1-2), 21–40.

Patel, F. (2007). *The Arab business world's ICT opportunity*. Arabian Business World.

Premkumar, G. (2003). A meta-analysis of research on information technology implementation in small business. *Journal of Organizational Computing and Electronic Commerce*, *13*(2), 91–121. doi:10.1207/S15327744JOCE1302_2

Riemenschneider, C. K., Harrison, D. A., & Mykytyn, P. P. Jr. (2003). Understanding it adoption decisions in small business: integrating current theories. *Information & Management*, *40*(4), 269–285. doi:10.1016/S0378-7206(02)00010-1

Sabbagh, K. (2003). *Closing the Digital Divide in the Arab World.* Retrieved July 23, 2009, from http://www.boozallen.com/publications/article/659082

Schubert, P., Fisher, J., & Leimstoll, U. (2007). ICT and Innovation in Small Companies. In *15th European Conference on Information Systems*, St. Gallen, Switzerland (pp. 1226-1239).

Schubert, P., & Leimstoll, U. (2006). The Importance of ICT: An Empirical Study in Swiss SMEs. In *19th Bled Conference eValues*, Bled, Slovenia.

Schubert, P., & Leimstoll, U. (2007). Importance and Use of Information Technology in Small and Medium-Sized Companies. *Electronic Markets*, *17*(1), 38–55. doi:10.1080/10196780601136799

Shiels, H., McIvor, R., & O'Reilly, D. (2003). Understanding the Implications of ICT adoption: Insights from SMEs. *Logistics Information Management*, *16*(5), 312–326. doi:10.1108/09576050310499318

Smallbone, D., North, D., Vickers, I., & Roper, S. (2001). Innovation and the Use of Technology in Manufacturing Plants and SMEs: An Inter-Regional Comparison. In *Proceedings 24th ISBA National Small Firms Conference: Exploring the Frontiers of Small Business,* Hinckley, Leicestershire (pp. 289-308).

Ssewanyana, J., & Busler, M. (2007). Adoption and Usage of ICT in developing Countries: Case of Ugandan Firms. *International Journal of Education and Development using ICT, 3*(3), 49-59. Retrieved march 13, 2009, from http://ijedict.dec.uwi.edu/viewarticle.php?id=349

Stroeken, J. H. M. (2001). The Adoption of IT by SMES: The Dutch Case. *Journal of Enterprising Culture*, *9*(1), 129–152. doi:10.1142/S0218495801000080

Temtime, Z. T., Chinyoka, S. V., & Shunda, J. P. W. (2003). Toward Strategic Use of IT in SMEs: A Developing Country Perspective. *Information Management & Computer Security*, *11*(5), 230–237. doi:10.1108/09685220310500144

UN E-Government Survey. (2008). *From e-Government to Connected Governance*. Document No. ST/ESA/PAD/SER.E/112. New York: United Nations.

UNCTAD. (2004). *ICT as an Enabler for Growth, Development and Competitiveness*. Retrieved March 13, 2008, from http://www.unctadxi.org/templates/Event____69.aspx

World Economic Forum and INSEAD. (2009). *The Global Information Technology Report 2008–2009.* Retrieved April 9, 2009, from http://www.mcit.gov.eg/General/Global%20IT%20Report%202008-092009331155142.pdf

Yeh, Q.-C., & Chang, A. J.-T. (2007). Proliferation of Computers among Taiwanese SMEs. *International Journal of Entrepreneurship and Innovation Management*, *7*(1), 51–73. doi:10.1504/IJEIM.2007.012173

Chapter 21
Supporting Companies Management and Improving Their Productivity through Mining Customers Transactions

Asem Omari
Jarash Private University, Jordan

ABSTRACT

Selling products or services online plays an important role in the success of businesses that have a physical presence, like a retail business. For many businesses, a retail website is an effective line of communication between the businesses and their customers. Even if the business does not present all of its products and services in the website, the website may be just what the customer needs to see to choose it over a competitor. Therefore, it is important to have a successful website to serve as a sales and marketing tool to participate in meeting the core requirements of the business. Clustering and classification are two important data mining techniques that are widely used to assign customers to different categories. Those categories are used to analyze customer behavior and interestingness. In this chapter, we use clustering and classification to support web designers to have better designed retail websites. This is done during the design phase by improving the structure of the website depending on the extracted patterns in a way that makes it easy for the website's navigator to find his target products in an efficient time, give him the opportunity to have a look at some products that may be of interest for him, and encourage him to buy more from the available products which will consequently increase the business's overall profit. This approach will open the eyes of business leaders to adapt new efficient technological tool that when invested in their organizations will improve the strategic goals and meet their basic requirements to be successful, productive, and competitive. The experimental work shows very promising results that can positively change the traditional techniques of the process of designing retail websites.

DOI: 10.4018/978-1-61692-016-6.ch021

INTRODUCTION

Recently, the web is becoming an important part of people's life. The web allows people to easily communicate and exchange ideas and views about any subject anywhere in the world. The web is a very good place to run successful businesses. Almost everything can be bought from online stores without the need to go to physical shops. In e-commerce, instead of having your business in a limited physical place and being limited to a sector of customers who are usually near to your store or business, you have it in the web. In e-commerce websites, you have the ability to sell, advertise, and introduce different kinds of services and products in the web. E-commerce websites have the advantage of reaching a large number of customers regardless of distance and time limitations. Furthermore, an advantage of e-commerce over traditional businesses is the faster speed and the lower expenses for both e-commerce website owners and customers in completing customers' transactions and orders. Creating a successful online business can be a very difficult and costly task if not taking into account e-commerce website design principles, web engineering techniques, and what e-commerce is supposed to do for the online business. Understanding the requirements of both e-commerce website owner and customer is an important aspect in building a successful e-commerce website. A successful website is a well-structured website. The website is well-structured from the user's point of view if it contains services that satisfy user's needs, if the user navigation is simplified, and if he can reach his target page in a short time without the need to make any search or to guess where his target page could be found. The authors in Ranganathan et al. (2002) found that *information content*, *design, security,* and *privacy* have an impact on the effectiveness of a website as well as on the online purchase intent of customers. *Security* and *privacy* were found to have greater effect on the purchase intent of customers.

On the other hand, from the point of view of the website owner, a website is well-structured if it participates in increasing the business overall profit, if it increases the user's trust in the business and its products, and participates in supporting the business marketing strategies. Therefore, it is important to develop and use tools that can guarantee to a high degree the quality of websites to meet the requirements of both website owners and users.

One of the effective used technologies for that purpose is data mining. Data mining is the extraction of useful patterns from large databases. Researchers attract much attention to data mining because of its wide applicability in many different fields (Kohavi et al. (2001)). Two major data mining techniques are classification and clustering. Classification, known as supervised learning, is the process of assigning objects to one of several predefined categories. In contrast to classification, clustering assigns objects into different groups (*clusters*) that are meaningful. The rules extracted using such data mining techniques can be used to support a variety of business related tasks. In our methodology, we get benefit from the patterns extracted through mining the business information system that records customers' transactions and profiles to support the design of the business's website that the transactions database belongs to. This is done during the design phase by improving the structure of the website depending on the extracted patterns in a way that makes it easy for the website's navigator to find his target products in an efficient time, give him the opportunity to have a look at some products that may be of interest for him, and encourage him to buy more from the available products which will consequently increase the overall profit of the business\company.

This chapter is structured as follows: In section 2, we introduce the knowledge discovery process and discuss data mining as it is considered the most important step in the knowledge discovery process and we discuss some of its business applications. In section 3, we discuss some related work to our approach. Then, in section 4, we give an overview about clustering and classification, and we show how we can use the extracted patterns from clustering and classification during the design phase to improve website's design structure. The experimental work is presented in section 5. An evaluation of the experimental work is presented in section 6. Finally, section 7, summarizes the main contributions of this chapter and identifies future dimensions to extend this work.

KNOWLEDGE DISCOVERY PROCESS

The enormous expansion of the volume of collected data from different data sources and fields yields to an increase of databases of all sizes and designs. However, it is obviously clear that the manual analysis of such amounts of data is impossible. For that reason, it is important to develop tools that can access and analyze such data to extract interesting knowledge that can be helpful in the decision making process. Knowledge discovery is a technique that can discover interesting information from such large databases. According to Fayyad et al. (1996),"*Knowledge discovery in databases (KDD) is the non-trivial process of identifying valid, novel, potentially useful, and ultimately understandable patterns in data*". The process is nontrivial means that it is not straightforward and some search methodology need to be followed. The extracted patterns should be novel or in other words unknown previously. They also have to be useful, this usefulness factor implies that the patterns can play a positive role in the decision making process. Finally, they must be understandable at least for the data analyst. The KDD process is interactive and iterative, involving a number of steps with many decisions made by the user (Fayyad et al. (1996)). Here we list the main steps of the knowledge discovery process (Lukasz et al. (2006)):

- **Understanding the Application Domain**: The knowledge discovery process begins by understanding the application domain and the goals of the data mining process. Previously unknown patterns that are useful and effective in the decision making process are expected to be gained.
- **Data Integration and Gathering**: In the data integration and gathering step the target data sets are gathered from different data sources for example from heterogeneous databases and data warehouses and combined in a suitable manner. At this step, the relevant data to the analysis process is targeted and retrieved from the data source(s).
- **Data Preprocessing**: Eliminating errors, ensuring consistency, solving the problem of missed and repeated data, and transforming the selected data to format that are appropriate for the data mining procedure, are the main tasks of this step.
- **Data Mining:** Data mining is the most important step in the knowledge discovery process in which different techniques are applied to extract interesting patterns. In this step, the appropriate data mining algorithm(s) or/and method(s) are decided to be applied on the target data. A brief discussion of data mining and its business applications is presented in the next two subsections.
- **Visualization**: To better understand and analyze the discovered knowledge, it is visually represented to the user using different visualization techniques.
- **Pattern Evaluation:** In this step, based on predefined measures, all interesting patterns representing meaningful knowledge are identified. It is common to combine some of these steps together. For example, the data integration and gathering and the data preprocessing steps can be combined together and considered as one preprocess-

ing step. Furthermore, most of those steps are often repeated iteratively to reach some satisfying level of the expected results. For example, in the data mining step the data analyst may repeat the data mining process by using another algorithm or method that could be more suitable for better and refined results of the knowledge discovery process. The data analyst can also jump within different steps. For example, if the data analyst is using some data mining algorithm and he want to use another algorithm that needs different data format, then he may go back to the data preprocessing step in order to convert the target data to the suitable format.

DATA MINING

Data mining is considered the most important step in the knowledge discovery process. Data mining is the process of extracting interesting patterns from large amounts of data (Jiawei Han J. and Kamber M. (2001)). It provides tools for automated learning from historical data and developing models to predict future trends and behaviors. Data mining has two main models. Predictive data mining model tries to predict unknown value or future trends or behaviors depending on other variables or historical values presented in the mined database (Hansen et al. (2002)). For example, an immunization dose against some virus may be given to a particular patient not because he is infected from that virus, but because his illness profile is very similar to another group of patients who were infected with the same virus. Descriptive data mining model tries to extract useful patterns that can describe the mined data and explore its properties. For example, in a grocery store database, it may be found that a large number of customers who buy product *A*, buy product *B* with. Data mining is widely used by different companies and organizations especially in the field of retail, finance, communication, science, and marketing. It enables these companies to gain information about sales behavior, customer satisfaction, and corporate profits. Using data mining, organizations can increase the profitability of their interactions with customers, detect fraud, and improve risk management. The patterns extracted using data mining help organizations make better and knowledge based decisions.

Data Mining Business Applications

Data Mining is becoming increasingly popular because of its wide applicability in many different fields. Data mining made substantial contributions to the success of different industries and application fields. In the following, we examine the applications of data mining in different business fields.

- **Data Mining in Customer Relationship Management**: Customer Relationship Management (CRM) tries to use all measures to understand customers and invest the extracted knowledge to implement marketing strategies, control production, and coordinate the supply chain. Data mining is one of those tools used by CRM to study customer behavior and interests and use the extracted knowledge to manage customers' life cycle, attract new customers, and retain good customers (Yen et al. (2006)). For example, by analyzing customer profiles, we can find the groups of customers who bought a particular product and encourage similar customers who have not bought that product to buy it. Furthermore, by studying the profiles of customers who have left the company, a special strategy can be built to retain customers who are expected to leave, because it is less expensive to retain an existing customer than to win a new one. The authors in (Chen et al. (2005)) employ a data mining tool in a credit card business to discover current spending patterns of customers and trends of the behavioral change to expand the customers' base and prevent loosing of customers.

- **Data Mining in Retailing:** Market basket analysis uses data mining techniques to analyze customers' transactions in a retail transaction database. The extracted knowledge can be used for cross-selling, store design, discount plans, and promotions. It is also useful for fast interaction with each new customer of the company. Although market basket analysis investigates shopping carts and supermarket shoppers, it is important to realize that there are many other areas in which it can be applied such as analysis of credit card purchases and telephone calling patterns.
- **Data Mining in Insurance:** Companies in the insurance industry collect enormous amounts of data about their clients such as information about customers' profiles, activities, and preferences. Applying data mining on such data might be useful in detecting and predicting fraud or risky customers and predicting which customers will get benefit from new services and policies (Liao S. et al. (2009)). It enables these companies to gain information about sales behavior, customer satisfaction, and corporate profits. Using data mining, organizations can increase the profitability of their interactions with customers, detect fraud, and improve risk management.
- **Data Mining in Telecommunications:** Usually, every telecommunication company has a database that records customers' transactions and contains other customer data such as billing information or customers' profiles, and additional data such as network load. Data mining can be used in the field of telecommunications to find customer groups that are highly profitable, decide which services or products should be offered to which customers, and find which kind of call rates that can increase the profit without loosing good customers (Eichinger et al. (2006)). Fraud detection techniques can also help in finding stolen mobile phones or phone cards.

RELATED WORK

Retail website design is a growing subject for many years due to the important role of websites in improving the efficiency of organizations, and supporting companies marketing strategies. In the website engineering process, some key processes and activities need to be followed in order to insure that the expected website will be reliable and performs well (Pressman (2005)). Those steps include requirements analysis, design, coding, testing, maintenance, and management. In (Murugesan et al. (2005)), the authors recommended several key steps for successful development and deployment of web applications such as understanding the system overall function and operational environment including business objectives and requirements and identifying the system main users and their typical profiles. A lot of research has been done to cover different website design techniques, and strategies. The work done by Dave Gehrke (1999) provides a survey of experts' recommendations of how to create an effective website from an e-commerce point of view. It investigates the determinants of an effective website. The survey indicated that the major categories of determinants are: page loading speed, business content, navigation efficiency, security, and marketing/customer focus.

The authors in (Troyer et al. (1998)) present a method for designing *kiosk* websites which are websites that provide information and allow users to navigate through that information. The method is based on the principle that the website should be designed and adapted to its users. It starts by identifying different classes of users and describe manually their characteristics, and their information requirements, and how could they navigate the website. Lohse et al. (1998) gives some recommendations and remarks on how to design retail websites. For example, stores that offer a FAQ's section have more visits than those without such a section and every web page must have consistent navigation links to move around on the website.

In general, there are two approaches for e-commerce websites design. The user-centered design focuses on user experience and user satisfaction by iterative prototyping, trial and error, and evolution. On the other hand, the usage-centered design focuses on improved tools supporting task accomplishment. Elaine Chou (2002) presents a technique for redesigning a large and complex website and provides usability practices and techniques. It provides some tips and practical issues and solutions for developing solid information architecture and for implementing web standards. The author indicates that the decisions about products and services to offer in the website are influenced by: The organization's strategic goals, the expertise of it, employees, past history, process, and infrastructure. An important aspect, with respect to the author, of redesigning a large and complex websites is knowing the target users. Creating user profiles and keeping them in mind help the redesign team focus on the core issues. This facilitates the identification of related pages or navigation patterns which can be used in web personalization (Mobasher et al. (2001)).

CLUSTERING AND CLASSIFICATION DURING THE DESIGN PHASE

Clustering is the process of partitioning a given population of events or items into sets of similar elements, so that items within a cluster have high similarity in comparison to one another, but are very dissimilar to items in other clusters (Han and Kamber 2001). In web usage mining there are two main interesting clusters to be discovered: usage clusters and pages clusters (Srivastava et al. (2000)). The authors in (Zhong et al. 2002) present an approach to cluster web pages to obtain high quality clusters of web pages and use those clusters to produce index pages, where index pages are web pages that have direct links to pages that may be of interest of some group of website navigators. In Koutri and Daskalaki (2003), clustering techniques are applied to web log file to discover those subsets of web pages that need to be connected and to improve the already connected pages. Velasquez, Yasuda, and Aoki (2003) use a clustering algorithm which identifies groups of similar sessions, allowing the analysis of visitor behavior.

In contrast to clustering, classification is dividing an existing set of events or transactions into other predefined sets or classes based on some characteristics. In web usage mining, classification is used to group users into predefined groups with respect to their navigation patterns in order to develop profiles of users belonging to a particular class or category (Srivastava et al. (2000)). The authors in (Fu, Creado, and Shih (2001)) propose an approach to reorganize a website based on user access patterns and the classification of web pages into two categories: index pages and content pages. Ishikawa et al. (2002) introduce the *System L-R* recommendation system which constructs user models by classifying the web access and recommends relevant pages to the users based both on the user models and the web content. Albanese et al. (2004) propose a web mining strategy for web personalization based on a novel pattern recognition strategy which analysis and classifies users taking into account both user provided data and navigational behavior of the users. They present the *Referrer Based Page Recommendation, RBPR*, that uses information about a visitor's browsing context (specially, the referrer *URL* provided by the *HTTP*) to suggest pages that might be relevant to the visitors underlying information needs.

Despite the effectiveness of web mining and specifically web personalization in improving websites, it costs a lot of maintenance efforts and suffers from different drawbacks. If we talk about retail websites of commercial companies which are companies that sells different kinds of products on the web, in order to make an effective maintenance to their websites, the companies have to wait at least one year in order to have a representative log file that reflects customer's transactions in their website. This amount of time is considered very large especially for the companies in which the time factor plays an important role in their success strategy, and has many competitors who can attract their customers if they have no solid marketing strategies in order to keep their customers as loyal as possible. On the other hand, most businesses gather information about internet customers through online questionnaires. But many customers choose not to complete these questionnaires because of the amount of time required to complete them as well as the lack of a clear benefit from completing them. Several companies use cookies to follow customers through the World Wide Web, but cookies are sometimes detected and disabled by web browsers and do not provide much insight into customer preferences (Shah (1998)). This is because customers are feeling that their profiles are not secure. For that reason, they usually give incorrect information about themselves (Reynolds (2004)).

An alternative approach for designing retail websites is improving the structure of the website during the design phase before being published. In our previous work (Omari and Conrad 2006), we investigated the usage of data mining to support website's designers to have better designed websites. We explained briefly different data mining techniques and showed how to use them in supporting website design. In Omari, Conrad, and Alcic (2007), we developed a new approach that measures the effectiveness of association rule mining in helping the website designer to improve the structure of the website in the design phase. Two website prototypes have been built. The first prototype was built by following the classical website design methods and recommendations. The other prototype was supported by the interesting patterns extracted by running association rule mining algorithms on a transactions dataset of a grocery store. The experiments showed that our method can reduce the navigation cost up to *90%* in some transactions.

Clustering and classification are two data mining techniques that play an important role in our approach. In this chapter, we use clustering and classification data mining techniques on the contents of the information system of a company or institution to solve the problem of building an ill-structured website for this company or institution. From the extracted patterns, the information need to be considered in the website building process are gained and invested in the process of website design which yields to a better designed retail website.

The main advantage of this method is that it reduces maintenance time and budgetary costs for websites if they are built taking into account the extracted interesting patterns from the transactions database of the company. This approach also permits the sales manager to focus on the core business and gives him a better view about his products and customers which is very helpful in designing retail websites. Our method can be beneficial for many companies and commercial institutions.

EXPERIMENTAL WORK

For the experiments, we used a dataset that represents customer transactions in an electronics store. The dataset contains information about customers' profiles, transactions, purchases, and store branches. The data set has a total of 3500 transactions. It contains the following attributes: *TransactionID, CustomerID, ProductID, Date_of_Purchase, Branch_Name, Customer_address,*

Figure 1. Standard Website Design

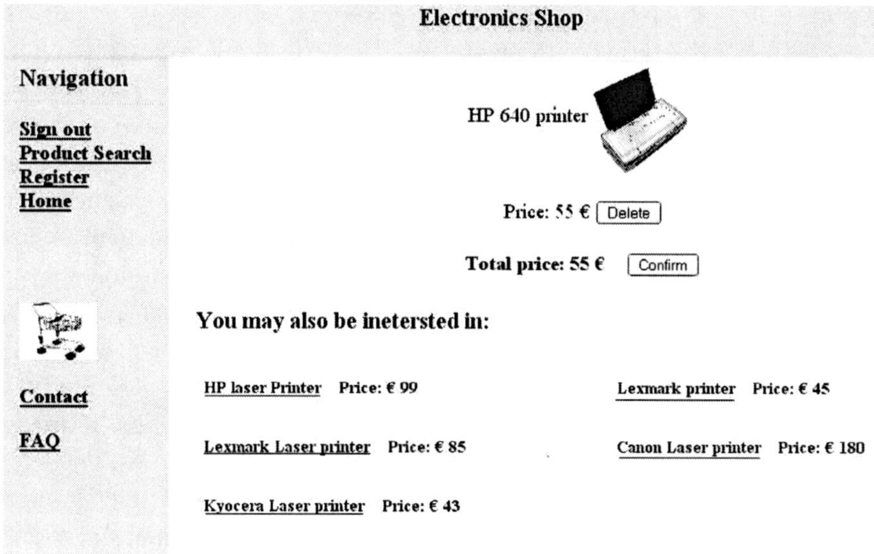

Customer_Sex, Customer_Age, and Customer_CreditCard_Rating. The following is a sample of two transactions from the data set:

- 12998, 1553, 85, 10, 1, 2004-10-02, Hamburg, Bramfeld, Male, 37, Good
- 13001, 1979, 80, 92, 201, 2005-10-07, Munich, Unterfoering, Female, 50, Bad

The first transaction with *12998 TransactionID* number is done by the customer who's *ID* number is *1553.* The electronics store, with its two branches in Hamburg and Munich, have a total of 250 different products. Every product has an *ID* number. This customer bought 3 products which have the *ID* numbers *85, 10,* and *1* respectively. The transaction was done in the second of October 2004 in *Hamburg* Branch. The customer is living in *Bramfeld,* and he is a *Male*, 37 years old, and has a *Good* credit card ratings.

A website for this store is decided to be built to give a good view about its work, to support and facilitate services introduced to customers, and to encourage customers was done in to buy more from its products. The website design process starts by identifying the store's goal from building this website. The website designer looks at the dataset and try to understand its structure, check out what kind of information are available in the dataset and whether those information should be presented in the website or not (Elaine Chou (2002)). Beside that information, the website designer considers some standards and recommendations adopted by website designers to have well-structured websites such as every page should be connected directly to the home page and every parent page should have direct links to its descendants (Lohse and Spiller (1998)). (Figure 1) shows the resultant elementary website design.

The website is well-designed with respect to website designers' standards. Every page has a consistent navigation link to move around in the website. When a user logs in, a number of random products are offered to him. When he visits some product page, a list of related products is introduced to him. Those products are related to the current product with respect to product type and manufacturer. For example, in (Figure 1), the customer chooses to buy *HP 640 Printer*. From that, a list of other printers and related products from the same manufacturer and other manufacturers are presented to the customer in order to be able to compare the same product from different manufacturers with respect to different attributes.

To improve the design of this retail website, we used different classification and clustering algorithms implemented in the data mining tool *WEKA* to mine the transactions dataset of the electronics store. WEKA (Waikato Environment for Knowledge Analysis) is a machine learning and data mining software tool written in Java and distributed under the GNU Public License A (Witten and Frank (2005)). The goal of the WEKA project is to *"build a state-of-the-art facility for developing machine learning techniques and to apply them to real-world data mining problems"* (Witten and Frank 2005). It contains several standard data mining techniques, including data preprocessing, classification, regression, clustering, and association rule mining.

For classification we used the *ADtree* and the *J48* algorithms. The *ADtree* is an implementation of Freund and Mason *Alternating Decision Tree* Algorithm (Comite et al. (2001)). Based on the work of Comite et al. (2001), *ADtree* is a learning algorithm for alternating decision trees that is based on boosting. Experimental results showed that it is competitive with boosted decision tree algorithms such as C5.0, and generates rules that are usually smaller in size and thus easier to interpret. In addition, these rules yield a natural measure of classification confidence which can be used to improve the accuracy at the cost of abstaining from predicting examples that are hard to classify. Furthermore, alternating decision trees give, in addition to classification, a measure of confidence which is called the classification margin. This measure gives a new evidence for the validity and usefulness of interpreting classification margins as measures of confidence.

J48 algorithm is an implementation of the *C4.5* decision tree learner. The algorithm uses the greedy technique to induce decision trees for classification (Quinlan (1999)). A decision-tree model is built by analyzing training data and the model is used to classify unseen data.

For clustering, we used the *EM* and the *SimpleKmeans* algorithms. The *EM* algorithm assigns a probability distribution to each instance which indicates the probability of it belonging to each of the clusters. *EM* can decide how many clusters to create by cross validation (we used this option in our experiments), or you may specify apriori how many clusters to generate. The *SimpleKmeans* algorithm clusters data using the *K-Means* algorithm. The *K-Means* algorithm takes the input parameter *k*, and partitions a set of *n* objects into *k* clusters so that the resulting similarity within the cluster is high but the similarity with other clusters is low. Cluster similarity is measured in regard to the mean value of the objects in the cluster (Han and Kamber (2001)). In the experiments, we used different numbers of clusters to be generated ranging from 2 to 10 clusters. After tuning the number of generated clusters, we found that 5 clusters is the most suitable number of clusters as it can give very descriptive results. After running the above mentioned algorithms, a lot of interesting patterns have been extracted. In all of the above algorithms, the extracted patterns were saved for visualization in order to ease the process of data analysis.

We summarized those interesting extracted patterns in (Figure 2). As we see in the flowchart in (Figure 2), we divided the customers with respect to their biographic information sex, age, and address into five classes. The first class is the *Male* customers living in *Hamburg* (*Cluster0*). The second class is the *Male* customers living in *Munich* (*Cluster1*). The third class is the *Female* customers who are living in *Hamburg* and greater than or equal 36 years old (*Cluster2*). The fourth class is the *Female* customers who are living in *Hamburg* but less than 36 years old (*Cluster3*). The last class is the *Female* customers living in *Munich* (*Cluster4*).

Each class has a list of products that may be of interest for its members. The products are ordered

Figure 2. A Summary of the Interesting Extracted Patterns

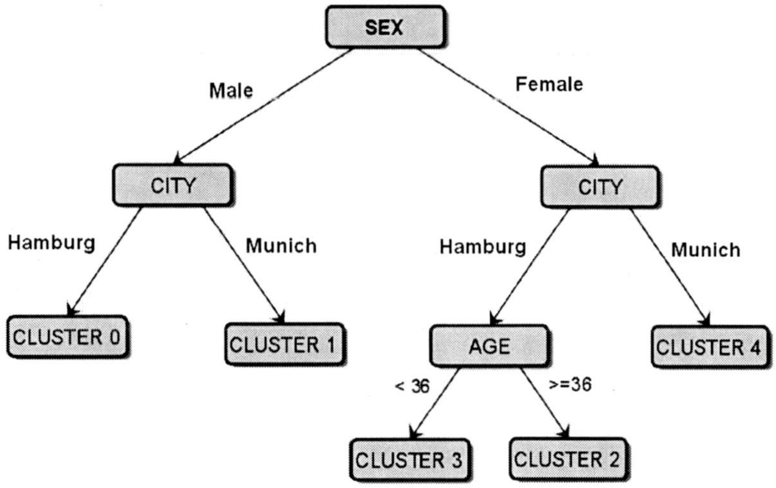

in the list with respect to buying frequency. The most frequently bought product is the first one in the list. On the other hand, the less frequently bought product is the last one in the list. In order to improve the standard website design in (Figure 1), we took into account the previously extracted patterns in the design process.

(Figure 3) shows a screen shot of the improved website design. In the process of building the new website design, we took into account the information about the clusters to be considered in the process of presenting a set of products to a specific customer. After the customer logs in, he is assigned to one of the clusters mentioned above (See Figure 2). From that, a list of products that may be of interest for him are introduced to him.

Through this process, we encourage the customer to buy more from the available products, give him the opportunity to have a look at some products that may be of interest for him. Further-

Figure 3. Improved Website Design

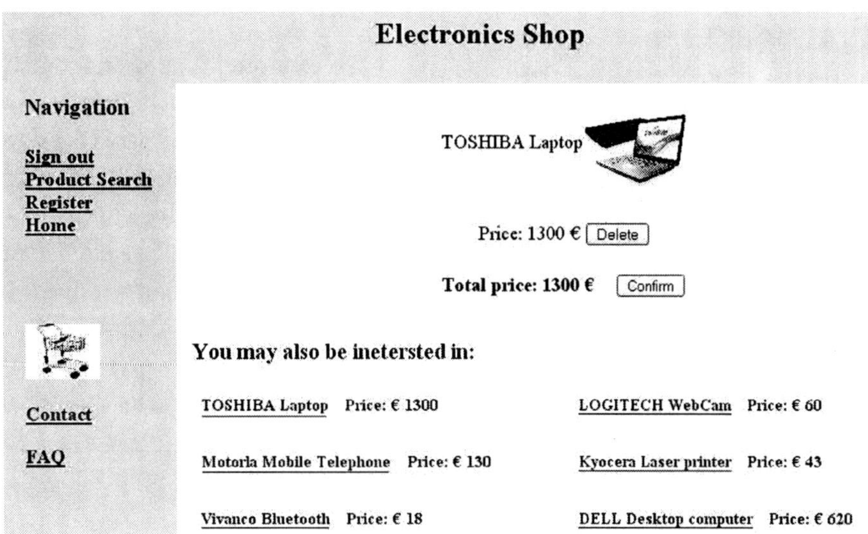

more, we ease the process of product search so that the customer can reach his target product in an efficient time and the navigation process will be optimized. This factor is very important in winning customers' loyalty and changing them to be frequent buyers. This is because, in most cases, if the customer did not find his target product in a specific time, he will give up and starts to search for another shop or provider in which he may find his target product in.

As a result, such interesting extracted patterns from clustering and classification can be used to design a well-structured retail website, plan marketing and advertising strategies which will consequently increase the electronics store overall profit. Furthermore, the main advantage of our method is that it reduces maintenance time and budgetary costs for websites if they are built taking into account such interesting patterns and customer buying habits that can be found in the transactions database in almost every shop or electronic store.

It also permits the sales manager to focus on the core business and gives him a better view about his products and customers which is very helpful in designing retail websites. This method will also participate in improving customer satisfaction and will encourage him to be a frequent buyer.

METHOD EVALUATION

In order to evaluate our method we implemented a simulation tool in *PHP.* The tool simulates the behavior of customers in both websites. We call the first website the standard website, which is built without taking into account patterns extracted from the electronics store transactions dataset using clustering and classification. On the other hand, the improved website is the one built taking into account interesting extracted patterns from the electronics store transactions dataset using clustering and classification techniques. In every transaction in the dataset, the customer has a list of products he wants to buy. Those products are considered as to be the set of all target products. Every product is represented by a page in both websites. We defined the session time $Time_c$ for some customer C to be the amount of time needed to buy all target products as follows:

$$Time_c = \underbrace{\sum_{i=1}^{m} (x_1 \cdot t_1)}_{\mathbf{X}} + \underbrace{\sum_{i=1}^{n} ((x_2 \cdot t_1) + t_2)}_{\mathbf{Y}}$$

where;

- X: The total time needed to reach a product that belongs to the offered list of products,
- Y: The total time needed to reach a product that does not belong to the offered list of products, in addition to the time needed to search for this product,
- m: Number of products that belong to the offered list of products,
- n: Number of products that do not belong to the offered list of products,
- $x1$: Number of web pages needed to reach the web page of a product belonging to the offered list of products,
- $x2$: Number of web pages needed to reach the web page of a product not belonging to the offered list of products,
- $t1$: Time needed to load a web page, and
- $t2$: Time needed to fill the search form.

For example, if some customer bought three products, two product belong to the offered list of products, and one product is outside the list of offered products. The overall time will be calculated as follows. Two seconds to load a web page ($t1$) and 7 seconds to fill the search form ($t2$). We set $x1$ to be 1 (i.e. the customer needs one web page to reach a product belonging to the offered list of products) and $x2$ to be 3 (i.e. the customer needs three web pages to reach a product not belonging to the offered list of products). The overall time will be calculated as follows:

Figure 4. Average Session Times Needed to Simulate Customers Transactions in Both Websites

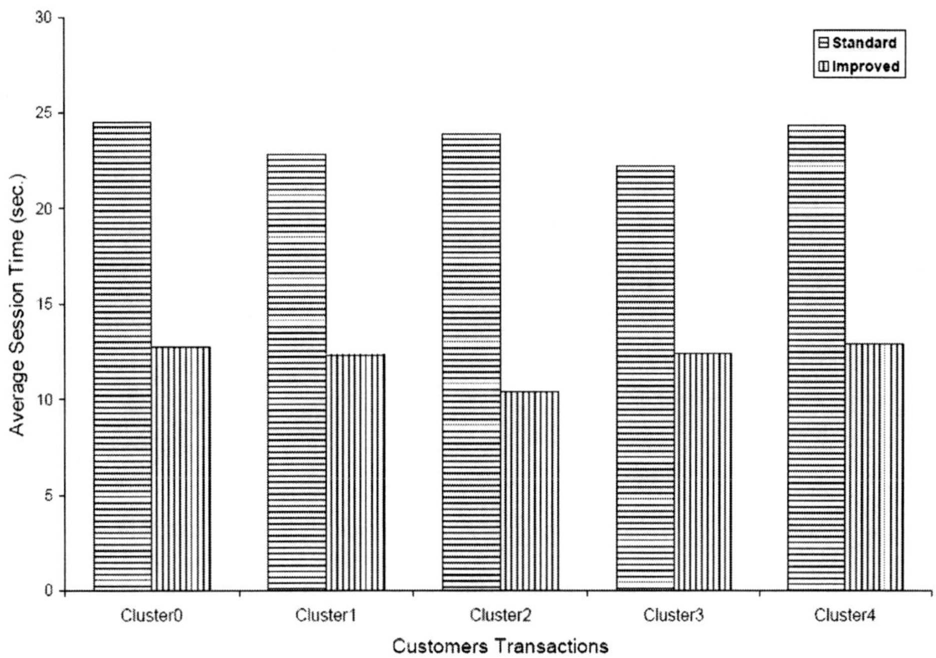

$$Time_c = \underbrace{\sum_{i=1}^{2}(2{\cdot}2)}_{\mathbf{X}} + \underbrace{\sum_{i=1}^{1}((3{\cdot}2)+7)}_{\mathbf{Y}} = 21\,\mathrm{sec}\,onds$$

Measuring the session time starts from customer *log in* time until buying the last product by clicking on *Confirm* button.

(Figure 4) shows the average session time needed to finish all customer transactions with respect to customers' clusters. The figure shows a clear difference between the session average times in both standard and improved websites. The session's average time of the improved website is reduced to 51% of the session's average time of the standard website.

(Table 1) shows a comparison between the efficiency of both websites with respect to transaction times where:

A: Number of transactions where Time (standard) > Time (Improved)
B: Number of transactions where Time (standard) = Time (Improved)
C: Number of transactions where Time (standard) < Time (Improved)

Besides evaluating the efficiency of both websites by simulating customer behavior in them, we made a manual evaluation by allowing a number of persons to navigate in both websites. A random of 50 transactions have been taken from the transactions dataset. Every person has been given a list of target products he needs to buy. In this case, the target products are the products that belong to a specific transaction of the chosen 50 transactions. Then, we allowed the users to use both websites (standard and improved) in order to search for their target products. After that, the sessions times were measured as previously mentioned for both websites.

(Figure 5) shows the resulted navigation time in both websites to complete the sessions of 50 transactions.

Table 1. A Comparison of Session Times within Different Clusters

Cluster	A	B	C
0	385	149	13
1	359	37	1
2	137	9	0
3	301	37	1
4	385	52	**3**

SUMMARY AND FUTURE WORK

In this chapter, with the help of clustering and classification, we introduced a method to design a well-structured retail website for some store. The extracted knowledge from transactions dataset of an electronics store are invested in the design phase to improve the design of the store's website that the transactions dataset belongs to. Many improvements and modifications can be done to the website's design, such as adding/modifying links and/or creating index pages. The experiments showed very promising results of our method that could be very effective in the process of designing retail websites. Our method will not only reduce the navigation costs but it also reduces the maintenance costs needed in the future. It also permits the sales manager to focus on the core business and gives him a better view about his products and customers which is very helpful in designing retail websites. This method will also participate in improving customer satisfaction and will encourage him to be a frequent buyer.

As a future work, we plan to develop a retail website design system that has a built-in data mining tool. The system takes customers transactions, profiles, and the requirements of the retail business owners as input and outputs a suggested prototype of the retail website.

Figure 5. Time Needed to Finish 50 Transactions Manually

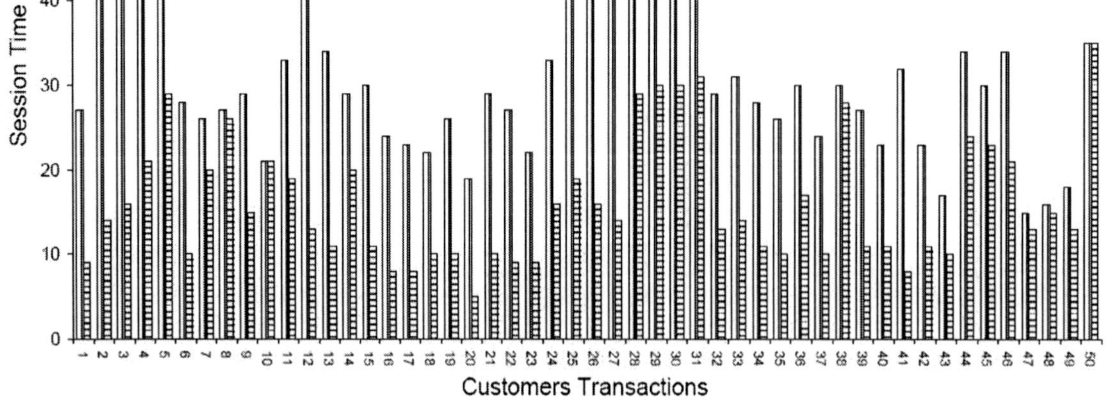

REFERENCES

Albanese, M., Picariello, A., Sansone, C., & Sansone, L. (2004). A Web Personalization System Based on Web Usage Mining Techniques. In *Proceedings of the 13th international World Wide Web conference on Alternate track papers andposters* (pp. 288-289). New York: ACM Press.

Chen, R., Wu, R., & Chen, J. (2005). Data Mining Application in Customer Relationship Management of Credit Card Business. In *29th Annual International Computer Software and Applications Conference COMPSAC* (pp. 39–40).

Chou, E. (2002). Redesigning a Large and Complex Website: How to Begin, and a Method for Success. In *SIGUCCS 2002: Proceedings of the 30th annual ACM SIGUCCS conference on User services* (pp. 22-28). New York: ACM Press.

Comite, F., Gilleron, R., & Tommasi, M. (2001). Learning multi-label alternating decision trees and applications. In G. Bisson (Ed.), *Proceedings of CAP'01: Conference en AP (prentissage Automatique)* (pp. 195-210).

Eichinger, F., Nauck, D., & Klawonn, F. (2006). Sequence Mining for Customer Behavior Predictions in Telecommunications. In M. Ackermann, C. Soares & B. Guidemann (Eds.), *Proceedings of the Workshop on Practical Data Mining at ECML/PKDD*, Berlin, Germany (pp. 3–10).

Fayyad, U., Piatetsky-Shapiro, G., & Smyth, P. (1996). An Overview. In *Advances in Knowledge Discovery and Data Mining* (pp. 1–34). From Data Mining to Knowledge Discovery.

Fu, Y., Creado, M., & Shih, M. (2001). Adaptive Web Sites by Web Usage Mining. In *International Conference on Internet Computing (IC 2001),* Las Vegas, NV.

Gehrke, D. (1999). Determinants of Successful Website Design: Relative Importance and Recommendations for Effectiveness. In *HICSS 1999: Proceedings of the Thirty-second Annual Hawaii International Conference on System Sciences* (Vol. 50, pp. 5042). Washington, DC: IEEE Computer Society.

Han, J., & Kamber, M. (2001). *Data Mining Concepts and Techniques*. San Francisco: Morgan Kaufmann Publishers.

Hansen, J., & McDonald, J. (2002). A generalized model for predictive data mining. *Information Systems Frontiers, 4*(2), 179–186. doi:10.1023/A:1016050803099

Ishikawa, H., Ohta, M., Yokoyama, S., Nakayama, J., & Katayama, K. (2002). On the Effectiveness of Web Usage Mining for Page Recommendation and Restructuring. In Chaudhri, A., Jeckle, M., Rahm, E., & Unland, R. (Eds.), *Web, Web Services, and Database Systems NODe 2002 Web and Database-Related Workshops* (pp. 253–267). Berlin: Springer-Verlag.

Kohavi, R., & Provost, F. (2001). Applications of data mining to electronic commerce. *Data Mining and Knowledge Discovery, 5*, 5–10. doi:10.1023/A:1009840925866

Koutri, M., & Daskalaki, S. (2003). Improving Web Site Usability through a Clustering Approach. In *10th International Conference on Human-Computer Interaction HCI,* Crete, Greece (pp. 11-19).

Liao, S., Chen, Y., & Tseng, Y. (2009). Mining demand change knowledge of life insurance market for new product development. *Expert Systems with Applications, 36*(5), 9422–9437. doi:10.1016/j.eswa.2008.12.053

Lohse, G. L., & Spiller, P. (1998). Electronic Shopping. *Communications of the ACM, 41*(7), 81–88. doi:10.1145/278476.278491

Lukasz, A., & Musilek, P. (2006). A survey of knowledge discovery and data mining process models source. *The Knowledge Engineering Review*, *21*(1), 1–24. doi:10.1017/S0269888906000737

Mobasher, B., Dai, H., Luo, T., & Nakagawa, M. (2001). Effective Personalization Based on Association Rule Discovery from Web Usage Data. In *WIDM 2001: Proceedings of the 3rd international workshop on Web information and data management* (pp. 9-15). New York: ACM Press.

Murugesan, S., & Ginige, A. (2005). Web Engineering: Introduction and Perspectives. In *Web Engineering: Principles and Techniques* (pp. 1–30). Hershey, PA: Idea Group Publishing.

Omari, A., & Conrad, S. (2006). On the Usage of Data Mining to Support Website Designers to Have Better Designed Websites. In *Advanced International Conference on Telecommunications and International Conference on Internet and Web Applications and Services (AICT-ICIW'06), Guadeloupe, French Caribbean* (pp. 171). Los Alamitos, CA: IEEE Computer Society.

Omari, A., Conrad, S., & Alcic, S. (2007). Designing a Well-Structured E-Shop Using Association Rule Mining. In *The 4th International Conference on Innovations in Information Technology, Dubai, United Arab Emirates* (pp. 9-14). Washington, DC: IEEE Communication Society.

Pressman, R. S. (2005). *Software Engineering: A Practitioner's Approach* (6th ed.). New York: McGraw-Hill.

Quinlan, J. R. (1999). *C4.5: Programs for Machine Learning*. San Francisco: Morgan Kaufmann Publishers.

Ranganathan, C., & Ganapathy, S. (2002). Key dimensions of business-to-consumer web sites. *Journal of International Management*, *39*(6), 457–465.

Reynolds, J. (2004). *The Complete E-Commerce Book: Design, Build and Maintain a Successful Web-Based Business*. San Francisco: CMP Books.

Shah, T. (1998). *Improving electronic Commerce Through Gathering Customer Data. School of engineering and applied science*. VA, USA: University of Virginia.

Srivastava, J., Cooley, R., Deshpande, M., & Tan, P. (2000). Web Usage Mining: Discovery and Applications of Usage Patterns from Web Data. *ACM SIGKDD Explorations*, *1*(2), 12–23. doi:10.1145/846183.846188

Troyer, O., & Leune, C. J. (1998). WSDM: A User Centered Design Method for Web Sites. *Computer Networks, 30*(1-7), 85- 94.

Velasquez, J., Yasuda, H., & Aoki, T. (2003). Combining the Web Content and Usage Mining to Understand the Visitor Behavior in a Web Site. In *Proceedings of the 3rd IEEE International Conference on Data Mining (ICDM 2003)* (pp. 669-672). Washington, DC: IEEE Computer Society Press.

Witten, I. H., & Frank, E. (2005). *Data Mining: Practical Machine Learning Tools and Techniques*. San Francisco: Morgan Kaufmann Publishers.

Yen, S., & Lee, Y. (2006). An efficient data mining approach for discovering interesting knowledge from customer transactions. *Expert Systems with Applications*, *30*, 650–657. doi:10.1016/j.eswa.2005.07.035

Zhong, S., Yang, Q., Zhang, H., Xu, X., Hu, Y., & Ma, S. (2002). Correlation-Based Web Document Clustering for Adaptive Web Interface Design. *Knowledge and Information Systems*, *4*(2), 151–167. doi:10.1007/s101150200002

Compilation of References

Abanumy, A., & Mayhew, P. (2005). M-government implications for e-government in developing countries: The case of Saudi Arabia. *European Mobile Government Conference*. Mobile Government Consortium International LLC

Abramowicz, W., Bassara, A., Filipowska, A., Wisniewski, M., & Zebrowski, P. (2006). Mobility implications for m-government platform design. *Cybernetics and Systems: An International Journal*, *37*(2-3), 119–135. doi:10.1080/01969720500428255

ADONIS. (n.d.). Retrieved from http://www.boc-group.com/documents/ products/bptrens_boc_adonis_ reportshort_eng.pdf

Agarwal, R., Krudys, G., & Tanniru, M. (1997). Infusing learning into the information systems organization. *European Journal of Information Systems*, *6*(1), 25–40. doi:10.1057/palgrave.ejis.3000257

Agrawal, R., & Srikant, R. (1995). Mining Sequential Patterns. In *11th International Conference on Data Engineering (ICDE 95)*, Taipei, Taiwan, IEEE Computer Society (pp. 3–14).

Agrawal, S., Chaudhuri, S., & Narasayya, V. R. (2000). Automated selection of materialized views and indexes in SQL databases. In *26th International Conference on Very Large Data Bases (VLDB 00)*, Cairo, Egypt (pp. 496–505).

Aiken, M., Vanjani, M., & Krosp, J. (1995). Group decision support systems. *Review of Business*, *16*(3), 38–42.

Ajzen, I. (1991). The theory of planned behavior. *Organizational Behavior and Human Decision Processes*, *50*, 179–211. doi:10.1016/0749-5978(91)90020-T

Ajzen, I., & Fishbein, M. (1980). *Understanding attitudes and predicting social behavior*. Englewood Cliffs, NJ: Prentice-Hall.

Ajzen, I. (1985). From intentions to actions: A theory of planned behavior . In Kuhl, J., & Beckman, J. (Eds.), *Action-control: From cognition to behavior* (pp. 11–39). Germany: Springer.

Al-A'ali, M., Al-Mahmood, S., & Al-Zobaidie, A. (2006). A study of user requirements for COTS - Computer off the shelf software solutions. *Software Quality Professional*, *9*(1), 32–39.

Alavi, M., & Leidner, D. E. (2001). Knowledge management and knowledge management systems: Conceptual foundations and research issues. *Management Information Systems Quarterly*, *25*(1), 107–136. doi:10.2307/3250961

Albanese, M., Picariello, A., Sansone, C., & Sansone, L. (2004). A Web Personalization System Based on Web Usage Mining Techniques. In *Proceedings of the 13th international World Wide Web conference on Alternate track papers and posters* (pp. 288-289). New York: ACM Press.

Alberts, C. J., Behrens, S. G., Pethia, R. D., & Wilson, W. R. (1999). *Operationally Critical Threat, Asset, and Vulnerability Valuation (OCTAVE) Framework*. Pittsburgh, PA: Carnegie Mellon Software Engineering Institute.

Al-But'hie, I. M., & Eben Saleh, M. A. (2002). Urban and industrial development planning as an approach for Saudi Arabia: the case study of Jubail and Yanbu. *Habitat International*, *26*(1), 1–20. doi:10.1016/S0197-3975(01)00026-1

Al-Farsy, F. (1986). *Saudi Arabia: A case study in development*. London: Keegan Paul International Limited.

Al-Gahtani, S. S., & Hubona, G., S., & Wang, J. (2007). Information technology (IT) in Saudi Arabia: Culture and the acceptance and use of IT. *Information & Management*, *44*, 681–691. doi:10.1016/j.im.2007.09.002

Al-Ghamdi, S. M. (2008). *International Business Practices in Saudi Arabia: Cultural effect*. King Fahd University of Petroleum & Minerals. Retrieved October 18, 2009, from http://faculty.kfupm.edu.sa/MGM/sghamdi/Dr_Salem_Al-Ghamdi/home.html

Al-Hawari, M. AL–Yamani, H., & Izwawa, B. (2008 February). Small Businesses' Decision to have a Website: Saudi Arabia Case Study. In *Proceedings of World Academy of Science, Engineering and Technology*, 27.

Allen, D., Kern, T., & Mattison, D. (2002). Culture, power, and politics in ICT outsourcing in high education institutions. *European Journal of Information Systems*, *11*(2), 159–173. doi:10.1057/palgrave/ejis/3000425

Al-Mahmood, S. (2004). *Managing software acquisition projects: Challenges and lessons. Unpublished master's project*. University of Bahrain, Kingdom of Bahrain.

Alonso, G., Casati, F., Kuno, H., & Machiraju, V. (2004). *Web Services, Concepts, Architectures and Applications*. Berlin: Springer-Verlag.

Al-Qirim, N. (2005). An Empirical Investigation of an e-commerce Adoption-Capability Model in Small Businesses in New Zealand. *Electronic Markets*, *15*(4), 418–437. doi:10.1080/10196780500303136

Al-Qirim, N. (2007). The adoption of eCommerce communications and applications technologies in small businesses in New Zealand. *Electronic Commerce Research and Applications*, *6*(4), 462–473. doi:10.1016/j.elerap.2007.02.012

Al-Qirim, N. (2007). A research trilogy into e-commerce adoption in small businesses in New Zealand. *Electronic Markets*, *17*(4), 263–285. doi:10.1080/10196780701635872

Al-Sudairy, M. A., & Tang, N. K. H. (2000). Information technology in Saudi Arabia's supermarket chains. *International Journal of Retail & Distribution Management*, *28*(8), 341–356. doi:10.1108/09590550010337292

Al-Yahya, K. (2009). Power-Influence in Decision Making, Competence Utilization, and Organizational Culture in Public Organizations: The Arab World in Comparative. *Journal of Public Administration: Research and Theory*, *19*(2), 385–407. doi:10.1093/jopart/mun005

AME Info - The ultimate Middle East business resource. (2005). *E-Commerce reaches new highs in Saudi Arabia*. Retrieved November 11, 2008, from http://www.ameinfo.com/61990.html

Anane, R., Freeland, R., & Theodoropoulos, G. (2007). e-Voting Requirements and Implementation. In *Proceedings of the 9th IEEE Int. Conf. on E-Commerce Technology and the 4th IEEE Int. Conf. on Enterprise Computing, E-Commerce and E-Services (CEC-EEE 2007)*.

Andam, Z. R. (2003). E-commerce and e-business. *Asia-Pacific e-primers*. Retrieved May 11, 2008, from http://www.apdip.net/publications/iespprimers/eprimer-ecom.pdf

Androutsellis-Theotokis, S., Karakoidas, V., Gousios, G., Spinellis, D., & Charalambidis, Y. (2005 October). *Building an e-Business Platform: An Experience Report*. Paper presented at the eChallenges 2005 Conference, Amsterdam, Netherlands.

Ang, S., & Cummings, L. L. (1997). Strategic response to institutional influence on information systems outsourcing. *Organization Science*, *8*(3), 235–256. doi:10.1287/orsc.8.3.235

Ang, S., & Straub, D. W. (1998). Production and transaction economies and IS outsourcing: A study of the U.S. banking industry . *Management Information Systems Quarterly*, *22*(4), 535–552. doi:10.2307/249554

Anonymous, . (1992). *The American Heritage Dictionary of the English Language*. New York: Houghton Mifflin Company.

Anonymous, . (1995). *Merriam-Webster's Collegiate Dictionary*. Springfield, MA: Merriam-Webster.

Antlova, K. (2009). Motivation and barriers of ICT adoption in small and medium sized enterprises. *E+M Ekonomie a Management*, 2, 140-155.

Aouiche, K., Jouve, P. E., & Darmont, J. (2006). Clustering-Based Materialized View Selection in Data Warehouses. In *10th East European Conference on Advances in Databases and Information Systems (ADBIS 06)* (LNCS 4152, pp. 81-95). Berlin: Springer.

Araujo, R. M. d., & Borges, M. R. S. (2007). The Role of Collaborative Support to Promote Participation and Commitment in Software Development Teams. *Software Process Improvement and Practice*, *12*(3), 229–246. doi:10.1002/spip.314

Argyris, C. (1986). Skilled incompetence. *Harvard Business Review*, *64*(5), 74–79.

Argyris, C. (1995). Action science and organizational learning. *Journal of Managerial Psychology*, *10*(6), 20–26. doi:10.1108/02683949510093849

Argyris, C., Putnam, R., & Smith, D. M. (1985). *Action science* (1st ed.). San Francisco: Jossey-Bass.

Ashrafi. R., & Murtaza, M. (2008). Use and impact of ICT on SMEs in Oman. *The Electronic Journal Information Systems Evaluation, 11*(3), 125-138. Retrieved from http://www.ejise.com

Aslam, M., Auer, S., Shen, J., & Herrmann, M. (2006). Expressing business process model as owl-s ontologies. In *2nd International Workshop on Grid and Peer-to-Peer based Workflows (GPWW 2006)* (pp. 400 - 415).

Assmann, D., & Punter, T. (2004). Towards partnership in software subcontracting . *Computers in Industry Journal*, *54*(2), 137–150. doi:10.1016/j.compind.2003.09.005

ATHENA Project. (n.d.). Retrieved from http://www.athena-ip.org

Atkinson, W. (2003). Buying software: Why you need to be involved. *Purchasing Journal, 132*, 22-23. Retrieved December 1, 2006, from http://www.purchasing.com

Attaran, M. (2004). Exploring the relationship between information technology and business process reengineering . *Information & Management*, *41*, 585–596. doi:10.1016/S0378-7206(03)00098-3

Aubert, B. A., Rivad, S., & Patry, M. (1996). A transaction cost approach to outsourcing behavior. *Information & Management*, *30*(2), 51–64. doi:10.1016/0378-7206(95)00045-3

Aubert, B. A., Rivad, S., & Patry, M. (2004). A transaction cost model of IT outsourcing. *Information & Management*, *41*(7), 921–932. doi:10.1016/j.im.2003.09.001

Avery, S. (2003). Sourcing software? An expert offers how-to tips. *Purchasing Journal, 132*(26), 28-29. Retrieved December 1, 2006, from http://www.purchasing.com

Avison, D., Lau, F., Myers, M., & Nielsen, P. A. (1999). Action Research. *Communications of the ACM*, *42*(1), 94–97. doi:10.1145/291469.291479

Azoff, M., Jones, T., Rodger, A., & Butler, G. (2004). *IT Performance Optimisation: Realising Best Value from IT Investments*. Hull, UK: Butler Direct.

Bacheldor, B. (2006, October 24). RFID Fills Security Gap at Psychiatric Ward. *RFID Journal*. Retrieved from http://www.rfidjournal.com/article/articleview/2750/1/1/

Bacheldor, B. (2007, August 21). RFID documents surgery at Huntsville hospital. *RFID Journal*. Retrieved from http://www.rfidjournal.com/article/articleprint/3572/-1/1/

Baghdadi, Y. (2004). ABBA: an architecture for deploying business-to-business electronic commerce applications. *Electronic Commerce Research and Applications*, *3*, 190–212. doi:10.1016/j.elerap.2003.09.006

Baldwin, G., & Larkin, M. (2008 January). Where did we put that wheelchair? *HealthLeaders*, 33-34.

Baldwin, J. R., Jarmin, R. S., & Tang, J. (2001). The Trend to Smaller Producers in Manufacturing in Canada and the US. *Statistics Canada Working paper*.

Ballon, P., & Walravens, N. (2008). Competing Platform Models for Mobile Service Delivery: The Importance of Gatekeeper Roles. In *Proceedings of the 7th International Conference on Mobile Business (ICMB '08)*, (pp. 102 – 111).

Bamber, E. M., Watson, R. T., & Hill, M. C. (1996). The effects of group support system technology on audit group decision-making. *Auditing: A Journal of Practice & Theory, 15*(1), 122-134.

Banerjee, D., Cronan, T. P., & Jones, T. W. (1998). Modeling IT ethics: A study in situational ethics. *Management Information Systems Quarterly*, *22*(1), 31–60. doi:10.2307/249677

Banks, T. (2006). *Web Services Resource Framework (WSRF)–Primer v1. 2*. OASIS Committee Draft.

Barclay, T., Gray, J., Ekblad, S., Strand, E., & Richter, J. (2006). Designing and Building TerraService. *IEEE Internet Computing, 10*(5), 16–25. doi:10.1109/MIC.2006.95

Barclay, T., Gray, J., & Slutz, D. (2000). Microsoft TerraServer: a spatial data warehouse. *SIGMOD Record, 29*(2), 307–318. doi:10.1145/335191.335424

Baril, X., & Bellahsène, Z. (2003). XML Data Management: Native XML and XML-enabled Database Systems . In *Designing and Managing an XML Warehouse* (pp. 455–473). Reading, MA: Addison Wesley.

Barkstrom, B. R., Hinke, T. H., Gavali, S., Smith, W., Seufzer, W. J., & Hu, C. (2003). Distributed Generation of NASA Earth Science Data Products. *Journal of Grid Computing, 1*(2), 101–116. doi:10.1023/B:GRID.0000024069.33399.ee

Barthelemy, J., & Geyer, D. (2005). An empirical investigation of IT outsourcing versus quasi-outsourcing in France and Germany. *Information & Management, 42*(4), 533–542. doi:10.1016/j.im.2004.02.005

Basili, V. R. (1989). Software Development: A Paradigm for the Future. In *Proceedings of the 13th Annual Computer Software and Applications Conference (COMPSAC)* (pp. 471-485). Washington, DC: IEEE Computer Society Press.

Basili, V. R., Caldiera, G., & McGarry, F. Pajerski. R., Page, G., & Waligora, S. (1992 May). The Software Engineering Laboratory - an Operational Software Experience Factory. In *Proceedings of the International Conference on Software Engineering* (pp. 370-381). Washington, DC: IEEE Computer Society Press.

Baskerville, R. L., & Siponen, M. T. (2002). An information security meta-policy for emergent organizations. *Logistics Information Management, 15*, 337–346. doi:10.1108/09576050210447019

Bassellier, G., & Benbasat, I. (2004). Business Competence of Information Technology Professionals: Conceptual Development and Influence on It-Business Partnerships. *Management Information Systems Quarterly, 28*(4), 673–694.

Bassellier, G., Reich, B. H., & Benbasat, I. (2001). Information Technology Competence of Business Managers: A Definition and Research Model. *Journal of Management Information Systems, 17*(4), 159–182.

Beatty, R. C., Shim, J. P., & Jones, M. C. (2001). Factors influencing corporate web site adoption: a time-based assessment. *Information & Management, 38*, 337–354. doi:10.1016/S0378-7206(00)00064-1

Beer, T., Rasinger, J., Höpken, W., Fuchs, M., & Werthner, H. (2007). Exploiting E-C-A Rules for Defining and Processing Context-Aware Push Messages. In *RuleML* (pp. 199-206).

Beeri, C., Eyal, A., Milo, T., & Pilberg, A. (2007) Query-based monitoring of BPEL business processes. In *Proceedings of the 2007 ACM SIGMOD international conference on Management of data,* Beijing (pp. 1122 – 1124). New York: ACM.

Behforooz, A., & Hudson, F. J. (1996). *Software Engineering Fundamentals*. New York: Oxford University Press.

Belderbos, R., Carree, M., Diederen, B., Lokshin, B., & Veugelers, R. (2004). Heterogeneity in R&D cooperation strategies. *International Journal of Industrial Organization, 22*, 1237–1263. doi:10.1016/j.ijindorg.2004.08.001

Bell, D. G., Kuehnel, F., Maxwell, C., Kim, R., Kasraie, K., Gaskins, T., et al. (2007). *NASA world wind: Open-source GIS for mission operations.*

Belsis, P., Kokolakis, S., & Kiountouzis, E. (2005). Information systems security from a knowledge management perspective. *Information Management & Computer Security, 13*(3), 189–202. doi:10.1108/09685220510602013

Belton, V., Ackermann, F., & Shepherd, I. (1997). Integrated support from problem structuring through to alternative evaluation using COPE and V.I.S.A. *Journal of Multi-Criteria Decision Analysis, 6*(3), 115–130. doi:10.1002/(SICI)1099-1360(199705)6:3<115::AID-MCDA140>3.0.CO;2-I

Benbasat, I., & Lim, L. H. (1993). The effects of group, task, context, and technology variables on the usefulness of group support systems: A meta-analysis of experimental studies. *Small Group Research, 24*, 430–462. doi:10.1177/1046496493244002

Bendoly, E., Rosenzweig, E., & Stratman, J. (2009). The efficient use of enterprise information for strategic advantage: A data envelopment analysis. *Journal of Operations Management, 27*, 310–323. doi:10.1016/j.jom.2008.11.001

Bertino, E., & Sandhu, R. (2005). Database security - concepts, approaches, and challenges. *IEEE Transactions on Dependable and Secure Computing*, *2*(1), 2–19. doi:10.1109/TDSC.2005.9

Beulen, E., & Ribbers, P. (2003). IT outsourcing contracts: Practical implications of the incomplete contract theory. In *Proceedings of the 36th Hawaii International Conference on System Sciences*.

Beyer, K. S., Chamberlin, D. D., Colby, L. S., Ozcan, F., Pirahesh, H., & Xu, Y. (2005). Extending XQuery for Analytics. In *ACM SIGMOD International Conference on Management of Data (SIGMOD '05)*, Baltimore, USA (pp. 503–514). New York: ACM.

Beyer, K. S., Cochrane, R., Colby, L. S., Ozcan, F., & Pirahesh, H. (2004). XQuery for Analytics: Challenges and Requirements. In *1st International Workshop on XQuery Implementation, Experience and Perspectives <XIME-P/>*, Paris, France (pp. 3–8).

Bianchi, A., & Phillips, J. G. (2005). Psychological predictors of problem mobile phone use. *Cyberpsychology & Behavior*, *8*(1), 39–51. doi:10.1089/cpb.2005.8.39

Bider, I., Johansson, L., Perjons, E., & Striy, A. (2006). *Activation of Knowledge in an Integrated Business Process Support/Knowledge Management System* (pp. 13–24). PAKM.

Bidgoli, H. (1996). A new productivity tool for the 90's: Group support systems. *Journal of Systems Management*, *47*(4), 56–62.

Bishop, M., & Wagner, D. (2007). Risks of e-Voting. *Communications of the ACM*, *50*(11), 120. doi:10.1145/1297797.1297827

Bjerke, B., & Al-Meer, A. R. (1993). Culture's consequences: management in Saudi Arabia. *Leadership and Organization Development Journal*, *14*(2), 30–35. doi:10.1108/01437739310032700

Boag, S., Chamberlin, D., Fernandez, M., Florescu, D., Robie, J., & Siméon, J. (2004). *XQuery 1.0: An XML Query Language*. W3C Working Draft. Retrieved from http://www.w3.org/TR/xquery/

Boehm, B. W. (1991). *Software Risk Management: Principles and Practices*. Washington, DC: IEEE Software.

Boehm, B. (2000). Requirements that handle IKIWISI, COTS, and rapid change. *IEEE Computer*, *33*(7), 99–102.

Boehm, B., Maiden, N., & Moore, M. (2004). Do we need requirements in COTS-based software development. In R. Kazman & D. Port (Eds.), *COTS-Based Software Systems: Third International Conference, ICCBSS 2004, Redondo Beach, CA, USA, February 1-4, 2004, Proceedings* (pp. 11-12). New York: Springer-Verlag.

Boley, H., Tabet, S., & Wagner, G. (2001). Design Rationale of RuleML: A Markup Language for Semantic Web Rules. In *Proceedings of the Semantic Web Working Symposium*, Stanford, 2001.

Bolin, S. (2004). *The Nature and Future of ICT Standardization*. Retrieved June 21, 2004, from http://www.sun.com/software/standards/natureandfuture_ICT.pdf

Bommel, P. v., Hoppenbrouwers, S. J. B. A., Proper, H. A. E., & Weide, T. P. d. (2006). Exploring modelling strategies in a meta-modelling context. In R. Meersman, Z. Tari & P. Herrero (Eds.), *On the move to meaningful internet systems 2006: Proceedings of Otm 2006 workshops* (LNCS 4278, pp. 1128-1137). Berlin: Springer.

Boresson C., J. (2005). *Good Enough! IT Investment and Business Process Performance in Higher Education*. Educause Center For Applied Research.

Borkar, V., & Carey, M. (2004). Extending XQuery for Grouping, Duplicate Elimination, and Outer Join. In *<XML 2004> Conference & Exhibition*, Washington, DC, USA (pp. 1–11).

Bostrom, R. P., & Heinen, S. (1977). MIS problems and failures: a socio-technical perspective, part 1: the causes. *Management Information Systems Quarterly*, *1*(3), 17–32. doi:10.2307/248710

Bouma, G. D., & Ling, R. (2004). *The Research Process* (5th ed.). Victoria, Australia: Oxford University Press.

Brereton, P. (2004). The software customer/supplier relationship. *Communications of the ACM*, *47*, 77–81. doi:10.1145/966389.966394

Brindley, C., & Ritchie, B. (2005). ICT Adoption by SMEs: Implications for Relationships and Management. *New Technology, Work and Employment*, *20*(3), 205–217. doi:10.1111/j.1468-005X.2005.00154.x

Briseno, A. G. (2009). *From m-euphoria to m-governance: Thinking about the potential of mobile technology*. Retrieved from http://blogs.worldbank.org/governance/from-m-euphoria-to-m-governance-thinking-about-the-potential-of-mobile-technology

British Computer Society. (2007 October). *Growing SMEs need IT*. Retrieved March 11, 2008, from http://www.bcs.org/server.php?show=ConWebDoc.15442

Brotby, W. K. (2009). *Information Security Management Metrics: A Definitive Guide to Effective Security Monitoring and Measurement*. Boca Raton, FL: Auerbach Publications. doi:10.1201/9781420052862

Brown, B., Green, N., & Harper, R. (2002). *Wireless world: Social, cultural and interactional issues in mobile communications and computing*. London: Springer.

Bruque, S., & Moyano, J. (2007). Organizational determinants of information technology adoption and implementation in SMEs: The case of family and cooperative firms. *Technovation*, *27*(5), 241–253. doi:10.1016/j.technovation.2006.12.003

Burke, K., Chidambaram, L., & Lock, J. (1995). Evolution of relational factors over time: A study of distributed and non-distributed meetings. In *Proceedings of the Twenty-Eighth Hawaii International Conference on System Sciences* (Vol. 4, pp. 14-23).

Burrows, J. (1999). Information Technology standards in a changing world: the role of the users . In *Computer Standards & Interfaces* (pp. 323–331). Amsterdam: Elsevier Science B.V.

Butler, G. (2004). *Managing Costs in IT: Achieving Best Value from IT Investments*. Hull, UK: Butler Group.

Butler, R. (1990). Decision-making research: Its uses and misuses. A comment on Mintzberg and Waters: 'Does decision get in the way.' . *Organization Studies*, *11*(1), 11–16. doi:10.1177/017084069001100103

Caldeira, M. M., & Ward, J. M. (2002). Understanding the Successful Adoption and Use of IS/IT in SMEs: an Explanation from Portuguese Manufacturing Industries. *Information Systems Journal*, *12*, 121–152. doi:10.1046/j.1365-2575.2002.00119.x

Canel, E. (1992). New social movement theory and resource mobilization: the need for integration . In Carroll, W. (Ed.), *Organizing Dissent: Social Movements in Theory and Practice* (pp. 22–51). Toronto, Canada: Garamond.

Capers, C., Bartels, A., Wilson, R., & Rugullies, E. (2001 November), *B2B Exchanges: Future Hopes, Current Doubts*. Booz Allen Hamilton and Giga Information Group.

Cardenas, A. F. (1975). Analysis and performance of inverted data base structures. *Communications of the ACM*, *18*(5), 253–263. doi:10.1145/360762.360766

Carr, M. J., Konda, S. L., Monarch, I. A., Ulrich, F. C., & Walker, C. F. (1993). *Taxonomy-Based Risk Identification*. SEI Technical Report SEI-93-TR-006. Pittsburgh, PA: Software Engineering Institute.

Carvallo, J., Franch, X., & Quer, C. (2008). Requirements engineering for COTS-based software systems. In *Proceedings of the 2008 ACM symposium on Applied Computing* (pp. 638-644). Ceará, Brazil: ACM.

Casassa Mont, M., Bramhall, P., & Pato, J. (2003). *On Adaptive Identity Management: The Next Generation of Identity Management Technologies*. Retrieved October 30, 2009, from http://www.hpl.hp.com/techreports/2003/HPL-2003-149.pdf

Cass, K., Heintz, T. J., & Kaiser, K. M. (1991). Using a voice-synchronous GDSS in dispersed locations: A preliminary analysis of participant satisfaction. In *Proceedings of the Twenty-Fourth Hawaii International Conference on System Sciences* (Vol. 3, pp. 555-563).

Cavoukian, A. (2008). *RFID and Privacy - Guidance for Health Care Providers* [Report]. Toronto, Canada: Information Privacy Commissioner of Ontario and Hewlett Packard Company.

Central Department of Statistics. (2005). *General Population Census and Housing*. Retrieved June 25, 2009, from http://www.cds.gov.sa/english/enewsectiondetail.aspx?id=63

Chalmers, D., & Sloman, M. (1999). A survey of quality of service in mobile computing environments. *IEEE Communications Surveys & Tutorials*, *2*(2).

Chan, M., Woon, I., & Kankanhalli, A. (2005). Perceptions of information security at the workplace: Linking information security climate to compliant behavior. *Journal of Information Privacy and Security*, *1*(3), 18–41.

Chan, C., & Swatman, P. (2002), Management and business issues for B2B eCommerce implementation. In *Proceedings of the 35th Hawaii International Conference on System Sciences*.

Chapin, D. A., & Akridge, S. (2005). How can security be measured? *Information Systems Audit and Control, 2*.

Chapman, S., & Schofield, W. N. (1998). Lifesavers and Samaritans: emergency use of cellular (mobile) phones in Australia. *Accident; Analysis and Prevention*, *30*(6), 815–819. doi:10.1016/S0001-4575(98)00034-7

Charette, R. N. (1989). *Software Engineering Risk Analysis and Management*. New York: McGraw-Hill.

Chau, P., & Hui, K. (2001). Determinants of Small Business EDI Adoption: An Empirical Investigation. *Journal of Organizational Computing and Electronic Commerce*, *11*(4), 229–252. doi:10.1207/S15327744JOCE1104_02

Checkland, P., & Holwell, S. (2004). *Information Systems and Information Systems-Making Sense of the Field*. Chichester, UK: John Wiley & Sons.

Checkland, P., & Scholes, J. (1990). *Soft System Methodology in Action*. Chichester, UK: Wiley.

Chen, C. C., Wu, J., Su, Y. S., & Yang, S. C. (2008). Key drivers for the continued use of RFID technology in the emergency room. *Management Research News*, *31*(4), 273–288. doi:10.1108/01409170810851348

Chen, A., Di, L., Wei, Y., Bai, Y., & Liu, Y. (2006). *An optimized grid-based, OGC standards-compliant collaborative software system for serving NASA geospatial data*.

Chen, R., Wu, R., & Chen, J. (2005). Data Mining Application in Customer Relationship Management of Credit Card Business. In *29th Annual International Computer Software and Applications Conference COMPSAC* (pp. 39–40).

Chong, S. (2008). Success in electronic commerce implementation: A cross-country study of small and medium-sized enterprises. *Journal of Enterprise Information Management*, *21*(5), 468–492. doi:10.1108/17410390810904247

Chou, E. (2002). Redesigning a Large and Complex Website: How to Begin, and a Method for Success. In *SIGUCCS 2002: Proceedings of the 30th annual ACM SIGUCCS conference on User services* (pp. 22-28). New York: ACM Press.

Chowdhury, B., & Khosla, R. (2007 July). RFID based Real Time Patient Management System. *Computer and Information Science*, 363-368.

Chudoba, K. M. (1999). Appropriations and patterns in the use of group support systems. *The Data Base for Advances in Information Systems*, *30*(3/4), 131–148.

Chung, C. W., Park, M. J., & Shim, K. (2002). APEX: an Adaptive Path Index of XML data. In *ACM SIGMOD International Conference on Management of Data (SIGMOD 02)* (pp. 121-132).

Cilingir, D., & Kushchu, I. (2004). E-government and m-government: Concurrent leaps by Turkey. In D. Remenyi (Ed.) *Proceedings of European Conference on E-Government (ECEG 2004),* Trinity College, Dublin, June 17-18 (pp. 813-821). Reading, UK: Academic Conferences International.

CITC - Communications and Information Technology Commission. (2007). *Internet in Saudi Arabia*. Retrieved October 14, 2009, from http://www.internet.gov.sa/learn-the-web/guides/internet-in-saudi-arabia

CITC - Communications and Information Technology Commission. (2008). *Internet Usage in the Kingdom of Saudi Arabia - Business establishments*. Retrieved November 4, 2008, from http://www.citc.gov.sa/

Clark, T., & Jones, R. (1999). Organizational interoperability maturity model. In *Proceedings of the 1999 Command and Control Research and Technology Symposium*. Newport, RI: United States Naval War College.

Clarke, J. (2004). Information Systems Strategy and Knowledge-based SMEs in the Australian Biotechnology Industry: Does IS need to reorient its thinking? In *15th Australian Conference on Information Systems*, Hobart, Australia.

Coase, R. H. (1937). The nature of the firm. *Economica*, *4*(16), 386–405. doi:10.1111/j.1468-0335.1937.tb00002.x

Collins, J. (2005, July 5). India adopts 865-867 MHz for RFID. *RFID Journal*. Retrieved from http://www.rfidjournal.com/article/view/1703/1/1

Comela-Dorda, S., Dean, J., Morris, E., & Oberndorf, P. (2002). A process for COTS software product evaluation. In *Proceedings of the First International Conference on COTS-Based Software Systems* (pp. 86-96). New York: Springer-Verlag.

Comite, F., Gilleron, R., & Tommasi, M. (2001). Learning multi-label alternating decision trees and applications. In G. Bisson (Ed.), *Proceedings of CAP'01: Conference en AP (prentissage Automatique)* (pp. 195-210).

Conklin, J., Selvin, A., Buckingham Shum, S., & Sierhuis, M. (2003). *Facilitated Hypertext for Collective Sense-making: 15 Years on from gIBIS.* Paper presented at the Proceedings of the 8th International Working Conference on the Language-Action Perspective on Communication Modeling (LAP'03), Tilburg, The Netherlands.

Cook, K. S. (1977). Exchange and power in networks of interorganizational relations. *The Sociological Quarterly*, *18*(1), 62–82. doi:10.1111/j.1533-8525.1977.tb02162.x

Cooper, B. F., Sample, N., Franklin, M. J., Hjaltason, G. R., & Shadmon, M. (2001). A Fast Index for Semistructured Data. In *27th International Conference on Very Large Data Bases (VLDB 01)*, Roma, Italy (pp. 341–350). San Francisco: Morgan Kaufmann.

Cortellessa, V., Crnkovic, I., Marinelli, F., & Potena, P. (2007). Driving the selection of COTS components on the basis of system requirements. In *Proceedings of the Twenty-second IEEE/ACM International Conference on Automated Software Engineering* (pp. 413-416). New York: ACM.

Costello, C. (2003). *Integrating Intelligence into the Business Process Management Framework.* Thesis: M.Sc. Applied Computing and Information Technology, National University of Ireland, Galway, 2003.

Council of Europe. (2004). *Electronic Governance Recommendation 15.* Strasbourg, France: Author.

Cox, J. (2008, August 25). RFID proving to be Rx for hospitals. *New World (New Orleans, La.)*, *25*(33), 24.

Creswell, J. W. (1997). *Qualitative Inquiry and Research Design: Choosing among five Traditions*. Thousand Oaks, CA: Sage Publications.

Cullen, S., Seddon, P., & Willcocks, L. (2005). IT outsourcing configuration: Research into defining and designing outsourcing arrangements. *Strategic Information Systems*, *14*(4), 357–387. doi:10.1016/j.jsis.2005.07.001

Curtis, B., Kellner, M. I., & Over, J. (1992). Process Modeling. *Communications of the ACM*, *35*, 75–90. doi:10.1145/130994.130998

Dacin, M. T., Oliver, C., & Roy, J.-P. (2007). The legitimacy of strategic alliances: An in-stitutional perspective. *Strategic Management Journal*, *28*, 169–187. doi:10.1002/smj.577

Damanpour, F. (1991). Organisational Innovation: A Meta-Analysis of Effects of Determinants and Moderators. *Academy of Management Journal*, *34*(3), 555–590. doi:10.2307/256406

D'Arcy, J., Hovav, A., & Galletta, D. (2009). User awareness of security countermeasures and its impact on information systems misuse: A deterrence approach. *Information Systems Research*, *20*(1). doi:10.1287/isre.1070.0160

Darie, C., & Bucica, M. (2006). WEB services connections . In *PHP5 and MySQL for Electronic Commerce* (pp. 506–534). Bucarest, Romania: Teora.

Darie, C., & Watson, K. (2006). Credit card transactions: creating customer accounts. In *Beginning ASP.Net 2.0 E-Commerce in C# 2005: From Novice to Professional* (pp. 593-624). New York: Apress.

Darie, C., & Watson, K. (2009). Creating customer accounts. In *Beginning ASP.Net E-Commerce in C# 2008: From Novice to Professional* (pp. 465-530). New York: Apress.

Darmont, J., Boussaïd, O., Bentayeb, F., Rabaseda, S., & Zellouf, Y. (2003). Web multiform data structuring for warehousing . In *Multimedia Systems and Applications* (*Vol. 22*, pp. 179–194). Amsterdam: Kluwer.

Darmont, J., Boussaïd, O., Ralaivao, J. C., & Aouiche, K. (2005). An Architecture Framework for Complex Data Warehouses. In *7th International Conference on Enterprise Information Systems (ICEIS 05)*, Miami, USA (pp. 370–373).

Das, T. K., & Teng, B.-S. (2000). A resource-based theory of strategic alliances. *Journal of Management*, *26*(1), 31–61. doi:10.1016/S0149-2063(99)00037-9

Davis, F., Bangozzi, R., & Warshaw, P. (1989). User Acceptance of Computer Technology: A Comparison of Two Theoretical Models. *Journal of Management science, 35*(8), 982-4.

Dawn, J., Podonik, P., & Dhaliwal, J. (2002). Supporting the E-business Readiness of Small and Medium-Sized Enterprises: Approaches and Metrics. *Internet Research, 12*(2), 139–195. doi:10.1108/10662240210422512

De Kervenoael, R., Palmer, M., & Cakici, N. M. (2010). Exploring civil servant resistance to m-government: A story of transition and opportunities in Turkey . In Abdel-Wahab, A. G., & El-Masry, A. A. (Eds.), *Mobile Information Communication Technologies Adoption in Developing Countries: Effects and Implications*. Hershey, PA: IGI Global.

Dedeoglu, A. O. (2004). The symbolic use of mobile telephone among Turkish consumers. *Journal of Euromarketing, 13*(2/3), 143–163. doi:10.1300/J037v13n02_08

DeFee, J., & Harmon, P. (2005). Business Activity Monitoring and Simulation . In *Workflow Handbook 2005* (pp. 53–74). Lighthouse Point, FL: Future Strategies.

Delaney, K. (2008). Tracing and profiling . In *Inside Microsoft SQL Server 2005* (pp. 57–103). Redmond, WA: Microsoft Press.

Deng, M., & Di, L. (2006). Utilization of latest geospatial Web service technologies for remote sensing education through GeoBrain sysem.

Depietro, R., Wiarda, E., & Fleischer, M. (1990). The Context for Change: Organisation, Technology, and Environment . In Tornatzky, L. G., & Fleischer, M. (Eds.), *The Processes of Technological Innovation* (pp. 151–175). Lexington, MA: Lexington Books.

Derzsi, Z., & Gordijn, J. (2006). A framework for business/IT alignment in networked value constellations. In T. Latour & M. Petit (Eds.) *Proceedings of the workshops of the 18th International Conference on Advanced Information Systems Engineering* (CAiSE 2006) (pp. 219–226). Namur, Belgium: Namur University Press.

Descy, E. D. (2006). The Wiki: True Web Democracy. *TechTrends, 50*(1), 4–5. doi:10.1007/s11528-006-7569-y

Dhillon, G. (1999). Managing and controlling computer abuse. *Information Management & Computer Security, 7*(4), 171–175. doi:10.1108/09685229910292664

Dhillon, G., & Backhouse, J. (2000). Information systems security management in the new millennium. *Communications of the ACM, 43*(7), 125–128. doi:10.1145/341852.341877

Dhillon, G., & Torkzadeh, G. (2006). Value-focused assessment of information system security in organizations. *Information Systems Journal, 16*, 293–314. doi:10.1111/j.1365-2575.2006.00219.x

Di, L., Zhao, P., Yang, W., Yu, G., & Yue, P. (2005). *Intelligent geospatial Web services.*

Dietz, J. L. G. (1999). Understanding and modeling business processes with DEMO. In J. Akoka, M. Bouzeghoub, I. Comyn-Wattiau & E. Métais (Eds.), *Proceedings of the 18th International Conference on Conceptual Modeling ER '99* (pp. 188-202). Berlin: Springer.

DiRomualdo, A., & Gurbaxani, V. (1998). Strategic intent for IT outsourcing. *Sloan Management Review, 39*(4), 67–80.

D'Mello, D. A., Ananthanarayana, V. S., & Santhi, T. (2008). A QoS Broker Based Architecture for Dynamic Web Service Selection. In *Proceedings of the Second Asia International Conference on Modeling & Simulation (AICMS 08)*, (pp. 101 – 106).

Doczi, M. (2002). Information and Communication Technologies and Social and Economic Inclusion. In *Information technology Policy Group, Ministry of Economic Development*, Manatu, Ohanga, NZ.

Döring, N., & Gundolf, A. (2005). Your Life in Snapshots. Mobile Weblogs (Moblogs) . In Glotz, P., Bertschi, S., & Locke, C. (Eds.), *Thumb Culture. The Meaning of Mobile Phones for Society* (pp. 211–224). Bielefeld, Germany: Transcript.

Douglas, B. (2008). Device to device communications . In *Programming Windows Embedded CE 6.0* (4th ed., pp. 469–535). Redmond, WA: Microsoft Press.

Dssouli, R., Saleh, K., Aboulhamid, E., En-Nouaary, A., & Bourhfir, C. (1999). Test development for communication protocols: towards automation. *Computer Networks, 31*, 1835–1872. doi:10.1016/S1389-1286(99)00063-8

Duan, Y., Mullins, R., Hamblin, D., Stanek, S., Sroka, H., Mavhado, V., & Araujo, J. (2002). Addressing ICTs Skill Challenges in SMEs: Insights from three country investigations. *Journal of European Industrial Training*, *26*(9), 430–441. doi:10.1108/03090590210451524

Dubelaar, C. (2005). Benefits, impediments and critical success factors in B2C e-business adoption. *Technovation*, *25*, 1251–1262. doi:10.1016/j.technovation.2004.08.004

Dutta, A., & McCrohan, K. (2002). Management's role in information security in a cyber economy. *California Management Review*, *45*(1), 67–87.

Dutta, S., & Coury, M. E. (2003). ICT Challenges for the Arab World. In *The Global Information Technology Report 2002-2003: Readiness for the Networked World* (pp. 116-131). New York: World Economic Forum/Oxford University Press.

eBusiness in Europe. (2008). *eBusiness Watch*. Retrieved from http://www.ebusiness-watch.org

Eccles, R. (1991 January). The Performance Management Manifesto. *Harvard Business Review*.

Edifecs. (2000). *Solving the B2B Ramp-up Challenge: Key to Realizing Widespread e-Commerce Adoption*. Research Report, Edifecs Inc.

eEurope. (2005). Retrieved from http://europa.eu/information_society/eeurope/

Egan, T., Clancy, S., & O'Toole, T. (2003). The Integration of E-Commerce Tools into the Business Processes of SMEs. *Irish Journal of Management* (pp. 139-152).

Eichinger, F., Nauck, D., & Klawonn, F. (2006). Sequence Mining for Customer Behavior Predictions in Telecommunications. In M. Ackermann, C. Soares & B. Guidemann (Eds.), *Proceedings of the Workshop on Practical Data Mining at ECML/PKDD*, Berlin, Germany (pp. 3–10).

Eisenhardt, K. M., & Schoonhoven, C. B. (1996). Resource-based view of strategic alliance formation: Strategic and social effects in entrepreneurial firms. *Organization Science*, *7*(2), 136–150. doi:10.1287/orsc.7.2.136

Elgin, D. (1981). *Voluntary Simplicity: Toward a way of life that is Outwardly Simple, Inwardly Rich*. New York: Morrow.

Ellis, S. (2008). The status of e-commerce in New Zealand. *Otago Marketing Review*, 1. University of Otago, New Zealand. Retrieved February 1, 2009 from, http://marketing.otago.ac.nz/OMR/img/Samuel%20Ellis%20June%202008.pdf

eMarketer. (2002). *Europe eCommerce: B2B & B2C*. Executive summary, eMarketer Inc.

Emarketer. (2007). *European E-Commerce on Pace to Reach €323 Billion in 2011*. Retrieved February 1, 2009, from http://www.emarketer.com/Article.aspx?id=1005231

Emerson, R. M. (1962). Power-dependence relations. *American Sociological Review*, *27*, 31–41. doi:10.2307/2089716

Ericsson, K., & Simon, H. (1993). *Protocol Analysis: Verbal Reports as Data*. Boston: MIT Press.

Ersala, N., Yen, D., & Rajkumar, T. (2002). Enterprise Application Integration in the electronic commerce world . *Computer Standards & Interfaces*, *2189*, 1–14.

Esbjornsson, M., Juhlin, O., & Weilenmann, A. (2007). Drivers using mobile phones in traffic: An ethnographic study of interactional adaptation. *International Journal of Human-Computer Interaction*, *22*(1-2), 37. doi:10.1207/s15327590ijhc2201-02_3

European Commission. (2004). *SME definitions*. Retrieved May 14, 2009, from http://europa.eu.int/comm/enterprise/enterprise_policy/sme_definition/index_en.htm.

Evermann, J. (2006). Organizational paradigms and organizational modelling. In T. Latour & M. Petit (Eds.) *Proceedings of the workshops of the 18th International Conference on Advanced Information Systems Engineering* (CAiSE 2006) (pp. 230–239). Namur, Belgium: Namur University Press.

Fairley, R. E. (1989). Risk Management: The Key to Successful Software Projects. In F. J. Mowle & P. F. Elzer (Eds.), *Proceedings of the 3rd IFAC/IFIP Workshop* (pp. 45-50). Oxford, UK: Pergamon.

Falk, M. (2001). Diffusion of Information Technology, Internet Use and the Demand for Heterogeneous Labor . In *European Association of Labour Economists*. Jyväskylä, Finland: EALE.

Faustmann, G. (1998). Enforcement vs. Freedom of Action, An Integrated Approach to Flexible Workflow Enactment. *SIGGROUP Bull*, *20*(3), 5–6.

Fayyad, U., Piatetsky-Shapiro, G., & Smyth, P. (1996). An Overview . In *Advances in Knowledge Discovery and Data Mining* (pp. 1–34). From Data Mining to Knowledge Discovery.

Fenz, S., & Ekelhart, A. (2009). *Formalizing information security knowledge.* Paper presented at the The 4th International Symposium on Information, Computer, and Communications Security, Sydney, Australia.

Ferguson, M. (2001). *e-Government- A strategic Framework for public services in the Information Age*. London: Society of IT Management.

Fillies, C., & Weichhardt, F. (n.d.). *On Ontology-based Event-driven Process Chains*. Retrieved from http://www.semtalk.com/pub/semtalkepk.pdf

Fink, D., & Disterer, G. (2006). International Case Studies: To what extent is ICT infused into the Operations of SMEs? *Journal of Enterprise Information Management*, *19*(6), 608–624. doi:10.1108/17410390610708490

Finnegan, D., & Currie, W. (2009). *A multilayered ap proach to CRM implementation: An integration perspective.* European Management Journal.

Fisher, J. A., & Monahan, T. (2008). Tracking the social dimensions of RFID systems in hospitals. *International Journal of Medical Informatics*, *77*(3), 176–183. doi:10.1016/j.ijmedinf.2007.04.010

Fitzke, J., Greve, K., M\üller, M., & Poth, A. (2004). *Building SDIs with Free Software-the deegree project.*

Fjermestad, J., & Hiltz, S. R. (1998). An assessment of group support systems experiment research: Methodology and results. *Journal of Management Information Systems*, *15*(3), 7–149.

Folmer, E., Hinderer, H., & Otto, B. (2003). The openXchange framework for ebXML-based business process integration . In Jardim-Gonçalves, R. (Eds.), *Concurrent Engineering: Enhanced Interoperable Systems* (pp. 447–453). Amsterdam: A. A. Balkema Publishers.

Forster, F. (2006). The Idea Behind Business Process Improvment. *BP Trends*. Retrieved from http://www.bptrends.com/publicationfiles/04-06-ART-PatternFramework-Forster.pdf

Fortunati, L., Katz, J. E., & Riccini, R. (2003). *Mediating the human body: Technology, communication, and fashion.* Mahwah, NJ: Lawrence Erlbaum.

Foster, K. R., & Moulder, J. E. (2000). Are mobile phones safe? *IEEE Spectrum*, ▪▪▪, 23–28. doi:10.1109/6.861774

Fowler, M. (2006). *UML 2.0 Distilled* (3rd ed.). Reading, MA: Addison Wesley.

Fraunholz, B. (2001) Project Management in the German Trade Sector – A (preliminary) framework for computer assisted management of Projects in Small and Medium Sized Enterprises. In *Proceedings of Australasian Conference on Information Systems,* Coffs Harbour, NSW, Australia.

Frederiks, P. J. M., & Weide, T. P. d. (2006). Information modelling: The process and the required competencies of its participants. *Data & Knowledge Engineering*, *58*(1), 4–20. doi:10.1016/j.datak.2005.05.007

Fu, S., Chieu, T., Yih, J.-S., & Kumaran, S. (2005). An Intelligent Event Adaptation Mechanism for Business Performance Monitoring. In *IEEE International Conference on e Business Engineering (ICEBE'05)*, Beijing, China, October 18-20.

Fu, Y., Creado, M., & Shih, M. (2001). Adaptive Web Sites by Web Usage Mining. In *International Conference on Internet Computing (IC 2001),* Las Vegas, NV.

Ganesh, M. (2006). *Introduction to Fuzzy Sets and Fuzzy Logic*. Upper Saddle River, NJ: Prentice Hall of India.

Gang, Y., Chanle, W., Jun, Y., & Shi, C. (2009). A QoS-Aware Model for Web Services Discovery. In *Proceedings of the First International Workshop on Education Technology and Computer Science (ETCS '09)* (Vol. 3, pp. 740–744).

Ganna, M., & Horlait, E. (2003). Policy-based service provisioning and users management using mobile agents . In Horlait, E., Magedanz, T., & Glitho, R. H. (Eds.), *Lecture Notes in Computer Science* (*Vol. 2881*, pp. 53–66). Berlin: Springer.

Garrety, K., & Badham, R. (2000). The politics of sociotechnical intervention: an interactionist view. *Technology*

Analysis and Strategic Management, *12*(1), 103–118. doi:10.1080/095373200107265

Gehrke, D. (1999). Determinants of Successful Website Design: Relative Importance and Recommendations for Effectiveness. In *HICSS 1999: Proceedings of the Thirty-second Annual Hawaii International Conference on System Sciences* (Vol. 50, pp. 5042). Washington, DC: IEEE Computer Society.

Gelete, S., Coscuellala, C., & Garcia, J. (2003). Agent assisted concurrent process engineering system for design support. In Jardim-Gonçalves, R. (Eds.), *Concurrent Engineering: Enhanced Interoperable Systems* (pp. 463–467). Amsterdam: A. A. Balkema Publishers.

GENESIS Project. (n.d.). Retrieved from http://www.genesis-ist.eu

Gerst, M., & Bunduchi, R. (2005). Shaping IT standardization in the automotive industry – the role of power in driving portal standardization. *Electronic Markets*, *15*(4), 335–343. doi:10.1080/10196780500302872

Ghiladi, V. (2003). The Importance of International Standards for Globally Operating Businesses. *International Journal of IT Standards and Standardization Research*, *1*(1), 54–56.

Ghyasi, A. F., & Kushchu, I. (2004). m-Government: Cases of developing countries. *Mobile Government Lab (mGovLab)*.

Glaser, T., & Pallas, F. (2007). *Information security and knowledge management: Solutions through analogies?* Retrieved October 30, 2009, from http://iv.tu-berlin.de/TechnBerichte/2007/2007-18.pdf

Godinez, V. (2007, April 29). RFID tracks hospitals devices: System improves heart facility's care. *Dallas Morning News*.

Goggin, G. (2008). *Mobile phone cultures*. London: Routledge.

GOI. (2002). National Health Policy. *Government of India*. Retrieved from http://mohfw.nic.in/np2002.htm

Goldman, R., & Widom, J. (1997). DataGuides: Enabling Query Formulation and Optimization in Semistructured Databases. In *23rd International Conference on Very Large Data Bases (VLDB 97)*, Athens, Greece (pp. 436–445). San Francisco: Morgan Kaufmann.

Golfarelli, M., & Rizzi, S. (1998). *A methodological framework for data warehouse design. In 1st ACM international workshop on Data warehousing and OLAP* (pp. 3–9). New York, USA: DOLAP.

Golfarelli, M., Rizzi, S., & Cella, I. (2004). Beyond Data Warehousing: What's Next in Business Intelligence. In *Proceedings of 7th ACM International Workshop on Data Warehousing and OLAP* (pp. 1-6).

Goodman, M. J., Tijerina, L., Bents, F. D., & Wierwille, W. W. (1999). Using cellular phones in vehicles. *Transportation Human Factors*, *1*, 3–42. doi:10.1207/sthf0101_2

Gordon, L. A., Loeb, M. P., Lucyshyn, W., & Sohail, T. (2006). The impact of the Sarbanes-Oxley Act on the corporate disclosures of information security activities. *Journal of Accounting and Public Policy*, *25*(5), 503–530. doi:10.1016/j.jaccpubpol.2006.07.005

Graham, I., Pollock, N., Smart, A., & Williams, R. (2003). Institutionalisation of E-Business Standards. In J. L. King & K. Lyytinen (Eds.), *Standard Making: A Critical Research Frontier for Information Systems, Pre-conference workshop for International Conference on Information Systems (ICIS 2003)*, December 12-14, 2003, Seattle, USA (pp. 1-9).

Grandon, E. E., & Pearson, J. M. (2004). Electronic commerce adoption: an empirical study of small and medium US businesses. *Information & Management*, *42*(1), 197–216.

Greene, J. (2005 September). Is your Hospital Ready for Radio Frequency Identification? Above Board Technology. *Trustee*, 30-32. H&HN. (2004 May). Beyond Bar Codes. *Hospitals and Health Networks Magazine*, 26. H&HN. (2005 June). Behind the Hype. *Hospitals and Health Networks Magazine*, 22-24.

Gregor, S., Fernandez, W., Holtham, D., Martin, S., Vitale, M., & Pratt, G. (2004). *Achieving Value from ICT: Key Management Strategies*. Canberra, Australia: ICT Research Study, Department of Communications, Information Technology and the Arts.

Gross, H.-G., Melideo, M., & Sillitti, A. (2005). Self-certification and trust in component procurement. *Science of Computer Programming*, *56*, 141–156. doi:10.1016/j.scico.2004.11.009

Gruber, T. R. (1995). Toward principles for the design of ontologies used for knowledge sharing. *International Journal of Human-Computer Studies*, *43*(5/6), 907–928. doi:10.1006/ijhc.1995.1081

Gruninger, M., & Fox, M. S. (1995 August). *Methodology for the Design and Evaluation of Ontologies*. Presented at the Workshop on Basic Ontological Issues in Knowledge Sharing, IJCAI-95, Montreal Quebec Canada

Gubbins, M. (2004). *Global IT spending by sector*.

Gudykunst, W. B. (1993). Toward a Theory of Effective Interpersonal and Intergroup Communication . In Wiseman, R., & Koester, J. (Eds.), *Intercultural Communication Competence*. Newbury Park, CA: Sage.

Gulati, R. (1998). Alliances and networks. *Strategic Management Journal*, *19*(4), 293–317. doi:10.1002/(SICI)1097-0266(199804)19:4<293::AID-SMJ982>3.0.CO;2-M

Gupta, H., & Mumick, I. S. (2005). Selection of Views to Materialize in a Data Warehouse. *IEEE Transactions on Knowledge and Data Engineering*, *17*(1), 24–43. doi:10.1109/TKDE.2005.16

Ha, I., Yoon, Y., & Choi, M. (2007). Determinants of adoption of mobile games under mobile broadband wireless access environment. *Information & Management*, *44*, 276–286. doi:10.1016/j.im.2007.01.001

Hackathorn, R. (2002). *Current Practices in Active DataWarehousing*. Retrieved from http://www.bolder.com/pubs/NCR200211-ADW.pdf

Hagedoorn, J. (2002). Inter-firm R&D partnerships: an overview of major trends and patterns since 1960. *Research Policy*, *31*, 477–492. doi:10.1016/S0048-7333(01)00120-2

Hall, S. (1990). Culture identity and diaspora . In Rutherford, J. (Ed.), *Identity: Community, Culture, Difference* (pp. 222–237). London: Lawrence and Wishart.

Hamade, S. N. (2009). Information and Communication Technology in Arab Countries: Problems and Solutions. In *Sixth International Conference on Information Technology: New Generations* (pp. 1498-1503).

Hammer, M., & Champy, J. (1996). *Business Reengineering, Die Radikalkur für das Unternehmen* (7th ed.). Frankfurt am Main, Germany: Campus Fachbuch.

Han, Y., & Youn, C.-H. (2009). A new grid resource management mechanism with resource-aware policy administrator for SLA-constrained applications. *Future Generation Computer Systems*, *25*, 768–778. doi:10.1016/j.future.2008.11.005

Han, J., & Kamber, M. (2001). *Data Mining Concepts and Techniques*. San Francisco: Morgan Kaufmann Publishers.

Hansen, J., & McDonald, J. (2002). A generalized model for predictive data mining. *Information Systems Frontiers*, *4*(2), 179–186. doi:10.1023/A:1016050803099

Hao, W., Gao, T., Yen, I.-L., Chen, Y., & Paul, R. (2006). An Infrastructure for Web Services Migration for Real-Time Applications. In *Service-Oriented System Engineering (SOSE'06), Second IEEE International Workshop* (pp. 41-48).

Harmer, J. A. (2003). Mobile multimedia services. *BT Technology Journal*, *21*(3), 169–180. doi:10.1023/A:1025175518841

Harrington, H. J. (1991). *Business Process Improvement: The Breakthrough Strategy for Total Quality, Productivity and Competitiveness*. New York: McGraw-Hill.

Harrington, S. J. (1996). The effects of codes of ethics and personal denial of responsibility on computer abuse judgments and intentions. *Management Information Systems Quarterly*, *20*(3), 257–278. doi:10.2307/249656

Harris, J. (2006). *Fuzzy Logic Applications in Engineering Science*. Berlin: Springer.

Harrison, R., & Shackman, R. (2007). Communications and messaging services. In *Symbian OS C++ for Mobile Phones Vol. 3, Application Development for Symbian OS v9* (pp. 605 649). Upper Saddle River, NJ: John Willey & Sons, Ltd.

Harrop, P. (2006). Rapid Adoption of RFID in Healthcare. In *RFID in Healthcare 2006-2016,* [White Paper]. Retrieved September 24, 2008, from http://www.idtechex.com

Harroud, H., & Karmouch, A. M. (2003). A Policy-driven personalized multimedia services for mobile users.

IEEE Transactions on Mobile Computing, *2*(1), 16–24. doi:10.1109/TMC.2003.1195148

Haynes, D., & Prakash, G. (1991). Introduction: The entanglement of power and resistance . In Haynes, D., & Prakash, G. (Eds.), *Contesting power: Resistance and everyday social relations in South Asia.*

Hazlett, S. A., & Hill, F. (2003). E-government: The realities of using IT to transform the public sector. *Managing Service Quality*, *13*(6), 445–452. doi:10.1108/09604520310506504

Head, M., & Yuan, Y. (2001). Privacy protection in electronic commerce - a theoretical framework. *Human Systems Management*, *20*, 149–160.

Heckman, R. (1999). Organizing and managing supplier relationships in information technology procurement. *International Journal of Information Management*, *19*, 141–155. doi:10.1016/S0268-4012(99)00005-5

Heeks, R. (2002). *Failure, Success and Improvisation of Information Systems Projects in Developing Countries. Institute for Development Policy and Management (IDPM)*. University of Manchester.

Heeks, R., & Stanforth, C. (2007). Understanding e-government project trajectories from an actor-network perspective. *European Journal of Information Systems*, *16*(2), 165–177. doi:10.1057/palgrave.ejis.3000676

Henbury, C. (2007). *Two definitions of agility*. Retrieved August 31, 2009, from http://www.cheshirehenbury.com/agility/twodefinitions.html

Hepp, M., & Roman, D. (2007 February). *An Ontology Framework for Semantic Business Process Management.* Presented at the 8th international conference Wirtschaftsinformatik 2007, Karlsruhe, Germany.

Heravizadeh, M., & Edmond, D. (2008), Making Workflows Context-Aware: A way to support knowledge-intensive tasks. In A. Hinze & M. Kirchberg (Ed.), *APCCM '08: Proceedings of the fifth on Asia-Pacific conference on conceptual modeling* (pp. 79–88).

Hevner, A., March, S., Park, J., & Ram, S. (2004). Design science in information systems research. *Management Information Systems Quarterly*, *28*(1).

HFM. (2006, August). RFID tracks ED overcrowding. *Health Facilities Management*, 8.

Hinkelmann, K., Probst, F., & Thönssen, B. (2006). Agile process management framework and methodolgy . In Abecker, A., Seth, A., Mentzas, G., & Stojanovic, L. (Eds.), *Semantic Web Meets e-Government*. Menlo Park, CA: AAAI Press.

Hirsch, F., & Kemp, J. (2006). Introduction to service oriented architecture . In *Mobile WEB Services* (pp. 21–25). Upper Saddle River, NJ: John Willey & Sons, Ltd.doi:10.1002/9780470017982.ch3

Hitchings, J. (1995). Deficiencies of the traditional approach to information security and the requirements for a new methodology. *Computers & Security*, *14*, 377–383. doi:10.1016/0167-4048(95)97088-R

Hofstede, G. (1980). *Culture's consequences: International differences in work-related values*. Beverly Hills, CA: Sage.

Hofstede, G. (1991). *Cultures and Organizations: Software of the Mind: Intercultural Cooperation and its Importance for Survival*. Cambridge, UK: McGraw-Hill.

Holak, S. L., & Lehman, D. R. (1990). Intentions and the dimensions of innovation: An exploratory model. *Journal of Product Innovation Management*, *7*(1), 59–73. doi:10.1016/0737-6782(90)90032-A

Holden, S. H., Norris, D. F., & Fletcher, P. D. (2003). Electronic government at the local level: Progress to date and future issues. *Public Performance & Management Review*, *26*(4), 325–344. doi:10.1177/1530957603026004002

Holliday, I., & Kwok, R. C. V. (2004). Governance in the information age: Building e-government in Hong Kong. *New Media & Society*, *6*(4), 549–570. doi:10.1177/146144804044334

Holm, J., Lähteenmäki, S., Salmela, H., Suomi, R., Suominen, A., & Viljanen, M. (2002). Best practices of ICT workforce management–a comparable research initiative in Finland. *Journal of European Industrial Training*, *26*(7), 333–341. doi:10.1108/03090590210432688

Holsapple, C. W., & Joshi, K. D. (2004). A formal knowledge management ontology: Conduct, activities, resources, and influences. *Journal of the American Society for Information Science and Technology*, *55*(7), 593–612. doi:10.1002/asi.20007

Holsapple, C. W., & Whinston, A. B. (1996). *Decision Support Systems: A Knowledge-Based Approach*. Minneapolis, MN: West Pub. Co.

Holsapple, C. W. (2003). Knowledge and its attributes . In Holsapple, C. W. (Ed.), *Handbook on Knowledge Management* (*Vol. 1*, pp. 165–188). Berlin: Springer.

Hoppenbrouwers, S. J. B. A., Lindeman, L., & Proper, H. A. (2006). Capturing modelling processes - towards the modial modelling laboratory. In R. Meersman, Z. Tari & P. Herrero (Eds.), *On the move to meaningful internet systems 2006: Proceedings of Otm 2006 workshops* (LNCS 4278, pp. 1242-1252). Berlin: Springer.

Hoppenbrouwers, S. J. B. A., Proper, H. A., & Weide, T. P. d. (2005). Formal Modelling as a Grounded Conversation. In G. Goldkuhl, M. Lind & S. Haraldson (Eds.), *Proceedings of the 10th International Working Conference on the Language Action Perspective on Communication Modelling (LAP`05)*, Kiruna, Sweden (pp. 139-155). Linköping, Sweden: Linköpings Universitet.

Horrocks, I., Patel-Schneider, P., Boley, H., Tabet, S., Grosof, B., & Dean, M. (2004). *SWRL: A Semantic Web Rule Language Combining OWL and RuleML*. Retrieved from http://www.w3.org/Submission/SWRL/

Horton, K., Davenport, E., & Wood-Harper, A. T. (2005). Exploring sociotechnical interaction with Rob Kling: five big ideas. *Information Technology & People*, *18*(1), 50–67. doi:10.1108/09593840510584621

Hoskins, R. (2006). *InfoLogix Announces HealthTrax RFID Asset Tracking Software for Hospital Mobile Assets Management*. Retrieved from http://www.bbwexchange.com/pubs/2006/02/11/page1395-98309.asp

Houghton, K. A., & Winklhofer, H. (2004). The Effect of Website and E-commerce Adoption on the Relationship between SMEs and Their Export Intermediaries. *International Small Business Journal*, *22*(4), 369–388. doi:10.1177/0266242604044305

Hulme, M., & Peters, S. (2003). Me, my phone and I: The role of the mobile phone. *3GSM World Congress*. Cannes, France: Teleconomy Research House.

Hümmer, W., Bauer, A., & Harde, G. (2003). XCube: XML for data warehouses. In *6th International Workshop on Data Warehousing and OLAP (DOLAP 03)*, New Orleans, USA (pp. 33–40). New York: ACM.

Iacocca Institute. (1991). *21st Century Manufacturing Enterprise Strategy, An Industry-Led View of Agile Manufacturing*. Bethlehem, PA: Leigh University.

Iacovou, C. L., Benbasat, I., & Dexter, A. S. (1995). Electronic data interchange and small organizations: Adoption and Impact of Technology. *Management Information Systems Quarterly*, *19*(4), 465–485. doi:10.2307/249629

IDABC European eGovernment Services. (n.d.). Retrieved from http://ec.europa.eu/idabc

IETF Network Working Group. (1999). *Policy framework architecture*. Retrieved September 2008, from http://tools.ietf.org/html/draft-ietf-policy-arch-00

IFX (Interactive Financial Exchange) Forum. (n.d.). Retrieved from http://www.ifxforum.org/home

Igabria, M., Zinatelli, N., Cragg, P., & Cavaye, A. L. M. (1997). Personal computing acceptance factors in small firms: a structural equation model. *Management Information Systems Quarterly*, *21*, 279–305. doi:10.2307/249498

Illuminas. (2006). *Net Impact Canada 2006*. Retrieved March 20, 2008, from http://www.netimpactstudy.com/ca/

Im, G. P., & Baskerville, R. L. (2005). A longitudinal study of information system threat categories: The enduring problem of human error. *The Data Base for Advances in Information Systems*, *36*(4), 68–79.

Information Technology Authority. (2008). *About ITA*. Retrieved March 15, 2008, from http://www.ittf.gov.om/english/about_ita.html

InnoVest Group. (n.d.). *The Technology Small and Medium-Sized Enterprises (SMEs) in Middle East Region*. Retrieved march 12, 2008, from http://www.theinnovest-group.com/43.html

Intel. (2003 October). *Collaborative RosettaNet Implementation: Intel and Fujitsu streamline e-Business automation across the supply chain*. Intel Information Technology White Paper.

INTEROP Network of Excellence. (n.d.). Retrieved from http://www.interopnoe.org

Ishikawa, Y. (2003). Concurrent Engineering: Part 1: Business requirements, life cycle activity, key agenda for success and challenge with ISO standards . In Cha, A. (Eds.), *Concurrent Engineering: The Vision for the Future Generation in Research and Applications* (pp. 523–532). Lisse, Portugal: Balkema Publishers.

Ishikawa, H., Ohta, M., Yokoyama, S., Nakayama, J., & Katayama, K. (2002). On the Effectiveness of Web Usage Mining for Page Recommendation and Restructuring . In Chaudhri, A., Jeckle, M., Rahm, E., & Unland, R. (Eds.), *Web, Web Services, and Database Systems NODe 2002 Web and Database-Related Workshops* (pp. 253–267). Berlin: Springer-Verlag.

ISO. (2003). *How conformity assessment works*. Retrieved June 2, 2003, from http://www.iso.org/iso/en/comms-markets/conformity/iso+conformity-02.html

ISO/IEC. (2005). *Information Technology - Security Techniques - Code of Practice for Information Security Management (ISO/IEC 27002)*. Geneva, Switzerland: International Organization for Standardization.

Jackson, N. F., Aiken, M. W. V., Mahesh, B. H., & Bassam, S. (1995). Support group decisions via computer systems. *Quality Progress*, *28*(5), 75–78.

Jamieson, D., Vinsen, K., & Callender, G. (2005). Agile procurement to support agile software development. In *3rd IEEE Intl. Conf. Industrial Informatics* (pp. 419-424). Perth: IEEE.

Jang, M., & Sohn, J.-C. (2004). Bossam: An Extended Rule Engine for OWL Inferencing. In *Rules and Rule Markup Languages for the Semantic Web. Third International Workshop* (*RuleML 2004*), Hiroshima, Japan (LNCS 3324, pp. 128-138). Berlin: Springer.

Jap, S., & Mohr, J. (2002). *Leveraging Internet Technologies in B2B Relationships*. California Management Review.

Jaquith, A. (2007). *Security Metrics: Replacing Fear, Uncertainty, and Doubt*. Upper Saddle River, NJ: Addison-Wesley.

JBoss. (2006). *JBOSS rules, conflict resolution*. Retrieved August 30, 2009, from http://legacy.drools.codehaus.org/Conflict+Resolution

Jeng, J., Flaxer, D., & Kapoor, S. (2004). RuleBAM: A Rule-Based Framework for Business Activity Management. In *SCC '04: Proceedings of the 2004 IEEE International Conference on Services Computing*, Washington, DC (pp. 262-270).

Jeppesen, S. L., Barfod, M. B., & Leleur, S. (2007, April 11). *Comparing a soft and hard multi-methodology approach: location of an IT company in the Oresund region*. Paper presented at the ISOneWorld 07, Las Vegas, USA.

Johnson, M. E. (2008). Information risk of inadvertent disclosure: An analysis of file-sharing risk in the financial supply chain. *Journal of Management Information Systems*, *25*(2), 97–123. doi:10.2753/MIS0742-1222250205

Johnson, M. E., & Goetz, E. (2007). Embedding information security into the organization. *IEEE Security & Privacy*, *5*(3), 16–24. doi:10.1109/MSP.2007.59

Johnston, D. A., Wade, M., & McClean, R. (2007, July). Does e-business matter to SMEs? A Comparison of the Financial Impacts of Internet Business Solutions on European and North American SMEs. *Journal of Small Business Management*, *45*(3), 354–361. doi:10.1111/j.1540-627X.2007.00217.x

Johnston, S., & Acquaah-Gaisie, G. (2001). Development via the Net in Oceania. In *Proceedings of the 3rd world conference of the Global IT Management*, Dallas, USA.

Joseph, C., Gunton, T., & Day, J. (2008). Implementation of resource management plans: Identifying keys to success. *Journal of Environmental Management*, *88*, 594–606. doi:10.1016/j.jenvman.2007.03.028

Journal, R. F. I. D. (2005). A summary of RFID standards. *RFID Journal*. Retrieved from http://www.rfidjournal.com/article/view/1335/1/129

Jouve, P., & Nicoloyannis, N. (2003). Kerouac: An algorithm for clustering categorical data sets with practical advantages. In *International Workshop on Data Mining Learning for Actionable Knowledge (DMAK 2003)*.

Juels, A. (2004). Financial Cryptography. *8th International Conference on Financial Cryptography* 2004, *Key West, FL, USA, February 9-12*, Springer LNCS 3110.

Junginger, S., Kuhn, H., & Bayer, F. (2004). Workflow-based Business Monitoring . In *WfMC Workflow Handbook*. Lighthouse Point, FL: Future Strategies.

Kaefer, F., & Bendoly, E. (2004). Measuring the impact of organizational constraints on the success of business-to-business e-commerce efforts: a transactional focus. *Information & Management*, *41*, 529–541. doi:10.1016/S0378-7206(03)00088-0

Kahn, M. (2008, June 25). RFID in hospitals could pose risks. *PC Magazine Online*.

Kahraman, C., Demirel Cetin, N., & Demirel, T. (2007). Prioritization of e-government strategies using a SWOT-AHP analysis: The case of Turkey. *European Journal of Information Systems*, *16*, 284–298. doi:10.1057/palgrave.ejis.3000679

Kankanhalli, A., Teo, H. H., Tan, B. C. Y., & Wei, K. K. (2003). An integrative study of information systems security effectiveness. *International Journal of Information Management*, *23*, 139–154. doi:10.1016/S0268-4012(02)00105-6

Kaplan, R. S., & Norton, D. P. (1992). The balanced scorecard: measures that drive performance. *Harvard Business Review*, *70*, 70–79.

Kaplan, R. S., & Norton, D. P. (1996). *Translating strategy into action: the balanced scorecard*. Boston: Harvard Business School Press.

Kaplan, R. S., & Norton, D. P. (2001). *The strategy-focused organization: how balanced scorecard companies thrive in the new business environment*. Boston, MA: Harvard Business School Press.

Kapurubandara, M., & Lawson, R. (2006). *Barriers Adopting ICT and E-commerce with SMEs in Developing Countries: An Exploratory Study in Sri Lanka*. Retrieved March 13, 2008, from http://www.collecter.org/archives/2006_December/07.pdf

Kartiwi, M. (2006). Case Studies of E-Commerce Adoption in Indonesian SMEs: The Evaluation of Strategic Use. *Australasian Journal of Information Systems, 14*(11).

Katsikas, S., & Mitrou, L. (2004). *Electronic Voting Systems, Final Deliverable*. e-business forum, Retrieved February 23, 2008, from http:// www.ebusinessforum.gr

Katz, J. E., & Sugiyama, S. (2006). Mobile phones as fashion statements: evidence from student surveys in the US and Japan. *New Media & Society*, *8*(2), 321–337. doi:10.1177/1461444806061950

Katz, J. E. (2003). *Machines that become us: The social context of personal communication technology*. New Brunswick, NJ: Transaction.

Kaushik, R., Shenoy, P., Bohannon, P., & Gudes, E. (2002). Exploiting Local Similarity for Indexing Paths in Graph-Structured Data. In *18th International Conference on Data Engineering (ICDE 02)*, San Jose, CA (pp. 129–140). Washington, DC: IEEE Computer Society.

Keller, F., & Wendt, S. (2003). *FMC: An Approach Towards Architecture-Centric System Development*. Paper presented at the 10th IEEE Symposium and Workshop on Engineering of Computer Based Systems, Pasadena, CA.

Kempster, S. J. (2007). Echoes from the past: An exploration of the impact of 'notable people' on leadership training. In *Academy of Management Annual Meeting Proceedings- Best Papers*, Philadelphia, PA.

Kern, T., & Willcocks, L. (2002). Exploring relationships in information technology outsourcing: The interaction approach. *European Journal of Information Systems*, *11*(1), 3–19. doi:10.1057/palgrave/ejis/3000415

Kesh, S., & Ratnasingam, P. (2007). A knowledge architecture for IT security. *Communications of the ACM*, *50*(7), 103–108. doi:10.1145/1272516.1272521

Khalfan, A. M., & Alshawaf, A. (2003). IS/IT outsourcing practices in the public health sector of Kuwait: A contingency approach. *Logistics Information Management*, *16*(3/4), 215–228. doi:10.1108/09576050310483817

Kiely, L., & Benzel, T. V. (2006). Systemic security management. *IEEE Security & Privacy*, *4*(6), 74–77. doi:10.1109/MSP.2006.167

Kimball, R., & Ross, M. (2002). *The Data Warehouse Toolkit: The Complete Guide To Dimensional Modeling* (2nd ed.). Hoboken, NJ: John Wiley.

Klein, H. (1999). Tocqueville in cyberspace: Using the internet for citizen associations. *The Information Society*, *15*(4), 213–220. doi:10.1080/019722499128376

Klein, H. K., & Myers, M. D. (1999). A set of principles for conducting and evaluating interpretive field studies in information systems. *Management Information Systems Quarterly*, *23*(1), 67–94. doi:10.2307/249410

Kling, R. (1999, January). What is Social Informatics and Why Does it Matter? *D-Lib Magazine*, 5.

Kling, R., & Iacono, S. (2001). *Information technology and organizational transformation: history, rhetoric, and practice*. Thousand Oaks, CA: Sage Publications.

Knapp, K. J., Marshall, T. E., Rainer, R. K., & Ford, F. N. (2006). Information security: Management's effect on culture and policy. *Information Management & Computer Security*, *14*(1), 24–36. doi:10.1108/09685220610648355

Knifsend, F., & Debb, J. (2005). Using BAM to Empower the Organization: Unifying Events and Processes. *Business Integration Journal.* Retrieved from http://www.alignjournal.com/index.cfm?section=article&aid=54

Knowledge Oasis Muscat. (2008). *About KOM.* Retrieved March 12, 2008, from http://www.kom.om/ev.htm

Koellinger, P. (2006). *Impact of ICT on Corporate Performance, Productivity and Employment Dynamics*. Berlin: European Commission Enterprise & Industry Directorate General.

Koh, C., Ang, S., & Straub, D. W. (2004). IT outsourcing success: A psychological contract perspective. *Information Systems Research*, *15*(4), 356–373. doi:10.1287/isre.1040.0035

Kohavi, R., & Provost, F. (2001). Applications of data mining to electronic commerce. *Data Mining and Knowledge Discovery*, *5*, 5–10. doi:10.1023/A:1009840925866

Kohli, R., & Devaraj, S. (2004, March). Realizing the Business Value of Information Technology Investments: An Organizational Process. *Management Information Systems Quarterly*, *3*(1), 55–69.

Kontio, J. (1994). *Software Engineering Risk Management: A Technology Review Report PI_4.1, A proprietary Nokia Research Center project deliverable*. Helsinki, Finland: Nokia Research Center.

Kontio, J., Englund, H., & Basili, V. R. (1996). *Experiences from an Exploratory Case Study with a Software Risk Management Method. CS-TR-3705, Computer Science Technical Reports*. College Park, MD: University of Maryland.

Kontio, J. (1995). *Promises: A Framework for Utilizing Process Models in Process Asset Management*. Licentiate thesis at Helsinki University of Technology.

Kontio, J., & Basili, V. R. (1996). Risk Knowledge Capture in the Riskit Method. In *Proceedings of the 21st Software Engineering Workshop*. Greenbelt, MD: NASA.

Kontio, J., & Basili, V. R. (1997). Empirical Evaluation of a Risk Management Method. In *Proceedings of the SEI Conference on Risk Management*. Pittsburgh, PA: Software Engineering Institute.

Kosanke, K., & Nell, J. (1999). Standardisation in ISO for enterprise engineering and integration. *Computers in Industry*, *40*, 311–319. doi:10.1016/S0166-3615(99)00034-2

Kotidis, Y., & Roussopoulos, N. (1999). Dynamat: A dynamic view management system for data warehouses. In *ACM SIGMOD International Conference on Management of Data (SIGMOD 1999)*, Philadelphia, USA (pp. 371– 382).

Kotok, A. (2002). *Standards-Based Methodology for U.S. E-Government Initiatives. Data Interchange Standards Association*. DISA.

Kotulic, A. G., & Clark, J. G. (2004). Why there aren't more information security research studies. *Information & Management*, *41*, 597–607. doi:10.1016/j.im.2003.08.001

Koutri, M., & Daskalaki, S. (2003). Improving Web Site Usability through a Clustering Approach. In *10th International Conference on Human-Computer Interaction HCI*, Crete, Greece (pp. 11-19).

Kowtha, N. R., & Choon, T. M. I. (2001). Determinants of website development: a study of electronic commerce in Singapore. *Information & Management*, *39*(3), 227–242. doi:10.1016/S0378-7206(01)00092-1

Kramer, M., Gregorowicz, A., & Iyer, B. (2008). Wiki Trust Metrics based on Phrasal Analysis. In *Proceedings of the 4th International Symposium on Wikis (WikiSym 2008)*, Porto, Portugal, September 8-10.

Kuan, K. K. Y., & Chau, P. Y. K. (2001). A perception-based model for EDI adoption in small businesses using a technology-organisation-environment framework. *Information & Management*, *38*(8), 507–521. doi:10.1016/S0378-7206(01)00073-8

Kurnia, S. (2008). Exploring e-Commerce Readiness in China: The Case of the Grocery Industry. In *Proceedings of the 41st Hawaii International Conference on System Sciences,* January 7-10, 2008.

Kushchu, I. (2007). *Mobile government: An emerging direction in e-government.* Hershey, PA: IGI Publishing.

Kushchu, I., & Kuscu, H. (2003). From e-government to m-government: Facing the inevitable. In *Proceedings of European Conference on E-Government (ECEG 2003),* Trinity College, Dublin, July 3-4 (pp. 253-260). Reading, UK: Academic Conferences International.

Lacity, M. C., & Willocks, L. P. (1995). Interpreting information technology sourcing decisions from a transaction cost perspective: findings and critique. *Accounting Management and Information Technology*, *5*(3/4), 203–244. doi:10.1016/0959-8022(96)00005-7

Lacity, M. C., & Willocks, L. P. (1998). An empirical investigation of information technology sourcing practices: Lessons from experience. *Management Information Systems Quarterly*, *22*(3), 363–408. doi:10.2307/249670

Lal, K. (2007). Globalization and Adoption of ICTs in Nigerian SMEs. *Science, Technology & Society*, *12*(2), 217–244. doi:10.1177/097172180701200203

Lam, W. (2005). Barriers to e-government integration. *The Journal of Enterprise Information Management*, *18*(5), 511–530. doi:10.1108/17410390510623981

Land, F. F. (2000). *Evaluation in a socio-technical context.* Paper presented at the Organizational and Social Perspectives on IT 2000, Aalborg, Denmark.

Lander, M., Purvis, R., McCray, G., & Leigh, W. (2003). Trust-building mechanisms utilized in outsourced IS development projects: A case study. *Journal of International Management*, *41*, 509–528.

Landt, J. (2001 October). Shrouds of Time: The history of RFID. *Association for Automatic Identification and Mobility*.

Lange, T., Ottens, M., & Taylor, A. (2000). SMEs and Barriers to skills development: A Scottish Perspective. *Journal of European Industrial Training*, *24*(1), 5–11. doi:10.1108/03090590010308219

Langley, A. (1999). Strategies for theorizing from process data. *Academy of Management Review*, *24*(4), 691–710. doi:10.2307/259349

Langley, A., Mintzberg, H., Pitcher, P., Posada, E., & Saint-Macary, J. (1995). Opening up decision making: The view from the black stool. *Organization Science*, *6*(3), 260–279. doi:10.1287/orsc.6.3.260

Larsen, E., & Rainie, L. (2002). *The rise of the e-citizen: How people use e-government agencies' web sites.* Washington, DC: Pew Internet & American Life Project.

Law, L. (1997). A matter of choice: discourses on prostitution in the Philippines . In Manderson, L., & Jolly, M. (Eds.), *Sites of Desire/Economies of Pleasure: Sexualities in Asia and the Pacific* (pp. 233–261). Chicago: University of Chicago Press.

Lawson, R., Alcock, C., Cooper, J., & Burgess, L. (2003). Factors Affecting the Adoption of Electronic Commerce Technologies by SMEs: An Australian Study. *Journal of Small Business and Enterprise Development*, *10*(3), 265–276. doi:10.1108/14626000310489727

Lee, K. (1996, June). Cooperative Standard-Setting: The Road to Compatibility or Deadlock? The NAFTA's Transformation of the Telecommunications Industry. *Federal Communications Law Journal*, *48*(3).

Lee, S. (2005). Efficiency analysis of controls in EDI applications. *Information & Management*, *42*(3), 425–439. doi:10.1016/j.im.2001.09.001

Lee, S., & Lim, G. (2003). The impact of partnership attributes on EDI implementation success. *Information & Management*, *41*, 135–148. doi:10.1016/S0378-7206(03)00043-0

Lee, S. C., Pak, B. Y., & Lee, H. G. (2003). Business value of B2B electronic commerce: the critical role of inter-firm collaboration. *Electronic Commerce Research and Applications*, *2*, 350–361. doi:10.1016/S1567-4223(03)00003-6

Lee, C. P., & Shim, J. P. (2007). An exploratory study of radio frequency identification (RFID) adoption in the healthcare industry. *European Journal of Information Systems*, *16*, 712–772. doi:10.1057/palgrave.ejis.3000716

Lee, N., & Cadogan, J. W. (2009). Sales force social exchange in problem resolution situations. *Industrial Marketing Management*, *32*(3), 355–372. doi:10.1016/j.indmarman.2008.02.002

Lee, S. M., Lee, S. G., & Yoo, S. (2004). An integrative model of computer abuse based on social control and general deterrence theories. *Information & Management*, *41*, 707–718. doi:10.1016/j.im.2003.08.008

Lengnick-Hall, M., Lengnick-Hall, C., Andrade, L., & Drake, B. (2009). Strategic human resource management: The evolution of the field. *Human Resource Management View*, *19*, 64–85. doi:10.1016/j.hrmr.2009.01.002

Lenk, K. (1997). Business process re-engineering in the public sector: Opportunities and risks . In Taylor, J. A., Snellen, I., & Zuurmond, A. (Eds.), *Beyond BPR in Public Administration* (pp. 151–163). Amsterdam: IOS Press.

Levina, N., & Ross, J. W. (2003). From the vendor's perspective: Exploring the value proposition in information technology outsourcing. *Management Information Systems Quarterly*, *27*(3), 331–364.

Levina, N., & Vasst, E. (2008). Innovating or doing as told? Status differences and overlapping boundaries in offshore collaboration. *Management Information Systems Quarterly*, *32*(2), 307–322.

Liao, S., Chen, Y., & Tseng, Y. (2009). Mining demand change knowledge of life insurance market for new product development. *Expert Systems with Applications*, *36*(5), 9422–9437. doi:10.1016/j.eswa.2008.12.053

Licker, P., & Motts, N. (2000). Extending the benefits of e-commerce in Africa: Exploratory phase. In *Proceedings, First Annual Global Information Technology Management World Conference*, Memphis, 11-13 June (pp. 115-118).

Lieshout, M. (1999, July). The Digital City of Amsterdam: between public domain and private enterprise. In *Social Learning regarding Multimedia Developments at a Local Level. The Case of Digital Cities* (pp.114). CITA-FUNDP, University of Namur.

Liming, S. D. (2003). Development requirements . In *Windows XP Embedded Advanced* (pp. 9–12). San Clemente, CA: RTC Books.

Lin, A., & Tong, A. (2008). Text-messaging culture of college girls in Hong Kong: SMS as resources for achieving intimacy and gift-exchange with multiple functions . In Goggin, G. (Ed.), *Mobile Phone Cultures* (pp. 158–170). London: Routledge.

Ling, R. S. (2004). *Mobile connection: The cell phone's impact on society*. San Francisco: Morgan Kaufmann.

Liyanage, J. P., & Bjerkebaek, E. (2006). Use of advanced technologies and information solutions for North Sea offshore assets: ambitious changes and socio-technical dimensions. *International Journal of International Technology and Information Management*, *15*(4), 1–10.

Lockamy III, A., & McCormack, K. (2004). The development of a supply chain management process maturity model using the concepts of business process orientation. *Supply Chain Management Journal, 9*(4).

Loh, L., & Venkatraman, N. (1992). Diffusion of information technology outsourcing: Influence sources and the Kodak Effect. *Information Systems Research*, *3*(4), 334–358. doi:10.1287/isre.3.4.334

Lohse, G. L., & Spiller, P. (1998). Electronic Shopping. *Communications of the ACM*, *41*(7), 81–88. doi:10.1145/278476.278491

Love, P., & Irani, Z. (2004, December). An exploratory study of information technology evaluation and benefits management practices of SMEs in the construction industry. *Information & Management*, *42*(1), 227–242.

Love, P. E. D., Irani, Z., Li, H., Cheng, E. W. L., & Tse, R. Y. C. (2001). An empirical analysis of the barriers to implementing e-commerce in small-medium sized construction contractors in the state of Victoria, Australia. *Construction Innovation*, *1*, 31–41.

Love, E. D., Irani, Z., & Edwards, D. J. (2004). Industry-centric Benchmarking of Information Technology Benefits, Costs and Risks for Small-to-Medium Sized Enterprises in Construction. *Automation in Construction*, *13*, 507–524. doi:10.1016/j.autcon.2004.02.002

Lu, X.-H. (2006). Critical success factors of inter-organizational information systems – A case study of Cisco and Xiao Tong in China. *Information & Management*, *43*, 395–408. doi:10.1016/j.im.2005.06.007

Lucas Henry, C. (1999). *Information Technology and the Productivity Paradox: Assessing the Value of the Investment in IT*. Oxford, UK: Oxford University Press.

Lucchetti, R., & Sterlacchini, A. (2004). The Adoption of UCT among SMEs: Evidence from an Italian Survey. *Small Business Economics*, *23*, 151–168. doi:10.1023/B:SBEJ.0000027667.55821.53

Luckham, D. (2002). *The Power of Events*. Reading, MA: Pearson Education Inc.

Lukasz, A., & Musilek, P. (2006). A survey of knowledge discovery and data mining process models source. *The Knowledge Engineering Review*, *21*(1), 1–24. doi:10.1017/S0269888906000737

MacCrimmon, K. R., & Wehrung, D. A. (1986). *Taking Risks*. New York: Free Press.

MacGregor, R., & Vrazalic, L. (2004). *Electronic Commerce Adoption in Small to Medium Enterprises (SMEs), A Comparative study of SMEs in Wollongong (Australia) and Karlstad (Sweden)*. Australia: University of Wollongong.

MacGregor, R. C., Bunker, D. J., & Waugh, P. (1998). Electronic Commerce and Small/Medium Enterprises (SMEs) in Australia: An Electronic Data Interchange (EDI) Pilot Study. In *Proceedings of the 11th International Bled Electronic Commerce Conference*, Slovenia, June

Mahnke, V., Overby, M. L., & Vang, J. (2005). Strategic outsourcing of IT services: Theoretical stocktaking and empirical challenges. *Industry and Innovation*, *12*(2), 205–253. doi:10.1080/13662710500087958

Mahnke, V., Wareham, J., & Bjorn-Andersen, N. (2008). Offshore middleman: transnational intermediation in technology sourcing. *Journal of Information Technology*, *23*(1), 18–30. doi:10.1057/palgrave.jit.2000124

Mähönen, P. (2000). The standardization process in IT – Too slow or too fast? In Jakobs, K. (Ed.), *Information Technology Standards and Standardization: A Global Perspective* (pp. 35–47). Hershey, PA: IDEA Group Publishing.

Malone, T. W. (2004). *The Future of Work: How the New Order of Business Will Shape Your Organization, Your Management Style, and Your Life*. Boston: Harvard Business School Publishing.

Marcelle, G. M. (2004). *Technological learning*. Cheltenham, UK: Edward Elgar.

Marcinkowski, S., & Stanton, J. M. (2003). *Motivational aspects of information security policies*. Paper presented at the IEEE International Conference on Systems, Man and Cybernetics.

Marques, V., et al. (2002). An architecture supporting end-to-end QoS with user mobility for systems beyond 3rd generation. In *Proceedings of IST Mobile and Wireless Telecommunications Summit 2002*.

Martin, L., & Matlay, H. (2001). Blanket approaches to promoting ICT in small firms: some lessons from the DTI ladder adoption model in the UK. *Internet Research: Electronic Networking Applications and Policy*, *11*(5), 399–410. doi:10.1108/EUM0000000006118

Martin, P. (2009). *The Recession and Migration: Alternative Scenarios*. Working Papers. International Migration Institute. James Martin 21st Century School. University of Oxford, UK. Retrieved October 17, 2009, from http://www.unitar.org

Martinsons, M., Davison, R., & Tse, D. (1999). The Balanced Scorecard: A Foundation for the Strategic Management of Information Systems. *Decision Support Systems*, *25*, 71–88. doi:10.1016/S0167-9236(98)00086-4

Martyr, J. W. (1985). *Cultural discontinuities and the transfer of management philosophies and practices With particular reference to Great Britain, and the Arab countries of the Arabian Gulf and Saudi Arabia*. Unpublished PhD Thesis. Uxbridge, UK: Brunel University.

Mathieu, P., & Verrons, M.-H. (2002). *A generic model for contract negotiation*. Paper presented at the AISB'02 Symposium on Intelligent Agents in Virtual Markets, Imperial College of Science, Technology and Medicine, University of London.

Matlay, H., & Addis, M. (2003). Adoption of ICT and e-commerce in small businesses: an HEI-based consultancy perspective. *Journal of Small Business and Enterprise Development*, *10*(3), 321–335. doi:10.1108/14626000310489790

Mattia, A., & Dhillon, G. (2003). Applying double loop learning to interpret implications for information systems security design, *IEEE International Conference on Systems, Man and Cybernetics* (Vol. 3, pp. 2521-2526).

Maurizio, M., Seaman, C. B., Basili, V. R., Parra, A. T., Kraft, S. E., & Condon, S. E. (2002). COTS based software development: Processes and open issues. *Journal of Systems and Software*, *61*, 189–199. doi:10.1016/S0164-1212(01)00147-9

Mcdonagh, P., & Prothero, A. (2000). Euroclicking and the Irish SME: prepared for e-commerce and the single currency. *Irish Marketing Review*, *13*(1), 21–33.

McEvoy, S. P., Stevenson, M. R., McCartt, A. T., Woodward, M., Haworth, C., & Palamara, P. (2005). Role of mobile phones in motor vehicle crashes resulting in hospital attendance: a case-crossover study. *British Medical Journal*. Retrieved July 12, 2005, from http://www.bmj.com/cgi/content/abstract/bmj.38537.397512.55v1

McGregor, C., & Eklund, J. (2008). Real-Time Service-Oriented Architectures to Support Remote Critical Care: Trends and Challenges. In *Proceedings of 2008 Annual IEEE International Computer Software and Applications Conference (COMPSAC)* (pp. 1199-1204).

McIvor, R., McHugh, M., & Cadden, C. (2002). Internet technologies: Supporting transparency in the public sector. *International Journal of Public Sector Management*, *15*(3), 170–187. doi:10.1108/09513550210423352

Meehan, M. (2002, January 1). Users Say Lack of IT Integration Hurts B2B. *ComputerWorld*. Retrieved from http://www.computerworld.com

Mehrjerdi, Y. Z. (2008). RFID enabled systems: a brief review. *Assembly Automation*, *28*(3), 235–245. doi:10.1108/01445150810889493

Mehrtens, J., Cragg, P., & Mills, A. (2001). A model of Internet adoption by SMEs. *Information & Management*, *39*, 165–176. doi:10.1016/S0378-7206(01)00086-6

Meier, W. (2002). eXist: An Open Source Native XML Database. In *Web, Web-Services, and Database Systems, NODe 2002 Web and Database-Related Workshops*, Erfurt, Germany (LNCS 2593, pp. 169–183). Berlin: Springer.

Meire, A. P., Borges, M. R. S., & Araújo, R. M. d. (2007). Supporting multiple viewpoints in collaborative graphical editing. *Multimedia Tools and Applications*, *32*(2), 185–208. doi:10.1007/s11042-006-0064-9

Meire, A. P., Borges, M. R. S., & Araújo, R. M. d. (2003). Supporting collaborative drawing with the mask versioning mechanism. In J. Favela & D. Decouchant (Eds.), *Proceedings of CRIWG 2003, Groupware: Design, Implementation, and Use*, Autrans, France, September 28 - October 2, 2003, (LNCS 2806, pp. 208-223). Berlin: Springer.

Melchert, F., Winter, R., & Klesse, M. (2004). Aligning Process Automation and Business Intelligence to Support Corporate Performance Management. In *Proceedings of the 10th Americas Conference on Information Systems*, New York, August 5-8 2004. Retrieved from http://aisel.aisnet.org/amcis2004/507

Melitski, J., Holzer, M., Kim, S., Kim, C., & Rho, S. (2005). Digital government worldwide: An e-government assessment of municipal websites throughout the world. *International Journal of E-government Research*, *1*(1), 1–19.

MENAFN. (2009). Middle East North Africa Financial Network – Mideast IT spend to Hit $50 b in 2009. *Khalij Times*. Retrieved March 6, 2009, from http://www.menafn.co

Mendling, J., & Neumann, G. (2005). A Comparison of XML Interchange Formats for Business Process Modelling . In *WfMC Workflow Handbook 2005* (pp. 185–198). Lighthouse Point, FL: Future Strategies Inc.

Mendling, J., & Nuttgens, M. (2006). XML interchange formats for Business Process Management. *International Journal of Information Systems and E-Business Management*, *4*(3), 217–220. doi:10.1007/s10257-006-0032-y

Merriam, S. B. (1998). *Qualitative research and case studies applications in education*. San Francisco: Jossey-Bass Publications.

Miles, M. B., & Huberman, A. M. (1994). *Qualitative data analysis: An expanded sourcebook*. Newbury Park, CA: Sage Publications.

Miller, S. J., Hickson, D. J., & Wilson, D. C. (1996). Decision-making in organizations . In Clegg, S. R., Hardy, C., & Nord, W. R. (Eds.), *Handbook of Organization Studies* (pp. 293–312). London: Sage Publications.

Milo, T., & Suciu, D. (1999). Index Structures for Path Expressions. In 7th International Conference on Database Theory (ICDT 99), Jerusalem, Israel (LNCS 1540, pp. 277–295). Berlin: Springer.

Ministry of Economy and Planning. (2008). *Saudi Arabia: Long-Term Strategy 2025*. Retrieved June 24, 2009, from http://www.mep.gov.sa/

Mintzberg, H., Raisinghani, D., & Theoret, A. (1976). The structure of 'unstructured' decision process. *Administrative Science Quarterly*, *21*(2), 246–275. doi:10.2307/2392045

Miranda, S. M., & Kim, Y. M. (2006). Professional versus political contexts: Institutional mitigation and the transaction cost heuristic in information systems outsourcing. *Management Information Systems Quarterly*, *30*(3), 725–753.

MIT CallTech. (2008). *Voting Technology Project*. Retrieved March 11, 2008, from http://www.vote.caltech.edu

Mitra, A., & Gupta, A. (2006). *Creating Agile Business Systems with Reusable Knowledge*. Cambridge, UK: Cambridge University Press. doi:10.1017/CBO9780511543432

Mitra, A., & Gupta, A. (2008). *Knowledge Reuse and Agile Processes: Catalysts for Innovation*. Hershey, PA: IGI Global.

Mitrou, L., Gritzalis, D., & Katsikas, S. (2002). Revisiting legal and regulatory requirements for secure e-voting. In *Proceedings of the 16th IFIP International Information Security Conference*, Egypt.

Mobasher, B., Dai, H., Luo, T., & Nakagawa, M. (2001). Effective Personalization Based on Association Rule Discovery from Web Usage Data. In *WIDM 2001: Proceedings of the 3rd international workshop on Web information and data management* (pp. 9-15). New York: ACM Press.

Mohamed, A., Ruhe, G., & Eberlein, A. (2007). Decision support for handling mismatches between COTS products and system requirements. In *Proceedings of the Sixth International IEEE Conference on Commercial-off-the-Shelf (COTS)-Based Software Systems* (pp. 63-72). Washington, DC: IEEE Computer Society.

Moldaschl, M., & Weber, W. G. (1998). The three waves of industrial groups: historical reflections on current research on group work. *Human Relations*, *51*, 347–388. doi:10.1177/001872679805100307

Molla, A., & Licker, P. S. (2005). Ecommerce adoption in developing countries: a model and instrument. *Information & Management*, *42*, 877–899. doi:10.1016/j.im.2004.09.002

Molla, A. (2005). E-Readiness and Successful E-Commerce Diffusion in Developing Countries: Results from a Cluster Analysis . In Kamel, S. (Ed.), *Electronic Business in Developing Countries: Opportunities and Challenges* (pp. 214–233). Hershey, PA, USA: Idea Group Publishing.

Morikawa, M. (2004). Information Technology and the Performance of Japanese SMEs. *Small Business Economics*, *23*, 171–177. doi:10.1023/B:SBEJ.0000032023.11566.4b

Morris, W. T. (1967). On the Art of Modeling. *Management Science*, *13*(12), B707–B717. doi:10.1287/mnsc.13.12.B707

Mörschel, I. (2003). Standardization of and for services: opportunities, risks, best practice. In K. Jakobs (Ed.), *Proceedings of the 8th Euras Workshop on Standardization,* Aachen, July 11-12, 2003 (pp. 59-60).

Moser, O., Resenberg, F., & Dustdar, S. (2008). Non-intrusive monitoring and service adaptation for WS-BPEL. In *Proceedings of the 17th international conference on World Wide Web, Beijing, 2008* (pp. 815-824). New York: ACM.

Moulton, R. T., & Moulton, M. E. (1996). Electronic communication risk management: A checklist for business managers. *Computers & Security*, *15*(5), 377–386. doi:10.1016/0167-4048(96)82560-0

Moynihan, G. P., Saxena, P., & Fonseca, D. J. (2006). Development of a decision support system for procurement operations. *International Journal of Logistical Systems Management*, *2*, 1–18. doi:10.1504/IJLSM.2006.008214

Mulpuru, S., Johnson, C., McGowan, B., & Wright, S. (2008). US eCommerce Forecast: 2008 To 2012. B2C eCommerce Expected To Top $300B In Five Years. *Forrester Research, Inc.* Retrieved February 1, 2009, from http://www.forrester.com/Research/Document/Excerpt/0,7211,41592,00.html

Mumford, E. (2003). *Redesigning Human Systems*. London: IRM Press.

Mumford, E. (2006). The story of socio-technical design: reflections on its successes, failures and potential. *Information Systems Journal*, *16*, 317–342. doi:10.1111/j.1365-2575.2006.00221.x

Mumford, E., & Weir, M. (1979). *Computer Systems in Work Design-The ETHICS Method: Effective Technical and Human Implementation of Computer Systems: A Work Design Exercise Book for Individuals and Groups*. London: Associated Business Press.

Murphy, R. (2004). Creating the contract - software sourcing. *Supply Management Journal, volume number unknown*, 30-31.

Murray, E. A. (1978). Strategic choice as a negotiated outcome. *Management Science*, *24*(9), 960–972. doi:10.1287/mnsc.24.9.960

Murugesan, S., & Ginige, A. (2005). Web Engineering: Introduction and Perspectives . In *Web Engineering: Principles and Techniques* (pp. 1–30). Hershey, PA: Idea Group Publishing.

Mutschler, B., & Reichert, M. (2006). Unleashing the effectiveness of process-oriented information systems: Problem analysis, critical, success factors, implications. *IEEE Transactions on Systems, Man, and Cybernetics*, *38*(3), 280–291.

Mutula, S. M., & Brakel, P. (2006). E-readiness of SMEs in the ICT Sectors in Botswana with Respect to Information Access. *The Electronic Library*, *24*(3), 402–417. doi:10.1108/02640470610671240

Myers, B., & Oberndorf, P. (2001). *Managing software acquisition: Open systems and COTS products*. Reading, MA: Addison Wesley.

Nachira, F., Chiozza, E., Ihonen, H., Manzoni, M., & Cunningham, F. (2002). *Towards a network of digital business ecosystems fostering the local development*. Retrieved May 26, 2008, from http://www.digital-ecosystems.org/doc/discussionpaper.pdf

Nadin, S. J., Waterson, P. E., & Parker, S. K. (2001). Participation in job redesign: an evaluation of the use of a sociotechnical tool and its impact. *Human Factors and Ergonomics in Manufacturing*, *11*(1), 53–69. doi:10.1002/1520-6564(200124)11:1<53::AID-HFM4>3.0.CO;2-F

Nagy, P., George, I., Bernstein, W., Caban, J., Klein, R., Mezrich, R., & Park, A. (2006). Radio Frequency Identification Systems Technology in the Surgical Setting. *Surgical Innovation*, *13*(1), 61–67. Retrieved from http://sri.sagepub.com/cgi/content/abstract/13/1/61. doi:10.1177/1553350606013001l0

Nahas, H. A., & Deogun, J. S. (2007). Radio Frequency Identification Applications in Smart Hospitals. In *Proceedings of the Twentieth IEEE International Symposium on Computer-Based Medical Systems (CBMS'07)*.

Nair, M. (2004). *Essentials of balanced scorecard*. New York: Wiley.

Nasiri, R., Moeini, A., & Abdollahzadeh, A. (2004). A New Approach Towards Procurement of Software Models Via Distributed Business Models. *The Journal of Supercomputing*.

Nassiri, R., & Moeini, A. (2007). The Essential of Business Software modeling in Successful ERP implementation. In *Proceedings of the 2007 Int'l conference on Software Engineering Research & practices (SERP 2007)*, USA.

Nassis, V., Rajugan, R., Dillon, T. S., & Rahayu, J. W. (2005). Conceptual and Systematic Design Approach for XML Document Warehouses. *International Journal of Data Warehousing and Mining*, *1*(3), 63–86.

Neely, A. (2005). Performance measurement system design: A literature review and research agenda. *International Journal of Operations & Production Management*, *25*(12), 1228–1263. doi:10.1108/01443570510633639

Nesamoney, D. (2004). BAM: Event-driven Business Intelligence for the Real-Time Enterprise. *DM Review*, *14*(3), 38–40.

Netherlands Tax and Customs Administration. (2005). *Benchmarking customs IT architecture. exploit commonality, manage variability*.

Neumann, P. G. (1995). *Computer-Related Risks*. New York: ACM Press.

Nissen, M. E., & Sengupta, K. (2006). Incorporating software agents into supply chains: Experimental investigation with a procurement task. *Management Information Systems Quarterly*, *30*, 145–166.

NIST. (2001 January). What is this thing called Conformance? *NIST*. Retrieved March 10, 2004, from http://www.itl.nist.gov/

Nonaka, I. (1994). A dynamic theory of organizational knowledge creation. *Organization Science*, *5*(1), 14. doi:10.1287/orsc.5.1.14

Nour, S. S. O. M. (2002). *ICT Opportunities and Challenges for Development in the Arab World.* WIDER Discussion Paper 2002/83. United Nations University/ World Institute for Development Economics Research. Retrieved October 10, 2009, from http://www.wider.unu.edu/publications/publications.htm

Nov, O. (2007). What Motivates Wikipedians? *Communications of the ACM, 50*(11), 60–64. doi:10.1145/1297797.1297798

Nucleus. (2002). *Microsoft BizTalk Server: A Nucleus Research Report.* Research report C30, Nucleus Research Inc. Retrieved from http://www.NucleusResearch.com

Nudurupati, S., & Bititci, U. (2005). Implementation and impact of IT-supported performance measurement systems. *Production Planning and Control, 16*(2), 152–162. doi:10.1080/09537280512331333057

O'Connor, M. C. (2005, August 25). Efficiencies Drive RFID adoption. *RFID Journal.* Retrieved from http://www.rfidjournal.com/article/articleview/1833/1/1/

O'Connor, M. C. (2006, November 26). Toronto area hospital kicks off asset tracking pilot. *RFID Journal.* Retrieved from http://www.rfidjournal.com/article/articleview/2848/1/1/

OASIS. (2007). *Web Services Business Process Execution Language (WS-BPEL) Version 2.0.* Retrieved August 31, 2009, from http://docs.oasis-open.org/wsbpel/2.0/OS/wsbpel-v2.0-OS.html

OASIS. (2007). *Web services reliable messaging (WS-1 ReliableMessaging) Version 1.1. OASIS Standard.* Retrieved March 2009, from http://docs.oasis-open.org/ws-rx/wsrm/200702/wsrm-1.1-spec-os-01.pdf

Ollner, J. (1988). *The Company and Standardization* (3rd ed.). Stockholm, Sweden: Swedish Standards Institution.

Ollson, H. H., Conchuir, E. O., Agerfalk, P. J., & Fitzgerald, B. (2008). Two-stage offshoring: A investigation of the Irish bridge. *Management Information Systems Quarterly, 32*(2), 257–279.

Olson, E., & Williams, P. (2001). E-Commerce with Web-Based Standards: A Case Study in Implementing RosettaNet Process Standards at Avnet, Inc. *PriceWaterhouseCoopers.* Retrieved April 2001, from http://www.rosettanet.org/RosettaNet/Doc/0/BMHE9II7VRK-K916EJ4DPI6I635/avnetwhitepaper.pdf

Oman Economic Review. (2007). *SME Forum –Making Life Easy.* Retrieved August 3, 2008, from http://www.oeronline.com/php/2007_dec/sme_forum.php

Omari, A., & Conrad, S. (2006). On the Usage of Data Mining to Support Website Designers to Have Better Designed Websites. In *Advanced International Conference on Telecommunications and International Conference on Internet and Web Applications and Services (AICT-ICIW'06), Guadeloupe, French Caribbean* (pp. 171). Los Alamitos, CA: IEEE Computer Society.

Omari, A., Conrad, S., & Alcic, S. (2007). Designing a Well-Structured E-Shop Using Association Rule Mining. In *The 4th International Conference on Innovations in Information Technology, Dubai, United Arab Emirates* (pp. 9-14). Washington, DC: IEEE Communication Society.

OMG. (2003 September). *UML 2.0 Diagram Interchange Specification.*

OMG. (2004). *UML 2.0 Superstructure Specification.* Retrieved December 20, 2005, from http://www.uml.org/

OMG. (2006). *Unified Modeling Language: Infrastructure.* Retrieved April 18, 2006, from http://www.uml.org/

Oostveen, A., & van den Besselaar, P. (2005). Trust, Identity, and the Effects of Voting Technologies on Voting Behavior. *Social Science Computer Review, 23*(3), 304–311. doi:10.1177/0894439305275852

Open Mobile Alliance. (2001). *WAG UAProf, version 20-Oct-2001.* Retrieved from http://www.openmobilealliance.org/tech/affiliates/wap/wap-248-uaprof-20011020-a.pdf

Oracle Corporation. (2006). *Oracle9i Data Warehousing Guide Release 2* (9.2). Retrieved from http://download-west.oracle.com/docs/cd/B10501 01/server.920/a96520/toc.htm

Osterwalder, A., & Pigneur, Y. (2002 June). *An e-Business Model Ontology for Modelling e-Business.* Presented at the Bled Electronic Commerce Conference, Bled, Slovenia.

Otsuki, M. (2002). *SMEs Supporting Systems in Saudi Arabia.* Retrieved February 1, 2009, from http://www.ssic2008.com/assets/files/

Ousterhout, J. (2000 October). Managing Trading Partners. *EAI Journal*, 89-92.

Ouyang, C., Dumas, M., Van der Aalst, W., & Ter Hofstede, A. (2006). From Business Process Models to Process-oriented Software Systems: The BPMN to BPEL Way. *BPMCentre.org*. Retrieved from http://is.tm.tue.nl/staff/wvdaalst/BPMcenter/reports.htm

Ozcan, Y. Z., & Kocak, A. (2003). Research note: A need or a status symbol? Use of cellular telephones in Turkey. *European Journal of Communication*, *18*(2), 241–254. doi:10.1177/0267323103018002004

Pagani, M. (2004). Determinant of adoption of third generation mobile multimedia services. *Journal of Interactive Marketing*, *18*(3), 46–59. doi:10.1002/dir.20011

Page, L. (2007, August). Hospitals tap into RFID to track patients and equipment. *Health Facilities Management*, 5–6.

Page, L. (2007 May). Hospitals tune into RFID – Testing gives way to implementation. *Material Management in Health Care*, 18-20.

Pahnila, S., Siponen, M. T., & Mahmood, A. (2007). *Employees' behavior towards IS security policy compliance.* Paper presented at the 40th Annual Hawaii International Conference on System Sciences, Hawaii.

Pappu, M., Singhal, R., & Zoghi, B. (2004 September). *RFID in hospitals: Issues and Solutions.* A report from the Consortium for the Accelerated Deployment of RFID in Distribution.

Park, B. K., Han, H., & Song, I. Y. (2005). XML-OLAP: A Multidimensional Analysis Framework for XML Warehouses. In *7th International Conference on Data Warehousing and Knowledge Discovery (DaWaK 05)*, Copenhagen, Denmark (LNCS 3589, pp. 32–42). Berlin: Springer.

Parker, M. M., & Benson, R. J. (1988). *Information Economics: Linking Business Performance to Information Technology*. Englewood Cliffs, NJ: Prentice-Hall International.

Parker, D. B. (1997). The strategic values of information security in business. *Computers & Security*, *16*, 572–582. doi:10.1016/S0167-4048(97)80793-6

Parker, C. M., & Castelman, T. (2007). New Directions for Research on SME-eBusiness: Insights from an Analysis of Journal Articles from 2003 to 2006. *Journal of Information Systems and Small Business*, *1*(1-2), 21–40.

Parker, M. C., & Castleman, T. (2006). A preliminary Meta-Analysis of SME –eBusiness Journal Publications: Current Trends and Future Research Opportunities Moving Beyond Adoption Factor Studies. Retrieved May, 1 2008, From, http://www.collecter2006.unisa.edu.au/

Pasmore, W. A. (1985). Social science transformer: the socio-technical perspective. *Human Relations*, *48*, 1–22. doi:10.1177/001872679504800101

Patel, F. (2007). *The Arab business world's ICT opportunity*. Arabian Business World.

Pato, J. (2003). Identity Management: Setting Context. Retrieved October 30, 2009, from http://www.hpl.hp.com/techreports/2003/HPL-2003-72.pdf

Pedrinaci, C., Domingue, J., & Medeiros, A. (2008). A Core Ontology for Business Process Analysis . In *The Semantic Web: Research and Applications*. Berlin: Springer. doi:10.1007/978-3-540-68234-9_7

Pedrinaci, C., & Domingue, J. (2007) Towards an Ontology for Process Monitoring and Mining. In M. Hepp, K. Hinkelmann, D. Karagiannis, R. Klein & N. Stojanovic (Eds.), *Semantic Business Process and Product Lifecycle Management. Proceedings of the Workshop SBPM 2007*, Innsbruck, April 7, 2007. Retrieved from http://CEUR-WS.org/Vol-251/

Pedrinaci, C., & Domingue, J. (2009). Ontology-based Metrics Computation for Business Process Analysis. *Workshop: 4th International Workshop on Semantic Business Process Management (SBPM2009) at The 6th European Semantic Web Conference (ESWC2009),* Heraklion, Greece. Retrieved from http://people.kmi.open.ac.uk/carlos/publications/ontology-based-metrics-SBPM09.pdf

Pedrinaci, C., Domingue, J., & Brelage, C. (2008). Semantic Business Process Management: Scaling up the Management of Business Processes. In *2nd IEEE International Conference on Semantic Computing (ICSC)*.

Pedrinaci, C., Lambert, D., Wetzstein, B., van Lessen, T., Cekov, L., & Dimitrov, M. (2008). SENTINEL: A Semantic Business Process Monitoring Tool. In *Workshop:*

Ontology-supported Business Intelligence (OBI2008) at 7th International Semantic Web Conference (ISWC2008), Karlsruhe, Germany. Retrieved from http://people.kmi.open.ac.uk/carlos/publications/obi2008.pdf

Persson, A. (2001). *Enterprise Modelling in Practice: Situational Factors and their Influence on Adopting a Participative Approach*. Unpublished PhD thesis. Department of Computer and Systems Sciences, Stockholm University.

Pestoff, V. A. (1999). Social empire and civil democracy in Sweden: developing a participatory welfare society in the twenty-first century. In W. E. Halal & K. B. Taylor (Eds.), *21st Century Economics*. London: Macmillan.

Pettigrew, A. M. (1990). Studying strategic choice and strategic change. A comment on Mintzberg and Waters: 'Does decision get in the way?' . *Organization Studies*, *11*(1), 6–11. doi:10.1177/017084069001100102

Pettigrew, A. M. (1985). Contextualist research and the study of organizational change processes . In Mumford, E. (Ed.), *Research Methods in Information Systems* (pp. 53–78). Amsterdam: North-Holland.

Phipps, I. (2000). New communications technologies: A conduit for social inclusion. *Information Communication and Society*, *3*(1), 39–68. doi:10.1080/136911800359419

Pillai, P. K. (2006). Saudi Arabia: 8th Five-year Plan (2005-2009). *Saudi Commerce and Economic Review*. Retrieved February. 1, 2009 from, http://zawya.com/story.cfm/

Plesea, L. (n.d.). The Design . *Implementation and Operation of the JPL OnEarth WMS Server*.

Pokorný, J. (2002). XML Data Warehouse: Modelling and Querying. In *5th International Baltic Conference (BalticDB&IS 02)*, Tallin, Estonia, Tallin Technical University (pp. 267–280).

Polanyi, M. (1962). *Personal Knowledge: Towards a Post-Critical Philosophy*. New York: Harper Torchbooks.

Ponisio, M. L., Sikkel, K., Riemens, L., & van Eck, P. (2008a). Combining visualisation techniques to understand cooperation in inter-organisational systems. *Journal of Systems and Information Technology*, *10*(2), 159–179. doi:10.1108/13287260810897774

Ponisio, M. L., van Eck, P., & Riemens, L. (2008b). Using critical problem solving to plan inter-organisational cooperation in e-customs. In *Proceedings of the International Association for Development of the Information Society (IADIS) International Conference e-Commerce 2008* (pp. 28–39). Amsterdam: IADIS Press.

Ponisio, M. L., van Eck, P., & Riemens, L. (2009). Ecustoms case study: mechanisms behind cooperation planning. In *Proceedings of the International Association for Development of the Information Society (IADIS) International Conference e-Commerce 2009*. Algarve, Portugal: IADIS Press.

Porter, M. E. (1985). *Competitive Advantage: Creating and Sustaining Superior Performance*. London: Collier Macmillan Publishers.

Porter, M. (2001, March). Strategy and the Internet. *Harvard Business Review*, 63–78.

Porter, L. W., Steers, R. M., Mowday, R. T., & Boultian, P. V. (1974). Organizational commitment, job satisfaction, and turnover among psychiatric technicians. *The Journal of Applied Psychology*, *59*, 603–609. doi:10.1037/h0037335

Premkumar, G., Ramamurthy, K., & Nilakanta, S. (1994). Implementation of Electronic Data Interchange: An Innovation Diffusion Perspective. *Journal of Management Information Systems*, *11*(2), 157–186.

Premkumar, G. (2003). A meta-analysis of research on information technology implementation in small business. *Journal of Organizational Computing and Electronic Commerce*, *13*(2), 91–121. doi:10.1207/S15327744JOCE1302_2

Pressman, R. S. (2005). *Software Engineering: A Practitioner's Approach* (6th ed.). New York: McGraw-Hill.

PriceWaterhouseCoopers. (1999, September 24). SME E-commerce Study (Final Report). *Asia Pacific Economic Cooperation (APEC)*.

Prins, J. E. J. (2001). *Designing e-government: On the crossroads of technological innovation and institutional change*. Amsterdam: Kluwer Law International.

Pyke, J. (2009) XPDL - The Silent Workhorse of BPM. *BPM.com*. Retrieved from http://www.bpm.com/xpdl-the-silent-workhorse-of-bpm.html

Qu, Y. (2007). *Sensemaking, Information Seeking and Retrieval: Supporting Representation Construction in Sensemaking*. Ann Arbor, MI: University of Michigan.

Quinlan, J. R. (1999). *C4.5: Programs for Machine Learning*. San Francisco: Morgan Kaufmann Publishers.

Qun, C., Lim, A., & Ong, K. W. (2003). D(k)-Index: An Adaptive Structural Summary for Graph-Structured Data. In *2003 ACM SIGMOD International Conference on Management of Data (SIGMOD 03)*, San Diego, USA (pp. 134–144).

Radice, R. A., Roth, N. K., O'Hara, A. C., & Ciarfella, W. A. (1985). A Programming Process Architecture. *IBM Systems Journal*, *24*, 79–90. doi:10.1147/sj.242.0079

Radwan, I. (2001). *Small and medium enterprise development: a vision for action in Saudi Arabia*. Paper prepared for the Economic Vision Conference Riyadh, Saudi Arabia. Retrieved January 28, 2007, from http://www.planning.gov.sa/

Rama Rao, T. P. (2001). E-Commerce and Digital Divide: Impact on Consumers. In *The Asia-Pacific: New Dimensions of Consumer Protection in the Era of Globalisation*, Goa, India. Retrieved October 3, 2008 from, http://www.iimahd.ernet.in/egov/documents

Ramasubbu, N., Krishnan, M., & Kompalli, P. (2005). A process maturity framework for managing distributed development. *IEEE Software*, *22*(3), 80–86. doi:10.1109/MS.2005.69

Ramsey, J. (1998 August). Developing an IT Strategy. *Computer Bits, 8*(8). Retrieved from http://www.computerbits.com

Ranganathan, C., & Ganapathy, S. (2002). Key dimensions of business-to-consumer web sites. *Journal of International Management*, *39*(6), 457–465.

Rao, H. R., & Chaudhury, A. (1996). A two-level investigation of information systems outsourcing. *Communications of the ACM*, *30*(7), 36–44.

Rao, D. N. (2006). *Saudi Arabia: The Emerging Economic Tiger of the Middle East*. Retrieved October 17, 2009 from, http://ssrn.com/abstract=935080

Rawashdeh, A., & Matalkah, B. (2006). A new software quality model for evaluating COTS. *Journal of Computer Science*, *2*(4), 2006.

Recker, J., & Mendling, J. (2006) On the Translation between BPMN and BPEL: Conceptual Mismatch between Process Modeling Languages. In T. Latour & M. Petit (Eds.), *Proceedings 18th International Conference on Advanced Information Systems Engineering* (pp. 521-532).

Remmert, M. (2004). Towards European Standards on Electronic Voting. In *Proceedings of the first International Workshop Electronic Voting in Europe–Technology, Law, Politics and Society*, Austria.

Research and Markets. (2009). *Turkey mobile operator forecast, 2009-2013*. Retrieved from http://www.researchandmarkets.com/reports/1087690/

Rettie, R. (2007). Mobile phones as network capital: Facilitating connections. *Mobilities*, *3*(2), 291–311. doi:10.1080/17450100802095346

Reynolds, J. (2004). *The Complete E-Commerce Book: Design, Build and Maintain a Successful Web-Based Business*. San Francisco: CMP Books.

Reynolds, D. (2007). *Jena2 inference support*. Retrieved August 31, 2009, from http://jena.sourceforge.net/inference/

Rheingold, H. (2002). *Smart mobs: The next social revolution*. New York: Perseus.

Riemenschneider, C. K., Harrison, D. A., & Mykytyn, P. P. Jr. (2003). Understanding it adoption decisions in small business: integrating current theories. *Information & Management*, *40*(4), 269–285. doi:10.1016/S0378-7206(02)00010-1

Rittgen, P. (2007). Negotiating Models. In J. Krogstie, A. Opdahl & G. Sindre (Eds.), *Proceedings of the 19th International Conference on Advanced Information Systems Engineering (CAiSE 2007)*, Trondheim, Norway, June 2007 (pp. 561-573). Berlin: Springer.

Riva, O., & Toivonen, S. (2007). The DYNAMOS approach to support context-aware service provisioning in mobile environments. *Journal of Systems and Software*, *80*(12), 1956–1972. doi:10.1016/j.jss.2007.03.009

Roark, D. C., & Miguel, K. (2006). Bar coding's replacement? *Nursing Management*, *37*(2), 29–31. doi:10.1097/00006247-200602000-00009

Rogers, E. M. (1995). *Diffusion of innovations* (4th ed.). New York: The Free Press.

Rosenberg, F., & Dustdar, S. (2005). Business rules integration in BPEL, a service-oriented approach. In *Proceedings of the 7th International IEEE Conference on E-Commerce Technology (CEC 2005)*.

Rosenkopf, L., Metiu, A., & George, V. P. (2001). From the bottom up? Technical committee activity and alliance formation. *Administrative Science Quarterly*, *46*(4), 748–772. doi:10.2307/3094830

Rosenthal, R. (2008). Saudi Arabia Vertical Markets 2008-2012 Forecast. *IDC Middle East and Africa*. Retrieved June 14, 2009, from http://www.idc-cema.com

RosettaNet. (2001). *Case Study: Arrow and UTEC replace EDI-based purchase order process with RosettaNet standards*. Retrieved February 20, 2004, from http://www.rosettanet.org/RosettaNet/Doc/0/D074294MUC4K-JD8GF7HQL8RE67/Arrow_case_study.pdf

RosettaNet. (2002). *Achieving Streamlined Operations Through Collaborative Forecasting and Inventory Management: STMicroelectronics E-Chain Optimization (eChO) Project*. Retrieved February 10, 2004, from http://www.rosettanet.org/RosettaNet/Doc/0/63NGGI61LP84P753UQ28VBMLA3/STMicroelectronics+White+Paper.pdf

RosettaNet. (2003). *Intel and Shinko to use RosettaNet standards to build forecase-to-cash procurement process*. Case study report. Retrieved from http://www.rosettanet.org/RosettaNet/Doc/0/FSG4VFMC6RA4B47H0FJB0N-NPED/IntelShinkoROICaseStudy.pdf

Ross, R. G. (2003). *Principles of the business rules approach*. Boston: Addison-Wesley Professional.

Rousseau, D. M. (1995). *Psychological contracts in organizations-Understanding written and unwritten agreements*. London: Sage.

Rowe, W. D. (1977). *An Anatomy of Risk*. New York: John Wiley & Sons.

Rukanova, B., van Slooten, K., & Stegwee, R. (2003). Beyond the Standard Development and the Standard Adoption. In K. Jakobs (Ed.), *Proceedings of the 8th Euras Workshop on Standardization*, Aachen, July 11-12 (pp. 133-143).

Rule, M. L. (2000). *The Rule Markup Initiative (RuleML)*. Retrieved from http://www.ruleml.org/

Rusu, L. I., Rahayu, J. W., & Taniar, D. (2005). A Methodology for Building XML Data Warehouse. *International Journal of Data Warehousing and Mining*, *1*(2), 67–92.

Rymer, J. R., & Moore, C. (2006). *The dynamic business applications imperative*. Retrieved August 31, 2009, from http://www.microsoft.com/presspassitanalyst/docs/09242007forresterdynamicbusiness.pdf

Rys, M. (2004). XQuery in Relational Database Systems. In *XML 2004 Conference and Exposition Proceedings (XML 2004)*, Washington, USA.

Sabbagh, K. (2003). *Closing the Digital Divide in the Arab World*. Retrieved July 23, 2009, from http://www.boozallen.com/publications/article/659082

Sabherwal, R. (1999). The role of trust in outsourced IS development projects. *Communications of the ACM*, *43*(2), 80–87. doi:10.1145/293411.293485

Sack, R. D. (1986). *Human territoriality: Its theory and history*. New York: Cambridge University Press.

Sajini, I. I. (2004). Effects of WTO on Small & Medium Enterprises. *Arab News*. Retrieved April 4, 2008, from http://www.arabnews.com/?page=1&section=0&article=38268&d=19&m=1&y=2004

Sander, S. (2008). *Knowledge management by wikis*. Universiteit Maastricht, Switzerland: Institute for Knowledge and Agent Technology.

Sanders, N. R. (2007). An empirical study of the impact of e-business technologies on organizational collaboration and performance. *Journal of Operations Management*, *25*, 1332–1347. doi:10.1016/j.jom.2007.01.008

Saxena, K. B. C. (2005). Towards excellence in e-governance. *International Journal of Public Sector Management*, *18*(6), 498–513. doi:10.1108/09513550510616733

Sayal, M., Casati, F., Dayal, U., & Shan, M.-C. (2002). Business process cockpit. In *Proceedings of the 28th Very Large DataBase (VLBD) Conference*, Hong Kong, China, 2002.

Sayar, A., Aktas, M. S., Aydin, G., Fox, G., & Pierce, M. (2005). *Developing a Web Service-Compatible Map Server for Geophysical Applications.* Paper presented at the Submitted to ACM-GIS Conference.

Scheer, A.-W. (1999). *ARIS - Business Process Modeling* (2nd ed.). Berlin: Springer.

Schubert, P., & Leimstoll, U. (2007). Importance and Use of Information Technology in Small and Medium-Sized Companies. *Electronic Markets*, *17*(1), 38–55. doi:10.1080/10196780601136799

Schubert, P., & Leimstoll, U. (2006). The Importance of ICT: An Empirical Study in Swiss SMEs. In *19th Bled Conference eValues*, Bled, Slovenia.

Schubert, P., Fisher, J., & Leimstoll, U. (2007). ICT and Innovation in Small Companies. In *15th European Conference on Information Systems*, St. Gallen, Switzerland (pp. 1226-1239).

Scupola, A. (2003). The Adoption of Internet Commerce by SMEs in the South of Italy: An Environmental, Technological and Organizational Perspective. *Journal of Global Information Technology Management*, *1*(6), 52–71.

Seminerio, M. (2000). B2B 2 The World. *eWeek*, *17*(35), 51-55.

Seo, Y., Ko, J., & Price, J. L. (2004). The determinants of job satisfaction among hospital a model estimation in Korea. *International Journal of Nursing Studies*, *41*, 437–446. doi:10.1016/j.ijnurstu.2003.11.003

Sergeant, J. (2000). *Presentation by the e-envoy of UK Online.* British Academy of Management Conference. Birmingham, UK: Aston University Business School.

Shah, T. (1998). *Improving electronic Commerce Through Gathering Customer Data. School of engineering and applied science.* VA, USA: University of Virginia.

Shaikh Ali, A., Rana, O. F., Al-Ali, R., & Walker, D. W. (2003). UDDIe: an extended Registry for Web services. In Proceedings of *The IEEE Symposium on Applications and the Internet Workshops, (SAINT 2003)*, pp. 85-89.

Sharma, G., & Sturges, P. (2007). Using ICT to help the poor access public services: An action research programme. *Information Development*, *23*(1), 15–24. doi:10.1177/0266666907075623

Sharma, S. K., & Gupta, J. N. D. (2004). Web services architecture for m-government: Issues and challenges. *Electronic Government*, *1*(4), 462–474. doi:10.1504/EG.2004.005921

Sharp, J. (2008). Creating and using a WEB service. In *Visual C# 2008 Step by Step* (pp. 623-645). Redmond, WA: Microsoft Press.

Sharpe, A., & McDermott, P. (2001). *Workflow Modelling: Tools for Process Improvement and Application Development.* Norwood, MA: Artech House.

Shiels, H., McIvor, R., & O'Reilly, D. (2003). Understanding the Implications of ICT adoption: Insights from SMEs. *Logistics Information Management*, *16*(5), 312–326. doi:10.1108/09576050310499318

Shin, K., & Leem, C. S. (2002). A reference system for internet based inter-enterprise electronic commerce. *Journal of Systems and Software*, *60*, 195–209. doi:10.1016/S0164-1212(01)00092-9

Shukla, A., Deshpande, P., & Naughton, J. F. (2000). Materialized view selection for multi-cube data models. In *7th International Conference on Extending DataBase Technology (EDBT 2000)*, Konstanz, Germany (pp. 269-284).

Simon, H. (1985). Human nature in politics: the dialogue of psychology with political science. *The American Political Science Review*, *79*, 293–304. doi:10.2307/1956650

Simon, H. A. (1976). *Administrative Behaviour* (3rd ed.). New York: Free Press.

Simpson, G. (2007, August 27). Hospitals need RFID injection. *ZDNetAsia*. Retrieved from http://www.zdnetasia.com/news/communications/0,39044192,62031433,00.htm

Siponen, M. T. (2000). A conceptual foundation for organizational information security awareness. *Information Management & Computer Security*, *8*(1), 31–41. doi:10.1108/09685220010371394

Siponen, M. T. (2001). Five dimensions of information security awareness. *ACM SIGCAS Computers and Society*, *31*(2), 24–29. doi:10.1145/503345.503348

Siponen, M. T. (2005). An analysis of the traditional IS security approaches: Implications for research and practices. *European Journal of Information Systems*, *14*, 303–315. doi:10.1057/palgrave.ejis.3000537

Siponen, M. T., & Iivari, J. (2006). Six design theories for IS security policies and guidelines. *Journal of the Association for Information Systems*, *7*(7), 445–472.

Siponen, M. T., & Vance, A. (2010). (forthcoming). Neutralization: New insight into the problem of employee information systems security policy violation. *Management Information Systems Quarterly*.

Sivashanmugam, K., Miller, J., Sheth, A., & Verma, K. (2005). Framework for Semantic Web Process Composition. *International Journal of Electronic Commerce*, *9*(2), 71–106.

Skall, M., & Rosenthal, L. (2000). *Conformance.* Presentation from the ebXML Tokyo Meeting in November, 2000.

Skalle, H., Ramachandran, S., Schuster, M., Szaloky, V., & Antoun, S. (2009). Aligning Business Process Manage ment, Service-Oriented Architecture, and Lean Six Sigma for Real Business Benefits. *IBM Redbooks*. Retrieved from http://www.redbooks.ibm.com/abstracts/redp4447.html

Smallbone, D., North, D., Vickers, I., & Roper, S. (2001). Innovation and the Use of Technology in Manufacturing Plants and SMEs: An Inter-Regional Comparison. In *Proceedings 24th ISBA National Small Firms Conference: Exploring the Frontiers of Small Business,* Hinckley, Leicestershire (pp. 289-308).

Smith, B. (1993, September). Making war on defects: Six-sigma design. *IEEE Spectrum*, 43–47. doi:10.1109/6.275174

Smith, H. J., & Hasnas, J. (1999). Ethics and information systems: The corporate domain. *Management Information Systems Quarterly*, *23*(1), 109–127. doi:10.2307/249412

Smith, H., & Fingar, P. (2003). *BPM's third wave, based on extracts from business process management: The third wave.* Retrieved October 19, 2009, from http://www.fairdene.com/processes/BPTrendsMay2003BPM-3SmithFingar.pdf

Söderström, E. (2008). Towards a general model of the B2B standards implementation process. In *Proceedings of the IADIS E-Commerce conference 2008*, Amsterdam, 22-24 July, 2008 (pp. 151-158).

Soliman, K., & Janz, B. (2004). An exploratory study to identify the critical factors affecting the decision to establish Internet-based inter-organisational information systems. *Information & Management*, *41*, 697–706. doi:10.1016/j.im.2003.06.001

Sourouni, A. M., Koussouris, S., Charalabidis, Y., Askounis, D., & Kalaboukas, K. (2007 December). *A generic process modelling approach for interoperable e-business transactions.* Paper presented at IADIS International Conference e-Commerce 2007, Algarve, Portugal.

Sparling, L., Cater-Steel, A., & Toleman, M. (2007). SME adoption of e-Commerce in the Central Okanagan region of Canada. In *18th Australasian Conference on Information Systems (ACIS 2007): The 3 Rs: Research, Relevance and Rigour - Coming of Age*, Toowoomba, Australia.

Srinivasan, A., & Te'eni, D. (1995). Modeling as Constrained Problem Solving: An Empirical Study of the Data Modeling Process. *Management Science*, *41*(3), 419–434. doi:10.1287/mnsc.41.3.419

Srivastava, J., Cooley, R., Deshpande, M., & Tan, P. (2000). Web Usage Mining: Discovery and Applications of Usage Patterns from Web Data. *ACM SIGKDD Explorations*, *1*(2), 12–23. doi:10.1145/846183.846188

Ssewanyana, J., & Busler, M. (2007). Adoption and Usage of ICT in developing Countries: Case of Ugandan Firms. *International Journal of Education and Development using ICT, 3*(3), 49-59. Retrieved march 13, 2009, from http://ijedict.dec.uwi.edu/viewarticle.php?id=349

Stacey, M., & McGregor, C. (2007). Temporal abstraction in intelligent clinical data analysis: A survey. *Artificial Intelligence in Medicine*, *39*(1), 1–24. doi:10.1016/j.artmed.2006.08.002

Stahl, B. C. (2005). The ethical problem of framing e-government in terms of e-commerce. *The Electronic . Journal of E-Government*, *3*(2), 77–86.

Stamper, R. (1991). The Semiotic Framework for Information Systems Research . In Nissen, H., Klein, H., & Hirschheim, R. (Eds.), *Information Systems Research:*

Contemporary Approaches and Emergent Traditions (pp. 515–517). Amsterdam: North-Holland.

Stattenberger, G., & Braun, T. (2001). QoS provisioning for mobile IP users . In Afifi, H., & Zeghlache, D. (Eds.), *Applications and Services in Wireless Networks*. New York: Hermes Science Publications.

Strassmann, P. A. (1990). *The Business Value of Computers: An Executive's Guide*. New Canaan, CT: Information Economics Press.

Straub, D. W. (1990). Effective IS security: An empirical study. *Information Systems Research, 1*(3), 255–276. doi:10.1287/isre.1.3.255

Straub, D. W., & Welke, R. J. (1998). Coping with systems risk: Security planning models for management decision-making. *Management Information Systems Quarterly, 22*(4), 441–469. doi:10.2307/249551

Strauss, A., & Corbin, J. (1998). *Basics of qualitative research techniques and procedures for developing grounded theory*. London: Sage.

Stroeken, J. H. M. (2001). The Adoption of IT by SMES: The Dutch Case. *Journal of Enterprising Culture, 9*(1), 129–152. doi:10.1142/S0218495801000080

Suchman, M. C. (1995). Managing legitimacy: Strategic and institutional approaches. *Academy of Management Review, 20*(3), 571–610. doi:10.2307/258788

Sundar, D. K., & Garg, S. (2005). M-governance: A framework for Indian urban local bodies. *European Mobile Government Conference*. Brighton, UK: Mobile Government Consortium International LLC

Suntinger, M., Obweger, H., Schiefer, J., & Gröller, M. (2008). The Event Tunnel: Interactive Visualization of Complex Event Streams for Business Process Pattern Analysis. In *IEEE VGTC Pacific Visualization Symposium 2008 (PacificVis),* Kyoto, Japan, March 5-7 2008 (pp. 111-118).

Supply Chain Digest (2009 May). The Greatest Supply Chain Disasters of All Time 2009. *Supply Chain Digest*.

Swann, P. (2000, December 11). *The economics of standardization*. Final report for Standards and Technical Regulations Directorate, Department of Trade and Industry, Manchester Business School.

Tan, J., Tyler, K., & Manica, A. (2007). Business- to – business adoption of ecommerce in China. *Information & Management, 44*, 3321–3351. doi:10.1016/j.im.2007.04.001

Tao, Y., & Lin, K. J. (2005). A broker-based framework for QoS-aware Web service composition. In *Proceedings of The 2005 IEEE International Conference on e-Technology, e-Commerce and e-Service (EEE'05)* (pp. 22-29).

Tarafdar, M., & Gordon, S. (2007). Understanding the influences of information systems competencies on process innovation: A resource-based view. *The Journal of Strategic Information Systems, 16*, 353–392. doi:10.1016/j.jsis.2007.09.001

Tarafdar, M., & Vaidya, S. D. (2004). Adoption of electronic commerce by organizations in India: Strategic and environmental imperatives. *Electronic Journal of Information Systems in Developing Countries, 17*(2), 1–25.

Taylor, H. (2006). Critical risks in outsourced IT projects: The intractable and the unforeseen. *Communications of the ACM, 49*(11), 75–79. doi:10.1145/1167838.1167840

Tayntor, B. C. (2006). *Successful packaged software implementation*. Boca Raton, FL: Auerbach.

Technology integration division. (2007). *Saudi Arabia in perspective: an orientation guide*. Defense Language Institute Foreign Language Center. Retrieved October 16, 2009, from ttp://fieldsupport.dliflc.edu/products/cip/saudi/

Telleria, K., Turner, T., & Bititci, U. (2002). Measuring and Improving Business Process Reliability. *International Journal of Business Performance Management, 4*(1), 76–94. doi:10.1504/IJBPM.2002.000109

Templeman, J. (2003). The.Net framework class library. In *Microsoft Visual C++.Net Step by Step, Version 2003*. Redmond, WA: Microsoft Press

Temtime, Z. T., Chinyoka, S. V., & Shunda, J. P. W. (2003). Toward Strategic Use of IT in SMEs: A Developing Country Perspective. *Information Management & Computer Security, 11*(5), 230–237. doi:10.1108/09685220310500144

Tennenholtz, M. (2004). Dynamic Voting. In *Proceedings of the 5th ACM Conference on Electronic Commerce - EC'04,* New York, USA, May 2004.

Teo, T., & Ranganathan, C. (2004, December). Adopters and non-adopters of business-to-business electronic commerce in Singapore. *Information & Management*, *42*(1), 89–102.

The University of Manchester. (2004). *Introducing The University of Manchester*. Manchester, UK: University of Manchester.

Theodorou, T., Violettas, G., & Georgiadis, C. K. (2008). Wiki-Dic: Implementing an e-Voting Application to Support User-generated Content. In *Proceedings of the IADIS E-Commerce International Conference (e-commerce 2008)*, Amsterdam, The Netherlands (pp. 209-214).

Theoharidou, M., Kokolakis, S., Karyda, M., & Kiountouzis, E. (2005). The insider threat to information systems and the effectiveness of ISO17799. *Computers & Security*, *24*, 472–481. doi:10.1016/j.cose.2005.05.002

Thomas, M., Redmond, R., Yoon, V., & Singh, R. (2005). A semantic approach to monitor business process. *Communications of the ACM*, *48*(12), 55–59. doi:10.1145/1101779.1101809

Thomas, K. (2008, May 30). Radio wrist tags that make for smoother operations, A technology for tracing consumer goods may help save lives and keep track of hospital equipment. *Financial Times (North American Edition)*, 12.

Thomke, S., & Fujimoto, T. (2000). The effect of front-loading problem-solving on product development performance. *Journal of Product Innovation Management*, *17*, 128–142. doi:10.1016/S0737-6782(99)00031-4

Thong, J. (1999). An integrated model of information systems adoption in small business. *Journal of Management Information Systems*, *15*(4), 187–214.

Thoren, C. (2004). The procurement of usable and accessible software. *Universal Access in the Information Society*, *3*, 102–106. doi:10.1007/s10209-003-0077-3

Tigre, P. B. (2003). Brazil in the age of electronic commerce. *The Information Society*, *19*(1), 33–43. doi:10.1080/01972240309476

TJX. (2007a). *Annual Report of 2006: The TJX Companies, Inc.*

TJX. (2007b, April 28). *Quarterly Report of The TJX Companies, Inc.* SEC Form 10-Q, for the Quarterly Period.

Toivonen, S. (2004). Hybrid Service Provision Model for Mobile Users: Prospects for the DYNAMOS Project. In Hyvönen, E., Kauppinen, T., Salminen, M., Viljanen, K., and Ala-Siuru, P. (Eds.): Proceedings of the *Web Intelligence Symposium of the Finnish Artificial Intelligence Conference (STeP 2004)*, (pp. 183-192).

Tornatzky, L. G., & Fleischer, M. (1990). *The Processes of Technological Innovation*. Lexington, MA: Lexington Books.

Tornatzky, L. G., & Klein, K. J. (1982). Innovation characteristics and innovation adoption–implementation: a meta analysis of findings. *IEEE Transactions on Engineering Management*, *29*(11), 28–45.

TOVE Ontology Project. (n.d.). Retrieved from http://www.eil.utoronto.ca/enterprise-modelling/tove/

Townsend, A. M., Whitman, M. E., & Hendrickson, A. R. (1995). Computer support system adds power to group processes. *HRMagazine*, *40*(9), 87–91.

Tozsa, I., & Budai, B. (2005). M-government in Hungary. *European Mobile Government Conference*. Brighton, UK. Mobile Government Consortium International LLC

Trechsel, A., & Mendez, F. (2005). *The European Union and E-voting*. London: Routledge.

Troyer, O., & Leune, C. J. (1998). WSDM: A User Centered Design Method for Web Sites. *Computer Networks*, *30*(1-7), 85- 94.

Tsoumas, B., & Gritzalis, D. (2006). *Towards an ontology-based security management*. Paper presented at the The 20th International Conference on Advanced Information Networking and Applications (AINA'06), Vienna.

Tuckman, B. W. (1965). Developmental sequences in small groups. *Psychological Bulletin*, *63*, 384–399. doi:10.1037/h0022100

Tufte, E. R. (1990). *Envisioning Information*. Cheshire, CT: Graphics Press.

Tufte, E. R. (1997). *Visual Explanations*. Cheshire, CT: Graphics Press.

Türksat. (2008). Retrieved from http://www.turksat.com.tr/english/v2/e-government-gateway

UBL (Universal Business Language). (n.d.). Retrieved from http://www.oasis-open.org/committees/ubl/

Uchiyama, H., Runapongsa, K., & Teorey, T. J. (1999). A progressive view materialization algorithm. In *2nd ACM International Workshop on Data warehousing and OLAP (DOLAP 1999)*, Kansas City, USA (pp. 36–41).

UN E-Government Survey. (2008). *From e-Government to Connected Governance*. Document No. ST/ESA/PAD/SER.E/112. New York: United Nations.

UNCTAD. (2004). *E-commerce and Development Report (2004)*. Retrieved October 18, 2009, from http://www.unctad.org/

UNCTAD. (2004). *ICT as an Enabler for Growth, Development and Competitiveness*. Retrieved March 13, 2008, from http://www.unctadxi.org/templates/Event____69.aspx

Unnithan, C., Smith, R., & Fraunholz, B. (2009). Maximising the Benefits of Radio Frequency Identification Technology (RFID) Integration in Clinical Contexts: a Linear Conduit. In *HIC'09 Conference*, August 19-21. Canberra, Australia: Health Informatics Society of Australia.

Valluri, S. R., Vadapalli, S., & Karlapalem, K. (2002). View relevance driven materialized view selection in data warehousing environment. In *30th Australasian conference on Database technologies*, Melbourne, Australia (pp. 187-196).

Van der Aalst, W. M. P., & Jablonski, S. (2000). Dealing with workflow change: identification of issues and solutions. *Computer Systems Science and Engineering*, *15*(5), 267–276.

Van der Aalst, W. M. P., & Weske, M. (2005). Case Handling: A New Paradigm for Business Process Support. *Data & Knowledge Engineering*, *53*, 192–162.

Van der Aalst, W., ter Hofstede, A., & Weske, M. (2003). Business Process Management: A Survey. In *Proceedings of the 1st International Conference on Business Process Management*. Berlin: Springer.

van der Sanden, W., & Sturm, B. (2000). *Informatie-architectuur: de infrastructurele benadering* (2nd ed.). Rosmalen, The Netherlands: Panfox/Ordina.

van der Spek, R., & Spijkervet, A. (1997). Knowledge management: Dealing intelligently with knowledge . In Liebowitz, J., & Wilcox, L. (Eds.), *Knowledge Management and Its Elements*. New York: CRC Press.

van der Torre, L., Lankhorst, M. M., ter Doest, H., Campschroer, J. T. P., & Arbab, F. (2006). Landscape maps for enterprise architectures. In E. Dubois & K. Pohl (Eds.), *Advanced Information Systems Engineering. 18th International Conference, CAiSE 2006* (LNCS 4001, pp. 351–366). Berlin: Springer-Verlag.

Vasilecas, O., & Bugaite, D. (2006) Business Rules Elicitation in the Process of Enterprise Information System Development. In *Eight International Conference on Enterprise Information Systems*, Paphos, Cyprus, May 2006.

Vedamuthu, A. S., et al. (2007). *Web services policy 1.5 – framework*. W3C Recommendation 04 September 2007. Retrieved February 2009, from http://www.w3.org/TR/ws-policy/.

Velasquez, J., Yasuda, H., & Aoki, T. (2003). Combining the Web Content and Usage Mining to Understand the Visitor Behavior in a Web Site. In *Proceedings of the 3rd IEEE International Conference on Data Mining (ICDM 2003)* (pp. 669-672). Washington, DC: IEEE Computer Society Press.

Venkatesh, V., Morris, M. G., Davis, G. B., & Davis, F. D. (2003). User acceptance of information technology: Toward a unified view. *Management Information Systems Quarterly*, *27*(3), 425–478.

Venkatesh, V., & Davis, F. D. (2000). A theoretical extension of the technology acceptance model: four longitudinal field studies. *Management Science*, *46*(2), 186–204. doi:10.1287/mnsc.46.2.186.11926

Venkatesh, V., Morris, M. G., Davis, G. B., & Davis, F. D. (2003). User acceptance of information technology: towards a unified view. *Management Information Systems Quarterly*, *27*(3), 425–478.

Verdon, D. (2006). Security policies and the software developer. *IEEE Security & Privacy*, *4*(4), 42–49. doi:10.1109/MSP.2006.103

Volkamer, M., & McGaley, M. (2007). Requirements and Evaluation Procedures for eVoting. In *Proceedings of the 2nd IEEE Int. Conf. on Availability, Reliability and Security (ARES'07).*

von Halle, B. (2002). *Business Rules Applied, Building Better Systems Using the Business Rules Approach.* New York: Wiley and Sons.

Vrdoljak, B., Banek, M., & Rizzi, S. (2003). Designing Web Warehouses from XML Schemas. In *5th International Conference on Data Warehousing and Knowledge Discovery (DaWaK 03)*, Prague, Czech Republic (LNCS 2737, pp. 89–98). Berlin: Springer.

W3C Mobile Web Initiative. (2005). *MWI device description working group.* Retrieved from http://www.w3.org/2005/MWI/DDWG/

W3C. (2006). *Web services policy attachment.* Retrieved from http://www.w3.org/Submission/WS-PolicyAttachment

W3C. (2007). *Composite Capability/Preference Profiles (CC/PP): Structure and vocabularies 2.0.* W3C Working Draft 30 April 2007. Retrieved from http://www.w3.org/TR/2007/WD-CCPP-struct-vocab2-20070430/

W3C. (2008). *W3C mobileOK Checker [Beta].* Retrieved from http://validator.w3.org/mobile/

Waldt, D. (2005). *Using XML and Databases: W3C Standards in Practice* [White Paper]. The Gilbane Report. Retrieved from http://www.x-hive.com

Walker, S. T. (1985). *Network security overview.* Paper presented at the IEEE Symposium on Security and Privacy.

Ware, C. (2000). *Information Visualization.* San Francisco: Morgan Kaufmann.

Warkentin, M., & Johnston, A. C. (2008). IT governance and organizational design for security management . In Straub, D. W., Goodman, S., & Baskerville, R. L. (Eds.), *Information Security: Policy, Processes, and Practices* (pp. 46–68). Armonk, NY: M.E. Sharpe.

Waterman, H., Marshall, M., Noble, J., Davies, H., Wakshe, K., Sheaff, R., & Elwyn, G. (2007). The role of action research in the investigation and diffusion of innovations in health care: The Pride Project. *Qualitative Health Research, 17*(3), 373–381. doi:10.1177/1049732306298976

Watjatrakul, B. (2005). Determinants of IS sourcing decisions: A comparative study of transaction cost theory versus the resource-based view. *The Journal of Strategic Information Systems, 14*(4), 289–415. doi:10.1016/j.jsis.2005.05.001

webMethods. (2003 February). *GEAR 6 RosettaNet Implementation Guide: Project Planning Guide* [Whitepaper].

Weilenmann, A. (2001). Negotiating use: Making sense of mobile technology. *Personal and Ubiquitous Computing, 5*(2), 109–122. doi:10.1007/PL00000015

Weippl, E. R., & Klemen, M. (2006). Implementing IT security for small and medium enterprises . In Warkentin, M. E. (Ed.), *Enterprise Information Systems Assurance and Systems Security.* Hershey, PA: Idea Group Publishing.

Werlinger, R., Hawkey, K., Botta, D., & Beznosov, K. (2009). Security practitioners in context: Their activities and interactions with other stakeholders within organizations. *International Journal of Human-Computer Studies, 67*(7), 584–606. doi:10.1016/j.ijhcs.2009.03.002

Whitman, M. E. (2004). In defense of the realm: Understanding the threats to information security. *International Journal of Information Management, 24*, 43–57. doi:10.1016/j.ijinfomgt.2003.12.003

Whitman, M. E., & Mattord, H. J. (2003). *Principles of Information Security.* Boston: Thomson.

Whitman, M. E. (2008). Security policy: From design to maintenance . In Straub, D. W., Goodman, S., & Baskerville, R. L. (Eds.), *Information Security: Policy, Processes, and Practices* (pp. 123–151). Armonk, NY: M.E. Sharpe.

Wicks, A. M., Visich, J. K., & Li, S. (2006). Radio Frequency Identification Applications in Hospital Environments. *Hospital Topics, 84*(3), 3–8. doi:10.3200/HTPS.84.3.3-9

Wieringa, R. (2007). *Research and design methodology for software and information engineers.* Internal report. Retrieved from http://www.cs.utwente.nl/~roelw

Wikipedia. (2007). *Public University.* Retrieved March 19, 2007, from http://en.wikipedia.org/wiki/Public_university

Wikipedia. (2008). *Web 2.0.* Retrieved March 16, 2008, from http://en.wikipedia.org/wiki/ Web_2#Definition

Willcocks, L., & Choi, C. J. (1995). Co-operative partnership and 'total' IT outsourcing: From contractual obligation to strategic alliance. *European Management Journal*, *13*(1), 67–78. doi:10.1016/0263-2373(94)00059-G

Willemain, T. R. (1994). Insights on Modeling from a Dozen Experts. *Operations Research*, *42*(2), 213–222. doi:10.1287/opre.42.2.213

Willemain, T. R. (1995). Model Formulation: What Experts Think about and When. *Operations Research*, *43*(6), 916–932. doi:10.1287/opre.43.6.916

Williamson, O. E. (1975). *Markets and hierarchies, analysis and antitrust implications: a study in the economics of internal organization* (1st ed.). New York: The Free Press.

Williamson, O. E. (1981). The economics of organization: The transaction cost approach. *American Journal of Sociology*, *87*(3), 548–577. doi:10.1086/227496

Williamson, O. E. (1993). *Opportunism and Its Critics* (*Vol. 14*). New York: Emerald Group Publishing Limited.

Wilson, D. C. (1982). Electricity and resistance: A case study of innovation and politics. *Organization Studies*, *3*(2), 119–140. doi:10.1177/017084068200300203

Witten, I. H., & Frank, E. (2005). *Data Mining: Practical Machine Learning Tools and Techniques*. San Francisco: Morgan Kaufmann Publishers.

Womack, J., Jones, D., & Roos, D. (2007). *The Machine That Changed the World: The Story of Lean Production--Toyota's Secret Weapon in the Global Car Wars That Is Now Revolutionizing World Industry*. New York: Free Press.

Wood, C. C., Banks, W. W., Guarro, S. B., Garcia, A. A., Hampel, V. E., & Sartorio, H. P. (1987). *Computer Security: A Comprehensive Controls Checklist*. New York: John Wiley & Sons.

Wood-Harper, A. T., Fok, L. M., & Kumar, K. (1987, December). *Methodologies for socio-technical systems (STS) development: a comparative review.* Paper presented at the 8th International Conference of Information Systems, Pittsburgh, USA.

World Economic Forum and INSEAD. (2009). *The Global Information Technology Report 2008–2009*. Retrieved April 9, 2009, from http://www.mcit.gov.eg/General/Global%20IT%20Report%202008-092009331155142.pdf

World Factbook, C. I. A. (2009). *Saudi Arabia*. Retrieved May 25, 2009, from https://www.cia.gov/library/publications/the-world-factbook/geos/sa.html

World Factbook, C. I. A. (2009a). *Saudi Arabia Economy 2009*. Retrieved October 14, 2009, from http://www.theodora.com/wfbcurrent/saudi_arabia/saudi_arabia_economy.html

World Trade Organization (WTO). (2005). *WTO General Council successfully adopts Saudi Arabia's terms of Accession*. WTO press releases. Retrieved November 5, 2008, from http://www.wto.org/english/news_e/pres05_e/pr420_e.htm

Wu, H., Wang, Q., Yu, J. X., Zhou, A., & Zhou, S. (2003). UD(k, l)-Index: An Efficient Approximate Index for XML Data. In *4th International Conference on Advances in Web-Age Information Management (WAIM 03)*, Chengdu, China (LNCS 2762, pp. 68–79). Berlin: Springer.

Xu, S., Zhu, K., & Gibbs, J. (2004). Global technology, local adoption: a cross-country investigation of Internet adoption by companies in the United States and China. *Electronic Markets*, *14*(1), 13–24. doi:10.1080/1019678042000175261

Yaar, A., Perrig, A., & Song, D. (2004). SIFF: a stateless Internet flow filter to mitigate DDoS flooding attacks. In *Proceedings of the IEEE Security and Privacy Symposium*, Pittsburgh, USA, May 2004 (pp. 130- 143).

Yang, C., Wong, D. W., Yang, R., Kafatos, M., & Li, Q. (2005). Performance-improving techniques in web-based GIS. *International Journal of Geographical Information Science*, *19*(3), 319–342. doi:10.1080/13658810412331280202

Yang, P., Cao, Y., & Evans, J. (2007). Web Map Server Performance and Client Design Principles. *GIScience & Remote Sensing*, *44*(4), 320–333. doi:10.2747/1548-1603.44.4.320

Yao, S. (1997). Approximating block accesses in database organizations. *Communications of the ACM*, *20*(4), 260–261. doi:10.1145/359461.359475

Yap, C. S., Soh, C. P. P., & Raman, K. S. (1992). Information systems success factors in small businesses.

Omega . International Journal of Management Science, 20(5), 597–609.

Yardley, D. (2002). *Successful IT project delivery: Learning the lessons of project failure*. London: Addison Wesley.

Yeh, Q.-C., & Chang, A. J.-T. (2007). Proliferation of Computers among Taiwanese SMEs. *International Journal of Entrepreneurship and Innovation Management, 7*(1), 51–73. doi:10.1504/IJEIM.2007.012173

Yen, S., & Lee, Y. (2006). An efficient data mining approach for discovering interesting knowledge from customer transactions. *Expert Systems with Applications, 30*, 650–657. doi:10.1016/j.eswa.2005.07.035

Yeom, G., & Min, D. (2005). Design and implementation of Web services QoS broker. In *Proceedings of The International Conference on Next Generation Web Services Practices (NWeSP 2005)* (pp. 454- 455).

Yildiz, M. (2007). The state of mobile government in Turkey: Overview, policy issues, and future prospects . In Kushchu, I. (Ed.), *Mobile Government: An Emerging Direction in E-Government* (pp. 252–268). Hershey, PA: IGI Publishing.

Yin, R. (1989). *Case study research: Design and methods*. Newbury Park, CA: Sage Publishing.

Yin, R. K. (2003). *Case study research, design and methods* (3rd ed.). Thousand Oaks, CA: Sage Publications.

Zeng, L., Lei, H., Dikun, M., Chang, H., Bhaskaran, K., & Frank, J. (2005) Model-driven Business Performance Management. In *IEEE International Conference on e-Business Engineering,* 18-21 October (pp. 295-304). Washington, DC: IEEE Computer Society.

Zhang, C., Naughton, J. F., DeWitt, D. J., Luo, Q., & Lohman, G. M. (2001). On Supporting Containment Queries in Relational Database Management Systems. In *ACM SIGMOD International Conference on Management of Data (SIGMOD 01)*, Santa Barbara, USA (pp. 425–436). New York: ACM.

Zhang, J., Wang, W., Liu, H., & Zhang, S. (2005). X-warehouse: building query pattern driven data. In *14th International Conference on World Wide Web (WWW 05)*, Chiba, Japan (pp. 896–897). New York: ACM.

Zhao, P., & Di, L. (2006). *Semantic Web service based geospatial knowledge discovery*.

Zhao, P., Yu, G., & Di, L. (2006). Geospatial Web Services. *Emerging Spatial Information Systems and Applications, 1*(1).

Zhong, S., Yang, Q., Zhang, H., Xu, X., Hu, Y., & Ma, S. (2002). Correlation-Based Web Document Clustering for Adaptive Web Interface Design. *Knowledge and Information Systems, 4*(2), 151–167. doi:10.1007/s101150200002

Zhu, K., Kraemer, K., & Xu, S. (2003). Electronic business adoption by European firms: a cross-country assessment of the facilitators and inhibitors. *European Journal of Information Systems, 12*(4), 251–268. doi:10.1057/palgrave.ejis.3000475

Zhu, K., & Kraemer, K. L. (2005). Post-Adoption Variations in Usage and Value of E-Business by Organizations: Cross-Country Evidence from the Retail Industry. *Information Systems Research, 16*(1), 61–84. doi:10.1287/isre.1050.0045

Zhu, K., Kraemer, K., & Xu, S. (2002). A cross-country study of e-business adoption using the technology-organisation-environment framework. In *Proceedings of International Conference on Information Systems*, Barcelona, Spain.

Ziman, J. (2000). *Technological innovation as an evolutionary process*. Cambridge, UK: Cambridge University Press.

Zolkiewski, J., & Littler, D. (2004). Future business relationships – traditional, electronic, virtual or hybrid? *Telematics and Informatics, 21*, 183–196. doi:10.1016/S0736-5853(03)00056-X

Zuquim, D., Guimares, G., & Felgar de Toledo, M. B. (2006). A Web service architecture providing QoS management. In *Proceedings of The Fourth Latin American Web Congress (LA-WEB '06)* (pp. 189-198).

About the Contributors

Eshaa M. Alkhalifa has obtained her BSc in Computer Science of the University of Bahrain, her MS in Artificial Intelligence from the University of George Washington, and her PhD in Cognitive Science from the University of Edinburgh in Scotland. She has published a number of books, and a large number of journal and conference papers. She is currently the Academic Vice President of the Royal University for Women. Her research interests including the utilization of Cognitive Science findings in increasing the efficiency of learning in general or elearning in particular.

***

Mansoor Al-A'ali finished his B.Sc. in Computer Studies from the University of Teesside, UK in 1982. He received his M.Sc. in Computer Science from the University of Aston in Birmingham, UK in 1984. He received his Ph.D. from the University of Aston in Birmingham, UK in 1989. Mansoor is currently working in the department of computer science at the University of Bahrain. Since 1989 he has been working as a consultant for a number of leading Bahraini organizations leading the design and quality assurance issues of major industrial computer systems. His research interests include: AI, computer ethics, COTS software, algorithms, software engineering and computers in education. He has over eighty refereed publications in these areas. Mansoor was the chairman of the department of computer science at the University of Bahrain from 1992 to 1995 and as the director of continuing education from 1996 to 2000.

Seema Al-Mahmood graduated with a bachelor's degree in office management from the University of Bahrain in 1998 and obtained her master's degree in computing in 2004 from the same university. She worked for nine years for the Bahrain Telecommunications Company as the information systems quality assurance and process improvement specialist. Her areas of interest are software engineering – COTS (Commercial of the Shelf) user requirements management and COTS software acquisition methodologies. She has published five research papers on this field.

Sabah Abdullah Al-Somali is a doctoral student in Operations and Information Systems at Aston University Business School. She received her MSc degree in e-business from Aston University in 2007 and an MBA from the Arab Academy for Science & Technology and Maritime Transport (AASTMT) in Alexandria, Egypt in 2004. She has practical experience as an IT specialist. Her research interests include ICT adoption and diffusion, technology acceptance and electronic commerce.

Rafi Ashrafi has over 20 years of teaching, research and consulting experience in academia and business in Canada and Middle East. He worked as a project manager with EDS and Alcatel and a consultant in IT Project Management in Canada. Rafi was also a Researcher and an Adjunct Professor at the University of Calgary, where he conducted research and taught graduate courses in the Haskyn School of Business and Schulich School of Engineering. Rafi has published over 40 research papers in international journal and conference proceedings. Currently he is Head of the Information Systems Department at the College of Commerce and Economics at Sultan Qaboos University in Oman.

Dimitris Askounis is Assistant Professor in the School of Electrical and Computer Engineering of the National Technical University of Athens (NTUA). He has been involved in numerous EU funded IT research projects since 1988 (ESPRIT, BRITE-EURAM, FP5, FP6) in the areas of computer integrated manufacturing, enterprise resource planning, decision support, knowledge management, quality management, business and data modelling, e-business, etc. He has also participated in several other EU-funded projects within the EUROPAID framework in CEEC, NIS and MEDA countries concerning management training, monitoring and evaluation of large projects, energy policy and planning.

Elarbi Badidi is currently an Assistant Professor of computer science at the College of Information Technology (CIT) of United Arab Emirates University. Before joining the CIT, he held the position of bioinformatics group leader at the Biochemistry Department of Université de Montréal from 2001 to July 2004. He received a Ph.D. in computer science in 2000 from Université de Montréal, Québec (Canada). Dr. Badidi has been conducting research in the areas of object-based distributed systems, bioinformatics, and Web services. He is a member of the IEEE, IEEE Computer Society, and ACM. He served on the technical program committees of many international conferences. His research interests include Web services and Service Oriented Computing, Middleware, and Bioinformatics data and tools integration.

N. Meltem Cakici is a Lecturer in Marketing at Gediz University, Izmir. She received her B.A. degree in Management from Bogazici University and Ph.D. in Marketing from Yeditepe University, Istanbul. She worked as a post doctoral fellow on a Tubitak project at Sabanci University, Istanbul. Her areas of interest are consumer behavior, marketing research, international marketing and retailing. She is paying particular attention on consumers' decision making process, cross-cultural studies on purchase and consumption patterns, ethical consumption and corporate social responsibility issues. Emerging themes and concepts in marketing, marketing's role in strategy development and marketing's relationship with other disciplines are also part of her research agenda.

Ben Clegg (PhD (De Montfort), BSc(Hons) and DIS Loughborough, CEng, DipM (Institute of Marketing), PGCHE (UCE), FHEA, MIET) graduated from Loughborough University with a degree in management science and a diploma in industrial studies. Simultaneously he completed a diploma in strategic marketing from the Chartered Institute of Marketing and a sponsored business student apprenticeship with GEC. He worked as a project manager for several years in the capital goods sector for GEC. He has conducted research at Portsmouth University and De Montfort University completing a PhD in systems engineering. He spent a year as a visiting scholar at Stanford University's Centre for Integrated Facilities Engineering (USA) continuing research into business improvement as well as working for a university spin-out company. He Joined Aston Business School in 2003; he consults, researches and teaches in the field of technology, strategy and operations. He is a reviewer for the many international journals and has held multimillion pound research projects from the UK government. He is a chartered engineer.

Jérôme Darmont received his Ph.D. in computer science from the University of Clermont-Ferrand II, France in 1999. He joined the University of Lyon 2, France in 1999 as an associate professor, and became full professor in 2008. He was head of the Decision Support Databases research group within the ERIC laboratory from 2000 to 2008, and has been director of the Computer Science and Statistics Department of the School of Economics and Management since 2003. His current research interests mainly relate to performance in database management systems and data warehouses (performance optimization, auto-administration, benchmarking...), but also include XML and complex data warehousing and mining, and medical or health-related applications.

Ronan de Kervenoael is a Lecturer in Marketing at Sabanci University and network Lecturer at Aston University. He received his Ph.D. from Sheffield University, UK. He has held position at Lancaster University, ITSM de Monterrey, and Manchester Universities. Ronan has a particular interest in choice and anti-choice investigating both consumers and within the supply chain actors through their everyday practice. His wider research interests lie under the umbrella of consumer behavior and retailing; the principal theme being the socio-spatial context of consumption. He is currently particularly interested in the Information Communication Technology change situation of emerging markets and associated strategies.

Pooya Khosraviyan Dehkordi is a faculty member of the technology and engineering department in Shahrekord Islamic Azad University of Iran. He got his B.S. in Computer Engineering (Software) from Najafabad Islamic Azad University, Iran. He has published several articles on optimization based on Fuzzy Logic, Cellular automata, Genetic Programming. His field of interest is Cellular Automata, Natural Language Processing, Software Engineering and Genetic Programming.

Larbi Esmahi is an Associate Professor of the School of Computing and Information Systems at Athabasca University. He was the graduate program coordinator at the same school during 2002-2005. He holds a PhD in electrical engineering from Ecole Polytechnique, University of Montreal. His current research interests are in e-services, e-commerce, multi-agent systems, and intelligent systems. He is an associate editor for the Journal of Computer Science, and the Tamkang Journal of Science and Engineering. He is also member of the editorial advisory board of the Advances in Web-Based Learning Book Series, IGI Global, and member of the international editorial review board the International Journal of Web-Based Learning and Teaching Technologies.

Daniela Feldkamp studied Computer Science at the University of Oldenburg, Germany, where she received the Diploma in 2006. Since then, she is working in the Information and Knowledge Management group of Prof. Dr. Knut Hinkelmann at the University of Applied Science Northwestern Switzerland. Because of her apprenticeship as a management assistant in wholesale and foreign trade, she is interested in doing application-oriented research and development in the area of agile enterprises. Additionally, she is interested in Knowledge Management, Business Rules and Workflow Management.

Bardo Fraunholz is a Senior Lecturer at Deakin University. He holds Professional Business Degree in Information Systems and Accounting (University of Trier, Germany) and GradDip in Legal studies specialising in IT, Media & Corporate Law from London (UK). He has lectured in the University of Koblenz, Germany, in enterprise modelling, project management, small business and knowledge management. He spent several years in the ICT sector managing/consulting with a number of projects involving mobile applications, SMEs, and e-learning. He has expertise in RFID based process integration in hospitals and has an interest in Web 2.0 based approaches that promote citizen engagement in democracies and environment sustainability.

Christos K. Georgiadis is an Assistant Professor at the Department of Applied Informatics, University of Macedonia – Thessaloniki – Greece. He received his Ph.D. in Information Systems Security - Access Control for Web Data Bases from the Aristotle University of Thessaloniki. His research interests include the areas of e-commerce and m-commerce technologies, e-security, and web services supporting technologies. Research productivity is summarized in various articles in cooperation with other researchers, in international journals and international conferences proceedings. He has participated in several Research Projects in Greece and in European Union related to information systems security and e-health. He is a reviewer of several international journals related to e-commerce (such as IJEB, JEIM, and JTAER). He is also a tutor of the Hellenic Open University. He is a professional member of ACM, and the SIGEcom.

Roya Gholami is a lecturer in Operations and Information Management Group, Aston Business School in Birmingham, UK. Her current research interests are IT business value, Green IT, Information Technology Adoption, Information Technology and Development. She has published in IEEE Transaction on Engineering Management, Information & Management, Journal of Global Information Management, Information Resource Management Journal, World Economy, Technovation and Electronic Journal of Information Systems in Developing Countries.

Ken H. Guo is a sessional lecturer and a PhD candidate in information systems at DeGroote School of Business, McMaster University. He received his M.Sc. in Business from the University of British Columbia and B.A. in Economics from Zhejiang University. He is a Certified Management Accountant (Canada) and a certified SAP consultant. His research interests include information security, identity theft, IT auditing, accounting information systems, and accounting. He teaches accounting information systems course at both MBA and undergraduate levels.

Ching-Cha Hsieh is currently an Associate Professor at the Department of Information Management, National Taiwan University. Her areas of research include Information Technology and Organizations, Business Transformation, Information Systems Planning and Design, Philosophy and Information System. In her 30-year professor career, Dr. Hsieh writes several books, including Information management. Currently, her focuses on eastern philosophy and Information system research.

Chunyang Hu is currently a PhD candidate in the School of Computer Science and Engineering at Beihang University. His research interests include Geospatial web service, web collaboration, service computing and semantic web. He received his MS degree in computer science from the University of Northwestern Polytechnic and is currently preparing his dissertation.

Cheng-Chieh Huang is currently a Ph.D. Candidate at the Graduate Institute of Information Management, National Taiwan University. His areas of research include Information Technology and Organization Change, Infomation systems outsourcing, Knowledge Management. Mr. Huang was a sr. consultant of Hewlett-Packard Taiwan, who consult and implement various outsourced projects. Currently, Mr. Huang work for an industry marketing and consulting company, as an ICT industry analyst, focuses on Information systems outsourcing and offshoring trends and strategies.

Farshad Kiyoumarsi is a professor of computer sciences at Shahrekord Islamic Azad University of Iran. He is the head of the technology and engineering department in this University. He got his Ph.D. computer science from Shahid Bahonar University of Kerman, Iran. He has published several articles on optimization based on Fuzzy Logic. His field of interest is artificial intelligence, Natural language Processing and Fuzzy Logic.

George Kourlimpinis after finishing his Electrical & Computer Engineer Diploma, has acquired two masters' degrees, one MBA in "Telecommunication Enterprises' Management" and one in "Fundamental & Applied Cognitive Science". Since 2005, he is a Ph.D. candidate and his research concerns knowledge-based systems and management methodological approaches to support the implementation of reengineering projects throughout their lifecycle. Apart from his academic interests he contributes to the specification, the design, the development and the deployment of numerous medium and large scale management information systems as well as to the implementation of research and consulting projects.

Dianfu Ma is Full Professor and dean of Computer Science and Engineering School at Beihang University, secretary-general of Computer Science and Technology Education Steering Committee of the Ministry of Education, vice president (chairman) of China Engineering Graphics Society, and currently serves on the editorial boards for Springer Transactions on Frontiers of Computer Science. He has served as an expert of whole team of Standards for Government Information Resource Catalog System and Exchange System. His principal area of research include network computing, distributed systems, E-government, and scientific computing visualization. Professor Ma undertook more than 10 scientific research projects including two National 863 high-tech programs, two sub subjects of the 973 programs, and programs funded by the Ministry of Science and Technology Foundation, the General Armament Department Research Foundation and the National Natural Science Foundation. Until now Ma has published more than 30 papers on the international conferences and domestic core journals.

Hadj Mahboubi was born on 17 March 1981 in Tlemcen Algeria. Since December 2008, he holds a PhD in computer science from the University of Lyon 2, France. He received his master degree from INSA Lyon in 2005 and his engineering degree in computer science in 2003 from the University of Tlemcen, Algeria. He was a research assistant in the University of Lyon 2, France. His is a post-doctoral researcher at Cemagref Clermont-Ferrand. His research interests lie in the field of XML data warehouse design and performance optimization.

Owen Molloy is a Senior Lecturer in Information Technology at the National University of Ireland, Galway, and a member of the Medical Informatics Research Group. Dr. Molloy is a specialist in the area of process management and extended value chain integration. His research is focused on the development of methodologies and systems to support the design and implementation of cross-functional business processes. This includes the design of value-stream modelling, optimisation and legacy system integration components to deliver real-time performance information to process-wide business intelligence dashboards. In his consulting work, he has provided expert facilitation and coaching in Lean Six Sigma to internal process improvement teams in a number of Irish and European organizations.

Spyridon Mouzakitis is an electrical and computer engineer and is currently finalizing his PhD. He has nine years of industry experience in conception, analysis and implementation of information technology systems. He has working experience as an IT Expert in public administrations and banking area. His current research is focused on decision analysis in the field of e-Business, enterprise interoperability and e-Government

Muhammad Murtaza is a Sultan Qaboos University (Oman) graduate specializing in Information Systems. He has also earned a Diploma in Software Programming from Higher College of Technology (Oman). He has been honored twice for academic distinction, once by H.M. Sultan Qaboos bin Said in 2007 and earlier by H.E. the Minister of Manpower in 2004. Also, he has co-authored a research on "Use and Impact of ICT on SMEs in Oman"; it was presented in The International Conference on Information Resources Management (Conf-IRM 2008) and published in the British Electronic Journal of Information Systems Evaluation (EJISE). Muhammad has served as the president of Information Systems Group in Oman for a year and currently, he works as the ICT Solutions Manager in one of the leading IT services companies in Middle East, overlooking software project implementations and architecting solutions. To contact Muhammad Murtaza, email him on muhd.murtaza@gmail.com.

Asem Omari has been working as an assistant professor in the department of Computer Science, Jerash Private University, Jordan since October 2008. Besides teaching different core computer science courses, Dr. Omari has been working as the director of Computer Center at the university. Dr. Omari obtained his PhD degree from the Institute of Computer Science at Heinrich-Heine University Duesseldorf, Germany in 2008. He obtained the Graduate Certificate in Computer and Information Sciences from the University of Michigan, Dearborn, USA in 2002. He completed his Bachelor degree in Applied Mathematics with programming and system analysis orientation from Jordan University of Science and Technology, Jordan, 1999. Since 2005 he has been researching in data mining and its applications in web design, marketing, medicine, traffic, and Arabic text mining.

María Laura Ponisio is Research Scientist at University of Twente (The Netherlands). Her research interests include inter-organizational networks, global software development and large object-oriented systems engineering. She received her Ph.D. in the area of software reverse engineering from the University of Bern (Switzerland), her Master in object-oriented software engineering from both Ecole des Mines de Nantes (France) and Vrije Universiteit Brussel (Belgium), and her Licentiate degree in Computer Science from UNLP, the National University of La Plata (Argentina). Dr Ponisio has work experience in industry and academia, including software systems development and database administration. Currently, she performs action research on inter-organizational networks and project management in international collaboration with private and public institutions.

Eugen Pop graduated the Faculty of Electronics and Telecommunications of the "Politehnica" University in Bucharest, Romania, in 1986. Since 1999 he is PhD in Telecommunications, in the Code

Division Multiple Access systems. In 1990 he joined the wireless communication department of the Electronic Research Institute in Bucharest, Romania, where afterwards he became the Head of Advanced Communications Laboratory. Now he is senior researcher in the IT&C department of the Automation Engineering Institute in Bucharest, Romania. The main direction of his R&D activity is the electronic services development and providing, through mobile communication networks. He collaborates with the European Technological Platform for Mobile and Wireless Communication, e-Mobility and with the World Wireless Research Forum. Dr Eugen POP also has various didactical activities at the Faculty of Electronics from the „Politechnica" University in Bucharest, Romania. He is author of books, many scientifical articles and papers at telecommunications international conferences.

John Psarras is Professor in the Department of Electrical and Computer Engineering of NTUA and the Head of NTUA-EPU, holding a Ph.D. degree on Multi-objective Mathematical Programming applied to energy and environmental systems (NTUA, 1989). He has been manager or senior researcher in numerous EC and national projects for over 25 years in the areas of energy policy (including climate change policy), national and regional energy planning, energy and environmental modelling, promotion of energy and environmentally friendly technologies, energy management, decision support and monitoring systems. In addition, he has a long professional record in capacity building, technology transfer and training in the fields of energy policy and planning, decision support systems analysis, sustainable energy technologies etc.

Lourens Riemens finished his study Software Engineering at the HIO Enschede in 1991. He started his working career at a small software company. In 1996 he joined the IT center of the Netherlands Tax and Customs Authority. Lourens performed several software engineering and architecture functions. Currently, he is a senior IT architect responsible for Customs IT systems. His main focus areas are customs enterprise architecture, architecture governance and architecture methods and techniques. In the area of Customs, Lourens performed several projects on national and international cooperation with other governmental agencies and trade, including a benchmarking study on e-Customs, and innovative projects on end-to-end supply chain security.

Peter Rittgen received a Master of Science in Computer Science and Computational Linguistics from University Koblenz-Landau, Germany, and a PhD in Economics and Business Administration from Frankfurt University, Germany. He is currently a Professor at the School of Business and Informatics of the University of Borås, Sweden. He has been doing research on business processes and information systems since 1997, especially in the areas Business and IT Co-design & Collaborative Modeling, Business Network Governance and Business Process Simulation & Improvement. Dr. Rittgen is the Vice-Chair of the AIS Special Interest Group on Modeling and Simulation (www.ModellingAndSimulation.org) and an Associate Editor of the Informing Science Journal and the ECIS. He is also a member of the editorial board of several international journals and serves on review committees for international journals and conferences. He published over 90 works including 2 edited books, 2 journal issues and 13 journal articles. For further details refer to http://www.adm.hb.se/~PRI/.

Claire Sheridan's research focuses primarily on the areas of process management and the development of technology models and frameworks for Business Process Management and Business Activity Monitoring. She has published a number of conference and journal papers in the areas of business process management. Since joining Accenture (UK) in 2007, she has been part of the Accenture Information Management Services (AIMS) division where she is aligned to the Business Intelligence group. She is an Information Management Consultant with Accenture Information Management Services (UK) and a specialist in the Business Intelligence domain, delivering projects across a number of domains from government to high-tech industry.

Nishant Singh is a Bachelor of Technology from Indian Institute of Technology, Kanpur. Born on 6th October, 1985 at Varanasi, he was always a keen student. With his profound interest in mathematical modeling and C/C++ during his intermediate, he chose to pursue his bachelors in Computer Science. During graduation he developed an interest in computer architecture and software engineering and Image Processing. To explore his interest in software engineering he did an internship at University of Applied Sciences and explored the areas of web services. Very satisfied, he still indulges in academic readings and contributions in the same. He did his undergraduate project in image processing in the field of Human Computer Interaction. Currently working in the computer architecture giant Intel he is pursuing his interest in computer architecture.

Ramanjit Singh has recently completed his PhD at Manchester Business School, University of Manchester. In addition to the PhD research, he has published a paper in the scientific inquiry journal, a report at the University of Trento, Italy, and five conference papers. He can be reached by email at raman.si@gmail.com.

Eva Söderström is an associate professor at the University of Skövde, Sweden. She earned her PhD in Computer and System Science from Stockholm University/Royal Institute of Technology in 2004, on the subject of B2B standards implementation. Her current research is focused on trust and standards for inter-organisational collaboration, through for example e-services and e-government services. She has led and participated in several national and international projects, and has published over 70 internationally reviewed publications.

Aikaterini-Maria Sourouni holds a Diploma in Electrical and Computer Engineer at National Technical University of Athens and is currently finalizing her PhD in the field of e-Government Knowledge Management and in particular in the area of Services Modeling methodologies to support governmental transformation projects with the use of semantic knowledge-based technologies. Her research interests comprise modeling and transformation of processes and services, business and government process reengineering, ontologies and semantic engineering as well as IT project management and monitoring. Apart from her academic activity, during the last four years, she has been involved in various projects related to e-Government and e-Business, process modelling, planning, management and implementation of IT projects.

Tryfon L. Theodorou is Director of Studies at the Pythagoras Institute of Vocational Studies – Thessaloniki – Greece. He is a Ph.D. candidate in the area of Information Systems Security – Development of Information Security Techniques Using Cryptographic Methods for Wireless Devices, at the Department of Applied Informatics, University of Macedonia – Thessaloniki – Greece. He received his MSc. in Artificial Intelligence – Knowledge Based Systems from the University of Edinburgh – Scotland and he also received his second MSc. in Applied Informatics from the University of Macedonia – Greece. His research interests include the areas of applied cryptography and information security, wireless networks, and e-commerce. Research productivity so far, is summarized in various articles in cooperation with other researchers, in international journals and international conferences proceedings.

Chandana Unnithan is an Associate Lecturer with Deakin University. She holds a degree in Arts/Commerce/Computer Sciences (Bangalore/Mumbai, India), an MBA as well as a Research Master's in Business Computing (RMIT University, Australia). She has held varied positions in the ICT industry, ranging from Business Analyst, Project Manager and Knowledge Manager with MNCs such as IBM and TATA. She has published widely in e-commerce, project management, mobile business applications, information systems and e-governance. Her doctoral research focuses on RFID integration in hospitals. She has expertise in health informatics and technology integration in hospitals. She has research interests in public health approaches to technology integration, inclusive approaches in democracies leveraging Web 2.0, and harnessing indigenous knowledge to build systems for environmental sustainability.

Pascal van Eck received his diploma in Computer Science (MSc degree) from the Free University of Amsterdam in April, 1995. From May, 1995 until January 2000, he worked as a research assistant at the Artificial Intelligence Department of the Free University on a PhD thesis on a formal, compositional semantic structure for the dynamics of multi-agent systems. Starting February, 2000, he works at the Information Systems Group of the Faculty of Computer Science, University of Twente, as an assistant professor. His research interests include IT governance and alignment of business and IT architectures at the enterprise level, with a focus on case studies in the Dutch financial services industry and large-scale transaction processing.

George Violettas is a Ph.D. candidate at the Department of Applied Informatics, University of Macedonia – Thessaloniki – Greece. He received his M.Sc. in Applied Informatics from that same University at 2008 and his B.Sc. in informatics from the Greek Open University at 2006. He is occupied as a general Manager in an IT company in Thessaloniki – Greece. His duties include presales, handling of corporate accounts, government contracts, and design of complex wireless networks & backhauls. His research interests include the areas of wireless security and positioning, applied cryptography and information security where his Ph.D. research is focused. Research productivity so far, is summarized in various articles in cooperation with other researchers, in international conferences proceedings.

Trevor Wood-Harper is a professor of Information Systems at Manchester Business School, University of Manchester. He has authored, coauthored, or coedited 20 books and proceedings, and has published over 200 research articles. He has supervised or co-supervised more than 30 Ph.D. students. He can be reached by email at atwh@mbs.ac.uk.

Yongwang Zhao is an assistant professor in the School of Computer Science and Engineering at Beihang University. He received his PhD degree in computer science from Beihang University and a bachelor degree in information management systems from the University of Beijing Information Science and Technology. His current research interests include service computing, model checking and science computing visualization.

Index

Symbols

3G mobile terminals 161
3G networks 159
3G standards 159

A

agency theories 306
agile manufacturing 1
application programming interfaces (API) 246
Auto-ID Center 122
automatic recognition 88

B

back-end systems 94
balanced scorecard (BSC) 47, 48, 54, 55, 56, 57, 59, 60
bar coding technologies 119
Bell Labs 28
blood transfusions 119
bottlenecks 24, 29
business activity monitoring (BAM) 24, 29, 30, 31, 32, 36, 39, 40, 44, 45
business activity monitoring (BAM) systems 24
business environment services 158
business intelligence (BI) 21, 22, 29, 33
business leaders 376
business marketing strategies 377
business modeling 199, 208, 256, 258
business models 199, 257, 258
business processes 1
business process execution language (BPEL) 1, 2, 3, 4, 6, 7, 8, 12, 13, 14, 17, 18, 19, 20, 21, 22, 29, 42, 43, 44, 45, 173
business process management (BPM) 21, 22, 24, 30, 33, 42, 43, 45, 46
business process management (BPM) systems 24, 30, 32, 33
business process models 200, 201, 257
business process re-engineering (BPR) 53, 92
business rule engines 2
business rules 1, 2, 3, 20
business rule systems 5
business-to-business (B2B) 86, 87, 88, 89, 90, 91, 92, 93, 95, 96, 97, 98, 99, 100, 101, 102, 103, 104, 105, 106, 110, 113, 114
business-to-consumer (B2C) 87, 102, 106, 327, 340, 343, 348
business-to-government (B2G) 106, 110, 113, 114
business to intermediaries (B2I) 106, 113, 114
business to software unified process (BSUP) 254, 256, 257, 258, 259, 260, 263, 265

C

call centre automation (CCA) 294
China Center for Resource Satellite Data and Applications (CRESDA) 225
CIA Triangle, the 268
civil administrations 139
civil servants 137, 138, 139, 141, 142, 144, 145, 146, 147, 148, 149, 150, 156, 157
client server architecture 158
clinical information processing platform (CLIP) 125
clinical information processing platform (CLIP) system 125
clustering algorithms 235
collaborative knowledge 185, 188, 190

collaborative modeling 199, 200, 204
collaborative modeling processes 200
collective sense-making 200, 204
commercial off-the-shelf (COTS) 288, 289, 290, 291, 292, 293, 294, 296, 297, 298, 299, 300, 301, 302, 303, 304, 305
commercial off-the-shelf (COTS) software 288, 289, 291, 292, 293, 294, 296, 297, 298, 299, 300, 301, 302, 303, 304
common base event (CBE) 30
common event infrastructure (CEI) 30
communications and information technology commission (CICT) 330
competitive business environments 88
complex event processing (CEP) 30, 39
component-based software engineering 291
component brokerage platforms 291
composite capabilities/ preference profiles (CC/PP) 175, 180, 182
configurational perspectives 308
consumer-generated media (CGM) 198
contract management software 290
corporate financial systems (CFS) 294
customer relationship management (CRM) 379
cycle time 26

D

database management systems (DBMS) 232, 233, 235, 246, 247, 248, 251
data mining 376, 377, 378, 379, 380, 382, 384, 388, 389, 390
data mining techniques 376, 377, 380, 382, 384
data warehouses 232, 233, 234, 235, 236, 248, 250, 378
define, measure, analyze, improve and control (DMAIC) 28, 29, 33
democratic work arrangements (DWA) 49
description logics (DL) 15, 16, 17
digital government 138, 139, 145, 149
digital government strategy 138
discretionary collaborative behavior (DCB) 289
double-loop learning 271, 277

E

e-business 106, 107, 108, 109, 110, 111, 112, 113, 115, 116, 159, 256, 327, 337, 339, 341, 342, 346, 349, 350, 353, 374
e-commerce 89, 103, 159, 313, 314, 315, 316, 317, 319, 326, 327, 331, 333, 334, 335, 336, 338, 339, 340, 341, 342, 343, 344, 345, 346, 347, 348, 349, 354, 377, 380, 381
e-commerce documents 89
e-commerce platform 313, 314, 319
e-commerce websites 377, 381
e-consultation 356
e-content 158, 166
e-content providers 158
e-customs 62, 63, 71, 73, 74, 75, 76, 77, 79, 80, 81
e-decision-making 356
e-dictionary 185
e-government 138, 140, 144, 145, 146, 148, 150, 152, 153, 154, 155
e-information 356
electronic customs 61, 71, 74, 76, 79
electronic data interchange (EDI) 89, 95, 102, 103, 104, 327, 347
electronic fund transfer (EFT) 327
electronic networks 61
electronic product code (EPC) 122, 125, 136
electronic product code (EPC) technologies 122
element index (E-index) 235
employee job satisfaction 56
encryption algorithms 267
endpoint reference (EPR) 222
engineering cycle 67, 68, 69, 70, 71, 84
enhanced data GSM environment (EDGE) 173
e-participation 355, 356, 357
e-participation index 356, 357
e-planning 61, 62, 63, 69, 70, 71, 72, 74, 75, 76, 77, 78, 79, 80, 81
e-polls 187, 188
e-readiness 355, 374
e-services 158, 161, 162, 163, 164, 165, 170, 171, 356
e-tools 356

European Interoperability Framework (EIF) 108
event-based process modelling 21, 33
event, condition, action (ECA) 4
e-voter profiles 195
e-voters 195
e-votes 187
e-voting 185, 186, 187, 188, 194, 195, 196, 197, 198
e-voting systems 187, 194, 195
extensible markup language (XML) 3, 21, 32, 35, 43, 44, 89, 108, 109, 110, 111, 113, 232, 233, 234, 235, 236, 237, 238, 241, 243, 246, 247, 248, 249, 250, 251, 252

F

for-profit organizations 47, 48, 57
fraud detection techniques 380
frequently-used path expressions (FUP) 234
fuzzy logic 254, 255, 261, 262, 263, 264, 265
fuzzy logic concepts 254, 255, 262, 263

G

general packet radio service (GPRS) 158, 159, 171, 173
geographic information system (GIS) 213, 214, 215, 229
Google Earth 215
Google proprietary file system (GFS) 215
graphical user interface (GUI) 111
greedy algorithm 235
greedy search 245
gross domestic product (GDP) 353, 355, 359
gross national product (GNP) 332
group decision support systems (GDSS) 208, 209
Gulf Cooperation Countries xv, xxiii
Gulf cooperation countries (GCC) 351, 352, 353, 355, 356, 357, 358, 359, 361, 370, 371, 372

H

healthcare providers 126
humanistic welfare paradigm 47, 57
human resource management 137, 143, 146
human resources 268, 270, 271
human resources management systems (HRMS) 294
hybrid execution models 7
hypertext markup language (HTML) 191, 222

I

identity management 268, 269
information and communication technology (ICT) 89, 101, 107, 137, 138, 141, 143, 144, 145, 146, 148, 149, 150, 152, 154, 156, 157, 327, 328, 331, 333, 338, 339, 340, 342, 343, 347, 348, 351, 352, 353, 354, 355, 357, 359, 360, 361, 362, 363, 364, 365, 366, 367, 368, 369, 370, 371, 372, 373, 374, 375
information and communication technology (ICT) adoption 351, 352, 354, 355, 357, 367, 371, 372, 375
information and knowledge management 107
information management 137, 146
information retrieval systems 235
information systems (IS) 107, 111, 266, 267, 268, 269, 271, 272, 273, 274, 275, 276, 277, 278, 279, 280, 281, 282, 283, 284, 285, 288, 289, 291, 292, 293, 294, 295, 296, 305, 306, 307, 308, 309, 310, 311, 312, 313, 317, 318, 321, 322, 323
information systems (IS) literature 307
information systems (IS) security 266, 267, 268, 269, 271, 272, 273, 274, 275, 276, 277, 278, 279, 280, 281, 284, 285
information systems (IS) security management 266, 267, 268, 269, 271, 272, 273, 275, 279, 280, 281
information technology (IT) 29, 30, 32, 45, 52, 57, 59, 61, 62, 63, 64, 65, 66, 68, 69, 70, 73, 74, 76, 78, 79, 80, 81, 82, 84, 86, 90, 92, 93, 102, 104, 107, 172, 208, 269, 273, 275, 276, 277, 278, 279, 280, 281, 282, 284, 285, 289, 290, 291, 292, 293, 297, 299, 300, 301, 302, 303, 305, 306, 307, 308, 309, 310, 311, 312, 313, 317, 318, 319, 320, 321, 322, 323, 355, 359, 361, 362, 363, 364, 367, 373, 374, 375
information technology (IT) architecture 69, 73

information technology (IT) capabilities 65
information technology (IT) consulting 208
information technology (IT) development 62, 64, 65, 66
information technology (IT) infrastructures 57, 65, 107
information technology (IT) outsourcing 306, 307, 308, 309, 310, 311, 312, 313, 317, 318, 319, 320, 321, 322, 323
information technology (IT) portfolios 65, 66, 76, 78
information technology (IT) security 269, 284, 285
information technology (IT) strategies 172
information technology (IT) suppliers 289, 293
information technology (IT) systems 29
infrared sensor networks 126
in-house development 288
innovation 2
interactive financial exchange (IFX) 108, 115
international markets 327
Internet 158, 159, 162, 165, 186, 187, 189, 190, 191, 192, 196, 197, 198, 212, 213, 214, 229
Internet enabled mobile phones 139
Internet information server (IIS) 192
Internet service providers (ISP) 190
Internet voting 186
inter-organizational business transactions 86, 105
inter-organizational networks 61, 62, 63, 64, 65, 66, 68, 69, 75, 77, 78, 81, 84
inter-organizational systems 61, 62, 63, 64, 68, 72, 73, 76, 83
IS/IT outsourcing 306, 307, 310, 311, 312, 313, 317, 318, 322
iWise 21, 32, 33, 34

K

key performance indicator (KPI) 27, 28, 30
King Abdulaziz City for Science and Technology (KACST) 330
KM influences 269, 270, 273
knowledge architecture 269, 284
knowledge discovery in databases (KDD) 378
knowledge management activities (KMA) 269
knowledge management (KM) 266, 267, 269, 270, 271, 272, 273, 274, 275, 276, 277, 278, 279, 281, 282, 283, 285
Knowledge Oasis Muscat (KOM) 357, 374
knowledge resources 269, 270, 271, 274, 277
knowledge sharing 107, 115

L

landscape maps 74, 75, 76, 78
Lean 25, 27, 28, 45, 46
Lean Six Sigma (LSS) 28

M

meteorological data 22
method for assessing software subcontractor process (MASS) 289
Middle East and North Africa (MENA) region 331
mismatch handling for COTS selection (MiHOS) 293
mobile communications 158, 159, 160
mobile communications networks 158
mobile devices 173, 174, 175, 176, 178
mobile government (m-government) 137, 138, 139, 140, 143, 144, 146, 147, 148, 149, 150, 151, 153, 154, 156, 157
mobile operators 158
mobile phones 137, 139, 140, 147, 148, 150, 151, 152, 153, 156, 328
mobile resources (m-resources) 141
mobile technological innovations 138
mobile technologies 138, 139, 140, 149, 150, 155
mobile users 158
modeling languages 201, 204, 208
modeling procedures 200
modeling support systems (MSS) 204, 205, 208, 209
modeling teams 202
Motorola 28
multimedia messaging service (MMS) 138, 140, 161
multi-objective, multi-criteria (MOMC) 53

N

natural language domain 201
networked readiness index (NRI) 357
new public management (NPM) 139
non-governmental organizations (NGO) 56, 139, 144
non-profit organizations 47, 48, 56, 57

O

object-oriented software systems 107
online businesses 377
online shops 327
ontologies 2, 5, 6, 7, 8, 16, 17, 19, 106, 107, 108, 109, 110, 111, 112, 113, 115, 116
OntologyManager 7
open mobile alliance (OMA) 173, 175
operating system resource management 137
organizational climate 56
Organization for Economic Co-operation and Development (OECD) 353
Organization of Petroleum Exporting Countries (OPEC) 328
outsourcing decision framework 306, 307, 310, 311, 312
outsourcing firms 307, 309, 315, 319, 320, 321
outsourcing vendors 309, 310, 320

P

personal digital assistants (PDA) 139, 158, 159, 160, 161, 163, 166, 169, 170, 171, 173
physical shops 377
policy decision point (PDP) 176, 179
policy enforcement point (PEP) 176, 179
policymakers 326
prescriptive perspective 307
process definition tools 1
process improvement 21, 22, 28, 44, 45
process modeling language 1
public insurance institutions 106

Q

quality of service (QoS) 172, 173, 174, 175, 176, 177, 178, 179, 180, 181, 182, 183
quality of service (QoS) brokers 174, 175
quality of service (QoS) service monitoring 172, 182

R

radio frequency identification (RFID) 118, 119, 120, 121, 122, 123, 124, 125, 126, 128, 129, 130, 131, 132, 133, 134, 135, 136
radio frequency identification (RFID) tags 118, 119, 121, 122, 123, 124, 125, 129
radio frequency identification (RFID) technology 119, 120, 121, 126, 129, 130, 133, 134
rational unified process (RUP) 254, 256, 265
real time location system (RTLS) 130, 132
real world 261
remote sensing imagery 212, 216
requests for proposals (RFP) 289, 292, 293, 295, 298, 299, 301, 312, 314, 315, 316, 317, 318, 320, 321, 324
research grants 57
resource dependency 306, 307
resource management 137, 138, 139, 141, 143, 145, 146, 147, 148, 149, 150, 157
resource management strategies 137, 138, 141
resource management systems 86, 266
resource models 257
retail businesses 376, 388
retail sectors 352
retail websites 376, 381, 382, 384, 386, 388
RHEA 2, 6, 7, 8, 13, 14, 15, 16, 17, 18
risk factors 260
Riskit 254, 255, 256, 257, 258, 259, 260, 261, 262, 263, 264, 265
Riskit method, the 254, 255, 256, 259, 263
risk management 254, 255, 256, 259, 261, 262, 263, 264
risk management methodology 254
RosettaNet 89, 92, 93, 103, 104, 105
rule engines 2, 6, 7, 8, 15

S

satellite remote sensing imagery 212
security management 266, 267, 268, 269, 271, 272, 273, 275, 276, 278, 279, 280, 281, 283, 284, 285
semantic web rule language (SWRL) 1, 2, 5, 6,

7, 15, 16, 17
service level agreement (SLA) 178, 179, 181, 182
service-oriented architecture (SOA) 2, 212, 216, 221
shareholder wealth 47, 48, 53, 55, 57
short message service (SMS) 138, 139, 140, 145, 153, 161
simple object access protocol (SOAP) 173, 180
single-loop learning 271, 277, 278
Six Sigma 25, 27, 28, 29, 35, 36, 37, 42, 43, 45
small and medium enterprises (SME) 106, 108, 326, 327, 331, 332, 333, 335, 336, 338, 339, 340, 341, 342, 343, 344, 345, 346, 347, 348, 349, 351, 352, 353, 354, 359, 360, 361, 363, 364, 365, 366, 367, 370, 371, 372, 373, 374, 375
Smartphones 158, 161, 163, 166, 169, 171, 173
social-political environments 307, 310, 311
social support systems 50
socio-technical balanced scorecard 47, 48, 55, 56, 57
socio-technical designs 48, 49, 50, 51, 52, 53, 60
socio-technical principles 47, 50, 51, 52, 53
socio-technical theory 47, 48, 49, 50, 51, 52, 56, 57
software applications 61, 73, 75, 76, 81
software development 254, 256
software supply chains 290
stakeholders 128, 129, 199, 203, 255, 256, 259, 262, 263
standards development organizations (SDO) 86, 90, 105
standards software organizations (SSO) 86, 90, 94, 105
standards user organizations (SUO) 86, 90, 92, 94, 105
statement of work (SOW) 295, 301
structured query language (SQL) 9, 10, 11, 17, 112, 191, 192, 214, 215, 237, 246, 247, 249
structured query language (SQL) server database 214
structured query language (SQL) servers 214, 215, 246
supervised learning 377
supply chain management 107
supply chains 290
systematic reasoning frameworks 61, 64

T

team-based modeling 199
technological systems 120
technology of accepted model (TAM) 354
technology-organization-environment (TOE) 326, 334
theory of planned behavior (TPB) 141, 354
theory of reasoned action (TRA) 141
Toyota Production System 28
tracking systems 125, 126, 129, 132
trading partner agreements (TPA) 93
transaction costs 306, 307, 308, 320
trust management 268

U

ultra high frequency (UHF) 121, 122, 124, 136
unified modeling language (UML) 76, 254, 257, 258, 260, 261, 264, 265
Uniform Code Council 122
uniform resource locators (URL) 213
universal business language (UBL) 108, 116
universal description discovery and integration (UDDI) 175, 178
universal mobile telecommunications system (UMTS) 158, 159, 160, 172
up-front investments 61
usage environment 68, 70
user-created content (UCC) 198
user-generated content (UGC) 198

V

very small enterprises (VSE) 106
virtual participation 186
voting models 186

W

Waikato Environment for Knowledge Analysis (WEKA) 384
Web 2.0 185, 187, 194, 195, 196, 197, 198, 212, 213, 228, 230, 232
Web 2.0-based service-oriented software para-

digm 228
Web 2.0 technologies 212
Web applications 187
Web coverage services (WCS) 213
web designers 376
web engineering techniques 377
Web feature services (WFS) 213
Web map services (WMS) 212, 213, 214, 216, 217, 222, 223, 224, 225, 226, 227, 228, 229
web measure index 355, 357
web ontology language (OWL) 1, 2, 5, 6, 7, 8, 12, 13, 15, 16, 17, 19
Web registries services (WRS) 213
Web services-based infrastructure 21
web services description language (WSDL) 173, 178
web usage mining 381
what you see is what I see (WYSIWIS) 200
wi-fi 173
wiki-based knowledge sharing 188
Wiki-Dic 185, 187, 188, 189, 190, 191, 192, 194, 195, 196
Wikipedia 185, 188, 196
wireless application protocol (WAP) 173, 176
wireless local area networks (WLAN) 158, 159, 161, 171
wireless networks 139, 173
word trade organisation (WTO) 326, 328, 333, 349, 350
workflow management systems 1
World War II 118
World Wide Web 107, 212, 230, 382, 389
World Wide Web Consortium (W3C) 173, 175, 177, 178, 182, 183

X

XML data 232, 233, 234, 235, 236, 246, 247, 249, 250, 251
XML data indexing 233, 234
XML data warehouses 232, 233, 234, 235, 236, 246, 247, 251, 252
XML documents 232, 233, 234, 235, 236, 237, 238, 247, 248, 251, 252
XML process definition language (XPDL) 21, 31, 42, 45
XML schemas 236
XQuery language 237, 246

LaVergne, TN USA
01 August 2010
191549LV00004B/3/P